Tawhidi Epistemology and its Applications: Economics, Finance, Science, and Society

Tawhidi Epistemology and its Applications: Economics, Finance, Science, and Society

By

Masudul Alam Choudhury

With contributions from T. Mariyanti, M. Shahadat Hossain and Jadi Suriadi

CAMBRIDGE
SCHOLARS
PUBLISHING

Tawhidi Epistemology and its Applications:
Economics, Finance, Science, and Society,
by M.A. Choudhury

This book first published 2014

Cambridge Scholars Publishing

12 Back Chapman Street, Newcastle upon Tyne, NE6 2XX, UK

British Library Cataloguing in Publication Data
A catalogue record for this book is available from the British Library

ISBN (10): 1-4438-5546-4, ISBN (13): 978-1-4438-5546-4

To all those who contemplate on the monotheistic design of the universe
by integrating Science and Religion

PROLOGUE

Behold, thy Lord said to the angels! I will create
"A vicegerent on earth." They said
"Will Thou place therein one who will make
Mischief therein and shed blood? –
While we do celebrate Thy praises
And glorify Thy holy (name)?"
He said: "I know what ye know not."

And He taught Adam the nature
Of all things; then He placed them
Before the angels and said: "Tell Me
The names of these if ye are right."

They said: "Glory to Thee: of knowledge
We have none, save what Thou
Hast taught us: in truth it is Thou
Who are perfect in knowledge and wisdom."

He said: "O Adam! Tell them
Their natures." When he had told them,
God said: "Did I not tell you
That I know the secrets of heaven
And earth, and I know what ye reveal
And what ye conceal?"

(*Qur'an*, 2:30-33)
Translation from Abdullah Yusuf Ali, 1946,
The Holy Qur'an, Text, Translation and Commentary,
McGregor & Werner, Inc., USA)

TABLE OF CONTENTS

**Part II:
Applications of *Tawhidi* Epistemology:
The Method of Circular Causation and Simulation
of the Wellbeing Objective Criterion**

LIST OF FIGURES

List of Tables

FOREWORD

This book is written by an internationally reputed researcher and professor with specialization in the mathematical treatment of various political economic issues with special focus on Islamic social economy and the world system. Professor Masudul Alam Choudhury's specialization makes him well-known in pioneering the *tawhidi* epistemology applied in economics and society. The significance of the *tawhidi* methodological worldview is reflected in the unity of the monotheistic law and the unity of the world-system in which the monotheistic law prevails. Professor Masudul Alam Choudhury has written many scholarly books and scientific journal articles. His focus has been in the particular area of epistemological critique of economic and social theory with special focus on the *tawhidi* methodology of unity of knowledge and unity of the world system in the generality and specifics of socio-scientific issues and problems.

Tawhidi methodology is unique and universal when premised on a carefully sought out and comprehensive epistemology. Religion and science together comprise the foundation of knowledge, process, and reality. Sociologists have long investigated the impact of religion on human behaviour. But economists have only recently attempted to investigate and define the linkages between religion and economic behaviour in subtle ways. Hence this book will be an excellent contribution for all those interested in understanding the functional nature of moral and ethical values drawn from the divine law embodied in the *Qur'an* and explained by the *Sunnah*. Such derivations find their home in economics and social theory and practice.

Such an approach and the *functional* ontological derivations as opposed to metaphysical indefiniteness are fundamental in understanding the theory and practice of *tawhidi* methodology drawn from the *Qur'an* and the *Sunnah*. Thereby, *Qur'anic* epistemology is essential to understand and invoke in every issue and problem of life. Professor Choudhury refers to this universal expanse of conception and application of the *tawhidi* episteme as the theory of 'everything'. The foundation of the purpose and objective of the Islamic law, referred to as *maqasid as-shari'ah,* is explained in this book to comprise the *tawhidi* epistemological worldview for understanding moral sustainability across the conception and functional ontology together with applications in 'everything'.

In this book, Professor Masudul Alam Choudhury has formalized the theorem of the unification of knowledge by the uniqueness of the universal law of monotheistic oneness that applies equally within and between socio-scientific systems. This universality of the tawhidi law of functional ontology within its episteme is true despite the perceived differences in the specifications of the problems underlying diverse socio-scientific systems and entities. In this methodological analytic, a theory of ethics treated as endogenous values pertaining to economic forces is different from the way economic theory treats ethics as external to the economic system.

In relation to such endogenous treatment of ethics in economics and social systems, some important mathematical properties of the *tawhidi* methodological worldview have been established. The proof of universality and uniqueness of the *tawhidi* methodological worldview and rigorous analysis are brought to bear on substantive socio-scientific issues. In essence, the metaphysical formalism of religion is transformed into functional formalism. This functional transformation of unity of knowledge is then made to functionally conceptualize and thus apply to specific issues of economics, finance, and society. The resulting material is for thoughtful and informed readers of all shades of scholarly persuasion, not limited to Muslims alone.

The book also presents subtle quantitative models that are treated empirically. This approach further expands the contributions of the *tawhidi* methodology to the applied and functional domains. The book thereby establishes both the conceptual and applied horizons of the monotheistic law on mundane problems and issues of 'everything'. This by itself is a bold and distinctive contribution *qua* materiality, encompassing thus a substantive integration of religion with a socio-scientific worldview. The result is a contribution not seen in any religious or socio-scientific study either in mainstream or Islamic literature in this area of highly scholarly investigation.

The content of the book is also extensively comparative in the review of the literature. This undertaking expands across epistemology in the field of philosophy of science, the scope of socio-scientific thinking, and moral reconstructive possibility of an ethically-benign world-system. Together with this there are deep applications in various areas of economics, finance, and society. These are epistemologically governed by unity of knowledge and unity of the induced world-system.

Throughout this book, Professor Masudul Alam Choudhury has aimed firstly, at fulfilling the gaps that exist in the available studies in Islamic economics and society. Secondly, the book, by its highly scholarly singularity of argumentation based on the *tawhidi* methodological worldview, stimulates further scope of scholarship, reflection, and inquiry on questions of significance in the area of monotheistic dynamics and socio-scientific analysis. All this is carried out in the book under a most rigorous analytical lens.

This is a *tawhidi* methodological lesson drawn from the *Qur'an* and the *Sunnah* for all the world-systems by their generality and specifics. The theory of systems and cybernetics abounds in unravelling the inherent analytical properties of the issues and problems investigated.

In regards to the substantive methodological and expanse of outlook that Professor Masudul Alam Choudhury has offered in this book, the contributory thought will be read and referred to for all times by ardent researchers, academicians, and practitioners who look beyond the narrow limits of vision.

Wassalam,
Chairman of
Ulama Council of Indonesia
Dr. KH. Ma'ruf Amin

PREFACE

The emergence of any socio-scientific body of knowledge requires firm logical, explanatory, and applicative epistemology as its methodology. Without an epistemological mooring there cannot be science, and therefore no socio-scientific knowledge. Upon such an epistemic foundation stands the methodological worldview. By this worldview the grand design of the world-system comes about, which can be established by a moral standard based on the methodological worldview. The establishment of the worldview and its grand design of the world-system embody the evaluation of the normatively reconstructed as against the prevalent states of knowledge, thought, and application. The totality of these defining elements comprising the methodology, theory, structure and function, altogether leading into application and inferences, makes up the phenomenological model.

The worldview and its constituent epistemological elements and functional ontological projections make up the entire study in this book. The book is divided into a first part on Theory and a second part on Applications. The emphasis in this book is on methodology. This takes up a cross section of approaches extending from the *Qur'an* and the authentic *sunnah* as the unfailing guidance of the Prophet Muhammad on the instructions of the *Qur'an*. The emergent pathway is towards the details of the socio-scientific generality and its specifics of issues, themes, and topics. The methodological approach is thus of an analytical nature. It embraces philosophy of science, mathematical orientation, and real-world issues and problems extending beyond the limits of economics, finance, science, and society, into the wider domain of their interdisciplinary embedding.

The starting point of the thesis is a quest for the knowledge, mind, and matter foundations of thought that initiate the phenomenological capability. Such is the challenge for the search and discovery of the foundation of holistic socio-scientific inquiry in the mould of interdisciplinary embedding.

Can the prevailing intellection in the variety of sciences render this possibility? The answer to that quest leads us to conclude that the inherited scholarship, and thereby its structure and function, cannot enable discovery of such holism. The quest then reaches out towards the functional nature of unity in and of everything (Barrow, 1991). This can only be found in that worldview which is unique and universal according to the technical understanding of these terms in accordance with the epistemology of unity of knowledge.

Such a cognizance of the generality and particulars of the multi-universal reality rests upon evolutionary learning processes that project reality from lesser to higher levels of understanding of the unified processes of being and becoming. But it also delineates the processes that differentiate between truth (primal and functional ontology of oneness) and falsehood (systemic conflict, individualism, and dualism). The *Qur'an* brings out these attributes of the ultimate reality of being and becoming in terms of its principles. These are, firstly, of multi-universal pairing (complementarities, participation, and thereby unity) between the good things of life as laid down by the purpose and objective of Islamic Law (*shari'ah*), known as *maqasid as-shari'ah*. Secondly, contrarily, the property of divisiveness is embodied in the character of methodological individualism, conflict, competition, and self-interest.

We begin our intellectual journey from and toward the *tawhidi* epistemic holism. In between this pathway there is the conscious cognizance of unity of knowledge and the unity of the morally constructed world-system.

Masudul Alam Choudhury

ACKNOWLEDGMENTS

This book is on the analytical deliberation of the central episteme of Islamic socio-scientific thought, *tawhid*, meaning the oneness of God and the unity of divine law at work in the unity of the generality and details of the world-system. *Tawhid* in this sense is the unique and universal message of the *Qur'an* to the entire world-system. This revolutionary worldview of Islamic socio-scientific thought, with its vista of advanced analytical inquiry derived from the *Qur'an*, the *sunnah*, the works of the great Islamic learned intellectuals, and contemporary comparative thought in the socio-scientific domain, started with the author now over twenty years ago. The focus here is on socio-scientific intellection encompassing economics, finance, science and society.

This *tawhidi* academic thought gained its first great momentum with the establishment of the Postgraduate Program in Islamic Economics and Finance (IEF) in Trisakti University, Jakarta, Indonesia in the year 2003. IEF undertakes advanced teaching and graduate and postgraduate research in the diverse areas underlining *tawhidi* epistemology and its applications in the contemporary world-system. In this institution today over one hundred students are currently pursuing their doctoral degree in various topics involving *tawhidi* epistemology and its applications. Select teachers knowledgeable in the *tawhidi* worldview are offering lectures to postgraduate students. The most advanced level of analytical intellection is used, including philosophy of science; mathematical, statistical and computer models; and various areas focusing on heterodox economics, finance, science, and society. Above all, the derivation of the methodology and methods of this heterodoxy is from the *Qur'an* and *sunnah,* combined with the thoughts of the Islamic learned masters and contemporary comparative thought. The focus is on the *tawhidi* foundation of this heterodoxy.

IEF was established by the meeting of minds and favourable circumstances offered by Trisakti University during the time of its inception. I owe this momentous event to my friend, the late Professor Sofyan Syafri Harahap of the Faculty of Economics, Trisakti University. The two of us were supported in Trisakti University by important persons like Professor Thoby Mutis, Rector of Trisakti University; Professor Yuswar Basri, Vice Rector of Trisakti University; and Dr. Tatik Mariyanti, Academic

Coordinator of IEF and Lecturer in Economics at the Faculty of Economics, Trisakti University. Their friendly academic support has increased over the years. Now IEF has its own establishment in the extension campus of Trisakti University with the Trisakti University Institute of Global Finance. IEF has by now produced ten PhD graduates, many Masters Graduates, and several more PhD graduations are continuing. These are the pioneers of the *tawhidi* epistemology and its applications to diverse areas of economics and finance in the field of comparative and heterodox socio-scientific thought.

My thanks are also due to the College of Economics and Political Science (CEPS) in Sultan Qaboos University (SQU) for approving my Summer Research Leaves to spend the time as Visiting Professor in various university departments overseas between 2010 and 2013. This opportunity enabled me to develop the reviewed book proposal and sample chapters that were approved by the notable academic publisher, Cambridge Scholars Publishing. My library work in Robarts Library of the University of Toronto and in the library of Saint Paul University, Ottawa, enabled me to draft some chapters of this momentous work.

I hope that this work, though of a deeply methodological, analytical, and applied nature in the field of *tawhidi* epistemology and its applications, will be a contribution to socio-scientific thought for *all* scholarship. By its very logical eminence, this book cannot and does not invoke parochial religious constrictions. Monotheism is a common belief of many religions.

I therefore render this book to scholarship among all good thinking people who pursue objectivity and reason for felicity to self and others. "Come my friends! It's not too late to seek a newer world."

Author

ABOUT THE AUTHOR

Masudul Alam Choudhury holds the Professorial Chair of Islamic Finance in the Institute of Islamic Banking and Finance, International Islamic University Malaysia. He is also the International Chair in the Postgraduate Program in Islamic Economics and Finance, Trisakti University, Jakarta, Indonesia. He earned his Masters and Doctorate Degrees in the field of political economy of human capital theory and economic growth at the University of Toronto. Earlier he was awarded the M.Phil. Degree in Mathematical Statistics, specializing in Econometrics, from Quaid-e-Azam University, Islamabad, Pakistan. He holds an earlier Bachelors of Science Honours Degree in Pure Mathematics from Dhaka University. Professor Choudhury took his retirement as Full Professor from Cape Bretn University, Nova Scotia, Canada, after twenty-two years of academi service.

Professor Masudul Alam Choudhury specializes, teaches, researches, and publishes in the field of epistemological problems of Islamic political economy and world-system, philosophy of science, and applications in diverse areas of economic theory. In these areas Professor Choudhury has published scholarly papers and books in reputed international outlets. His treatment is oriented to the study of *Qur'an* and *sunnah* along with comparative studies on the related topics. His contributions use the methodology and methods of philosophy of science, mathematics, economic theory, and applications. He is an original pioneer of Islamic economics in North America.

His selected publications are, *Socio-Cybernetic Study of God and the World-System* (IGI-Global, 2013), *Islamic Economics and Finance: an Epistemological Inquiry* (Emerald, 2011); *The Universal Paradigm and the Islamic World-System* (World Scientific Publications, 2007); *An Advanced Exposition in Islamic Economics and Finance* (Edwin Mellen Press, 2004); *The Islamic World-System, a Study in Polity-Market Interaction* (Routledge Curzon, 2004); *Explaining the Qur'an, a Socio-Scientific Inquiry*, 2 volumes (Edwin Mellen, 2003); *The Islamic Worldview, Socio-Scientific Perspectives* (Kegan Paul, 2000); *Comparative Economic Perspectives: Occidental and Islamic Perspectives* (Kluwer Academic, 1999); *Studies in Islamic Science and Polity* (Macmillan, 1998); *Reforming the Muslim World* (Kegan Paul, 1998); *Studies in*

Islamic Social Sciences (Macmillan, 1998); Money in Islam (Routledge, 1997); The Principles of *Islamic Political Economy, A Methodological Inquiry* (Macmillan & St. Martin's, 1992); *The Foundations of Islamic Political Economy* (Macmillan & St. Martin's, 1992); *Islamic Economic Co-operation* (Macmillan, 1990); *Contributions to Islamic Economic Theory, A Study in Social Economics* (Macmillan & St. Martin's, 1986); 5 volumes entitled *Science and Epistemology in the Qur'an* (with individual volume titles) (Edwin Mellen, 2006). Besides, Professor Choudhury has contributed many scholarly papers in international refereed journals. He is the editor of the specialized SCOPUS journal entitled, *Humanomics, International Journal of Systems and Ethics* (Emerald, now publishing volume 31).

INTRODUCTION

The epistemic use in evolutionary epistemology in this work is to unravel the conceptual, supported by the formal, followed by the empirical nature of real-world issues. Two steps are taken. These are followed by their continuity across systems spanning the dimensions of knowledge, space, and time.

The substantive matter to understand is the formalization of evolutionary epistemology in the light of *tawhid*, the monotheistic law in Islam. The imminent pursuit is then applied to specific topics and case studies in economics, finance, science, and society.

The total ontological experience of knowledge exists at two levels. Firstly, there is the premise of its universality. This acquires the nature of self-referencing in terms of stated laws of unity of knowledge. The derived Primordial Ontology explains various states of socio-scientific systems. Among these are the relationally cooperative and participatory (unity by participation and complementarities) ones on the one hand. Oppositely, there are the states of conflict and competition; differentiation of knowledge by the marginalism hypothesis.

The first ontological level is termed here as Primordial Ontology of the divine essence. Primordial Ontology therefore means existence of Being in the domain of the attributes of divine oneness. It is unravelled in the law of monotheism – not in the nature of oneness of God, though this remains the divine quiddity. According to the principle of *tawhid*, the existence of divine quiddity alone is not sufficient to understand the function of the monotheistic law in the scheme and order of things. The unravelling of the monotheistic law on the structure and function of the unified world-system as the Sign of God is essential for a complete phenomenological understanding of reality.

Secondly, *Primordial* Ontology is formalized into *Functional* Ontology by explaining and applying the *tawhidi* methodological worldview to specific problems taken from the general category of all evolutionary systems with different forms of learning behaviour. Among these are the relationally cooperative, participatory, and pervasively complementary ones. Oppositely, there are the competing, conflicting, and differentiating ones.

The principal problem that this book addresses is this: How is *Primordial* Ontology made to correspond with *Functional* Ontology to explain the working of *tawhid* in the experiential world-system? This is the same as saying: How is the monotheistic law argued to be universal and unique by way of its self-referencing, derived from precepts, and made operational by way of evolutionary epistemology of unity of knowledge? Here, mathematical formalism is used and the language is of philosophy of science.

Finally, real world transmission of the above unity between Primordial and Functional Ontology is explained by its continuity across systemic continuums spanning the dimensions of knowledge, space, and time. The continuity of the underlying analytic that integrates Primordial Ontology and Functional Ontology across systems and across the dimensions of knowledge, space, and time is referred to as the *tawhidi* phenomenological worldview.

The phenomenological model, to be developed in depth and emphasized in every chapter, is formally presented in the following way:

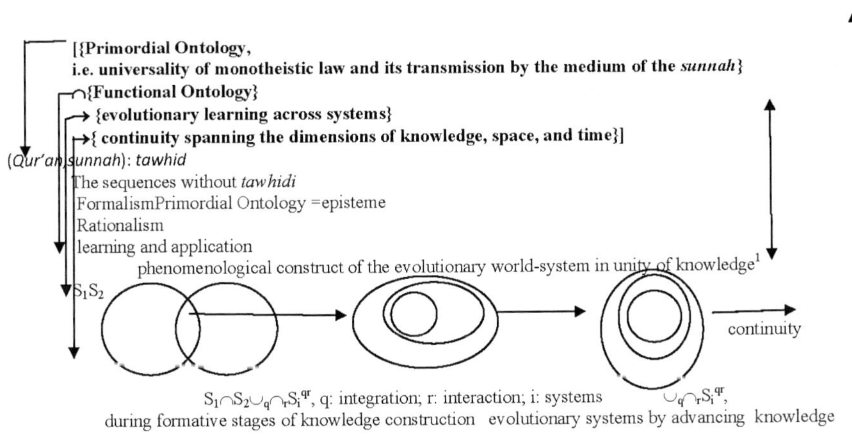

Figure I: A summary of *tawhidi* phenomenological model identifying Primordial and Functional Ontologies

Formalism

The phenomenological model will be formalized and repeated throughout this work as the groundwork of integrating Primordial Ontology and Functional Ontology. One of these without the other is a perspective of rationalism, not of the unified Mind-Matter worldview according to *tawhid*. In this Introduction, too, we give the early formalism of the *tawhidi* phenomenological worldview according to its epistemic framework.

Any event in the *tawhidi* super-space happens in the dimensions of knowledge ($\theta \in$Primordial Ontology), space ($\mathbf{x}$), and time (t as datum). Therefore, a vector (also matrix, tensor) of variables and their relations are denoted by, $\mathbf{x} = \mathbf{x}(\theta;t)$. A monotonic positive transformation of θ is a wellbeing function, say $W(\mathbf{x}(\theta;t))$. To prove such monotonic transformation we write,

$$d\mathbf{x}/d\theta \Rightarrow dW(\mathbf{x})/d\theta > 0$$

Take the wellbeing function in the following product form:

$W(\mathbf{x}) = \Pi A.x_i^{\alpha i}$, all the variables and parameters on the right-hand side are θ-induced.

$$\ln W(\mathbf{x}) = \Sigma_i \ln A + \Sigma_i \alpha_i.\ln x_i$$

By the monotonic positive transformation property between W and θ we obtain the following expression. Note the indicated signs of the terms,

$$dW/W = d\theta/\theta = \Sigma_i \alpha_i.(dx_i/x_i)^+ + \Sigma_i x_i.(d\alpha_i/d\theta)^+ + (dA/d\theta)^+$$

This expression can be written in terms of growth rates, $g(.) > 0$, as,

$dg(\theta)/d\theta = \Sigma_i(\alpha_i.dg_i/d\theta)^+ + \Sigma_i(dx_i/d\theta)^+.(d\alpha_i/d\theta)^\pm + x_i.(d^2\alpha_i/d\theta^2)^\pm + (d^2A/d\theta^2)^\pm$as being positive or negative.

This is the case of the early stages of explaining *tawhidi* evolutionary learning processes. Such stages are represented in Figure I.

In the special case of advanced *tawhidi* evolutionary learning it is possible that,

$$dg(\theta)/d\theta = \Sigma_i(\alpha_i.dg_i/d\theta)^+ + \Sigma_i(dx_i/d\theta)^+.(d\alpha_i/d\theta)^+ + x_i.(d^2\alpha_i/d\theta^2)^+ + (d^2A/d\theta^2)^+ > 0. \quad (I.2)$$

This case is shown in expression (1) by evolutionary symmetrical spheres of n-dimensions, n increasing but remaining finite in order to convey the socio-scientific commensurate meaning of events happening in the continuity of knowledge, space, and time.

Summary

In understanding this book in respect of *tawhidi* epistemology and its applications to the universal ‘everything’, the most important characterizations to follow are, firstly, the organic relational meaning of unity of knowledge and the world system interpreted in knowledge, space, and time in the light of the law of monotheism. Secondly, the application of *tawhidi* epistemology is studied in respect of its methodology in evaluating and constructing the world-system in terms of unity of knowledge. This characterization is represented by pervasive complementarities or relational participation. This phenomenon is explained by the pairing of the variables and entities in the generality and specific issues and problems studied. The method that reveals this perspective of unity of knowledge is presented as circular causation. This method is derived from the purpose and objective of the *shari'ah*, known as *maqasid as-shari'ah* in reference to the *tawhidi* methodological worldview. The *tawhidi* epistemological foundation comprises the *Qur'an*, the Prophetic guidance (*sunnah*), and critical examination of the historical contributions of the learned Islamic scholars. These points are elaborated in this work by way of conceptualization and application using rigorous scientific approaches.

PART I:

THEORY AND CONCEPTS: EPISTEMOLOGICAL CONTENT

CHAPTER ONE

METHODOLOGICAL INTRODUCTION: *TAWHID* AND THE WORLD-SYSTEM

Objective

The objective of this chapter is to undertake a substantive definition and explanation of various concepts that characterize the idea of consciousness according to *tawhid* and the resulting formalism of the *tawhidi* phenomenological model. *Tawhid* means the episteme of oneness of God, and its explanation in terms of the divine law of monotheism that translates its unification role into diverse world-systems and into the relations between them. Various concepts and terms linked to the comprehensive meaning of *tawhid* and their explanations are presented in this chapter, though in rudimentary form. They will be substantively developed in the chapters that follow. The totality of the interrelationships between these concepts, and their dynamic intra-systems and inter-systems across evolutionary learning processes, set up the domain upon which a formalism will be undertaken, applications carried out, and analyses done. In light of the entirety of the *tawhidi* phenomenological model with its internal socio-scientific properties, this research manuscript will develop the substantive socio-scientific accomplishment in the concept of wellbeing and its understanding as a revolutionary worldview.[1]

In this manuscript a comparative study of the precept of *tawhid* and its world-system will be undertaken in comparative and contrasting perspectives. The *tawhidi* worldview will be revealed in the subsequent chapters as a socio-scientific revolution in thought and application aimed at a moral reconstruction of an unethical world-system. In the understanding

[1] We will understand by the concept of worldview *verbatim* the following, given by Smart (2000, p. 2): "The study of religion and ideologies can be called 'worldview analysis'. In this we try to depict the history and nature of the symbols and beliefs that have helped form the structure of human consciousness and society. This is the heart of the modern study of religion. As a phrase, 'worldview analysis' conveys a sense of attempted objectivity, and indeed it is for that reason a relatively modern phenomenon."

and delineation of the extended world-system by its intellection, formalism, and applications, the emergent revolutionary socio-scientific worldview of *tawhid* is substantively different from much of received socio-scientific worldview and the prevalent approach to understanding the socio-scientific worldview in the absence of the epistemological methodology. Finally, this chapter concludes with a summary of the goals of all the chapters to be included in this book.

The tenor of the whole book is a combination of textual presentation with analytical and mathematical tracts. Socio-scientific theory and concepts, diagrams, and quantitative empirical analyses are offered. Both conceptual intellection and quantitative empirical work are employed for specific issues. Policy analysis in the framework of *tawhidi* epistemology and its formalism in terms of the *tawhidi* phenomenological model are studied by the method of circular causation. This is carried out by specific country and institutional case studies.

Qur'anic exegesis leading to the extended meaning of *tawhid*: Oneness of God in relation to its epistemological construction of knowledge and the knowledge-induced world-system

Tawhid and the monotheistic law

Tawhid summarily means oneness of God. But simply by this ontological metaphysic it is not possible to understand the role that God plays in the created order. The created socio-scientific order comprises wholly the human intellection process in 'everything'. A particularity of this domain is the world-system that is constructed out of the organization of the extant thought and application. Thus the substantive meaning of *tawhid* comprehends not only the primordial existence, absoluteness, and non-partnership attribute of God in creation, but with God remaining the uncreated being. Besides these attributes, God and the world-system, what is termed as the created domain of 'everything' (Barrow, 1991) is the centrepiece of a substantive study of *tawhid* in reference to the monotheistic law. This is to assert that God does not descend on earth or in anything as a corporeal agent of being and change. Only the attributes of God are transmitted by the monotheistic law into the construction of the fullest extent of 'everything' in the light of *tawhid*. This creatorship is now understood both as having the attribute of God as the One (non-partnership in creation), and in terms of God's monotheistic law transmitted in everything as the attribute of oneness.

The monotheistic law establishes the non-partnership of God's command in creation as the Absolute Being, the sole Creator. Such a principle that remains without partnership and is extensively ingrained in the generality and details of things and intellection regarding the world-system must universally and uniquely be the monotheistic law of the oneness of God. Yet, God assumes no corporeal manifestation – neither by cognition nor in shape or form – in the design of relationships of the monotheistic law with the details and generality of the created world-system. Besides, the action of God on creation in respect of His absoluteness and non-partnership is instantaneous by command, God's will. Thereby, God creates out of nothing, except by His command of absolute knowledge. Such a law, though, when tried for comprehension of the human and physical worlds, demands recognition of simultaneity between the law and comprehension of the being of existence. Thus God creates by His command; and this simultaneously brings about intellect and form. The *tawhidi* induced world-system is established instantaneously with the divine command.

The perfection of knowledge in God as Creator and Sustainer and the continued incompleteness of knowledge in human and physical schemes, establishes the humble acceptance of human imperfection in knowledge. This is true both of knowledge and its induced effects in creation. The result then is an evolutionary learning process towards gaining knowledge. Consequently, there arises an evolutionary world-system of being, in relation to the incompleteness of knowledge, as knowledge gets manifested in the evolutionary learning process-oriented universe.

Regretfully, such an epistemological perspective of the *tawhid*-centred socio-scientific universe has been abandoned in contemporary times. Nonetheless, that was the centrepiece of knowledge and understanding of creation in the thought of the great scholastic Islamic thinkers. On this theme, Buchman (1998, p. xviii) writes regarding Imam Ghazzali's masterpiece, *Niche of Lights*: "While the book could stand by itself with little or no introduction, it may be helpful to elucidate the general '*tawhid*-centred' worldview of twelfth-century Islam. People today – Muslims and non-Muslims alike – usually hold drastically different assumptions on the nature of existence than those held by al-Ghazzali and most of his contemporaries." The revival and fresh quest for the *tawhid*-centred epistemological intellection, and its application to the generality and particulars of the world-system in detail, continues on for rediscovery. Such a search and rediscovery in substantive analytical content is the theme of this book.

The *qur'anic* world-system in the light of *tawhid*

The world-system of the *Qur'an* comprises manifest and hidden pairs – that is, complementary relational universes of generality and particulars – of 'everything'. Such complementary pairing in everything is an organic relational fact. It exists for both the truth realm and the falsehood realm, but in disjoint realities. These two realms, according to the *Qur'an,* manifest their realities by different forms of dynamics. Such dynamics describe the inner and evolutionary constructs of the respective world-systems in both truth and falsehood, respectively.

The world-system spanned by the monotheistic law becomes the realm of the Signs of God in everything. The direct relationship between the primordial prevalence of the monotheistic law of oneness as mentioned above, and the realm of truth and falsehood reveals creation of everything in its respective mould of oneness. Through reflection on the Signs of God that are manifest in terms of the good things of life, the evident conclusion is to see the truth of oneness that alludes to the transcendent law of oneness.

But the primacy of the monotheistic law is equally true in the domain of falsehood. What is the explanation for this latter case? The manifestation of oneness, as the organic process in the action of becoming, plays itself in the falsehood domain by the unique property of this realm to abide in rationalism. There follow the manifestations of methodological individualism, methodological independence of relations, by conflict and rivalry, also referred to as competition. The falsehood realm can thereby be described as the integrated evolutionary process of such attributes that create ethical and social differentiation in the human world and in the non-human world. This is likewise true of differentiated thought, action and organization. It is true also in intellectual abstraction of reality and its material configuration. Thereby, the entire world-system is comprehended by such attributes of falsehood. In consequence we have the two disparate knowledge-induced and de-knowledge-induced world-systems.

The *Qur'an* rejects the attributes of the latter in the truth realm. Goodness is therefore defined by the paired organic relationship of unity of being and becoming. That is, reasoning and materiality of human existence abides permanently either in truth or in falsehood as distinct forms of reality. Falsehood is defined by the pairing of organic relationship between entities that cause their subsequent dissociation by rivalry, conflict, and illogicalness. Such consequences exist in reasoning, thought, institutions and application. Such opposing kinds of world-systems between truth and falsehood perpetuate in the history of the world-system and its details.

Relational epistemology and the world-system according to *qur'anic* exegesis

In the end, we derive the relational epistemology of the evolutionary learning universe of unification in knowledge, intellection, and construction. This is to comprehend and apply the epistemological worldview of unity of knowledge that arises uniquely from the monotheistic law. It equally explains the dynamics of truth and falsehood by the same principle of oneness of relationship. But truth and falsehood remain opposing realities in such an epistemological explanation. God's creation is thereby the continuum of the Signs of God in the order of everything. This comprises truth and falsehood. The *world-system* as manifestation, intellection, and creative potentiality of the Signs of God is referred to in the *Qur'an* as *alameen*. The *Qur'an* (1:2) declares in this regard: "Praise be to God, the Cherisher and Sustainer of the Worlds (*alameen*)". In the same chapter the *Qur'an* (1:7) declares: "The way of those on whom You have bestowed Your Grace, those whose (portion) is not wrath, and who do not go astray." Combining these two verses yields the possible exegesis that *alameen* is the completion of the opposite realities mentioned here.

Besides, the generality of these verses (*ayat*) is all-inclusive of intellection and materiality. On this fact in the same chapter the *Qur'an* (1:5) declares: "You do we worship, and your aid we seek". This explains *tawhid* as knowledge and the representation of the knowledge-induced world-system, all according to the epistemology of unity of knowledge. Furthermore, there is the invocation to God to establish the truthful path of both intellection and the world-system: "Show us the straight path" (*Qur'an*, 1:6).

Altogether, we understand the attribute of divine praise to be the endless recognition and bestowing of thanks, and awesome assertion of the richness of knowledge and its constructive power in the world-system by means of perfectly separating truth from falsehood in everything. It is this beatific recognition of the world-system separately in truth and falsehood, and conscious separation between these two realities, that entirely defines *tawhid* in terms of the monotheistic law of divine oneness. By comprehending truth and falsehood as the possibilities of the total reality, the precept of *tawhid* explains everything as Signs of God (*ayat Allah*).

The comprehensive meaning of God is as Creator and Sustainer, who is devoid of partnership in creation. He creates all by Himself without material limitations and in the full command of His Will. This divine attribute is laid out in Chapter 112.[2] This chapter establishes the primordial attributes of God as Creator. The primordial and functional attributes of God through the monotheistic law are brought out in the *Qur'an* (2:255).[3] The attributes laid down in this verse (called *ayat al-kursi*, the verse of the Throne) has a distinctive relationship between the ontological *tawhidi* primacy and the monotheistic law in action.

Ayat al-kursi points out the corporeal actions of God in terms of worldly attributes. Such attributes are called *sifat* in *qur'anic* exegesis. They form an inseparable part of the comprehensive meaning of Islamic monotheism. *Tawhid* conveys the meaning of oneness of God in terms of the primordial attributes of God, and its worldly functional manifestations through the monotheistic law. But since God in every way is non-created, non-corporeal, non-cognitive, and non-formal in His primal ontological Being, the *ayat al-kursi* as a result cannot convey any worldly attributes from the primordial attributes of God, the One and Only. Hence the *sifat* pointed out in *ayat al-kursi* can only be interpreted as the attributes of the monotheistic law that are ordained by God's singular will of command and action through the monotheistic law into the world-system. The active consequences bring about wellbeing in everything.

In the chronological order of revelation of the *Qur'an* to the Prophet Muhammad, the chapter named Purity (*Ikhlas)* as a Makkan revelation preceded the chapter named The Heifer (*Baqarah*) in which appears the *ayat al-kursi* verse. This sequence of revelation establishes the process of primordial order from understanding *tawhid* as declaration of belief (*shahadah*) in the heart to declaring the manifestation of *tawhid* as *sifat*, which is then followed by its functioning in the world-system. Thereby, *tawhid* is reflected as the monotheistic law of action in the world-system.

However, after the completion of the revelation of the *Qur'an*, the message was declared ever after as universal in the dimensions of

---

[2] *Qur'an* (112:1-4), *Ikhlas*, Purity (of Faith): "Say: He is God, the One and Only; God, the Eternal, Absolute; He begets not, nor is He begotten; and there is none like unto Him."

[3] *Qur'an* (2:255): "God! There is no god but He, – the Living, the Self-subsisting, Eternal. No slumber can seize Him nor sleep. His are all things in the heavens and on earth. Who is there can intercede in His presence except as He permits? He knows what (appears to His creatures as) Before or After or Behind them. Nor shall they compass aught of His knowledge, except as He wills. His Throne does extend over the heavens and the earth, and He feels no fatigue in guarding and preserving them for He is the Most High, the Supreme (in glory)."

knowledge, space, and time.[4] Hence, no distinction in the continuity of meaning, except for historical narrative of revelation, must be upheld between the Makkan and Madinan revelations in the context of *qur'anic* universality. There is no need now to keep the sequential ordering of Makkah to Madinah revelations for the construction of the *tawhidi* worldview. Discourse, exegesis, and understanding of *qur'anic* knowledge can be recursive between Makkah and Madinah, as long as the sole primacy and goal of convergence for all purpose is from and toward *tawhid*. Thus we have a circularity of organic unification within the *tawhidi* worldview between its primal precept and the induced world-system. This organic unification results in knowledge formation directed towards human wellbeing as its objective criterion. Wellbeing is the objective and measurable criterion conveying goodness (*maslaha*) and establishing truth as distinct from falsehood (*furqan*).

The extended exegesis carried out here is in conformity with the Islamic discursive methodology. This point is found in Shah Waliullah (trans. Jalbani, 1985), who was a traditionalist in *qur'anic* exegesis. But he nonetheless explained the methodology of *qur'anic* exegesis in the following words: "... if you want to see a sample in the Muslim community then look at the vile scholars (*ulama' sui*). ... They have developed the habit of blind imitation of their predecessors and have turned away from the plain text of the *Qur'an* and the *Tradition*. They have taken the result of unwarranted thinking, improper rigidity, and baseless inferences of the theologians as an authority and have callously neglected the teaching of the sinless law-giver."

In more recent times, Rippin (2006) wrote on the views of modernists like Fazlur Rahman (1980. See Rippin p. 279 in (ed.) McAuliffe, 2006): "[Fazlur Rahman] argues that contemporary Muslim scholarship on the *Qur'an* faces two main problems: the lack of a genuine feel for the relevance of the *Qur'an* today, which prevents presentations in terms adequate to the needs of contemporary society, and a fear that such a presentation might deviate on some points from traditionally received opinions."

Thus there is need to awaken fresh scholarship that agrees between the traditional understanding and the emergence of the *qur'anic* exegesis on modern themes. However, the revolutionary breakthrough of such *qur'anic*

---

4 The last verse revealed in the *Qur'an* (5:3) marking the completion of Islam in the light of *tawhid* is, "This day have those who reject Faith given up all hope of your religion. Yet fear them not but fear Me. This day have I perfected your religion for you, completed my favor upon you, and have chosen for you Islam as your religion".

scholarship can be found by basing the *tawhidi* epistemology as the premise of discourse. This is because *tawhid* is unequivocally the keynote element of the *Qur'an* in connection with its ontological and worldly conception.

The emergent *tawhidi* phenomenological model would then prove to be a revolutionary breakthrough in the realm of socio-scientific thought. The emergence of the *tawhidi* phenomenological model with its universal worldview will indeed be non-cumulative in nature (Kuhn, 1970). Such a new exegetic emergence will prove to be the scientific basis on one hand for the occidental philosophy of science, and on the other hand, will serve to patch up the Muslim divide between the traditionalists and modernists. The new epistemological socio-scientific inquiry provides an approach that establishes unified rapprochement between the Muslim fissures (Choudhury, 2006). This is also how the Muslim epistemologists (school of *kalam*) and their scholastic thought on various issues of science and society will converge with those of the Muslim rationalists (*mutakallimun*).

The present work is in this realm of new exegetic thought invoking *tawhid* for the reconstruction of socio-scientific thought on the epistemological basis of unity of knowledge. Here is where *tawhid* enters lock, stock and barrel, occupying the centrepiece in the revolutionary global socio-scientific scene.

***Qur'anic* universality of the *tawhidi* worldview in the dimensions of knowledge, space, and time: towards the understanding of a *tawhidi* phenomenological model**

Therefore, the precept of continuity of the monotheistic law is ascertained over the continua of knowledge, space, and time. These three realms form the complete dimensions of *alameen* (the *qur'anic* complete world-system). Events, which are Signs of God (*ayat Allah*), take place in the domain of these combined dimensions. The combination of the epistemology of *tawhid* with its knowledge endowment to the heart, mind, and matter universes; and finally, to the construction of the *tawhidi* world-system, constructs God's creation. Creation comprises multiverses that are spanned by the Signs of God existing in pervasive unity of knowledge. Such is *alameen*, the *qur'anic* world-system. It forms the conscious universe and its extant intellection.

This is the idea of consciousness in the scheme and order of everything. Consciousness takes place in the framework of *tawhid*, now understood as the oneness of God unravelling itself through the dynamics and function of the monotheistic law in the unity of all things. The realm of all things comprehends intellection and reasoning, and the construction of the moral socio-scientific order by raising it from a fallen state of darkness, and ushering it into light.

The *tawhidi* derived meaning of the purpose and objective of the *shari'ah: maqasid as-shari'ah*

A good part of this book will deal with the methodological development of what is referred to as the purpose and objective of the Islamic law (*shari'ah*) as derived from the *Qur'an* and the *sunnah*. The domain of *shari'ah* is extended beyond personal and public affairs into the affairs of everything. In this extensive way of understanding the *shari'ah,* there is the distinctive place of the entire socio-scientific order in terms of the total intellection relating to it. However, such is not the way in which Muslims usually understand the meaning of the purpose and objective of the *shari'ah*, termed the *maqasid as-shari'ah*. On this matter, it is indeed surprising to find that Ramadan (2004, p. 47-51) did not refer to such an original context of extension of the *maqasid as-shari'ah*. Ramadan did not mention the great theme of *maqasid as-shari'ah* in his book that is published by a leading Islamic academic centre, the Islamic Foundation in Leicester, UK. Likewise, Guessoum (2009) failed to go deep beyond just a mention of the *tawhidi* project into a fresh scientific epistemological inquiry. Guessoum, in his historical narrative, rather than a methodological work (p. 110), simply writes: "In its scientific version, this philosophy is to put in the framework of *tawheed* (unity/unicity/unification), which in that optic proclaims not just that God is one but also that all existence and all history (of nature and of humanity) stems from that unicity or unity".

This book not only continues on the first ever fundamental project of *tawhid* and the unified world-system opened up, established, and formalized by this author, yet not mentioned by Guessoum; it also forms a significantly further development of that revolutionary scientific worldview of the *Qur'an* and the *sunnah*. This book elevates that *tawhidi* scientific inquiry in respect of the generality and particulars of the world-system to significantly great heights. It brings this methodological worldview to the service of the entire scientific community of now and the future, for discourse, criticism, and the advancement of new vistas of thought.

Yet it is only by the extensive understanding of this purpose and objective of the *shari'ah* that the central parts of the *Qur'an* and the *sunnah* can be understood. Indeed, the very first element of *maqasid as-*

shari'ah is on upholding the Islamic religion; that is, the episteme of the *tawhidi* worldview over all things. *Tawhid* brings out the holistic nature of creation in organic unity with diversity. This encompasses the *tawhidi* worldview. Only through such a vast comprehension of the *shari'ah* is it possible to have interaction between the great meanings of the divine law (*sunnat Allah*), the *sunnah* of the Prophet (*sunnat al-Rasul*), and the affairs of the world-system (*alameen*).[5] The end result reaches between abstraction and unravelling.

In fact, the authenticity of any Prophetic sayings (*ahadith*), which indeed were codified nearly two hundred years after the Prophet, must be checked in reference to the *Qur'an*.[6] This means that the *ahadith* cannot be reduced except to the principal themes of the *Qur'an*. Of these is the principle theme of the divine law,[7] which extends across the world-system in its abstraction and unravelling.

The second most important implication of the generalization of the *maqasid as-shari'ah* in the intellection that overarches everything between abstraction and unravelling, is its relevance for the general system of study of the world-system, both in its generality and particulars. Indeed, the *tawhidi* worldview, by its grand design of unity of knowledge and the unity of the knowledge-induced world-system, is a vastly unified cybernetic holism left for gradual understanding by the phenomenological combination of the heart, mind, and matter (Choudhury, 2013). Those scholars writing in the field of a critical examination of the *shari'ah* have pointed out the partial equilibrium and partial-system orientation of the existing Muslim understanding of the *shari'ah* as a partial worldview (Weeramantry, 2001; Hassan, 2002; Coulson, 1984). Indeed, the *shari'ah* fell into such dysfunctional problems by the intrusion of the traditional interpretive (*fiqh*) approach made by the traditionalists in denial of the whole intellection process. The result was a heavily personified development of administrative impositions often based on opinion rather than the natural law of justice and balance (*mizan*) as in the *Qur'an* (Kung, trans. Bowden, 2007, pp. 208-212).

---

[5] *Qur'anic* knowledge as the praises of God the One and Creator is summed up in the verse (1:2): Praise be to God, the Cherisher and Sustainer of the Worlds (*alameen*).

[6] *Qur'an* (53:2-5): "Your companion (Muhammad) has neither gone astray nor has erred. Nor does he speak of (his own) desire. It is only a Revelation revealed. He has been taught (this *Qur'an*) by one mighty in power (Gabriel)."

[7] *Qur'an* (48:23): "(Such has been) the practice (approved) by God already in the past: no change will you find in the practice (approved) of God."

Such is a sign of decadence of reasoning in the realm of Islamic intellection. There was thus no strong development in the direction of positive and normative law as we find in the history of thought (Schumpeter, 1968). Consequently, there was no development of fresh conceptions and applications from the general-system foundations of the *shari'ah*. The departure of the *shari'ah* from the overarching theory of the law underlying the *shari'ah* was an untenable development. For if, in the systemic sense, the social world is interrelated keenly by complementarities with the other cosmological world of wholeness, the legal theory of the *shari'ah* must address both of these areas of intellection in a holistic way. Such formalism would be nearer to the *maqasid as-shari'ah*.

The *maqasid as shari'ah* thus rests on the socio-scientific arrangements of belief and action relating to the following precepts: upholding *tawhid* (religion); protection of reason; intertemporal protection of the family; guarantee of the basic needs of life; and protection of property rights. In the sense of sustainability caused by evolutionary learning processes spanning paired systems, the *maqasid as-shari'ah* establishes its socio-scientific effects of balance (*mizan*) intertemporally.

Contrary to *maqasid as-shari'ah*, the Muslim world has today taken to the catchphrase of '*shari'ah*-compliance' as a sheer product-development legitimating of financial instruments in the eyes of certain Islamic learned scholars (*ulemas*) and modernists. They belong to opposite extremes of the Islamic schools interested primarily in the commercialization of the *shari'ah* and not in its intellection. One can refer to Meera (2006), Mufeedh Choudhury (2009), and Usmani (2004) to understand the critical evaluation of the present-day restricted *fiqh* approach to the *shari'ah*.

Muslim intellection in the emergent discipline of Islamic finance following the demise of Islamic economics, as it is understood by the traditionalists and modernists, has resulted merely in imitated modelling of mainstream arguments. The epistemological values of the emergent discipline to discover its operational values in the economic, financial, and socio-scientific disciplines have totally failed. The universal resilient worldview of Islam, far from being raised and discovered as a scientific revolution, has now devolved in the hands of novices, causing sheer disciplinary imitation (Choudhury, 2011a).

We will inquire into these problems in the light of the tawhidi phenomenological worldview of its epistemological unity of knowledge and unity of the knowledge-induced world-system. But in this sense, the tawhidi worldview and its phenomenological methodology is a calling for all mankind. Religious exclusivity is annulled.[8]

Tawhidi consciousness leading to the concept of a *tawhidi* phenomenological model

We can now derive the meaning of consciousness in respect of the *tawhidi* worldview. Consciousness is knowledge of the complete reality caused by the circular evolutionary interrelationship between the following three premises in terms of unity of knowledge: First, belief commences from the human heart. Secondly, the heart then meets the sensation of the mind. This comprises the initiation of reasoning. Thirdly, the world is opened up to the cognitive capability. By this circular organic linkage, the world-system reverts to its connection with the *a priori* position of the heart once again. Upon this integration follows the re-combining of the *a priori* with the *a posteriori* states of reasoning through the medium of the mind. The world-system is once again integrated with the *a posteriori* station of knowledge-induction and reconstruction by the epistemology of unity of knowledge. The emergent problems of this circular interconnection span both the generality and particular issues of the world-system. Any socio-scientific event is the result of sensibility occurring in these three stations of consciousness.

We equate the heart with primal knowledge in respect to belief (*shahadah*) in the *tawhidi* epistemological worldview. The mind is the premise of derived knowledge from the primal *tawhidi* epistemology. Derived knowledge enables the realization of the unified world-system. Matter, as the world-system, is configured in the dimensions of space and time. Thereby, according to the *tawhidi* worldview, consciousness in everything circularly combines with the dynamics of evolutionary and creative reproduction of knowledge and the associated world-system through the circular interconnection of events that occur and evolve in the dimensions of knowledge, space, and time.

The same meaning remains valid in the circular relationship of reproduction of de-knowledge (falsehood) by interrelating belief in the law that is opposed to the monotheistic law. From the negation of the monotheistic law (rationalism) comes about the derived de-knowledge in rationalistic intellection. Thereby comes about the construction and

---

[8] The *Qur'an* (96:1-5), on this universality of its message (*tawhid* and knowledge) to all the worlds, declares the following first four verses of revelation: "Proclaim! (or read)! In the name of your Lord and Cherisher, who created – created man, out of a (mere) clot of congealed blood: Proclaim! And thy Lord is most bountiful, -- He Who taught (the use of) the Pen, -- Taught man that which he knew not."

continuity of the rationalist world-system, which now is interpreted as the divided or conjectured world-system (Campbell, 1988). Such a rationalist world-system, by being opposed to the law of oneness in everything, acquires the attributes of methodological individualism, independence, conflict and rivalry. Such dichotomies by conflict, competition and mutual independence, altogether cause continuous demarcation and divisions between intellection, events, and the generated artefacts of cognition and observation. Such differentiating attributes remain pervasive in a rationalist world-system (Buchanan, 1999).

Now, between the epistemologies of unity of monotheistic knowledge and of differentiation in de-knowledge, the *tawhidi* phenomenology can be understood as the recognition of the totality of the experience of perceiving a phenomenon under investigation in every detail of the world-system. We refer to the emergent unified totality of the *tawhidi* worldview as the episteme.[9]

The total *tawhidi* reality starts from the derivation of worldly knowledge of unity from the primal source invoking *tawhid* (*Qur'an* and *sunnah*). This stage is followed by simulation of the positive state of knowledge by the epistemology of *tawhidi* unity of knowledge in the construction of a certain stage of the unified world-system taken up in its generality and particulars. Finally, the continued relationship between *tawhid* as ontology, together with the monotheistic law and knowledge and the world-system, is sustained by degrees of inter-causal recursion between its primal attributes and the manifest elements, and the abstractions along the evolution of experience in unity of knowledge and its induction of the unifying world-system and issues under study. However, *tawhid, Qur'an*, and *sunnah* are not recreated in such recursive relations. It is just the progressive knowledge of these sources that is revived and recalled for fresh invocation on re-emergent evolutionary learning in unity of knowledge, and its induction of the issues and problems of the inquired world-system.

---

[9] Episteme is defined by Foucault (trans. Sheridan, 1972, p. 191) in the following words; we accept this definition as our understanding of the totality of functional relationship between knowledge, cognition and world-system: "By *episteme* we mean ... the total set of relations that unite, at a given period, the discursive practices that give rise to epistemological figures, sciences, and possibly formalized systems ... The episteme is not a form of knowledge (*connaissance*) or type of rationality which, crossing the boundaries of the most varied sciences, manifests the sovereign unity of a subject, a spirit, or a period; it is the totality of relations that can be discovered, for a given period, between the sciences when one analyses them at the level of discursive regularities."

According to the relational epistemology of the evolutionary learning universe, *tawhidi* consciousness is a divine attribute induced in this realm by way of both of the following experiences: *tawhid* as the monotheistic law is embedded in the essence of things, and intellection of mind caused by the interconnected heart, mind, and matter circularity, as explained earlier. Such a holistic experience of the world-system in its generality and particularity is referred to in the *Qur'an* as *tasbih*.[10] Indeed, it is because of this common existence of consciousness in heart, mind, and matter that the interrelationship between them enables our knowledge of the world-system to be recycled as positive and normative phenomena. The result then is a conceptual explanation and quantitative policy-theoretic application of the precepts in real experience.

An example here is of combining the *tawhidi* dynamics of unity of knowledge with the *functional* ontological (Gruber, 1993) formalism of market process with a well-defined wellbeing objective criterion. In this book, we will define the market process as a grand ecology, presenting in it the exchange mechanism of dynamic preferences on choices that determine specific things of exchange. Thus a general-system with evolutionary learning equilibrium dynamics is invoked to explain the evolutionary dynamics of the grand ecology of markets. Such dynamics are induced by knowledge-flows that are derived from the epistemological premise of *tawhid*.

The wellbeing function is in turn defined by the complex integration of dynamic preferences, the determination of knowledge-induced goods and services (e.g. environmentally friendly goods, consumption and production in moderation), prices, incomes, technology and other relevant variables. The learning complementarities between these diverse things in the grand ecological wellbeing criterion of the market process form a generalized systemic perspective. Thereafter, specific deconstructions are made for specific multi-market cases. Yet the same kind of dynamics of evolutionary learning system is applied to the particular cases of integrated multi-markets in the good things of life (*fadl al-azim/hayat at-tayyibah*).[11]

---

[10] *Qur'an* (59:24): "He is Allah, the Creator, the Inventor of all things, the Bestower of forms. To Him belong the Best Names. All that is in the heavens and the earth glorify Him. And He is the All-Mighty, the All-Wise."

[11] The following *qur'anic* verse (8:29) combines knowledge with blessings in the wellbeing criterion of truth against falsehood as a general precept that can be applied now to the principle of market process as a great ecology to render the good things of life: "O you who believe! If you obey and fear Allah, He will grant you *Furqan* (a criterion to judge between right and wrong), will expiate for you your sins, and will forgive you; and *Allah* is the Owner of the Great Bounty."

The generalized market system with its particulars found in deconstructed multi-markets, all being induced by knowledge derived from the epistemology of *tawhid*, has internal (intra-systemic) and external (inter-systemic) dynamics pertaining to evolutionary equilibriums. This is a technical area to study and analyse for a deeper study of the nature of the *tawhidi* evolutionary learning worldview in world-system issues. In it are embedded the natural and social system properties that govern the emergent *tawhidi* phenomenological model (Choudhury, 2011b, 2006a).

The *tawhidi* phenomenological model

Firstly, one must note the substantive properties of such a model. What are the attributes that characterize the *tawhidi* phenomenological model? The *tawhidi* worldview is comprehensively based on the Prophet Muhammad's experience between Makkah and Madinah. This experience is ever after followed by the seamless *tawhidi* integration in universalizing the emergence of the *tawhidi* worldview in everything. The phenomenological model thus commences its structure and function from the primal epistemology of *tawhid* in knowledge derivation. We will explain in this book that the comprehensive meaning of *tawhid* encompasses first its primal ontological premise. This premise then yields the worldly knowledge-flows as a functional criterion of unity of knowledge. The primal epistemological premise of *tawhid* in its attribute as the monotheistic law will be substantively established and explained in this book in reference to the primal epistemological sources, the *Qur'an* and the *sunnah*.

At this point we simply understand that, to be *functional* ontology, the *tawhidi* ontological premise must be capable of firstly moulding the monotheistic law into derived worldly unity of knowledge. This functional transformation holds the *tawhidi* premise to be a mathematical super-topology. The super-topological concept is well-defined in the meaning of super-cardinality of the super-topological mathematical entity. Its elements need not have dimensions, forms and commensurateness (Rucker, 1982a). This epistemological stage yields the meaning of the absolute and pure essence of God, as according to the *Qur'an* chapter *Ikhlas* (Purity). This was mentioned earlier and in a footnote.

Secondly, the medium of the Prophetic guidance (*sunnah*) and the exegetic discourse of the learned, and the extended participation of the community, together form the functional ontological premise of knowledge derivation arising from the primal epistemology. Such a discursive stage relating to the *qur'anic* verses (*ayat*) and the *sunnah* forms the *qur'anic* exegesis. The experience of discourse is continuously carried out by the Islamic institution of consultation (*shura*) on the basis of deriving meaning by using consciousness (*tasbih*), and understanding all of these out of the primal sources of the *Qur'an* and the *sunnah*.

As in the case of a restricted meaning of the *shari'ah* by the *fiqh* tradition, so too has the greater meaning of the *shura* (consultation) remained confined by both traditional and modern Muslims. Surprisingly, even on this matter of the *shura* in the light of its great extant of possibility in the entire cosmic meaning, the prolific author Tariq Ramadan (2004, pp. 81-97) has remained silent on the relationship that *tasbih* bears to the *shura* as a learning process through the project of learned discourse based on the foundational epistemology of the *Qur'an* and the *sunnah*. This intellectual experience is known as *ijtihad*. It emerges from the *shura* as a learning medium in combination with *tasbih*. It is not necessarily traditional *fiqh*. We will refer to the evolutionary learning combination of *shura* with *tasbih* in discovering meaning of intellection (*ijtihad*) arising from the *Qur'an* and the *sunnah* as *tasbih-shura*.

Yet revelation made the Prophet resort to the most subtle imagery of thought. The *qur'anic* verse (32:17) supports the *hadith al-qudsi* in *Sahih Bukhari*: "Abu Huraira reported *Allah's* Apostle saying: Allah has prepared for His pious servants that (Heaven) which no eye has ever seen, and no ear has ever heard, and no human heart has ever perceived; but it is testified by the Book of *Allah*. He then recited: 'No soul knows what comfort has been concealed from them, as a reward for their (good) Deeds.'" (*Qur'an*, 32:17).

The ambivalence of some Muslims to reflect on the greater scope of the *shari'ah*, the *tasbih-shura*, *ijtihad*, and in this way, on the vista of the *tawhidi* methodological worldview, has failed both the Islamic world and every other quest for intellection in unity of knowledge. This aspect of the prevailing Islamic scholarship marks the character of methodological independence, methodological individualism, and disciplinary differentiation of modern-day intellectual orientation. Present-day Islamic intellection has sadly inherited this approach in contradiction to the unified worldview of *tawhid*. That is, in spite of *tawhid* being the keynote of the *Qur'an* and the *sunnah*, this has been slighted in Islamic socio-scientific inquiry.

Overview of the coverage of *tawhidi* phenomenological worldview in this book

This book will refer to such a discursive experience concerning the generality and particulars of socio-scientific issues as the *shura-tasbih* learning process, coincident with the interactive, integrative, and evolutionary (**IIE**) learning process that we will explain at length. Search and discovery of knowledge-induced possibilities in this sense takes place via the medium of investigation based on the inseparable combination of the *Qur'an*, the *sunnah*, and *shura-tasbih* based discourse. The resultant learning process in this comprehensive sense is referred to as *ijtihad*. In such a discursive learning experience the traditional approach to interpretation (*fiqh*) is replaced by continuous and seamless recourse to the *Qur'an* and the *sunnah* in every case in the first place. The rules and interpretations arising from the fundamental source of *tawhidi* epistemology are next discussed for deriving worldly unity of knowledge in relation to the particular issues under investigation. Because of the intrinsic organic relationship between the multi-system learning and learning induction of the world-system, the investigative and extended approach of the *shura-tasbih* abides for both the social and natural sciences, and thereby, for the entire socio-scientific domain.

Thirdly, from the combination of the primal epistemological invocation followed by its functional ontological derivation of worldly knowledge-flows and rules in generality, and then particularized by the discursive medium to details, there comes about the structuring of unity of organic relations between the variables of the issues under investigation. The *tawhidi* epistemological principles taken in their *a priori* premise are thus induced in the *a posteriori* search and discovery of the selected variables that mark the good things of life. The *a priori* and the *a posteriori* reasoning recursively interact. Thus interacting, they unify and evolve across the evolutionary learning processes.

Fourthly, from the above-described dynamics of knowledge production and its induction of the variables in the issues under investigation, there arises an evaluation of the prevailing socio-scientific states. The 'as-is' state of evaluation is followed by the normatively simulated possibility of the same problem in its multi-dimensional perspectives. The total evaluation stage in the two perspectives – from estimation to simulation – leads to evaluation of the criterion-of-wellbeing function. Such a criterion is referred to in the *Qur'an* as *Furqan*: the criterion of discerning truth from falsehood.

Following the evaluation by simulation to attain a certain degree of complementarity (unity) in accordance with the rules of *maqasid as-shari'ah* between the selected variables, there comes about an evolution in the subsequent learning process. The evaluative learning dynamics of wellbeing in any given process carries the evolution into a new process of a similar type. In between the previous and the emergent evolutionary learning process is the recalling of the *tawhidi* worldview to initiate the new evolutionary learning process in unity of knowledge and sustain it. Such evolutionary learning processes continue forward and across by way of intra- and inter- systemic interaction (I), integration (I), and creative evolution (E). We abbreviate this total learning process by calling it the **IIE**-learning process.

The large-scale and small-scale universes of *tawhidi* phenomenological model

The large-scale evolutionary learning universe of the *Qur'an* progresses from *tawhid* in the Beginning to *tawhid* in the End. The End marks the Great Event of the hereafter (*akhira*). Consequently, the large-scale evolutionary learning universe from *tawhid* in the Beginning to *tawhid* in the End forms a closed super-topological universe with super-cardinal dimensions of knowledge, space, and time. See the appendix of this chapter for a technical explanation of super-cardinality, super-space, and super-topology. Knowledge and the wellbeing attained from the knowledge-induced world-system are maximal at these two points of abstraction. In the world-system the same entities are evolutionary. No optimality and steady-state equilibriums of the objective goals exist. In this way, the concept of infinity is replaced by that of super-cardinality of the closure -- *tawhid* to *tawhid* from the Beginning to the End in the hereafter.

On the other hand, the temporal progress of the evolutionary learning universe marks small-scale universes that are embedded in the large-scale learned universe. This explains particulars being embedded in the generality of the *tawhidi* unified universe as a whole. Such an embedding of small-scale universes in the unique large-scale universe explains evolutionary equilibrium dynamics by the process of learning in the continuum of learning processes. But for the closed large-scale structure there is a unique equilibrium. It is precisely attained by way of the closed and compact nature of the super-topology of the mapping – *tawhid* to *tawhid* in the hereafter through the evolutionary learning processes of the world-system.

That which is true of the purely evolutionary learning processes is equally true of the associated knowledge-induced variables of the simulated wellbeing function as the criterion called *Furqan*. Therefore, all the properties of evolutionary learning are induced in the variables of the objective wellbeing function. The implication is a deep one. The co-evolution of knowledge-flows, in concert with their knowledge-induced vector of variables, all occurring in pairs, implies interaction, integration and creative evolution in every evolutionary learning process – both intra- and inter-system. Besides, the meaning of pairing occurs both within and between knowledge-flows and the knowledge-induced variables. Consequently, no less than one consensual knowledge-variable gained from interaction leading to complementarities or participative consensus, and two socio-scientific variables, must minimally enter the evaluation of the wellbeing function.

While the above properties of the total evolutionary learning multiverse system will be substantively studied in this book for the knowledge-induced phenomena underlying conceptualization, cognition and application, the opposites of this evolutionary universe are the de-knowledge induced multiverses. The dynamics of the de-knowledge universes are procedurally similar to that of the *tawhidi* phenomenological model. However, the evolutionary characteristic of the de-knowledge multiverses is shown by continuous evolution into the development of states of demarcation, conflict, competition, methodological individualism, and independence between the variables and their entities.

The de-knowledge universe studied by the self-same *tawhidi* phenomenological model

The de-knowledge universe will also be studied. But for extensive coverage of the de-knowledge theme in the light of *tawhid,* see Choudhury (2000). A de-knowledge multiverse is thereby characterized by any of the following phenomena: There could be (1) a monotonic positive revealed relationship between de-knowledge values and the unwanted elements in the eyes of *maqasid as-shari'ah.* (2) There is a negative relationship between the *maqasid* variables and de-knowledge values. (3) There is simply no knowledge-flow in the system. The investigated study remains neutral to knowledge. Such a state is conveyed by states of an optimal objective criterion and steady-state equilibrium, where learning ceases. Innovation has ended.

Contrarily, in the *tawhidi* knowledge-induced multiverse system there is only one possibility. This is the positive relationship, albeit by different degrees in the simulated state of evaluation of the wellbeing criterion. The simulated version of the wellbeing function is always in terms of the complementary variables according to *maqasid as-shari'ah*.

The knowledge and de-knowledge systems are opposing and disjoint manifestations. The de-knowledge system runs contrary to the *tawhidi* unity of knowledge. It represents the universal design of rationalism. The properties of the knowledge-induced and de-knowledge induced universes are mathematical in nature. They will be studied in this book (both textually according to the *Qur'an* and the *sunnah*) and analytically (by the use of topological mathematics and otherwise).

An example of the *tawhidi* methodology's application to both the knowledge and de-knowledge perspectives of the total phenomenological model is the question of trade-versus-interest transactions in the *Qur'an*.[12] We can offer at least three formulations for this relationship in terms of the wellbeing function in these variables.

Firstly, we can invert the interest rate variable and combine it with the real rate-of-return variable. By doing so, we have the price vector denoted by [(interest rate)/(rate of return)]. We then make the real output variable depend upon this price relative to the wellbeing function. We postulate that in the long-run, a relative increase in the [(rate of return)/(interest rate)] price will increase real output, and decrease it otherwise, provided the real output is linked with the good things of life (the *maqasid as-shari'ah* goods). The knowledge variable in this relationship is measured as a ranking of the degree of complementarities between the relative price and the real output.

The wellbeing function has the estimated and simulated normative variables – the {[(rate of return in trade) relative-to-(real rate of interest)] – and the real output}. The wellbeing function itself is a monotonic functional of the knowledge-value ranked by the degree of complementarities as observed between the other two variables. This kind of representation of the wellbeing function and its derived relationship between real output of *maqasid*-choice and price relative, [(real rate of return)/(real interest rate)], is a category of the purely *tawhidi* knowledge-induced problem.

Secondly, in the case of a de-knowledge function, the relationship can be either of the following cases: (1) a negative relationship – thus marginalism – between *maqasid*-goods and the relative price as [(real rate of interest)/(rate of return on trade)]. The de-knowledge calibration in this case assumes negative or decreasing calibrated knowledge-values as

[12] *Qur'an* (2:275): "Those who devour usury will not stand except as stands one whom the Evil One by his touch has driven to madness. That is because they say: 'Trade is like usury". But God has permitted trade and forbidden usury….."

complementarities along with the rise in the degree of marginalism. (2) A positively calibrated de-knowledge relationship exists between an increase in the real output of non-*maqasid* goods and the relative price: [(real rate of interest)/(real rate of return in trade)].

Thirdly, the presence of knowledge-flows or de-knowledge-flows is zero in the wellbeing function. This is the case of optimality and steady-state equilibrium of resource allocation in mainstream economics. It is the usual characteristic of orthodox economic theory. However, it is this very steady-state equilibrium concept that Shackle (1971) remarks as being the end of novelty by the end of relational and discursive experience. Such a predictive situation of the economic universe is fictive.[13] The wellbeing function now shows these variables to be in competition, and resource allocation to be defined by marginal rate of substitution – the case of de-knowledge.

The *tawhidi* phenomenological model will thus be completely specified for the generality of the large-scale evolutionary learning universe, its particulars, and in contrast to the opposing parallel universe of de-knowledge. The *tawhidi* phenomenological model can thus be defined by the pervasive knowledge of unity of being and becoming, across the evolutionary learning universe in knowledge-flows and its induced variables according to the *maqasid as-shari'ah*. This model has its intrinsic properties of epistemological derivation of worldly knowledge-flows by *a priori* reference to the *Qur'an* and the *sunnah*. Thereby emerges the discursive medium for determining the structure of the issues under investigation.

The wellbeing criterion is thereby evaluated by pervasive unity of knowledge and unity of the knowledge-induced variables of the simulated form of the wellbeing criterion. Thereby, the same characteristics of evolutionary learning processes continue along path-dependent trajectories or across inter-systemic trajectories. Phenomenology, as the study of

---

[13] Shackle (1971) writes in this regard: "Equilibrium is a solution, and there is, in the general frame of thought, no guarantee that a problem which presents itself, unchosen and undesigned by us, will have any solution, or that it will not have infinity of solutions. In either case, there is no prescription of conduct". Shackle continues on to critique the concept of reason and rationality, which are taken as the foundations of neoclassical methodology of price determination. He writes: "But if we wish to claim that reason by itself is a sufficient guide for conduct, we need to claim, not that reason can find novelty, but that it can find *all* novelties and thus exhaust novelty. Only when novelty is eliminated and all is known can reason be the sole guide of conduct. It is only in the timeless fiction of general equilibrium that reason can prevail alone."

systemic consciousness made up of recursive interrelationship between epistemology, cognition, application, and sustained continuity, is thus integrated from the beginning to the end of the knowledge-induced issues across interacting, integrating and evolutionary processes.

Interaction, integration, and evolution (IIE) in *tawhidi* phenomenological model

In the *tawhidi* phenomenological model the concepts of interaction, integration and evolution are defined in a subtle way as derived from the *Qur'an* and applied to the generality and particulars of investigated socio-scientific issues. Throughout this book we take the *Qur'an* and the *sunnah* as the starting point of conceptualization and quantitative application. That is because of the epistemological primacy of *tawhid,* which is derived foundationally from the *Qur'an* and the *sunnah* as the *a priori* texts. This is the exclusively and singularly exogenous reference to intellection on *tawhid* as the monotheistic belief combined with law spanning from the Beginning to the End of evolutionary learning experience.

Every other relational entity in the *tawhidi* phenomenological model is endogenous in nature. This must be so, since the strongest evidence of the Signs of God's oneness in the order of things is pervasive complementarity by way of organic symbiosis between variables and entities. Only after the primal epistemological derivation of concepts, theory, and application do other various developments come about out of the rational process of intellection brought to bear on the *tawhidi* worldview on the issues under investigation and discourse.

In the history of scientific development, Archimedes would say: Give me a fulcrum and I will rule the world. Leibniz said: Give me a geometrical point and I will describe the universe. In *tawhidi* worldview, the epistemology of *tawhid* as the functioning of the monotheistic law explains the socio-scientific 'everything'. Taking stock of the phenomenological description between exogenous and endogenous functional entities, we obtain the world-system as a pervasively relational epistemological order. Within this learning world-system only, there abide the phenomenological characteristics of interaction, integration, and evolution.

The same properties do not characterize the solely exogenous premise of *tawhid* in the Beginning and the End (the hereafter) of creation. *Tawhid* does not belong to learning and material process order. Rather, *tawhid,* as God's Will and Law, generates details of all worldly processes by its divine ordainments, yet comprehends the world-system in a consistent and logical way. Evolutionary learning process and its relationship with cognitive processes is a permanently simulated experience attained by intra-systemic and inter-variable causality, though without need for sequencing between interaction, integration, and evolutionary learning. Let us examine this point briefly here, leaving additional details for the later chapters of the book.

Interaction

The *Qur'an* has established the institution of the *shura* (consultation) for human interaction as well as the phenomenon of diversity in the order of things to unravel the Signs of God and Pure Oneness through the intermediation of the Prophet Muhammad's guidance (*sunnah*).[14] Consequently, both human (*shura*) and natural (*tasbih*) interactions are meant to establish the principle of unity in diversity across the entire active and phenomenological domain of reality. In this book we will take *shura* and *tasbih* as indivisible experiences, for the reason that, as the *Qur'an* declares, there is intrinsic purpose (*tasbih*) in creation; and it is for the human reason and discourse (*shura*) to understand this purpose.[15] Hence we will refer to this inseparable experience by the term *shura-tasbih*. This is a comprehensive conception of consciousness, which comprises the realm of phenomenology.

Interaction, then, is the starting point of worldly knowledge creation derived from the epistemology of the creative exogeneity of *tawhid*. Such worldly knowledge derivation, comprising both truth and falsehood, forms the basis of the *maqasid as-shari'ah* in their contrasting meanings. The

---

[14] *Qur'an* (42:52-43): "And thus have We, by Our command, sent inspiration to you; You knew not (before) what was Revelation, and what was Faith; but We have made the (*Qur'an*) a Light, wherewith We guide such of Our servants as We will; and verily you do guide (men) to the Straight Way – the Way of God, to Whom belongs whatever is in the heavens and whatever is on earth. Behold (how) all affairs tend towards God!"

[15] The *Qur'an* (44:38-39) declares on universal purpose of creation: "We created not the heavens, the earth, and all between them, merely in (idle) sport: We created them not except for just ends: and most of them do not understand." On *shura* with submission to God as would be to extend the domain of worship as *tasbih* (*qur'anic* consultation) the *Qur'an* (42:38) declares: "Those who hearken to their Lord, and establish regular prayer; and who (conduct) their affairs by mutual consultation; who spend out of what We bestowed on them for sustenance." On the *tasbih* (contemplative) portion of discoursing with the universe the *Qur'an* (41:53) declares: "Soon shall We show them Our Signs in the (furthest) regions (of the earth), and in their own souls, until it becomes manifest to them that this is the Truth. Is it not enough that your Lord does witness all things?"

singular purpose is to bring out the truth. Indeed, central to all discursive experience in Islam is *tawhid* as the monotheistic law and its multifaceted manifestations as the Signs of God. Thus creative purpose and phenomenology in the Islamic worldview translates into conscious understanding of *tawhid* as both divine Oneness and the monotheistic law in action. On this theme the *Qur'an* lays down the grand design of the *shura-tasbih* process of knowing and moral construction of the world-system.[16]

Thus interaction occurs firstly at the level of deriving the exegesis of the general meaning of *qur'anic* verses, the *sunnah*, and collectively participated interpretations by the learned in the light of the *Qur'an* and the *sunnah*. Such a knowledge-deriving process is termed as *ijtihad*. It is conducted in the midst of *shura-tasbih* pursuit in reference to the fundamental premises, the *Qur'an* and the *sunnah*. The result then is not necessarily the solving of the problem at issue. Rather, it is to derive the general understanding of the rules that ensue from the *qur'anic* exegesis. Such is the stage of rule-setting (*ahkam*). The rule-based epistemic knowledge is next made to form the worldly knowledge-flows pertaining to specific issues under discussion.

The emergent knowledge-flows then induce the variables that define the issues under consideration. This stage too is a vastly interactive process in the domain of worldly systemic construction by organic interrelationship of complementarities and participation according to the primal epistemology of *tawhidi* unity of knowledge and unity of the world-system induced by such knowledge.

In the contrasting model as well, there is the polarity of relationship between knowledge and de-knowledge; and there is interactive behaviour to replace de-knowledge by knowledge.[17] Finally, since the *tawhidi* phenomenological model reaches across the dimensions of knowledge, space, and time, interaction appears at every stage of the evolutionary learning processes. Concerning a similar point, the great mathematical

---

[16] The combination of *shura-tasbih* process of learning in the midst of *tawhid* is declared by the *Qur'an* (51:20-23) as a universal fact: "On the earth are Signs for those of assured Faith, as also in your own selves: will you not then see? And in heaven is your sustenance, as (also) that which you are promised. Then, by the Lord of heaven and earth, this is the very Truth, as much as the fact that you can speak intelligently to each other."

[17] *Qur'an* (10:32-33) on the evidence of truth against falsehood: "Such is God, your real Cherisher and Sustainer: Apart from Truth what (remains) but error? How then are you turned away? Thus is the Word of your Lord proved true against those who rebel: Verily they will not believe."

philosopher of science, Professor Alfred North Whitehead, wrote: "Accordingly the general potentiality of the universe must be somewhere; since it retains its 'proximate relevance' to actual entities for which it is unrealized. This 'proximate relevance' reappears in subsequent concrescence as final causation regulative of the emergence of novelty. This 'somewhere' is the non-temporal actual entity. Thus 'proximate relevance' means 'relevance as in the primordial mind of God.'" (eds. Griffin and Sherburne, 1979, p. 46).

Integration

Yet, in the *tawhidi* worldview, interaction cannot be continuous and pervasive in continua of being and becoming unless it goes through a relational unifying experience. That is, in the human world, interaction – by way of discourse at the primal level of derivation of knowledge followed by the worldly derivation of knowledge-flows; and simultaneously the construction (concrescence) of the knowledge-induced world-system; and the interactive manifestations in the phenomenological order – results in evolutionary temporary equilibriums. This is the socio-scientific consensus of being and becoming at any process level evolving into further evolutionary processes across the dimensions of knowledge, space, and time.

Integration is a term chosen for its relevance in the philosophy of science. Like the property of interaction in the *tawhidi* phenomenological model, integration also signifies its knowledge-induced unification property in the unity of being. This happens both out of human participation, and by way of intrinsic unification of entities within the grand design of the universe. Thus, learning equilibrium is the inherent nature of the social world and the socio-scientific world-system. Incidentally, the Nobel Laureate of theoretical physics, Professor Schrödinger, used to say that fundamental particles are highly politicized entities. That is, they are interactive by consciousness.

But such equilibrium states are not steady-states. Evolutionary change by interaction continuously transforms their states of being and becoming into newly learnt states. Thereby, new knowledge-flows in this intrinsic sense of evolutionary learning in both the human world and the physical world interact to unravel fresh knowledge-flows, and thereby freshly knowledge-induced cognitive and material states. While interaction means participation and pairing in the midst of diversity, the interactive dynamics impact upon integration in the state of learning equilibrium towards realizing unity of knowledge. Interaction thus leads into integration as formation of dynamic states of unity of knowledge and results in continued evolutionary learning.

Evolution

The continua of interaction leading to integration as intra-systemic processes result in the evaluation of the intra-process world (hence particular phenomena). The simulated world of evolutionary learning post-wellbeing evaluation registers the evolution of new knowledge-flows and the consequential unified socio-scientific possibility.

The epistemological origin is recalled at the beginning of every new process of the **IIE**. In other words, the same experience of deriving fresh knowledge-flows automatically arises from the recollection of the *tawhidi* epistemological roots by way of invoking this fundamental epistemology in the presence of the learned discursive community. The rest of the conceptual, interpretive, participatory, and complementary nature of the second phase of evolution emerges. New evaluation of emergent wellbeing functions is done firstly by way of empirical 'estimation'. 'Estimation' yields the state of the world 'as is'. The 'estimation' phase is next followed by an empirical 'simulation' stage in the moral construction of the *tawhidi* world-system. Such an evolutionary learning marks interaction which in turn leads to integration in any given process. Interaction and integration evolve into the epistemological regeneration of fresh knowledge-flows and the rebirth of fresh interaction leading to integration – and thereby, into creative evolution in labyrinths of new learning processes.

In any given learning process, the complete course of interaction leading into integration and being evaluated by the wellbeing function marks the intra-systemic learning process. The evoking of *tawhidi* epistemology at the restart of fresh rounds of evolutionary learning marks the fresh evolutionary process arising out of the previous one. This completes the interaction leading to integration and onwards into evolution. Such a learning process is the intra-systemic and inter-systemic characterization of the evolutionary dynamics. The emergent processes out of such internal learning evolve into process-wide learning, and combine newer socio-scientific sub-systems.

All of these phases of experience characterize the same kind of learning dynamics of interaction, integration, and creative evolution. This full characterization of a learning process defines the dynamic elements of the *tawhidi* phenomenological model from the Beginning to the End of the universal entirety occurring in the dimensions of knowledge, space, and time.[18] The *Qur'an* has thus totally encompassed all the properties of interaction, integration, and creative evolution from which the *tawhidi* phenomenological model is derived. The passage from *tawhid* in the primordial super-topological space merges with the Hereafter at the End in the very large-scale learning universe. Within this learning worldview, the process of evolutionary learning characterized by intra-systemic interaction leading to integration and onwards into evolution is repeated by evolution in every process of the same kind of dynamics across intra-systemic and inter-systemic processes. Such is the phenomenon of temporality in the small-scale material, cognitive, and formalized universes of continued reciprocal unification within the large-scale universe of primordial *tawhid*-to-*tawhid* in the hereafter.

The method of circular causation embedded in the interactive, integrative, and evolutionary characterization of the *tawhidi* phenomenological model

The evaluative content of the *tawhidi* phenomenological model in respect of the episteme of unity of knowledge is the wellbeing function. The evaluation exercise goes through two phases, as mentioned earlier. First, there is the 'estimation' stage of the wellbeing function in terms of the positivistic relationship between the selected variables for a given issue

---

[18] On the dynamics of integration the *Qur'an* (36:36) has given its great principle of universal pairing. The meaning of pairing is unification for serving the unique objective and goal of *tawhid* in the order of things: "Glory to God, Who created in pairs all things that the earth produces, as well as their own (human) kind and (other) things of which they have no knowledge."

The *Qur'an* (4:59) establishes the cardinal principle of integration in resolving disputes: "O you who believe! Obey God, and obey the Apostle, and those charged with authority among you. If you differ in anything among them, refer it to God and His Apostle. If you do believe in God and the Last Day: That is best, and most suitable for final determination."

In reference to the pairing of the universe as diverse systems of interaction and integration the *Qur'an* declares (13:3): "And it is He Who spread out the earth, and set therein mountains standing firm. And (flowing) rivers: and fruit of every kind He made in pairs, two and two: He draws the Night as a veil over the Day. Behold, verily in these things there are Signs for those who consider!" The reflective understanding of pairing in the intellection domain is included in this last portion of the verse.

In reference to the creative evolution unraveling *tawhid* as monotheistic law in 'everything', the *Qur'an* (30:11) declares: "It is God, Who begins (the process of) creation; then repeats it; then shall you be brought back to Him."

and problem. The result of estimation is to examine the degree to which complementarities exist or not between the selected variables. Such variables arise in reference to the *maqasid as-shari'ah*. The method of reading the interaction is done by inter-relating each variable with the rest of the variables. Thus all the inter-variable relations emerge in their circularly related equations. The emergent system of circular causation variables is solvable in the variables by virtue of the endogenous relationships between the variables. Thus a temporary equilibrium solution of the system exists.

Integration of the interactive relations is thus established in a given process. Interaction and integration between the selected variables in their estimation stage thus exist in the circular causation system of relations between the variables in their positivistic states.

In the case of weak or negative complementarities – such as marginalism in the case of a neoclassical-type competing relationship between alternatives – then simulation is carried out. This is done by changing the estimated coefficients of the circular causation equations into normatively desired values in the light of *maqasid as-shari'ah*. Such multiple cases of simulated possibilities exist within a given process in the evolutionary learning processes. There comes about as a result of such simulacra a history of evolutionary learning processes and the worldly concrescence according to these. Fitzpatrick (2003) and Hawking (2010) write on such functional learning phenomena.[19]

Every given simulated state of the predictor variables of the transformed circular causation system of equations implies policy-theoretic institutional and resource related consequences. In any given process, the simulated results for the predictor variables are attained. But with the knowledge-induced impact by way of building up the effective complementarities between the variables, the additional policy-theoretic variables are selectively included in an augmented list of new variables. The evolutionary process now enters from the state of evaluation in a given learning process to the subsequent process of evolutionary learning. The dynamic relations of interaction, integration, and evolution remain identical to the previous process but have now become *inter*-processes.

---

[19] Fitzpatrick (2003, p. 128) writes on such simulacra of evolutionary learning processes: "everything is a reproduction of other reproductions. Society explodes in on itself and we cannot liberate ourselves from the *simulacra*…"
Hawking (2010, p. 80): "Feynman showed that, for a general system, the probability of any observation is constructed from all the possible histories that could have led to that observation. Because of that his method is called the 'sum over histories' or 'alternative histories' formulation of quantum physics".

Such results can also be extended by the development of a particular *intra*-system dynamics into *inter*-system dynamics of estimator-type predictor variables in econometrics (Johnston, 1984) using the circular causation method.

Merging *tawhidi* epistemology with *tawhidi* ontology in the *tawhidi* phenomenological model with endogenous dynamics

We will summarize the meanings of the captioned terms from philosophy of science used in this book for the construction of the *tawhidi* monotheistic worldview, its conception, methodology, and applications. The first of these issues brings out the comparative use of the following concepts in this book:

1. *Epistemology*: The *tawhidi* theory of knowledge is the absolutely primordial and ineluctable precept of oneness of God as the *a priori* premise of knowledge. This *a priori* premise coexists with the precept of the monotheistic law in the *a posteriori* derivation of worldly knowledge-flows. This kind of relational continuity and recursive feedback between the *a priori* and the *a posteriori* as axiomatically explained, establishes the basis of a comprehensive Islamic belief. It is reflected in the unified worldview in 'everything' as explained by *tawhidi* knowledge, both in generality and in its particulars taken up in the details. *Tawhidi* epistemology thereby explains knowledge formation. Knowledge so formed then enters the totality of continuous relations between *a priori* reasoning and *a posteriori* reasoning concerning formation of worldly knowledge-flows arising from the *tawhidi* monotheistic law. The relationship between the primal *tawhidi* epistemology, its origin for derivation of worldly knowledge-flows, and the simultaneous emergence of the knowledge-induced world-system, recursively returns to the *tawhidi* recalling every time in the **IIE**-learning process. Such a recursive process projects the meaning and practice of systemic sustainability of evolutionary learning.[20]

2. *Phenomenology*: This means the study of consciousness in turning the ontological aspects of learning to formalism. Thus the *tawhidi* epistemology is extended from the ontological level (*a priori*) to the

[20] *Qur'an* (42:53): "The Path of *Allah* to Whom belongs all that is in the heavens and all that is in the earth. Verily, all matters at the end go to *Allah* (for decision)."

derivation of worldly knowledge-flows, and is thereby brought to bear upon the construction of the cognitive and corporeal aspects of the issues under investigation in the knowledge-induced unified world-system (*a posteriori*). The endogenous observer then comprehends events in the conscious world-system. Events in such a comprehensive universe of *a priori* and *a posteriori* linkage occur in the realms of the heart, mind, and matter spaces. Such holistic experience establishes the conscious, that is, phenomenological world-system of events. The emergent events are now interpretable by the *tawhidi* epistemology.

The *tawhidi* meaning of phenomenology in terms of the epistemology of unity of the monotheistic law is different from the conception given by Husserl (see Hammond et al. 1991, pp. 1-13) in regard to his lament on the moral decadence of occidental science. Husserl wanted to unify science between the *a priori* and *a posteriori* domains of reasoning, forming inference. Yet the project did not succeed.

The problem of differentiation between the unitary and rationalist phenomenological worldviews happens due to the Kantian type *a priori* reasoning, which Husserl wants to integrate with *a posteriori* reasoning. Yet he cannot get this right because of the permanent dichotomous place of deductive and inductive philosophy in rationalism. Rationalism can at best place the *a priori* and the *a posteriori* within competing reasoning domains by the process of self-determination. Dichotomy between these two regions of reasoning, and thereby, between deductive and inductive reasoning, is entrenched in the rationalist philosophy of socio-scientific knowledge.

If then, God is to be inducted into the rationalist version of Husserl's theory of phenomenology as the study of mind-matter consciousness of being then, God must remain exclusively in the realm of the transcendental ego. Dichotomy between God and the divine law on the one hand, and the perceptual world of cognitive realism on the other hand, is the inevitable consequence of any rationalist reasoning. This kind of polarization of reasoning is contrary to the permanent organic unity we find in the *tawhidi* phenomenological worldview.

3. *Ontology*: In this book we have used the meaning of ontology in its *functional* concept (Gruber, 1993; Maxwell, 1962). For example, the *a priori* precept of *tawhid* as God's oneness is explained by means of the ontology of the monotheistic law. Likewise, the *qur'anic* exegesis is explained by way of the medium of Prophet Muhammad's guidance. Prophetic guidance assumes the role of ontological transformation of primal *tawhidi* epistemology into the experiential world-system in respect

of its generality and particularity of issues and details. By adopting this meaning of the ontological, the nature of relational coexistence between the *a priori* and the *a posteriori* in the dimensions of knowledge, space, and time, and thereby in the realm of the heart, mind and matter spaces, reaches between the epistemological and the phenomenological scopes. This unified experience then becomes recursive by evolutionary learning in unity of knowledge.

4. *Universality and uniqueness*: In a specific chapter of this book, we will establish the idea of universality and uniqueness of the *tawhidi* unified worldview in the realms of the heart, mind, and matter spaces by explaining their relational functionalism using the *tawhidi* phenomenological model. Phenomenology is now understood as the inter-causal and overarching systemic experience of *tawhidi* epistemology that is enabled by ontological functionalism of the *sunnah* and the learned discourse as mediums of discourse. The *tawhidi* phenomenological model is now understood as the grand design of the inherent dynamics that well-define the evolutionary learning processes of a world-system premised in the unity of knowledge.

5. *Circular causation*: The inherent dynamics of the *tawhidi* phenomenological model are characterized, and both quantitatively and empirically engaged, by the principle of pervasive complementarities representing simulated pairing between the variables selected in accordance with *maqasid as-shar'iah* to attain levels of simulated wellbeing. The method used to realize this quantitative and empirical formalism is called the method of circular causation.

All of the above-mentioned stages of formalizing the *tawhidi* worldview in unity of knowledge and unity of the knowledge-induced world-system in its generality and particulars are derived from the *Qur'an* and the *sunnah*. The exegetic interpretation (*tafsir*) and derivation of these stages based on *qur'anic* verses will follow. This forms the experience of discourse by the learned community in the process of deriving worldly knowledge-flows from the foundational *tawhidi* epistemological roots of knowledge. Interestingly, we note that the connector linking the *Qur'an* and the *sunnah* together comprises *a priori* foundations and the *ijtihad* combined, using *shura-tasbih* (integration of *a priori* and *a posteriori*) as its discursive learning medium. This medium is the carrier of the discursive correspondence. The *shura-tasbih* experience via *ijtihad* carries the *a priori* reasoning into the *a posteriori* reasoning, and circularly by interrelations. The *a priori* and *a posteriori* interconnect recursively over continuous evolutionary learning processes.

A formal expression of the *tawhidi* phenomenological model

The *tawhidi* phenomenological model thereby formalizes the systemic and evolutionary learning process – a process that spans all experiences in the universe across the dimensions of knowledge, space, and time by the following ontological transformation:

> $O(T\rightarrow (\theta,\mathbf{x}(\theta))$. Here O denotes the heart, mind, matter transformation (denoted by $\rightarrow$) by the process of deriving knowledge in connection with the knowledge-induced world-system $\{\theta,\mathbf{x}(\theta)\}$. The symbolization encapsulates the totality of the *tawhidi* phenomenological model.

T denotes the super-cardinality of the super-topology of (Ω,S). T comprises the foundational epistemology denoted by (Ω,S), where, Ω denotes the super-cardinal knowledge space of the *Qur'an*. S denotes the functional ontological transmission of Ω by the *sunnah* (S) into the space of learned discourse by way of *shura-tasbih* and *ijtihad.*

> $\{\theta\}$ denotes the knowledge-flows derived from the epistemological origin of (Ω,S).

$\mathbf{x}(\theta)$ denotes the vector or higher categories of mathematical representations – matrices and tensors, and complex inter-variable and inter-causal relations – to signify unity of the *tawhidi* epistemologically knowledge-induced (by θ) variables and entities.

Finally, any complex monotonic transformation (order preserving) of $O(T\rightarrow (\theta,\mathbf{x}(\theta))$[21] also defines levels of consciousness in the evolutionary learning form of the *tawhidi* phenomenological model.

---

[21] Monotonic positive transformation implies: $O(T\rightarrow (\theta,\mathbf{x}(\theta)) \Rightarrow F[O(T\rightarrow (\theta,\mathbf{x}(\theta))]$ $\Rightarrow$ by the property of order-preserving continuous mapping, $F_{ij}\{[\cup_i\cap_j O_{ij}(T\rightarrow (\theta,\mathbf{x}(\theta))_{ij}] \Rightarrow [\cup_i\cap_j F_{ij}(O_{ij}(T\rightarrow (\theta,\mathbf{x}(\theta))_{ij}))$; with $dF_{ij}((\theta,\mathbf{x}(\theta))_{ij})/d\theta ij > 0$ for each $i = 1,2,3,\ldots, n_1$; $j = 1,2,3,\ldots,n_2$; and therefore, $dF(\theta,\mathbf{x}(\theta))/d\theta > 0$, for each variable of the vector $\mathbf{x}(\theta)$.

The same implication is extendable to the case of de-knowledge (rationalism). Symbols now are denoted by asterisk. The difference though is that, $\cup_i\cap_j O_{ij}(T\rightarrow$

In the end, it is the epistemological beginning of the *tawhidi* reconstructive worldview of the socio-scientific order that plays the centrally permanent role in developing its phenomenological model.

The importance of the epistemological beginning has not been recognized in most substantive developments of the Islamic socio-scientific worldview. Thereby, a scientific revolution, as would be expected in Islamic economics, finance, science and society, has long been delayed. Yet today the socio-scientific disciplines find new awakenings on fresh epistemological grounds. On this point, Albert Einstein (undated) wrote to his friend Niels Bohr: "Science without epistemology is – insofar as it is thinkable at all – primitive and muddled". Hawking (2010) is still today unsettled in his conviction of an epistemological origin that can define the whole of the natural universe. But even here, there remains a caveat of the natural universe being dissociated from the social universe.

Nevertheless, the intellection of a revolutionary Islamic worldview in socio-scientific inquiry still advances with a dim future, unless the *tawhidi* epistemology becomes the lynchpin of the new structure of scientific explanation. On the great importance of the *tawhidi* epistemological relevance in Islamic worldview, Ghazzali (trans. Marmura, 1997, p. 217) wrote: "Whoever combines both virtues, the epistemological and the practical, is the worshipping 'knower', the absolutely blissful one. Whoever has the epistemological virtue but not the practical is the knowledgeable [believing] sinner who will be tormented for a period, which [torment] will not last because his soul has been perfected through knowledge but bodily occurrences had tarnished [it] in an accidental manner opposed to the substance of the soul. ..... He who has practical virtue but not the epistemological is saved and delivered, but does not attain perfect bliss."

$(\theta',\mathbf{x'}(\theta'))_{ij} = \phi$; or $\lim_{\theta'}[\cup_i\cap_j O_{ij}(T\rightarrow (\theta',\mathbf{x'}(\theta'))_{ij}] = \phi$. Hence, $[\cup_i\cap_j F'_{ij}(O_{ij}(T\rightarrow (\theta,\mathbf{x}(\theta))_{ij}) = [\cup_i F'_i(O_i(T\rightarrow (\theta',\mathbf{x'}(\theta'))_i]$ forms a separable function. This is the indication of methodological individualism and methodological independence between variables and functions. These are the signs of phenomenological analysis in rationalism either by assumption (neoclassicism) or limit (e.g. Popper's conjectural universe). $dF'(\theta',\mathbf{x'}(\theta'))/d\theta' > 0$ (rationalist limiting dynamics); $dF'(\theta',\mathbf{x'}(\theta'))/d\theta' = 0$ as in the neoclassical economic case of non-relationship at the optimal and steady-state equilibrium of resource allocation. At such points, $\theta' = 0$; $\theta = 0$.

Note that, T determines both truth (epistemic unity by T_1) and falsehood (rationalism by T_2). T as the *tawhidi* epistemology comprises $T_1 \cup T_2 = T$; such that $T_1 \cap T_2 = \phi$.

The analytical intellection of this book is to establish the fact that the mornings of new socio-scientific thought belong to the new, more extended and comprehensive epistemological inquiry. The *tawhidi* epistemological approach presents this possibility through its comprehensive phenomenological model, and its inner dynamics and systemic methods of analysis and applications for moral construction of the socio-scientific world-system.

The precepts of universality and uniqueness of (Ω,S)

Universality

The substantive terms, 'universality' and 'uniqueness' are used often in the book to explain many terms that are connected with the *tawhidi* phenomenological concepts. We will develop these concepts by methodological discussions and analytics invoking importantly the theory of self-referencing applied to the imagery of disseminating *qur'anic* meanings. Topological mathematics will be used on the *tawhidi* super-topological space having super-cardinal dimensions (uncountable and unbounded nature). At this point of the *Methodological Introduction* it is sufficient to explain these substantive terms descriptively only.

The concept of universality can be summarized by invoking the definition of *tawhidi* phenomenology in terms of the symbolization, $O(T\rightarrow(\theta,\mathbf{x}(\theta))$ and its complex monotonic transformations according to the *tawhidi* unitary worldview. Such a given relationship determined along the evolutionary learning path describes the interactive, integrative and evolutionary character of the one-system investigative issues of a world-system. Its wellbeing objective function is evaluated by the circular causation method of estimation-to-simulation possibilities across simulacra.

An expanding and spanning evolutionary dynamic with interaction and integration formalizes the phenomenological model for multi-systems and multiverses with the same kind of intra-systemic and inter-systemic dynamics. The wellbeing function is now a multi-systemic criterion that is evaluated by the endogenously interacting, integrating and evolutionary variables using the extended form of the circular causation method. It is true though, that in spite of the multi-systemic bundling of the diversified system-specific wellbeing indexes, the convergence of objective of all such wellbeing indexes (*maslaha*) is for the common moral, ethical, and social good in the light of the *tawhidi* epistemology of unity and balance. That is because all of human intellection across the socio-scientific universe must ultimately serve human wellbeing through the *tawhidi* primal objective.

Universality also carries two further properties. Firstly, the *a priori* reasoning and the *a posteriori* reasoning are relationally unified by their inter-causality. Consequently, the following kind of recursive relationship by variables, and their complex relations (transformations) and entities exist:

> *a priori* (*tawhidi* epistemology) → *a posteriori* (knowledge-induced world-system) → *a priori* (by recalling the *tawhidi* epistemology) → *a posteriori* (knowledge-induced world-system in evolutionary learning processes) → occurs continuously across continua of open spaces (no closure) →.... → hereafter (grand closure of the learning universe: Great Event).

Such a structure of reasoning and learning in unity of knowledge by the principle of complementarities (*qur'anic* universal pairing) and evolution of learning (*qur'anic* re-origination in the dimensions of knowledge, space and time)[22] applies equally to abstraction and cognitive and material orders. The socio-scientific entirety is comprehended in the knowledge, space, and time dimensions.

Finally, on the theme of universality, the *tawhidi* phenomenological model is equally applicable to the epistemology of truth and the epistemology of falsehood (de-knowledge) by way of its circular causation and endogenous nature of inter-causal and inter-variable relations. Examples of de-knowledge are rationalism, methodological individualism, neoclassicism, social Darwinism, Marx's and Popper's dialectics (Popper, 1988), and so on. De-knowledge is equated with falsehood because of its ineptness to explain the vast extent of knowledge and the knowledge-induced world-system premised on the epistemology of unity of knowledge. Consequently, many a limitation, inconsistency, and illogical inference arise from the intellection and application of rationalist thought (Farrell, 1996).

The difference between the two worldviews in the *tawhidi* phenomenological model is this: Primal epistemic knowledge regenerates unity of knowledge and regenerates its endogenously-induced unified entities continuously across continua of world-systems. The same model

---

[22] *Qur'an* (29:19): "See they not how God originates the creation, and then repeats it. Verily this is easy for God."

Also there is the *qur'anic* verse (71:17-18): "And God has produced from the earth, growing (gradually), and in the End He will return you into the (earth), and raise you forth (again at the resurrection)?"

explains de-knowledge in terms of its endogeneity of differentiated forms. In other words, the world-system of de-knowledge evolves by differentiated forms, structures, and functions.

Uniqueness

The universality essence of the *tawhidi* phenomenological model explains the structure, function and applications of issues in *any* and *every* world-system in a comprehensive way that is unique to the model. The same kind of an address to the theme of universality cannot be afforded by any other system, as of de-knowledge, since it is not possible for rationalism or its genre to derive a world-system by its generality and particulars in terms of the ontological functionalism of monotheism in relation to the issues of the world-system. Thereby, there is no other explanation for the coexistence in reasoning between the *a priori* and the *a posteriori* concepts. In such a contrary system, God remains a metaphysical being. The functionality of the law of monotheism cannot be induced into the living world-system.

Likewise, the emergence of the endogenous path-dependent evolutions of de-knowledge carries forward and repeats the nature of methodological independence and methodological individualism. The world-system as an evolutionary bundle is seen as the continuous characterization of such differentiated evolutionary paths. But each evolutionary path becomes increasingly independent and individuated of the others. The method of circular causation evaluates the world-system in its given 'as is' state. There is no pressing aspiration in this system to develop consciousness for endogenously self-governing moral and ethical change. That is because there is no fixed epistemological premise, except of multiple rationalist choices.

Consequently, in the absence of an endogenous self-governed consciousness arising out of monotheistic epistemology as the only axiomatic premise, policies and institutions are of one of two kinds: Firstly, they are exogenously induced in the system, as is the case in much of macroeconomic and technological choices. Secondly, they are induced in the system through the flow of learning innovation and information. As is the case in Lucas' (1975) rational expectations theory; Schumpeter's (see Gafford, 2009) growth model; Romer's (1986) endogenous growth model; and Hayek's (1990) knowledge model, the postulates of resource scarcity and competition behaviour remain intact. These conditions perpetuate the methodological competition, individualism, and bifurcated path-dependency model. The result then is reversion of the rationalist epistemological foundations of socio-scientific theory (Lawson, 2003).

The rationalist epistemology remains permanent in the mainstream socio-scientific worldview. However, by accepting such a rationalist worldview we completely omit the vast scope of human nature and aspiration for a comprehensive inclusion of choices and decision-making along with moral and ethical values (Choudhury, 2011c).

Summary of chapters in the book

The chapters of this book altogether lay down the challenging epistemological perspectives of rediscovering the heart, mind, matter interrelationship of the socio-scientific worldview of *tawhid* in terms of the monotheistic law. This book accomplishes this project by a vast intellection in analytical formalism and the exegetic explanation of the *Qur'an* and *sunnah* combined with comparative study of the philosophy of science, while addressing specific issues and problems of economics, finance, science and society. Following the conceptual delineation of the epistemological, ontological, and phenomenological conceptions, the comprehensive *tawhidi* phenomenological model is applied to theoretical and applied issues of economics, finance, science, and society.

The *tawhidi* groundwork is thus brought into this book as an original epistemological worldview for socio-scientific understanding. It forms the original contribution of the author and a selected number of colleagues in the socio-scientific conceptualization and applications of the *tawhid*-centred inquiry. As this book progresses in its chapters, the principal areas presented in this chapter of *Methodological Introduction* are extensively developed with erudition, rigor, and depth.

The conceptual part of the book is followed by a cogent number of applications in specific issues of economics, finance and society. The emergent epistemological inquiry now becomes a contribution for the global scholarly and practitioner community. At the end of this book, this accomplishment will be evident in respect of the emergent currency of thought for the Islamic worldview, the heterodox worldview, and the morally reconstructed mainstream worldview. The emphasis will be on the economic, financial, and social world-systems under study by the *tawhidi* phenomenological model of unity of knowledge.

Technical Appendix: Concept of Super-Cardinality

In Figure 1.A1 let, a_i denote sets along the surfaces marked by systems S_i. From this set, which is of an intra-systemic kind, we obtain the limiting value, say a_i^* of denumerable points of S_i; i = 1,2,... Every such point is an event intra-system, and hence is characterized by $(\theta, x(\theta); t)$. This is implied and not expressed here with the intra-systemic events $\{a_i\}$.

We write all this as,

$$a_i^* = \lim \{a_{i1}, a_{i2}, \ldots\} \text{ intra-systems, } i = 1,2,\ldots \qquad (1A1)$$

Intra-system events are combined with evolutionary inter-systemic events in interactive, integrative, and evolutionary learning trajectories. Thereby, we show in Figure 1A1 the following evolutionary sets (Rucker, 1982b):

$$a_0 = a_0$$
$$a_1 = \{a_0, a_1(a_0)\}$$
$$a_2 = \{a_0, a_1(a_0), a_2(a_0, a_1(a_0))\}$$
$$\ldots\ldots\ldots\ldots\ldots\ldots\ldots\ldots$$
$$a_n = \{a_0, a_1(a_0)\} \qquad (1A2)$$

The limiting value of such evolutionary trajectories as shown in Figure 1A1 on a given S_i surface is given by,

$$a_i^{**} = \lim(\theta \to_S \Omega)\{a_i = \{a_0, a_1(a_0), a_2(a_0, a_1(a_0)), \ldots\ldots$$
$$a_n(a_0, a_1(a_0), a_2(a_0, a_1(a_0), \ldots a_{i-1}(_{a0})\} \qquad (1A3)$$

The non-null intersection between $\{a_i^*\}$ and $\{a_i^{**}\}$ is denoted by, $\{a_i^*\} \cap \{a_i^{**}\} = a_i^{***}$. Furthermore along the evolutionary path overarching intra-systems and inter-systems, the set

$$\cup\{a_i^*\} \cap \{a_i^{**}\} = a_i^{****} \neq \phi. \qquad (1A4)$$

In terms of evolutionary knowledge-flows, $\{\theta\}$ derived from *tawhidi* epistemology premised on the *Qur'an* (Ω) and the *sunnah* (S), we write,

$$(d/d\theta)[\cup\{a_i^*\} \cap \{a_i^{**}\} = a_i^{****}] > 0. \qquad (1A5)$$

Furthermore,

$$\lim (\theta \to_S \Omega \equiv (\Omega, S)) \, [(d/d\theta)[\cup\{a_i^*\} \cap \{a_i^{**}\} = a_i^{****}] \subseteq \Omega. \qquad (1A6)$$

The dimension of this limiting space is larger than any finite space. Hence we refer to such a space as super-space. The dimensionality in $(\theta, x(\theta), t)$ – knowledge, space, time – is referred to as super-cardinality.

Any subset of the (knowledge, space, time) super-space preserves the same property as expression (1A5). Hence, by its super-cardinality, (Ω, S) is super-topology. Included in it, is itself as super-topology. Any subset of (Ω, S) and of relations defined by this super-topology forms a topology. The difference though is this:

$$\text{Super-cardinal topology } \Omega \rightarrow_S \rightarrow \theta \rightarrow \text{World-System} \tag{1A7}$$

$\rightarrow$ relational continuity across continua $_S\rightarrow\Omega$ super-cardinal topology (closure of the unbounded super-topology)

But any subset of the closure has a finite cardinality.

Thus super-cardinality and its consequences on super-space, and super topology are unique properties and are universal in the sense of the overarching unbounded closure of *tawhidi* universe (*alameen*).

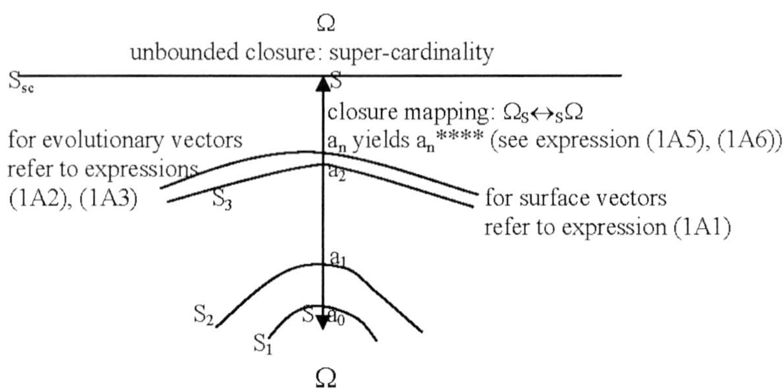

Figure 1A1: Super-cardinal (S_{sc}) super-space and super-topology of the *tawhidi* knowledge, space, and time dimensions

The evolutionary learning equilibriums intra-system, combined with inter-system dynamics, as in expressions (1A5) and (1A6), are shown in Figure 1A2. This diagram is repeated in several other places in this book to explain evolutionary learning equilibriums according to the episteme of unity of knowledge arising from imperfect states of evolutionary learning in unity of knowledge to better states of such evolutionary learning. See initially Figure IA1 in this case.

A conical cross section of the evolutionary learning spaces (topologies) and their dynamics is shown below.

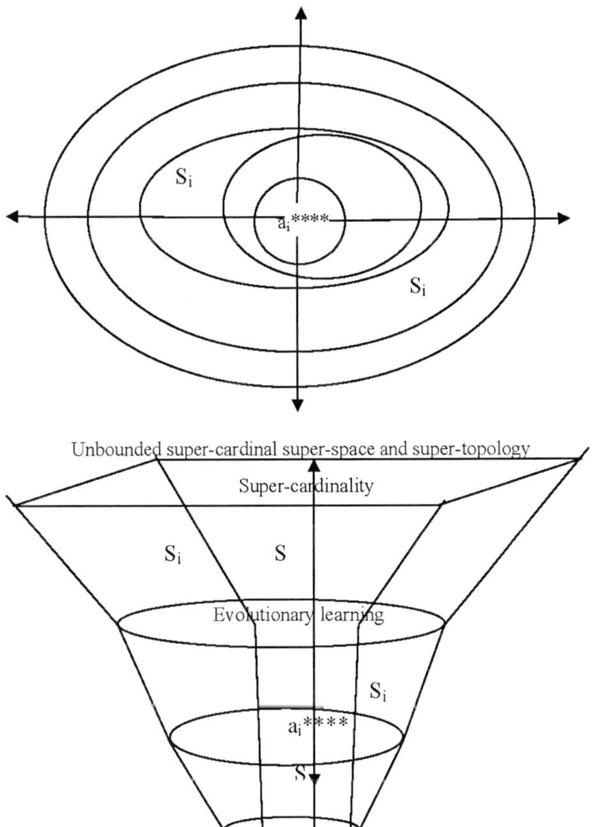

Figure 1A2: Evolutionary learning equilibriums moving towards super-cardinality

References

Barrow, J.D., 1991, "Laws", in his *Theories of Everything, the Quest for Ultimate Explanation*, pp 12-30, Oxford University Press, Oxford, Eng.

Buchanan, J.M., 1999, "The domain of constitutional economics", in his, *The Logical Foundations of Constitutional Liberty*, Indianapolis, IN, Liberty Fund.
Buchman, D., (trans.), 1988, *Al-Ghazzali Niche of Lights,* Brigham University Press, Provo, Utah.
Campbell, D.T., 1988, "Evolutionary epistemology", in Radnitzky, G. & Bartley, W.W. III (eds.), *Evolutionary Epistemology, Rationality, and the Sociology of Knowledge*, pp.47-89, Open Court, La Salle, IL.
Choudhury, M.A., 2000, *The Islamic Worldview, Socio-Scientific Perspectives*, Kegan Paul International, London, Eng.
—. 2006a, "Evolutionary equilibrium in learning spaces of unity of knowledge", *The Middle East Business and Economic Review*, 18(2), 39-53.
—. 2006b, "Development of Islamic economic and social thought", in Kabir. M. H. & Lewis. M., (eds.), *Handbook of Islamic Banking*, Edward Elgar Publishing Company, London, Eng.
—. 2011a, "So thirty years after – where do Islamic economics, finance, and banking stand?" in his *Islamic Economics and Finance: an Epistemological Inquiry*, pp. 233-264, Bingley, UK: Emerald Publications.
—. 2011b, "On the existence of evolutionary learning equilibriums", *Journal for Science*, 16, 68-81.
—. 2011c, "A critique of economic theory and modeling: a meta-epistemological general-system model of Islamic economics", *Social Epistemology*, 25(4), 423-446.
—. 2013, *Socio-Cybernetic Study of God and the World-System*. IGI-Global Inc., Philadelphia, PA.
Choudhury, Mufeedh, U. A., 2009, *Money, Finance, and the Real Economy in Islamic Banking and Finance: Perspectives from the Maqasid as-Shari'ah*, unpublished MSC dissertation, Department of Economics, University of Stirling, Stirling, UK.
Coulson, N.J., 1984, *Commercial Law in the Gulf States: The Islamic Legal Tradition*, Graham & Trotman, London, Eng.
Einstein, A., n.d., "The laws of science and the laws of ethics", in his *Lectures in Physics*, Philosophical Library, New York, NY.
Farrell, F.B., 1996, "Disenchantment of the world and of subjectivity", in his *Subjectivity, Realism and Postmodernism*, pp. 1-4, Cambridge University Press, Cambridge, Eng.
Fitzpatrick, T., 2003, "Postmodernism and new directions", in Alcock, P. Erskine, A. & May, M. (eds.), *Social Policy*, pp. 125-133, Blackwell, Oxford, Eng.

Gafford, J., 2009, "Innovation, competition, and growth: Schumpeterian ideas within a Hicksian framework", in Cantner, U. Luc Gaffard, J. & Nesta, L. (eds.), *Schumpeterian Perspectives on Innovation, Competition, and Growth*, pp. 7-24, Springer, New York, NY.

(Imam) Ghazzali, A.H. trans. by Marmura, M.E., 1997, *The Incoherence of the Philosophers*, Brigham Young University Press, Provo, Utah.

Gruber, T.R., 1993, "A translation approach to portable ontologies", *Knowledge Acquisition*, (5)2, 199-200.

Guessoum, N., 2011, *Islam's Quantum Question*, I.B. Taurus, London, Eng.

Hammond, M. Howarth, J & Keat, R., 1991, *Understanding Phenomenology*, Basil Blackwell, Oxford, Eng.

Hassan, H., 2002, "Contracts in Islamic law: The principles of commutative justice and liberality", *Journal of Islamic Studies*, (13)3, 257-297.

Hawking, S.W. and Mlodinow, L., 2010, "Alternative histories", in his *The Grand Design*, pp. 80, 82, Transworld Publishers, London, Eng.

Hayek, F.A., 1990, reprint, "The use of knowledge in society", in Spechler, M.C. (ed.), *Perspectives in Economic Thought*, pp. 183-200, McGraw-Hill, New York, N.Y.

Husserl, E. trans. by Lauer, Q., 1965, *Phenomenology and the Crisis of Philosophy*, p. 155, Harper & Row Publishers, New York. Particularly note the comment on the perceived absence of ethical roots in Occidental scientific inquiry.

Johnston, J., 1984, "The k-variable linear model", in his *Econometric Methods*, pp. 193-198, McGraw-Hill Book Co., New York, NY.

Kuhn, T.S., 1970, *The Structure of Scientific Revolution*, University of Chicago Press, Chicago, IL.

Kung, H. trans. by Bowden, J., 2007, *Islam, Past, Present & Future*, One World, Oxford, Eng.

Lawson, T., 2003, "Competing theories and policies within post-Keynesianism", in his *Reorienting Economics*, Routledge, London, Eng.

Lucas, R.E. Jr., 1975, "An equilibrium model of the business cycle", *Journal of Political Economy*, 83, pp. 1113-44.

Maxwell, G., 1962, "The ontological status of theoretical entities", in Feigl, H. & Maxwell, G. (eds.), *Minnesota Studies in the Philosophy of Science, Vol. II: Scientific Explanation, Space and Time*, pp. 3-27, University of Minnesota Press, Minneapolis, Minnesota.

McAuliffe, J.D., 2006, *The Cambridge Companion to the Qur'an*, Cambridge University Press, Cambridge, Eng.

Meera, A.K.M. & Larbani, M., 2006, "Part I: Seigniorage of fiat money and the *maqasid al-shari'ah*: the unattainableness of the *maqasid*", *Humanomics, International Journal of Systems and Ethics*, (22)1, pp. 17-33.

Popper, K., 1988, "Natural selection and the emergence of mind", in Radnitzky, G. & Bartley, III W.W., (eds.) *Evolutionary Epistemology, Rationality, and the Sociology of Knowledge*, pp. 139-54, Open Court, La Salle, IL.

Rahman, F., 1980, *Major Themes of the Qur'an*, Bibliotheca Islamica, Minneapolis, Minnesota, USA.

Ramadan, T., 2004, *Islam, the West and the Challenges of Modernity*, The Islamic Foundation, Leicester, UK.

Romer, P.M., 1986, "Increasing returns and long-run growth", *Journal of Political Economy*, 94, pp. 1002-1037.

Rucker, R., 1982a, "Large cardinals", in his *Infinity and the Mind*, Bantam Books, New York, NY.

—. 1982b, "Excursion I: the transfinite cardinals", in his *Infinity and the Mind*, pp. 239-286, Bantam Books, New York, NY.

Schumpeter, J.S., 1968, "The scholastic doctors and the philosophers of natural law", in his *History of Economic Analysis*, Oxford University Press, New York.

Shackle, G.L.S., 1971, *Epistemics & Economics*, Cambridge University Press, Cambridge, Eng.

Usmani, M. T., 2004, *An Introduction to Islamic Finance*, Maktaba Ma'Ariful Qur'an, Karachi, Pakistan.

Waliyullah, S. trans. by Jalbani, G.N., 1985, *Al-Fauz Al-Kabir Fi Usul Al-Tafsir, The Principle of Qur'an Commentary*, National Hijra Council, Islamabad, Pakistan.

Weeramantry, C.G., 2001, *Islamic Jurisprudence, an International Perspective*, The Other Press, Kuala Lumpur, Malaysia.

Whitehead, A.N., 1979, "Fact and form", in Griffin, D.R. & Sherburne, D.W. (eds.), *Process and Reality*, pp. 39-60, The Free Press, New York, NY.

CHAPTER TWO

THE COMPARATIVE *QUR'ANIC* EPISTEMOLOGICAL QUESTIONS

In this chapter, the interconnected ontological, epistemological and ontic (evidential) problem in the philosophy of science is investigated from the contrasting worldviews of the *Qur'an* and the Occident. The objective here is to investigate whether an epistemology of monotheism of the like of the *tawhidi* worldview can be found in Occidentalism to explain similar attributes of unity of knowledge and the world-system.

The *Qur'an* lays down the epistemological foundation of Islamic socio-scientific thought. This is different from the rationalist origins of Occidentalism. This contrasting problem of philosophy of science in terms of conceptualization and empiricism is studied on one hand in reference to some principal occidental references, and on the other by reference to the *Qur'an*. The building blocks of an Epistemological, Ontological and Ontic (EOO) model for delineating the *qur'anic* worldview of a socio-scientific world-system are thus developed. In all of these investigations the worldview of the *Qur'an* is shown to centre on and to be formalized by the ultimate foundation of all knowledge uniquely and universally. This is the oneness of God, interpreted here also as the unity of monotheism, the divine law. This is referred to as *tawhid*.

Contrary to *tawhid* is the root of rationalism that belongs to the order of a form of Kantian dichotomy of knowledge, which in essence is unified, but exists as heteronomy in Kantianism. This chapter thus lays down a first-of-its-kind original investigation on the *tawhidi* foundation of Islamic epistemological thought concerning moral law, science, and the world-system taken in general and in its particulars.

The emergence of scientific thought and its use in the development of a consistent socio-scientific outlook requires an epistemology. There can be no science without a fundamental inquiry into the nature and roots of knowledge. The search for the roots of knowledge leads to a divergence of views on the 'perception' of knowledge itself according to different vintages of beliefs, cultures and norms. The problem to address then is whether it is possible to establish a body of scientific beliefs for all of life and thought that can lead knowledge into a unified whole, trans-culturally and trans-religiously. This precept of the unification of knowledge through a universally acceptable, axiomatic, and systemically pervasive comprehension of the entire scientific order, be that of the natural or the social sciences, is what we will refer to here as the socio-scientific worldview (see the reference section captioned *Notes with References* on Popper, Lakatos, Kuhn, von Mises, Hayek, Choudhury).

The principal characteristic of the worldview is conscious negation of the pluralistic episteme that has been inherited by the academic disciplines through norms alien to a unified systemic conception of the universe and its parts. On positivistic grounds, the domain of the worldview is one of unifying all systems of thought, institutional behaviours, and individual preferences, on the basis of a unique foundation, axiom, and methodology, notwithstanding the differences of issues and problems that differentiated systems may address.

It is thus the formulation of this unique axiom and methodology, its application to various socio-scientific systems, and the analytics of its unshakeable worldview that constitute the main objectives of this chapter.

Epistemology and ontology perceived in occidental thought

Occidental culture and norms started in their conscious lineage back to Greek philosophy (Vermont et al, 1995). This is the perception of life that upholds atomism, whereby the world of material and non-material forms is seen as a realization of rationalism and individualism. Plato and Aristotle explained reason as being derived from the ethical and moral worth of a political order comprising perfectly ethical individuals – the ethically perfect social whole (Barker, 1959; Erguden, 1987).

In his *Republic*, Plato signified the good society in terms of the Good State formed by individual membership of this good society and imbued by the traits of the ultimate Good in the sense of the Socratic conception of goodness. Thus, Plato emphasized the transformation of the individual into a *perfect* moral being in the midst of the Good State. The Good State is seen as an ideal collection of perfectly ethical individuals.

In Aristotle's *Politics*, one finds a unifying approach to the study of ethics and politics. Man is again seen as the embryo of the Good Society, formed out of the inculcation of traits of goodness and justice. But it is the State in the midst of the individual that is seen to realize these moralizing precepts. With the process of advance in the moral transformation of mankind in the midst of the State, Aristotle's great transformation sees growing interconnectedness in the realm of thought and behaviour inducing moral self-actualisation.

What then are the epistemological questions in Plato and Aristotle, as in most other Greek thinkers, that colour the distinctness of occidental belief, culture and norm? In their formulations, the individual self-motivated and socially transformed being is realized by a continuous recourse to individualism and rationalism, for the State has no other means of deriving its moral law. Either the cultural norms or the law of the sovereign king, or the will of the individuated self, formulates the law of ethics under which the state and society must carry out their affairs. What one finds then in such a derivation of a rationalistic doctrine of the democratic order is the epistemological basis for the individuated roots of rationalism. Thereafter, this is collectivised into an organized form. But the realm of rationalism so extended by individualistic patterns of search or social collectivism is a pluralistic *norm* by the very essence of individualism grounding rationalism in this domain. Hence, all such searches result in differentiated new *thought* rather than convergence to a given premise of knowledge.

Knowledge emanating from the monotheistic core on the other hand denotes the most irreducible premise of reasoning and thought. Irreducibility here means the limit of intellectual search for truth or falsehood as antonyms that can accept no further deconstruction by individualist claims. On the other hand, such an irreducible deconstruction is neither microscopic nor macroscopic in nature. It comprehends both. Thus the essence of knowledge is unification across all systems of thought by the very method of interconnecting the micro and macro in one all-embracing form within the generalized holistic model. The result is the discovery of a methodology that addresses the study and application of the most irreducible element of a holistic world-system in which particular sub-systems emulate the nature and foundation of knowledge of the generalized world-system. The actualised methodology remains undifferentiated across all systems.

In the perspective of Greek philosophy of morality, the individual, and the state, such an epistemological issue means the merging of the individual and the state: a unique derivation of the moral law and self-actualisation within the moral domain of self in the primal order. All virtues are realized by the elements and the whole that is the state, according to the plane of the abiding, never changing, evanescent law enacted by the most enlightened individuals. The Greek concept of rationalism thus relegates its staying power to this ever-reducible deconstruction of reality. In this way, the meaning of unification between ethics and politics, and between the individual and the state, becomes an undefined link in the never-ending chain of the cause and effect relationship.

This cause and effect relationship, which extends from its metaphysical primordial essence to the state of manifestations in the realm of reality, is never realized in relation to the epistemologically incomplete nature of Greek and occidental reasoning and thought *ad infinitum*. Hence, knowledge is not possible in such open-ended and ever-evolving systems. With this non-convergent attribute it is equally impossible to discover unification either of knowledge, reasoning, or thought as these get intertwined with the growing interconnectedness between cause and effect in the relational world-system.

Occidental belief, culture and norms as derived and perpetuated from their roots in Greek thought have configured both its material and non-material nature according to the non-convergent and open-ended form of dialectical evolution. Perceptions rule supreme in this case. Perceptions are mentalist sensations of the lower order of mind. Russell writes on the Bergsonian idea of perception as follows (Russell, 1990): "'Pure perception', he says, 'which is the lowest degree of mind -- mind without memory -- is really part of matter, as we understand it.'" Hence, the physical world like the social world in occidental perception is structurally embedded in this formal division between perception-forming rationalistic individualism and the essential roots of monotheistic knowledge, which remains evasive.

One can further take Kantian philosophy in respect of the epistemological question to prove the impossibility of unification of knowledge and thought in occidental belief, culture and norm. Perception in Kantian philosophy belongs to the *a posteriori* world of empirical entities. Perceptual entities do not form essential reality. Kant sees essence to be embedded in what he refers to as the critical imperative. This is Kant's transcendental order of the *a priori* experience. But here too, Kant does not refer to the transcendental as the *T*ranscendent. Consequently, all *a priori* experiences are determined in the realm of perceptions, causing rationalism. The entire argument regarding the impossibility of premising on the epistemological roots in such an incomplete and random search for knowledge, now causes the Kantian *problematique* of rationalism (Friedrich, 1977).

This Kantian problem is further deepened in reference to the ontological and ontic aspects of reality, as developed by Descartes (1954), Hume (1988a, 1988b) and Heidegger (1962). The ontological method of philosophical analysis is based upon the bestowing of explanation to the cause of the *act of be-ing*. Like Kant, who placed all substantive predominance on *a priori* reasoning for forming perceptions manifested in the empirical consequences, but relegated the empirical essence of matter as being non-substantive, so also the *functional* ontological (Gruber, 1993) approach explains the empirical facts *post-hoc* by constructing the premise that describes perceptions. The ontological method is thus a reprieve of Kant's *a priorism* by the deductive method of reconstructing the explanatory basis of the ontic form.

The ontic investigation, in the words of Sherover (1972), "would be one concerning particular facts, actual specific occurrences, and empirical generalizations from them. An ontological investigation, on the other hand, as a Kantian transcendental investigation, would be directed toward the general, universal, and necessary grounds upon which, or limits within which, any ontic, or empirical, experience can occur. The transcendental or ontological is thus logically prior to, and renders possible, empirical or ontic objects or events."

Epistemological problem in occidental philosophy of science

By a similar reference, we will refer to the purely Kantian-type and ontological-type metaphysical entities as the epistemic verities. Just as the ontic is claimed by occidental philosophers to be confined to the evidential world, so also the epistemic will be treated as being confined to the *a priori* realm of primordial forms. The epistemic and the ontic are thus separated independently from each other by these two parts of reality that are dichotomised in occidental culture and norm. Reality according to transcendental metaphysics is to be found *exclusively* in the epistemic; and according to reductionist philosophy of science, it is to be found in the ontic (Sherover, 1972). The philosophy of science of all vintages in occidental culture and norm has proceeded in the midst of such a pronounced dichotomy. It presents itself in the division of religion from the sciences during the Age of Enlightenment. It continues on to prevail over the dichotomy between rationalism and the Transcendent Law, and in its methodological separateness between the micro and macro perspectives of socio-scientific reality.

In mathematics and physics for example, such dichotomous methodological rendering was earlier proven by the impossibility of the Kantian-type of *a priori* thought to comprehend non-Euclidean geometry and its subsequent developments. That is, *a priori* reality could not be correctly perceived in the realm of the cognitive experiential order of the mind as found in Euclidean geometry. Quantum Physics and the latter-days generalized unified field theory questioned the dichotomous nature of analysis of physical reality. For instance, the Principle of Complementarities in Atomic Physics rejects mutual independence between waves, particles, positions, and momentum. Instead, it claims that there are analytical complementarities between these to form a complete physical reality (Bohr, 1961).

Yet the explanation of physical reality by failing to invoke the fundamental epistemological question remains too distant from the integrative principle of the epistemic and the ontic in the light of a unified precept of reality. Relativity Physics, for example, understood this unification problem (Maxwell, 1962; Breuer, 1990), but could not disentangle itself from the axiom of universal constants, in which there is the assumption of the constancy of the velocity of light. The subsequent development of the Relativistic Simultaneity Principle explaining convertibility between time and events in any fixed geometrical frame of reference was riddled with the problems of specifying an isotropic space-time structure. Einstein (1960) had to axiomatically create this assumption in order to endow symmetric properties to the relativistic constructed universe. In spite of this assumption, Infeld (1951) has shown that variations in the 'universal constant' of the equation of the geodesic of space-time curvature in an Einstein-Minkowski-Friedman type universal equation can lead to an indeterminacy problem of the curvature itself. These are fundamental problems of modern physics in respect of cosmology, cosmogony, and unification of physical fields.

The consequential problems arising from these multiple views of the universe and the questioning of the axiomatic foundation of physics, lead to two deep problems of occidental epistemology. These problems are firstly, the question of appropriateness of the axiomatic premise, which involves the Kantian-type *problematique* with the *a priori* nature of universal constants. Secondly, the problem of unification theory in physics still remains distant because of its un-unified understanding of the epistemic and ontic interrelationship (Carnap, 1966; Hicks, 1979).

The dichotomy between the epistemic and the ontic premises causes dissociation between cause and effect in reasoning. Yet the understanding of this interconnection is the most crucial part of a unified socio-scientific reality to be found in the epistemology of monotheism and its unified world-system.

In Husserl's (1964) phenomenology for example, one discovers this deepening methodological chasm. The problem of phenomenology is essentially one of discerning a description of physical reality by combining perceptions with experiences. Like Kant, according to Husserl the all-embracing Transcendent belies cognisable possibility. Hence, such an experience is taken out of scientific relevance. The consequential perception in reasoning and thought now falls victim to the dichotomous nature of the socio-scientific world-system, its rationalist law, inferences and rules. Hammond et al. (1991) write in this regard as follows:

> Husserl objects to this division between a world which can be known and a world which cannot be known. Like Kant, Husserl rejects the idea of what transcends *all* experience as a possible object of knowledge, because it is impossible to experience; but, unlike Kant, he wants to eliminate such a concept from having any role to play in knowledge.

In the end, socio-scientific inquiry in Occidentalism resides in a system of logical relationship as perceived by the temporal dimension of rationalism. What is comprehended in the perceived world is what has been the object of rationalistic cognition; what can be comprehended in the perceived world is subjected to a set of logical relationships. The precincts of knowledge are the undefined, random and competing domains formed by individualistic rationalist reasoning. This kind of reasoning can be certified by power (as in Hellenic State). It can be won by popular support of a hegemonic scientific community (institutional democracy). It can be promoted by the strength of resources (funding and pedagogy in occidental science). According to Russell, as explained by Sainsbury (1985), "numbers, classes, the self, the physical world, space, time and events are not 'genuine entities' but rather 'logical constructions' or 'logical fictions'."

Epistemological problems in occidental philosophy of economics

The sheer recourse to a rationalistic foray in the construction of logical types while delimiting the potential of the Transcendent in such a logical construction is at the root of moral neutrality in occidental socio-scientific thought. Such a moral neutrality or ethical exogeneity is most pronounced in received economic doctrines.

What makes the moral neutrality so pronounced in economics is the severance of social justice from the economic question of efficiency, or treating the two as competing values while the same attitude to values is also transmitted to the institutional framework. In this regard, the two most important agents of the economic system being consumers and producers, the role of government in the economy is to establish harmony in their wellbeing. Thereby the connection between these agents is brought about by the formalization of a social wellbeing objective that is endowed by its appropriate socio-economic variables and policy variables.

The role of the government and development institutions is to formulate and implement policies and programmes, regulate the production and pricing mechanism, undertake joint ventures and constructively transform the preferences of consumers, technological choices and production menus of the producers in the light of social policies. Social justice represented by distributive equity becomes an important target for governments to promote. Yet in the midst of all these virtues, the social goals and market efficiency remain competing opposites; trade-offs. This is the permanent perspective of received economic theory.

1. Microeconomic problem

In the context of such a trade-off we find the economic agents independently playing competing roles in the principal functions of any economic activity, namely, consumption, production, and distribution. The economic formalism in this regard works as follows:

The product market determines its supply of goods by supply prices and outputs that are determined not by the demand side, but by the marginal cost conditions of the firms in either perfect or imperfect conditions (Mansfield, 1985). Consumer demand (hence, market demand) in the product market is determined by conditions of the demand side of price formation as given by the marginal consumer utilities of the goods. Supply price equates demand price to establish equilibrium price and output in the context of these two independent sides of price determination. Subsequently, costs are minimized, profits are optimised, and individual utilities are maximized simultaneously. This is the nature both of the partial and general economic equilibriums in markets.

When imperfect competition prevails, economic theory still assumes the same kinds of market clearance dynamics and profit-maximization conditions, with the exception of differences in demand and supply elasticity and regulated pricing conditions. Consequently, in orthodox neoclassical economic theory, the market is a system of exchange between competing agents, within and across buyers and sellers, who act in their independent focus of objectives. Methodological individualism and the axiom of economic rationality are upheld in such a perfect or imperfect market order.

The first methodological problem to arise from the above-described kind of market exchange is the incompatibility of the underlying perspectives on prices in the two cases. For, if exchange is demand-driven, then demand prices would predominate. Now, all possible supply prices, p_s, must be determined by all possible demand prices, p_d. Thus, $p_s = p_s(p_d)$, with $\partial p_s/\partial p_d > 0$. Furthermore, the supply function, S(.) is such that, $q_s = S(p_s) = S(p_s(p_d))$, where, q_s denotes the quantity supplied at price p_s. Likewise, it can be argued that for the demand side, $q_d = D(p_d(p_s))$.

From these relations we obtain the excess demand function, $E = E(p_d,p_s)$. Subsequently, $dE/dp_d = (\partial E/\partial p_s).(dp_s/dp_d) + (\partial E/\partial p_d)$. Now since $(\partial E/\partial p_s) > 0$, $(\partial E/\partial p_d) > 0$, and $dp_s/dp_d > 0$, all these conditions are attained because of market equilibrating conditions, yet it is impossible for $dE/dp_d < 0$, the condition otherwise required for market equilibrium to exist.

Likewise, it can be shown that it is impossible for $dE/dp_s < 0$ (Henderson & Quandt, 1958). Therefore, the only way that a market equilibrium can exist in either the Walrasian or the Marshallian sense is to *assume* that market equilibrium price exists, but without explaining the underlying process of price adjustment, even though this may negate the existence of market equilibrium. The existence of market equilibrium and the underlying behaviours of pricing and objective functions thus become axiomatic premises of economic theory. This rules out the possibility of integrating the demand and supply pricing mechanisms, and thereby explaining the underlying behavioural relationships in anything other than the competitive nature of markets. This furthermore emanated from the postulate of methodological individualism of maximizing behaviour (Shackle, 1972; Parsons, 1964).

The above kind of indeterminacy of market equilibrium in the ontological (relational process explanation of the existence of equilibrium) sense is found to occur in the factor market and the monetary sector as well. In the factor market, a Pareto optimal general equilibrium result necessitates that the consumers' rate of commodity substitution between the supply of factors and the demand for commodities must equal the corresponding factor marginal products. That is, factor prices will be determined proportionately to the consumers' rate of commodity substitution. Hence, factor prices become indeterminate corresponding to the indeterminacy between demand and supply prices of goods as explained earlier. This point also implies that the marginal productivities of factors remain unobservable quantities. Hence, factor prices cannot be determined in terms of marginal product as suggested by the general equilibrium result. These points are formalized by Henderson and Quandt (1958).

In the monetary sector, the price of money (finance) is taken to be the interest rate, which measures a speculative value of uncertainty, whereas money is used to transact goods/services that attain actual prices. Thus, the economic return on money must be the return on the good/service, which is a function of the price of the latter. How then can interest rate be taken as a price of money replacing the objective value in terms of the prices of goods/services? There is a problem of inconsistency here, which is not resolved in the ontological meaning of the quantity theory of money or in the Keynesian liquidity preferences and the LM-curve (Veneiris & Sebold, 1977).

Indeed, with such an axiomatic assumption, market prices like consumer prices cannot be observed. We thus encounter the problem of observing an *a priori* axiomatic rationalism (Etzioni, 1988). Contrarily, given the different moulds of pricing and exchange behaviour in the market system, such as pure co-operation, mixed competition and co-operation, 'satisfying' behaviour of consumers and firms, and polity-market interactive decision-making, it then becomes impossible to associate any realism with the theoretical and institutional experiences of neoclassical economy according to competitive behaviour. Here the ontological premise of neoclassicism does not convey economic reality. Thus, both the epistemic and the ontic experiences of market economy as perceived in mainstream economics are foreign to the essentially co-evolutionary interactive and integrative functions of agents in alternative forms of market systems (Fischer, 1986).

2. Macroeconomic problem

What we have shown in terms of the microeconomic problem is equally true of macroeconomics. But here a second compounded nature of the problem arises. Behaviour in microeconomics does not reflect itself at the macroeconomic level. Aggregation in consumption, production and distributional functions of a market economy do not form the price level of aggregate demand for goods and services at the macroeconomic level. In other words, the macroeconomic level is totally independent of, insulated from, and neutral to, any ethical perceptions at the microeconomic level.

Consequently, we find that by working in this form of insulated system, all efforts to reorganize the economic system towards social justice have failed. This class of failures includes the Marxist notions of exchange value and use value of labour: The classical economic school equates all exchange value to the notion of normal prices, and the neoclassical school equates both exchange value and use value to the common objective equilibrium price (Cole, 1966). We know from the literature that the Hegelian influence in Marxist economics and the latter days' neoclassical reformulation of Marxist economics by Oscar Lange have shown that Marx had no new contribution by way of an epistemological economic methodology (Lange, 1938).

The micro- and macro-economics of Austrian and Keynesian origins are developed in Marxism as under Wicksell (1935), von Mises (1962), Hayek (1967), and Keynes (1936, 1973), in either of the following aggregation scenarios: Firstly, individual and firm-specific aggregations of preferences are used to yield consumption, production and distributional menus. This is the case explained by the Austrian school and the new institutionalism of the social choice vintage (Wicksell, 1935; von Mises, 1962; Hayek, 1967; Feiwel, 1987). This paradigm is also shown as the Marxist problem of transformation of values into prices. Secondly, no such aggregation is assumed and the individualistic micro-orientation is replaced by the analysis of perceived relations among the activities of consumption, production, and distribution, without assuming behavioural preferences. Here we have the Keynesian economic epistemology and its reformulation in the social welfare framework (O'Donnell, 1989).

In all cases of economic methodology, we find the legacy of the Kantian-type dichotomy and irresolution between the epistemic and ontic verities. Equally we find that the sub-setting of the rationalistic nature of economic reasoning leads to perpetual instability and incoherence between reality, economic behaviour and social institutions (Gonick, 1987). This is the legacy of the Hegelian dialectics. It assumes an accentuated form in Karl Popper's refutation and conjecture methodology imported into economics.

Perception as opposed to knowledge evolves in the midst of this kind of incongruence between essence and form. The distinction between microeconomic and macroeconomic reasoning dichotomises economic reality. This otherwise should be unified in order to address the questions of both economic efficiency and distributive justice simultaneously, rather than in a substituting trade-off perspective of either microeconomic or macroeconomic analysis.

Summary of methodological orientation in the social and natural sciences

The impossibility of realizing knowledge

The nature of irreconcilability between various epistemological questions of economics and its irresolution at the level of microeconomics and macroeconomics creates fundamental methodological problems in economics. One such predominant methodology is that given by Popper.

Boland (1991) points out that Popper's refutation and conjecture hypothesis in the philosophy of science is not applicable to tautological facts that establish themselves by self-referencing. If this is the case, it is difficult to see either through the natural science or social science doctrines how a worldview can be established on the basis of the Transcendental Truth in occidental thought. The self-referential nature of the Transcendent Truth makes this truth pervade *all* systems as cause and effect, epistemic-ontic circular causation and continuity of unified reality, but which need not lend to direct cognitive verification. Its verification and logical nature comes from the descriptions and interrelationships that it generates, explains, and perpetuates across varied systems. Hence, the same kind of temporality emerges in Popper's refutation hypothesis as in Hegelian and Darwinian forms of dialectics and organisms, respectively (Hegel, 1956; Choudhury, 2009).

It is equally devoid of universality, although it pronounces the derivation of specific theories from more universal categories of theories. Yet this form of theory derivation leaves out of its purview the possibility of a Transcendental Truth, lapsing thus into the Kantian *problematique* and Husserl's problem in phenomenology on the impossibility of attaining knowledge. In such a contradiction between completeness, continuity, universality and unification on the one hand, and epistemic-ontic duality, methodological individualism and systemic independence on the other hand, evolutionary economics degenerates simply into mutative processes. The result does not yield socio-scientific interrelationship and convergence. Knowledge remains impossible by way of inter-variable causality. Only rationalist perceptions prevail.

Islamization of the socio-scientific order

We have now come to establish that the over-riding socio-scientific epistemological question must address the simultaneity issue of the epistemic and the ontic parts of unified reality in the light of a circular causation and continuity model involving cause and effect circularity in socio-scientific relations. We have shown that the possibility of attaining knowledge depends upon the unified reality in the epistemic-ontic complementary mould. This perspective carries with it two singularly universal precepts.

These are: firstly, the uniqueness of the axiomatic premise that encompasses, without differentiation, all systems of reasoning and thought taken separately between the monotheistic (*tawhidi*) oneness between the good things of life (unity of knowledge); and the same between the contrary things of life (unity of de-knowledge as a manifestation of differentiation, conflict, independence, and methodological individualism). The latter are manifestations of the rationalist order of reasoning, thought, and world-system construction.

Secondly, the unique methodology of the epistemic-ontic circular causation and continuity model of unified reality prevails across all systems. The socio-scientific order is thus seen as interactive, integrative and co-evolutionary in reference to this unique methodology of unity of knowledge, although different systems may deal with different verities of problems. Besides, the methodology and the underlying method of circular causation apply to both the systems of unity of knowledge and to differentiated ones taken up in their separate categories, respectively.

The axiom and methodology of the epistemic-ontic circular causation and continuity model of unified reality

We now go on to explain the axiom and methodology, and hence the worldview of the epistemic-ontic circular causation and continuity model of unified reality. We present its model description as follows (Choudhury, 2006a).

Let the concept of the stock of knowledge be defined as the optimal, uncreated form of the primordial essence of existence. This verity neither can be nor needs to be empirically configured. Yet its verification comprises the logical, comprehensive, testable, and inferential relations of reality. However, this stock of knowledge can be explained by taking recourse to the real world relations. The universe in its entirety, and hence in its specificity of systems, is then seen as a topological entity (Barrow, 1989; Barrow 1991; Reichenbach, 1958).

Being a topology, its existence is defined by the properties of its subsets. Thus, with Ω as the given *stock of knowledge*, it is mapped 'onto' the whole of the topology (Maddox, 1970), T giving $T(\Omega)$ maps 'onto' the subsets of T denoted by T_i giving $T_i(\Omega)$. Hence, $\cup_i[T_i(\Omega)] \subset T(\Omega)$;

$\cap_i[T_i(\Omega)] \subset T(\Omega)$. These properties mean that the entire topology, T, is spanned by the totality of all its subsets of knowledge, and there is integration among these subsets to yield a knowledge-induced consensus, which forms part of the knowledge-induced topology. Only relations, as they are affected by the knowledge variable, matter in this topology. When the primordial stock (or topologically complete stock) Ω is so mapped into the temporal order to give a good definition to forms and their relations, then $T_i(\Omega)$ becomes a *flow of knowledge*. We will henceforth denote this knowledge-flow by $\theta_i \in T_i(\Omega)$.

The implication is then clear. The primordial stock contains the sum of its flows across systems i =1, 2, …, whereas, $\theta_i \in \mathbf{R}$ meaning knowledge flows across the real continuous space and across all dimensions of such spaces, such as Euclidean, non-Euclidean, super-manifolds ($\mathbf{R}^\infty$) (Gray, 1989; Dewitt, 1992). But Ω being the primordial, and thereby, uncreated *stock of knowledge* with topologically explainable functions, is such that, $\Omega \in$ super-manifold having super-cardinality (Cantor, 1955; Rucker, 1983; Dewitt, 1992). Consequently, the Cardinality of $[\cup_i\{\theta_i\}] << $ Super-cardinality of $[\Omega]$. In the topological meaning of these systems of knowledge-flows, the relations governed by them form mathematical, measurable and continuous functions. Hence, knowledge-flows and the functions induced by them in $\mathbf{R}^\infty$ are all mathematically integrable and analytic (Choudhury, 2000; Kline, 1990). This property enables the process of relating Ω to θ_i and vice-a-versa.

The complementation part of Ω in T is $\Omega\sim$, which we will call 'de-knowledge' (falsehood or ignorance), such that, over all possible evolution of knowledge, Ω in $\mathbf{R}^\infty$, $\Omega\cap\Omega\sim = \phi$. $\Omega\sim$ is characterized by its own subsets and flows of 'de-knowledge', as for the case of Ω.

Besides, in between Ω and $\Omega\sim$ there is the region of irresolution, denoted by P, which is neither Ω nor $\Omega\sim$ clearly, until a clear specification has been made between these categories for the socio-scientific issues in question. P is legion in human experience but is well-determined between Ω and $\Omega\sim$ by the progress of knowledge. P is referred to in Islamic terminology as *mubah* (indeterminacy of a rule, *ahkam*). Such a progress of evolutionary knowledge is activated by interactions, j =1,2,...N, in the universal and embryonic sense among agents, systems and their variables. Thus, $P_{ij} = P_{ij}(\theta_{ij}\cup\theta\sim_{ij})$ denotes the class of perceptions that depend upon the temporary state of knowledge-flows or 'de-knowledge-flows' in the agent/system/entity denoted by 'i' at the jth interaction. As interactions proceed, integration between systems sets in with the convergence of P to either one or the other of Ω or $\Omega\sim$ through its determination.

Thus,

$$\lim(j\text{-}\!\!\rightarrow N)[P_{ij}] = \Omega_{iN}, \text{ when } P_{iN} \cap \theta\sim_{iN} = \phi; \text{ or } \quad (2.1)$$
$$\{\theta\sim_{iN}, \text{ when } P_{iN} \cap \theta_{iN} = \phi, N \in \aleph \text{ (the natural number system).}$$

The attainment of θ_i either directly, or through the above-mentioned convergence process of P, points to a critical juncture of knowledge formation. This explains the simultaneity between interaction and integration. Simultaneity taken across all systems and interactions means the unification of knowledge by the stock of knowledge, Ω, across systems. This primordial stock of knowledge that so unifies reality uniquely in all systems and causes evolutionary knowledge to appear is the system of the divine law.

In Islam the divine law is derived from the *Qur'an* and the authentic guidance of the Prophet Muhammad (*sunnah*). These sources form the definitive premise for establishing the unity of knowledge in terms of the monotheistic law and it is explained and applied for all varieties of the socio-scientific order. The essence of irreducibility and the unifying premise of this complete, uncreated, primordial stock of knowledge, which explains and is in turn explainable (although not measurable except functional in the super-cardinal topological sense) is referred to in the *Qur'an* as *tawhid*, the Oneness of God.

The axiom of the *tawhidi* precept is thus the Oneness of God, monotheism, in the context of its comprehension and application of the divine law (*sunnat Allah*). The methodology of the *tawhidi* precept is based on the possibility and unification of knowledge, Ω, through the plane of evolutionary knowledge values, θ_i, as interaction and integration proceed. This simultaneity between interaction and integration across agents and systems of thought occurring through systemic interrelations is known in Islamic literature as *ijtihad*. It forms the third pillar of the Islamic epistemological inquiry through the learned participants in deriving knowledge, rules and norms from the fundamental sources of the *Qur'an* and the *sunnah*.

The pervasiveness and dynamic evolution of θ_{ij} through sequences of *ijtihad* by invoking the divine law in every detail of life by circular interaction and responses between agents, entities, variables and systems, form the interactive, integrative and co-evolutionary cause-and-effect interrelationships of the most embryonic form. They encompass society, political economy, politics, markets, and the scientific order. Hence, the methodology of the epistemic-ontic circular causation and continuity model of unified reality comes into life by the cause-effect *inter-*

relationships between the evolutionary knowledge domains, their cognitive transformations of the socio-scientific order and the regeneration of knowledge-flows by circularly causal *inter*-relationship through further evolutionary learning by discourse (*ijtihad* and *shura*).

The epistemic nature of the knowledge premise is brought about by the primacy of the Islamic law (*shari'ah*) in acquiring knowledge as the realization of relational phenomena within the context of the universal topology Ω of such systemic relations. The epistemic nature of such knowledge leads to the ontological flows of θ_i and the ontic realization of cognitive forms. The circular causation between these epistemic and ontic parts is established by the regeneration of further increases in the epistemological rendering through evolutionary knowledge arising from the ontic reality, which is endowed by the knowledge-induced cognitive power. The circular causation is made continuous by the dynamics of *ijtihad* and the *shura-tasbih* learning process in terms of interaction between and integration across agents, entities and systems. At each of these points of re-launching the *ijtihadi* and *shuratic* process, there are strings of rules, which we call the *qur'anic ahkam*. They bestow fresh life to the flows of knowledge on the understanding, interpretation, and application of the *shari'ah*. Thus, the epistemic-ontic circular causation and continuity model of unified reality is established as a distinct departure and an antidote to the occidental field of rationalist perceptions in thought.

Formalizing the epistemic-ontic knowledge model

We will now formalize the cause-effect relations of the epistemic-ontic circular causation model of unified reality in the following way:

Let, $\mathbf{x}(\boldsymbol{\theta}_{ij})$ denote the vector of socio-scientific variables induced by the vector of knowledge-flows, $\boldsymbol{\theta}_{ij}$ across agents/entities/systems, $i = 1,2,..,N_1$, and interaction $j = 1,2,..,N_2$. We then convert these socio-scientific variables into their objective functions, $f_{ij} = f(\mathbf{x}(\boldsymbol{\theta}_{ij}))$. Such mathematical functionals form the social wellbeing functions of diverse Islamic world-systems (Choudhury, 1991a): the polity-market processes of an Islamic approach to sustainable development (Ansari & Choudhury, 1994), and matter-energy relations in physics.

The chain of cause-effect interrelationships between the derived evolutionary knowledge and the cognitive forms of the socio-scientific order is described in Figure 2.1.

$$\ldots\theta_{11}\rightarrow_{f11}\mathbf{x}_{11}\rightarrow_{g11}\theta_{12}\rightarrow_{f12}\mathbf{x}_{13}\rightarrow\ldots\rightarrow_{f1N}\theta_{1N1}\rightarrow\ldots \quad (2.2)$$
$$\ldots\theta_{21}\rightarrow_{f21}\mathbf{x}_{21}\rightarrow_{g21}\theta_{22}\rightarrow_{f22}\mathbf{x}_{23}\rightarrow\ldots\rightarrow_{f2N}\theta_{2N1}\rightarrow\ldots$$
$$\ldots\ldots\ldots\ldots\ldots\ldots\ldots\ldots\ldots\ldots\ldots\ldots$$
$$\ldots\theta_{n1}\rightarrow_{fn1}\mathbf{x}_{n1}\rightarrow_{gn1}\theta_{n2}\rightarrow_{fn2}\mathbf{x}_{n3}\rightarrow\ldots\rightarrow_{fnN}\theta_{nN1}\rightarrow\ldots$$
$$\ldots\ldots\ldots\ldots\ldots\ldots\ldots\ldots\ldots\ldots\ldots\ldots$$

where, $f_{ij}(\theta_{ij}) = \mathbf{x}_{ij}$, $g_{ij}(\mathbf{x}_{ij})=\theta_{ij}$. That is, $g_{ij}\bullet f_{ij} > 0$, i =1,2,...N1; j =1,2,..., N2

Figure 2.1: The chain of cause and effect interrelationships in the epistemic-ontic circular causation and continuity model of unified reality

The material consequences of knowledge values are shown to have positive relationships with the regenerated quanta of knowledge-flows (Choudhury & Nadvi, 1992). Hence, g_{ij} and f_{ij} are invertible, continuous, measurable functionals in each other's domains (Chichilnisky, 1982). This result signifies the interactive nature of evolutionary knowledge-flows both between themselves and in terms of the interconnectedness that knowledge generates through its ontic forms in the socio-scientific order.

The interaction and integration denoted by,

$(\lim(j\rightarrow N2)[(\theta_{ij},\mathbf{x}_{ij})] = (\theta_i^*,\mathbf{x}_i^*)$, i = 1,2,..,N1.,
(N1,N2) $\in \aleph$ (natural number system) signify the intra-systemic interactions-integration simultaneity.

Furthermore, the above functionals also establish inter-systemic simultaneity between interaction and integration. Here the mathematics becomes complicated and can be formalized by tensor analysis. For details, the technical reader may refer elsewhere (Choudhury, 2006b, Gel'fand, 1961). On a simplified note, if we denote by $\theta_{ii'...j}$ the inter-systemic knowledge functional, then,

$$f_{ii'...j}'(\theta_{ii'...j},\mathbf{x}_{ii'...j}(\theta_{ii'...j'})) = f_{ii'...j}, \quad (2.3)$$
for i,i',...= 1,2,..N1. j=1,2,..,N2, then,
$\int[f_{ii'..j}d\theta_{ii'..j} <<$ Supercard. $[\Omega]$.

For practical purposes we note that, it is only possible to mathematically integrate across complex systems within finite limits. Hence, a finite mathematical integral equivalent of the above contour integral can be taken. This proves the result that the knowledge-flows are both derived from and mapped back 'onto' the *stock* of knowledge, both temporally and primordially in the topological sense of deriving logical relationships and proving their existence in the socio-scientific order.

The primordial *stock* of knowledge we have shown here is the uncreated and complete knowledge stock.[1] The implications of the knowledge-flows forming a subspace of the *tawhidi* topology are several (Choudhury, 1991b reprinted 2011a).

Firstly, in the *tawhidi* socio-scientific order, the objective functionals shown above do not follow an optimisation criterion. Rather, a better method for such systems is the simulative methodology over $(\theta_{ij},\mathbf{x}(\theta_{ij}))$.

Secondly, the integration of θ_{ij} over a subspace of θ suggests that Ω is explainable by topological analysis but not directly. This proves the possibility of attaining knowledge in the epistemic-ontic circular causation and continuity model of unified reality; and not merely leaving knowledge to perception, as in the case of 'de-knowledge'. Thirdly, since primordial knowledge equals a full and complete knowledge *stock*, which according to the *Qur'an* will be manifest in the hereafter (*akhira*), this precept holds a fundamental meaning for knowledge-flows and the constructed world-system according to the *tawhidi* worldview (Qadri, 1990; Faruqi, 1977; Yadegari, 1984; Al-Din, 1991; Choudhury, 1992a).

The central place of knowledge-flows as both the input and output of the circularly and continuously regenerated socio-scientific order with functionals for the knowledge-induced material and relational forms (ontic) of the relational transformations underlying such forms (ontology) means that morals and ethics become endogenous elements of the *tawhidi* worldview. The meaning of endogeneity is conveyed by the cause-effect linkage manifesting pervasive complementarities (participation), epistemic-ontic circularity and continuity, and regeneration of knowledge-flows through the discursive *ijtihadi* process based on continuously evolved *qur'anic ahkam* as knowledge evolution rises from lesser to higher degrees of its realization followed by its corresponding cognitive forms.

Thus, unlike the occidental philosophy of the sciences that we have investigated above, the *tawhidi* worldview presents a totally polar approach to questions of social justice, economic efficiency and the scientific concept of complementarities and unified field theory. We shall examine these concepts now.

---

[1] *Qur'an* (42:12): "To Him belong the keys of the heavens and the earth: He enlarges and restricts the Sustenance to whom He will; for He knows full well all things."

The epistemic-ontic circular causation and continuity model of unified reality applied to Islamic political economy

Social choice in Islamic political economy in the framework of the knowledge model is developed by means of interactive preferences between polity and the market system. The concept of polity is taken here in its most embryonic and pervasive meaning, commencing from the grassroots and proceeding upwards to higher echelons of decision-making and participation. The polity of this kind is formed of representatives from all interest groups in society having the sound knowledge of the *shari'ah* and endowed by attributes of integrity as manifestation of divine essence (*fitra*), God-consciousness (*taqwa*). Minority representation (*dhimmi*) can also be included (Doi, 1984). Such a representation forms an extensive linkage with the research, scientific, educational, and other necessary groups in society at large. They collectively deliberate upon and come up with consensual rules for the problems at hand. Such rules are derived by a combination of analytical methods and facts and are formulated on the basis of specific *qur'anic ahkam* (rules) that can be formulated in reference to the *Qur'an*, the *sunnah* and the *ijtihadi* and *shuratic* process. The result is the collective and socially representative set of preferences of this embryonic and pervasive polity (*shura*) in concert with human experiences on the specific issues at hand.

The rules (*ahkam*) are developed and delivered through the medium of institutions, and implementation of policies and programmes. Examples here are institutions supportive of the *shura*, policies of elimination of interest rates, institution of profit-sharing with economic co-operation, the institution of *zakat* or wealth taxation, and policies on the control of waste called *israf* in the *Qur'an*. These are then received by the market system (ecological order) as ethical inputs for conscious use. The impact of such rules through appropriate institutions is expected to transform the consumer preferences and production menus, and bring about co-operative mechanisms in the economic relations between households and owners of capital who generate distribution and ownership among all in a market venue. This is the idea of moral consciousness. In it economic efficiency is gained by complementarities between the choice of technology, the types of goods produced, and the evolution of human capital in accordance with the co-operative industrial democracy of the workplace and the changing ethically induced preferences of consumers on the one hand, and profitability motives of the producers, on the other hand.

In this way, the input of knowledge through rules rendered by polity finds its response from the market venue where individuals, households, labour and enterprises, big, medium and small, react to the preferences of polity and respond. Such responses form integrative knowledge formation and perpetuate the dynamics of the embryonic and pervasive *shuratic* process. Responses could be of various kinds. They could pronounce acceptance and reinforcement of earlier policies and their further development. They could call forth revisions and changes or abandonment of the adopted rules. In every case, a fresh round of interactive preferences between polity and the market system regenerates the process and leads it into an *ijtihadi* consensus followed by repetitive evolution on the same scale of processes.

In the broadest sense of the word, this is the nature of social consensus representing an *ijma. Ijma* may represent majority consensus, but not necessarily unanimity. *Ijma* represents the integrative process generated by interactions, *ijtihad* and *shura* out of studying the problems of the embedded world-systems (*tasbih*). Interactions leading to integration are followed by co-evolution according to the complementary order of pairing between entities in the world-system.

In this *shuratic* process, the joint preferences of the agents of change are defined by $(\succ_p \cap \succ_m)(\theta_{ij})$, where $(\succ_p)$ denotes the preferences of polity as specifically defined here in terms of its universal decision-making nature in the Islamic socio-scientific order. $(\succ_m)$ denotes the preferences of the market system (ecological order). But only the joint preferences can be induced by the knowledge variables, θ_{ij}, for the reason that θ_{ij} is the realization of the interaction-integration-co-evolution principle of socio-scientific complementarities.

Now, since the complementarities must work across evolutionary fields of knowledge-flows and knowledge-induced forms inter-systems and intra-systems, therefore, there logically comes about complementarities between economic efficiency and distributive equity in this framework. The entire neoclassical idea of marginal rate of substitution, trade-off, opportunity cost, incongruence of pricing and preference formation in the milieu of methodological individualism, independence and atomistic competition (perfectly competitive markets), are replaced by the principle of complementarities in the co-evolutionary interactive-integrative world-system.

This means the possibilities of co-operation between participants exist in the Islamic political economy, even though such arrangements are governed by the response of the market-driven preferences with induced knowledge-flows for the mutual wellbeing. For example, it would be illogical to substitute unskilled labour for skilled labour, when unskilled labour as participants in an enterprise can form a co-operative. Another example is the augmentation by *zakat* expenditure of marginal start-up ventures for the needy to gain financial feasibility of such marginal enterprises. In all such ventures, resource allocation among alternatives improves the social wellbeing of the participants, brings about linkages between enterprises and economic sectors, universalises ownership through workplace democracy, integrates skilled and unskilled labour, and establishes a *dynamically evolved* basic needs regime of enterprise and development through participation and discourse.

Hence, the social wellbeing evaluation model of such ventures is based on the co-operative behaviour of mutual wellbeing, profitability and diversification, rather than on substitution and competition.

The concept of moral consciousness in the epistemic-ontic model

At this point, it seems relevant to present a brief note on the concept of moral consciousness. The profitability of an Islamic enterprise rests on profit-sharing under a model of economic co-operation. Such is a participatory economy. This in turn is a function of several factors: owner-worker incentive to launch joint ventures; co-operative decision-making in the enterprise; common preferences toward mutual benefit to own assets in the firm and thus to generate profits; participative linkages between various firms and sectors for marketing the goods. In all of these, the principles of *ahkam* formation on specific matters and their simulation in a universally simulative way, form the discursive basis of knowledge evolution in the interactive-integrative milieu. Now rationality becomes a realization by mutual preferences to establish complementarities for the benefit of wellbeing and profitability. This in turn transmits the mutually interactive preferences among agents/entities/systems across the political economy.

It is thus seen that the principle of moral rationality, market order, self-interest and targets of profitability as grounds for economic efficiency are not ruled out. However, such individualistic motivations are activated through a co-operative medium based on a knowledge simulation that must, in a natural way (not through policy imposition), cause social benefits of production, distribution, and consumption to occur. Hence, social justice, distributive equity and economic efficiency and growth are treated simultaneously in the complementary participative processes.

Formalization of social wellbeing function by the epistemic-ontic model

The social choice menu of the Islamic word-system is based on the same meaning as the epistemic-ontic circular causation model. This is now seen to actualise through the embryonic and pervasive medium of the *shuratic* process (Choudhury, 1990; Kamali, 1989; Arif, 1985). We have seen above that functionals of the n-tuples, $(\theta_{ij},x_{ij}(\theta_{ij}))$, being continuous and mathematically measurable functions with non-zero Jacobian matrices, are well-defined entities. They are mathematically integrable and differentiable functions (Adams, 1987).

A special case of these functionals is the Social Wellbeing Function. Let this be expressed by, $W = W(\theta_{ij},\mathbf{x}_{ij}(\theta_{ij}))$, with the interactive preference set, $Pr.=\{(\succ_p \cap \succ_m)\}(\theta_{ij})$. That is, θ_{ij} qualifies all the bracketed preference maps. Let the recursively interactive relations between the socio-scientific variables, $\mathbf{x}_{ij}(\theta_{ij})$ and θ_{ij}, be given by $G = G(\theta_{ij},\mathbf{x}_{ij}(\theta_{ij}))$, $i = 1,2,..,N_1$; $j = 1,2,.. N_2$.

W(.) has a finitely cardinal mathematical measure conveying an objective level of social wellbeing attained from any process of interaction and integration, and hence by knowledge-flows arising from the *shuratic* process. The instances of integration among the agents of the embryonic and extensive *shuratic* process, which includes the market order, are temporary points of social consensus (*ijma*) – evolutionary learning equilibriums. These are temporary in the sense that they give rise to fresh new levels of social consensus resulting from continuous knowledge simulation on the basis of continuing *ijtihad* and *ijma* on both generality and specifics across a range of issues as they arise. This bears the mark of the Islamic discursive dynamics. This property of W(.), whose evaluation follows estimation and simulation rather than the optimising nature of the social welfare function in mainstream economics, subjected to the constraints of G(.) and Pr., points out that there are at best locally temporary equilibriums attained by analytical simulation and social consensus. No globally stable equilibriums can exist as knowledge evolution proceeds (Choudhury, 1992b).

The epistemic aspect of the social choice model involves the simulation of the *shari'ah* rules (*ahkam*) by the discursive polity (*shura*). The epistemic aspect is denoted by $(\theta_{ij};\succ_p)$. This generates an ontic effect on the market system (ecological order) as signified by $\{\mathbf{x}_{ij}(\theta_{ij});\succ_m\}$. The epistemic and the ontic are now circularly interlinked in endless continuity by polity-market interactions explained by $\{\theta_{ij},\mathbf{x}_{ij}(\theta_{ij});\succ_p \cap \succ_m\}$, with $G = G(\theta_{ij},x_{ij}(\theta_{ij}))$. Integration following the interactions is explained by the simulation of $W(\theta_{ij},\mathbf{x}_{ij}(\theta_{ij}))$ over the domains of $\{\theta_{ij},\mathbf{x}_{ij}(\theta_{ij}\};\Im_p\cap\Im_m))$ with $G(\theta_{ij},\mathbf{x}_{ij}(\theta_{ij})) = G$. It can finally be noted that the interactive preferences 'Pr' are subject to evolution with the evolution of knowledge-flows, thus signifying that opportunities and choices open up endlessly in this evolutionary epistemic-ontic form of knowledge-induced socio-economic order.

The epistemic-ontic (E-O) circular causation and continuity model in natural sciences

The E-O model is a universal one in terms of its axiom of *tawhid* and its methodology of unification of knowledge across all systems. This knowledge model can explain the example of energy creation in space-time as many other scientific facts in new methodological ways.

According to the entropy theory of the Second Law of Thermodynamics and the theory of Dark Matter in the universe, there is an irreversible process of energy dissipation and disorder arising from this non-conservation of energy. This phenomenon cannot be explained by Einstein's fundamental equation of conservation of energy and mass (Riordan & Schramm, 1990). The energy that is dissipated is either lost in the splitting of particles reaching the proximity of the event horizon around an ergosphere of the black hole, of which one part of the split particles falls into the black hole and escapes conservation, forming negative energy (Wald, 1992). Likewise, the energy that is released by increasing entropy, as claimed by the Second Law of Thermodynamics, is converted into heat and is lost. There is growing magnitude of such entropy losses of energy in the form of heat with changes in the universe over time.

In both of the above explanations of non-conservation of energy with inherent physical interactive processes continuously taking place in the universe, the concept is one of uselessness of the lost energy by its conversion into super-gravity or heat form. Non-conservation here does not mean that the total stock of particle/wave equivalent of energy is dissipated. The magnitude of non-conservation is thus equal to the universal physical disutility of matter.

In the E-O knowledge model no such concept of disutility holds except in the case of de-knowledge. But by way of mathematical disjointedness between the knowledge and de-knowledge sub-spaces of *tawhidi* topology, it is strictly necessary that every quantum of knowledge be measurable, and hence, be continuous. Consequently, every quantum of de-knowledge must also be measurable and continuous. However, there will exist functional transformations of such situations, such as the significance of increasing and decreasing returns, respectively. Thus, the sub-spaces of knowledge and de-knowledge are unbounded or bounded by their own independent cardinalities, respectively.

The energy dissipation concept of physical science is now replaced in the knowledge model by the process of continuous sifting between knowledge and de-knowledge, as interaction, integration and co-evolution advance. Along with this, the determination of temporarily indeterminate perceptions between knowledge and de-knowledge sub-spaces is realized. Thus, the concept of energy dissipation is now replaced by adding points to the de-knowledge sub-space. In this way, the universally systemic whole proceeds towards two perfectly independent and disjoint nexuses of topological relations. The universe evolves through *inter*-relationships within the two disjoint nexuses along paths that form trajectories of the same or differentiated dimensions. Such families of trajectories may be termed the *tawhidi* nexus of trajectories (Choudhury, 2006a).

The disjoint nature of the nexus categorizing independence between the relations of truth and the relations of falsehood (de-knowledge) forms the universal principle of conservation as utility or disutility of physical forms, waves, particles, energy and matter. The unification of knowledge (hence, of de-knowledge) within its independent nexus of trajectories, formed through inter-systemic and intra-systemic interaction (removal of perceptions) and integration (forming independence between knowledge and 'de-knowledge') is the grand principle of complementarities in the E-O knowledge model.

In the formal form, one of the $(g\bullet f)(\theta_{ij})$ compound ($\bullet$) functions in the chain of relations shown earlier, becomes the topological relation(s) of energy as interpreted by the E-O knowledge model. The underlying interaction and integration can be explained likewise. The objective simulation criterion of the social wellbeing function mentioned earlier, now applies in its own right to the knowledge-induced energy model. This result from social sciences into natural sciences proves the uniqueness and universality of the *tawhidi* axiomatic foundation and the E-O methodology as derived from *qur'anic ahkam*, to all systems.

The epistemic-ontic (E-O) model compared to theories of knowledge in the Islamic literature

The epistemic-ontic circular causation and continuity model of unified reality is derived from *qur'anic ahkam*. We summarize here that, the epistemological question is derived from the *tawhidi* foundation of the

Qur'an. The unique system of unification as oneness and its systemic integration is derived from the *qur'anic* message of balance, purpose and felicity centred on the realization of God from end to end of the universe, across all systems, in the primordial state, and in the hereafter. The possibility of ontic regeneration of knowledge premised in the flow form is derived from the understanding of the Signs of God in the universe. The concept of the *stock of knowledge* is derived from the uncreated nature of the *Qur'an* and the manifestation of the full truth and supreme felicity attainable in the hereafter, which the *Qur'an* emphasizes unequivocally. The evolutionary knowledge precept of thought and life is derived from the *qur'anic* principle of consultation in its most embryonic and pervasive form as a medium to unravel, comprehend, and apply the tenets of the divine law. This medium is the *shura* acting as a process of knowledge formation and its circular causal *inter*-relations of unified reality in the evidential world-system. Thus, to derive the E-O model directly and independently from the *Qur'an*, only the *qur'anic ahkam* are relied upon. This approach endows the E-O model *prima facie* to be based on the roots of the revealed law alone, not on rationalism. No Islamic syllogism can thus be developed with an Islamic claim that depends upon any epistemological premise other than *tawhid*. Thus, no such enunciation, as either the predominance of reason or the notion of complementarities between revelation and reason, is invoked in the development of the E-O model. All formative rules of reasoning, thought and life are initially and continuously generated from the *qur'anic ahkam*.

Reason-essence, called *fitra*, is the medium for exciting, comprehending, and applying the *qur'anic ahkam*. The E-O model unequivocally maintains that the only basis of knowledge in Islam is the revealed law of monotheism, with reason simply being a product of the revealed law. Within the revealed law is also subsumed the non-conflicting unison between the *Qur'an* and the authentic *sunnah*. However, it is revealing to note here that the E-O model shows profound conformity with the ideas of some of the great Islamic philosophers and scientists. But because of its singular root in the *qur'anic ahkam* the E-O model contradicts the rationalist philosophers not in the idea of knowledge evolution as a dialectical process, but in the sense of the rationalistic dialectics relating to form and spirit in their dualistic role found in the rationalist philosophers (Nasr, 1978).

On this subject matter, first we note the theory of knowledge given by Ibn al-Arabi. He says that knowledge can be derived from two sources and there is no third. Chittick explaining this idea presented by Al-Arabi in his *Futuhat*, writes (Chittick, 1989):

> The first way is by way of unveiling. It is an incontrovertible knowledge which is actualized through unveiling and which man finds in himself. He receives no obfuscation along with it and is not able to repel it.....The second way is the way of reflection and reasoning (*istidlal*) through rational demonstration (*burhan `aqli*). This way is lower than the first way, since he who bases his consideration upon proof can be visited by obfuscations which detract from his proof, and only with difficulty can he remove them.

Ibn al-Arabi's unveiling of knowledge is indeed a forerunner of the idea of evolutionary knowledge-flow that occurs in the human soul and then represents itself in the mind, and thereby in the unified world-system. In regards to the inseparable centricity of *tawhid* in all such flows, which means the derivation of knowledge-flows from the stock, Ω, Al-Arabi explained, in Chittick's (op cit, 1989, edited) words, "Useless knowledge is that which is disconnected from its source and origin, i.e. from the divine reality. Any knowledge outside of *tawhid* leads away from *Allah*, not toward Him. But knowledge within the context of *tawhid* allows its possessor to grasp the interconnectedness of all things through a vast web whose centre is the divine. All existent things come from *Allah* and go back to Him." This concept of knowledge also establishes the circularity and continuity of the E-O model of unified reality with *tawhid* as its axiomatic foundation.

Imam Shatibi's theory of wellbeing for the public purpose (*maslaha*) as derived from Imam Malik's idea of public preferences (*istihsan*) is found to underlie the formalization of the social wellbeing objective criterion of the Islamic political economy in the E-O model (Masud, 1984). The non-utilitarian theory of the public purpose by Shatibi and Malik implies two properties of the social wellbeing objective. Firstly, *al-maslaha-wal-istihsan* cannot be limited by tangible hedonic preferences derived from consumer satisfaction levels. The absence of self-interested preferences cannot therefore introduce methodological individualism and independence in the consumers (decision-makers) of *al-maslaha-wal-istihsan* social wellbeing function. Aggregation of Benthamite-type utility indices of independent consumers cannot construct the *maslaha* function. The *al-maslaha-wal-istihsan* goods, being non-utilitarian goods, must be augmented with social felicity. In the E-O model such felicities are direct functions of knowledge-flow values. Consequently, a simulated type of the social wellbeing function of the E-O model is a logical corollary of the *al-maslaha-wal-istihsan* model (Choudhury, 1993; Zarqa, 1980).

Syed Qutb's (1974) idea of systemic knowledge-flows agrees partially with the E-O knowledge model. In his definition of knowledge, "Knowledge is complete comprehension and interaction with this comprehension, in the depths of the soul and conscience, which is then followed by action in harmony with them." The departure of the E-O model from Syed Qutb's model appears when the former is found not to aim at a philosophy of metaphysics. Rather, it pertains to the philosophy of science and its theoretical-empirical wholeness (the epistemic-ontic). The implication of Qutb's theory in this relation is one-directional from knowledge to cognition to world. At face value this agrees with the E-O model, for both the input and output of this system is knowledge-flow. Hence, knowledge breeds knowledge. But the important difference is in relation to the medium of knowledge-induced felicity that forms the ontic premise to regenerate further knowledge. This kind of dynamic is not seen in Qutb's theory (Mousalli, 1990).

The E-O model is not in complete accord with Imam Ghazzali's views on epistemology. The difference occurs due to the overly psychological and individuated level of knowledge possibility in Ghazzali's *Ihya*, which would then lead to the comprehension and application of the *shari'ah* in social life. This is also the view held by the lateral aggregation principle of social utilitarianism. In recent times it is shared by the neoclassical theory of social choice (Feiwel, 1987; Arrow, 1951; Ghazzali trans. Faris, 1966). In the E-O knowledge model instead, the simple aggregative nature of social choices is replaced by interactive preferences. The individual is introduced as an agent in this interactive preference milieu to which he contributes and from which he learns.

Other contemporary writers who have written on Islamic epistemology and the philosophy of science, such as Nasr (1968), al-Attas (1990), Manzoor (1991), and Sardar (1988), have either leaned on Hellenic philosophising to characterize a *tawhidi* idea of Islamic science or have written on the need for investigating Islamic epistemology, but not on its constructive and developmental framework for the Islamic socio-scientific order, keeping in view the analytics gained from such *qur'anic* worldview.

Parting with pluralism in the epistemic-ontic model of unified reality

The fissure and total dissimilarity of the E-O knowledge model from *all* occidental epistemological questions and philosophies of science is similarly carried over to the oriental epistemological question as well. In occidental scientific/philosophical norms and culture we have seen dualism as the sole difficulty preventing the unification of knowledge and reality. In the oriental norm and culture, dualism takes the form of pluralism. The problem of One-Many either as an association of similar things or as the unity of all things in the light of the Absolute, is not compatible with the mapping of the Oneness Precept 'onto' the world-systems.

The mapping of the Absolute 'onto' everything is a once-and-for-all, complete, and predestined relationship. Thus, its static relation to another thing is endowed in each entity and system of the universe. Now K_i can map 'onto' two systems, say A_1 and A_2, in two possible ways. But in either of these cases the functional relation so determined remains unchanging:

$$\Omega \rightarrow \theta_i,\ A_1 \cap A_2 = \phi;\ \text{thus } \theta_i \rightarrow A_1 \text{ and/or } \theta_i \rightarrow A_2 \text{ independently}; \quad (2.4)$$
$$\text{or}, \{A_i \cap Aj\} = \phi;\ i,j = 1,2.$$

In either of these cases, the mapping, once realized, completes its function and no further dynamics of the A_i-sets are possible with the advance of θ_i. If A_i are similar things, then $\theta_i \rightarrow A_1 \cap A_2 = A_1 = A_2$, with simply a scalar difference between the A_i-sets. This is a tautology in the temporal world. In neither of these cases is the principal idea of evolutionary knowledge apparent through which the universe unifies. In the case of the multiplicity of disjoint relationships among systems into which θ_i maps itself, the effect would be to make this disjoint relationship rigid and unchangeable. For this reason, Lovejoy refers to this form of the One-Many problem as "monistic or pantheistic pathos" (Rucker 1983).

The pluralism caused by dualism and multiplicity, as reflected in the entire system of norms and cultures of occidental and oriental perceptions of science and philosophy is thus eliminated in the *tawhidi* worldview in the midst of its pervasive principle of unity of knowledge. In this chapter this principle is explained by formalizing the E-O model. The dynamic of unity of knowledge according to the *tawhidi* worldview is found to be a process of organic unification through circular causation *inter*-relationships, which carry with them the unique axiomatic *tawhidi* premise and its E-O methodology. Both of these are derivations directly from the *qur'anic ahkam*.

Conclusion

The epistemological question remains an unresolved one in the comprehension of the occidental socio-scientific order. As for the occidental norm and culture of science, this has deepened in the fold of dualism, which has uniformly influenced the epistemological *problematique* in the natural and social sciences. Even if physics were to unify the four forces of nature in the near future (Hawking, 1980), the deeper and central meaning of epistemology – that is, how to endogenously mould the ethical values with the ontic domains of thought and life – remains an evasive issue from the sciences. This is what we have referred to as the nature of ethical neutrality or ethical exogeneity of the entire system of occidental social and natural sciences.

Equally, the epistemological question suffers from a deepening sense of pluralism in the oriental norms and culture. The perspectives here are simply a repetition of the occidental epistemological view in a pantheistic form. Hence, attempts to discover the epistemology of science are replaced in the oriental framework by the epistemology of metaphysics, wherein the individual, society and science cannot present their interactive and integrative relational manifolds. One thus comes to the conclusion that such pluralistic systems represent repetitive social Darwinism, Kantianism and Popper's legacy in the philosophy of science across multiple segmented systems.

The epistemic-ontic circular causation and continuity model of unified reality makes intra-system and inter-system unification the governing methodology of its axiomatic premise of unity of knowledge. This is that of *tawhid*. *Tawhid* by itself is not configured materially in systems. Rather, the monotheistic law inherent in *tawhid* makes the socio-scientific systems develop flows of derived knowledge through systemic discourse and complementarities (participation) from the fullness of the *tawhidi* stock. These manifestations of knowledge-flows and their circularly continuous interactive and integrative *inter*-relationships between agents, entities, and relations in systems, regenerate knowledge-flows and evolve them to the point of their cumulative manifestation. This terminally cumulative reality is of a topological nature, not an observed one. It thus establishes the meaning of the epistemological premise of unified reality and makes this possible in world-systems in terms of derived knowledge and relations. Hence, the answer to the epistemological question in the *tawhidi* worldview is an affirmative one: knowledge is possible and realizable, yet dynamic by virtue of circular causation and continuity in evolutionary learning spaces.

Such a conclusion is the inevitable analytical result of the E-O knowledge as derived from the *qur'anic ahkam*. It is shown here to hold the high-water mark of epistemological possibility in the socio-scientific order. All past and present Islamic epistemologists do not necessarily share such an approach to derivation and universal characterization of the E-O model. We have referred to a few of them in this chapter.

Furthermore, the assertion of the impossibility of knowledge in the Islamic framework has continued on in contemporary times, with Idris (1987) and Rahman (1988) as examples. The possibility of knowledge in the Islamic epistemological context always means that it can never be optimal either in the sense of comparison with fullness of knowledge – which is God's alone and which is used as the epistemological premise in our study – and also in the sense of the inherent incompleteness of knowledge as it advances from lesser to higher degrees of cumulative enhancement. In this simulation sense, such knowledge advancement can never be complete, absolute or perfect in the cognitive order of existence.

The consequences of such an incompleteness of knowledge (as compared with the indelible completeness of divine knowledge) find their expression in the paradigm and models that emanate from such an epistemological meaning of incompleteness. Optimal models of science and economics in particular, are replaced in such a case, with simulation models that acquire the features of process in the context of our interactive, integrative and evolutionary learning model (**IIE**).

Author Notes

The quantity theory equation has a *post-hoc* error in terms of its indeterminacy of causal relations between prices and money supply. See Laidler, D., 1989, "The quantity theory is always and everywhere controversial - why?" *Atlantic Canada Economic Association Papers*, 1; Desai, M., 1989, "Endogenous and exogenous money", in Eatwell, J. Milgate, M. and Newman, P., (eds.) *New Palgrave: Money,* W.W. Norton, New York, NY; Choudhury, M.A., 1991, "The endogenous theory of money and Islamic capital markets", *Journal of Economic Cooperation Among Islamic Countries*, 12.

The idea of praxeology in economics as the foundations of economic science at the microeconomic and macroeconomic levels is presented by the Austrian economist von Mises. Few Muslim scholars of the past and present have dwelled on the explicit treatment of *tawhid* in the natural and social science methodology.

References

Notes: on Popper, Lakatos, Kuhn, von Mises, and Choudhury. The concept of the worldview is opposed to those of paradigm and normal science given by Kuhn, T.S.,1970, *The Structure of Scientific Revolutions*, University of Chicago Press, Chicago, ILL.; the idea of scientific research program by Lakatos, I., 1978, *The Methodology of Scientific Research Programmes,* Cambridge University Press, Cambridge, Eng.; the idea of falsification by Popper, K.R., 1972, *Conjectures and Refutations: The Growth of Scientific Knowledge*, Routledge and Kegan Paul, London, Eng.; and the idea of theory (e.g. praxeology) by von Mises, L., 1966, *Human Action: A Treatise on Economics*, Contemporary Books, Chicago, ILL. For the concept of worldview see Choudhury, M.A., 1993, *Comparative Development Studies: In Search of the Worldview* (Macmillan Press Ltd., London, Eng. & St. Martin's Press, New York, NY.

Adams, R.A., 1987, *Calculus of Several Variables*, Addison-Wesley Publishers Ltd., Don Mills, Ont. Canada.

Ansari, M.I. & Choudhury, M.A., 1994, "The idea of sustainable development in Islam", *The Journal of Development Studies*, XI:1.

Arif, M., 1985, "Toward the *shari'ah* paradigm of Islamic economics: the beginning of a scientific revolution", *The American Journal of Islamic Social Sciences*, (2:1).

Arrow, K.J., 1951, *Social Choice and Individual Values*, John Wiley & Sons, New York, NY.

Barker, E., 1959, *The Political Thought of Plato and Aristotle*, Dover Publications, Inc., New York, NY.

Barrow, J.D., 1989, "The Mathematical Universe", *World and I Magazine*, May.

—. 1991, In this regard a non-mathematical discussion of the philosophies of mathematics and its universal structure is given by J.D. Barrow, *Theories of Everything, the Quest for Ultimate Explanation*, Oxford University Press, Oxford, Eng.

Bohr, N., 1961, *Atomic Theory and the Description of Nature,* Cambridge University Press, Cambridge, Eng.

Boland, L.A., 1991, *The Methodology of Economic Model Building, Methodology After Samuelson*, Routledge, London, Eng.

Breuer, R., 1990, For a discussion of the constraint of physics on universal constants see R. Breuer, *The Anthropic Principle, Man as the Focal Point of Nature*, Birkhauser, Boston, MA.

Cantor, G., trans. Jourdain P.E.J., 1955, *Contributions to the Founding of the Theory of Transfinite Numbers*, Dover, New York, NY.

Carnap, R., 1966, This is essentially a problem of causality and effect in physics. See, Carnap, R., "Causality and determinism", in *Philosophical foundations of Physics*, edited by Gardner, M., Basic Books, Inc. New York, NY.

Chichilnisky, G., 1982, "Structural instability of decisive majority rules", *Journal of Mathematical Economics*, vol. 9.
Chittick, W.C., 1989, *Sufi Path of Knowledge*, State University of New York Press, Albany, NY.
Choudhury, M.A., 1990, "Islamic economics as a social science", *The International Journal of Social Economics*, (17:6).
—. 1991a, "Social choice in an Islamic economic framework", *The American Journal of Islamic Social Sciences*, (8:2).
—. 1991b, "The *tawhidi* precept in the sciences", *MAAS Journal of Islamic Science*, (7,2); reprinted in Iqbal, M. (ed.), 2012, *Studies in the Islam and Science Nexus Volume I*, Ashgate, London, Eng.
—. 1992a, "*Book Review: Islamization of Knowledge: A Methodology,* by I. al Din Khalil", *The American Journal of Islamic Social Sciences*, (9:3).
—. 1992b, *The Principles of Islamic Political Economy*, Macmillan, London, Eng. & St. Martin's Press, New York, NY. Issues on existence and stability of equilibrium are formalized.
—. 1993, *The Unicity Precept and the Socio-Scientific Order*, The University Press of America, Lanham, MD.
—. 2000, *"Contrasting models of knowledge and 'de-knowledge'"*, Chapter 10 of in his, *The Islamic Worldview*, Kegan Paul International, London, Eng.
—. 2002, *"The key concepts in understanding qur'anic methodology, Chapter 3* of his, *Explaining the Qur'an*, The Edwin Mellen Press, Lewiston, NY. Here is Cantor's extension formalized by M.A. Choudhury.
—. 2006a, *Circular Causation Model in the Koran*, Vol. 3 of his, *Science and Epistemology in the Qur'an, in 5 Vol.s,* The Edwin Mellen Press, Lewiston, MA, USA.
—. 2006b, *Science and Epistemology*, op cit. Tensor characterization of such *tawhidi* nexuses of trajectories is formalized.
—. 2009, "Dialectics in socio-scientific inquiry: Islam contra occident", *International Journal of Sociology and Social Policy*, (29:9/10), pp. 498-511.
Choudhury, M.A., and Nadvi, M.A., 1992, "Critical examination of the concept of Islamization of knowledge in contemporary times: Ismail Faruqi and Fazlur Rahman", *Humanomics*, (7:5).
Cole, G.D.H., 1966, *The Meaning of Marxism,* The University of Michigan Press, Ann Arbor, Michigan.

Descartes, R., 1954, "Discourse on method", reprinted in Commins, S. & Linscott, R.N. (eds.), *Man and the Universe: The Philosophers of Science,* The Pocket Library, New York, NY.

Dewitt, A., 1992, *Supermanifolds,* Cambridge University Press, Cambridge, Eng.

Doi, R.I., 1984, *Shar'iah, the Islamic Law,* Ta Ha Publishers, London, Eng. for a discussion of *dhimmis* (the protected ones) in the Islamic state.

Einstein, A., 1960, *Relativity, The Special and the General Theory,* Methuen, London, Eng.

Erguden, A., 1987, "Scientific knowledge in Aristotle's posterior analytics", *Journal of Human Sciences,* (VI:2).

Etzioni, A., 1988, *The Moral Dimension, Toward a New Economics,*The Free Press. Various kinds of rationalism are discussed.

Faruqi, B.A., 1977, *The Mujaddid's Conception of Tawhid,* Idarah-i Adabiyat-i-Delhi, Delhi, India.

Feiwel, G.R., 1987, *Arrow and the Foundations of the Theory of Economic Policy,* Macmillan Press Ltd., London, Eng.

Fischer, C.C., 1986, "The Nature and implications of a process conception of rationality based on social learning", *Forum for Social Economics,* Spring.

Friedrich, C.J., (ed.), 1977, *The Philosophy of Kant: Immanuel Kant's Moral and Political Writings,* The Modern Library, New York, NY.

[Imam] Ghazali, trans. Faris, N.A., 1966, *The Book of Knowledge,* Shah Muhammad Ashraf, Lahore, Pakistan.

Gel'fand, I.M., 1961, *Lectures on Linear Algebra,* Interscience Publishers, Inc., New York, NY.

Gonick, C., 1987, "Economic theory and ideology", in his, *The Great Economic Debate,* James Lorimer & Co. Publishers, Toronto, Ont. The institutional impact of neoclassical, Keynesian and other economic theories can be read.

Gray, J., 1989, *Ideas of Space: Euclidean, Non-Euclidean and Relativistic,* Clarendon Press, Oxford, Eng.

Gruber, T.R., 1993, "A translation approach to portable ontologies", *Knowledge Acquisition,* (5:2), 199-200.

Hammond, M. Howarth, J. & Keat, R., 1991, *Understanding Phenomenology,* Basil Blackwell, Oxford, Eng.

Hawking, S.W., 1980, "Is the end in sight for theoretical physics?", Cambridge University Press, Cambridge, Eng.

Hayek, F.A., 1967, *Studies in Philosophy, Politics and Economics,* The University of Chicago Press, Chicago, ILL.

Hegel, G.W.F., 1956, *The Philosophy of History*, Dover Publications, Inc., New York, NY.

Heidegger, M., 1962, *Being and Time*, trans. Macquarrie, J. and Robinson, E., SCM Press, London, Eng.

Henderson, J.M., & Quandt, R.E., 1958, *Microeconomic Theory, A Mathematical Approach*, McGraw-Hill Book Co., New York, NY.

Hicks, J., 1979, *Causality in Economics,* Basil Blackwell, Oxford, Eng. Problem of causality and effect in economics is discussed.

Husserl, E., 1964, *The Idea of Phenomenology*, trans. Alston, W.P. & Nakhnikian, G., Martin Nijhoff, The Hague, Netherlands.

Hume, D., 1988a, *An Enquiry Concerning Human Understanding*, Prometheus Books, Buffalo, NY.

—. 1988b, *Treatise on Human Nature*, edited by Bigge, S., Oxford, University Press, Oxford, Eng.

Idris, J.S., 1987, "The Islamization of the sciences: its philosophy and methodology", *The American Journal of Islamic Social Sciences*, (4:2).

Infeld, L., 1951, "General Relativity and the structure of our universe", in Schilpp, P.A., (ed.) *Albert Einstein: Philosopher-Scientist*, Tudor Publishing Co., New York, NY.

Kamali, M.H., 1989, "*Siyasah shari'ah*", *The American Journal of Islamic Social Sciences*, (6:1).

Keynes, J.M., 1936, 1973, *The General Theory of Employment, Interest and Money*, Macmillan for the Royal Economic Society, London, Eng.

Khalil, Al-Din, 1991, *Islamization of Knowledge: A Methodology,* Occasional Papers Series, The International Institute of Islamic Thought, Herndon, VA.

Kline, M., 1990, "The Foundations of the real and transfinite numbers", in *Mathematical Thought From Ancient to Modern Times, Vol. 3*, Oxford University Press, New York, NY. Here is a translated version of Cantor's formalization of transfinite numbers.

Lange, O., 1938, *On the Economic Theory of Socialism,* The University of Minnesota Press, Minneapolis, Minnesota.

Maddox, I.J., 1970, *Elements of Functional Analysis*, Cambridge University Press, Cambridge, Eng. Topological concepts are given here.

Mansfield, E., 1985, *Microeconomics,* W.W. Norton, New York, NY.

Manzoor, S.P., 1991, "Human ecology and the quest for a universal science", *MAAS Journal of Islamic Science*, (7:2).

Masud, M.K., 1984, *Islamic Legal Philosophy: A Study of Abu Ishaq al-Shatibi's Life and Work*, Islamic Research Institute, Islamabad, Pakistan.

Maxwell, G., 1962, "The ontological status of theoretical entities", in Feigl, H. & Maxwell, G. (eds.), *Minnesota Studies in the Philosophy of Science, Vol. III: Scientific Explanation, Space and Time,* University of Minnesota Press. Minneapolis, Minnesota.

Moussalli, A., 1990, "Sayyid Qutb's view of knowledge", *The American Journal of Islamic Social Sciences*, (7:3).

Naquib al-Attas, S.M., 1990, "Islam and the philosophy of science", *MAAS Journal of Islamic Sciences*, (6:1).

Nasr, S.H., 1968, *Science and Civilization in Islam,* Harvard University Press, Cambridge, MA.

Nasr, S.H., 1978, *An Introduction to Islamic Cosmological Doctrines*, Shambhala, Boulder, CO.

O'Donnell, R.M., 1989, *Keynes: Philosophy, Economics and Politics,* Macmillan Press Ltd., London, Eng.

Parsons, T., 1964, *The Structure of Social Actions,* The Free Press of Glencoe, New York, NY.

Qadri, C.A., 1990, *Philosophy and Science in the Islamic World,* Routledge, London, Eng.

Qutb, S., 1974, *Fi al Tarikh Fikrah wa Minhaj*, Dar al Shuruq, Cairo, Egypt.

Rahman, F., 1988, "Islamization of knowledge: a response", *The American Journal of Islamic Social Sciences*, (5:1).

Reichenbach, H., 1958, "The most general properties of space and time", in *The Philosophy of Space and Time*, trans., by Reichenbach, M. & Freund, J., Dover Publications, Inc., New York, NY.

Riordan, M. & Schramm, D.N., 1990, *The Shadows of Creation, Dark Matter and the Structure of the Universe,* W.H. Freeman & Co., New York, NY.

Rucker, R., 1983, *Infinity and the Mind, the Science and Philosophy of the Infinite*, Bantam Books, New York, NY.

Russell, B., 1990, "Bergson", in his, *A History of Western Philosophy*, Unwin Paperback, London, Eng.

Sainsbury, R.M., 1985, "Ontology", in his, *Russell,* Routledge and Kegan Paul, London, Eng.

Sardar, Z., 1988, *Islamic Futures, the Shape of Ideas to Come*, Pelanduk Publications, Petaling Jaya, Malaysia.

—. 1984, "Islamisation of knowledge or the westernisation of Islam?" *Inquiry*, (1:7).

Shackle, G.L.S., 1972, *Epistemics and Economics, A Critique of Economic Doctrines*, Cambridge University Press, Cambridge, Eng.

Sherover, C.M., 1972, *Heidegger, Kant and Time*, Indiana University Press, Bloomington, IN.

Venieris, Y.P. & Sebold, F.D., 1977, *Macroeconomic Models and Policy,* John Wiley & Sons, New York, NY.

Vermont, J-P., trans. Lambert, C. & Fagan, T.L., 1995, *The Greeks*, The University of Chicago Press, Chicago, IL.

von Mises, L., 1962, *The Ultimate Foundation of Economic Science: An Essay on Method,* Van Nostrand, New York, NY.

Wald, R.M., 1992, *Space, Time and Gravity: The Theory of the Big Bang and Black Hole,* The University of Chicago Press, Chicago, ILL. Penrose Process on ergodic energy splitting is discussed.

Wicksell, K., 1935, *Lectures on Political Economy Vols. 1 and 2,* Routledge and Kegan Paul, London, Eng.

Yadegari, M., 1984, "Shariati and the reconstruction of social sciences", *The American Journal of Islamic Studies*, (1:1).

Zarqa, M.A., 1980, "Islamic economics: an approach to human welfare", in Ahmad, K., *Studies in Islamic Economics*, The Islamic Foundation, Leicester, U.K.

CHAPTER THREE

THE NATURE OF SOCIO-SCIENTIFIC PROCESS STUDY IN THE *QUR'AN*

Religion and science are at a meeting point when premised on a carefully sought out and comprehensive epistemology. This is the message of this Chapter. In it, the universal and unique methodology that meaningfully enables religion and science to converge into an organic holistic relationship, is premised on the episteme of oneness of God, monotheism (*tawhid*). But when understood in terms of the unity of the socio-scientific world-system, the episteme of oneness of God is taken up as the unity of knowledge that is contained in the divine law. Thus there is an inseparable circular causal interrelationship between God, the world-system, and the hereafter. Such a comprehensive holism is explained in terms of an epistemological methodology that grounds the new pervasively complementary perspective of relations between socio-scientific entities, which are taken up in their diversities and details. Such a methodology becomes the worldview when it is proven to be universal and unique within its interactive, integrative, and evolutionary properties. The continuous circular cause-and-effect of the unity of divine law organically relating with the world-system in explicated ways forms the evolutionary learning universe of the *Qur'an* and its methodology, termed *tawhid*, oneness of God. The *Qur'an* excites the ponderous mind on this theme through its verses on the conscious evolutionary learning universes of mind and matter. The episteme of *tawhid* through its reflective extension of the meaning of organic unity in the order of things forms a universal reality that is different from other epistemological and ontological ideas of the mainstream received philosophy of science and society. This chapter highlights this difference while formulating the methodology of a unified socio-scientific universe as explained by *tawhid*.

The *Qur'an* is a divine book of knowledge. It presents knowledge as the divine essence of the oneness of God, referred to as *tawhid*. This word is derived from the generic *qur'anic* term, *ahad*, meaning divine oneness in the sense of there being no partnership with God in any shape, form or implication, either directly or indirectly in the entire of creation. *Tawhid* as the ultimate reality also means God's absolute, complete and perfect state of knowledge that creates, governs and prevails over all the universes solely by itself. The *Qur'an* refers to such perfection of God's attributes in terms of His Creatorship and Sustenance of the universes in the verse:

> Verily this is a Revelation from the Lord of the Worlds: With it came down the Spirit of faith and truth – to thy heart and mind that you (Muhammad) may admonish in the perspicuous Arabic tongue. (26:193-95).

In this regard, God also refers to Himself as the Light of the Heavens and the Earth (*Qur'an*, 24:35).

The Qur'an and the knowledge-centred worldview: briefly delineating the praxis

Qur'anic world-systems

The complete, perfect, and absolute nature of divine knowledge, never changing but ever enriching the universes of self and others, and over which the Creator sublimely rules, is the meaning of the unity of knowledge in its primordial form. From this stock of knowledge, knowledge-flows emanate. Knowledge-flows then determine the *qur'anic* world systems (*alameen*) that explain life, existence and comprehension of true reality. In this sense, divinely derived knowledge-flows are inter-causally linked with human cognition, comprehension, intellection, and thereby relations and inferences. While the acts of comprehension, intellection and inference are commands of the human order, the relational functions exist across human, animate and inanimate orders. However, it takes the human mind to search, discover and unravel the inner depths of organic relations between the animate and inanimate domains as well as between those that fill the human domain.

Thereby, the primal existence of the divine stock of knowledge creates universes that remain permanently premised on this fundamental divine unity of knowledge. From this primal premise of knowledge appear knowledge-induced worlds, their entities, systems, domains, and relations. Such processes and entities learn pervasively within and across their own and other interrelated world-systems. An extensively relational order is thus born out of such learning on the framework of unity across diverse systems and relations, actions and responses. Such a framework of unity of knowledge is conveyed by the epistemology of *tawhid* as the essence of oneness in its perfection, completeness, and the absolute nature of the divine law in the order and scheme of all things. For studies on Islamic epistemology from a historical Islamic perspective and in terms of a *qur'anic* lexicographical approach see Bakar (1991) and Al-Edrus (1990).

The *Qur'an* points to such over-arching learning and relational processes that span all systems of creation in terms of unity across diversity. Knowledge-flows and their induced systems and relations are causally bound together by the unique law of divine oneness that is *tawhid*. We have the following verse from the *Qur'an* in this regard:

> And in the earth are tracts (diverse though) neighboring, and gardens of vines and fields sown with corn, and palm trees – growing out of single roots or otherwise: watered with the same water, yet some of them We make more excellent than others to eat. Behold, verily in these things there are Signs of those who understand! (13:4).

One can also refer to the Chapter of The Bee (*Nahl*), which expounds with instilling depth on the meaning of relational orders caused by the conscious invocation of divine oneness as the epistemology of learning worlds with diversity and complementarities within and among themselves.

On the theme of submission of the animate and inanimate worlds to divine will – that is, to the law of unity – the *Qur'an* says:

> Do they not look at God's creation, (even) among (inanimate) things, – How their (very) shadows turn around, from the right and the left, prostrating themselves to God, and that in the humblest manner? And to God pays obeisance all that is in the heavens and on earth, whether moving (living) creatures or the angels: for none are arrogant (before their Lord). They all revere their Lord, high above them, and they do all that they are commanded. (16:48-50).

Furthermore, the *Qur'an* says on the divinely conscious process of creation:

> It is God Who begins (the process of) creation; then repeats it; then shall you be brought back to Him. (30:11).

The creative nature of knowledge-centred world-systems

The implication of the creative process emanating from and returning to the ultimate source of oneness is continuous, throughout knowledge, space and time. The same process also establishes the closed nature of the evolutionary learning universes in terms of the ultimate reality, which is the hereafter (*akhira*). The *Qur'an* equates the event of the hereafter with confirmation of faith, and refers to it as the equivalent part of the purpose of creation in truth. The event of the hereafter (*akhira*) is thus referred to as the Great Event (*Naba ul-Azim*) (*Qur'an*, 77) or the True Reality (*Al-Haqqah*) (*Qur'an*, 69).

Being premised on the same theme of the intrinsic and conscious nature of unity in creation, the intellection of human faculties is invoked through reflective contemplation (tafakkur). Such contemplation extends over the entire creation beyond mere human domains of reflection. The Qur'an says in regard to the intrinsic consciousness of tawhid in inanimate creation:

> Moreover He comprehended in His design the sky, and it had been (as smoke): He said to it and to the earth: "Come you together, willingly or unwillingly." They said: "We do come (together), in willing obedience." (41:11).

In regard to reflective contemplation and the observant disposition of the human world to *tawhid* the *Qur'an* says:

> Behold! In the creation of the heavens and the earth and the alteration of Night and Day, – there are indeed Signs for men of understanding, – men who celebrate the praises of God, standing, sitting, and lying down on their sides, and contemplate the (wonders of) creation in the heavens and the earth, (with the thought): "Our Lord! Not for naught have You created (all) this! Glory to You! Give us salvation from the Penalty of the Fire." (3:190-91).

A comprehensive understanding of this verse extends its meaning to the entire fold of human cognition, intellection, and reflective empiricism, while being centrally premised and causally determined by divine law (monotheism). It also links both the episteme of divine knowledge and the experiential creative order with the proof of purpose in all of these. This purpose is then brought to relate to the ultimate reality of the hereafter (*akhira*). Thus the meaning of extensively unifying interactions among various domains of realities under the premise of the divine unity of knowledge is induction of all such realities or entities by the signs of God (*ayat*). The meaning of *qur'anic* world-systems (*alameen*) is thereby derived under the praxis of the divine unity of knowledge.

The above brief discussion in this introductory section initiates the nature of Islamic socio-scientific inquiry. This inquiry is relates to searching for and discovering a methodology of the grand and permanent, unique and universal praxis of unity of knowledge as the epistemology of *tawhid* that is explainable in *all* world-systems. This is the idea of the 'theory of everything'. This absolute and unique essence of the *tawhidi* episteme that brings about the fundamental role of divine unity into the experiential world and makes this reality explainable in the framework of unity across diversity has categories of its unravelling. Knowledge-flows and their induced forms in *qur'anic* world-systems commence and continuously return to the divine source of unity. Between these periods of commencement and return there is the intellectual process of creative learning in the ensuing unifying world-systems. Such a process is a vastly relational and unifying order across diversity of domains, relations, and systems. The process of forming such interrelationships and realizing their evolution by the advance of the knowledge of unity in experiential domains reflects the dynamics of knowledge-flows in such universes, once they are derived from the source of *tawhid* and continuously return to the same episteme. This phenomenon is continuous across the continua of knowledge, space, and time in which events happen.

The *Qur'an* refers to this dynamic knowledge-induced movement, the repetitive re-origination in the framework of unity and unification of knowledge, as *khalqin jadid* (creative evolution) or *khalaqa thumma yu'id* (creation and returning). These *qur'anic* phrases mean creatively re-originated orders arising by the command and will of God, thus premising such evolutions on the unity of divine laws. The *Qur'an* says in this regard:

> See they not how God originates creation, then repeats it: truly that is easy for God. (29:19).

The dynamic process of discovering unity in the world-systems after commencing from the *tawhidi* epistemology and configuring the world-systems (domains and systems) on the basis of that very epistemology for confirmation and assertion forms a total belief system. The resulting evolution of knowledge-flows over the totality of knowledge, space, and time, both revealed and hidden, culminates into the hereafter. This is also an indication of the *qur'anic* reference that our ultimate return is to God in the hereafter. It means the culmination of all universal knowledge-flows back to the stock from which it is continuously emanating in living experience. The *Qur'an* says in this regard:

> It is God Who begins (the process of) creation; then repeats it; then shall you be brought back to Him. (30:11).

The thought process and the world-system derived from the organization of such a knowledge-centred worldview together comprise the unique praxis of all systems of life and thought. Such knowledge-centred systems convey the *qur'anic* meaning of worlds and world-systems: the *alameen*. Now there remains no distinction between the praxis of the natural sciences, social sciences and human sciences. They are all unified together by this fundamental epistemology of unity. Unity pervades in all systems and thus unifies them uniquely by this epistemology. Upon such a unification process rests the ultimate purpose of existence and reality. It is to understand the purpose and the grand unified structure of the universe and all there is in it, by means of the most reduced principle, a principle that cannot be further reduced. This irreducible principle is of the oneness of God at the Beginning as at the End in the hereafter. In this regard the *Qur'an* says:

> And verily unto Us (belong) the End and the Beginning. (92:13).

A process-oriented systems view of qur'anic praxis

A systemic view of pervasive interrelationships among the tenets of the *tawhidi* worldview now emerges. The tenets of such a system are first the fundamental epistemology of fundamental unity of knowledge. Secondly, there emanate knowledge-flows from the fundamental epistemology for the construction of knowledge-induced world-systems along with the associated thought processes, reflective action and response in and through such diverse but unified world-systems. Thirdly, there is the process of creative evolution of the same knowledge-centred order towards its cumulative, full, and optimal realization in the hereafter.

These systemic interrelationships are borne out in many ways and are well explained by the interaction, integration (unification), and creative evolution (*khalqin jadid*) processes caused by circular interrelationships among three *qur'anic* tenets, which are the premises of the Supreme Truth. The principle and integral tenet is the epistemology of *tawhid* (*haqq ul-yaqin*). Next to follow is the domain of knowledge-flows within world-systems emanating from that epistemology (*ilm ul-yaqin*). These are followed by the use of the two tenets in the organization of *qur'anic* world-systems as being unified and creatively evolutionary while enabling reflective empiricism and inferences to arise as creative responses once they are premised on the truth actions of the knowledge-flows (*ayn ul-yaqin*).

Such a circular interrelationship maintains *haqq ul-yaqin* as the exogenous, permanent, and immutable invariant in every learning process caused by the epistemology in developing continuously relational creativity between *ilm* and *ayn* of the *tawhidi* worldview. The processes of interrelationships remain permanently endogenous in nature. The only exogenous position is given to the singularly complete premise of *tawhid* as the fundamental epistemology in all kinds of *qur'anic* reasoning and world-systems.

The complex nature of qur'anic world-systems

Since the circularly repeating endogenous interrelationships among *ilm* and *ayn* are creatively dynamic and diversely evolutionary in form with the immutable centricity of *tawhid* as *haqq ul-yaqin*, the interrelationships in this systemic order are therefore of a complex nature. Yet order, harmony, balance and equilibrium are all maintained, but only within the non-linear meaning of complexity. Complexity is bestowed by the ever-widening function of knowledge-flows in initiating the emergent knowledge-induced unified forms as caused by interaction and integration among such knowledge-flows and forms. Even in Heaven (*Jannah*), the creative evolution stabilizes and continues on in knowledge-induced continuum of praises of God.

The above forms of endogenous interrelationships among *ilm ul-yaqin* and *ayn ul-yaqin* with the singularly exogenous epistemic centricity of *haqq ul-yaqin* (*tawhid*) are explained in Figure 3.1. Figure 3.1 is to be understood as a cross-sectional view of a conic evolution of the base comprising *ilm ul-yaqin* and *ayn ul-yaqin*, while the vertex of the cone, *haqq ul-yaqin* remains invariant. This geometry is not a commensurate one in essence due to the immeasurable nature of divine knowledge as stock. Hence the vertex is explained here by the 'open' point belonging to a super-manifold topology.

Topology is a non-dimensional method of pure mathematics, used particularly for explaining relational forms that may be entities or otherwise. The method of topology is chosen here over other mathematical methods in order to appropriately address the non-dimensional but pervasively relational nature of divine essence (*fitra*) in the order of things that comes about simply by the intervention of the monotheistic law.

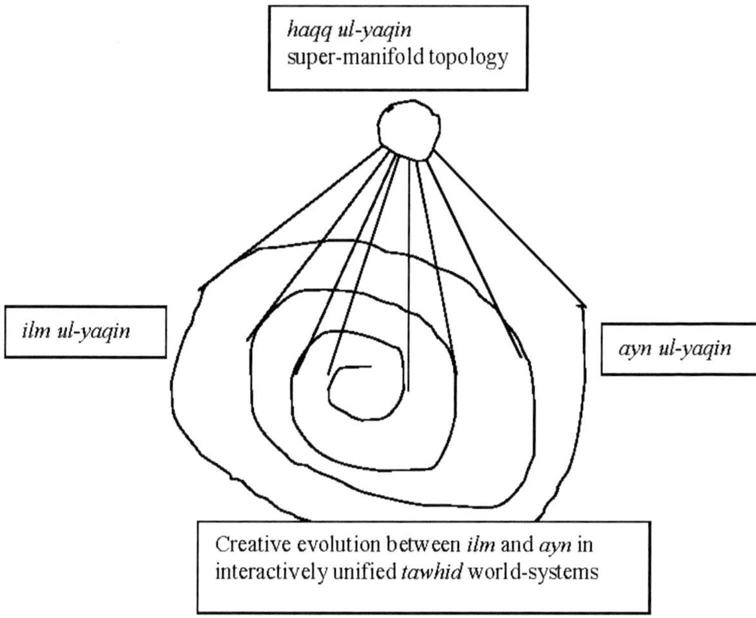

Figure 3.1: Evolutionary interrelationships in the *Qur'anic* world-system

Super-manifold is a hyper-topology in which numerical measurability is replaced by relational correspondences of 'complete' types that span all possible world-systems. Hence, if the world-systems can be delineated by topological spaces and mappings then a super-manifold as the diverse combination of such spaces and correspondences belong to the nexus of all of them. When such a nexus of interrelationships is comprehensive, then it is also complete. The limit of the super-manifold is reached. Completeness across the diversity of relationships across all possible combinations among such pervasive interrelationships is possible only in a perfectly unified world-system that evolves in its own unique praxis. This is the *knowledge-induced* worldview. But this same episteme also determines the 'mathematical opposite' space of relations. This is the domain of *de-knowledge*. It must also belong to the super-manifold by way of reinforcing the ineluctable proof of the unity of knowledge as truth in the *tawhidi* worldview by virtue of its contrast with the falsehood of disintegrative rationalism found in the mathematical opposite of truth, which is *de-knowledge*.

Certain outstanding questions

Even while we are delineating a worldview premised on *tawhid*, certain outstanding questions remain to be addressed. Such questionable areas are as follows: how can the *tawhidi* praxis become the epistemology of a world-system that is distinct from the scientific philosophy of the occidental world-system? Is not much of the clamour of modernity, science and technology, power and prowess taking place in the occidental order? These are questions that must be addressed in the light of the kinds of interactively unified evolutionary knowledge-induced world-system projected in Figure 3.1. They are then to be taken up in relation to a variety of conceptions, systemic diversity, issues and problems, analytical details and applications that arise in and through the *tawhidi* worldview. Such realizations represent combinations of interrelating tenets of a knowledge-centred worldview that is fired by reflective empiricism. The continuity between knowledge-flows and their induced forms enables reasoning, actions, responses and creative dynamics of evolution to move into more of the same kind. Such organisms of the *tawhidi* world-systems remain endogenously interactive in reference to the epistemological permanence of *tawhid*.

Further questions arise. Is there reason to believe in the permanence of modernity and its scientific validity that has appeared in the West over the last two hundred years? Is there a serious critique of the received philosophy of science in terms of essentialism rather than rationalism? Is there reason to be sceptical about the emergence of a truly integrated science and society, which is a socio-scientific order that can be premised on the *tawhidi* epistemology after these two hundred years of science, technology, economics and political power in the West? In other words, was *tawhid* not always permanently entrenched within the diverse problems of mind and matter – except that we see its *conscious* resurgence as a distinct civilization process that came with the advent of Islam, and subsequently delineated the age of Islamic scholasticism? Can such a worldview again mark human future?

We are then led to ask the resulting question: what will be the future threshold of such a new global transformation if it arises? Will this be determined by a continued show of scientific and technological feats and their global transference, or will it be determined by addressing the great and impending moral and social issues on which the wellbeing of humankind and the world truly rests?

We are now led to assert that the means of addressing the future and the total environment of humans, both morally and ethically, would implicate a new methodological conception, understanding, and application of science and technology. Within this very unique praxis will come about the interactive unification of these disciplines across a diversity of systems. The result as well will be to make this methodological approach creatively dynamic between actions and responses spanning all human experience in relation to unified world-systems (*alameen*).

Thus the concept of a *socio-scientific* order is a domain of intellection that interactively integrates (unifies) diverse issues and problems by a unique methodology. Such a unifying methodology becomes the praxis of all verities of world-systems – science, technology, and the social order with its extensive ecological and cosmological meaning and relations with other domains. Such is the meta-function of the knowledge-centred world-system, premised on the fundamental unity of knowledge as the epistemology of a coherent and unique praxis in the study of the relational socio-scientific order involving God, man, environment, science and society.

The last two hundred years of Western modernism is to be questioned on the premise of this singular praxis of unity of knowledge across systems of thought and action. The occidental survival and acceptance as a human artefact is also to be questioned on the same premise. Behind these affirmations relating to the inevitable consequences of Western mind-matter relationships that have remained insensitive to the endogenous role of the ethical and moral forces in it, is the recognition that the unitary worldview is permanently entrenched in reality. Nonetheless it was hitherto rejected by a distorted culture of science, thought, social action and response.

Briefly contrasting the qur'anic worldview with rationalism

To understand the background and the past and future prospects of the culture of science, technology, society, and the treatment of the mind-matter dichotomy in Western thought, actions and responses, a brief examination of occidental thought is taken up here. It is contrasted with the *qur'anic* epistemic worldview of unity of knowledge.

At the outset it is important to note the exogenous nature of the universally determining role of *tawhid* in all experiential domains. These domains are endogenously characterized by the *tawhidi* law. To discuss this topic we must first carefully define the place of human reason in the understanding of truth. The question begs for serious consideration. Is reason a primordial entity that is required to understand *tawhid* and the role of the divine law (*sunnat Allah*) in creation? Contrarily, is reason as *fitra* – a natural essence – a created essence that is realized spontaneously at the *moment* when a relational complexity ensues through interactions between the divine law and the consequential knowledge-induced events? In the *tawhidi* world-system such a consequential and relational outcome would be of the interactive, integrative, and evolutionary type (**IIE**).

The emergence of the Western mind in Greek thought

In reference to the subject matter of this chapter, it is sufficient for us to have a cursory view of divinity and the world in Greek thought in which both the Muslim rationalists and subsequently their heirs, the occidental world, have their epistemological roots. The details of life, such as economy, society and science (the physics of the Greeks) were tied intrinsically to a peculiar connection between God and the world (Vermont, 1995).

To the Greeks, God was earthly-born, as required by human need. Hence it was an earthly God of needs and was thus relative in scale and scope. This gave rise to many gods, each taking dominion over a particular function of human relations as they exist and have evolved over space and time. Yet, there was an unbridgeable distance between God and the world. Such limitations as sickness and weakness, joy and defeat, the ups and downs of life's variegated patterns, did not affect the gods as they did the humans. Yet the Greek gods were relationally tied to human actions and relations. This is a conception of gods being pantheistic in nature and multiple in origin.

The Greek concept of ethics and values in mundane affairs emanated from a perfect order of the gods. This kind of concept took an earthly meaning of the relations assumed to exist between particular gods in their domains and consequent human affairs. In this way, human relational order in the picture of a god-centric Greek universe took up a rationalist fervour. Divinity was relinquished to such a relativistic understanding of God as divine and in terms of his relationship with human actions and propensities.

The pantheism and material relativism of Greek thought was a forerunner of the evolutionary dynamics of a rationalist mind. This attribute became part and parcel of Western dialectic culture. Likewise, the banishing of God as the substantive lawgiver, so that divine law does not act upon the world, yet having an exogenously numinous existence, is the continued message of Western socio-scientific epistemology premised on rationalism. Paradoxically, the same kind of rationalist epistemological thinking was inherited by the Muslims. Muslim rationalism, called *kalam*, gave rise to an exegesis that was incompatible with the understanding of *tawhid* as the singular monotheistic law, along with its dynamic functions in constructing the worldview of unity of knowledge and its induction of the unified world-system.

The mingling of Greek thought with the Muslim and Western minds that were copying it, is therefore not difficult to understand. Each of these schools, by choosing a rationalist understanding of the divine origin, made the divine order either dysfunctional in a numinous epistemological sense or left it to erroneous pantheistic conceptions. None of these approaches can be any part of the *qur'anic* worldview, wherein God is the absolute one without partnership in the act of creation and its sustenance, the everlasting creator and sustainer of the universes. God is the ultimate lawgiver above the limitations of the created worlds. The emergent worldview created by divine law is thus natural and consistent, unmarred by fault. The divine law is thereby explainable in relation to world-systems. God is above earthly attributes. Yet He is the lawgiver, whose divine law is the essential part of reality and around which world-systems are established, organized, explained and evolved by knowledge-flows premised on monotheism.

A comparative perspective continued: the emergence of the Western mind in Immanuel Kant's metaphysics and the impossibility of knowledge-flows therein

The Western mind claims that, even in its best moral representation, morality, goodness, truth and God, only appear in the form and meaning determined by 'objective' reason. If this is so, then reason, which determines 'objectivity', can manifest in one of two forms. Either reason is an original essence, which once created by God, has ever since its creation been left to function in the universe of and by itself. The other understanding is that reason is the primal basis for determining the objective relationship between God, universal law, and human affairs.

The first of the preceding two claims represents the standpoint of non-Islamic scholastics and Muslim rationalists. It is reflected in Aquinas's *Summa Theologiae* (Aquinas, reprinted 1946), particularly in the way that Aquinas dealt with Ibn Sina's concept of the use of the 'number one' to explain the principle of divine unity.

With respect to the above-mentioned original function of reason, Immanuel Kant posed his problem of autonomy and heteronomy. Autonomy constituted Kant's assertion that God is an objective Creator, who endowed humans with will, which in turn formed objective reason. The problem of heteronomy is one of incompatibility in assimilating God (and hence the divine law) within human affairs. In the case of heteronomy, the freedom of human will to reason is lost by dissociating it from the moral premise, and causing it to exist as material reality alone. Kant considered this to be a desire, and thereby, contradictory to the freedom of will.

Kant (reprinted 1963, p.80-81) wrote on the relationship between God and the moral law in a perspective, which interrelated will and reason:

> A clear exposition of morality of itself leads to the belief in God. Belief in this philosophic connexion means not trust in a revelation, but trust arising from the use of the reason, which springs from the principle of practical morality.

Kant continues,

> Religion is the application of the moral laws to the knowledge of God, and not the origins of morals. For let us imagine a religion prior to all morality: then this would imply a relation to God, and would therefore consist in recognizing Him as a mighty lord whom we should have to placate. All religion assumes morality, and morality cannot, therefore, be derived from religion...

The concepts underlying such 'reasoned' beliefs on the relationship between moral law (God) (autonomy), the material or cognitive world (heteronomy), and the freedom of will to determine and know the moral law, are dichotomous philosophic wrangling. They distort the essence of unity that underlies the interrelationships as explained in Figure 3.1. Kant's meaning of reason is therefore not a created essence as it is in Islam, as *fitra*. Rather, it is a determiner of morality prior to being a created essence. It must therefore appear either as a primordial created essence that subsequently has separated itself from its need for a continuously conscious relationship with God and the divine law, or it assumes a state of heteronomy that is determined solely by humanly reasoned concepts of freedom, goodness and truth.

The autonomy of science from religious and moral epistemology in the West was powerfully transformed by Immanuel Kant's philosophical thought at the turn of the Eighteenth Century (Enlightenment). Among many others, Kant wrote his three major pieces inquiring into the question of the possibility of knowledge. In his Groundwork for the Metaphysic of Morals, also appearing as a shorter work, Metaphysical Foundations of

Morals, Kant wrote on the relationship between the moral law and the freedom of reason to know and exercise the moral law.

In his well-known example on analytic and synthetic reasoning for developing analytical relations, Kant said that if a relation or event A was an element of another similar event, B, then A and B are analytic phenomena to each other. He explained an element C not in A and B as synthetic, which may have an external, that is exogenous, relationship with A and B.

The above case when seen from the pervasively *tawhidi* knowledge-induced endogenous interrelationships between knowledge (*ilm*) and observation (*ayn*), as in Figure 3.1, must be an endogenously interrelated organic whole. Yet nothing in the *qur'anic* world-system remains independent of the primordial *haqq*, not even Evil is determined independently of the divine law as command on the opposite of Truth. Consequently, all relations are 'analytic' in the *tawhidi* world-system except *tawhid* itself, which remains the exogenous primordial existent and thereby determines creation and its diverse world-systems. Yet in the case of Kant's example, there exist pervasively exogenous relations between all of the entities.

First, examining the *qur'anic* perspective, the *Qur'an* declares (2:255) in the following verse on the universality of the *tawhidi* law in all phenomena:

> God! There is no god but He, –the Living, the Self-subsisting, Eternal: neither slumber can seize Him nor sleep. His are all things in the heavens and on earth. Who is there to intercede in His presence except as He permits? He knows what (appears to His creatures as) before or after or behind them. Nor shall they encompass aught of His knowledge except as He wills. His Throne does extend over the heavens and the earth, and He feels no fatigue in guarding and preserving them for He is the Most High, the Supreme (in glory).

The preceding verse amply spotlights the supremely creative command and act of God. He has created reason as universal essence of the divine law (*fitra*) in the first place. But since God incessantly creates, governs, and guides the universes (*alameen*) by His law, the relationship of essence to creation is forever renewed. Reason is thereby created at the spontaneous *moment* of such renewed relationships. Such relationships are dynamic and within human understanding, social action, and response, involving the material and cognitive worlds. They are manifested in and through the knowledge-flows that God bestows as He wills at the spontaneous *moment* of the emanating relations in the *ilm-ayn* domain, and which follows by His command. That is, the spontaneous moment is when reality is determined by the *tawhidi* epistemology.

Within such a relationship there can be no abhorrence of desire as in the context of Kant's meaning, if the relationships are determined by divine command. An example is the natural desire to gain God's blessings in Heaven (*Jannah*), which goes with all the material and sensual bestowing of *Jannah* in corporeal form. Indeed, the moral law of the *Qur'an* premised on *tawhid* and completely manifested in the hereafter, comes about through the cumulative evolutionary processes of the incessantly and pervasively learning world-systems. The event of the hereafter thus marks the culmination of the pervasively emanating processes of interrelationships in the *ilm-ayn* domains both of the revealed and hidden types and is determined by the *tawhidi* epistemology.

We now return to Kant's philosophy and note that, in the presence of the dichotomy between his analytic and synthetic configurations of relationships, and in Kant's depiction of knowledge separated between autonomy and heteronomy, knowledge in its flow-form is riddled with uncertainty. This is the meaning of knowledge *failing to be attained* in given states of relationships.

Kant writes on his dichotomous perception of pure reason and practical reason (reprinted 1949, p.25):

> This, then, is a question which at least calls for closer examination, and does not permit any off-hand answer: whether there is any knowledge that is thus independent of experience and even of all impressions of the senses. Such knowledge is entitled *a priori*, and is distinguished from the empirical, which has its sources *a posteriori*, that is, in experience.

Kant's *a priori* knowledge denotes pure reason and marks his domain of freedom. The *a posteriori* denotes practical reason and has no validity in the formation of freedom and what is sensible. Kant says in this regard (reprinted 1949, p. 25):

> In what follows, therefore, we shall understand by *a priori* knowledge, no knowledge independent of this or that experience, but knowledge absolutely independent of all experience. Opposed to it is empirical knowledge, which is knowledge possible only *a posteriori*, that is through experience.

Now, when the function of freedom and human will, premised in pure reason as the moral law, is combined with the above-mentioned dichotomous condition of knowledge-flows, we obtain the following relation within Kantian reasoning. We find it contradictory to the tenets that can make holistic knowledge possible.

According to Kant the following is true (Table 3.1):

Table 3.1: The impossibility of knowledge-flows in Kantian metaphysics

Objectivity (A):	Subjectivity (B):	Inference:
Let, {a} belonging to A be all The moral maxims and laws. Moral law is absolutely independent of the senses and empiricism. This is *a priori* knowledge.	Let, {b} belonging to B be all the empirical maxims and laws. Empirical law (practical law) premised on desire and hence non-sensible. This is *a posteriori* knowledge.	A and B are synthetic, not analytical. Thus{a}, {b} are synthetic, not analytical. Thus there exists no causality between any or all of A and B.

From the Islamic point of view, Kant was so mistaken in his categorization of what is objective and subjective, that he thought of prayers and human supplications to God as being purely subjective experiences. He considered prayer as being based on the craving of self for human needs, wants and desires, which he equated with acts outside the moral domain. Kant wrote in this regard (quoted in 1963, p. 99):

> To wish to converse with God is absurd; we cannot talk to one we cannot intuit; and as we cannot intuit God, but can only believe in him, we cannot converse with him. The uses of prayer are thus only subjective.

Kant goes on (p. 101):

> Prayer appears to be a presumptuous act and an act of distrust in God. It seems to imply distrust in God's knowledge of what is good for us. Continuous, unremitting prayer may be construed as an attempt to coerce God by constant begging into granting our desires.

Kant thus made man the yardstick of morality and left God out of his equation of causality respecting a divine moral law that presents itself to the world. Kant's conception of God and the sciences thus rests on the rationalistic understanding mind-set. He writes (quoted in 1949, p. 318):

> Much as my words may startle you, you must not condemn me for saying: every man creates his God. From the moral point of view… you even *have*

> to create your God, in order to worship Him as your creator. For in whatever way … the Deity should be made known to you, and even…if He should reveal Himself to you: it is you … who must judge whether you are permitted [by your conscience] to believe in Him, and to worship Him.

Kant furthermore carried this humanistic and rationalistic basis of the philosophy of science into all of cosmology. He wrote (quoted in 1949, 261):

> Two things fill the mind with ever new and increasing awe and admiration the more frequently and continuously reflection is occupied with them; the starred heaven above me and the moral law within me. I ought not to seek either outside my field of vision, as though they were either shrouded in obscurity or were visionary. I see them confronting me and link them immediately with the consciousness of my existence.

In *qur'anic* terms on the other hand, prayer is a communication with God invoking His mercy through human submission to His will and possibility. Prayer is thus an individual power that integrates the individual with the greater social purpose. By the institution of prayer the personality and disposition of the believer are increasingly heightened to moral possibility within the social whole. The mosque and congregational prayers are thus much more highly recommended than individual prayer, but without the exclusion of the latter.

On the matter of prayer as experience in developing the Islamic personality and communal realization, the *Qur'an* asks the believers to pray more intensely in times of affliction. Besides, for the yearning desire of Heaven and divine bliss as the supreme blessing, the *Qur'an* declares (3:194):

> Our Lord! Grant us what Thou did promise unto us through Your Apostles, and save us from shame on the Day of Judgment: For You never break Your promise.

The communal and social sense of prayer in Islam enters the core of natural and social phenomena through the awareness of the faculty of knowledge to see, understand, act and respond. This is the basis of consciousness by reflective observation (*tafakkur*). The individual becomes socially determined and makes the community see and act positively in the light of moral and material perspectives. Such is a consequence of the knowledge-induced model of the *Qur'an* in the *haqq-ilm-ayn* interrelationships within the socio-scientific order. Its relational aspect across pervasive unification of diverse systems, agents and socio-scientific variables was explained by means of Figure 3.1.

On the other hand, the debility of Western thought in all the sciences has been the pervasive inference that the real world does not explain divine reality. Once divinely created, the universe with its purpose of existence, are left to evolve independently. This is a concept contrary to the meanings of *tawhid al-uluhiyyah* (God as Creator) and *tawhid al-rububiyyah* (God as Cherisher and Sustainer).

Kantianism and a generalized Western mind-set derived from the metaphysical ideas of Kant also contradict the causation of a pervasively relational universe. Such a learning universe is made possible by the continuous emanation of knowledge-flows and their induced forms. All these are derived from the episteme of the divine law. This kind of dynamics makes us move nearer to the *tawhidi* worldview through our experiences in world-systems. Divine law is thus transformed from numinous nature into reasoned and practical implements. Such an epiphenomenon (observed manifestation or argumentation for explaining reality) happens through the function of the *sunnah* and the *hadith*, which constitute the guidance and practices of the Prophet Muhammad on the *qur'anic* law. They are carriers of the divine law into action and further understanding of the dynamics of the monotheistic law. This theme of the *tawhidi* knowledge-centred interaction was explained by the *ilm-ayn* interrelations. See Figure 3.1.

The impossibility of attaining knowledge-flows in Kantian metaphysics is due to the absence of causality as shown in the inference of Table 3.1. The possibility of knowledge-flows, on the other hand, is caused by the functional causality between the *a priori* and the *a posteriori*. It is this very function that induces the *qur'anic* perspective of the world-system by its attributes of the signs of God (*ayat Allah*) and completely explains creation and creation theory by means of *ayat Allah*.

The emergence of Western mind in David Hume's metaphysics and the impossibility of knowledge-flows therein

On the opposite side to Kant was David Hume's concept of knowledge. Hume presented a philosophical perspective of Western modernism based on sensate ontological origins of thinking and reasoning. He stipulated such a sensate premise of the origin of reasoning, knowledge, and thought. Hume thereby opposed deductive reasoning and reference to all forms of 'metaphysical' elements. According to Hume, these would have included divine origins of knowledge as well. Hume thereby premised all of knowledge on 'ontic' (evidential) experimental grounds but included in this the important place of relations among cognitive forms. The word 'ontic' here means the experiential, cognitive, and material effects of sensate ontological reasoning or evidences.

To Hume, the deciphering of knowledge meant well-defined conceptions of memory, impression, imagination, relations, modes and substances. Thus, through these elements of the human possibility to attain reason and construct a philosophical order, Hume reduced the mind-and-matter relationship purely to the level of human reason as the origin. This too, he premised on human imagination, memory, and the continuity of forms and relations in space-time domains. With the divine law divorced from his sensate ontological reasoning and by the primacy of human reason premised on impression, imagination, ideas and relations according to the corporeal concept of forming reason, Hume intensified the inductive source of rationalist philosophy.

Hume wrote (quoted in 1992 reprint p.1):

> All the perceptions of the human mind resolve themselves into two distinct kinds, which I shall call Impressions and Ideas.... Those perceptions, which enter with most force and violence, we may name impressions; and under this name I comprehend all our sensations, passions and emotions, as they make their first appearance in the soul. By ideas I mean the faint images of these in thinking and reasoning.

On the universally extended sensate ontological premise of Hume's reasoning he wrote (op cit. p. xvi):

> And as the science of man is the only solid foundation for the other sciences, so the only solid foundation we can give to this science itself must be laid on experience and observation.

Furthermore, (op cit. p. xvii):

> For me it seems evident, that the essence of the mind being equally unknown to us with that of external bodies, it must be equally impossible to form any notion of its powers and qualities otherwise than from careful and exact experiments, and the observation of those particular effects, which result from its different circumstances and situations. And tho' we must endeavour to render all our principles as universal as possible, by tracing up our experiments to the utmost, and explaining all effects from the simplest and fewest causes, 'tis still certain we cannot go beyond experience; and any hypothesis, that pretends to discover the ultimate

> original qualities of human nature, ought at first to be rejected as presumptuous and chimerical.

The above narration clearly establishes the ultimate source of ontic (evidential) phenomena to which Hume assigned the roots of knowledge. It is also clear that the source of divine unity of knowledge, which is explainable in Islam but beyond the realm of rationalism, cannot be incorporated in Hume's extension of the relational order into the universal knowledge-induced domains. Such an extensive relational domain is the topology of all forms of knowledge and their induced forms.

Hume's relational order is categorized as simple and complex. His complex form is simply a causal assemblage of simple forms. Hence, linearly separable forms and the meaning of causality between interacting forms are not substantively integrated in forming complex forms. There is only a lateral aggregation of simple forms to cause complex forms. This kind of systemic complexity is equivalent to the view of the Greeks of antiquity and, later on, that of civil libertarianism that the ethical social order is made up of an ethically perfected lateral aggregation of social preferences arising from ethically perfect individual preferences. Society was construed as the lateral addition of ethically ideal individuals, yet ethics was being understood according to the rationalist concept.

Hume wrote in regards to his concept of causally determined complex forms in relation to simple forms (op cit. p. 13):

> Amongst the effects of this union or association of ideas, there are none more remarkable, than those complex ideas, which are the common subjects of our thoughts and reasoning, and generally arise from some principle of union among our simple ideas. These complex ideas may be divided into Relations, Modes, and Substances.

Hume's concepts of modes and substances in themselves are also a collection of simple ideas. He wrote (op cit. p. 16):

> The idea of a substance as well as that of a mode, is nothing but a collection of simple ideas that are united by the imagination, and have a particular name assigned them, by which we are able to recall, either to ourselves or others, that collection.

Hume's concept of 'relation' exists in association with the infinite divisibility of space and time. His universe reflects unity within which every part is infinitely reducible. A relation in such an infinitely divisible order is a linear concept of interconnectedness by means of contiguity and continuity.

It is impossible in such a system for the *tawhidi* topology, T, to reflect T in the hereafter, without being interconnected with an infinite number of times in some sense through a reduction of T within the world. Such a concept is contrary to the *tawhidi* worldview, where all forms of relations can exist. Within these relations, T in the primordial reflects T in the hereafter of and by itself. Into this large-scale relationship we introduce the meaning of world-system induced by the same large-scale relationship. We thereby have two self-sustaining and complete relationships in the *tawhidi* worldview. These are "T in the primal to T in the hereafter", and "T in the primal to T in the hereafter through the relations of the world-systems induced by the emergent knowledge-flows emanating from T".

However, in the comparability conception of "T to T" there is identity of mapping here in the sense of super-cardinality and not infinity, as we have briefly referred to (Choudhury, 1995) and will explain further. In Hume's relational conception, such comparability in the cardinal sense is necessary within the infinite divisibility of space and time. The concept of 'relation' to Hume is therefore an atomistic one. It is the result of aggregating together infinitely reduced forms into a collective.

Comparative perspective continued: the emergence of the Western mind in rationalism according to Karl Popper and the impossibility of knowledge therein

Popper (2004) thought and wrote concerning the philosophy of science of a conjectural-though-evolutionary learning universe. Within this structure of scientific model lies the meaning of dialectics and modernism using the dialectical perspective of social transformation. Modernism is characterized by its intrinsic attribute of change, instability, conjectures and refutations according to a dialectical movement of thought and the recursive understanding of underlying conflict, mutation, and group synthesis. Such dialectical attributes of modernism delineate the biology of falsification and natural selection in which Popper thought and wrote. Modern scientific epistemology generalizes these attributes and biological functions equally in the natural and the social sciences. The same methodology is brought to bear upon institutional thinking and individual and group behaviour. The first kind is to be found in civil libertarianism, neo-liberalism, and democracy (Hayek, 1967; Sullivan, 1989). The second kind is to be found in neoclassical economic thought, public choice theory, social choice and social contract theory and systems theory (Capra, 1983).

The frontrunner of falsification theory in the sciences was Karl Popper (1998). Popper's theory of rationalism premised falsification as his claimed foundation of modernism is briefly examined below. Within this concept we can critically evaluate the philosophy of science and human behaviour in relation to the world as perceived in occidental thought.

According to Popper, truth can never be known. He (1998) wrote, "Truth is not manifest." Hence there can never be an essentialist approach to the discovery of knowledge. All that is possible is a dialectical movement of conjectures and the refutation of theories. Scientific theories are not established by experiment and observation; rather, they emanate from conjecture, which is then subject to experimentation and observation. Since there is no 'essentialist' basis of theory formulation in Popper, there can be no movement of the dialectical process towards gaining knowledge of Truth. Scientific theory is thus seen to evolve through fields of conjecture and refutation *ad infinitum*.

In his critique of 'the ultimate explanation of essences' Popper asserts (1998, p.103-4):

> The scientist cannot succeed in 'finally establishing the truth of theories beyond all reasonable doubt. Truly scientific theories cannot describe the 'essences' or the 'essential nature' of things – the realities which lie behind the appearances.

Thus Popper goes on to reject the epistemology, which he calls the divine state of true knowledge. Instead, he favours the development of scientific philosophy as conjecture, subject to conceptualization, experimentation, inference and change. Popper refers to this pattern of evolution as the recurrence of open-ended phenomena *ad infinitum*. The evolving phenomena are not subject to any orderly pre-conditions in their development, although all knowledge remains interconnected in Popper's space-time continuum.

One finds that not even in the temporal field of knowledge-evolution within world-systems, as explained by the *tawhidi* knowledge-induced model, can Popper's falsification hypothesis be tenable. The *tawhidi* knowledge-induced model is premised on the unification of knowledge as the episteme. It produces sensation, organization, necessary conditions, operational instruments, guidance and creative evolution in knowledge-induced world-systems. Thereby, unification within and across systems, agents and relations in diversity becomes the governing attribute of a knowledge-centred worldview. This is a perspective quite contrary to Popper's hypothesis of evolution of the mind in phases of open-ended conjectures that do not need to remain unified.

Analytical problems are compounded when rationalism, with its separable group conflicts, establishes hegemony of self-determination in Popper's dialectical processes. A sense of unifying relations exists within progressively more isolated groups that assume their natural selection. Yet the emerging conflicts and dialectics cause the atomism of such conflicting groups (reprinted Darwin, 1963; Popper 1988). Such a process occurring in continuum breaks up the natural selection groups into ever-smaller self-determining and conflicting groups. The limit of this process of disintegration is the non-interacting, and thus, dissociated state of methodological individualism. This ensuing perspective is articulated in Popper's words (p.341):

> Accordingly, the belief in the empirical existence of social wholes or collectives, which may be described as *naïve collectivism*, has to be replaced by the demand that social phenomena, including collectives, *should be analyzed in terms of individuals and their actions and relations.*

Such characteristics of Popper's model are quite contrary to the pervasively unifying relational order and balance of unifying world-systems in the *tawhidi* knowledge-centred worldview.

The domain of rationalism formed by the complex and chaotic open-ended search for meaning derived from falsification causes world-systems and their inherent phenomena to be unsettled and unpredictable. Within this reigns the perpetual movement of conflicting agents and systems as atomistic self-interested competitors. Methodological individualism with simply a temporary glimmer of unity within natural selection is the pervasive state of affairs in Popper's dialectical world and also in Darwinism. Unity of organism and knowledge is thus totally supplanted by the pervasiveness of atomism arising out of complexity and chaos between conflicting organisms (Choudhury, 1999).

In such an open ended chaotic world of complexity, since predictability and stability are sacrificed, knowledge becomes impossible. The human mind evolves dialectically towards ever more conflicting situations of rationalistic quests. On these grounds Popper explains his idea of evolution of the liberal mind (1998, p.352):

> The Western rationalist tradition, which derives from the Greeks, is the tradition of critical discussion – of examining and testing propositions or theories by attempting to refute them. *This critical rational method must not be mistaken for a method of finally establishing truth; nor is it a method, which always secures agreement.* Its value lies, rather, in the fact that participants in a discussion will, to some extent, change their minds, and part as wiser men.

It is clear from this statement that liberal order is not a process that manifests absolute truth. Popper clearly maintains this view when he writes, "Truth is not manifest". Popper (1998, reprinted) thus noted Kant's propensity for making man the rationalist lawgiver of morality both in science and society.

Liberal and democratic order is a rationalist evolutionary process of discourse that is based under the principle of conflict, agreement, and newer conflict. This is the basis of the conjectures and refutations that become the dialectical wisdom and processes of the occidental mind, thought, and action in every field of human endeavour. It is entrenched in the occidental philosophy of the natural and social sciences and in human behaviour. Quite the opposite of this process is that of discourse leading to unity and the further evolution of the same kind of unification processes in all sciences. Such is the pervasive perspective in the knowledge-centred worldview derivable from the *Qur'an*. The emanating praxis is unique to the *Qur'an*.

Comparative perspective continued: the emergence of Western mind in rationalism according to Karl Marx and the impossibility of knowledge therein

Marx's dialectical concepts were borrowed from Hegel to explain his materialistic premise of historicism. Like Hegel, Popper and Kant's models, Marx's model of social and historical change was of the process-oriented type. All of them wrote on the phenomenon of intrinsic knowledge-sharing that occurs in nature. Yet this attribute of complexity and process in scientific and social methodology does not make the writers' epistemologies similar to the unifying worldview of the *tawhidi* worldview.

The differences between these two streams of mind-set remain polar and widely apart. Thereby, the two mind-sets engender different praxes of thought, organization, and experience. They build upon different sensations carrying altogether contrasting implications in our scientific, social, political and behavioural understanding of world-systems. Included in such a social spectrum is the study of political economy, which assumes a widely interactive and systemic framework in Islamic political economy. We have referred to this collected ensemble of diverse disciplines that can be uniquely addressed by the same methodology of the unity of knowledge in the socio-scientific order. Hence the importance here is to note the place of that common methodology which they all share. The presence of this unique methodology in all disciplines enables them to interact, unify (integrate), and evolve creatively under the force of knowledge-flows in the *tawhidi* world-system.

Let us briefly examine the Marxist process-oriented dialectical methodology. It is succinctly explained in the words of Resnick and Wolff (1987, p.6-7):

> Marxian theory, then, recognizes no single reality or absolute truth or epistemological standard that can serve to validate one theory as against another. For Marxian theory, validations occur within theories as they subject various statements to their differing criteria of truth. Marxist theory sees itself as one among many different theories, each of which conceptualizes its reality differently and tests its conceptualizations differently. Reality for Marxian theory is a totality comprising contradictions in theory interacting with contradictions within all the other processes that constitute that totality. Marxian theory specifies that interaction as over-determination. Marxian theory also recognizes, of course, that other theories conceptualize all these matters differently; they take different epistemological positions.

Problems emanating from the process-oriented characterization of Marxist dialectics render such a conceptualization utterly dysfunctional for unifying social and scientific organisms, both within themselves and across systems. Marxist theory runs into a logical contradiction that renders Marx's, and thereby Hegel's ideologies of organically interacting systems and of the notion of World Spirit (Hegel, 1956), null and void. Let us examine this assertion closely.

If the case is that each sub-system of an organic whole comes to acquire its own competing epistemology through conflict that makes the sub-systems dissociate and evolve independently of the rest, finally seeking their own independent epistemologies, then at best, limited interactions can exist. Over the process of evolution, which is an essential characteristic of all the theories we have examined above, as well as of Marxist theory of knowledge, emanation of the independent systems out of competition and conflict becomes a pervasive phenomenon. Consequently, there is a semblance of social Darwinism in Marx and Hegel's dialectics.

Any theory of substantive interaction must then be replaced by a permanent semblance of conflict, competition, and independence among the emerging systemic entities in Marxist, Hegelian, and the other above-mentioned doctrines. This is due to the fact that, if sub-systems as processes emanate from initial interaction and then depart into separate organisms, the parent organism eventually becomes irrelevant in the evolution. The structure of the evolutionary process and of any systemic organism is then characterized by a series of mutually separable sub-processes.

Against this inevitable consequence of systemic process-based evolution, the question of equilibrium assumes two forms. Both of these are possible. First, in the state of its limited initial evolution, there is disequilibrium arising out of conflict among the entities of a given system or sub-system. Such an initial state is followed by temporary equilibriums associated with the emerging independent states of entities in nature. But by pervasiveness of conflict, independence and individuation of such states and sub-processes, the temporary evolutionary equilibriums remain embedded in a 'global' disequilibrium trajectory. The picture is that of an endogenous equilibrium nature of bifurcating trajectories, which by themselves remain in permanent disequilibrium due to inner conflicts. The second characterization of Marxist-type evolutionary equilibriums within the permanent disequilibrium states of emerging trajectories is of the open-ended conjectural nature, like that of Popper's. In this case, the disequilibrium trajectories are increasingly multiplied and the chaotic nature of complex forms enhanced. The result is a complete loss of predictability and stability in Marxist scientific and social constructs. The same is the result of conjecture and refutation of the open-ended universe of Popper and the rationalist nature-centred worldview of Kant.

Both on the basis of his over-determinist epistemology and the rationalist origin of this theory, Marx was like Kant in believing that the empirical sensations cannot develop theory. Only an underlying essence in nature that can be rationally conceptualized, explained, and tested out becomes the *a priori* premise of Marxist epistemology. From what has been explained earlier, the proof of disconnected thinking befogs Marx's empty claim of process and interactions. That is because the interactive processes between any two, and thus among multiple entities cannot reproduce themselves once a separation between the sub-processes has occurred. Consequently, all further evolution of such sub-processes occurs by independent epistemologies of their own. In the ultimate state of atomism arrived at through such pervasive states of competition, conflict, individualism and independence, there finally remains no interactive, integrative and evolutionary learning power in such atomistic states.

An analytical explanation of over-determination epistemologies

In this regard let us consider three entities, A, B, and C, interrelated in the following ways: $A \Leftrightarrow B \rightarrow$ state of $A(E_1) \cap B(E_2)$, where, E_1 and E_2 are the resulting different epistemologies associated with the emergent independent entities, A and B. This is despite the fact that, initially and locally, it may be that $(E_1 \cap E_2) \in E$, a parent epistemology, and thereby, $(A \cap B) \in A^*$, a parent organism.

Now if we treat C in the same manner as A and B, any dissociation with either of these will lead to a similar independence of state with the remaining entity. Thus in the long run, it is impossible that C can come back to interact with A *and* B.

Furthermore, in the open-ended universe of many emanating entities and trajectories we will notice, $E' \in \{E_1, E_2, ..., E_n\}$, such that, E' is defined by the basis vectors, $\{E_1, E_2, ..., E_n\}$. That is, any $E' = \Sigma_{i=1}^{n} a_i.E_i$, is true in the (n+1)-dimensional space. Now E' is expressed in terms of a set of mutually independent vectors of the n-dimensional space. The argument can be carried forward to repeat itself for higher dimensional spaces, there being no predictable change in such a process of evolution according to the principle of conjecture, refutation, conflict, independence, and chaotic complexity in all such spatial evolutions.

The Marxist concept of progression along mutually separable and independent entities as a result of biological conflict and competition while maintaining this feature within temporary sub-processes and as generalized in all conjectural spaces, is well articulated by Lucaks (1968 reprint). He writes (noted in Resnick & Wolff op cit, p. 71):

> The materialist-dialectical conception of totality means first of all the concrete unity of interacting *contradictions* --- secondly, the systematic relativity of all totality both upwards and downwards (which means that all totality is made of totalities subordinated to it, and also that the totality in question is, at the same time, over-determined by totalities of *a higher complexity* ...) and thirdly, the historical relativity of all totality is *changing, disintegrating, confined to a determinate, concrete historical period.*

Comparative perspectives continued: the essence of Darwinism entrenched in rationalism

Darwinism in one form or another is entrenched in the epistemology of rationalism. It has thus spread its competing and marginalizing consequences of competing entities both in the natural and social sciences. Such a perspective of marginalism is the abiding characteristic of conflicting opposites in all categories of things, be these good or bad. Marginalism is contrary to complementarity. Thus the stronger conclusion of Darwinism regarding marginalism against pervasive complementarity is also found entrenched in the epistemologies of both the natural and social sciences. In the occidental epistemological context we now have a tripartite interrelationship. In this, rationalism links up with Darwinism, and these two link up with the marginalist hypothesis. Such a case is strongly manifested in neoclassical economic theory (Sen, 1977) and the Darwinian process view of science (Hull, 1988).

Let us examine how, according to Darwinism, anthropology establishes local interactions followed by intergenerational competition between natural selections. By local interactions we mean within and across contiguous generations. The idea of generations itself is not necessarily time-bound. In the context of knowledge, the ever-changing perspective of knowledge-flows causes a continuous shift in generations, though not always impetuously. The model of perpetual learning as the unified knowledge-centred worldview that is presented in this chapter, will criticize the intergenerational competition model as being premised in this uniquely continuous phenomenon of 'global' competition, marginalism, individualism, rationalism, and thereby Darwinism. This implication of continuity of the marginalist property cannot be understood in the discrete time-bound model of intergenerational change.

Darwin (quoted in 1936, p. 52) explains natural selection in the following words (italics provided by author):

> Again, it may be asked, how is it that varieties, which I have called incipient species, become ultimately converted into *good and distinct species*, which in most cases *obviously differ from each other far more than do the varieties of the same species*? How do these groups of species, which constitute what are called *distinct genera*, and which differ from each other more than the species of the same genus arise? All these results … follow from *the struggle for life. Owing to this struggle*, *variations, however slight* and from whatever cause proceeding, if they be in any degree profitable to the individuals of a species, in their infinitely complex relations to other organic beings and to their physical conditions of life, *will tend to the preservation of such individuals, and will generally be inherited by the offspring*. The offspring also, will thus have a better chance of surviving, for, of the many individuals of any species which are periodically born, but *a small number can survive*. I have called this principle, by which each slight variation, if useful, is preserved, by the term Natural Selection, in order to mark its relation to *man's power of selection*.

Darwin (op cit. Chapter V) goes on to elaborate upon his natural selection principle to explain intergenerational growth of species in the following way. The genus of varieties arises from a parent. They change and diverge over generations seeking their own survival. Eventually, after a period of maintaining the character of survival for the fittest of their parents, the descendants finally part to have their own divergent existences. In the process it is possible that many varieties would have become extinct.

Darwin does talk favourably about diversification of species and this as a condition for their prolonged survival. But intergenerationally, the power of diversification is shown to decline for certain groups of individuals in the genera, and causes their extinction. It is thereby difficult to read from Darwin the substantive difference between the implications of diversification and divergences when natural selection is induced into the explanation of 'survival of the fittest'. The family tree model presented by Darwin shows divergences, and thereby, survival by extinction to occur intergenerationally.

Darwin also writes on the need for diversification to withstand competition. Nevertheless, if competition is not entrenched in Darwin's intergenerational model, then evolution into new and distinct genera is not possible. Thus only competition causing and emanating from natural selection must be the permanent character of Darwin's intergenerational evolutionary model. Diversification in Darwinism is a mere prescription for resistance to competitive destruction.

The local nature of interaction is essentially the limiting intergenerational diversification and strength that a particular genus holds in connection with the character of its parents. The global nature of interaction diverges from such a view with the rise of competing and divergent natural selection species. This limited interaction being replaced by the globally marginalist characteristic of the evolutionary genus is a dialectical attribute of all rationalistic behaviour. Its dynamics will be explained in this work. In the plethora of developments that ensue in the process view of the sciences, economy, institutions and society, the multiplicity of such individuated developments by divergences rather than by complementarity becomes the sign of global individualism as the abiding character of rationalism and its created orders.

Inference from the examination of rationalist doctrines of dialectical processes

It is quite obvious now that the principal division between the rationalist doctrines of organic processes and a *tawhidi* methodology in science, society, organization and behaviour is marked by the permanent absence of organic unity of knowledge in rationalism and the fundamental and pervasive existence of this principle in the *tawhidi* worldview. The consequences of this difference are devastating. The entire mode and method for developing reasoning, thought, actions and responses between the above two views of life and praxes are completely opposite to each other. The methodology of occidental science, society, organization and self, remains partitioned and pluralistic. Hence systems of thought and discipline interact only temporarily at best in a rationalistic mental construct. Yet occidental thought is always in the quest for the unity of sciences.

On the other hand, the knowledge-centred methodology of *tawhid* is unique for all disciplines. Only the problems, issues, and tools (or methods) of analysis vary between these disciplines. We have pointed out that methodology is different from theory. The knowledge-centred worldview of the *Qur'an* is based on its unique epistemology. It is thereby immutable, contrary to what the relative meaning of theory would imply. Methodology is powerfully embedded in the *tawhidi* epistemology. It is this unique methodology of the unity of knowledge across all fields of thought and its explanatory power in such fields that makes the unification of knowledge and the unity of the knowledge-induced world-systems possible.

As was shown in Figure 3.1, the unification of the disciplines is made possible simply by applying the epistemology of the unity of knowledge and its dynamic effects in and across all the disciplines. This implies that the interrelations within and between human world-systems and cosmic world-systems appear and evolve not by the physical transformation of one physical entity into another one. Rather, there is a constant sharing of knowledge-flows premised on the episteme of unity and the unique explanatory power of this methodology between the domains. This is the relational aspect of the cosmic whole in knowledge-centred totality.

Consequently, the *tawhidi* knowledge-centred worldview is contrary to all traces of Darwinism, conjecture, refutation and dialectics. Thereby, semblances of competition and conflict are replaced by the principles of pervasive complementarities across diversity and by consensus formation. This marks the abiding characteristic of the *tawhidi* way of explaining both the precepts and fields for explaining both truth and of falsehood.

In the field of falsehood characterized by conflict, competition, methodological individualism, and independence, the same unique *tawhidi* methodology is applied to explain the existence of temporarily endogenous equilibriums within long-run evolutionary trajectories of disequilibrium behaviour emerging from chaotic complexity. In the case of truth, whose attributes are explained by the organic unity of knowledge, complementarity, diversity, and consensus formation in creatively evolutionary fields of knowledge, one can always learn from the instruments and guidance of the divine law through shared experiences of unifying world-systems. A glimpse of this methodology was given in Figure 3.1.

Truth versus rationalism in brief

The methodology and model of rationalism that are entrenched in all of occidental thought, institutional order, social action and responses is contrary to the methodology shown in Figure 3.1. Such characterization of occidental roots of rationalism is explained in Figure 3.2.

The explanation of both truth and rationalism (falsehood) by the same unique *tawhidi* epistemology shown in Figure 3.2 is established in reference to the *Qur'an*. When *Iblis* (Satan) was expelled from the garden of bliss by God after he tempted the Prophet Adam and his wife, Hawa, *Iblis* begged for respite from God for his deceitful act. Satan was given respite for his evil, which he would exercise over the transgressors of truth, but he would be unable to do so with the true believers. In this regard, the verse states (15:36-37):

> (*Iblis*) said: 'O my Lord! Give me then respite till the day the (dead) are raised.' (God) said: 'Respite is granted thee – till the Day of the Time Appointed.

The opposing character of systems in the tawhidi worldview and rationalism

Although rationalism and the *tawhidi* worldview of the unity of knowledge both prescribe a systems-based process-oriented methodology, the above inference points out an entirely different construction of the theories of man, machines, science, technology, society, and the cosmos between the two polar praxis. Polarity between the two kinds of understanding and sensations is expressed emphatically in the words of Capra.

Capra (1983, p. 302) wrote,

> Detailed study of ecosystems over the past decades has shown quite clearly that most relationships between living organisms are essentially co-operative ones, characterized by coexistence and interdependence, and symbiotic in various degrees.... This insight is in sharp contrast to the views of the Social Darwinists, who saw life exclusively in terms of competition, struggle, and destruction. Their view of nature has helped to create a philosophy that legitimates exploitation and the disastrous impact of our technology on the natural environment. But such a view has no scientific justification, because it fails to perceive the integrative and co-operative principles that are essential aspects of the ways in which living systems organize themselves at all levels.

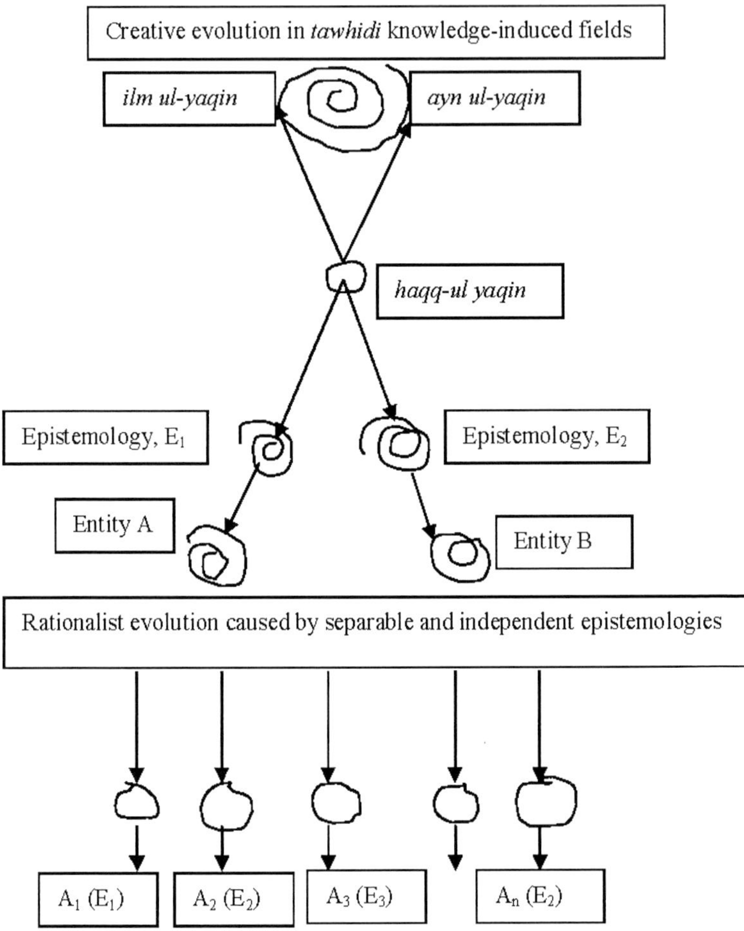

$\cap_i A_i (E_i) = \phi$, i=1,2,….n. Thereby, $\{E_i\}$ is a set of basis of vectors in n-dimensional space of A_i (E_i). In the (n+1)-dimensional space of vectors, $A_{n+1}(E_{n+1}) = \Sigma_{i=1}{}^{n} A_i(E_i)$, as a linear combination of the basis of vectors, which are independent in the n-dimensional space. The case can now be generalized. The end result is atomism of these emerging trajectories of conflicting, separable and independent epistemologies and their socio-scientific spaces. This marks the emergence of methodological individualism.

Figure 3.2: Treatment of falsehood by the *tawhidi* knowledge-centered methodology

To consider the *tawhidi* unity of knowledge more deeply, this methodology totally rejects the place of competition and marginalism between organic categories when premised on the unitary epistemology. In the perpetual conflict between truth and falsehood, the rule is not one of competition between truth and falsehood. Rather, it is to pursue the fixed goal of the truth paradigm. Thereby, the two trajectories of truth and falsehood evolve in evolutionary world-systems in distinct ways of their own kinds. They remain permanently polarized to each other, given however, that they are both explained uniquely by the dynamics of the *tawhidi* methodology, as referred to above (Choudhury, 2000) and learnt progressively, not optimally.

This point of singularity between the two polar and opposing praxes of life is brought out both in the *Qur'an* and the *sunnah*. Regarding the uncertain rambling of rationalist thought, even in its most tempting form, the *Qur'an* (51:10-11) declares:

> Woe to the falsehood-mongers, – those who (flounder) heedless in a flood of confusion.

Also there is the *qur'anic* verse (10:18):

> And they worship besides God things that hurt them not nor profit them, and they say: "These are our intercessors with God," Say: 'Do you inform God with that which He knows not in the heavens and on the earth?' Glorified and Exalted be He above all that they associate as partners with Him!"

Furthermore the *Qur'an* (40:66) declares:

> Say: 'I have been forbidden to invoke those who you invoke besides God, – seeing that the Clear Signs have come to me from my Lord; and I have been commanded to bow (in Islam) to the Lord of the Worlds.

Although this very verse refers to the mission of the Prophet Muhammad by the principle of universality of *qur'anic* verses, it is extended to apply to all believers in general. Yusuf Ali (1942) commenting on this verse writes, "When we bow to the Real and Everlasting, we are automatically saved from falling victims to the false and evanescent."

In a *hadith* (a saying of the Prophet Muhammad) on these matters, narrated by the Prophet's companion, Abu Huraira, the people of the scripture used to read the Torah in Hebrew and then explain it in Arabic to the Muslims. The Messenger said to the Muslims (Sahih Al-Bukhari, Vol. 9, *hadith* No. 460):

> Do not believe the people of the scripture, nor disbelieve them, but say, 'We believe in *Allah* and whatever is revealed to us, and whatever is revealed to you.'

Also, narrated by Abdullah, a companion of the Prophet, the Prophet said (Sahih Al-Bukhari, Vol. 6, *hadith* No. 24):

> "Whoever dies while still invoking anything other than *Allah* as a rival to *Allah*, will enter the Hell Fire."

The above and further evidence from the *Qur'an*, the *sunnah*, and the *hadith* unequivocally establish the undiluted purity of the *Qur'an* in establishing its meaning and worldview by referring to itself regarding the oneness of God. This is the challenging methodology of self-referencing in socio-scientific theory and practice. The theme will be developed at length in this work. It is to be found nowhere in received occidental and other pluralistic philosophies of the sciences.

Conclusion

This chapter is concerned with discovering the methodology shown in the *tawhidi* knowledge-centred worldview of the *Qur'an* in a way that can be explicated to form a unique epistemological foundation of the *qur'anic* praxis for explaining all socio-scientific phenomena. The *tawhidi* knowledge-centred worldview emerges as a substantive methodology of a nature quite contrary to the epistemology of all received bodies of thought in the natural and social sciences. The *qur'anic* methodology so derived will be shown to apply uniquely in a logical way to both the natural and social sciences. Thus the terminology of the *tawhidi* knowledge-centred foundations of the socio-scientific order is used.

While establishing the *qur'anic* knowledge-centred worldview by principally referring to the *Qur'an* with due reference to the *hadith* and *sunnah*, and claiming its uncompromising distinction from a rationalistic philosophy of the sciences and human behaviour, an extensive study of received philosophies of the sciences is undertaken. Within this critical approach real problems of human thought and experience are addressed. Some of these issues and problems are of a mundane nature. They explain the nature of the *qur'anic* world-systems.

While developing a general system-outlook of the *qur'anic* worldview the central methodological questions are made to revolve around the praxis of the *tawhidi* worldview. Upon this worldview, this chapter points out rules and explanations after researching the principal Islamic epistemological sources. These are namely the *Qur'an* and the *sunnah*.

References

Al-Edrus, S.M.D., 1992, *Islamic Epistemology, an Introduction to the Theory of Knowledge in al-Qur'an*, Secretariat for Islamic Philosophy and Science, Penang, Malaysia.

Aquinas, T., 1946, "The existence of God in things", "The infinity of God", "The eternity of God", "The unity of God", "Of God's knowledge", in *Summa Theologiae.* Vol. 1, pp. 1-11, 30-34, 40-45, 46-48, 72-86, Benziger Brothers, Inc., New York, NY.

Bakar, O., 1991, *Tawhid and Science, Essays on the History and Philosophy of Islamic Science*, Secretariat for Islamic Philosophy and Science, Kuala Lumpur, Malaysia.

Buchman, D. trans., 1998, *Al-Ghazzali Niche of Lights,* Brigham University Press, Provo, Utah.

Capra, F., 1983, "The systems view of life", in his, *The Turning Point*, Flamingo, London, Eng.

Choudhury, M.A., 1995, "Belief and knowledge formation in the *tawhid*i superspace", in his, *The Epistemological Foundations of Islamic Economic, Social and Scientific Order*, Vol. VI of 6 vols. Chapter 2, Statistical, Economic and Social Research and Training Center for Islamic Countries, Ankara, Turkey.

—. 1999, "Globally interactive systems", in his, *Comparative Economic Theory, Occidental and Islamic Perspectives*, Chapter 3, Kluwer Academic, Norwell, MA.

—. 2000, "The *Qur'anic* model of knowledge: the interactive, integrative and evolutionary process", in his, *The Islamic World View*, Chapter 3, Kegan Paul International, London, Eng.

Darwin, C., 1936, *Descent of Man* (or *Origin of Species*), Modern Library, New York, NY.

Ghazzali, A.H. (Imam) trans. by Buchman, D., 1998, *The Niche of Lights*, Brigham Young University, Salt Lake City, Utah.

—. (Imam) trans. by Marmura, M.E., 1997, *The Incoherence of the Philosophers*, Brigham Young University Press, Provo, Utah.

Ghazzali, A.H. (Imam) trans. by Karim, M.F. n.d., *Ihya Ulum-Id-Din* in 5 Vols., Sh. Muhammad Ashraf, Lahore, Pakistan. See Vol. 4 explaining the various stages of attaining belief on *tawhid*.

Hayek, F.A., 1967, "The principles of liberal social order", in his, *Studies in Philosophy, Politics and Economics*, The University of Chicago Press, Chicago, IL.

Hegel, G.W.F. trans. by Sibree, J., 1956, *The Philosophy of History*, Dover Books, New York, NY.

Hull, D.L., 1988, *Science as a Process, an Evolutionary Account of the Social and Conceptual Development of Science*, University of Chicago Press, Chicago, IL.

Hume, D., 1992, "Of the understanding", in his, *Treatise of Human Nature*, Prometheus Books, Buffalo, NY.

Kant, I. ed. by Friedrich, C.J., 1949, "Critique of pure reason"; also see, "Critique of judgment", in *The Philosophy of Kant*; "Reason within the limits of reason"; "Idea for a universal history with cosmopolitan content", in *The Philosophy of Kant*, Modern Library, New York, NY.

Kant, I. trans. by Infeld, L., 1963, "The general principle of morality"; also see "Natural religion"; "Prayer", *Kant's Lectures on Ethics*, Hackett Publishing Co., Indianapolis, IN.

Lucaks, J., 1968, *Historical Consciousness*, Harper & Row Publishers, New York, NY.

Popper, K., 1988, "Natural selection and the emergence of mind", in Radnitzky, G. & Bartley III, W.W. (eds.), *Evolutionary Epistemology, Rationality and the Sociology of Knowledge*, Open Court, La Salle, IL.

—. 1998, *Conjectures and Refutations: The Growth of Scientific Knowledge*, Routledge & Kegan Paul, London, Eng.

—. 2004, *The Logic of Scientific Discovery*, Routledge, London, Eng.

Resnick, S.A. & Wolff, R.D., 1987, *Knowledge and Class, A Marxian Critique of Political Economy*, The University of Chicago Press, Chicago, IL.

Sen, A., 1977, "Rational fools: a critique of the behavioural foundations of economic theory", *Philosophy and Public Affairs*, 6.

Sullivan, W.M., 1989, "The contemporary crisis of liberal society", in McCullough, H.B. (ed.), *Political Ideologies and Political Philosophies*. Wall & Thomson, Toronto, Ont.

Vermont, J-P. trans. by Lambert, C. & Fagan, T.L., 1995, *The Greeks*, The University of Chicago Press, Chicago, IL.

CHAPTER FOUR

A *TAWHIDI* EPISTEMOLOGICAL CRITIQUE OF THE PROJECT OF *ISLAMIZATION* OF KNOWLEDGE

After undertaking a critical review of the state of religious and socio-scientific thought, even after invoking the *tawhidi* critical approach in this, the critical question remains: How well has the Muslim mind done in this epistemological inquiry, essential as it is for gaining a substantive Islamic socio-scientific meaning? Our standpoint extensively explained thus far in this book, and to be further carried forward, has shown that there cannot be an Islamic intellectual enterprise without a substantive epistemological foundation on the *tawhidi* methodology and worldview. Equally, there must be sound socio-scientific analytical basis for such a foundational inquiry. Finally, these two approaches must be amenable for application on rigorous analytical grounds.

Such claims of course never mean that what is being formalized and presented in this way as a *tawhidi* methodological worldview derived from the *Qur'an*, the *sunnah*, and the discursive enterprise of the learned, is in any way the final construct of the *tawhidi* epistemological worldview. The attempt in this book on the theme of *tawhidi* methodology and its application with deep socio-scientific investigation is a quest for truth along the path of evolutionary learning towards understanding unity of knowledge. This quest embraces the unity of the generality and the details of the world-system, and related issues. The comparative scholarship is upheld while the *Qur'an*, the *sunnah*, and the learned Islamic edicts remain foundational.

Introduction

Every scientific theory and development of scientific thought depends importantly on its abstraction of the world as the scientists see it. This means to premise scientific inquiry on its epistemology as primordial as this can be. On this point Einstein (1954, p. 473) wrote: "Scientific thought is a development of pre-scientific thought. As the concept of space was already fundamental in the latter, we must begin with the concept of space in pre-scientific thought."

By a similar argument, the Islamic scholastics have established the centrepiece of all worldly inquiries as being premised on the epistemology of unity of knowledge (Al-Attas, 1989). Such epistemic unity has been explained in terms of the cardinal value of the Islamic socio-scientific worldview. This is termed *tawhid*, the Oneness of God in the sense of the ontological primordial existence of God carried forward by the monotheistic law. Thus the precept of *tawhid* includes the organic symbiosis of oneness presented by the monotheistic law in the scheme of things. These two aspects of epistemic unity together comprise the epistemological premise of unity of knowledge in Islamic monotheism, *tawhid*. Thus the complete intellection of *tawhid* as monotheistic oneness relates to the integration of God's oneness (*tawhid* in its ontological primacy) in the understanding of the generality and the specifics of the world-system, even in the minutest of details.[1]

Tawhid as the comprehensive worldview is the primal axiom. In terms of the monotheistic law, *tawhid* forms the basis of its epistemology that is premised on unity of knowledge. This is how the meaning of *tawhid* is used in this chapter. The *Qur'an* says in this regard (96:1-5): "Read: In the name of your Lord Who created, created man from a clot. Read: And your Lord is the Most Bounteous. Who taught by the pen, taught man that which he knew not."[2]

---

[1] Why is *tawhid* the logical and scientific episteme as also the worldview of both ontological and phenomenological consequences in explaining the socio-scientific 'everything'? It is because *tawhid* offers a formalism that explains in detail *both* truth and falsehood. *Tawhid* is thus the ontological combined with the functional understanding of the total reality comprising both truth and falsehood. Metaphysical shadows of belief and faith are abandoned in this comprehensive conception of unity of knowledge overarching 'everything', i.e. truth and falsehood. See a further footnote later on regarding this substantive issue.

[2] The comprehensive meaning of *tawhid* presented in the *Qur'an* is conveyed by the passage of knowledge emanating from the monotheistic law. Such immanent knowledge is then carried from the ontological level of belief and faith in the oneness of God to the functional level of divine oneness that is presented by the impact of monotheism as law on the unity of the world-system and its details. The comprehension of this total episteme is by knowledge and towards regeneration of knowledge. The verses of the *qur'anic* Chapter entitled, *Read* (*Iqra, Qur'an,* Chapter 96) conveys the functional role of the medium of knowledge in the

The early thinkers on the *qur'anic* worldview delved deeply into the *Qur'an* and in the conveyance of the meaning of its verses through the practices and sayings of the Prophet Muhammad (*sunnah*). The *Qur'an* and the *sunnah* are followed in the Islamic epistemological practice by learned discourse (the *shura,* narrowly meaning consultation) on the issues at hand (*ijtihad*).[3]

In this regard, the principal thought of the great scholastic thinker that we will examine in this chapter is of Abdul Hameed Al-Ghazzali. His works in this area are too many to mention here. See Ghazanfar & Islahi (1990, pp. 381-403) for a comprehensive review.

Ijtihad and *shura* as the medium of discourse on diverse issues in the light of *tawhid* and the world-system are established in and by the Islamic learned community. Discourse relating to *tawhid* and the issues of the organically related world-system[4] are launched by the learned Islamic community to derive and establish meanings out of the *qur'anic* verses on the epistemological understanding of the issues under investigation. *Tawhid* as the moral and functional law of monotheism conveys and structures the organic unification of the world-systems being premised on the moral law. This is a fact that overarches the entire Islamic community irrespective of being *sunnis* or *shi'as*, two sects of Muslims.

The debates and disagreements that lay in the discursive practices of *shura*, *ijtihad*, and *fiqh* (interpretation) on socio-scientific issues from the

---

understanding of the comprehensive meaning of *tawhid* and the unified nature of the world-system. Note also that the verses of the Chapter *Read* (*Iqra*) must never be limited to the meaning of reading and writing as casual acts. Rather, the meaning is all-encompassing in the realm of knowledge, its epistemology, phenomenology, and extensive understanding across 'everything'. On this point, Yusuf Ali (1946) writes: "The object understood being God's Message." This is *tawhid*.

[3] The traditional meaning of *shura* as consultation is extended here to discourse. That is because the purpose of the *shura* (likewise *ijtihad*) as knowledge-generating process involves the understanding of the deeper meanings of the processes inherent in the socio-scientific discourse induced by elements of the monotheistic law. This is the essence of matter that we have derived from the *Qur'an* to explain consciousness as *tasbih*. These implications of the discursive meaning of the *shura* as process of epistemological learning can be read off the *qur'anic* verses (42:49-53).

[4] The unified world-system is referred to in the *Qur'an* as *alameen* whose creator and sustainer is God. The *alameen* presents unity of being in everything by the functioning of the monotheistic law. The *Qur'an* (1:1) declares: "Praise be to God, the Lord of the *Alameen*."

qur'anic and *sunnah* points of view, which is the matter that interests us in this chapter, is a sign of the discursive practice. The *Qur'an* and the *sunnah* have endowed such a practice on the participants from all sides.[5] Qadir (1990, p.73) writes well on this point: "According to Amir Ali, the great object of the Muslim philosophers was 'to furnish the world with a complete theory of the unity of the cosmos which would satisfy not the mind only, but also the religious sense. And accordingly they endeavoured to reconcile the ethical and spiritual with the philosophical side of science'."

Such an exercise on the functional relationship between the *Qur'an*, the *sunnah*, and learned discourse on the generality, diversities, and details of the world-system is an extensive one. It invokes intellection in the domain of incessant learning. Such evolutionary learning invokes the knowledge of organic oneness that is conveyed by the law of *tawhid* in relation to the generality and details of issues of the world-system.

Organic learning of and by the relational understanding cannot be completed in temporal experience; and it is present in 'everything' and everywhere incessantly.[6] The *Qur'an* establishes this openness of the immanent search, discovery, and evolution of knowledge in and of the learning world-system by relational unity without end. The *Qur'an* thus builds and explains the openness of evolutionary learning within and across the diversity of systemic oneness in 'everything' in terms of this epistemic knowledge. It then continues on to study the knowledge induction of the world-system in its generality and specifics.

The study of the learning world-system in and by the *tawhidi* law thus explains reality in the dimensions of knowledge, space, and time.

---

[5] *Qur'an* (4:50): "O you who believe, Obey God, and obey the Apostle and those charged in with authority among you. If you differ in anything among yourselves, refer it to God and His Apostle, if you do believe in God and the Last Day: That is best, and most suitable for final determination." This is a command adhered to both by Sunni and Shi'a sects of Muslims.

[6] The *Qur'an* mentions the continuous reorigination in learning and knowledge. These are the *qur'anic* cardinal attributes derived from the *tawhidi* worldview. The imminent phenomenology is expressed by the *qur'anic* terms as 'pairing (*jauz al-karim*) in everything (signifying organic relational orders); reoriginative socio-scientific orders (*khalqin jadid*); continuums (*alameen*); and the Great Event of completion of learning towards *tawhid* in the Beginning and the End, the Hereafter (*Naba ul Azim*)'. With these and many similar verses of the *Qur'an*, the scientists of all persuasions can now interactively integrate these precepts into an interconnected generalized worldview of being and becoming. Such is the nature of knowledge-induced system and cybernetics network. It forms the generalized system perspective of the knowledge-induced entirety.

Knowledge, space, and time together occupy the formal precincts of conception, explanation, and application according to the *tawhidi* law of monotheistic oneness in 'everything'. This essence is now studied in its organic learning perspective of relational unification. The emergent phenomenology is a vastly scientific endeavour. It establishes the scientific core of the *tawhidi* evolutionary learning worldview. See Choudhury (2011c) for details of the mathematical formalism of evolutionary learning equilibriums explained by the inherent models and dynamics.

The system and cybernetic universe of *tawhid* is thus summarized as the realm of unity of knowledge as its episteme. In it, knowledge of relational oneness by the monotheistic law proceeds incessantly across the processes of evolutionary learning in the entirety of knowledge, space and time. Such a universe transcends the universe of sheer space-time. Space-time is a limited dimensional view of the universe. Rather, such a limited conception of the universe is embedded. In the substantive sense of *tawhid*, the system embedding occurs within the overarching universe of knowledge, space, and time. The understanding and configuration, significance and application in the dimensions of knowledge, space and time substantially change the systemic and cybernetic formalism of the universe. In this chapter, we have focused on the socio-scientific world-system of the yet more overarching universe. We refer to such a unified sub-universe governed by the *tawhidi* law as the *tawhidi* world-system.

Objective

This chapter is an original contribution to the theme of the *tawhidi* (monotheistic) Scientific Research Program (SRP) that is conceptually formalized in terms of the evolutionary theory of Islamization of knowledge. Such an evolutionary learning theory that interactively integrates the epistemology of monotheism (*tawhid*) found in the *Qur'an* to the general and specific issues and problems of the world-system is an original field of intellection. It has not been taken up in any leading understanding of the theme of Islamization of knowledge. Such an intellectual void is true of both the Islamic classical and modern literature on the theme. Consequently, a system and cybernetic worldview of *tawhid* in action in the unity of the world-system as an interactive, integrative, and evolutionary process (**IIE**-process) of relational unity, has not been invoked. The functioning of the *tawhidi* law in the generalized system and the cybernetic worldview of unity of knowledge as its episteme remains absent. The true nature of relationship between knowledge and the socio-scientific worldview could not be understood and derived from the *tawhidi* praxis.

The objective of this chapter is to formalize the *tawhidi* meaning of knowledge and present its intellectual character on how the monotheistic law is transmitted to the world-system towards formalizing relations that explain organic unification and the emergent applications. The chapter presents a methodological worldview as the phenomenology of the integrative mind and matter relations in evolutionary epistemology.

Hence, while the derivation of the methodology is purely *qur'anic* in essence, taking along with this the prophetic guidance (*sunnah*), it is also formal and analytical in nature. Hence the epistemological and the formal precepts together establish the explanation and application of the resulting formal model of monotheistic unity of knowledge. It is applied to the generalized and specific issues of various unified and socially embedded world-systems. Such is the phenomenological representation of the system and cybernetic formalism that *tawhidi* unity of knowledge establishes.

Nature of knowledge in the Qur'an

To understand the nature of knowledge endowed by the *Qur'an* to the world-system, the meaning of knowledge as an ontological essence must be first understood. This initial quest for knowledge in the phenomenological sphere of the *Qur'an* is from and of the oneness of God. Following the many peripatetic Islamic philosophers, including significantly Abu Hamed Muhammad Ibn Muhammad Al-Ghazzali (1058 CE-1111CE), the functional meaning of the oneness of God is taken as the manifestation of the organic *pairing* of the universe and its details by the medium of the monotheistic law. *Tawhid* comprehends the oneness of God in belief and its implication on the unity of the knowledge-induced world-system. In this way, the meaning of *tawhid* is explained in the sphere of its universal functioning by epistemic unity of knowledge.

Yet in this chapter *tawhid* in its functional form is represented *not* in terms of the *ontological being* of God. God by ontological belief and intellection is incommensurate in shape, form, conception, attribute, and functionality. Therefore such an understanding of the primordial existence of God cannot be used in formal analysis. Rather, the meaning of monotheistic oneness as the completion of the absolute and perfect knowledge without partnership (duality and multiplicity), but remaining incommensurate in any dimension, is manifested in the organic form of relational unity in the cognitive world. The precept thereby is contrary to the phenomenology explained by Heidegger (trans. Hofstadter, 1988). The organic process of becoming cognitive beings invokes the relational and evidential (ontic) states of learning in the experiential world-system by its generality and specifics of issues and problems. Indeed, 'Being' in any ontological concept cannot convey the Purity (*Iqhlas*) of God. Rather, being is the result of the becoming of the world-system, which is realized by the induction of the monotheistic law of unity, the *tawhidi* law.

Thus the cardinal principle of Islamic belief, namely consciousness, meaning understanding and embracing the oneness of God, is manifested in the organic becoming of beings in worldly experience. *Tawhid* is thus manifested through and learnt via the universe in its attribute of consciousness of understanding by the learning process in unity of knowledge. The *Qur'an* refers to this learning process in terms of the interminable capacity to comprehend the organic unity of knowledge of *tawhid* as monotheistic law. This law functions in the order and scheme of creation. Such attributes of knowledge and knowing are conveyed by the extended understanding of the *qur'anic* phrase, *khalqin jadid*, meaning reoriginated creations taken over continua of experiences (17:49). The reoriginative positivism that alerts consciousness to understand the functioning of *tawhid* in the beings of the world-system, is pointed out in verse (29: 19-22). The created universal state of continuous worship, which man endeavours to know by searching, is implied in verse (17:44). The *Qur'an* introduces the idea of the learning universe in terms of its *pairing* ontology of being and becoming in 'everything' and everywhere in the dimensions of knowledge, space and time. We note this property of universality underlying the pairing universe in the *qur'anic* verse (36:36).

The phenomenological model of knowledge and its induction of the world-system according to the *Qur'an*

The *Qur'an* classifies the elements of the concept of knowledge and its relationship with the world-system. This comprises the *qur'anic* phenomenological model of unity of knowledge in relation to the world-system. Figure 4.1 presents this model.

The sequences (1-5) in figure (4.1) comprise the continuity of the learning process across 'everything' and everywhere in a world-system comprising many world-systems as unified orders. Each of these has the common episteme of learning by unity of knowledge. Yet even as the embodiment of knowledge is through unity, the experiential facts may reveal the contrary in terms of relations between the differentiated variables, their non-complementary relations, and the competing entities of the specific world-system under study. In such a state, the same process evaluation of inter-variable relations can unravel differentiations and trade-offs instead of the desired unity of knowledge. Out of such conflicting trade-offs, the *tawhidi* formulation invokes the moral reconstruction of the differentiated inter-variables relations. Such an evaluation process resolves the nature of differentiation to better states of relational unification in degrees of unity of being realized through simulation and discourse. Such a transformation of the differentiated world-systems in terms of specifics and totality characterizes the moral-social reconstruction. It characterizes the combinations of the two integral functions, that is 'estimation' followed by 'simulation', to gain better perspectives of inter-variable and inter-causal unity of knowledge. The episteme and the moral reconstruction of the world-system convey the meaning of *tawhidi* consciousness.

1		2		3		4		5 (4.1)
tawhid (monotheistic law: *Qur'an*)	→	Unraveled to the world-system through the guidance of the Prophet Muhammad (*sunnah*)	→	Discourse on the unraveling of *tawhid* as functional ontology of rules of life	→	Learning as pairing in world-systems	→	The Hereafter
	↓			↓		↓		↓
Fundamental Episteme Initiation of Knowledge			→	Discursive worldly derivation of rules of experience	→	Processes of knowing: being and becoming	→	Equivalence to *tawhid* at the End by closure of the openness of learning processes

Figure 4.1: Structure of the *qur'anic* phenomenological model of the learning world-system premised in the episteme of unity of knowledge

Firstly, there is the discursive medium that engages in extracting rules in the light of the *qur'anic* law through the *sunnah*. This is the stage of deriving rules from the monotheistic law of *tawhid*. The institution engaging in such a derivation of rules from the *tawhidi* law is called the *shura*. Its investigative pursuit is called *ijtihad*, meaning the derivation of rules from the fundamental epistemic sources.

The second fundamental element of knowledge derivation through the discursive process in the *shura* discourse (consultation) exercising *ijtihad* is called *tasbih* (60:24). The meaning of *tasbih* conveys the worshipping nature of unification of knowledge and the understanding of *functional* ontological forms according to the *qur'anic* principle of '*pairing*' (uniting, symbiosis, and synergy by organic complementarities and participation by entities). Such pairing characterizes the representative variables by their unifying (also complementary and participative) interrelations concerning the issues and problems under study.

In this chapter we will combine this *paired* nature of the knowledge-forming process of the *Qur'an* and refer to it as *tasbih-shura* (*TS*), as in earlier chapters. *TS* marks the intrinsic experience of learning in unity of knowledge and the unified world-system. *TS* forms the basis of *qur'anic* consciousness in its active functioning in the world-system.

The Islamic phenomenology of unity of knowledge and its impact on the moral-social reconstruction of the unified world-system is thus cast in the framework of a logical, consistent, and *functionally* ontological (Gruber, 1993) model of being and becoming in reference to the axiomatic episteme of unity of knowledge (*tawhid*). All properties of the emergent learning process-oriented general-system model, erected upon the *qur'anic* phenomenological worldview, generate the dynamics of the synergistic relations. Yet the ultimate exogenous axiom is solely *tawhid* as monotheistic oneness of God, the moral law, and the world-system in the *tawhid*-world-system-hereafter completeness of the universal learning processes (the **IIE**-processes as explained in earlier chapters). *Tawhid* forms the irreducible and ultimate axiom to hold on to in the description of the unified mind-matter world-system by generality and its specifics, both studied by the *qur'anic* consciousness.

Meaning of knowledge in the context of *tawhidi* phenomenology

We therefore inquire: What is the substantive meaning of knowledge in the context of such a phenomenological system and cybernetic worldview? The meaning can be best unravelled by way of the *tawhidi* functionalism in the *qur'anic* phenomenological model. This is now explained by Figure 4.2.

--- Phenomenology of the learning world-system and specifics in unity of knowledge ----

The completeness→ ontological→ ontological→ functional→ inductive→ recursive continuity

The completeness of knowledge as episteme of unity of being and *becoming tawhid* as axiom treated mathematically as super-cardinal topology (Rucker, 1983a) causing relational property but not measurability and is not relational of itself

ontological mapping of formal law into rules

ontological formulation: discursively derived rules

functional ontological formalism in deductive reasoning leading to abstraction of reality

inductive

recursive continuity of evaluation of deductive formalism for moral-social reconstruction inference to inter-relations between variables

(4.2)

----- Fundamental ----
Absolute Epistemology:
Axiom

--- relativism----------
functional ontological Formalism of rules and ideas and relations:

post-evaluation and of functional formal ontological rules moral-social reconstruction of specific issues in the light of *tawhidi* law

------------------------ Derivation of Epistemic Knowledge based on deductive reasoning leading to formal ontological construction as abstraction of reality ------------ Evaluation and ----- continuity in learning processes integrating deductive and inductive reasoning: moral and social reconstruction

evolutionary epistemology knowledge, time, space intra-and inter-systemic continuum

----- axiomatic derivation and continuity of *tasbih-shura* ----
TS experience Islamic discursive society

construction of the knowledge-induced world-system and its specifics ------------- continuity →

Figure 4.2: The meaning of knowledge in the framework of *tawhidi* phenomenology

A review of the literature on the Islamic characterization of knowledge: the project of Islamization of knowledge

In the aforementioned schematic explanation of the idea of knowledge, I have left out the deeply mathematical details that embody the entire phenomenological model of unity of knowledge, and the emergent unified world-system and its specifics that arise on particular problems under study in the light of the mind-matter complementarities. That is relational unification. However, the learning processes depicted in Figures 4.1 and 4.2 present the author's formal characterization of the Islamization-of-knowledge project.

In the context of the epistemology of unity of knowledge in this chapter (Choudhury, 1993), Islamization means an evolutionary epistemological explanation of junctures of moral-social change, wherein mind and matter, i.e. thought and events, interact to establish new epistemological socio-scientific realities in reference to the *tawhidi* worldview. Islamization is characterized by such immanent processes of learning in unity of knowledge. These learning processes have a multi-universal nature (cybernetic systems), existing in the continuum of (knowledge, space, and time) dimensions. They sustain the emergent Islamization of knowledge and education, knowledge and life, by the substantive *tawhidi* evolutionary dynamics (Choudhury, 2011a).

Islamization of knowledge and education is an idea for which many have endeavoured in the light of Islamic epistemology and human resource development. Such efforts have been less than effective in contributing any significant idea of advancement to scholarship as it presently stands. The main failure of the Islamization project has been its inability to understand the logical formalism and functioning of the *tawhidi* worldview of the *tasbih-shura (TS)* relationship in the scheme and order of the worldly issues (specifics) and in the cosmological entirety (cybernetic generality). This totality comprises the multiverse concept.

Instead, Islamization has remained a nominal Islamic appendix rather than an epistemologically original Islamic inquiry. Likewise, Islamization of education, a subset of the knowledge domain, which is phenomenological in the entire socio-scientific thought, has produced non-substantive increment in mainstream books and paraphernalia of education. There is just an ostensible Islamic garb.

On the other hand, those who aimed at an epistemological reconstruction of Islamic thought have dwelled only on the metaphysical aspects. This has yielded no fresh insight into the formalism of knowledge, thought, and designs of the world-system in which the fundamental episteme of unity of knowledge functions through its rich dynamics. In the end, the Islamic universities, Islamic institutions, such as the Islamic Development Bank, the Islamic Research and Training Institute, and the many Islamic banks along with scholarly pursuits in recent times have simply impelled Muslims to return to the scientific crux of sheer modernity – but not to the *tawhidi* epistemological origins in the *Qur'an*.

One may refer here to the following glimpses in regard to our criticism: In his defence of the thoughts of Al-Attas, Daud (1998a) establishes an utterly metaphysical epistemic concept. There is a total absence of the formal and analytical dynamics of the epistemological worldview of *tawhid* in the construction and working of the world-system and its specifics in the light of the *tawhidi* phenomenological methodology (Daud, 1998b). The same implications are found in Al-Attas' views on the contemporary education field with particular reference to Malaysia (Daud, 1998c).

Faruqi (1982a) failed in the same sort of project, leaving his book entitled *Tawhid* to speculative wishes rather than substantive analytics and foundational issues with applications. Faruqi (1982b) promoted Islamization of the mainstream textbooks in university educational programs. There was no demand on the *qur'anic* epistemological originality to establish Islamization of knowledge. Rahman (1988) contested this approach to Islamization of knowledge.

Choudhury (2006) has pointed out that in the entire area of economic and social thought, contemporary Islamic scholars have failed to incorporate a substantive study of the *tawhidi* methodological worldview in the form of epistemological analytics and its function. Yet this inclusion remains most essential in the *qur'anic* originality to Islamization of knowledge.

Like Rahman, Sardar (1984) raised intellectual criticism against the idea of Islamization of knowledge and education. He objected to the way that this project has been carried out with clamour in the receiving circles. Such polemical clamour has had no significant contribution to the world of learning and academia. The pursuit could otherwise be premised on the new epistemological birth of knowledge in a socio-scientific scope of the *tawhidi* overarching worldview.

Indeed, without epistemology there can be no science. Science without epistemology is no more than a muddled form of thinking. Such a message was conveyed by Einstein to his colleague Neils Bohr (1985). On the same theme in Islamic science and philosophy, Nasr (1968; see also Qadir, 1990) proceeds in the following way: Nasr like Husserl (1965) is indeed dismayed with the moral decadence of Occidental science. He attributes this moral decadence to the excessive secularization of science that has excluded the divine element from it. In a similar tone, Husserl thought of the transcendental ego that remains absent in the secularization of science. Nasr premises Islamic science on metaphysics. Metaphysics in turn is an ontological meaning of *tawhid* understood only in terms of God's attributes and essence, not in terms of the divine law in action. That ontological primordial part is the metaphysical attribute as laid down in the chapter of the *Qur'an* named "Purity", *Iqhlas* (*Qur'an*, Chapter 112).

But the metaphysical approach leaves out the phenomenological methodology of *tawhid* that connects the ontological with the world-system through the monotheistic law of organic oneness of unity of knowledge. Such a dynamic of the monotheistic law is not cultivated by Nasr. In this regard, Qadri (1988, p. 147) writes, "metaphysics may be said to constitute the inner dimension of the *shar'iah*, which directs and determines the activities and the goals of human life". But how is the socio-scientific world-system governed in the framework of a scientific methodology of *tawhid*? Nasr remains silent on this ground, except for the exercise of gnosis in metaphysical scientific speculation. Hence, Nasr has not been successful in establishing the scientific functional methodology and methods for the epistemic and applied constructs of the *tawhidi* epistemological socio-scientific worldview.

In Guessoum's (op cit, p.111) words on Nasr's position in science, "Existence is one, and all phenomena are partial reflections of it. *Tawhid* then also implies the unity of truth and knowledge, the unity of creation, the unity of life and the unity of humanity. Consequently, in Nasr's view, the goal of all Islamic sciences, from mathematics to medicine, is to reveal that unity and the 'interrelatedness of all that exists'" (Nasr, 1987, p. 22). Such claims are similar to Choudhury's (1983), which are presented in this and other chapters of this book with methodological substance through the stage of early inception as paradigm. Choudhury's paradigm was initiated earlier than Nasr's philosophical views. Yet since he first wrote, Nasr could not give functional dimensions to his philosophy. Thus Nasr's academic philosophy did not bear any scientific result.

Our present chapter progresses in this direction of ontology complementing the functioning of the world-system taken in its generality and details. This chapter thereby embarks on and deepens the theme of the *tawhidi* phenomenology. It does not simply limit itself to the metaphysical ontology of epistemic oneness of God.

Imam Ghazzali's phenomenology of knowledge

Next we reconstruct Figures 4.1 and 4.2 in Figure 4.3 to present Imam Ghazzali's phenomenology in regards to knowledge and education in Islam. Ghazzali shed importance on the micro-level moral, social, and ethical values of individual self towards forming a good society, market economic system, and institutional order; all of these through the application of the Islamic law (*shari'ah*), considered as the best moral law.

Still, the *methodology and dynamics* of the *tawhidi* epistemological worldview remained absent at this level. Ghazzali's contribution, despite pointing out the importance of *tawhid* and the *shari'ah* in human experiences, remained focused on *tawhid* at the metaphysical level. The nature of holistic system and cybernetics in which the epistemological general-system model could have been formulated in Ghazzali's peripatetic thought to represent the unification worldview of *tawhid,* was left out.

We have argued in this chapter that the ontological argument dealing with the topic of being and becoming cannot be attributed to God *per se* in terms of a process model. God as an *ontological being* can at best be an axiom of assumed existence without commensurateness in any shape, form or representation. Hence it is impossible to assign process-driven attributes to God as an ontological being. In other words, there is no meaningful relation between say, the attribute of 'seeing' by God and the human act of seeing. Likewise, there is no such relationship between God as the *M*erciful and human beings as *m*erciful. There is no relationship between the Absolute and Perfect knowledge of God and the created knowledge of the world and the human experience gained by it.

In the process model of *tawhidi* dynamics, God enters the scene of action and responses in models of circular causation of unity of knowledge and the worldly beings. This happens by way of the worldly functionality of the divine law of monotheism. Functionalism is realized by transmission of the *qur'anic* knowledge by the *sunnah* of the Prophet Muhammad and the discourses of the Islamic learned. Consequently, *tawhid* as fundamental epistemology (Figure 4.2) is translated into the completeness and absoluteness of the divine law of monotheism. This is relationally extracted via 'bits' from the *qur'anic* law through the medium of the *sunnah* and the discourse based on *TS*-dynamics across continuums of evolutionary epistemology. This is the phenomenology of knowledge explained in Figures 4.1 and 4.2. Consequential models and inferences are thereby developed in the form of a process model of organic learning.

The same is not possible in the metaphysical construction of God's Purity taken in its metaphysical meaning only, separated from its relationship with the world-system. Even the following two cases are impossible to interpret and use in the phenomenological process model of learning: (1) God is One. There cannot be any tenable interpretation of the invincible principle of monotheism by configuring God by the number 'one'. God is 'One' in terms of the absence of partnership with God in creation. The implication then is the total embodiment of the divine law in 'everything' and everywhere. (2) 'Neither slumber nor sleep overtake

God'. This *qur'anic* statement too is impossible to interpret in any ontological *being*-state of God, except to invoke the being and becoming of creation as it unfolds by the embodiment of the divine law in it. The divine law never fails to act.

The same ontological problem is cast in the following argument: If we hold God as a metaphysical ontological being, and then take parts of this ontological God, inevitably metaphysics would drown in the One-Many problem (Rucker, 1983b). The entire *qur'anic* meaning of God is then negated.

Thus only the divine law can be understood in 'bits' of knowledge-flows derived from the epistemological core. The human comprehension of the divine law cannot be comprehended in terms of God as a metaphysical being. Indeed, God cannot be taken into 'bits'. The divine law of monotheism when so enabled by its transmission through 'bits', becomes useable in the learning-process only. This phase marks the moral-social reconstruction of the world-system and its specifics through the *functional* ontology of the *sunnah* and the discursive intervention of the learned society. This intermediation carries the *tawhidi* law to the world-system. Such a process transmission is pointed out in Figure 4.2.

The epistemological dynamics of *tawhid* are now set alive and are creative in the learning world-system, which is washed by the law of organic oneness (*tawhid* = monotheism as unravelled and explained). The *Qur'an* establishes such an understanding of God and the world-system explained by the monotheistic law, instead of submerging the mind into the impossible task of knowing the metaphysical ontology of God as One.

Therefore, when Imam Ghazzali classified knowledge into stages of its realization, he ascended from the heart and soul into the heights of unravelling the heart and mind to know the world.[7] Ghazzali's

[7] In this overarching domain of knowledge taken out of the *Qur'an*, Ghazzali is a peripatetic thinker who has combined the ontological with the phenomenological consequences of the knowledge of unity of being and becoming. He thus extended the all-embracing domain of events of the world from the constricted space-time structure to the *res extensa* of the knowledge, space, and time structure. Ghazzali thus took the domain of phenomenology out of rationalism (and not rationality, as reason is incorrectly construed) to the all encompassing domain of belief and faith. This kind of overarching experience modern science cannot and does not want to embrace for a consistent study of the holistic entirety.

On this matter Ghazzali confronted Ibn Rushd (Averroes) and Ibn Sina (Avicenna) on their mistakes to place God within a process order of causation. That is God does not have terminal attributes in the (knowledge, space, time)-dimensions. Revelation supplements rational knowledge (reason). Rationalism on

classification of knowledge is now explained in Figure 4.3. Ghazzali's phenomenological model is premised on a perfect nature of the knowledge model towards which the heart, soul, and self, rise to attain certainty. Ghazzali envisions seventy veils of unravelling knowledge while coming closest to God, the Ultimate Certainty. The last of such stages is of *fana*. This stage means self-annihilation as moral self-actualization in meeting the consciousness of God as One.

Ghazzali explains the gaining of knowledge of *tawhid* by the unravelling the heart, soul and mind to the kernel of a coconut (Karim, n.d.). A man who simply hails God as the One (*tawhid* in its initial expression) is a believer, yet he is in the lowest rungs of true belief. This state of belief is like the outer kernel of the coconut. In the second stage, the believer sees the inside of the coconut. Subsequently, the believer continues on to see the oil of the coconut. This stage marks the growing consciousness moving into purity. The stages of cognitive evolution move across seventy stages of evolutionary knowledge of *tawhid*.

In the delineation of knowledge formation, our *tawhidi* epistemological model resembles that of Ghazzali's. The difference is substantively on the origination and continuity of our *tawhidi* worldview through the passage of human imperfection and incompleteness of knowledge. This does not allow for knowing the divine law of monotheism in its perfection. Human knowledge in the learning process-oriented phenomenology can simply simulate an idea of reality in *tawhid*. The emergent mind-matter unification in the *tawhidi* phenomenological model would then proceed on to worldly applications. This would acquire empirical and inferential evolutionary designs of the moral-social reconstruction of the world-system.

Our *tawhidi* epistemological model thus explains and formalizes both of the opposite phenomenological models, namely of knowledge and 'de-

---

the other hand, conveys man's incomplete understanding of reality by separating *a priori* reasoning from *a posteriori* reasoning.

Being so different from reason, rationalism is classified with falsehood, and therefore abandoned as unacceptable in the grand design of knowledge *parri passu*. Fakhry (2004, p. 295) writes on this point of Ghazzali: "Al-Ghazzali was therefore right to argue that 'with respect to whatever lies outside the scope of human cognitions, it is necessary to resort to Scripture ... In all such cases, revelation necessarily supplements rational knowledge."

In his masterful argumentations in philosophy and belief, Ghazzali simply held up *tawhid* as the sole axiomatic basis of argumentation. Such an approach is surely of the spirit of scientific analysis. It is therefore incorrect to interpret that Ghazzali was against the rationalist processes of understanding reality. Ghazzali simply emphasized the meaning of complementarities between revelation and reason.

knowledge' (rationalism). In the end, a process model of simulated learning replaces the metaphysical conception of the perfect state. This latter state is characterized by the *optimum primus* of human craving for reaching Ghazzali's devotional state of self-annihilation, *fana*. Attainment of such a sublime state of knowledge and self-actualization is beyond human possibility.

Contrasting Ghazzali's phenomenology with the *tawhidi* evolutionary learning model of Islamization of knowledge

Despite a striking similarity in the epistemological sense between Ghazzali and our model, the two phenomenological perspectives lead to different mechanisms in explaining the process of knowing existents. For Ghazzali, the process towards knowing existents is based on the five stages of knowing (Karim, n.d. p. 21). These are "namely, the sensory, imaginative, intelligential, cogitative (or ratiocinative) and prophetic faculties". These are attributes of knowledge formation embodied in stage I within the bracketed term [.] in Figure 4.3. Yet the progress of knowledge from stage I to its impact on the design of stage II in Figure 4.3 is not within the domain of Ghazzali's phenomenology. For instance, the interaction between the world-system and its specific issues are not explained to generate new rounds of knowledge-flows, once the fundamental epistemology continues to impact upon the continuity of the learning processes, and recursively between knowledge derivation and its impact on the world-system.

Ghazzali's phenomenological worldview explains the creation of knowledge in its original stages by the divine will. The divine will as law continues on to be present in the world-system. Our model shows that knowledge-flows and their impact on the states of the world-system are always primordially created by the recalling of the fundamental epistemology of *tawhid*. Yet in the initiation of learning processes, the knowledge-induced world-system generates fresh rounds of knowledge. These progressively advance further comprehension of *tawhid*, and so on.

While Ghazzali's phenomenology relies on deductive reasoning *per se*, our model has a unifying continuity between deductive and inductive reasoning, *a priori* and *a posteriori* reasoning, inasmuch as each learning process evolves out of the previous one by continuously recalling the fundamental epistemology of *tawhid*. Such recalling re-originates the next learning process between newly generated knowledge-flows and the consequential emergent states of the world-system relating to specific issues and problems. The evolutionary learning processes regenerate in the continua of knowledge, space and time.

This difference between the two phenomenological models of knowledge-induced reality also results in another consequence. Ghazzali's knowledge-domain only appertains to the *human* cogitation of knowing and its sensory attributes. Our knowledge-model extends learning to *all* worlds – 'everything' (Barrow, 1991). Hence in our model, knowledge and its impact on the plethora of world-systems are intra-system and inter-systems across multiverses. Consequently, the knowledge of *tawhid* is embodied in 'everything' everywhere. It is of human pursuit to know and benefit from knowledge-flows in epistemic unity to unravel the nature of unity ('*pairing*') in the generality and details of the world-system. In our model, the *tawhidi* worldview is axiomatically premised on an organic form of relational unity between all good things of life as determined by *maqasid as–shari'ah*, be these animate or inanimate. In our model, the fallen world that is not so unified due to its departure from knowledge induction and abidance by the *maqasid as-shari'ah*, is capable of reconstruction towards unity of knowledge through the processes of being and becoming.

Ghazzali's systemic model of learning rising towards *fana* is an optimal model of knowledge-induced worldly situations. Our model as a continuously learning model across continua denies optimality. It replaces the impossibility of optimal states by the objectivity of simulation across simulacra of possibilities resulting in moral-social reconstructions of *tawhidi* unity of being and becoming. Such is the perspective inherent in *tasbih-shura (TS)* evolutionary learning in unity of knowledge.

An interpretation of other classical and modern views on Islamization of knowledge in the *tawhidi* context of evolutionary learning worldview

The focus of this chapter is on the understanding of the concept of Islamization of knowledge in terms of the dynamics of evolutionary learning premised on the epistemology of *tawhid* and its unifying consequences in the world-system. This comprises the unified system and cybernetic world-system by systemic symbiosis on the premise of unity of knowledge. We will now maintain this focus by considering some salient features of Ibn Khaldun and Mawdudi and other understanding of Islamization of knowledge.

Figure 4.3: Imam Ghazzali's classification of knowledge

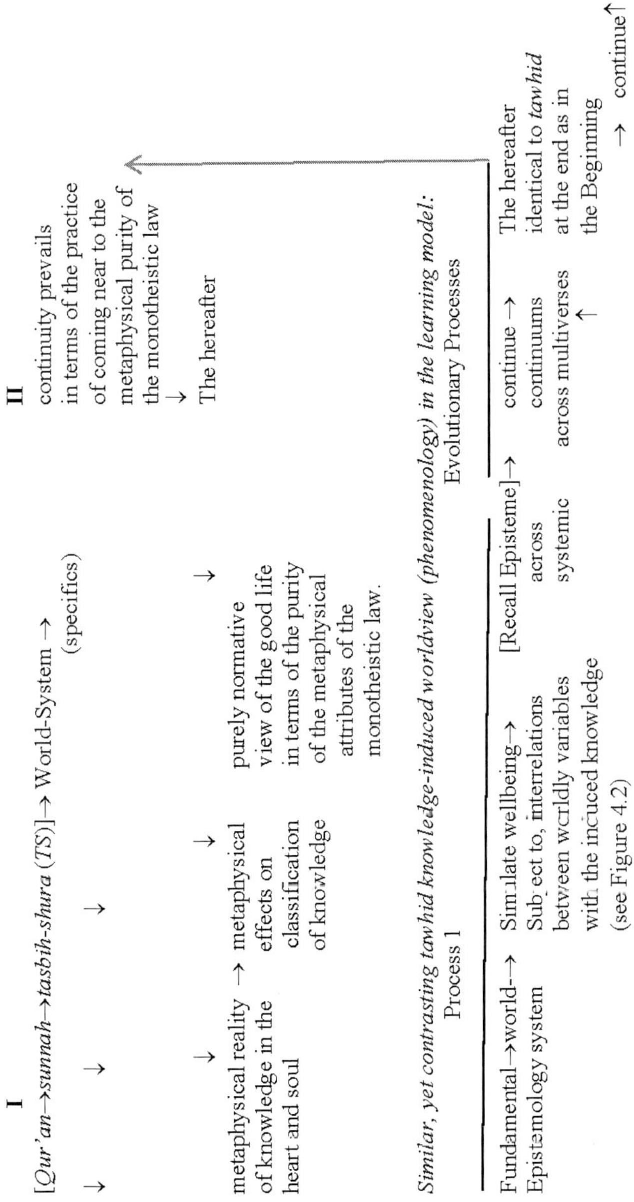

Legend: The fundamental epistemology denotes the completeness and absoluteness of the monotheistic law (*tawhid*) as super-cardinal (non-commensurate, only relational) topology (Maddox, 1970). The *sunnah* as *functional* ontological mapping carries 'bits' of knowledge-flows as understanding derived from the monotheistic law through the *sunnah* and learned discourse, generating ethical rules out of the law. Such rules, combined with the world-system issues, form the knowledge-induced '*paired*' variables, relations, and entities of the world-systems (specific issues). The vector of variables is brought into simulation by their '*paired*' (complementary, symbiotic) interrelations in the wellbeing criterion in order to estimate the degree of unity of knowledge established by complementary interrelations between the knowledge-induced variables. The moral-social reconstruction of thought and the world-system in the *tawhidi* worldview follows the inherent relational concept of *tawhidi* unity of knowledge.

Ibn Khaldun's *magnum opus*, the *Muqaddimah* (Rozenthal, 1968; Mahdi, 1964), comprising the sociology of history, attempted to describe the rise and fall of civilization in terms of its passage that rises from the rudimentary stages of *asabiyya* (community) into evolution to *umran* (city state) and onwards to *hadara* (civilization). Yet the solidarity to community and religion fades away along the path of this social transformation as politico-economic pressure to maintain an increasingly complex social order introduces conflicts between the urban and village organizations of the state – *asabiyya* and *umran*, respectively. In the end, the increasing politico-economic pressure of complexity spells out the decadence of the state, leading further to its distressed signal in civilization dynamics.

Ibn Khaldun limited his study of the historical process of social evolution to an observation of North Africa of his time. Thereby, Ibn Khaldun did not provide a universal theory of social evolution and of historical change in his *Muqaddimah*. The consequence of this limited outlook of historical and social change resulted in the inability of *Muqaddimah* to explain the fall and rise of a social order along the advancing path of its creative evolution. A revolutionary contribution made to this path of creative evolution is by knowledge. Knowledge remains undiminished. In the evolutionary learning path of social change its path is marked by incessant progress of socio-scientific wellbeing. Thus by the theory of knowledge a decadent social order is capable of rising to its moral-social reconstruction. This cyclical nature of evolutionary learning was not explained in *Muqaddimah* and in the philosophy of history according to Ibn Khaldun (Mahdi, op cit). Consequently, the theme of Islamization of knowledge in terms of its evolutionary dynamics could not be explained by Ibn Khaldun.

Islamization in Mawdudi and Iqbal

Turning to recent times, Maulana Mawdudi's Islamic ideas contributed to the field of Islamization of Knowledge (Wikipedia, http://en.Wikipedia .org/wiki/Jamaat-e-Islami). Yet, in line with the political and social outlook of the Jamaat-e-Islami political movement in Pakistan established by Maulana Mawdudi and his colleagues, the originality in knowledge development based purely on the *Qur'an,* remained paramount. Consequently, the nature and philosophy of knowledge and education in Occidentalism could not be the basis of Islamization of knowledge. In the pure state of the idea, this was an honest manifestation of the philosophy underlying the political movement. However, the problem of such a purist outlook lies in its inability to establish a universal theory of the Islamization dynamics out of the *Qur'an* for the whole socio-scientific intellectual process. Such a totality would be equally acceptable to Muslims and others. Yet the *Qur'an* bestows such a worldview that remains universal, just as it is possible to unite the rationalist classical Islamic school (*kalam*) and the epistemologists (*mutakallimun*) in the unique *tawhidi* mould of thought (Choudhury, 2006).

Sir Muhammad Iqbal (1934) was one such pioneer who moulded the universal *qur'anic* worldview into western philosophy and also invoked in it *qur'anic* thought. In his cosmopolitanism, Iqbal upheld the potential of integrating some of the dialectical nature of historical change between the *Qur'an* and the western idea of historicism that became central to the explanation of social transformation in Hegel's philosophy of history. An important precept that Iqbal extracted from the *Qur'an,* and used to integrate it with the dialectical theory of social and historical change, was creative re-origination (*khalqin jadid*). See Choudhury (2002) for a detailed development of the derived theory of historicism from the *Qur'an*.

In this chapter, this precept of evolutionary learning in unity of knowledge is a keynote for deriving and establishing the *qur'anic* precepts of *pairing* (relational unification) and creative re-origination in the evolutionary learning process that is causally related to the dynamics of Islamization of knowledge. These are the essential attributes of a learning system and cybernetic unified worldview.

Some knowledge-induced socio-scientific examples

The objective of this section is to highlight the possible attention to specific issues that can be invoked to study the methodology and model of evolutionary learning in the context of Islamization of knowledge. As mentioned in this chapter, such a methodological approach to the study and formalization of the general and specific problems of Islamization of knowledge addresses the socio-scientific theme. That is, to study general and specific problems in the light of the consciousness of *tawhid* applied to the rigorous formalization of scientific thought and its application vis-à-vis the grand design of unified system and cybernetic.

Social justice by the wellbeing function (*maslaha*) in the inherent system and cybernetic design of organic interrelations

An example here of the social order examined in the light of our phenomenological model of unity of knowledge is the theory of justice and freedom that must govern social preference formation in an Islamic social contract. Imam Shatibi looked into this important topic in his theory of *maslaha wal-istihsan* (preference formation for public purposes) (Shatibi trans. Draz, u.d.). *Maslaha* revealed the single most important function of the Islamic state as that of transforming and realizing social preference in accordance with the *maqasid as-shari'ah,* the purpose and objective of the Islamic law pertaining to choices in economy, institutions, and society, and in the extensive domain of socio-scientific study.

Social contractarianism concerning human ecology is an example of social justice in its wide meaning. It encompasses the extensive domain of interaction between human communities and ethics, environment and the global order (Hawley, 1986). Since such interactive preferences are the result of the formation of knowledge out of participation between institutions, markets, individuals, households, businesses, communities and the environment, the overarching epistemology of monotheism governs this kind of knowledge formation and its induced variables, entities, and relations. The very creatively dynamic feature of the learning process methodology makes the resulting preference formation dynamic. Such preferences form the extensive basis of Islamic social choice, and thus of the participatory worldview of *shura* institution and *tasbih-shura* heart-mind-matter praxis on worldly matters.

Such is the initiating premise of Islamic social contract in the theory of *maslaha* given by Imam Shatibi (Choudhury, 1993; Masud, 1984). To Imam Shatibi, *ijtihad* and *ijma* were premised on the uniqueness of the *tawhidi* worldview. But learning comprehension of the *tawhidi* worldview evolved dynamically through knowledge formation as flow (see Figure

4.3). The emergent learning process moving onwards in sequences of evolutionary epistemology could not therefore be static.

Syed Qutb's understanding of embodied knowledge in the cosmic order (Mousalli, 1990) is similar to our *tasbih-shura* dynamics of integrating the essence of knowledge between mind (*res cogitans*) and matter (*res extensa*). In other words, Syed Qutb explained that the systemic world of matter has embodied knowledge like human beings have. But such intrinsic knowledge appears by way of causation in inter-variable and inter-causal relations. Without such interactive dynamics, knowledge would remain innate and inactive in the mind-matter world.

This chapter has explained that the irrevocable premise of knowledge derivation being the *Qur'an* and the *sunnah,* its universality stretches across the dimensions of knowledge, space and time. Hence by the relational causality between heart, mind and matter, that is *tasbih* and *shura,* knowledge is activated for the purpose of a generalized universal explanation concerning the scheme of things. Thereby, Islamization of knowledge in its dynamic concept cannot be independently realized without the dynamic evolutionary learning experience.

Understanding economic fundamentals in *tawhidi* evolutionary epistemology

The economy as an *independent* domain of human needs and actions and responses in mainstream theory is replaced in the learning world-system by the study of problems of the economic nature. Such problems can only be understood by interaction between multitude of forces in the economy with their embedding in society, science, morality and ethics at given points of time by given attained knowledge-flows. Behaviour is still the starting point of such an embedded economy as a social organism. Yet such behaviour is manifest in the formation and aggregation of preferences of individuals interacting with institutional, government, and all social domains. Such aggregations at any economic stage cannot be linear. Contrarily, complex preferences are formed by the impact of dynamic socio-economic forces that enter the learning processes at every stage of the social embedding.

Markets as ethical venues for realizing preferences that form consumer and market demand, and production menus that form supply, are not ethically *wertfrei* systems of exchange of goods at revealed prices. Thus demand and supply are only nice concepts that are made to exist in mainstream economics, but only in the absence of the interactive dynamics causing embedding to occur and to continuously change in the embedded social magna of circular causes and effects.

The socio-scientific multiverse design in the knowledge-induced entirety

Interesting similarities also arise, albeit with substantively different meanings and interpretations, from specific socio-scientific phenomena. One of these quests is the nature of scientific inquiry. An apparent one, but with not much similarity in this area, is Hawking's characterization of scientific theory. Hawking (1988, pp. 10-11) writes:

> The eventual goal of science is to provide a single theory that describes the whole universe. However, the approach most scientists actually follow is to separate the problem into two parts. First, there are the laws that will tell us how the universe changes with time….. Second, there is the question of the initial state of the universe. Some people feel that science should be concerned with only the first part; they regard the question of the initial situation as a matter for metaphysics or religion. They would say that God, being omnipotent, could have started the universe off any way he wanted. That may be so, but in that case he also could have made it develop in a completely arbitrary way. Yet it appears that he chose to make it evolve in a very regular way according to certain laws. It therefore seems equally reasonable to suppose that there are also laws governing the initial state.

Socio-scientific reasoning in the *tawhidi* worldview starts by the sole axiom of the oneness of God and the divine law, and its purposeful, explainable, and applicative consequences in the world-system taken up in both generality and specifics. Thus the substantive meaning of organic unity of the world-system explained by the fundamental episteme of unity is by the oneness of the divine law and its functional ontology spanning multi-universes of relational world-systems.

Hawking's initial condition and law are essentially and infallibly premised on the oneness of the divine law and its organic moral-social reconstruction of science and society taken together interactively. From such interactions arise knowledge-flows representing the *tawhidi* characterization of unity (integration) in all phenomena. That is in the domain of 'everything' (Barrow, 1991).

The *tawhidi* universe is thereby premised on the (knowledge, space, time)-dimensions, with knowledge-flows emanating from the fundamental episteme of oneness (see Figure 4.3). Such knowledge-flows then induce the events in the learning space through complexity. Yet such a knowledge-induced characterization of event is unlike Hawking's. The whole of the scientific view that characterizes the universe is premised simply in space-time structure. The moral and ethical social construction of the socio-scientific order in the learning multiverse comprises vastly interacting, integrating, and evolutionary world-systems. These span science and society in the generalized model of system and cybernetic applying to complexly interrelated world-systems.

We then answer the question: 'How did we get here at a stately point of time in our existence?' The *tawhidi* worldview answers this question by its fundamental reference to the epistemic axiom firstly. It then analyses, proves and explains the geometrical coordinate of existence in reference to a plethora of learning processes that are causally linked with interaction, integration, and evolution of knowledge-induced events taken in their diversity. We have therefore evolutionary histories that brought us here across learning processes, as defined here. The *Qur'an* mentions such evolutionary universes formed by induced learning processes. The mind is invoked to comprehend, observe, and reflect on *tawhidi* epistemic oneness in such '*paired*' universes. This is the basis of the principle of pervasively complementary multi-universes.

Hawking & Mlodinow (2010, p 80) write about similar learning (probabilistic general system) histories: "...for a general system, the probability of any observation is constructed from all the possible histories that could have led to that observation. Because of that (t)his method is called the 'sum over histories' or alternative histories' formulation of quantum physics." For this profound assertion of Feynman's description of the probabilistic learning universe (Choudhury, 2011b), there cannot be linear aggregation of histories in the learning multi-universes. Instead, there are complexly interrelating and evolving learning geodesics (Kupka & Peixoto, 1993). These exist as subspaces of the multi-universal manifold and share the same universal and unique law of organic unity of being and becoming. The multi-universe is then formed by a nexus of learning histories in systems and cybernetics.

Conclusion

This chapter has presented knowledge as an epistemological category wherein 'everything' self-actualizes in *tawhid*, the monotheistic law of unity of knowledge in relation to the world-system and its Great Event of the hereafter (*Qur'an*, 78:1-5). This is the perpetual evolutionary learning history of the heart, mind, and matter relations; likewise of the *tasbih-shura* learning process. The chapter has thereby interconnected knowledge, education, and the world-system by the generality and specifics of issues using the epistemic premise of oneness. The emergent epistemic and phenomenological model of unity of knowledge and of the unified world-system is found to have its holism in the *Qur'an* according to the Islamic worldview of monotheistic oneness. We called this the phenomenological model of unity of knowledge and its induction of the unified world-system to comprise the *tawhidi* worldview.[8]

This chapter has brought out the *tawhidi* worldview, its selected application in the real-world case, and has compared and contrasted it with several other scholarly contributions in Islamization of knowledge. The important case to study was the phenomenology of Islamization of knowledge in contemporary times. In the end, the salient features of the *Tawhidi* Scientific Research Program (TSRP) have been introduced to reflect and build upon by others. The learning processes of systemic interaction, integration, and creative evolution (**IIE**) framed the multi-universal grand design of its system and cybernetic structure and formalism in knowledge, space, and time. Such a *tawhidi* worldview framed an alternative formulation of the idea of Islamization of knowledge.

References

Al-Attas, S.M.N., 1989, "Islam and the philosophy of science", pp. 1-36, International Institute of Islamic Thought, Kuala Lumpur, Malaysia.

Al-Faruqi, I.R., 1982a, *Tawhid: Its Implications for Thought and Life*, International Institute of Islamic Thought, Herndon, VA.

—. 1982b, *Islamization of Knowledge: General Principles and Workplan*, The International Institute of Islamic Thought, Herndon, VA.

Barrow, J.D., 1991, *Theories of Everything, the Quest for Ultimate Explanation*, Oxford University Press, Oxford, Eng.

Bohr, N., 1985, "Discussions with Einstein on epistemological issues", in H. Folse (ed.), *The Philosophy of Niels Bohr: The Framework of*

[8] Foucault (see Sheridan, p. 191, 1972) gives a succinct explanation of the terminology, 'episteme': "By *episteme* we mean … the total set of relations that unite, at a given period, the discursive practices that give rise to epistemological figures, sciences, and possibly formalized systems … The episteme is not a form of knowledge (*connaissance*) or type of rationality which, crossing the boundaries of the most varied sciences, manifests the sovereign unity of a subject, a spirit, or a period; it is the totality of relations that can be discovered, for a given period, between the sciences when one analyses them at the level of discursive regularities."

Complementarity, North Holland Physics Publishing, Amsterdam, the Netherlands.

Choudhury, M.A., 1983, "Educational planning and economic development in Islamic perspective", *Muslim Education*, (1)1.

—. 1993, *The Unicity Precept and the Socio-Scientific Order*, The University Press of America, Lanham, MD, USA.

—. 2002, "Historicism", in his, *Explaining the Qur'an*, Book I, pp. 184-219, The Edwin Mellen Press, Lewiston, New York.

—. 2006, "Development of Islamic Economic and Social Thought", Hassan, M.K. & Lewis, *M.* (eds.) *Handbook of Islamic Banking*, Edward Elgar Publishing Company, London, Eng.

—. 2011a, "Knowledge and life: comparative Islamic development perspectives", *International Journal of Education, Education and Development*, (2)1, 1-17.

—. 2011b, "A probabilistic model of learning fields". *The Journal of Muamalat and Islamic Finance Research*, (7)1.

—. 2011c, "On the existence of evolutionary learning equilibriums", *Journal of Science*, 16, pp. 1-13.

Daud, W.M.N.W., 1998a, "Metaphysical worldview", *The Educational Philosophy and Practice of Syed Muhammad Naquib Al-Attas, an Exposition of the Original Concept of Islamization*, pp. 33-68, International Institute of Islamic Thought and Civilization, Kuala Lumpur, Malaysia.

—. 1998b, "On knowledge and knowing", *The Educational Philosophy and Practice of Syed Muhammad Naquib Al-Attas, an Exposition of the Original Concept of Islamization*, pp. 69-120, International Institute of Islamic Thought and Civilization, Kuala Lumpur, Malaysia.

—. 1998c, "Islamization of contemporary knowledge: theoretical dimensions and practical contributions", *The Educational Philosophy and Practice of Syed Muhammad Naquib Al-Attas, an Exposition of the Original Concept of Islamization,* International Institute of Islamic Thought and Civilization, Kuala Lumpur, Malaysia.

Einstein, A., 1954, "The problem of space, ether, and the field in physics", in Commins, S. & Linscott, R.N. (eds.), *Man and the Universe: The Philosophers of Science*, pp. 473-485, Pocket Books, Inc., New York, NY.

Fakhry, M., 2004, "The Arab-Spanish interlude and the revival of peripateticism", in his, *A History of Islamic Philosophy*, pp. 267-302, Columbia University Press, New York, NY.

Gel'fand, I.M. & Shenitzer, A., 1961, "Introduction to tensors", *Lectures on Linear Algebra*, pp. 164-185, Interscience Publishers, Inc. New York, NY.
Ghazzali, Abu Hamid M. (Imam) 1966, *The Book of Knowledge*, N.A. Faris (trans.), Shah Muhammad Ashraf, Lahore, Pakistan.
Ghazanfar, S.M. & Islahi, A.A., 1990, "Economic thought of an Arab scholastic, Abu Hamid al-Ghazzali", *History of Political Economy*, (22)2, 381-403.
Gruber, T.R., 1993, "A translation approach to portable ontologies", *Knowledge Acquisition*, (5)2, 199-200.
Guessoum, N., 2011, *Islam's Quantum Question*, I.B. Taurus, London, Eng.
Hawking, S.W., 1988, *A Brief History of Time, From the Big Bang to Black Holes*. Bantam Books, Inc., New York, NY.
Hawking, S.W. and Mlodinow, L., 2010, *The Grand Design*. Transworld Publishers, London, Eng.
Hawley, A.H., 1986, *Human Ecology*, The University of Chicago Press, Chicago, IL.
Heidegger, M. trans. by Hofstadter, A., 1988, "The thesis of modern ontology: the basic ways of being are the being of nature (res extensa) and the being of mind (res cogitans)".*The Basic Problems of Phenomenology*, pp. 122-225, Indiana University Press, Bloomington & Indianapolis, IN.
Husserl, E. trans. by Lauer, Q., 1965, *Phenomenology and the Crisis of Philosophy*, p. 155, Harper & Row Publishers, New York. Particularly note his comment on the perceived absence of ethical roots in Occidental scientific inquiry.
Ibn Khaldun trans. by Rozenthal, F., 1958, *Muqaddimah, an Introduction to History*, in 3 volumes, Routledge & Kegan Paul, London, Eng.
Iqbal, M., 1934, *The Reconstruction of Religious Thought in Islam*, Oxford University Press, Oxford, Eng.
Kakutani, S., 1941, "A generalization of Bouwer's fixed point theorem". *Duke Mathematical Journal*.(8)3, 457-459.
Karim, F., n.d. *Imam Ghazzali'sIhyaUlum-Id-Din*, Shah Muhammad Ashraf, Lahore, Pakistan.
Kupka, I.A.K. & Peixoto, M.M., 1993, "On the enumerative geometry of geodesics". Hirsch, M.W. Marsden, J.E. Shub, M. (eds.), *From Topology to Computation: Proceedings of the Smalefest*, pp. 243-253, Springer-Verlag, New York, NY.
Maddox, I.J., 1970, *Elements of Functional Analysis*, Cambridge University Press, Cambridge, Eng.

Mahdi, M., 1964, *Ibn Khaldun's Philosophy of History*, University of Chicago Press, Chicago, IL.

Masud, M.K., 1994, *Shatibi's Theory of Meaning*, Islamic Research Institute, International Islamic University, Islamabad, Pakistan.

Mousalli, A., 1990, "Sayyid Qutb's view of knowledge", *American Journal of Islamic Social Sciences*. (7)3, 315-35.

Nasr, S.H., 2003, *Science and Civilization in Islam*, Islamic Texts Society, Cambridge, UK. Also published by Harvard University Press, Cambridge, MA, USA, 1987)

Qadir, C.A., 1990, "The renaissance of philosophical knowledge in the Islamic World", in his *Philosophy and Science in the Islamic World*, pp. 135-150, Routledge, London, Eng.

Rahman, R., 1988, "Islamization of Knowledge: A Response". *American Journal of Islamic Social Sciences*, (5)1.

Rucker, R., 1983a, "Large cardinalities", *Infinity and the Mind, the Science and Philosophy of the Infinite,* Bantam Books, New York, NY.

—. 1983b, "The one and the many". *Infinity and the Mind, the Science and Philosophy of the Infinite*, Chapter 5, Bantam Books, New York, NY.

Sardar, Z., 1984, "Islamisation of Knowledge, or the Westernisation of Islam?" *Inquiry*, (1)7.

[Imam] Shatibi, trans. AbdallahDraz. (u.d.). *Al-Muwafaqat Fi-Usul Al-Shari'ah*. Al-Maktabah Al-Tijariyah Al-Kubra, Cairo, Egypt.

Wikipedia, http://en.wikipedia.org/wiki/Jamaat-e-Islami. "Jamaat-e-Islami".

CHAPTER FIVE

TAWHID, RELIGION AND ECONOMICS: PROBLEMS OF INTEGRATION AND THE *TAWHIDI* ALTERNATIVE

An important field of human intellection on *tawhid* and the construct of the unified world-system is economics. Combining *tawhid*, economics, and the scientific method in a logical framework of inquiry, bestows a socio-scientific outlook to a logical study of science and religion. Such an approach also yields a substantive study of economics and religion in the *tawhidi* framework. By such an approach we shear away religion from an abstruse meaning in human life, experience, and application. Indeed, the worldly integration of the monotheistic law in a universal way is the be-all and end-all of the *tawhidi* worldview. But this premise of *tawhidi* universality can be acceptable only if the symbiotic interrelationship between *tawhid* as monotheism is coherently integrated in a conceptual and workable way both at the level of epistemology and its application. Thus carrying on from the epistemological foundation of *tawhid* as unity of knowledge arising from the divine law and its constructive bearing on the unified world-system taken by generality and details, we now undertake the scientific treatment of *tawhid* as monotheistic religion in economics. Economics is thus studied as a specific sub-system of the generalized socio-scientific world-system. Our approach once again is of a comparative nature. The purpose here is to discover the socio-scientific validity of the *tawhidi* worldview and methodology within the specific sub-system of economics.

The research question

Religion and economics, likewise religion and science and society, have long remained isolated domains of human intellection, belief, and behavior. The result has thus been a differentiated and incomplete worldview of human reality. Human reality is to be premised on the overarching meaning and substance of the total wellbeing. Wellbeing here means the degree of interconnectedness in the relations between religion, science, and society by way of their mutual embedding. In such a case, the emergent field of holistic understanding leads to the formalism of an embedded field of moral-social inquiry encompassing religion and the socio-scientific 'everything' (Barrow, 1991). The resulting formalism assumes an epistemological meaning. By the extensive embedding that arises across diverse systems, the resulting formalism invokes concepts of uniqueness and universality of its epistemic methodology that has profound explanatory power for the socio-scientific 'everything'.

We will explain in this chapter that traditional religious inquiry on the scheme of things has either premised its episteme on a numinous understanding of God and the world as separated identities, or has caused the problem of irrelevance of God in explaining the world-system. An integrated understanding of God and the world-system in its details has not dawned. In formalism, there also remains the need for explaining any form of embedding as a methodological approach. Such a methodological approach has not occurred to enable an integrated and embedded study of religion and economics; more widely religion, science, and society.

The parting knell of religion and economics (science) can thus be expressed in the quote: "Give unto Caesar what is Caesar's (materiality); and unto God what is God's (spirituality)" (Lewis, 2010). The prevailing methodology in the study of religion and economics (science) fails to establish an integrated worldview with an ontological formalism that otherwise would unify religion and other disciplines by a unique and universal epistemological methodology.

Objective

The objective of this chapter is to break out of the methodological divisiveness and search for an epistemology that unifies the disciplines by a unique methodology. Emulating Foucault, we refer to this totality of the overarching methodology as an episteme[1]. Ours is the search for the episteme of unity of knowledge between interdisciplinary systems. It is

[1] Foucault (see Sheridan,1972, p. 191) defines the word *episteme* as follows: "By *episteme* we mean ... the total set of relations that unite, at a given period, the discursive practices that give rise to epistemological figures, sciences, and possibly formalized systems ... The episteme is not a form of knowledge (*connaissance*) or type of rationality which, crossing the boundaries of the most varied sciences, manifests the sovereign unity of a subject, a spirit, or a period; it is the totality of relations that can be discovered, for a given period, between the sciences when one analyses them at the level of discursive regularities."

explained in terms of organic unification of the elements in the emergent knowledge-induced world-system that combines the inter-disciplines[2].

The issue in this chapter is this: Socio-scientific reality as the domain of total human experience is not a collection of its dissociated parts. Thus religion and economics (spirituality and materiality, respectively) cannot answer the total objective of wellbeing as an integrated balance if they are treated as independently segmented domains of human action. On the other hand, mere wishful thinking on the desired integration between spirituality and materiality does not suffice for a methodological work. Rigorous and viable formalism based on sound epistemological grounds, analytical and applied in nature, is necessary. Along with this, the new methodology must be able to extend the immanent theory and application across open domains of inquiry. Thereby, religion and economics come to inherit their integrative study by the same methodology. An organic relational approach as the expression of the episteme of unity of knowledge is thereby made possible between these domains (Choudhury, 2011a). This is the intent of the chapter in building up an appropriate integrative methodology of interdisciplinary systemic embedding.

[2] The *world-system* comprises the totality of all unraveling universes that embed in each other by relational dynamics. In the world-system there prevails an ontological formalism that governs it, giving it meaning, shape, form, explanation, and application. In the religio-scientific conception of the socio-scientific entirety the causality is like this: World-System, WS = $\{(\mathbf{X},\mathbf{Y})_s[\theta\in\Omega]\}$, together with all possible monotonic positive functional transformations of the knowledge-induced tuple of variables, $\{\mathbf{X},\mathbf{Y}\}_s$. This is true intra-systemic and inter-systemic categorization, denoted by ‘s’. $\{\mathbf{X}\}_s$ denotes the space of variables. $\{\mathbf{Y}\}_s$ denotes the totality of functional transformations of $\{\mathbf{X}\}_s$ intra-systems and inter- systems denoted by ‘s’. $(\mathbf{X},\mathbf{Y})_s$ are induced by knowledge-flows $\{\theta\}$ in a unique way that explains the broad picture and its specifics in what we refer to as the universal way. $\{\theta\}$-knowledge values are derived by consciousness, discourse (interaction), and consensus (integration). These attributes are derived from the super-space of the governing ontology, which is denoted by Ω. The super-topology as open mapping defined on the super-space of Ω (Rucker, 1982) includes all possible functional transforms in the world-system (WS). That is both truth and falsehood are comprehended in the light of the moral law. This form further comprises all kinds of related variables, their interdependencies, and functional transformations. The usual topological properties of mathematical union and intersection, nullity and universality of topological sub-spaces apply (Maddox, 1970).

Review of the literature

Our review of the literature will cover those intellectual aspects that might address our search for integration between the disciplines towards explaining a holistic formal methodology. See the Appendix for a non-parametric representation of methodological unification between the disciplines (economics and religion) as interactive, integrative, and creative evolutionary systems (**IIE**).

Looking at the classical axiomatic nature of economics, Nelson (2001) intends to use the economic postulates of rationality, efficiency, investment and growth under certainty as conditions for attaining a well-functioning perfectly competitive economy that reduces transaction cost. The argument made is that, if individuals were religiously honest in their behaviour, the result would be minimum transaction cost. This would lead to the attainment of the postulates of a perfectly competitive market economy. Consequently, the objectives of utility maximization and profit maximization yielding normal profits with efficient production at the minimum level of average cost of production would all be emanating from good religious behaviour in economic dealings. Such religious behaviour would explain the perfectly rational individual of economic theory.

Based on such implications, the new institutionalists inferred (Nelson, pp. 208-209) "an awkward compromise rejecting neoclassical assumptions but employing the same analytical formalism long favored by the neoclassicals". In reference to the neoclassical methods of economic calculation, the argument is further made that, if religious values induce lower average cost of producing cultural, social and ethical capital than merely physical capital, at least of some sorts, then the economic choice for religious capital would result in efficient investment and growth. By proceeding along the lines of traditional neoclassical economic assumptions operating in the religious sphere of utilitarian behaviour and production and costs, the economists subsume religion within classical and neoclassical economic explanation. The end result is the study of religion *as* economics.

The widest possible difference and discontent remains between religion and economics in terms of methodology, methods, objectives, and application. If religion is to transcend into a social enterprise and not be limited to the individual moral wellbeing alone, then this approach calls for a methodology of assimilation, decision-making, and aggregation from the individual to the societal level. Zweig (1991) attributes this task to theology as the social premise of extending religious values to society at large. He writes (p. 3-49): "It is theology that seeks to address and change social institutions, not just individuals. It is therefore theology that extends the bounds of traditional religious discourse to dialogue with social science, to better understand society and the role of religion in it."

By the theological approach, religion introduces the theme of aggregation and extension of individual preferences, beliefs, behaviours and choices to the social level. On the other side, economics of social choice has not settled the theory of social aggregation of this kind. The lateral aggregation of individual preferences to form social preference is a mistake. Social order is greater in the measure of valuation than the lateral aggregation of individual preferences.

Even in the case of Arrow's (1951) postulate of social choice theory, aggregation is not possible without the presence of a dictator to announce the end of the game of making social choice (Wolff, 1977). The presence of a dictator is realized by introducing the postulate of irrelevant preferences. The presence of dictator to announce the end of a social choice game, and the postulate of irrelevant preferences, are together needed to affect the formulation and maximization of the social welfare function.

Now between economics and religion there is no socially acceptable method to realize perfect participation among all decision-makers as individuals in order to solve the aggregation problem by an equitable participatory social game. Consensus in the social choice game is enforced, not self-governed by consciousness, as religion would otherwise aspire for.

The fact of the matter is that neither can the postulates of economic theory work by its utilitarian methodology of aggregation nor can religion adhere to the traditional economic postulates. The postulates of economic rationality, efficiency, and optimal resource allocation and maximization of objective functions, as in the case of welfare maximization, utility maximization, profit-maximization, and minimization of transaction cost, are irrelevant methods for integrating religion and economics. An altogether new ontological approach is now needed to fuse together the formal domains of religion and science. Nelson (2001, pp. 229) writes on this issue: "In short, economists would not have much to lose in turning back in their methods of inquiry to the approaches of the old historical and institutional school. They may think they would be losing their scientific value, but it would be more correct to say that they would be abandoning their scientific hypocrisy".

The ontological problem in methodologically integrating religion and economics

A.N. Whitehead

The ontological problem of religious philosophy is explained emphatically by Whitehead (eds. Griffin & Sherburne, 1979, p. 43) in the following words:

> The ontological principle asserts the relativity of decision; whereby every decision expresses the relation of the actual thing, for which a decision is made, to an actual thing by which that decision is made. It constitutes the very meaning of actuality. An actual entity arises from decisions for it, and by its very existence provides decisions for other actual entities which supersede it. Thus the ontological principle is the first stage in constituting a theory embracing the notions of 'actual entity,' 'giveness', and 'process'.

Thus the full realization of the ontological problem is the situating of *Being* in the context of a process of phenomenological *Becoming*. The ontological situate is the coordinate point of the knowledge-induced topology of the world-system wherein the following relationship holds in perpetuity of the learning worldview:

$R \rightarrow_p \{\mathbf{X},\mathbf{Y}\}_s[R] \rightarrow_p$ continuity of learning processes based on the episteme of rationalism R. (5.1)

I. Kant

The symbol 'R' given in expression (5.1) comprises multifaceted human speculative experience. Hence it is differentiated by methodical independence, methodological individualism, and competition. R is not unified in scope, and its application configures a differentiated world-system. The multifaceted speculative nature of R is a direct derivation from the problem of heteronomy poised by Kant between his *a priori* realm of pure reason and *a posteriori* realm of practical reason. Upon such an intrinsic Kantian dichotomy of reason, which characterizes R, Kant writes on his dichotomous perception of pure reason and practical reason (reprinted 1949, p.25):

> This, then, is a question which at least calls for closer examination, and does not permit any off-hand answer: whether there is any knowledge that is thus independent of experience and even of all impressions of the senses.

> Such knowledge is entitled *a priori*, and is distinguished from the empirical, which has its sources *a posteriori*, that is, in experience.

Kant continues to write of the problem of dichotomy in reasoning (reprinted 1949, p. 25):

> In what follows, therefore, we shall understand by *a priori* knowledge, no knowledge independent of this or that experience, but knowledge absolutely independent of all experience. Opposed to it is empirical knowledge, which is knowledge possible only *a posteriori*, that is through experience.

M. Heidegger

Along similar lines of understanding the ontological theory of consciousness, namely phenomenology, there can be associated the idea of the supernatural category, the *Dasein* of Heidegger (trans. Hofstadter, 1988). *Dasein* takes the place of rationalism in moving this episteme into its becoming of being, the ontic category of a personified identity. Like Whitehead's idea of ontological functionalism of being, so also *Dasein* creates the ontic category as the personified consciousness of the rationalist process of social construction. Now, to situate the result of the process of becoming into the location of the ontic as being, is to observe and understand phenomenon. The ontological function as the consciousness of knowing phenomenon is termed as phenomenology.

The process denoted by $\rightarrow_p$ in driving R into its social construction of materiality is denoted by $\{\mathbf{X},\mathbf{Y}\}[R]$, together with its functional transformations. These steps together comprise phenomenology as consciousness that is embedded in R and is conveyed to the world-system and its details in the context of R.

D. Hume and I. Kant

A similar view of the dichotomy of reasoning and belief in God was expressed by Hume (1960) through his inductive categorization of knowledge that remains contrary to the deductive reasoning of Kant.[3] In

[3] Hume wrote in regards to such dichotomy (1960 reprinted, pp. 8-9)): "The ancient philosophers, though they often affirm, that virtue is nothing but conformity to reason, yet, in general, seem to consider morals as deriving their existence from taste and sentiments. On the other hand, our modern inquirers, though they also talk much of the virtue of beauty, and deformity of vice, yet have

the end, the resulting problem of demarcation caused inductive reasoning to remain independent of deductive reasoning. This kind of partitioning of the otherwise integrated nature of reasoning is itself a form of heteronomy. While Kant aspired, unsuccessfully though due to the problem of heteronomy (Carnap, 1966), for the ultimate moral ego in human experience, Hume (1992) completed the demarcation of the *a priori* from the *a posteriori*. Thereby, the deductive and inductive reasoning, and logical positivism and normative potentiality were all dichotomized from each other.

On the moral imperative of unification *res extensa,* Kant (quoted in 1949, 261) wrote: "Two things fill the mind with ever new and increasing awe and admiration the more frequently and continuously reflection is occupied with them; the starred heaven above me and the moral law within me. I ought not to seek either outside my field of vision, as though they were either shrouded in obscurity or were visionary. I see them confronting me and link them immediately with the consciousness of my existence."

On the clear separation between inductive and deductive reasoning for all of science, Hume (1992, p.1) wrote: "All the perceptions of the human mind resolve themselves into two distinct kinds, which I shall call Impressions and Ideas ….. Those perceptions, which enter with most force and violence, we may name impressions; and under this name I comprehend all our sensations, passions and emotions, as they make their first appearance in the soul. By ideas I mean the faint images of these in thinking and reasoning."

To Hume the deciphering of knowledge meant well-defined conceptions of memory, impression, imagination, relations, modes and substances. Through these elements of the human possibility to attain reasoning and construct a philosophical order, Hume took the mind and matter relationship purely as the origin of reasoning. This too he premised on human imagination, memory, and the continuity of forms and relations in space-time dimension. Contrary to the divine law divorced from his ontological reasoning, and by the primacy of reason premised on impression, imagination, ideas and relations according to the corporeal concept of reasoning, Hume intensified the inductive source of rationalist philosophy.

The problematique of Kant and Hume on the question of religion and economics lies in the domain of explanatory forms comprising variables

---

commonly endeavoured to account for these distinctions by metaphysical reasonings, and by deductions from the most abstract principles of the understanding".

and their functional relations that integrate the two disciplines: Kant's heteronomy and his assertion of the rationalist perception of the moral law, transcending God, causes dichotomy between God and the ethical law for economic explanation (Smart, 2000). The embedding between religion and economics is then rent asunder. The possibility of an integrated methodology is lost. To Hume the meanings of truth, beauty, falsehood, and rejection were based purely on sensate phenomena. These meanings have nothing to do with the religious basis of the moral law.

Hume's primacy of knowledge based on reason *qua* rationalism presents the problem of subjectivity of a rationalist perception[4]. Thus the methodological integration of religion and economics remains impossible by the differentiated nature of the divine law and the sensate. Such dichotomy left Mind and Matter to be speculatively determined by rationalist persuasion alone.

Inference drawn from speculative philosophy on the nature of integration between religion and economics

The circular causation methodology has been a powerful formalism to test, assert or correct for the presence or loss of complementarities between the

[4] Knowledge K is given by, K = f(I,X), where f is a function of impressions {I} and sensate materiality {X}. Since I is defined by X, therefore I = F(X). The speculative nature of such relations is conveyed by the randomness of {I,X,F}. The values of this sequence are caused by the primacy of R (reason as perception caused by rationalism). Thereby, there exists the compound functional (foF) generating knowledge K(R): K(R) = (foF)(X)[R].

Such a functional can be disaggregated at the individual level, that is micro-level, and then aggregated at the macro-level. At the micro-level, we can associate I with individual preferences; X with goods and services; K with information flow; and (foF) as processes that transform economic meaning into 'objective criteria'. The microeconomic example of K(R) is the ordinal nature of utility function in consumption (or cardinal expected utility in risk and return of investment), given impression (I) as preference by datum.

At the macroeconomic (aggregate) level there is no method of aggregation arising from the microeconomic level, except by the use of the utilitarian postulates of irrelevant preferences and the existence of a dictator. Such postulates defy the integrated nature of the world-system of participation (unity by pairing). Hume's rationalist basis of reasoning like Kant's by heteronomy thus lead into speculation of knowledge formation resting on R. The result is individualism by methodical independence between variables, systems, categories, agents, goods, and their forms of quantitative relations.

variables in the light of the rules derived from the law of unity of knowledge. In economics, the circular causation method was used by Myrdal (1958). But the method has not become popular in economics overall (Toner, 1999). That is because economics does not treat pervasively endogenous relations between variables. There are always externally induced and exogenous policies and extraneous variables in economic models. In the religious, sociological, and philosophical literature we also find faint presence of the circular causation method; but it exists in the concept of simulacra – simulation over simulation continuously (Fitzpatrick, 2003).

The circular causation idea has been used in theological thought but contrary to purpose. Thomas Aquinas placed the whole universal design to rest on God from the beginning to the end. He then construed the working of the universe in everything according to this feature of ontology and being. The entire *Summa Theologia* presents the expounding of this divine design of creation. While God lies in a process as Creator, He exists as the sole and exogenous creator of everything. The divine law is thereby a super-space like Ω. Yet there is no S as *functional* ontology to carry primal knowledge of unity (metaphysical ontology) onto the world-system. The divine law thus becomes dysfunctional in the affairs of the world-system.

An early version of Kantian heteronomy thereby exists in *Summa*. Therefore, despite the aspiration for the divine construction of the universal design, the ontology of unity could not be realized in a methodological way. The absence of the divinely assigned mapping, 'S', causes 'S' to assume a rationalist form. As a result, the part of phenomenology given by $[\Omega \rightarrow_R \{\theta\}]$ is realized by the rationalist speculative process. Consequently, the constructed and construed world-system remains premised on $\bar{R}$.

An example of Aquinas' duality in regards to God and the World due to the presence of rationalist belief results in his comment on the rate of interest. While the classical Bible abhors interest-based transaction, Aquinas considered the market rate of interest to be permissible (Blaug, 1968). Such a statement was a contradiction between belief and practice. In the end, not the divine text, but the rationalist viewpoint, ruled over the doctrine of permissibility of interest rate on financial transactions.

The circular plan, as of circular causation, remained a worldly process in the *Summa*. The divine law, just as in Kantian heteronomy, remained numinous for the world-system. On the circular plan of religion and the world-system, Thomas Aquinas' idea of circular causation in *Summa* is explained by Torrell (2005, p. 27-36): "The work (*Summa*) is in fact constructed according to a circular plan that draws the reader into the 'going-out-from-returning-to' (*exitus-reditus*) movement, which is that of the entire universe coming from God to creation and returning to him as its final end." In the absence of a mapping like 'S', the *exitus-reditus* rests on speculation by its rationalist roots.

Lately, a similar dynamic perception is found in the writings of Lonergan (see Hosinski, 1987, pp. 63-78): "Lonergan draws his notion of 'finality' in the dynamic structure of becoming from the correspondences to the notion of being as the unifying drive in knowing. Just as the notion of being drives and unifies the process of knowing, so does finality drive and unify becoming." One can note the similarity of the circular causation relations in the phenomenological process of Figure 5.1 with the mechanism construed by Lonergan.

Yet despite the similarity indicated above, Lonergan placed the study of God within a *process* (Vertin, 1987). In doing so, rationalism once again supplanted the divine origin of knowledge and law affecting the world-system in the phenomenological model of Figure 5.1. Kant's heteronomy is brought back into this picture of phenomenology. Thereby, a rationalist conception of truth and goodness replaces the divine text. Contrarily, in the case of the ontological origin of unity of knowledge by the divine text, the moral law is mapped onto the world-system through the super-topological mapping S along with the participation of a discursive community (Figure 5.1).

Lonergan (1908, 1999, 2001) has contributed profoundly to other fields of scientific knowledge. But his contributions in economics, mathematical logic, and phenomenology do not utilize any element of his ideas in theological philosophy. Consequently, one finds the two differentiated streams of intellection, one in hardcore science and economics and the other in religious thought. These two streams of thought evolve independently of each other. This is the stark representation of two independent streams -- of rational and religious evolution of thought that do not synergize with each other. It is a mark of methodological independence between the disciplines and the form of compartmentalization of knowledge that marks our modern world. Such a worldview requires repair and replacement by the essentially evolutionary learning epistemic worldview, as it is derived, formalized, explained, and applied by the epistemology of unity of knowledge between systems, and their variables and entities. We have presented in this chapter the phenomenological model of the unified worldview and the world-system based on the epistemology of unity of knowledge.

Lonergan's kind of reversion of thought is always into rationalism in every case that we have noted (Doron & Monsour, trans. Shields, 2011).

These are namely, an economic approach to religion, or rationalist speculation of the ontological problem of religion in embracing the economic problem. The gap in integration between religion and economics is caused by the absence of the worldly element of the divine law in deriving rules in cogent ways and by structured methodology and social approach. Yet the essential province of the divine epistemological root is never ignored in continuity.

An example in this case is the moral adage: Give unto your neighbour what you desire for yourself. The statement is not a practical rule as derived from the law of *equality*. The humanly practical element of *equity* contrary to *equality* is absent in this moral adage. Distribution of economic resources in the global neighbourhood is a matter of equity to satisfy basic needs of all. And yet such equitable distribution of resources must establish the right to private ownership. Private ownership does not solve social resource allocation by equality. But moral consciousness can make resource allocation solve the equity question.

Likewise, according to Weberian Protestant ethic, charity is restricted within the limits of enabling a productive and frugal community. Beyond this limit, charity can disengage able persons from active economic activity and self-reliance. Here too we note that the sheer general law of love and charity remains undefined by a precision of rules to exercise altruism.

Contrarily, the divine law is not a sheer statement of general values. It also carries with it the precise *rules* for enacting the general *law*.[5] In one

---

[5] As an example, in the Islamic Law (*shari'ah*) there is something referred to as the *purpose and objective* of the *shari'ah* -- the *maqasid as-shari'ah* (Doi, 1984). This has its criterion based on the injunctions of the *Qur'an* and the Prophetic practices (*sunnah*) along with social discourse on the derivation of rules based in the general framework of the *maqasid as shari'ah*. Thereby, distribution and equitable ownership and sharing of resources while being the general law, is governed by the specific rule of avoidance of interest rates as impediments to fair and equitable distribution and shared ownership in society at large.

Likewise, the mandatory distribution of wealth in the alleviation of poverty and deprivation, the uplift of human resources and a frugal participatory community, are set by the charitable instrument called *zakat*, the due distribution to the needy at 2.5% of wealth. *Zakat* is levied as a specific rule on attaining the general *qur'anic* law that states: "In your wealth is a share of the poor".

The *zakat* principle and the interest-rate policy, mandatory though, are specified for implementation through social discourse in structured ways. The mapping 'S' in the phenomenological model, along with the discursive medium of the learned participants, is the way to assign specified rules to the general law of goodness and unity. Mathematically, the characterization here is topologically

sense, the need for rules derived from the general law that enters the generalized phenomenological model, is similar to the inductive nature of critical realism advanced by Lawson (2009).

Morality, ethics, religion and economics

Recently the search for a theory of endogenous relationship between ethics and economics has drawn serious interest in the economic literature (Sen, 1992). But from our study of Kantian type heteronomy and the rationalist foundation of the moral law it becomes evident that the endogenous integration of the moral law, and thereby, of integrating religion with economics, becomes impossible. Consequently, ethics is derived from the rationalist domain of humanism. This is different from ethics that are derived from the foundational premise of the moral law in religious ontology.

Smart (2000, pp. 114-116) writes on Kantian understanding of autonomy or independence of morals that transcend direct Godly vision. Kantian categorical imperative "implies that we can by reason establish what is right and wrong; morality does not have any external source, not even

---

contained in Ω. Along the way of its deduction, the *shari'ah* is shown as the net result of the following process (Choudhury, 2011b):

Shari'ah is usually construed to be a law governing worldly affairs. But the universal implication of the phenomenological model given by Figure 5.1 extends the domain of the *shari'ah* to 'everything'. In other words, the unified and participatory nature of organic relations in the evolutionary learning domains invokes the methodological interrelationship between heart, mind and matter by circular causation. With this comprehensive meaning and functionalism, the *shari'ah* is defined by (1) the foundational core, (Ω,S), remaining exogenously outside Process; and (2) the evolutionary learned periphery of $\mathbf{z}(\theta)=\{\theta,\mathbf{X}(\theta),t,W(\mathbf{X}(\theta)\}$, occurring in perpetuity of (knowledge, space, and time)-structure. The consequence of the compounded two functions causing integration between Religion and Materiality (Economics) is denoted by L[.].

1 2

FOUNDATIONAL EVOLVED PROCESSES RECURSIVELY REPEATING IN PERPETUITY (5.1)

$L[(\Omega,S) \rightarrow \{\theta\} \rightarrow \{\theta, X(\theta),t\}$; CC simulation $W(\mathbf{X}(\theta)) \rightarrow$ continuity] $\cong$ *Shari'ah*

Law ; specific rules ; application to the world-system in specific cases ; sustainability across evolutionary learning phases

↓ ↓ ↓ ↓

Epistemology: unity of knowledge *maqasid as-shari'ah* ; functional ontology: normative specific rules reconstruction formalism towards wellbeing ; application: sustainability ; recursive continuity

Figure 5.1: The phenomenological model of unity of knowledge and its causal effect on the generalityand specifics of the world-system (economics)

God. It derives, as I have said, from each person as his or her own moral legislator."

This implication of Kant's categorical imperative drifting to the domain of practical reason (*a posteriori*) solely, apart from the functionalism of God (*a priori* reason), brings into economic reasoning that which Marx treated as the problem of over-determination (Resnick & Wolff, 1987). Every different culture, people, and economic category will then derive its own meaning of morality and ethics from differentiated understanding that the rationalist mind bestows on individual and group choices. The possibility for universality of a discoursed moral law is disabled.

Contrarily, the pre-assignment of the meaning and nature of morals by the source of the divine law must be of the universally and naturally acceptable type, nothing cumbersome. An example is the simple meaning of monotheism (absolute creatorship without partnership, *tawhid*) against the concept of trinity as a concept of three in one. Consequently, ethics as derived from the law of unity would be the only way of proposing the methodology of endogenous relationship between morality, ethics and economics. Such is the method of deontological preferences in social choice formation that Sen (1992) writes on.

Ethics, as derived from the moral law of monotheism (*tawhid*), is different in meaning and application than the rationalist meaning, transcending God as monotheism. The precept of monotheism (*tawhid*) precedes that of morality. Its text then gives meaning to morality. Ethics thereafter flows from the monotheistic law of morality.

An example in this regard is global ethics (Commission on Global Governance, 1995). Barbara Ward reflects upon such ethical value for the human future:

> The most important change that people can make is to change their way of looking at the world. We can change studies, jobs, neighborhoods, even countries and continents and still remain much as we always were. But change our fundamental angle of vision and everything changes – our priorities, our values, our judgments, our pursuits. Again and again, in the history of religion, this total upheaval in the imagination has marked the beginning of a new life – a turning away of the heart, a 'metanoia', by which men see with new eyes and understand with new minds and turn their energies to new ways of living.

Within such a global ethical vision, the self-reliant development for the South is designed by the South Commission (1990, p. 13). It writes as follows: "To sum up: development is a process of self-reliant growth, achieved through participation of the people acting in their own interests as they see them, and under their own control." Such a definition of development is very much of the rationalistic mould, premised on methodical independence of each country's individualism and self-interest.

But now we change the meaning of development vis-à-vis the meaning of global ethics derived from the monotheistic perspective of unity of knowledge. We would then define self-reliant development as a process of extensive participation in the global community according to collective social interest that is premised on the principle of unity of global ethics, which is derived epistemologically from the law of unity of knowledge between systems.

Many other examples can be found that show if ethics and economics are to be endogenously integrated into a holistic theory and application, then the partitioned worldview emanating from rationalism cannot enable such integration to happen. This points out that at the very inception, the methodology of integration between religion and materiality (economics) requires the epistemology of the fullest degree of inter-causal participation. This state arises strictly from the principle of systemic complementarities by organic unification (pairing). Since rationalism cannot attain such a unique and universal premise of unity of knowledge, upon which the world-system and its details can be constructed, we have then to turn to the phenomenology generated strictly by the monotheistic law. This was depicted in Figure 5.1.

Worldly rules derived from the monotheistic law and their applications

We provide here a few examples in respect of the above-mentioned ethical rule derived from the moral law of strict monotheism (*tawhid*) contrary to a rationalist epistemological approach. Such examples are invoked despite the fact that the call of religion to goodness and truth against falsehood and evil is indeed to be found in the rationalist approach.

One example is of the abolition of the rate of interest (*riba*) for purposes of attaining resource mobilization, distribution of wealth, generating ownership, equity, empowerment and entitlement among the rich and poor. Abolition of *riba* is an enabling instrument of the moral law. On the other hand, the rationalistic basis of religious law says nothing on the matter of abolition of interest rate.

Note the following two processes are contradictory paths of economic relations with different religious values:

(1) Based on rationalism and the religious inclination in rationalism:

nominal i↑⇒P↑⇒Y_R↓⇒I↓⇒r↓⇒L↓⇒D↓ (5.2)
⇒ economic and social linkages (complementarities)↓
⇒ marginalist condition of resource allocation
⇒ hence, methodological individualism↑.

(2) Based on the monotheistic law of unity of knowledge (*tawhid*) in relation to the unified world-system:

i = 0 ⇒ I↑↑⇒r↑⇒ Y_R↑⇒P↓⇒L↑⇒D↑ (5.3)
⇒ economic and social linkages (complementarities)↑
⇒ marginalist condition disappears
⇒ methodological individualism disappears
⇒ hence pure participation as the economic signature of unity of knowledge between inputs and goods
increases.

i denotes nominal interest rate;
I denotes gross investment;
r denotes rate of return on spending (I);
Y_R denotes real income;
P denotes price level;
L denotes mobilization of labour force (employment; labour force participation
rate);
D denotes distribution of income, wealth, and resources (equity, entitlement,
ownership, empowerment)

The fullest extent of complementarities between the good possibilities, signified also by extensive participation, conveys the sure sign of fusion of unity of knowledge as derived from the attribute and tenets of the monotheistic law. The complementary attribute equally applies to the specifics of the generalized world-system. They are represented by their characteristic variables symbolizing the issues under study. The case (2) (expression 5.3) based on the representation of monotheistic unity of knowledge in the form of pervasive participation and complementarity is the apt consequence of economic and social sustainability. In the phenomenological model of evolutionary learning of Figure 5.1, sustainability is explained by a recursive and progressive relationship continuing in perpetuity. Thus case 2, when placed in the phenomenological context, is regenerated by a recursive relationship occurring in perpetuity along the humanly constructed endogenous development path.

The role of Bishops' Pastoral Letters vis-à-vis *Centesimus Annus* (CA)

The Bishops' Pastoral Letters on the state of the North American economy during the hyperinflationary period of the eighties is an example that, despite its noble objectives, remained silent on the central effect of interest rate on economic and social adversities.

Kantian perspective of CA

Centesimus Annus (also other papal encyclicals noted as companions of CA)[6] (http://faculty.cua.edu/pennington/Law111/PapalSocialEncyclicals.htm) placed a great deal of concern on the plight of workers during the times of unbridled capitalism that deprives the workers of their rights. The same philosophy and its consequences would also prevail for the problems of social inequality within and between nations in today's age of global capitalism and for the plight of the abject poor. The same extension applies to the case of loss of empowerment and entitlement in an age of continued financial uncertainty, instability, and deprivation.

But what was the epistemological premise of *Centesimus Annus* in respect of the evolutionary learning model of sustainability of ethics and morality? Does *CA* present a systemic sense of continuity and pervasiveness of its reconstructive thought across the evolutionary learning dimensions of knowledge, space and time? This perspective we have argued, otherwise bridges the dichotomous gaps of reasoning in Kantian heteronomy.

Kant was indeed a moralist of the Western World. His works influenced many, of which one was the Catholic Church at the time of the Eighteenth Century Enlightenment (Makkreel, 1990). Thus the Kantian philosophy of 'authentic theodicy' in his heteronomy deeply enters the

---

[6] Leo XIII, Encyclical Letter *Rerum Novarum* (May 15, 1891): *Leonis XIII P.M. Acta*, XI, Romae 1892, 97-144. Pius XI, Encyclical Letter *Quadragesimo Anno* (May 15,1931): *AAS* 23 (1931),177-228; Pius XII, Radio Message of June 1, 1941: *AAS* 33 (1941), 195-205; John XXIII, Encyclical Letter *Mater et Magistra* (May 15, 1961): *AAS* 53 (1961), 401-464; Paul VI, Apostolic Epistle *Octogesima Adveniens* (May 14, 1971): *AAS* 63 (1971), 401-441.

theme of *CA* vis-à-vis social, economic, financial and institutional contractarianism.

Labour-capital socioeconomic conflict in CA

On the issue of labour-capital relationship, *CA* throughout depicts this as a permanent binary conflict of the times of oppressive capitalism. On this matter *CA* writes:

> The Pope and the Church with him were confronted, as was the civil community, by a society which was torn by a conflict all the more harsh and inhumane because it knew no rule or regulation. It was *the conflict between capital and labour,* or — as the Encyclical puts it — the worker question. It is precisely about this conflict, in the very pointed terms in which it then appeared that the Pope did not hesitate to speak.

Toward resolving this conflict between labour and capital, and likewise in another instance between capitalism and socialism, the Papal Encyclicals prescribed a return to Christian values. On this matter *CA* wrote:

> In a certain sense, it was a struggle born of prayer, and it would have been unthinkable without immense trust in God, the Lord of history, who carries the human heart in his hands. It is by uniting his own sufferings for the sake of truth and freedom to the sufferings of Christ on the Cross that man is able to accomplish the miracle of peace and is in a position to discern the often narrow path between the cowardice which gives in to evil and the violence which, under the illusion of fighting evil, only makes it worse.

The problem posed by the Church was cast in the ontological mystery of the Original Sin for which Christ laid down his life. Yet this event did not bring in laws with specific rules to abide by in the functioning of the world-system. Christ is not known to have brought laws with him for the juridical and economic conduct of society. Thus no clear rules could arise from the religious basis of law. Yet it remained the social order and its social, economic, and political misdeeds that had to be reformed by the divine law with specific rules.

Thus this missing link between the ontological precept of God and the world-system manifested the Kantian heteronomy. The gap could not be filled in by the tenets of the divine law presented in the cast of worldly laws and instruments, except by rationalist laws and instruments acting independently of the religious premise. On this matter *CA* writes:

> In this regard, *Rerum Novarum* points the way to just reforms which can restore dignity to work as the free activity of man. These reforms imply that society and the State will both assume responsibility, especially for protecting the worker from the nightmare of unemployment. Historically, this has happened in two converging ways: either through economic policies aimed at ensuring balanced growth and full employment, or through unemployment insurance and retraining programmes capable of ensuring a smooth transfer of workers from crisis sectors to those in expansion.

We note from this extract that ethical social policies and social structures are determined as usual -- independently of any presence of the divine law in action. Instead, the social intervention is by the rational artefacts of individuals and institutions. In these abide many contradictions. There is no connection between the tenets of the divine law and the emanating conduct derived from the divine law for the conduct of a good social and economic order.

The economic and financial implications of Kantian heteronomy in CA

Take the case of our theme discussed above, namely, economic stabilization being impossible in the presence of interest rates. Interest rates rupture the much-needed unifying function between money, finance, and the real economy to deliver economic and social justice through the endogenous process of systemic interrelations. In such endogenous exchange process, markets and governments would learn in co-determination with each other. In the absence of such organic complementarities, the Kantian heteronomy between the *a priori* and the *a posteriori*, between *noumena* and phenomena, between God and the world-system, between deductive and inductive reasoning, abides fully.

Basing their arguments of dualism between markets and social values, there are those who consider such alienation and competition between these sectors of human experience as being inevitable. Consequently, ethics and morality in economy, society, state and global politics, although so often voiced in *CA*, remains a purely rationalistic institutional project. It is independently treated as a humanistic one. On this matter *CA* writes:

> The State must contribute to the achievement of these goals both directly and indirectly. Indirectly, and according to the *principle of subsidiarity,* by creating favourable conditions for the free exercise of economic activity, which will lead to abundant opportunities for employment and sources of wealth. Directly, and according to the *principle of solidarity,* by defending

the weakest, by placing certain limits on the autonomy of the parties who determine working conditions, and by ensuring in every case the necessary minimum support for the unemployed worker.

The rationalist element in CA

CA was incorrect in yet another area of its argumentation concerning the issue of rationalism, entrenched as it remains in Kantian heteronomy. That is, rationalism is of the humanly engineered origin, and God has a different ontological premise of argumentation for the world-system. Then in such divine law, God must be a law-giver with well-defined laws and ways that are brought into the world-system to unite the ontological with the ontic (evidence). Yet in the social characterization explained above, this is not the case. Thus God and His divine law remain insulated ontological precepts, disconnected from the world-system as endogenous relations. In its dichotomous moral and material states, God after creation has left the world to evolve by itself. Only murmurs of humanistic feelings abide in the bosoms of good-thinking men.

Conclusion

For a long time now religious philosophy has been struggling to find a methodology that would establish the integrated worldview of religion and the world-system (economics). The methodology remains in abeyance because of the prevailing academic ineptness to get out of rationalism and rationalist religious philosophy and move into ontological unity of knowledge as an episteme methodologically formalized.

In conclusion, this chapter has noted that in the overarching epistemology of monotheism (*tawhid*) as unity of knowledge and bestowing a theory of 'everything' (Barrow, 1991), the foundation of faith needs to answer the question of continuity of meanings of material causation in the universal totality of knowledge, space and time. Such inter-causality establishes the foundation of faith as having an organic relationship with the world-system. Such an approach to epistemological inquiry must be able to decipher uniquely and universally the meanings of truth and falsehood as disjoint realities. That epistemological approach must be able to integrate the *a priori* with the *a posteriori* reasoning by a learning process across continuums of complementary analytical and ontic formalisms. Such formalisms comprise the *functional* ontological ones. These are necessary for explaining total reality by critical realism, and not to be limited to particular ones, or to be differentiated between specifics (Maxwell, 1962; Lawson, 2003).

This quest for the overarching epistemology, which we have launched in this chapter, when applied to the state of the world economy today, brings out certain structural problems of economic theory. According to the epistemology of unity of knowledge that we have propounded, the endogenous ethical and learning dynamics of economic theory suggests that the dichotomies between ethics and economics, between microeconomics and macroeconomics, and indeed between religion and science, were wrong.

But so also the microeconomic foundation of macroeconomics is equally flawed. Within this field of intellectual inquiry, economic paradigms such as rational expectations hypothesis and general equilibrium in welfare economics are problems. The central problem in all these areas is the overly neoclassical or aggregate (Keynesian or monetarist) leanings. Neoclassical economic theory as deductive reasoning has poor inductive power. The deductive and the inductive do not integrate into a unified evolutionary learning process-based economic reasoning. For example, Keynesianism (Dasgupta, 1987) and monetarism (Friedman, 1953) are based on inductive reasoning, and are thereby removed from the ethical moorings of deductive reasoning. The ethico-economic origin arising from moral roots belongs methodologically to the field of microeconomics. Thus the deductive and inductive points of reasoning, and the microeconomics and macroeconomics, cannot connect by circular causality between them in received economic and scientific reasoning.

Such a differentiation between deductive and inductive reasoning, and between the *a priori* and *a posteriori* reasoning, has also invaded pure scientific theories. The differentiation between Relativity Physics and Quantum Mechanics is the most prominent evidence of the breach (Penrose, 1989). Likewise, in Popper's (1998) form of conjectures and scientific refutations, the silence on unity of knowledge between forms, entities, and their inter-causal relations has caused the loss of ethical directions in science. Husserl (1970) lamented on such a state of moral emptiness in the pure natural sciences. Finally, even Godel's (1965) rejection of self-referencing according to his theorem of incompleteness of the arithmetical system, which was a rejection of the claim of the finality of mathematical machinery given by Russell and Whitehead (1910-13) in their *Principia Mathematica*, is great, yet it is subject to questioning. Godel's denial of self-referencing leaves out the theme of unity of knowledge in explaining the possibilities of the socio-scientific universe

(Choudhury & Zaman, 2009) in the unbounded domain of super-cardinal super-topology.

Conclusively therefore, the rationalist socio-scientific epistemology is bereft of the overarching epistemology of unity of knowledge and the world-system. Prevalent theories and their empirical and institutional pursuits cannot therefore, succeed in analysing and reconstructing the economic, financial and social worlds into a cohesively relational unity for the sustainable common human future. Reasoning, theories, institutions, policies and entities need to acquire their essential nature of inter-causally embedded ensembles.

The intrinsic nature of creative experience in the learning universe invokes the inexorable embedding of our experiences with the divine law. Without this, neither a meaning of reality, continuous and complete, nor the meaning of goodness as knowledge, the sublime endowment, can be found. On this ultimate faith dimension of the universal socio-scientific explanation Gulen writes (2006, p. 148-49):

> We use 'the horizon of hope' to mean traveling beyond the visible dimension of existence, and considering existence as an interrelated whole in the absence of which things and events cannot be perceived as they really are. Nor can its essence and relation with the Creator as well as the relation between them and humanity be grasped. Scientific disciplines that conduct their own discourse largely in isolation from one another and the prevailing materialistic nature of science that has compartmentalized existence and life cannot discover the reality of things, existence, or life.

Technical Appendix: Non-Parametric Representation of what Integration between Economics and Religions Means in the Evolutionary Learning Methodological Worldview

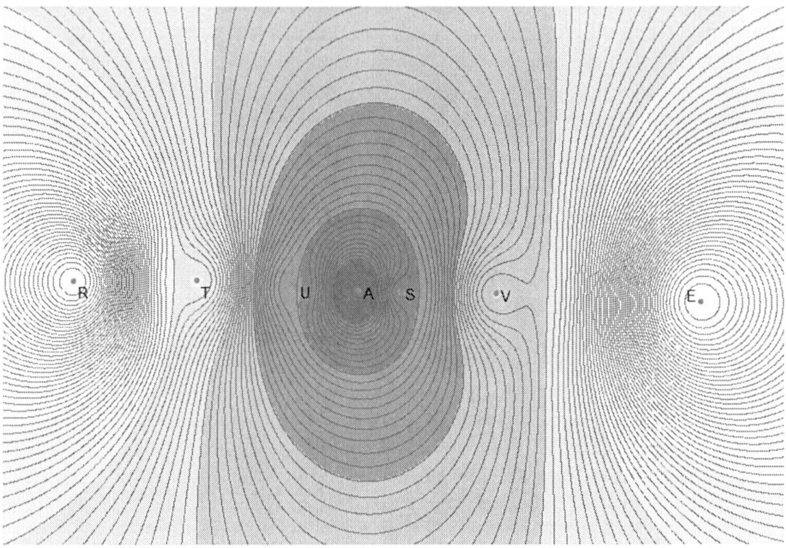

Figure 5A1: From non-integration to integration between Religion and Economics as inter-disciplines when embedded in the epistemology of unity of systemic knowledge as methodology[7]

Explanation

Spatial Domain Analysis (SDA) is a specialized subproject of the Geographical Information System. It is applied here to socio-scientific topography involving economics and religion, both being governed by the epistemology of unity of knowledge. In actual practice the SDA forms a pervasive field of numbers that arise as all possible estimated and simulated values of coefficients representing inter-causal relations between selected variables as of the inter-systemic wellbeing function. The wellbeing function relates to the study of integration between economics

[7] My thanks are to Professor M. Shahadat Hossain of the Department of Computer Science, Chittagong University for improvising on Figure 5A1 in the SDA form.

and religion as two inter-disciplinary systems. The pervasive field of numbers next allows simulated choices of improved and revised numerical values of the estimated coefficients in order to build on the principle of complementarities between the inter-causal variables of the wellbeing function. The underlying method in such integration out of interaction, thereby growing outwards into evolutionary learning processes is circular causation. Although numbers are invoked in actual estimation and simulation by the SDA method, in our case, the representation remains non-parametric and hence illustrative.

The origins of **E**conomics and **R**eligion denote those of initially disjoint systems. The improvising of the epistemology of unity of knowledge (*tawhidi* methodology) causes the disjoint systems to become knowledge-induced. Now the circular causation method works, causing progress towards greater integration by the interactive, integrative, and evolutionary learning processes. The regions extensively denoted by TU and VS move toward their complementary integration in the region around A. The evolutionary SDA waves as shown signify the progressing **IIE**-processes wherein estimated values of inter-variable relational coefficients represent non-parametric simulations to gain on unity of systemic knowledge as the epistemology. The method underlying the immanent dynamics of the inter-causal relations between the selected variable is circular causation.

References

Arrow, K.J., 1951, *Social Choice and Individual Values*, John Wiley & Sons, New York, NY.

Barrow, J.D., 1991, "Laws", in his, *Theories of Everything, the Quest for Ultimate Explanation*, pp. 12-30, Oxford University Press, Oxford, Eng.

Blaug, M., 1968, "Introduction: has economic theory progressed?", in his, *Economic Theory in Retrospect*, Richard D. Irwin, Inc., Homewood, ILL. Read regarding Thomas Aquinas on financial interest.

Carnap, R., 1966, "Kant's synthetic a priori", in his, *Philosophical Foundations of Physics*, Gardner, M. (ed.), Basic Books, Inc., New York, NY.

Centesimus Annus, (http://faculty.cua.edu/pennington/Law111/PapalSocialEncyclicals.htm)

Choudhury, M.A., 2011a, "A meta-epistemological general-system model of Islamic economics", *Social Epistemology*, (25)4.

—. 2011b, "The dynamics of the *shari'ah* and the world-system", *The Journal of King AbdulAziz University,* (23)2.

Choudhury, M.A. & Zaman, S.I., 2009, "Self-referencing as socio-scientific methodology in contrasting paradigms", *Kybernetes, The International Journal of Systems & Cybernetics*, (38)6, 994-1008.

Commission on Global Governance, 1995, "Global Civic Ethic", in *Our Global Neighbourhood, a Report of the Commission on Global Governance*, Oxford University Press, New York, N.Y.

Dasgupta, A.K., 1987, "Marginalist challenge", in his, *Epochs of Economic Theory*, pp. 74-98, Basil Blackwell, Oxford, U.K

Doi, A.R., 1984, *Shari'ah*, Ta Ha Publishers, London, Eng.

Erasmus Journal for Philosophy and Economics, 2009, "Cambridge social ontology: an interview with Tony Lawson", (2)1,100-122.

Fitzpatrick, T., 2003, "Postmodernism and new directions", in Alcock, P. Erskine, A. & May, M. (eds.), *Social Policy*, pp. 125-133, Blackwell, Oxford, Eng.

Foucault, M. trans. by Sheridan, A.M. 1972, *The Archeology of Knowledge and the Discourse on Language*, Harper Torchbooks, New York.

Friedman, M., 1953, *Essays in Positive Economics*, University of Chicago Press, Chicago, ILL.

Godel, K., 1965, "On formally undecidable propositions of *Principia Mathematica* and related systems", in M. Davies (ed.), *The Undecidable*, Raven Books, New York.

Gulen, M.F., 2006, *Toward Global Civilization of Love & Tolerance*, The Light, Inc., Somerset, New Jersey.

Heidegger, M. trans. by Hofstadter, A., 1988, "The thesis of modern ontology: the basic ways of being are the being of nature (res extensa) and the being of mind (res cogitans)", in *The Basic Problems of Phenomenology*, pp. 122-224, Indiana University Press, Bloomington & Indianapolis, IN.

Hosinski, T., 1987, "Lonergan and a process understanding of God", in Fallon, T.P. & Riley, P.B. (eds.), *Religion and Culture: Essays in Honor of Bernard Lonergan, S.J.*, pp. 63-78, State University of New York Press, Albany, N.Y.

Hume, D., 1960, "Principles of morals", in his *An Enquiry Concerning the Principles of Morals*, The Open Court Publishing Co., La Salle, ILL.

—. 1992, *An Enquiry Concerning Human Understanding*, Prometheus Books, Buffalo, USA.

Husserl, E. trans. by Lauer, Q., 1970, *Phenomenology and the Crisis of Philosophy*, p. 155, Harper & Row Publishers, New York. Particularly note his comment on the perceived absence of ethical roots in occidental scientific inquiry.

Kant, I. trans. by Friedrich, C.J., 1949, "Religion within the limits of reason alone", in Friedrich C.J., (ed.), *The Philosophy of Kant*, pp. 365-411, Modern Library, New York, NY.

Lawson, T., 2003, "An evolutionary economics?", in his, *Reorienting Economics*, pp. 110-140, Routledge, London, Eng.

Lewis, B., 2010, "Religion and politics in Islam and Judaism", in his *Faith and Power, Religion and Politics in the Middle East*, pp. 39-54, Oxford University Press, Oxford, Eng.

Lonergan, B., 1908, "The pure process", and "Equilibria of the mechanical structure", in McShane, P.J. (ed.), *Collected Works of Bernard Lonergan, for a New Political Economy*, University of Toronto Press, Toronto, ON.

—. 1999, "An essay in circular analysis" in Lawrence, F.G. Byrne, P.H. and Heflong Jr. C.C. (eds.), *Collected Works of B. Lonergan, Macroeconomic Dynamics*, University of Toronto Press, Toronto, ON.

—. 2001, "The general character of mathematical logic", in McShane P.J. (ed.) *Collected Works of B. Lonergan, Phenomenology and Logic*, University of Toronto Press, Toronto, ON.

Maddox, I.J., 1970, *Elements of Functional Analysis*, Cambridge University Press, Cambridge, Eng.

Mater et Magistra, (http://faculty.cua.edu/pennington/Law111/PapalSocialEncyclicals.htm)

Makkreel, R.A., 1990, Teleological ideas and the authentic interpretation of history", in his, *Imagination and Interpretation in Kant*, pp. 130-153, The University of Chicago Press, Chicago, ILL.

Maxwell, G., 1962, "The ontological status of theoretical entities", in Feigl, H. & Maxwell, G. (eds.), *Minnesota Studies in the Philosophy of Science, Vol. II: Scientific Explanation, Space and Time*, pp. 3-27, University of Minnesota Press, Minneapolis, Minnesota.

Myrdal, G., 1958, "The principle of cumulation", in Streeten, P. (ed.), *Value in Social Theory, a Selection of Essays on Methodology by Gunnar Myrdal*, pp. 198-205, Harper & Brothers Publishers, New York, NY.

Nelson, R.H., 2001, "Efficient religion", in *Economics as Religion (from Samuelson to Chicago and Beyond),* Pennsylvania State University Press, pp. 230-260.

Nelson, R.H. 2001, "A new economic world", n *Economics as Religion (from Samuelson to Chicago and Beyond,* pp. 208 – 229, Pennsylvania State University Press, Pennsylvania, PA, USA.

Octogesima Adveniens, (http://faculty.cua.edu/pennington/Law111/PapalSocialEncyclicals.htm)

Penrose, R., 1989, *The Emperor's New Mind*, Oxford University Press, Oxford, Eng.

Popper, K., 1998, *Conjectures and Refutations: The Growth of Scientific Knowledge*, Routledge & Kegan Paul, London, Eng.

Quadragesimo Anno, (http://faculty.cua.edu/pennington/Law111/PapalSocialEncyclicals.htm)

Rerum Novarum, (http://faculty.cua.edu/pennington/Law111/PapalSocialEncyclicals.htm)

Resnick, S.A. & Wolff, R.D., 1987, *Knowledge and Class, A Marxian Critique of Political Economy*, The University of Chicago Press, Chicago, IL.

Rucker, R., 1982, "Large cardinals", in his, *Infinity and the Mind*, pp. 273-286, Bantam Books, New York, NY.

Russell, B. & Whitehead, A.N., 1910-13, *Principia Mathematica*, Cambridge University Press, New York, NY.

Sen, A., 1992, "Conduct, ethics and economics", in his, *On Ethics & Economics*, pp. 88-89, Basil Blackwell, Oxford, UK.

Smart, N., 2000, "The nature of morality", in his *Worldviews*, pp. 114-116, Prentice Hall, Upper Saddle River, New Jersey.

South Commission, 1990, *The Challenge to the South*, Oxford University Press, Oxford, Eng.

Toner, P., 1999, "Gunnar Myrdal (1898-1987): circular and cumulative causation as the methodology of the social sciences", in his, *Main Currents in Cumulative Causation, the Dynamics of Growth and Development*, Chapter 5, Macmillan Press Ltd., Houndmills, Hampshire:

Torrell, J.P. (trans.) by Gueven, B.M. 2005, "A circular plan", in *Aquinas' SUMMA, Background, Structure, and Reception*, pp. 27-36, The Catholic University of America Press, Washington, D.C.

Vertin, M., 1987, "Is God in Process?" in Fallon, T. P. & Riley, P.B., (eds.), *Religion and Culture: Essays in Honor of Bernard Lonergan*, pp. 45-63, State University of New York Press, Albany, N.Y.

Whitehead, A.N., 1979, "Fact and form", in his, *Process and Reality*, (eds.), Griffin, D.R. & Sherburne, D.W., pp. 39-60, The Free Press, New York, NY.

Wolff, R.P., 1977, *A Reconstruction of a Critique of a Theory of Justice: Understanding Rawls*, Princeton University Press, Princeton, NJ.

Zweig, M., 1991, "Economics and liberation theology", in his edited, *Religion and Economic Justice*, pp. 3-99, Remple University Press, Philadelphia, PA.

CHAPTER SIX

METHODOLOGICAL INTRODUCTION TO *TAWHID* IN RELATION TO THE WORLD-SYSTEM: COMPARATIVE PERSPECTIVES IN ECONOMICS, FINANCE, SOCIETY AND SCIENCE

Background of the research question on *Tawhid*

Tawhid means oneness as the primal attribute of God. Every Muslim and non-Muslim believes in the oneness of God as the cardinal attribute of their religion, be this Islam or any other. Yet the understanding of *tawhid* in its ontological, epistemological, and phenomenological relationship in the articles of faith and its relationship with the world-system is not easily comprehended. This is equally true of Muslims and non-Muslims. Consequently, the substantive meaning of monotheism in relation to God, self, the world, and the ultimate closure of knowledge and temporal order in the hereafter (*akhira*) is not understood. Only a casual reference is made to this substantive knowledge premise. The failure and the gradual decline of interest and pursuit in the intellectual world of the substantive understanding of monotheism as the unity of organic relationship explained by invoking the structure and functionalism of scientific knowledge, caused the gradual abandonment of the study of the monotheistic law in hardcore scientific inquiry.

Such an abandonment of the monotheistic essence from the core of scientific and worldly inquiry caused a fading away on several fronts of intellection. In the age of scholasticism the departure occurred firstly due to the inability of the churchmen to explain the growing challenges towards understanding both the abstraction and the material reality that arose during the Eighteenth Century Enlightenment. This paucity of knowledge in the then apprehended meaning of the monotheistic essence and the analytical world-system, caused the dichotomy between church and science (Schumpeter, 1966). The growing dichotomy subsequently received the full force in every quarter of human activity, institutions, and socio-scientific relations. It entered the domain of knowledge and education; of culture and politics; and of science, morality, ethics, economics and society, altogether forming the differentiating pillars of the mental construct and its application in the realms of practice and enforcement of the monotheistic law. Such growing division between religion and the social and scientific order has now permanently marked the whole of human thought, practice, and application. Even the scientific application of religion has been disabled due to that primal failure on the part of the churchmen to explain scientific phenomena by the edicts of monotheism. Vice-a-versa, it was equally necessary to explain monotheism by the edicts of science and analytics. Such a circular causality between monotheism and science does not mean the acceptance of a final and unchangeable epistemology of science, which as if once unbarred remains the unquestionable finality for all times. This belief is itself questionable even after age-old reliance on scientific facts as the supreme knowledge.

Scientific theories have been changing by the force of abstraction and experimentation for a long time now. Yet certain scientific facts have remained unquestioned despite the dynamic nature of scientific inquiry. Examples are legion. Of special note is the failure of establishing a sound methodology that will integrate ethics endogenously in scientific theory. This was a broader dream of Einstein (Bohr in Folse, 1985). No methodology has been established to integrate the micro-universe phenomena with the macro-universe phenomena, in spite of the grandiose works of Penrose (1989) on Quantum Gravity. The essential program of systemic unification between relativity physics and quantum physics has stalled in the absence of a viable methodology to explain, formalize, and yield such a methodology of unity of social and scientific knowledge. The Vienna Circle (Neurath, Carnap & Morris, 1970) tried in this direction but failed. This was particularly due to two factors: Firstly, a generalized formalism to integrate ethics with scientific theory could not be conceptualized, let alone application of ethics in a troubled world, except for giving structuralism to the study of ethics (Edel, 1970). Secondly, specialization not only narrowed down the scope of science and economic study to logical positivism, rather, to invoke God and the divine law in scientific study was considered scientific blasphemy (Pheby, 1988).

In economics, the dynamic preference formation in rational choice theory, and the resulting effects on social choice theory, could not be explained outside the paradigm of economic rationality and transitivity of preferences. Heterodox economics has seriously questioned these static conditions of the growth of economic thought as sheer scientific thought. Lawson (2003) has revived a quest for new and functional ontological beginnings of economic reasoning. In the name of specialization, scientific and social inquiry has receded into a narrowed down domain that excludes a systemic, and therefore complex and endogenous, interrelated study of morality, ethics, culture, and values from the social and scientific calculus. Consequently, the treatment of technology and choices by interactive dynamic preference formation, except for the distant linear aggregation of utilitarian social choice, has remained benign in the study of economics, science and society. Now for example, there is no positive circular causation possible between distributive justice and economic efficiency to link these up in the presence of the prevailing core axiom of economic science, namely scarcity of resource and competition for scarce resources to maximize certain so-called 'objective functions' under rational choice at any given point of time.

On the other hand, economics suffered from the contesting schools of Keynes and the Keynesians (Hunt, 1979) on one side, and Friedman and the monetarists on the other side. Keynes, though a rationalist believing in economic rationality to solve the ethical problem signified via government expenditure, deficit financing, and the spending problem versus the saving problem (Ventelou, 2005), was yet a normative thinker. He was swayed by the ethical thought of G.E. Moore (1903) concerning the extraneous elements of a theory of probability concerning economic events. Friedman (1989) oppositely was a champion of the role of money in the economy. His prescription to economic stabilization with stable prices and economic growth was the private market solution. In this, the quantity of money played the central role by measuring the quantity in accord with the exchange demand of the economy. Ethics to Friedman descended to market competition and economic efficiency. Only ethical positivism in this sense mattered against the normative view towards ethical reconstruction.

On the issue of economic epistemology, the contested views of Keynes and Friedman, and with a whimper of this debate in many others, could not expand the horizons of economics as a science into the cybernetic synergy of religion and related values. Among these other works are those by Hayek (1976), von Mises (1976) as the Austrian economic epistemologists, Sen (1988), and the evolutionary economists like Myrdal (1958), Schumpeter (1961), Georgescu-Roegen (1981) in economic process, and North (1981) on economic institutions.

The economic aggregation and behavioural theory coming out of Lucas subjected macroeconomics to the neoclassical form of rational choice and static preferences towards framing the rational expectations hypothesis.

Nordhaus delineated aggregate behaviour in relation to economics and politics also in reference to rational choice theory. Arrow's social choice theory is a replica of utilitarianism arising from the transitivity assumption of rational choice. Arrow allows dictatorial termination of a discursive game, but leaves the agent of termination undefined. Hayek and von Mises of the Austrian School of Economics stand out as economic epistemologists based on the axiom of economic rationality as was Keynes as an economic philosopher (O'Donnell, 1989). Consequently, justice and institutions being important elements in their thought, these took up only economic meanings. Economics was attempted to be made a hand maiden of ethics. Yet the idea of social justice was seen as mirage in the market system.

The works of Myrdal, Schumpeter, and Georgescu-Roegen were a combination of the Austrian form of evolutionary economics and an evolutionary epistemology affecting economic theory. For example, Myrdal's concept of 'the wider field of valuation' introduced the importance of cultural values in the form of a dual economic reasoning. Yet it could not formulate an abiding general theory of economics based on the ethical idea. The evolutionary economic thought of Boulding (1971) went in this direction to incorporate ethics and values as part of a general theory of economic science. Yet the endogenous nature of resource formation, ownership, and distribution remained subjected to the postulate of scarcity of resources, and thus annulled the endogenous nature of creative evolution.

Schumpeter and North's evolutionary institutions do not point out any definite normative goal towards which the political economy of transformation and technological future ought to be directed. Thereby, a narrative study of economic history overshadows the theory of normative change and social transformation.

Sen's theory of ethics and economics is a new development. It incorporates deontological preferences in developing a phenomenological perspective of dynamic preferences and economic behaviour away from rational choice theory. Sen's theory like Arrow's, is not time-and-preference dynamic. Consequently, a theory of change cannot be empirically viable to study a normative future of change with ethics endogenously embedded in economics. The very most important theory of endogenous ethics in economic, social, and scientific worldview is still to materialize. One wonders why the project has not been realized thus far.

In the light of the monotheistic inclusion in a theory of 'everything' that would expand the scope and deepen the explanatory power of science, economics, finance and society, we must break down the wall of impermeability that divides the monotheistic methodological worldview from that of science and the social entirety. This totality we refer to as the field of human intellection. It includes of a general, unique and universal theory for everything in the form of an evolutionary learning system. We refer to such a methodological unified totality as the socio-scientific order. Its methodology is premised on the epistemology of unity of knowledge. The realm of this socio-scientific unification is governed by textual laws and their applications out of the good things of life. The good things of life are the unifying ones in abstraction and materiality out of the life-sustaining regime of moral actualization. The moral foundation of the immanent methodological worldview thereby, generates ethical endogeneity in an organic relationship, as by evolutionary learning in processes across systems.

The permanent problem of heteronomy in mainstream socio-scientific inquiry

The divisive wall of intellection in systemic discontinuity between micro and macro aspects of socio-scientific inquiry; and most critically, the impossibility to integrate the monotheistic law in mainstream socio-scientific thought is due to the permanence of what is termed heteronomy of the Kantian type. The problem of heteronomy is not simply of a philosophical nature. Its identical effects of divisiveness between disparate types of socio-scientific reasoning are found in economics, finance, and social orders (Choudhury, 2010).

The meaning of heteronomy can be derived from the words of Kant (reprinted 1949, p.25): "This, then, is a question which at least calls for closer examination, and does not permit any off-hand answer: whether there is any knowledge that is thus independent of experience and even of all impressions of the senses. Such knowledge is entitled *a priori*, and is distinguished from the empirical, which has its sources *a posteriori*, that is, in experience."

Kant continues on to write of the problem of dichotomy in reasoning (reprinted 1949, p. 25): “In what follows, therefore, we shall understand by *a priori* knowledge, no knowledge independent of this or that experience, but knowledge absolutely independent of all experience. Opposed to it is empirical knowledge, which is knowledge possible only *a posteriori*, that is through experience.”

Heteronomy is thus the epistemological problem of dichotomy between *a priori* reason and *a posteriori* reason; likewise between deductive reasoning and inductive reasoning; and thereby also between normative analysis and logical positivism. Kant’s problem of heteronomy is explained by Carnap as the divided understanding between the moral imperative and the material world-system. This also beacons the meaning of intellectual rationalism. The epistemological dichotomy in reasoning can be explained as follows: A synthetic gap exists between the metaphysical order of pure reason that is contained in the *a priori* domain, and the material world of concrescence that is embodied in *a posteriori* domain.

Consequently, even though much desired in Kant's critical moral imperative, and arising from the *a priori* domain, such an imperative cannot be mapped *onto* the *a posteriori* domain and vice-a-versa. Inter-causality becomes impossible. All this is due to there not being a well-defined correspondence by the enactment of an overarching law and rules uniquely governing the *a priori* and the *a posteriori* reasoning domains. To resolve this problem, morality becomes embodied in human rationalism as the sole determiner. The divine law of pure reason becomes impossible for positive action in its metaphysical form. It becomes dysfunctional in the material world; and is replaced by a rationalist interpretation of the moral and ethical imperatives (Kant, trans. Friedrich, 1949). At the end, monotheistic law failed to be integrated in mainstream socio-scientific intellection. Besides, the endogeneity of the moral and ethical law had to be dispensed with.

Endogeneity in socio-scientific reasoning between *a priori* and *a posteriori* domains formalizes by way of functional ontological approach a seamless circular continuity between them. An example would provide an explanation of this. A policy variable is taken to be exogenous, and hence normative. Thus an ethical perspective is carried forward by policy variables to affect socioeconomic change that is endogenous in nature. However, policy variables, being exogenous, are not affected by a set of endogenous variables. Heteronomy exists between the policy and socioeconomic variables in this sense of the dichotomy between positivistic reasoning (endogenous socioeconomic variables) and normative variable (exogenous policy variable). To create continuous endogeneity, the policy variables must be turned into endogenous variables. This can happen by a change in the structure of decision-making between government as institution and the socioeconomic system. Such decision-making becomes participative. Thereby the imminent conditions that affect socioeconomic variables also affect policy-variables and institutions.

In respect of society and economics we can refer to Sztompka's (1991) model of endogenous continuity as historical processes evolving over time and regenerating social structures, agencies, and agents through the intervening mediums of operation, praxis, and action. Likewise it is true of a continuous function between these elements over time, say structure (y_{1t}), agencies (y_{2t}), agents (y_{3t}) through the regenerated inputs of operation (x_{1t}), praxis (x_{2t}), and action (x_{3t}). The continuous function involving these variables is written as, $F(y_{1t},y_{2t},y_{3t},x_{1t}.x_{2t},x_{3t})$ = parameter. The properties of continuity and differentiability of this function in terms of the stated variables establishes the well-known implicit functions theorem of differential calculus (Baldani, Bradfield & Turner, 2005). Every variable can now be written by inter-causality in terms of the other variables. Thus all the variables get endogenously interrelated. In the list of variables would be the participatory policy variables. Now no variable remains exogenous in nature.

Heteronomy in the world of economics and finance globally

Another example from economics and finance in the global economic situation is the case of differentiation between money and the real economy. Kantian heteronomy with its differentiation between *a priori* and *a posteriori* analysis, noumena and phenomena, pure reason and practical reason, reflect the condition of separation of the monetary sector from the real economy. This is manifest in all features of capitalism and capitalist globalization. The financial instruments, in the midst of this dichotomy, lose their participatory function due to the holding back of resource mobilization by the rate of financial interest in bank savings.

Figure 6.1 explains the above problem of Kantian differentiation both in respect of the epistemological questions of science and religion, and for the broken links between money, finance and real economy. This subject matter is then explained to be capable of study within monotheism and its relationship with the economic and financial world-system. Kant's theoretical construct, failing to apply to the organic need for methodological synthesis between the moral law and materiality, deny the immanent causality to prevail.

This kind of formal consequence is utterly destructive for modern socio-scientific reasoning and its application to facts. The entire domain of the sciences has always claimed an isolated existence of its own, separated from any endogenous theory of morality, ethics and sociality in it. Even when social Darwinism is invoked to explain process in scientific theory (Hull, 1988), then competition, conflict, methodological individualism and biological differentiation are found to fully colour the organic relational domains. Now symbiosis in socio-scientific processes is meant to explain instead, the continuum of endogenously embedded forces of competition, conflict, methodological individualism and differentiation (Holton, 1992).

We note here that, in accordance with the implications of Kantian heteronomy regarding the ruptured relationship between money, finance and real economy, there is no mechanism that can make the system of production and risk diversifications 'learn' adaptively to recursively establish unity of knowledge. Such feedback recursive relations establish unity of knowledge in the form of circular causation. Thereby the state of heteronomy is annulled. The implication of Kantian heteronomy in this case is that, although the *a priori* knowledge has its moral imperative, it remains causally disjoint from *a posteriori* reason and the moral law. Hence the moral law as intellectual formalism, and the instruments and social arrangements as functional ontological artefacts to bring about complementary linkages between the *a priori* and the *a posteriori* domains, remains absent. As long as there is no substantive theory for avoidance of interest and its replacement by participatory financing instruments, the endogenous relationship between money, finance and real economy cannot be formalized by a cogent methodology and its application.

The result of Kantian dichotomy and the resulting problem of lack of synthesis, that is, the ineluctable problem of heteronomy by Kantian reasoning applied as a case in economics and finance, is caused by the mainstream economic postulate of resource scarcity. Kantian rationalism is now seen to enhance this constriction in the augmenting of resources causing widening systemic differentiation. 'Learning' cannot now be extensively realized, as it should be by its endogenous sustainable nature of inter-causal relations between the ethical choices everywhere (Primavesi, 2000).

Thus there remains the pressing epistemological need to examine, study, and implement a new perspective based on the endogenous nature of unity of knowledge and of its induction on the world-system (Hubner, 1985). In this context, the monotheistic law becomes applicable on the question of money, finance, and the real economy. This gives an example of a primal way of cancelling the debilitating problem of heteronomy caused by the presence of interest rates as the price that drives financial resources away from the real economy into bank savings. Annulment of the problem of heteronomy in both the monotheistic issue of unity of knowledge across systems, and the cancelling of its debilitating effect on establishing the endogenous relationship between *a priori* and *a posteriori* reasoning, are essential requirements for the effective working of the monotheistic law in its conceptual and evidential results. This is argued presently with respect to the particular problem of economics, finance and the real economy.

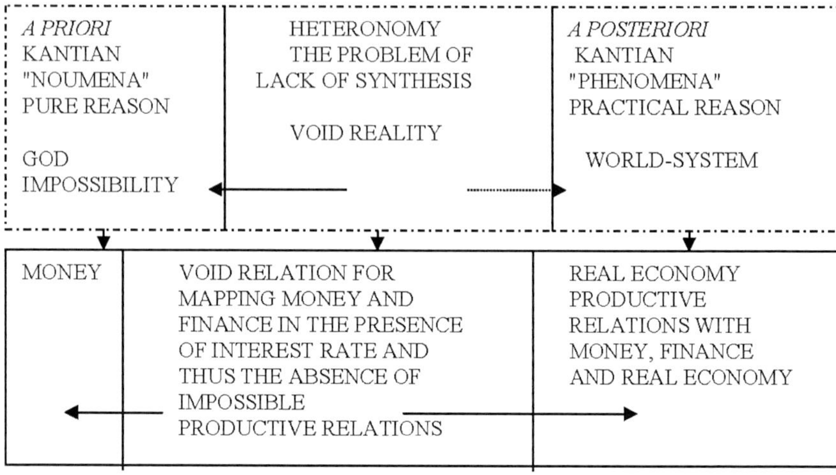

Figure 6.1: Socioeconomic effect of the problem of Kantian heteronomy

Heteronomy as the key problem in the development of the monotheistic epistemology of unity of knowledge: a contrasting study between Kant and Ghazzali

Like Kant's moral imperative as the foundation of his epistemology in *a priori* (pure reason) reasoning, Imam Ghazzali, in the history of Islamic peripatetic thought concerning monotheism and the world-system, had similar moral ideals (Choudhury, 1997). Yet the difference between Kant and Ghazzali lies in the transmission of thought from the *a priori* to the *a posteriori*. Kant left these two sides in the problem of heteronomy, there being no well-defined mapping that would carry *a priori* reasoning to *a posteriori* reasoning, and thus to cause an organic unity between these two.

Ghazzali depicted the advance of knowledge rising upwards from the first level of a mere utterance of the monotheistic declaration of *tawhid* by the tongue (*shahadah*), to its advance through seventy levels of deepening human surrender to this monotheistic cardinal principle empowering belief. The last of these stages of ascent was the realm of bliss resting in knowledge and purity. Ghazzali called this point of bliss *'fana'*. It is the state of self-actualization that Ghazzali said can be gained in the optimal state of mingling with God in that state of purity. Ghazzali thus established the continuous path of learning towards the blissful advance. The continuous actualization of the world, self, and the end point of *fana* leading to the terminal point of worldly life in the hereafter marked the continuous version of Ghazzali's advance through seventy veils of knowledge. The human realm of cognition and experience moves into bliss through the subtle combination of knowledge, belief, and action (the world) (Ghazzali (trans.) by Karim, u.d., p. 237, edited):

> What is *Tauhid* (monotheism)? Know O readers, that God –reliance is a door out of the doors of faith. All the doors of faith are not kept in order except with knowledge, condition, and action. Out of these three elements, God-reliance is born. Knowledge is the basis, action is its fruit.

Ghazzali thus integrated the heart and soul with mind and matter as worlds, and the hereafter as the final test of moral actualization. In this regard, Buchman (1998, p. 38) translates on Ghazzali:

> Knowledge is above faith, and tasting is above knowledge; [this] because tasting is a finding, but knowing is a drawing of analogies, and having faith is a mere acceptance through imitation.

Ghazzali thereby originated the power and possibility of realizing the world-system on the texts of foundational knowledge, the *Qur'an,* and the guidance of the Prophet Muhammad called the *sunnah*. There was thus this media to well-define the transmission of knowledge to the world-system. Thereby, *a priori* reasoning was linked with *a posteriori* reasoning. The problem of heteronomy could not exist. Ghazzali transcended the problem of Kantian heteronomy. And this intellectual feat has the most extensive consequences in the entire realm of socio-scientific reasoning, intellection, construction, and application between the functional meanings of monotheism and the various aspects of heteronomy. We have exemplified this deepening and expansive problem in terms of money, finance, and the real economy, and micro and macro dimensions of socio-scientific thought. Much on this socio-scientific *problematique* of thought and reasoning will follow.

Yet for all the significant contribution of Ghazzali to epistemology, his line of intellection remained one-directional – from the revealed monotheistic law to the moral construction of thought, reasoning, and the world-system in its generality and particulars. We do not find in Ghazzali any explanation of the other part that completes the meaning of knowledge as the comprehension and consciousness based on unification in the midst of causality. Unification means circular causality, not simply the determination of the world in a one-directional effect of the moral law.

Wehr (1976) and Macdonald (1987, 8:704) write on the meaning of *tawhid* (see Buchman, op cit. p. xxxi): "*Tawhid* is an Arabic noun that literally means 'unification and union'. It is derived from a verb which means 'to make one, to unite, to unify." In Islamic theology it has come to mean "belief in the unity of God; the profession of the unity of God; and monotheism." The socio-scientific implication we derive from these explanations of the cardinal root of knowledge in Islamic monotheism that Ghazzali professed, is the two-way circular organic unification of knowledge, and likewise, circular-causal unification of the knowledge-induced relational world-system on the basis of the episteme of unity of the monotheistic law (*tawhid*). Ghazzali could not accomplish this task of inter-causal unification by relational dynamics.

Yet Ghazzali did refer to the cause-effect circular causality, except between material entities. The questions that beg for explanation in Ghazzali's limitation of the cause-effect circularity to temporal causes alone are these: Firstly, how does the return of *tawhid* to itself at the Great Event[1] of the hereafter explain the circular causality of this large scale universe of 'everything'? Secondly, what initiates the process-oriented evolutionary learning in the circularity between causes and effects?[2] How is this dynamic explained in the context of the closure (attaining learning equilibriums) and openness of evolutionary learning (intra-systemic and inter-systemic evolutionary epistemology) (Choudhury, 2012)?

These questions cannot be answered in reference to the epistemology of unity of knowledge unless the questions of the large-scale universe and the circular causations within it are regenerated by the continued action of the primal ontological cause. Such a dynamic explains the *tawhidi* continuity in the world-system as the active law until the hereafter. Yet God and monotheism are not within the inter-causal relations. Hence they are not rendered to processes in the dynamics of being and becoming. By delaying the answer to these subtle questions, the project of unification of knowledge and the knowledge-induced world, remained incomplete. This is despite the rationalist ideas to render evolution to an uncharted path caused by the random human will.

---

[1] *Qur'an* (78) *Naba ul-Azim*.

[2] *Qur'an* (57:3): "He is the First and the Last, the Evident and the Immanent: and He has full knowledge of all things."
Qur'an (92:16): "And verily unto Us (belong) the End and the Beginning."
Qur'an (42:53): "The Way of God, to Whom belongs whatever is in the heavens and whatever is on earth. Behold (how) all affairs tend towards God!"

Figure 6.2 summarizes the kinds of reasoning in the three different epistemological viewpoints towards understanding reality, namely, Kant, Ghazzali, and *tawhidi* circular causation dynamics.

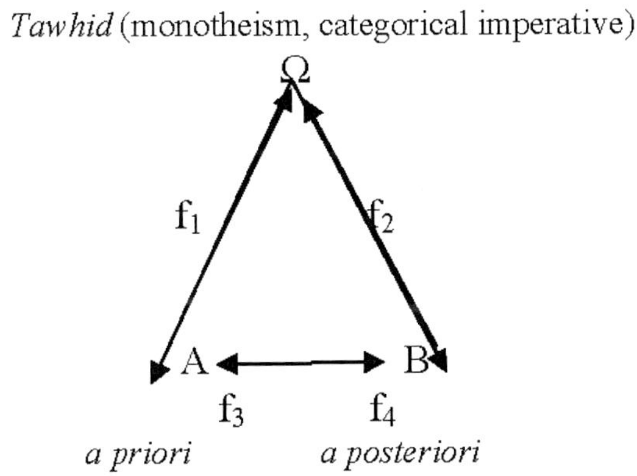

Figure 6.2: Comparative and contrasting epistemologies between Kantian heteronomy and Ghazzali's peripatetic thoughts and the *tawhidi* explanation

1. *Kantian heteronomy*: Functional mappings $f_1(\Omega)$, $f_2(\Omega)$, $f_4 \bullet f_3$ and $f_3 \bullet f_4$ are undefined. Consequently, $f_3 \bullet f_1$ is undefined; $f_4 \bullet f_2$ is undefined. The result is that, the mappings f_1, f_2. f_3, f_4 are independent of each other and separable functional maps.
2. *Ghazzali's causality*: f_1 is well-defined; f_4 is well-defined. Therefore, $f_4 \bullet f_1$ is well-defined. Besides, $f_3 \bullet f_4$ and $f_4 \bullet f_3$ of the material world of inter-causality are well-defined. Yet the reverse mappings $f_3^{-1} \bullet f_2^{-1}$ and $f_4^{-1} \bullet f_1^{-1}$ are not well-defined.
3. Tawhidi circular causation dynamics: All the functions as shown are well-defined. Consequently, $f_3^{-1} \bullet f_2^{-1}$ and $f_4^{-1} \bullet f_1^{-1}$ are well-defined. Yet because of the permanent incompleteness of evolutionary knowledge, circular causality will leave gaps in our consciousness and applications, and thereby, in the moral construction of the world-system. Therefore, $(f_2 \bullet f_3) \bullet (f_3^{-1} \bullet f_2^{-1}) = f_2(f_3 \bullet f_3^{-1}) \bullet f_2^{-1} = f_2(a.I)f_2^{-1} = a.I \bullet (f_2 \bullet f_2^{-1}) = a.I \bullet b.I = a.b.I \neq I$, because of this parallax effect of incompleteness of knowledge on knowledge regeneration and the consequential development of the unified world-system, happening either on the positive or negative scale of evolutionary learning (conversely de-learning). For this reason of the dynamics in the evolutionary learning processes, the coefficients 'a' and 'b' are functions of knowledge-flows arising

from the monotheistic epistemological of unity of knowledge and unity of the knowledge-induced world-system.

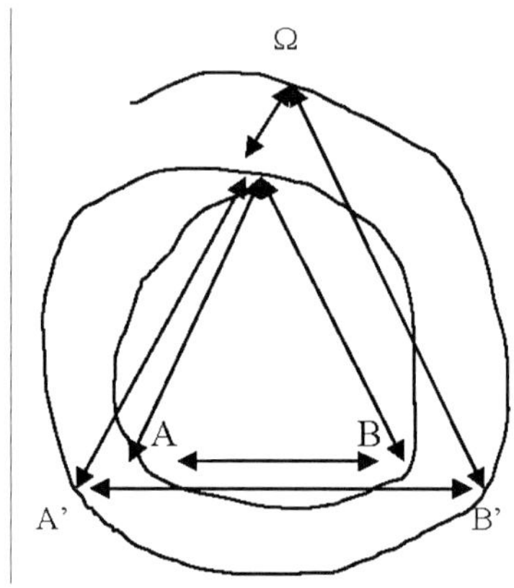

Figure 6.3: Evolutionary learning processes under circular causation caused by the monotheistic law

Figure 6.3 depicts this last case of evolutionary learning, and thus the *tawhidi* circular causation dynamics on the phenomenological plane of unity of knowledge and the unified world-system.

Opening up the scientific research program of *tawhid* and the monotheistic epistemology of unity of knowledge and its concrescence in the unified world-system

We now build on the substantive research issues that underlie the analysis of Figures 6.2 and 6.3. The scientific research program that emanates from the underlying inquiry negates, firstly, the Kantian heteronomy that otherwise spreads thoroughly in modern perspectives of science and society. Secondly, the research program completes the incomplete causality underlying Ghazzali's one-directional correspondence between the monotheistic law and its concrescence. Thirdly, the completeness by the *tawhidi* methodological worldview of Ghazzali's *problematique* of causality, and the logical annulment of Kantian heteronomy, enable the monotheistic law to attain unity of knowledge and unification. This is true in both the general and particular issues of the world-systems relating to 'everything'.

The establishing of the scientific research program of *tawhidi* epistemology requires a detailed explanation and scientific delineation of each of the following steps in the light of the *Qur'an*. The *Qur'an* is explicated by the guidance of the Prophet Muhammad on the *qur'anic* meanings in details.

Firstly, the functional ontology (Gruber, 1993; Maxwell, 1962) of the *Qur'an* and the Prophetic guidance, the *sunnah*, will be established as a super-cardinal topology. Corresponding to this, the topological mappings defined on the super-cardinal topology attain mathematical conception.[3]

Secondly, the primal derivation of knowledge addressing the general system pertaining to the problems and issues under study is to be explained. The meaning of the purpose and objective of the Islamic law, the *maqasid as-shari'ah*, is to be established in reference to the primal *functional* ontology.

Thirdly, the knowledge-flows as rules derived from the *maqasid as-shari'ah*, which is in turn derived from the *tawhidi* ontological origin in respect to a particular set of problems under study, will be explained.

Fourthly, the functional ontology of the derived knowledge-flows representing the epistemology of unity of knowledge as derived from the *tawhidi* premise through the medium of the *maqasid as-shari'ah*, is induced in the organization of the specific problem and issue of the world-system under study. Such an investigation enables the attainment of the normative moral transformation in the light of *tawhid*.

Fifth, the *tawhidi* knowledge-induction of the variables of the specific problem under study is formalized as a generalized model of evaluating the wellbeing criterion. Wellbeing conveys the measure of the degree of unity of relations by complementarities and participation between the variables in the problem under study. The emergent simulation of the wellbeing criterion under the episteme of unity of knowledge is carried out by the circular causation relations between the variables of the wellbeing objective function.

Sixth, the ending of the given process of evaluation of the wellbeing, as the criterion of empirically measuring the degree of complementarities or substitutions as required in the light of the *maqasid as-shari'ah* between the selected variables, is carried into the next process of evolutionary learning. The foundational *tawhidi* episteme is recalled to restart the next and subsequent co-evolutionary learning processes in continuity and across continuums of knowledge, space, and time.

Seventh, the continuity of the learning processes through their variegated experience between truth and error is shown to end in the hereafter

---

[3] See also the appendix to Chapter 1 for concepts on topology, super-cardinality, and super-space mapping on super-cardinal topology.

(*akhira*). The hereafter is thus equated with the Great Event of the fully unravelled *tawhid* at the end as it was in the beginning of creation.

Figure 6.4 shows that, *tawhid* as episteme (Foucault, trans. by Sheridan, 1972)[4] is the totality of the three cells shown:

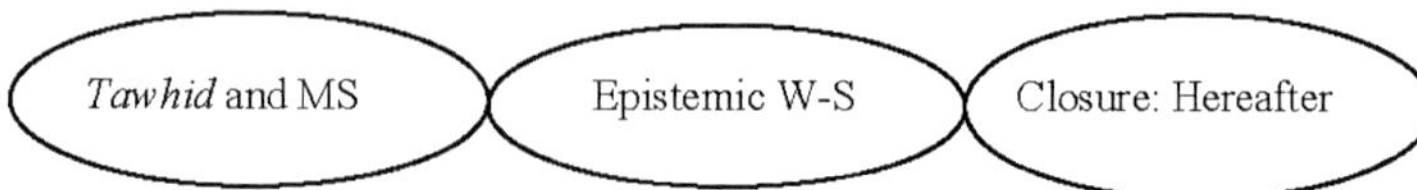

$\Omega \rightarrow_S$ $(\theta \rightarrow \text{W-S}(\theta))$ $\rightarrow$ continuity until $\rightarrow_S \rightarrow \Omega$

Thus: $[(\Omega,S) \rightarrow (\theta,\mathbf{x}(\theta);\ W(\mathbf{x}(\theta))]_1 \rightarrow$ co-evolution of $[.]_1$ into process $2 \rightarrow (\Omega,S)$

MS: *maqasid as-shari'ah*; W-S: specifics issues of world-system in the light of *tawhid.*

Figure 6.4: The continuous loops of interrelations along the *tawhidi* unified worldview

Establishing the primal functional ontology of *tawhid* and MS

(Ω,S) is the super-cardinal space of all relational mappings across 'everything'. This totality comprises both the truth domain and the falsehood domain over which the *qur'anic* law prevails as the criterion between truth and falsehood. In this regard, the *Qur'an* (8:29) declares, "O ye who believe! If ye fear God, He will grant you a Criterion (to judge between right and wrong)…"

Furthermore, in respect to the fullness of both knowledge $\{\theta\}$, and the oppositeness of de-knowledge (falsehood) $\{\bar{\theta}\}$, both being determined in the primal ontology of the monotheistic law (the *Qur'an*), the *Qur'an* (25:1-2) states: "Blessed is He Who sent down the Criterion to His Servant, that it may be an admonition to all creatures – He to Whom belongs the dominion of the heavens and the earth: … no son has He begotten, nor has He a partner in His dominion: It is He Who has created all things, and ordered them in due proportion." These verses establish the

[4] Foucault on episteme: Foucault (see Sheridan,1972, p. 191) defines the word *episteme* as follows: "By *episteme* we mean … the total set of relations that unite, at a given period, the discursive practices that give rise to epistemological figures, sciences, and possibly formalized systems … The episteme is not a form of knowledge (*connaissance*) or type of rationality which, crossing the boundaries of the most varied sciences, manifests the sovereign unity of a subject, a spirit, or a period; it is the totality of relations that can be discovered, for a given period, between the sciences when one analyses them at the level of discursive regularities."

conjoint functions of the *tawhidi* worldview in the absolute oneness of being and the relational becoming of the world of mind and matter *res extensa* on the basis of the *tawhidi* relational praxis governing both good *and* bad.

The universal role that the ontological mapping 'S' plays irrevocably in mapping the *qur'anic* monotheistic law onto the world-system can be read off the following *qur'anic* (25:6) verse: "Say: 'The (*Qur'an*) was sent down by Him Who knows the mystery (that is) in the heavens and the earth: verily He is oft-forgiving, Most-Merciful."

Yet for all, de-knowledge has its determination in and by the *Qur'an*. It has no independent power of existence. In this regard the *Qur'an* (7:16-18) affirms: "He (*iblis*) said: "Because thou hast thrown me out of the Way, lo! I will lie in wait for them on Thy Straight Way: Then will I assault them from before them and behind them, from their right and their left: Nor wilt Thou find in most of them, gratitude (for Thy mercies)." (God) said: "Get out from this (paradise), disgraced and expelled. If any of them follow thee, -- Hell will I fill with you all."

The primal ontology of the monotheistic law in (Ω,S) bears the essence of universality and uniqueness by virtue of its capacity to explain *both* truth and falsehood as contrasting domains of reality. Anything in between these two opposites are aberrations that soon disappear in temporal experience as knowledge advances, and thereby, well-defines truth while it identifies falsehood opposite to truth.[5] These verses establish knowledge as mercy, and de-knowledge as darkness of the heart, mind, and the world. Thereby monotheism annuls rationalism as the ground for knowledge by its self-created vision of reality that does not understand the purpose and order that is ingrained in creation as unity of being and becoming. This is manifest in 'everything' as a system and cybernetic grand design of the multi-universes (Choudhury, 2014 forthcoming). The result then is the annulment of heteronomy in human understanding of unified reality. The domain of knowledge, comprehension and consciousness is then extended beyond the space-time limitation of reality to the knowledge-space-time structure encompassing 'everything' by the monotheistic law.

Importantly, in this final overarching universality of the monotheistic law that annuls the rationalist postulate of heteronomy, is the mapping of super-cardinality of Ω by the transmission medium of the *sunnah* (S). The

---

[5] *Qur'an* (3:7): He it is Who has sent down to thee the Book: In it are verses basic or fundamental (of established meaning); they are the foundation of the Book; others are allegorical. ...... and those who are firmly grounded in knowledge say: "We believe in the Book; the whole of it is from our Lord:" and none will grasp the Message except men of understanding."

problem of dichotomy of synthesis, as in Kant, is now resolved by this bridging of the relational mappings. They form the topology of all monotheistic rules that emanate from Ω and are carried through by the well-defined mapping S. Thus $S(\Omega) \subset \Omega$, with the closure property of the large-scale multi-universe of the seen and unseen; abstract and revealed. Yet all these are causally interrelated by the organism of the monotheistic episteme. The closure property is thus given by the *Qur'an* as, $\Omega \rightarrow S(\Omega) \rightarrow \Omega$.

This mathematically 'complete' but not terminally 'compact' topological mapping in the sense of unbounded domain of Ω establishes universality of law, relations, form, and explanation of the multi-universes by inter-entity unifying causality. Such a mapping having the power of explaining both knowledge and 'de-knowledge', that is truth and falsehood, or monotheism and rationalism, respectively, explains the nature of the rationalistic folds of thought, functions, and structures. On the contrary, rationalist mappings, governed as they are by rationalism everywhere, cannot explain the kind of *tawhidi* mapping given above. Rationalism thereby cannot access the completeness realm of monotheism. In the technical appendix to this chapter we elaborate on the mathematical proof of the above attributes of universality and uniqueness of $\Omega \rightarrow S(\Omega) \rightarrow \Omega$. The *Qur'an* (92:13) declares in regards to this completeness of the monotheistic closure: "And verily unto Us (belong) the End and the Beginning."

A commentary of this last verse in the light of the fullness of knowledge and the evolutionary learning of all temporal things can be derived from Ghazzali's explanation of the verse (trans. Karim, n.d. p. 247): "He is the First in comparison with the things created as all things come from Him in seriatim one after another. He is the Last in comparison with the things that will remain, as they will return from stage to stage till they return to God. That is the end of their journey. So He is the First of the past things and He is the Last of the future things."

A further extension can be made of the meanings of the monotheistic continuity between the first and the second, and thereby by evolutionary epistemology arising from circle 1 of Figure 6.4. The small-scale universes are embedded in the large-scale universe. Because these sub-universes (world-systems) are members of the total multi-dimensional universe of creation, and because the latter is a super-cardinal topology, every member of this topological super-space is, therefore, a topological subset. Consequently, the dynamics of evolutionary learning in the large-scale universe, namely the string depiction, $\Omega \rightarrow S(\Omega) \rightarrow \Omega$, is repeated in the small-scale and the infinitesimal inter-event cases. The *tawhidi* phenomenology thus transcends from (Ω,S) in respect of any event, to (Ω,S), along the evolutionary learning processes as they emerge and continue across continuums of (knowledge, space, and time)-structure. Such a topological continuity of an evolutionary learning character in monotheistic unity of knowledge is asserted by the *Qur'an* (1:1-2): "In the name of God, Most Gracious, Most Merciful, Praises be to God, the Cherisher and Sustainer of the Worlds" (*Alameen*). We will now explain this important second circle of Figure 6.4 in itself and in relation to the (Ω,S)-circle.

Maqasid as-shari'ah in relation to the *tawhidi* primal ontological box

The purpose and objective of Islamic law (*shari'ah*) is the functional derivation of rules out of the monotheistic law aimed at the wellbeing of all. Wellbeing measures the degree of complementary relations between human beings and the world-system. Such unified relations convey the service to *Allah* by way of the monotheistic law as denoted and explained in (Ω,S). The notation for such an epistemic relationship of *maqasid as-shari'ah* with the primal *tawhidi* premise is denoted by $(\Omega,S)\rightarrow\{\theta^*\}$. Here (Ω,S) stands for the completion of the overarching mapping of the super-cardinal topological super-space by the mapping S, such that the following mappings apply: $S(\Omega) \subset \Omega$, both in the small-scale events and the large-scale multi-dimensional universe. $\{\theta^*\}$ is the general derivation of rules out of the primal sources, the *Qur'an* and the *sunnah,* to understand the grand generalized perspective of the *qur'anic* meaning of unity of knowledge in studying the issues at hand. The medium in such a derivation of the generalized *qur'anic* worldview is the *sunnah*. The result then is to understand, decipher, and interpret, the generalized meaning of the issues under consideration in the light of the *Qur'an* and the *sunnah*.

A conclusion that naturally arises from the understanding of the *maqasid as-shari'ah* in its direct link with the *Qur'an* and the *sunnah* towards developing the interpretive capacity of the general perspective surrounds the topic of *fiqh*; interpretive knowledge. *Fiqh,* despite its critical importance in understanding the general and specific issues at hand in the light of the *Qur'an* and the *sunnah,* must return every new investigation on such matters to continuous reference to the primal ontological sources of Islamic knowledge. All human interpretations developed over time can at best serve as assistance and reference, rather than fixed traditions. *Fiqh* therefore needs to be continuously renewed in the epistemological light of *tawhid* in reference to the *Qur'an* and the *sunnah*.

The problem that has arisen from the traditional conception and practice of *fiqh* as the benchmark for an old and legalist aspect of interpretations, has reduced the scope of both *fiqh* and its influence on the development of the *shari'ah*. Today, instead of focusing on the epistemological wealth of knowledge and generalization of the *maqasid as-shari'ah*, and *fiqh*, the *shari'ah* has become a set of edicts on legal contracts. The field of *fiqh* and *shari'ah* has narrowed into personal law, and public affairs (*muamalat*). In the midst of their deepening in these areas alone, the *shari'ah* has not been able to encompass the greater scope of the monotheistic law that generalizes the relations between God, individual, the mind, the world-system, and creates the multi-dimensional abstraction, discourse, and analysis.

The legal contractual nature as opposed to the generalized system of the *shari'ah* is pointed out by Hassan (2002) in relation to business and social ethics. Hassan points out a clear absence of a holistic approach to social ethics involving business or otherwise. Such imperfection of the humanly developed theories of *shari'ah* contracts in different and segmented contracts (*'aqd*) is due to the failure of Islamic scholarship to formulate a generalized universal theory of contracts in the *shari'ah*, be this in personal law or in the law of contracts pertaining to commercial dealings. Instead of a universal and holistic understanding and formalism of a theory of integrated social contracts, scholars have evolved a segmented idea of contracts instead. The result has been contradictions, inefficiencies, and impossibilities in the development and application of business social ethics by a theory of business ethics that is embedded in the interactive dynamics of economy, finance, science, and society.

A better picture of social business ethics, one that would flow from a universal and unified theory of contracts in Islam, could have some of the inner contradictions and conflicts between Islamic financing instruments. For example, the law of avoidance of financial interest (*riba*) is not well integrated with the financing mode of cost-plus pricing in real assets (*murabaha*). The idea of fair profit-sharing ratios between partners in a profit-sharing contract (*mudarabah*) and equity-participation (*musharakah*) remains a problematic concept. The idea of a Diversified Pooled Fund to meet the goals of the *maqasid as-shari'ah* is replaced by a plethora of secondary financing instruments characterized as *shari'ah*-compliant. Yet these segmented instruments miss the epistemic foundation of *maqasid as-shari'ah* in the general-system sense of social ethics and morality. Such is also the concern expressed by Coulson (1984) and Schacht (1964) in respect of their understanding of the Islamic law of *contracts*, contrary to a unique and universal generalized law of *contracts* that can be rendered by the *maqasid as-shari'ah*.

The legal and contractual nature of *shari'ah* being limited to personal, commercial, and public affairs, has resulted in the ignorance of the Islamic community to develop the *tawhidi* type relational overarching linkages between the world and the cosmic generality. For instance, there has not arisen a treatise in modern times except of the learned scholars of the Islamic scholasticism on the theme of justice as balance (*mizan*). Bayrakli (1992) writes on Farabi's theory of justice to span horizontally in *muamalat*, and vertically in relation to the cosmic order. In the *tawhidi* perspective, we consider the domain of *shari'ah* both horizontally and vertically by evolutionary circular causation between these dimensions in the entirety of the world-systems across (knowledge, space, and time)-structure. This last part is the scientific research program that we are formalizing in this work.

The general-system perspective of the *shari'ah* also leaves another important note. That is, since diversity in unity is a hallmark of the *tawhidi* episteme, simply limiting the *maqasid as-shari'ah* to its five traditional implements is not enough. These five are (i) protection and advancement of Islamic religion (monotheism); (ii) protection of reason; (iii) protection of the family; (iv) protection of progeny; (v) protection of property rights. Rather, there are countless other diversities within these given principal parts of the *maqasid as-shari'ah*. The *Qur'an* unravels such countless diversities as signs of God (*ayath-Allah*) (59:24)[6]. From these diversities arise lessons of learning corresponding to the countless many beatific names of *Allah*, called *Asma al-Husna* and the moral construction of the world-system.

Imam Ghazzali can be understood as conveying the same idea of emanation of meanings according to the emergence of knowledge in its continuous-flow form, enabling ever higher flights towards truth (*tawhid*). He wrote (trans. Karim, u.d., p. 245):

> When knowledge was puffed up in his heart, his oil was enkindled. Then light upon light came to him. Then knowledge said to him: Value this moment greatly. Open your eyes, so that you may find the path. When he opened his eyes, he found the pen of God as described. It is not made of reed, it has got no head. It is incessantly writing in the mind or soul of men. He said being surprised at it: What a good thing is knowledge.

---

[6] *Qur'an* (59:24): "He is God, the Creator, the Evolver, the Bestower of Forms (or Colors). To Him belong the Most Beautiful Names….."

Conclusion: Emanation of *tawhidi* world-system in the midst of the monotheistic law

The *Qur'an,* by its explanation of the monotheistic centred and completion of knowledge as the result of circularly causal interaction, integration, and evolutionary phenomenology, annuls heteronomy understood as the separated *a priori* and *a posteriori* domains of reasoning. The consequence then is a holistic, seamless, and continuous interrelationship by unity of knowledge inducing the unified world-system in its generality and particulars. Such a phenomenology with the epistemological basis and its constructive description of the world-system are summarized in the *Qur'an* by the precept of *alameen.* Centred in the *alameen* is the evanescence of the monotheistic law: "Praise be to God, the Lord of the universes" (*Qur'an*, 1:2).

The emergent world-system forms a unified combinatory of diverse sub-systems that are paired together in the light of complementarities and participation as the observed signs of God in the order of reality. The combinatory of interactive, integrative and evolutionary systems (**IIE**) is explained by the *qur'anic* verses (*Qur'an*, 13: 1-5).[7] Here we can categorize the following sub-systems. These together unify the organic interrelations to form a unified world-system with diversity in unity between them. The result is the attainment of wellbeing of all by the dynamics of the monotheistic law of oneness in action.

Consider the sub-system S_1, heavens and cosmology endowed by knowledge in the (knowledge, space, and time)-dimensions.

---

[7] *Qur'an* (13:1-4): "A.L.M.R. These are the Signs of the Book: that which has been revealed unto thee from the Lord is the Truth; but most men believe not. God is He Who raised the heavens without any pillars that ye can see; is firmly established on the Throne (of Authority); He has subjected the sun and the moon (to His Law)! Each one runs (its course) for a term appointed. He does regulate all affairs, explaining the Signs in detail that you may believe with certainty in the meeting with your Lord. And it is He Who spread out the earth, and set thereon mountains standing firm, and (flowing) rivers; and fruit of every kind He made in pairs, two and two: He draws the Night as a veil over the Day. Behold, verily in these things are Signs for those who consider! And in the earth and tracts (diverse though) neighbouring. And gardens and vines and fields sown with corn and palm trees – growing out of single roots or otherwise watered with the same water, yet some of them We make more excellent than others to eat. Behold, verily in these things there are Signs for those who understand!"

Sub-system S_2 denotes earthly topography, again defined by the knowledge-centricity of the monotheistic law.

Sub-system S_3 denotes the ecological and sustainable environmental dimensions of the richness of God's favour on mankind.

Sub-system S_4 denotes extended diversity of divine favours on mankind and the world-system.

Each of these sub-systems is shown to overarch the paired multi-universes for the sole purpose of gaining wellbeing. Wellbeing is maximized in the conscious realization of the moral values only at the Great Event of the hereafter.

The crowning principle over all such paired, that is, participatory and complementary, diversities in explaining the unity of the world-system by the dynamics of consciousness as knowledge, is declared as the Throne (*Istawa*) of God in sole authority. This is the principle of *tawhid.* It governs the generality and details of unity of knowledge and unity of the knowledge-induced (conscious) world-system.

The evolutionary function of unity of knowledge as the epistemology of *tawhid* is explained by the principle of unravelling reality to human comprehension. Revelation of the *Qur'an* commenced with the first four verses of the chapter named *Iqra*, meaning Read – in the Name of your Lord. The fourth verse declares the evolutionary dynamics of knowledge from the source of *tawhid* in the *Qur'an*: "Proclaim! (or Read!) in the name of thy Lord and Cherisher, Who created …. He Who taught (the use of the Pen), -- taught man that which he knew not." Knowledge and learning are thereby evolutionary processes of the highest order of moral construction comprising the conscious understanding of the monotheistic law, *tawhid*, by its functions in the multi-dimensional universe.

By combining the above-mentioned verses explained here, the study of the conscious multi-universe induced by knowledge, and thereby, with divine mercy and balance, can be signified by,

$$S(\theta) = \cup_j \cap_i S_{ij}(\theta). \tag{6.1}$$

This expression next yields the wellbeing criterion of unity of knowledge and its induction of the unified world-system comprising the interaction ($\cup_j$) and integration ($\cap_i$) of the sub-systems $\{S_{ij}(\theta)\}$. The wellbeing function is expressed as,

$$W = W(\cup_j \cap_i S_{ij}(\theta)) = W(\mathbf{x}(\theta)). \tag{6.2}$$

W(.) is evaluated by circular causation methods in terms of the variables of the vector- $\mathbf{x}(\theta)$. That is, $\mathbf{x}_s = f_s(\mathbf{x}_s'(\theta))$; s = 1,2,… n number of inter-causal variables. $\mathbf{x}'(\theta)$ denotes the intra-system and inter-system variables of the vector- $\mathbf{x}(\theta)$. Finally, the wellbeing function can be expressed in its empirical form as the knowledge function, $\theta = F(\mathbf{x}(\theta))$. The evolutionary property is signified by the condition, $dF(\mathbf{x}(\theta))/d\theta > 0$ in its simulated form of positive relationship between knowledge-flows, $\{\theta\}$, while correcting for the variation of signs in the estimated coefficients of the circular causation relations to attain inter-variables balance by complementarities, and thus participation.

In regards to the big picture of social evolution including the socio-scientific evolutionary theory premised on unity of knowledge, the verses of *Iqra* (Read!) establish the evolutionary socio-scientific worldview of *tawhid* in action. Such a *qur'anic* exegesis goes beyond the limited, though profound understanding of the divine description of the human reproductive process. The exegesis of the verses can now be organized as follows to bring out the socio-scientific *tawhid*-centred worldview:

Verses 1-5 explain the fundamental power of *tawhid* in all of creation, specified to the human reproductive process but extended to the advent of human society.

Verses 6-17 denote the description of the events of the world-system that are variegated between truth and falsehood in the choices by free human will.

Verses 18-19 denote returning back to God, with the stock of knowledge against 'de-knowledge'. This is the ultimate determination of total reality. It marks the episteme of our total existence. It seals the sure reality of truth overwhelming all of falsehood: "Nay, heed him not: But bow down in adoration, and bring thyself the closer (to God)" (*Qur'an*, 96, 19). Abdullah Yusuf Ali (1946, p. 1763) comments on this concluding verse of the chapter *Iqra* (edited): ".... For God is always close to him – closer to him than his jugular veins[8]. Man's humility and adoration remove him from being an insolent rebel on the one hand, and on the other, prepare his will to realize his nearness to God."

Thus in the end, in reference to Figure 4.4, the *tawhidi* phenomenological worldview has now been completed by the above-mentioned *qur'anic* exegesis. The stages of the small-scale and large-scale universes embedded in 'everything' are now organized as follows: (1)

[8] (*Qur'an*, 50:16): "It was We Who created man, and We know what dark suggestions his soul makes to him: for We are nearer to him than (his) jugular vein." Thus *tawhid* is evanescent everywhere and in 'everything'.

tawhid is engrained in the monotheistic law. (2) The monotheistic law is the criterion of the world-system between truth (knowledge) and falsehood (de-knowledge). (3) The closure of the multi-dimensional universes returns the large-scale (knowledge, space, and time)-dimensions to *tawhid* in the end as in the beginning.

Technical Appendix: Mathematical Excursions on the Concepts of Uniqueness and Universality

Concept of super-cardinality leading to the precepts of uniqueness and universality of the *tawhidi* epistemological methodology

In the mathematical theory of transfinite cardinals, it is shown that there can be several classes of numbers each with their own sequences of members. Hence, if ‘n’ is a class of numbers of any system (natural, rational, irrational, etc.) then this class can be further subdivided into subclasses, which repeat the process in progressions. Each such class of numbers must then be inexhaustible. Hence, a number can be assigned by induction for every number of these classes. This is the concept of infinity as belonging to that class of numbers. George Cantor (1955) denoted this concept of the dimension of transfinite numbers by N_0, the smallest class of transfinite cardinal numbers having its own measure of infinity. We call N_0 the cardinality of n. However, for 2^n numbers for different values of n, the number of transfinite cardinal classes that can be generated is greater than the cardinality of N_0. Likewise, for $(2^n)^n$ numbers the cardinality must be greater than the cardinality of 2^n, hence much greater than the cardinality of n, and so on. Each of the classes of numbers in the set, $\{n, 2^n, (2^n)^n, ...\}$ has an infinity of its own. But these infinities are in an ascending range, signifying that the cardinality of these classes of numbers is increasing. Thus there is a way in mathematics to rank the magnitude of infinities by means of comparing cardinalities of classes of transfinite numbers.

If this concept of transfinite cardinals was used for ranking the evolving spaces of knowledge, all moving perpetually towards the *tawhidi* universal super-space of knowledge, then each of the subspaces of $T(\theta)$ can be seen as having exactly the cardinalities arranged in increasing magnitudes. The infinity for $T(\theta)$ in the language of cardinalities is thus the highest cardinality of all the evolutionary epistemologies.

Now to make this highest cardinality functionally useful to establish the type of correspondences between the $T(\theta)$ super-space and the temporal order, say $A_i(\theta) \in T(\theta)$, $i = 1,2,...$, all that we need to do is treat $T(\theta)$ as a real space of highest cardinality. Let us denote this by $(2^N)^{...(\text{power of } \infty)}$. Now any correspondence between $T(\theta)$ and $A_i(\theta)$ is not in terms of the infinity of $T(\theta)$ but in relation to the cardinality $(2^N)^{...(\text{power of } \infty)}$. We define the cardinality of $T(\theta)$ as $\text{Card}.T(\theta) = \text{supremum}.\{\text{card } N_0, \text{card},2^{No}, \text{card}.(2^{No})^{No}, ... (2^{No})^{...(\text{power of } \infty)}\}$. Furthermore, card.$N_0$, card.$2^{No}$, etc. form increasing cardinalities of the subsets $A_i(\theta) \in T(\theta)$, i = 1,2,....

Now define the functions, t: card.$T(\theta) \rightarrow \{card.A_i(\theta)\}$, so that it would now be possible to find Neighbourhood$\{t(card.T(\theta))\} \in \{card.A_i(\theta)\}$, but it is impossible to define an 'onto' mapping, $t':\{card.A_i(\theta)\} \rightarrow card.T(\theta)$. This is the same thing as saying that, the mind-space of $T(\theta)$ is too vast to be comprehended fully by temporal reality, but itself can comprehend perfectly all of temporal reality. The *shari'ah* is at point here. The *shari'ah* is the worldly perfection of divine law in the realm of all human thought. But only a portion can be comprehended through the exercise of knowledge-flows in the $A_i(\theta)$ realm. Only when $T(\theta)$ is attained in the hereafter, will the perfection of the *shari'ah* dawn in that reality. God in His incommensurate vastness will unravel to mankind the fullest extent of the wisdom and essence of *tawhid*. In temporal life, our comprehension and thus our exercise of the *shari'ah* derived from the *tawhidi* worldview would always remain imperfect, incomplete, and thereby evolutionary, not optimal.

When the relationship of knowledge and infinite reward is seen in the context of Card.$T(\theta)$, then for purposes of generating interrelationships between $T(\theta)$ and $A_i(\theta)$, the concept of infinity must mean a transfinite cardinal with infinite cardinality as the supremum of all other ascending cardinalities. We refer to this upper limiting cardinality of the *tawhidi* topology as *super-cardinality*. In this context it is logical to see now that the infinity in rewards for acts of goodness returned to the believer in the hereafter is a reality and not a mathematical tautology of infinity.

When we take the concept of infinity in relation to the supremum of cardinalities, we solve the problem of infinities in equations transforming the various forces of nature into a unified field. The most difficult infinity arises when gravity is combined with the other forces of nature. It then becomes increasingly necessary to move away from the quantum and relativistic mix (quantum gravity) to address the unification problem involving gravitational force. The alternative to us is the formulation of mathematical axioms of initial conditions that would subsequently play topological relations between systems of realities in all fields of knowledge over the (knowledge, space and time)-dimensions.

The *tawhidi* manifestation of such a structure as explained above shows that the $A_i(\theta)$ may denote different precepts of realities in such a field over knowledge, space and time. This approach would allow unification to take place under the choices of all classes of functions that satisfy the two-way mappings as shown above by t and t'. Hence, if t' exists, then $t_1'^{\circ}t_2'^{\circ}t_3'^{\circ}$.... would define the compound mapping of the sequence of mappings like 't' over expanding sets of $A_i(\theta)$ with expanding cardinalities. Likewise, $t_1{}^{\circ}t_2{}^{\circ}t_3{}^{\circ}$.... would define the compound mapping of t from $T(\theta)$ 'onto' $A_i(\theta)$.

According to the above *qur'anic* verse, since goodness is recompensed beyond measure, $(t_1'^{\circ}t_2'^{\circ}...)^{\circ}(t_1^{\circ}t_2^{\circ}...) = (t_1'^{\circ}t_1)^{\circ}(t_2'^{\circ}t_2)^{\circ}...\neq 1$, because of the differences in cardinalities between the subsets $A_i(\theta)$ and between $T(\theta)$ and $A_i(\theta)$, i = 1,2,... Also note that there can be infinitely many combinations among the mappings t'_j and t_k's; j,k=1,2,.... This result signifies that the choices of methods and directions to attain the supreme felicity of the hereafter are infinitely many, but all are based on the interactive, integrative, and evolutionary (**IIE**) relations explaining circular causality between the $A_i(\theta)$ subsets and the $T(\theta)$ mind-space. This means that, given the tenets of the *shari'ah*, only its hard core of the *tawhidi* precept and the *sunnah* (Prophetic guidance) need to be maintained immutable. Apart from this fundamental epistemology of *tawhid*, the *Qur'an* gives freedom to exercise multitude of alternative approaches towards understanding, applying, and enhancing the causal relationships between $A_i(\theta)$ and $T(\theta)$.

We show the above universal epistemic-ontic circular causation interrelationships between $A_i(\theta)$ subsets and the $T(\theta)$ set in Figure 6A.1. The multiplicity of the t'_j and t'_k mappings and their compounding is shown in the lattices.

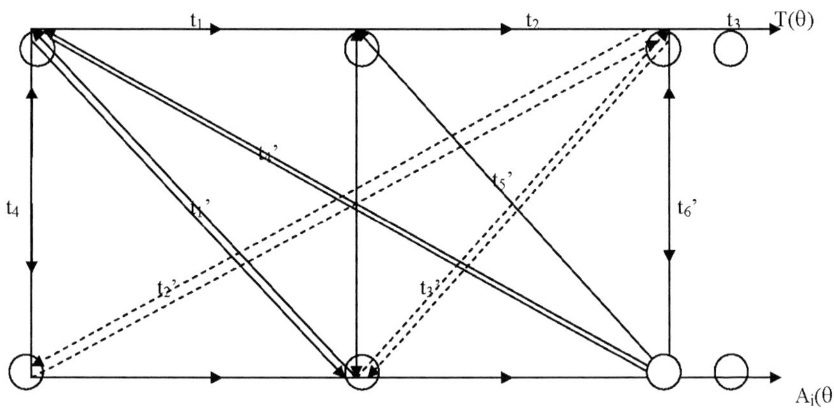

Figure 6A1: Lattices of compound mappings between $A_i(\theta)$ and $T(\theta)$

It needs to be noted that, since neither t nor t' comprises complete mappings between $A_i(\theta)$ subsets and $T(\theta)$ space, the infinity of compound mappings must suggest that there is endless openness in the mathematical structure of $T(\theta)$-space. This is a perception that has also been given by Godel (1965) in his Incompleteness Theorem of Mathematical Systems. But because every one of such possibilities assumes cardinality in the set of increasing cardinalities, the problem of infinity is removed from these relationships by transforming all such infinities into classes of numbers and functions with cardinalities having different orders of infinities. All that matters now is to give a good definition of the series of interrelationships in terms of the compound mappings as shown.

Finally, it can be noted that in the system of transformations herein implied, there is no relevance of time when mappings are between t and t', that is, between what ordinarily would seem to be infinite sequential time. Hence, the interrelationships must now be explained in terms of events and relations rather than time. Such events and relations are the realizations of and by the *shari'ah*. In other words, events and time are determined by the pre-existence of *tawhidi* knowledge-flows inducing them. The timeless nature of such mappings and the replacement of the time-concept by the knowledge-event relational concept also establish the permanence of the *shari'ah* over (knowledge, space and time)-dimensions. In the above *qur'anic* verse this fact is pointed out by the statement, "They will abide therein forever". This abidance is realized in the hereafter, that is, upon realizing $T(\theta)$ by the fullness of the *tawhidi* stock of knowledge bestowing the supreme felicity (wellbeing).

Topology

Being a topology (Maddox, 1970), the existence of knowledge-induced events is defined by the properties of the subsets of such events. Thus, with $\{\theta\}$ as the given *stock of knowledge*, and θ being the flow of knowledge, it is mapped 'onto' the whole of the topology, T, giving $T(\theta)$ maps 'onto' the subsets of T denoted by T_i giving $T_i(\theta)$. Hence, $\cup_i[T_i(\theta)] \subset T(\theta)$; $\cap_i[T_i(\theta)] \subset T(\theta)$. These properties mean that the entire topology, 'T', is spanned by the totality of all its subsets of knowledge, and there is integration among these subsets to yield a knowledge-induced consensus, which forms part of the knowledge-topology. Only relations, as they are affected by the knowledge variable, matter in this topology. When the primordial stock (or topologically complete stock) $\{\theta\}$ is so mapped into the temporal order to give good definition to forms and their relations, then $T_i(\theta)$ becomes a functional of the *flow of knowledge*, $\{\theta\}$

The topological mapping on the super-cardinal space of monotheistic law, understood now as the super-space, that is a space with super-cardinality comprising all laws affecting abstraction and corporeality, is defined on the *tawhidi* super-cardinal space. The definition of $T(\theta)$ means the transcendental evolutionary bundles of all relational mappings as is shown in Figure 6A.1 by its multi-dimensionality. The *Qur'an* (10:31) declares in this regard: "Say:

'Who is it that sustains you (in life) from the sky and from the earth? Or who is it that has power over hearing and sight? And who is it that brings out the living from the dead and the dead from the living? And who is it that rules and regulates all affairs?' They will soon say, 'God'. Say, 'Will ye not then show piety (to Him)?'"

The *Qur'an* (10:32) further declares in respect to the ultimate completeness of the super-cardinal space of divine monotheistic knowledge in (Ω,S): "Such is God, your real Cherisher and Sustainer: Apart from Truth, what (remains) but error? How then are ye turned away?"

Universality and uniqueness of *tawhidi* worldview

On the matter of Truth and Falsehood as functional ontological domains in the light of the *tawhidi* worldview, here is a topological formalism:

We prove here the following theorem.

> The episteme of unity of knowledge represented by pervasive systemic complementarities is both unique and universal in explaining the nature of systemic unity and methodological individualism. Contrarily, the model of methodological individualism cannot explain the worldview of unity of knowledge.

Let $\{\theta\} \in (\Omega^T,S^T) \subset (\Omega,S)$ for systems, s = 1,2,..,N. T denotes the system of wellbeing conveying entities. Yet both complementarities of wellbeing and methodological individualism are comprised in (Ω,S).

$\Rightarrow \cup_{\text{interaction}}\{\mathbf{x}(\theta),\theta\} \subset (\Omega^T,S^T)$; the interactive or diversity condition;

$\cap_{\text{integration}}\{\mathbf{x}(\theta),\theta\} \neq \phi \subset (\Omega^T,S^T)$, the integrative condition,

$\cup_{\text{interaction}}\cap_{\text{integration}}\{\mathbf{x}(\theta),\theta\} \neq \phi \subset (\Omega^T,S^T)$, interactive and integrative condition

These are the properties of subsets belonging to (Ω,S), which because it is denumerable and non-commensurate, forms a super-space (Rucker, 1983).

Because of methodological individualism in the Falsehood domain denoted by ~,

$\cup_{\text{interaction}}\cap_{\text{integration}}\{x\sim(\theta\sim),\theta\sim\} = \phi \subset (\Omega\sim,S\sim) \subset (\Omega,S)$ as Falsehood facts.

Since these facts form a super-space within (Ω,S), we denote it by (Ω^T,S^T), such that, $(\Omega\sim,S\sim)\cap(\Omega^T,S^T) = \phi$; and $(\Omega\sim,S\sim)\cup(\Omega^T,S^T) = (\Omega,S)$.

Because $\{\mathbf{x}\sim(\theta\sim),\theta\sim\} \in (\Omega\sim,S\sim)$ and $\{\mathbf{x}(\theta),\theta\} \in (\Omega,S)$, therefore, $\{\mathbf{x}(\theta),\theta\} \cup \{\mathbf{x}\sim(\theta\sim),\theta\sim\} \in (\Omega^T,S^T) \cup (\Omega\sim,S\sim) = (\Omega,S)$

Therefore, (Ω,S) explains both the domains of truth and falsehood.

Contrarily, starting from $(\Omega\sim,S\sim)$ primordially yields,

$$\cup_{\text{interaction}} \cap_{\text{integration}} \{x\sim(\theta\sim),\theta\sim\} = \phi \notin (\Omega^T,S^T) \text{ but } \phi \in (\Omega\sim,S\sim).$$

Therefore, neither (Ω^T,S^T) nor $(\Omega\sim,S\sim)$ can explain total reality. Only (Ω,S) explains total reality.

Consequently, (Ω,S) is universal in explaining 'everything'.

(Ω,S) is unique because neither (Ω^T,S^T) nor $(\Omega\sim,S\sim)$ by themselves can explain total reality.

References

Baldani, J. Bradfield, J. & Turner, R.W., 2005, *Mathematical Economics*, 129-131, Thomson, Canada.

Bayrakli, B., 1992, "The concept of justice (*Adl*) in the philosophy of Al-Farabi", *Hamdard Islamicus*, (V)3.

Bohr, N., 1985, "Discussion with Einstein on epistemological issues", in H. Folse Ed. *The Philosophy of Neils Bohr: The Framework of Complementarity*, North Holland Physics Publications, Amsterdam, the Netherlands.

Boulding, K.E., 1971., "Economics as a moral science", in Glass J.F. & Staude J.R. (eds.), *Humanistic Society*, Goodyear Publishing Co. Inc., Pacific Palisades, CA.

Buchman, D., 1998, *Al-Ghazali The Niche of Lights*, Brigham Young University Press, Provo, Utah.

Cantor, G., ed. by Jourdain, P., 1955, *Contributions to the Founding of the Theory of Transfinite Numbers*, Dover, New York, NY.

Choudhury, M.A., 1997, The epistemologies of Ghazzali, Kant and the alternative, formalism in unification of knowledge applied to the concepts of markets and sustainability", *International Journal of Social Economics*, (24)7/8/9, 918-940.

—. 2010, "Unity of knowledge versus Kant's heteronomy with reference to the problem of money, finance, and real economy relations in a new global architecture", *International Journal of Social Economics*, (37)10, 764-778.

—. 2014, *The Socio-Cybernetic Study of God and the World-System,*, Ideas Group Inc., Philadelphia, PA., USA.

Coulson, N.J., 1984, *Commercial Law in the Gulf States: The Islamic Legal Tradition*, Graham & Trotman, London, Eng.

Edel, A., 1970, "Science and the structure of ethics", in Neurath, O. Carnap, R. & Morris, C. (eds.), *Foundations of the Unity of Science*, University of Chicago Press, Chicago, ILL.

Friedman, M., 1989, "The quantity theory of money", in Eatwell, J. Milgate, M. & Newman, P. (eds.), *New Palgrave: Money*, pp. 1-40, W.W. Norton, New York, NY.

Georgescu-Roegen, N., 1981, *The Entropy Law and the Economic Process* Harvard University Press, Cambridge, MA.

Godel, K., 1965, "On formally undecidable propositions of *Principia Mathematica* and related systems", in Davis, M (ed.), *The Undecidable*, Raven Press, Hewlett, NY.

Gruber, T.R., 1993, "A translation approach to portable ontologies", *Knowledge Acquisition*, (5)2, 199-200.

Hassan, H., 2002, "Contracts in Islamic law: The principles of commutative justice and liberality", *Journal of Islamic Studies*, (13)3, 257-297.

Hayek, F.A., 1976, *Law, Legislation and Liberty, the Mirage of Social Justice, vol. 2*, The University of Chicago Press, Chicago, ILL.

Holton, R.L., 1992, *Economy and Society*, Routledge. London, Eng.

Hubner, K. trans.) by Dixon, P.R. Jr. & Dixon, H.M., 1985, "Foundations of a universal historistic theory of the empirical sciences", in his *Critique of Scientific Reason*, pp.105-122, The University of Chicago Press, Chicago, IL.

Hull, D.L.,1988, *Science as a Process, an Evolutionary Account of the Social and Conceptual Development of Science*, University of Chicago Press, Chicago, IL.

Hunt, W.H., 1979, *The Keynesian Episode, a Reassessment*, Liberty Fund Inc., Indianapolis, Indiana, USA.

Kant, I. trans. by Friedrich, C.J., 1949, "Religion within the limits of reason alone", in Friedrich, C.J., (ed.), *The Philosophy of Kant*, pp. 365-411, Modern Library, New York, NY.

—. trans. by Infeld, L., 1963, "The general principle of morality"; also see "Natural religion", "Prayer", in *Kant's Lectures on Ethics*, Hackett Publishing Co., Indianapolis, IN.

Karim, F., u.d, *Imam Ghazali'sIhyaUlum-Id-Din*, Shah Muhammad Ashraf, Lahore, Pakistan.

Lawson, T., 2003, "An evolutionary economics?" in his, *Reorienting Economics*, pp. 110-140, Routledge, London, Eng.

Lucas, R.E. Jr., 1975, "An equilibrium model of the business cycle", *Journal of Political Economy*, Vol. 83, pp. 1113-44.
Macdonald, D.B., 1987, "*Tawhid*", in E.J. Brill, *First Encyclopaedia of Islam*, E.J. Brill, New York.
Maddox, I.J., 1970, *Elements of Functional Analysis*, Cambridge University Press, Cambridge, Eng.
Maxwell, G., 1962, "The ontological status of theoretical entities", in Feigl, H. & G. Maxwell, G. (eds.), *Minnesota Studies in the Philosophy of Science, Vol. II: Scientific Explanation, Space and Time*, pp. 3-27, University of Minnesota Press, Minneapolis, Minnesota.
Moore, G.E., 1903, *Principia Ethica*, Cambridge University Press, Cambridge, Eng:
Myrdal, G., 1958, "The principle of cumulation", in Streeten, P. (ed.) *Value in Social Theory, a Selection of Essays on Methodology by Gunnar Myrdal*, pp. 198-205, Harper & Brothers Publishers, New York, NY.
North, D. C., 1981, "A theory of institutional change and the economic history of the Western World", in his, *Structure and Change in Economic History*, Chapter15, W.W. Norton, New York.
O'Donnell, R.M., 1989, "Some philosophical background", in his, *Keynes: Philosophy, Economics & Politics*, pp. 11-28, Macmillan, London, Eng.
Penrose, R., 1989, *The Emperor's New Mind*, Oxford University Press, Oxford, Eng.
Pheby, J., 1988, *Methodology and Economics, A Critical Introduction*, Macmillan, London, Eng.
Rucker, R., 1983, "Transfinite Cardinals", in *Infinity and the Mind*, Bantam New Books, New York, NY.
Schacht, J., 1964, *Introduction to Islamic Law*, Clarendon Press, Oxford, Eng.
Schumpeter, J.A., 1961, *The Theory of Economic Development*, Harvard University Press, Cambridge, Mass.
Schumpeter, J.S., 1966, "The scholastic doctors and the philosophers of natural law", in his, *History of Economic Analysis*, Oxford University Press, New York, NY.
Sen, A., 1988, "Conduct, ethics and economics", in his, *On Ethics & Economics*, pp. 88-89, Basil Blackwell, Oxford, UK.
Sztompka, P., 1991, *Society in Action, The Theory of Social Becoming*, The University of Chicago Press, Chicago, IL

Neurath, O. Carnap, R. & Morris, C., (eds.), 1970, *Foundations of the Unity of Science*, Chicago, ILL: University of Chicago Press. This is the work of the Vienna Circle.
Ventelou, B., 2005, "Economic thought on the eve of the General Theory", in *Millennial Keynes*, Chapter 2, M.E. Sharpe, Armonk, New York.
Von Mises, L., 1976, *The Ultimate Foundation of Economic Science*, Sheed Andrews & McMeel, Kansas City, Kansas.
Wehr, H., 1976, *A Dictionary of Modern Written Arabic*, Cowan, J. M. (ed.), Ithaca, Spoken Language Services, New York.

CHAPTER SEVEN

THE *TAWHIDI* METHODOLOGY OF ISLAMIC ECONOMICS AND FINANCE AND ITS INSTITUTIONAL IMPLICATIONS

Background

There is a debate that has been being waged for a considerable time now by so-called Islamic economists and finance experts calling for resorting completely to mainstream methods and models of these fields with some *fiqhi* colouring to them. *Fiqh* means canonical Islamic jurisprudence or rules of the *shar'iah*, the Islamic law, based on religious interpretation. *Fiqhi* inferences colour what the protagonists would like to qualify as 'Islamic'. The retrogressive results have been that Islamic financial institutions, most importantly the Islamic Development Bank and many Islamic banks with exclusive and dual windows, have embraced this mechanistic approach to what they call Islamic financial activities. There are multiple methodological errors in such an approach to what has come to be referred to as 'Islamic Economics' and 'Islamic Finance' and the many themes they comprise. In the end, the result of the intellectual enterprise leaves the observer in a deep predicament of intellectual poverty and loss of self-reliance toward establishing a *qur'anic* worldview transcending both mainstream imitation (*taqlid*) and also sheer *fiqhi* (legalistic interpretive) origin of Islamic thinking.

In regards to the latter case, Asad (1987) writes: "In consequence, our current theology (*kalam*) and canonical jurisprudence (*fiqh*) now resemble nothing so much as a vast old-clothes shop where ancient thought-garments, almost unrecognizable as to their original purport, are mechanically bought and sold, patched up and re-sold, and where the buyer's own delight consists in praising the old tailors' skill."

Such problems multiply during the new millennium even with the rise of post-modernist questioning in intelligentsia and with deepening Islamic crises with the Western World. We want to address this problem of the Muslim predicament as it is premised in the mainstream mould against the backdrop of what otherwise can be truly an Islamic approach and worldview. Our focus in this regard will continue on to be on problems of economics, finance, institutions, social order, and the world-system (Choudhury, 2004a).

Objective

This chapter argues that the submissive attitude and advice on equating the Islamic and mainstream *methodologies* and empirical approaches, thereby calling for adopting mainstream *methods* of analysis, constitutes a flawed reasoning. Instead, reverting to Islamic economics and finance as an embedded study in the ethico-epistemology of divine oneness as the foundation of Islamic law is the principal objective of this chapter. This critical examination is built up by an examination of the idea and practice of Islamic economics and finance and their institutional implications in present times. Epistemological issues are examined in the socio-scientific reconstruction of what this chapter surmises should be the true methodology in Islamic economics, finance, and institutionalism.

Critical methodological issues of Islamic economics and finance

This chapter makes a major difference between the concepts of *Method* and *Methodology*. Choudhury (1999) explains that methodology and methods are interrelated scientific primitives. They are together used for understanding praxis and applying it to inferential consequences of the methodological premise via the use of the corresponding analytical methods.

The original praxis is invariably epistemological in nature. Epistemology is subsequently integrated by a scientific discursive approach with ontology, and thereafter, with the ontic (evidential) domain of analysis, application, and policy formulation. Methods belong to the *functional* ontological (Gruber, 1993) formalism and ontic domains (forms) (Heidegger transl. by Hofstadter, 1988). In these domains the epistemic premise of methodology becomes analytical and applicable.

Yet, in the absence of the epistemological methodology it is possible for methods to be used independently of the ontological and ontic (evidential) understanding. When this is the case, methods fail to have substantive relevance to epistemic methodology. Methods then exist merely as procedural approaches for formalism and analysis. There is no demand in such an approach to for methods to comply with methodology.

Choudhury (1999, op cit, p. 348) writes, "Methods can exist without methodology as was explained in the case of the reductionist design of rationalism. But methodology cannot exist without self-determined methods. Such methods must be derived from the essence of the methodology itself. Methods must be such instruments that mobilize the ontological-epistemological nature of divinely unified systems into explanatory relations." We will explain the difficulties that are encountered in such academic ventures from the Islamic side.

Contrary to the above assertion, we find distancing of the prevailing Islamic socio-scientists from any substantive reference to the *qur'anic* worldview. The epistemology of oneness of the divine law (*tawhid*) has remained absent in formulating the inter-causal understanding of unification of knowledge in issues of world-systems. The epistemological methodology embedded in ontology and ontic learning domains of world-system study remains unknown. Consequently, there remains an utter vacuum in the construction of the Islamic phenomena vis-à-vis its epistemology, the world, and the ontological reconstruction of a socio-scientific normative worldview, which can then convert itself into logical positivism (Choudhury 1998).

Within the broad arena of human inquiry there are massive unanswered questions that span methodology, methods, and both normative and positive construction in the light of the *Qur'an* and the *sunnah* (guidance of the Prophet Muhammad). Without the fundamental epistemological reference there cannot be an authentic building block of the Islamic revolutionary paradigm of its socio-scientific worldview. Within this worldview is the embedded field of Islamic economics, finance, and institutionalism as a subset of study. It is precisely for this intellectual inadequacy of the notion of Islamic economics and now Islamic finance! – that the last seventy years of their existence and the last thirty years of Islamic banking and Islamic development finance organization such as the Islamic Development Bank, have produced no positive challenge and transformation in the Muslim World as it slips into decadence.

An example of ambivalence of Islamic goals in Islamic financing institutions

As an example, the ambivalence of the goal of Islamic intellectual and world-system to the *Qur'an* is proven by a cursory and unplanned use of Islamic charity for human uplift. A haphazard approach exists despite much table talk on the issues of human development at the drawing boards of the Islamic development forums and Islamic banks.

Tables 7.1 and 7.2 point out that allocation in charity as prescribed by the *shari'ah* (2.5% of net wealth) has not met this required level. On the contrary, such allocations dropped from a mere 1.89% of shareholders' wealth in the year 2000 to a meagre 1.42% in the year 2001 - within a year. This performance spells out a meagre picture on one of the critical goals of Islamic financing, which is poverty alleviation by productive transformation of the poor charity-recipients.

On the financing side, the lure for short-term returns on questionable secondary financing outlets is either negligible or questionable. This is shown in Table 7.1 and by the questionable nature of the secondary instruments as marked by (*). In *ijara*, this forward pricing of future rent-setting is like an interest-rate set on future cash-flows. In the securities markets, the capitalization of cash-flows is done by the discounting methods and the use of LIBOR rates. These rates are seriously questionable in the Islamic financing perspective. In fact, such rates stand for shadow interest-rates.

In Table 7.2 we note a flaw in reading the efficiency ratios. For instance, for the needy and poor-returns, there is no meaning in comparing poor and needy funds with the 'total in charity'. The [charity/shareholders' spending] ratio remained low and declined between the years 2000 and 2001. Besides, the share of the needy and poor in charity income as a proportion of shareholders' wealth is far less than the required threshold for zakat payment (2.5 %).

Likewise, the high ratios of retained earnings are in fact a weak sign for the activities of Islamic banks. According to the Islamic philosophy of financing assets in the real economy, Islamic banks ought to show lower rates of the retained earnings. The implication then would be an effective mobilization of depositors' funds into Islamic spending. That is how the rate of interest can be lowered down by replacing loan capital with share-capital and depositors' funds. The result then would be to bring about effective linkages between money, finance, and the real economy. Such is the practical implication of the episteme of unity of knowledge. In the absence of such organic inter-causal unity of relations, Islamic banks remain in permanent misunderstanding on the issue of Islamic financial transformation in the light of the episteme of unity of knowledge and the unified world-system. The epistemic principle is represented in this specific case of complementary linkages between money, finance and the real economy by the use of development-financing instruments.

The Islamic development-financing portfolio is very weakly diversified. There has not been any increase, but rather diminished investment in the primary PLS of profit-sharing (*mudarabah*). Almost all the funds are going into equities (*musharakah*) and mark-up financing (*murabaha*), and into securities in the secondary financial market. The efficiency ratios of Table 7.2 do not bring out the true status of the social effects of Islamic bank financing. The social effects in fact remain very weak. One can see this case by the high ratios of private depositors' returns and the high (equity/liability) ratios. In spite of this financing state, there is weak social impact and a perceived failure in realizing the social benefits from Islamic financing in the face of their questionable validity.

In another case as well, the weakness and ethical failure of Islamic bank financing have been noted. The Organization of Islamic Conferences has recently handed over its global Islamic charitable funds of $3billion for management by the BMB Fund under the asset management theory and model suggested by Rayo Withanage. But consider the percentage of this Zakat Fund: $3billion out of the total of $700billion value of Islamic capital market assets. The capital market funds are expected to grow to 4 trillion dollars in the next few years. The zakat-ratio then would be between 0 and 0.42 percent. So what kind of awareness towards the much-clamoured for social objectives of Islamic banking and finance can be upheld in the face of such poor showing? Besides, OIC's feeling is that the BMB Fund Management as custodian of the OIC global charitable funds will "(position) itself as an institution that marries mainstream and eastern capabilities". Such an aspiration marks exactly the problem of perpetuating the kind of mainstream theory, ideas, model, and management that we have critiqued. Islamic banks have thus shied away from publishing data on their zakat and waqf allocations, not to speak of the charitable funds as a whole.

The above empirical facts point out that Islamic banks to date have failed to attain the participative complementarities between the economic and social goals. The complementary kind of organic embedding of relational unity between all good things of life arises from the episteme of unity of knowledge and of its knowledge-induced perspectives of the world-system. This is the essential principle underlying the Islamic worldview, and thereby, Islamic economics, finance, banking, and the social order. Such kinds of complementary interrelations between the *shari'ah*-driven possibilities mark the *functional* ontology of unity of knowledge. Such a *functional* ontology forms the ethico-epistemological premise of the Islamic worldview that we explain in this chapter. Such an ethico-epistemological premise is the be-all and end-all of the Islamic worldview. It equally grounds economics and finance as well as society and science.

Figure 7.1 depicts the knowledge-induced embedding of systems according to the ever-expanding discursive impact of learning in *tawhidi* unity of knowledge on issues of the world-system. This though is not the nature of Islamic financing prevailing today.

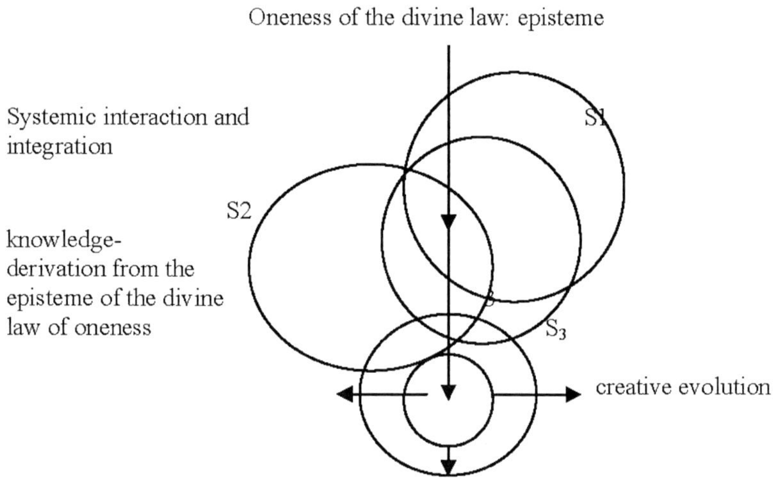

Figure 7.1: Systemic expression of evolutionary knowledge-induced unity of knowledge as episteme

Table 7.1: Financial Indicators for a major Islamic Bank (US Dollars)

	2001	**2000**
Total Investment	35,658,989	23,260,739
Total Liabilities	71,406,905	64,653,836
Retained Earnings	6,936,026	4,788,361
Shareholders' Equity	60,999,688	59,063,352
Total Income	17,045,580	12,978,254
Net Income	1,908,463	1,302,685
Return on Unrestricted Investment Accounts (Depositors' Share of Income)	11,063,139	8,142,705

Selected Investments			
Mudarabah (*sukuk* Leasing)	1,000,000	1,000,000	0.00%
**Ijara*	8,489,624	481,628	1662%
Sukuk Salam	1,940,000	1,940,000	0.00%
Musharakah	3,376,927	2,443,696	38.19%
Istisna	1,142,737	1,400,665	-18.41%
Real Estate	8,793,419	8,793,419	0.00%
In Related Companies	4,935,083	4,935,005	0.00%
**Securities*	5,973,342	1,718,681	247.55%
Managed Funds	1,947,857	2,487,645	-21.70%
Total Investments	35,658,989	23,260,739	53.30%
Charity Allocation			
Total	311,527	334,330	-6.82%
Total charity/ shareholders income	2.81%	4.11%	
Poor & Needy	157,570	152,123	
Poor & Needy: Percentage of shareholders income:	157,570/11,063,139 1.42%	152,123/8,142,705 1.89%	

Table 7.2: Efficiency Ratios (Percentages)

	2001	**2000**
Depositor' Return/ Total Investment	31.02 85.42	35.00 } Equity/Total 91.35 } Liability
Retained Earnings/ Total Investment	19.45	20.59
Poor & Needy/ Net Income	8.26	11.68
Poor & Needy/ Total Charity	50.57	45.50

Sources for Tables 7.1 and 7.2: A Major Islamic Bank (anonymous)

For published data of the Islamic Bank Bangladesh (IBBL Annual Report, 2008), a bank that is rated as being the best one internationally according to the Global Finance Forum, *murabaha* (mark-up financing) financing comprised almost 51 per cent of total financing in the year 2007. PLS financing (*mudarabah* and *musharakah*) held a distant 0.13 per cent financing ratio. No data on social spending (Islamic *zakat* and *sadaqah* on the needy) are available in the bank balance sheets or otherwise. This is one of the persistent problems of lack of disclosure and transparency of Islamic banks in declaring their social spending and assets. If we approximate microenterprise development financing as a rough representation of a kind of social spending, the ratios held by the Islamic Bank Bangladesh were as follows: 0.02 per cent of total investment in 2007, and 0.005 per cent in 2006. These are despicable figures on social spending. In spite of these low social standings and in the absence of transparency and disclosure and the inadequacy of the balance sheets of Islamic Bank Bangladesh on charitable spending, its ROE-ratio (return on equity) stood at a high 13.42 per cent in 2006 and 13.00 per cent in 2007. The conclusion is reinforced: Such efficiency ratios while they speak out in favour of shareholders' returns and wealth position, are not representative of the social and ethical meaning of Islamic economics, finance, and financial institutions.

In the case of Islamic banks in Indonesia, published data (Bank Indonesia, 2009) indicate slightly better but still questionable financing trends for microenterprises. Medium and small scale microenterprise (MSMEs) financing ranked at approximately 15 per cent of total financing in 2008, up from approximately 9 per cent in 2007. Yet Islamic financing of rural sector projects ranked between 4.00 and 4.50 percentages between the years 2006 and 2008. The return on equity (ROE) was a large 37 percent to 68.85 percent between 2006 and 2008. Thus, once again the inadmissibility of Islamic bank reporting in respect of the ethical social context remains unchanged.

In the case of Malaysian Islamic banks, published data show that the Islamic banks' social financing ('community, social and personal services') stood at 0.69 percent in January 2005 and 0.91 per cent in December 2005. This ratio decreased to 0.88 percent in March 2006. Given the high watermark of Malaysian Islamic banks in Islamic banking and finance in the secondary financing markets, the social financing figures shown in their consolidated balance sheets auger poorly for the ethical and social objective.

The trend towards secondary financing, significantly away from the main basis of Islamic participatory financing, which are the profit-loss instruments comprising M1 = *mudarabah*; *musharakah* = M2, *murabaha* = M3, with a concentration on M3 at the expense of PLS-portfolio diversification, can be seen from Table 7.3 below:

Table 7.3: Percentage share of Islamic profit-loss sharing financing instruments and secondary financing instruments

	Total	M1	M2	M3	Secondary Instruments
June 2006	100	0.12	0.40	9.22	90.26
Dec 2005	100	0.05	0.24	12.25	87.46
Dec 2004	100	0.32	0.44	19.58	76.66
Dec 2003	100	0.39	0.54	22.48	76.59

Sources: Malaysian Islamic financing data posted in the internet.

The inference derived from Islamic bank financing in the ethical front

Over the expanse of time from 2001 to present the Islamic bank financing facts point out a clear pattern. This is that Islamic financial institutions are evolving along a line of activities based on a mechanistic understanding of the *shar'iah* (Islamic law). In fact, the *shar'iah* conception based on learning dynamics did not evolve in Islamic banks by a participatory discourse of the learned with diverse agencies of the Muslim community. There is no effective process in place in the Islamic institutions to understand the foundational methodology of the Islamic worldview. This is unity of the divine law (*tawhid*) in action in the world-system in all details of problems and issues. The *shura*, Islamic consultative medium, which generates an extensive learning process spanning all of human order including science and complex discourse, is not a mechanistic institutional consultation. Rather, the *shuratic* (of the *shura*) learning process is premised on knowledge reproduction by developing insight into the intellection process of unity of knowledge integrated with intellectual discourse. These two guidelines together evolve directions and rules on how the episteme of unity of knowledge can be actualized in the problems and issues at hand (*Qur'an* 42: 38, 49-53).

A sheer literal interpretation of a particular injunction of the *shar'iah* to safeguard shareholders' wealth, and thus the preservation of the net worth of the Islamic institution, despite being a necessary condition of justice, fairness and accountability, remains devoid of purpose and objective of the *shar'iah* (*maqasid as-shari'ah*) This happens when the understanding of complementary and inter-causal relations between different parts of the economic, financial and social order for attaining wellbeing is not understood as belonging distinctively to the episteme of unity of the divine law in action along with issues of the world-system. The resulting state of trade-off in resource allocation and decision-making vis-à-vis mainstream economic roots of the prevailing thinking in Islamic economics and finance is contrary to the principle of the paired universe presented by the *Qur'an* (36:36). The *qur'anic* pairing of entities in world-systems is the defining basis of the principle of pervasive complementarities across diversity. In the absence of such understanding and applying the principle of Islamic transformation, Islamic economics and finance and the Islamic organizations have lost their way into competition for resources, marginal rate of substitution and trade-off between economic and social goals as are found in mainstream economics.

The true nature of Islamic economic and financial studies

The above set of arguments gives an illustrative example, though not meant to be exhaustive in the many details that can be objectively launched against the present state of Islamic economics and finance and their institutional practice. The situation leads to a critical review. We reiterate here the nature of Islamic economic and financial studies in a different light in reference to the *Qur'an* and the *sunnah* as the basis of the *tawhidi* epistemology. By *tawhidi* epistemology we mean the epistemology of organic unity enabled by divine knowledge in relation to the schemes of the world-system. Such a relational formalism is studied here in respect of economics, finance, and institutions.

We need therefore to examine the nature of Islamic economics as an interdisciplinary paradigm that explains interaction over the domains of moral guidance, laws, and their impulses in the issues of world-systems. These elements are evolved according to discursive impulses and processes. Such interactive learning systems as *processes* have remained outside mainstream economic analysis. Mainstream economic doctrine, not the epistemological worldview of unity of knowledge, has been thoroughly imported into the intellection of Islamic Economics and Islamic Finance. Such an imitation rendered Islamic economics and finance incapable of being any different from mainstream economic and financial ideas, wherein deep methodological concerns abound. The *fiqh* (legal interpretation) tradition has succumbed to this catching-up rush in the midst of capitalist globalization and the inadequate kind of human resource that today engineers the Islamic institutions and their intellection processes.

The substantive question of interaction, integration, and creative evolution by organic learning between diverse issues of the embedded social, economic, and scientific systems in accordance with the epistemic oneness, is fundamental in understanding the nature and logic of economic behaviour and Islamic transformation in embedded systems with endogenous circular causations. Such learning processes equivalently reflect the unity of divine knowledge working in the particular sub-systems by the Islamic worldview. Such a knowledge-centred process model transcends the level of the individual and family. It spreads into society, markets, economy, institutions and the global order (Choudhury, Umar and Al-Ghamdi, 2003). A discursive society and participative complementary organic world-system ensues. The meaning of discursive society underlying a participatory worldview was exalted by Foucault (1993).

Without the *tawhidi* episteme spearheading Islamic economic, financial, and social investigations, and thereby, the delineation and analysis of the emergent problems, there cannot emerge Islamic reasoning regarding the abolition of interest rate, money, finance, and real economy linkages. The embedded formalism in respect of the good things of life shape and form the institutional, social and Islamic orders. Consequently, in the absence of *tawhidi* epistemology, the mainstream model of money and macroeconomics will continue to prevail in Islamic economics and finance. The mainstream microeconomics of Islamic behaviour will prevail. Yet the *tawhidi* and mainstream approaches of Islamic economics and finance are fundamentally contrary.

Other Islamic economists in this group have continued on to force deductions from the works of the scholastic Islamic scholars to fit into the mainstream model and thought. In this regard see Oslington (2003) for a criticism of Ghazzanfar and Islahi (1990) in their modernist characterization of scholastic works, especially of Imam Ghazzali's.

Contrary to the above situation, the Islamic world-system is established and its analytics constructed on the basis of the *tawhidi* methodological worldview in the episteme of unity of divine knowledge spanning inter-systems and intra-systems. Such systems continuously interact, integrate, and evolve. They thus learn in concert with the existential phenomenon of discourse, participation, linkages, and creative evolution. These properties of the learning processes delineate the worldview of unity of the divine law in relation to the unified nature of complementary issues in the world-systems. Discourse conveys the dynamics of the *shuratic* process. *Functional* ontology (Maxwell, 1962) is the formal way of abstracting the implications of the paired universe of pervasive learning in unity of knowledge.

How to get there?

Firstly, education along the lines of the *tawhidi* epistemology of global change, with particular emphasis placed on the dynamics of money, finance, and real economy, must instil such awareness and education at the intellectual and practitioning levels. The Islamic Research and Training Institute (Jeddah, Saudi Arabia) in concert with seats of higher education in the Muslim World and the Islamic banks ought to spearhead such discourses with the right kind of leadership and human resource. Such approaches do not exist presently.

Secondly, a conglomerate of pilot projects can be established. Examples here are realizing diversity of processes interrelating primary goods with agrarian and manufacturing production. Such interfaced goods would be developed and traded internationally. In international trade, the gold standard will become the basis of inter-communal trade agreement in the Muslim World. The Islamic Development Bank (IDB) can establish such a pilot mechanism on the basis of maintaining the institutionalism of 100 per cent reserve requirements monetary system between the central bank and the Islamic banks in the trading countries (Choudhury, 1997). Such a pilot project can be subsequently expanded to include many traded items of similar kinds of diversified goods.

There will be a special need to protect such expanding segmented markets of goods, services, and financial instruments. This can be done by targeting specific markets for trade promotion in goods and services generated in the pilot project and traded by the support of 100 per cent reserve requirements monetary system with the gold standard (Choudhury & Hoque, 2004).

A value-contract will be established between the central bank and the commercial bank on holding a residual (small) amount of gold, which IDB will guarantee to the central banks. This gold stock will support the 'residual' amount of un-mobilized currency (say the IDB Dinar in the gold standard) that may remain unutilized after a maximum quantity of available money with Islamic banks is mobilized into the real sector (i.e. in market transaction, trade, and development) using Islamic financial instruments. This 'residual' amount of the IDB Dinar needs to be backed up by a quantity of gold that will be sufficient to assign value to the unit of currency in circulation in the real economy. In this way, financial resources are mobilized in markets, trade and development bringing about their social and ethical effects. Consequently, the quantity of gold required for shoring up the value of currency in circulation will be small even as resource mobilization remains inversely proportional to the quantity of gold required to shore up the residual un-mobilized financial resource. The amount of gold held in the central bank for shoring up the value of residual un-mobilized monetary resource would thus be inversely related to the speed and quantity of money mobilized into the real economy. On the structure of 100 per cent reserve requirement monetary system see Choudhury (2004b). On the gold standard respecting 'residual' quantity of gold required to lubricate market exchange, trade and development see Mydin (2004) and Mydin and Larbani (2004).

A small amount of gold is required to maintain the value of monetary circulation in the real economy

Here is a formal explanation of the gold-backing of currency in circulation.

Let total of monetary resources R = Rc + Re;
Rc: money unmobilized and thus with central bank;
Re: money mobilized into the real economy.
Let G: quantity of gold required to shore the total monetary resource (stock Rc and flow Re).

Thus, R/G = Rc/G + Re/G.
Or, Rc/G = R/G – Re/G.
Rc/G = a, the money/gold ratio determined by the Central Bank according the size of Rc.
Thus, log R – log G = log a – (log Re – log G) = log a – log Re + log G
Or, log R + log Re = log a + 2log G.
Or, in the form of rates of change (^): R^ + Re^ = 2G^
That is Rc^ + Re^ + Re^= 2G^
When money resource is *fully mobilized* into the Real Economy Rc^ + Re^ = 0
Thus Re^=2G^.
Write, G^/Re^ = $\varepsilon_{G|Re}$ = ½.
Therefore, what amount of gold needs to be increased to shore the value of a unit of increase in Re = 1/2?

The time-change in this elasticity equals zero. Thus the response to a change in the increase of gold to protect an increase of a unit of Re mobilized in the real economy is negligible when R is fully mobilized into the real economy.

Obviously, the above result is true also in the case of partial mobilization of monetary resources into the real economy. The amount of G remains small to zero in the Central Bank under the condition of partial to full mobilization of monetary resources into the real economy. The elasticity is a constant 1/2. The rate of change in the proportionate time-rate of variation in G is small to zero with the increase in the monetary resource mobilization into the real economy.

Conclusion

After so many years of talking about Islamic economics and finance, there remains a great gap in true Islamic intellection in the scholarly field that Islamic Economics and Finance can otherwise potentially give to the academic world at large. Thus far, it is only the goals of capital formation, business survival, and profit-making in an intensifying global financial competition agenda and protection of shareholders' wealth in Islamic banks that have activated the motivations and activities of the Islamic financing institutions and development organizations. Islamic economics and finance has remained a 'normal' science. Rather, what it ought to be is a 'scientific revolution' (Kuhn, 1970) so as to give something new to the world of learning and practice.

Likewise, on the academic front the absence of the epistemological worldview in Islamic economics and finance has failed to study ethics and economics as a substantive ethico-economic scientific theme (Edel, 1970) of Islamic economics and finance. This failure is due to subservience of Islamic economics and finance to mainstream thought. Yet, mainstream economic thought is already subject to questioning on the theme of ethics. Consequently, the human resources of Islamic economics and finance are lost to the mainstream worldview. They are increasingly taken away from the *tawhidi* methodological worldview. Upon this, the Islamic revolutionary ideas ought to be premised. The vision, understanding, and use of Islamic economics, financial instruments, and Islamic institutions have been misplaced. New and fresh visions of intellectual pursuit and applications are required.

References

Asad, M., 1987, *This Law of Ours*, p. 11, Dar Al-Andalus, Gibraltar.

Bank Indonesia, 2008, *Indonesian Islamic Bank Outlook 2009*, Islamic Banking Directorate, Jakarta, Indonesia.

Choudhury, M.A., 1997, *Money in Islam*, Routledge, London, Eng.

—. 1998, *Studies in Islamic Social Sciences*, Macmillan, London, Eng.

—. 1999, "Methodological Conclusion", Chapter 21 of his, *Comparative Economic Theory: Occidental and Islamic Perspectives*, Kluwer Academic Publishers, Norwell, MA.

—. 2004a, *The Islamic World-System: A Study in Polity-Market Interaction*. London, Eng: Routledge.
—. 2004b, "Islamic political economy", *Review of Islamic Economics*, (13)1.
Choudhury, M.A. & Hoque, M.Z., 2004, *An Advanced Exposition in Islamic Economics and Finance*. Lewiston, Edwin Mellen Press, Maryland, USA.
Choudhury, M.A. Umar, Y. & Al-Ghamdi, M., 2003, "*Ummatic* globalization versus neoclassical capitalist globalization". *Review of Islamic Economics*. (12)1, 5-45.
Edel, A. 1970, "Science and the structure of ethics". Neurath, O. Carnap. R. & Morris, C. (eds.) *Foundations of the Unity of Science*, Vol.II, Nos. 1-9, Chicago, ILL: The University of Chicago Press, 273-378.
Foucault, M. trans. by Sheridan, A.M., 1972, *The Archeology of Knowledge and the Discourse on Language*, Harper Torchbooks, New York, NY.
Ghazzanfar, S.M. and Islahi, A.Z., 1990, "Economic thought of an Arab Scholastic, Abu Hamid al-Ghazali", *History of Political Economy*, (22)2, 381-403; reprinted in S.M. Ghazzanfar (ed.), 2003, *Medieval Islamic Economic Thought, Filling the "Great Gap" in European Economics,* 23-44, Routledge, London, Eng.
Gruber, T.R., 1993, "A translation approach to portable ontologies", *Knowledge Acquisition*, (5)2, 199-200.
Heidegger, M. trans. by Hofstadter, A., 1988, *The Basic Problems of Phenomenology*, Indiana University Press, Bloomington & Indiana.
Islamic Bank Bangladesh, *Annual Report 2007*, Islamic Bank Bangladesh (IBBL), Dhaka, Bangladesh.
Kuhn, T.S., 1970, *The Structure of Scientific Revolution*, University of Chicago Press, Chicago, IL.
Maxwell, G., 1962, "The ontological status of theoretical entities". Feigl, H. & Maxwell, G. (eds.), *Minnesota Studies in the Philosophy of Science, Vol. II: Scientific Explanation, Space and Time*, pp. 3-27, University of Minnesota Press, Minneapolis, Minnesota.
Mydin, A.K., 2004, *The Theft of Nations*, Pelanduk, Kuala Lumpur, Malaysia.
Mydin, A.K. & Larbani, M., 2004, "The Gold Dinar: the next component in Islamic economics, banking and finance", *Review of Islamic Economics*, (8)1, 5-34.
Oslington, P., 1995, "Economic thought and religious thought, a comment on Ghazzanfar and Islahi". *History of Political Economy*, (2)4, 781-5. Reprinted in S.M. Ghazzafar ed. op cit.

PART II:

APPLICATIONS OF *TAWHIDI* EPISTEMOLOGY: THE METHOD OF CIRCULAR CAUSATION AND SIMULATION OF THE WELLBEING OBJECTIVE CRITERION

CHAPTER EIGHT

CIRCULAR CAUSATION METHOD OF *TAWHIDI* METHODOLOGY: EVALUATING WELLBEING AND SUSTAINABLE DEVELOPMENT

In the light of the monotheistic methodology of *tawhid* in the order and scheme of things, this chapter now explains how this epistemology is applied by the method of circular causation. Circular causation as an applied method arises from the *tawhidi* methodological worldview.The selected examples given here are illustrative of the great deal of further applications that can be examined at length and in substantive details (Choudhury, 2011). Indeed, circular causation proves to be a most powerful and innovative method to evaluate the objective criterion of the wellbeing function, first in terms of 'estimating' the state of the socioeconomic problem under study 'as is' in the prevailing world situation. Estimation is then followed by the empirical study of the state of the world 'as it ought to be'. This is the 'simulation' stage in the normative perspective of *tawhidi* episteme of unity of knowledge. Simulation as the empirical reconstruction of the state of the world-system as it 'ought to be' by generality and particulars when induced by the *tawhidi* epistemic worldview. Thus 'estimation' followed by 'simulation' comprises the total empirical components of the method of circular causation in thesetwo-stages of 'evaluation' of the wellbeing objective criterion function.

Objective

The principal objective of this chapter is to formalize the socio-scientific application of the monotheistic law yieldingthe *tawhidi* epistemology of unity of knowledge. As an example, we will study the specific case of poverty alleviation in relation to economic development in Indonesia. This is done by means of simulating the wellbeing function in growth, poverty, and price level as variables, with the use of the circular causation method. The circular causation method of simulating wellbeing is explained by a comparative study of the literature in the field of development and in the light of distributive equity and economy relationship. The method then yields the social and economic implications upon which relevant policies can be formulated. The chapter also explains how endogenous ethical relations, referred to as ethico-economic in nature are used to present a pervasively complementary and thus participatory picture of sustainable development.

In conclusion, we explain that the principle of complementarity in its endogenous ethico-economic sense arises uniquely from the understanding and application of the monotheistic law as a socio-scientific methodology for the study of relationally organic complementarities. This approach equivalently yields the study of participatory worldview in unity of knowledge. Such an analytical method cannot be found in the entire development literature otherwise. Contrarily, economic development is always studied in mainstream economics in terms of the following postulates: scarcity of resources, competition, optimization, steady-state equilibrium, marginal rate of substitution, opportunity cost, and a static view of resource allocation between competing ends. On the other hand, the properties of evolutionary learning are characterized by the pervasively complementary nature of the interactive, integrative, and evolutionary learning processes (**IIE**-processes). Now a participatory picture of development is opposed to that in mainstream economic theory due to the substantive change in the ontological socio-scientific orientations.

Background

Our starting point is to formulate a *functionally* ontological model of the world-system in the light of the epistemology of unity of knowledge (Gruber, 1993). What does this epistemic foundation of socio-scientific reasoning mean? Its foundation lies on a scientific understanding of the most irreducible roots of unity of being and its ontological representation in the universe of creative becoming. The search continues to discover where such a functionally ontological premise can be found and that can be applied in every discipline and shade of thought. The contention is that the unity of being and becoming upon which the ultimate foundation of knowledge and its representation lies, is explained by the monotheistic law. No other premise can be found that renders such a meaning of organic and systemic unity. Consequently, the scientific understanding of such a functionally ontological unity of knowledge in being and becoming of reality, as it is comprehended and then represented in evidences, is the essentially credible proof of the oneness of the monotheistic law. The span of the ontological comprehension is the result of integration between credible belief and its application in all aspects of reality. The ultimate nature of the monotheistic law is therefore, not a figment of the imagination or an irrational belief system. Instead, it comprises the ultimate premise of the true order of a total phenomenology of 'everything' (Barrow, 1991).

A full and entire comprehension of the monotheistic law in such a final shape is not possible due to human limitations. Therefore, the world-system in its entirety under the impact of the monotheistic law at work is not possible at any given instance. Yet the unravelling of the process rising into higher levels of certainty of knowledge and the knowledge-induced world-system taken in its generality and specifics, represents the evolutionary learning path. Such evolutionary learning paths build upon the episteme of unity of knowledge and its creative function in evident and explained reality. This kind of continuous unravelling and proof in belief and evidence that is in the unification of the knowledge-induced micro-universes interfaced with the macro-universes proves itself in 'everything'.

The creative evolutionary learning is manifest by the organic unification of diverse possibilities. Such possibilities are sanctioned by the monotheistic law. Yet they are evaluated through the process of enlightened discourseand analysis that examine the prevailing and possible degrees of socioeconomic pairing between variables. In this process, while knowledge and evidence prevail, there is no coercion in reaching a consensus. The immanent intellection involves the interaction between the heart, mind, and matter. The continuous process of intellection in gaining knowledge carries with it a definite goal and the meaning of closure of the final and total systemic and cybernetic universe that knowledge investigates.

The emergent total phenomenology comprises abstraction, formalism, application and continuity of evolutionary learning processes towards attaining a definite objective criterion. The most generalized perspective of this objective criterion spans human intellection of the organically unifying universes and entities under investigation. In this way, there is a well-defined structure and function that reflect a comprehensive phenomenology in the continuity of epistemic unity across the continuums of 'everything'.

The structure shows interaction (I) as a matter of collective discourse and search across diversity of possible epistemic paths of unity of knowledge spanning the entire socio-scientific world-system pertaining to the growth of knowledge. Discursive interaction in the spirit-mind-matter domain leads to an attained level of integration (I). Interaction to integration (I) takes place out of discourse on the generality and its specific issues. This I-to-I experience is followed by co-evolution (E) of similar processes of creative learning functionally defined by the process of interaction leading to integration, and then evolution. The resulting process-oriented totality of the learning structure is now encapsulated in the **IIE**-learning processes of unity of knowledge that build on the positive and reconstructed normative nature of the issues and problems under investigation.

Two kinds of unification experience are inherent in the **IIE** structure. **IIE** continuously recalls the epistemic core of unity of knowledge to continue on the evolutionary learning processes. The first experience is of abstraction. It involves the heart and mind toward understanding systemic (organic) unity of being and becoming. This experience is equivalent to the derivation of knowledge from the epistemic premise of unity of knowledge (*tawhid*). The next experience is the impact of epistemic unity on the (re)constructed world-system and its study of specific issues. Such a (re)constructed world-system and its specifics comprise the knowledge-induced material entities of the total world-system. Hence the structure and function of the phenomenological model of unity of knowledge organically interconnect the primordial ontological oneness in the normatively evaluated and constructed material world-system. This state of knowledge reflects the dynamics of unity of knowledge in the world-system.

Circular causation and wellbeing objective in the phenomenological model of epistemic unity

The representation of evolutionary learning processes in unity of knowledge, which is of the form of abstraction, and then this property being induced into the issues and problems under investigation, involves organic inter-causal relationships between the variables and entities. Such interrelations convey the meaning of systemic complementarities and participation. Such a property is system-pervasive and expansionary by way of the evolutionary learning dynamics driven by the episteme of unity of knowledge.

Such organic interrelations are characterised by circular causation. Its meaning is further conveyed by the continuity in cause-effect inter-causality that remains incessant and pervasive by recursive inter-relations between the variables and entities and their regenerated relations. The recursive relations mark evolutionary learning by inter-variable and inter-entity/variable causality. In ethical language, truth breeds truth; falsehood breeds falsehood.[1]

The monotheistic law is thus defined by the phenomenological system shown in Figure 8.1. Such a representation forms the permanent and the most pervasive form, structure, and function of the learning universe and its systemic components. It is confirmed and reaffirmed by co-evolutionary learning through the method of circular causation in the **IIE**-process model.

---

[1] $A1^+ \cap A2^+ = A3^+ \neq \phi$, as truth statement, with A1 and A2 as truth statements. Likewise, $T(\cap A3^+)$ = domain of truth comprising truth statements, with T(.) being positive monotonic transformation of truth statements.

$B1^- \cap B2^- = B3^- = \phi$ or non-ϕ, as distinct from truth statements, with B1 and B2 as false statements. Likewise the functional transformation (F(.)), denoted by , $F(\cap B3^-)$ = domain of false statements. F is a positive monotonic transformation establishing the truth of false statements.

Furthermore, $A1 \cup A2$; $B1 \cup B2$ maintain these properties. But the following is true: $A3 \cap B3 = \phi$, the null space in the state of certain knowledge (truth exclusive of falsehood). Consequently, every pair of truth and falsehood forms a null set. Thereby, $(A1 \cup A2) \cap (B1 \cup B2) = A1 \cap (B1 \cup B2) \cup A2 \cap (B1 \cup B2) =$
$[(A1 \cap B1) \cup (A1 \cap B2)] \cup [(A2 \cap B1) \cup (A2 \cap B2)] = \phi$, identically.

These results prove that, while there are pervasive complementarities between truth-conditions of the world-system, there is also pervasiveness of complementarities among falsehood conditions of the world-system. Yet there is pervasive nullity between truth and falsehood.

Truth and falsehood are defined in respect of these properties of their domains *and* in terms of the appropriateness of the good and bad choices determined by the moral law of epistemic oneness. An example of the contrary situations is the pervasive methodological individualism of neoclassical economic theory, and the pervasive system orientation of complementarities of the monotheistic law. Likewise, there is the open-ended conjecture of Popper's universe with evolutionary processes but no final learnt objective functional.

On the other hand, we have the evolutionary learning universe of circular causality addressing simulation of the wellbeing objective with pervasive inter-variables and inter-entities causality, but having a final closure in the ultimate learnt universe called the Great Event of the hereafter. This marks the self-actualization of the most complete domain of accumulated knowledge. This is true in terms of intra-systemic dynamics -- that is, within a given process -- where no final optimality and equilibrium exists. This property is also true of the inter-systemic enveloping of interactive and integrative universes forming the grand systems. In and by these processes, no terminal optimality and steady-state equilibrium can exist due to perturbations and non-linearity of inter-causal relations.

The circular causation model is established by the following formalism:

'Evaluation' of wellbeing function, $W=W(\mathbf{x}(\theta))$ (8.1)
subject to, $x_i(\theta) = f_i(\theta,\mathbf{x}'(\theta))$;
$\theta = F(\mathbf{x}_i(\theta)) \cong W(\mathbf{x}(\theta))$.
$i = 1,2,..,n$

Ω denotes the primal text of the monotheistic law. This is the *Qur'an*. From it, via the Prophetic guidance and a discursive experience of the Islamic learned ones, the foundation of Islamic law (*shari'ah*) is derived.

S denotes the transmission of the monotheistic law into its understanding by guidance. In Islam this comprises the guidance of the Prophet Muhammad, termed the *sunnah*(S).

$[(\Omega \rightarrow S) \cong (\Omega,S)]$ denotes the *primal functional* ontology.

θ^* denotes the primal reference to the monotheistic law on the generality, but notyet the specifics of a problem and issue under study. For example, a theory of justice as a general worldview is carried next to the specific treatment of the issue of just resource allocation as distributive equity. We write, $\theta^* \in (\Omega,S)$. Likewise, the general theme of justice as balance within the wellbeing criterion is carried over to study the particular problem of poverty alleviation in respect of participative development.

f_1 denotes the transmission of the general moral principle by the phenomenology of the worldly-system under study.

(Ω,S,θ^*) denotes the primal functional ontology as $\theta^* \in (\Omega,S)$.

In Islamic epistemology the primal foundation comprises the *Qur'an* (Ω), the *sunnah* (*S*), and the knowledge of those in authority to undertake authoritative interpretation (denoted by θ^*). (Ω,S,θ^*) altogether through the discursive function of f_1 comprises the objective and purpose of the *shari'ah*, which is termed as *maqasid as-shari'ah*.

θ denotes the knowledge-flow derived by way of the **IIE**-learning processes pertaining to any given process. Such evolutionary learning processes carry the repeated into new knowledge-flows, $\theta \in (\Omega,S,\theta^*)$.

$\mathbf{x}(\theta)$ denotes the knowledge-induced vector or matrix of variables of the problem under investigation in the light of epistemic oneness.

$x_i(\theta)$ denotes any of the ith component of the vector/matrix, $\mathbf{x}(\theta)$, $i = 1,2,..,n$.

$\mathbf{x}'(\theta)$ denotes the vector/sub-matrix excluding ith. component; $i = 1,2,..,n$.

In all of these symbols the time factor as a recorder of events can be included as t(θ).

Furthermore on the wellbeing objective function

The wellbeing function, W(.), is the objective criterion for evaluating the degree of epistemic oneness (relational complementarity and participation). It thereby acts as an index, as functional ontology, explaining the inter-variable participatory relations among **x**(θ) as vector or matrix of variables. The system of inter-causal relations is represented by expression (8.1).

In the end, the functional similarity between W(.) and θ in given **IIE**-learning processes is established. The equivalence of the meanings between W(.) and 'θ' implies that, while W(.) bears the conceptual meaning of organic inter-causal unity of relations in terms of the epistemic oneness, the expression for 'θ' in any specific evolutionary learning process denotes the empirical version of W(.).

W is evaluated in terms of the circular causation **x**(θ)-variables. These variables feed into the process-specific θ-function in two stages. 'Evaluation' means the following stages of empirical quantification: Firstly, the system in expression (8.1) is 'estimated'. Here 'estimation', as the statistical exercise, conveys the positive state of the world 'as is'. Secondly, the moral/ethical reconstruction takes the form of statistical plus institutional discursive 'simulation' of the system of equations in expression (8.1).Simulation is done by appropriate changes in the coefficients of the estimated model to convey a semblance of complementarities between the variables as they 'ought to be'. As an example, there is an inverse relationship between spending activity and interest rate. Here the inter-variable complementarities by way ofinter-causality are shown between spending as one variable and the inverse of the rate of interest as the other complementary variable. In this sense, spending increases as the rate of interest declines and vice-a-versa. That is, the spending variable is positively complementary to the inverse of interest rate, and vice-a-versa between real rates of return and interest rates.

The epistemological derivation of such a rule is from the *Qur'an*. Between the good things as identified by the moral text and implicated in the *maqasid as-shari'ah*, there is another example of complementarity. This is the meaning that is opposite to the mainstream economic concept of marginal rate of substitution. An example is the conflict between labour and capital in the allocation of scarce production resources. The conflict represented by the marginal rate of substitution between labour and capital of mainstream economics is changed into positive complementarities between these productive factors by changing the production structure and inducing in this endogenous technological change. The latter is the case of application of the *tawhidi* relational methodology of unity of knowledge.

The 'estimated' θ-value (simulated in expression 8.1)as the wellbeing index gives a numerical positive value indicating the level of interrelationship (degree of complementarities or absence of this) between the variables in the circular causation relations. Yet the simulation ofθ-value takes a different approach from that of evaluation of the wellbeing criterion.

Let θ_{new} denote the 'simulated' normative value of social reconstruction based on inter-variable complementarities. Evaluation of the wellbeing function, as explained in respect of unity of knowledge expressed by inter-causal and inter-variable complementarities via the route of estimation into simulation, can be carried out intra-system as by the given time-period. It can be carried out inter-systems, as over evolutionary learning processes. These points on methods of estimation and simulation for evaluation of the wellbeing function using circular causation relations are brought out in the Statistical Appendix.

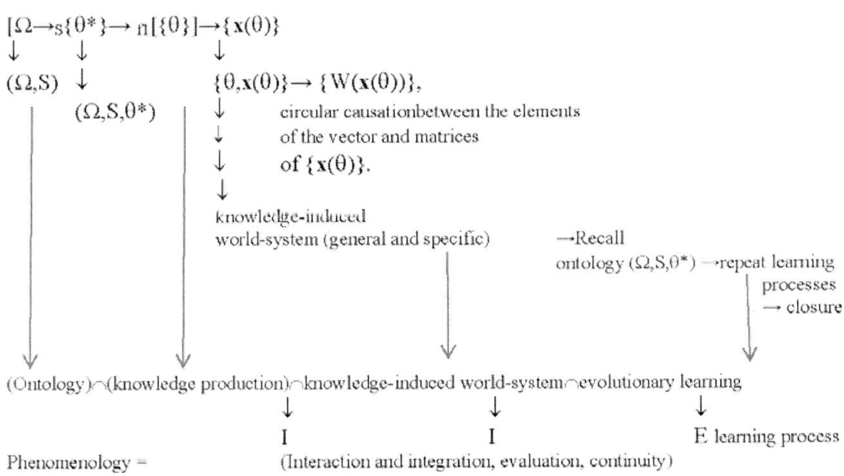

Figure 8.1: Phenomenological representation of the epistemic model of unity of knowledge

Inter-systemic extension of circular causation with wellbeing

By a further extension of expression (8.1) we can include the analytical implications of inter-systemic **IIE**-learning processes. An extreme but beautiful example is that of a keen sense of relationship between Man and the Cosmos. On this theme Kant (1949, p. 261) wrote his ponderous words: "Two things fill the mind with ever new and increasing awe and admiration the more frequently and continuously reflection is occupied with them; the starred heaven above me and the moral law within me. I ought not to seek either outside my field of vision, as though they were either shrouded in obscurity or were visionary. I see them confronting me and link them immediately with the consciousness of my existence."

In the light of the above inter-systemic implications of circular causation in 'evaluating', that is 'estimating' followed by 'simulating' the wellbeing function, we write,

$$\text{Evaluate } W = \Pi_{ij} W_{ij}(\mathbf{x}_{ij}(\theta_{ij})). \tag{8.2}$$

i = 1,2,..,n; j=1 (starred heaven),2(moral law)

Select i = 1(energy), 2(resource allocation), 3(mathematical knowledge)

(i,j) implies meanings like: Energy is embedded in space discovery for energy (x_{11}); and in the sense of energy explained in the monotheistic law as environmental resource for the sustenance of humanity (x_{12}).[2]Resource allocation takes place in the cosmos for the discovery of energy for spending in complementary material(x_{21}) and human needs (x_{22}). Mathematical knowledge, as of abstract analytical knowledge, is used to study both the cosmos (x_{31}) and the moral law (x_{32}). Energy and resource allocations are functions in both of these domains.

On this point wrote Albert Einstein (n.d.): "It is the privilege of man's genius, impersonated by inspired individuals, to advance ethical axioms which are so comprehensive and so well founded that men will accept them as grounded in the vast mass of their individual emotional

---

[2] The *Qur'an* on iron, the human world, and the divine law (57:25): "And We sent down Iron, in which is (material for) mighty war, as well as many benefits for mankind, that God may test who it is that will help, unseen, Him and His apostles: For God is full of Strength, exalted in Might." Furthermore in the Qur'an (57:1) is the following verse declaring the relationship between the heavens and the earth (entirety) by way of *tawhid*: "Whatever is in the heavens and on earth, let it declare the Praises and Glory of God: For He is the Exalted in Might, the Wise."

experiences. Ethical axioms are founded and tested not differently from the axioms of science. Truth is what stands the test of experience."

Thus by the method of circular causation, the total wellbeing functional can be written as,

$$W(\mathbf{x}(\boldsymbol{\theta})) = \cup_{interaction}\cap_{integration}\{\Pi_{ij}W_{ij}(\mathbf{x}_{ij}(\boldsymbol{\theta}_{ij}))\} \quad (8.3)$$
$$\text{Here, } \mathbf{x}(\boldsymbol{\theta}) = \cup_{interaction}\cap_{integration}\{x_{11},x_{12},x_{13},x_{21},x_{22}, x_{23}\}[\boldsymbol{\theta}_{ij}];$$
$$\lim [\cup_{interaction}\cap_{integration} \{\boldsymbol{\theta}_{ij}\}] = \theta$$

Thus $W(\mathbf{x}(\theta))$ is well-defined in terms of interaction and integration along the **IIE**-learning processes for any given process related to the $(\mathbf{x}_{ij},\boldsymbol{\theta}_{ij})$-vector or matrix (Choudhury and Hossain, 2006) in the circular causation system. The representation now takes up a matrix form. The formalism in the footnote shows that the ultimate treatment can be reduced to that of interactive-integrative variables by rows (i) and columns (j). Thus the final set of variables within (intra-systems) forms the vector $\{x_1, x_2, x_{3.}\}[\theta_{1.},\theta_{2.},\theta_{3.}]$.

Likewise, the final set of variables across(inter-) systems is denoted by $\{x_{.1},x_{.2}\}[\theta_{.1},\theta_{.2}]$. Furthermore, there is equivalence in either recording the variables over systems or systems across given sets of variables. In the end in these two cases, the reference vector arising from the inter-systemic and inter-variable causal matrix is denoted by,

$$\mathbf{x}(\theta) = \{x_{1.},x_{2.},x_{3.},x_{.1},x_{.2}\}[\lim [\cup_{interaction}\cap_{integration} \{\boldsymbol{\theta}_{ij}\}=\theta].$$

The inter-system circular causation in its matrix form followed by 'estimation' and 'simulation' of the wellbeing function, as explained earlier, is now complete.[3] Expression (8.3) now takes the form of

[3] The **IIE**-learning process in terms of inter-systemic variables can be represented in the following matrix:

Interaction &→ integration *variables*		*Process system knowledge-flows* 1	2	1	2	interactively-integrated variables by systems		
	1	x_{11}	x_{12}	θ_{11}	θ_{12}	$x_{1.}$	↔	$\theta_{1.}$
	2	x_{21}	x_{22}	θ_{21}	θ_{22}	$x_{2.}$	↔	$\theta_{2.}$
	3	x_{31}	x_{32}	θ_{31}	θ_{32}	$x_{3.}$	↔	$\theta_{3.}$
Interactively-Integrated systems		$x_{.1}$	$x_{.2}$	$\theta_{.1}$	$\theta_{.2}$	$\mathbf{x}(\theta)$	$\leftrightarrow\theta = \lim [\cup_{interaction}\cap_{integration} \{\boldsymbol{\theta}_{ij}\}]$	

Double arrows indicate cause-effect circularity between 'θ' and $\mathbf{x}(\theta)$ across evolutionary learning processes both intra-system and inter-systems.

expression (8.1), given the system-specific explanation of details. The continuous process orientation of evolutionary learning in unity of knowledge is as explained by Figure 8.1.

Our next point is to explain how the monotheistic law works in the inter-systemic worldview of circular causation understood as a method. The conditions for the embedded endogenous relations of organic unity by learning are explained firstly, by the pervasive organic unity between variables and systems. Secondly, the choices in generating the organic unity by pervasive complementarities and participation must be appropriate in the context of the monotheistic law.

In reference to the above-mentioned example of Man-Cosmos relationally-unified causality, we note that the governing epistemology over all of the inter-system variables in the matrix explanation of the organic interrelations between variables is the vector,

$$\lim [\cup_{\text{interaction}} \cap_{\text{integration}} \{\theta_{ij}\} = \theta.$$

As by the Kantian example, the Man-Cosmos interrelationship is extended to the common consciousness in both of these two systems. This consciousness grounds the dynamics of the moral law, the monotheistic law, by way of the ontological function as explained in Figure 8.1. Hence, the order of Man-Cosmos relationship is now extended to the causal interrelationship between the Monotheistic Law, Cosmos, Man, and further on into the closure in the Great Event of the hereafter (*akhira*). This inter-causal unified interrelationship now assumes a circular nature.

An event in respect of these dimensions happens in the intersection, $\{(\Omega,S,\theta^*)\}\cap\{(\theta,\mathbf{x}(\theta)) \in [(\text{Cosmos}\cap\text{Man})\in(\text{Space-Time})]\}$. In this form, the relationship means that, while(Ω,S,θ^*) as the epistemic knowledge domain determines the rest, it is also the evolutionary knowledge-flows $\{\theta\}$ arising out of the evaluation of the world-system in unity of knowledge that generates a progressively greater depth of comprehension of (Ω,S,θ^*). This recurrent experience in unity of knowledge takes place continuously in continuums of 'everything' in the dimensions of knowledge, space, and time. In this way, the limited space-time universe and its structure and function have been extended into the full-scale universe of knowledge, space, and time. In this complete picture, only knowledge remains the primal cause in determining events. Time acts as the recorder, not as the cause of the occurrence of events.

The meaning of the dimension of time in the totality of knowledge, space, and time universe

An event in this kind of universe, pervasively governed by knowledge, is denoted by $\{\theta \in (\Omega, S, \theta^*), \mathbf{x}(\theta), t(\theta)\}$.Now what is meant by the notation, $t = t(\theta)$? This means that time is a human psychological entity. Its existence depends upon the prior existence of a knowledge-induced event. Such an idea of the relationship between knowledge and time is like the treatment of time and event in the relativistic space-time universe. About this matter Einstein (trans. Lawson, 1954, p. 155) wrote: "There is no such thing as an empty space, i.e. space without field. Space-time does not claim existence on its own, but only as a structural quality of the field."

An example of the relationship between knowledge and time can be found in resource allocation: If a historical time period is marked by competition and marginalism, then that historical epoch is governed by an episteme contrary to epistemic unity in resource allocation. Such an epoch is independent of knowledge induction. On the other hand, if the historical epoch is marked by coordination and embedding avoiding methodological individualism and methodological independence, then such an epoch is governed by the consciousness of unity of knowledge. Historical (time) consciousness (Lucaks, 1968) thus depends on the occurrence and continuity of evolutionary patterns between knowledge or 'de-knowledge', and the corresponding nature of materiality and intellectual abstraction, respectively.

Properties of the wellbeing function in the dimensions of knowledge, space, and time

This last case of conscious systemic evolution provides the following property of the objective criterion of evaluation and change. This means the 'evaluation' of the wellbeing function, subject to circular causation relations in their states of 'estimation' followed by 'simulation' of the estimated equations to gain systemic unity of knowledge. Simulation comes about and continues by recursive interrelationship between consciousness, application, and regeneration of learning processes. The structure of **IIE**-process model now fits well into this category of the epistemic knowledge-induced model of the world-system.

In the light of the above remarks we can express the wellbeing function equivalently in terms of θ-function as follows:

$$W(\theta, \mathbf{x}(\theta), t(\theta)) = A(\theta, t) + \theta(\theta, \mathbf{x}(\theta), t(\theta)) \quad (8.4)$$

Here $A(\theta,t)$ is a learning parameter of the wellbeing function.

$\theta(\theta,\mathbf{x}(\theta),t(\theta))$ denotes the θ-induced function of $(\theta,\mathbf{x}(\theta),t(\theta))$

The following results will hold true:

$$dW/d\theta = dA(\theta,t)/d\theta + 1 > 1; \quad (8.5)$$

That is, $dW/d\theta = dA(\theta,t)/d\theta + \Sigma_i(\partial\theta/\partial x_i(\theta)).(dx_i(\theta)/d\theta) > 1.$ (8.6)

In reference to the coefficientsα_i of the regression equation for θ-function in the circular causation equations, we can write,

$$dW/d\theta = dA(\theta,t)/d\theta + \Sigma_i\alpha_i.(dx_i(\theta)/d\theta) > 1 \quad (8.7)$$

See appendix for more details in this regard.

Thus there is always increasing returns-to-scale in the wellbeing function by knowledge induction.

In case, $\Sigma_i\alpha_i = 1$, it is still obviously true that expression (8.5) will hold. $i = 1,2,..,n$

The meaning of endogenous and complex relations in non-linear circular causation system

The coefficients of expression (8.4) and of every equation in the circular causation system (8.1) and of its systemic extension in expression (8.3) are functionally induced by θ-values. Consequently, all variables and coefficients belong to probability fields of evolutionary learning denoted by continuously changing θ-values in the simulation results of the circular causation relations. Consequently, endogeneity and complexity arise in the non-linear forms of such simulated relations. Bertuglia and Vaio (2005, p. 269) explain this nature of non-linearity in their words: "The fundamental characteristic of complexity is the fact that, in the study of the evolution of dynamical systems that complexity deals with, the nature of the system in question is usually irrelevant. In the vision proposed by complexity, we can identify forms and evolutive characteristics common to all, or almost all, systems that are made up of numerous elements, between which there are reciprocals, non-linear interactions and positive feedback mechanisms. These systems, precisely for this reason, are generally called complex systems."

Besides, the circular causation interrelations implied by the characteristics of 'numerous elements, between which there are reciprocals, non-linear interactions and positive feedback mechanisms', means that each variable learns from other ones. This is due to the common impact of θ-values on each and all of such variables. Besides, the wellbeing equation and its simulation implies further feedback causation of the variables on the regeneration of recursive knowledge-flows, the θ-values. Consequently, every variable including the θ-variable and the estimation followed by simulation values become pervasively endogenous in the emergent inter-variables and inter-system simulacra.

The interesting point to note here is that all policy variables and institutional variables such as corporate governance, and ethical variables such as of corporate social responsibility, are transformed into endogenous variables. Yet the interaction between all such endogenous variables in the system of circular causation relations makes the system endogenous as well as complex and non-linear.

This fact can be seen from the following formalism in the circular causation method. We recall here the simulation aspect of circular causation relations. Coefficients are represented by $\{\alpha_i^*,\alpha^*_{ij},\beta_i^*\}$. Predictors of simulated dependent variables are denoted by $\{x^*_i\}$. Finally, the simulated knowledge function, which is equivalent to the wellbeing function, is denoted by Θ.

$x^*_i = \alpha_i^* + \Sigma_j\alpha_j^*.x_j(\theta) + \beta_i^*.\theta$; i = 1,2,…,n number of variables; j = 1,2,…,m number of variables excluding the ith variable. (8.8)

From the simulated vector$\mathbf{x}^*(\theta)$ generated by the series of equations as in expression (8), a new wellbeing function is generated. In it a recursive and discursive set of $\{\alpha_i^*,\alpha^*_j,\beta_i^*\}$-values determines the $\mathbf{x}^*(\theta)$-vector. The same simulacra continues on by generating new sequences of evolutionary tuple like $\{\Theta,\mathbf{x}^*(\Theta^*)\}$across the simulacra of evolutionary learning processes. Over these simulacra the index of wellbeing is given by,

$$\Theta = F(\mathbf{x}^*(\theta^*)), \quad (8.9)$$

Here F(.) assimulated functional acquires dynamic form by recursive and discursively determined coefficients in the F-functional. In this way, the interactive and integrative nature of the F-functional in the presence of circularly interrelated (integrative and integrative) dynamic coefficients and simulated predictors over evolutionary learning simulacra makes the F-functional complex and endogenous in the learning variables and coefficients. $\{\theta^*\}$ denote evolutionary sequences of knowledge-flow variables.

At the end of, say, Nth rounds of **IIE**-processes of repeated simulations of individual process-oriented wellbeing functions (say $f_r(.)$, r = 1,2,3,…,N) taken separately, the compounded (denoted by •) Θ-functional at the Nth terminal simulacra would be denoted by,

$$f_N \bullet f_{N-1} \bullet f_{N-2} \bullet \ldots\ldots \bullet f_1 = F_N \quad (8.10)$$

Any of the separate process-oriented f-functional is determined by intra-system simulated values of $\{(\alpha_i^*,\alpha^*_j,\beta_i^*),\mathbf{x}^*(\theta_i^*)\}$, acrossN sequential processes. Each process is characterized by intra-process, inter-variable causality in the circular causation relationships. Thereby,

$$F_N = F_N[\cup_{interaction}\cap_{integration}\{(\alpha_i^*,\alpha^*_j,\beta_i^*),\mathbf{x}^*(\theta_i^*)\}]_N, \quad (8.11)$$

Here interaction and integration followed by evolutionary learning take place within and across (N-1) processes. Through the continuous dynamic effects of inter-variable and inter-causal recursion and discursiveness through the **IIE**-processes in the field $\{(\alpha_i^*,\alpha^*_j,\beta_i^*),\mathbf{x}^*(\theta_i^*)\}$, the complex and endogenous nature of organic interrelationships are generated in the light of the relational episteme of unity of knowledge. The circular causation method is the phenomenological representation that empirically configures the epistemology of unity of knowledge in the form of pervasive complementarities (participation) between inter-causal variables. The phenomenological consequences are transmitted continuously across continuums of intra-systemic and inter-systemic cause-effect-cause recursions, as N number of processes evolve towards the very large scale universe.

That is,

$$[\Omega \rightarrow_S \rightarrow \{\text{knowledge-induced unity of the world-system, } \{\theta,\mathbf{x}(\theta)\} \rightarrow_S \rightarrow \Omega] \quad (8.12)$$

Expression (8.12) forms a pervasively complex and endogenous chain of organic relations of unity of knowledge explained by the **IIE**-learning processes in 'everything'.

We can construct specific forms of the rthf-functional of the whole system of circular causation equations, say as,

$$f_r = f_r(z_r(\theta_r^*)=(\alpha_i^*,\alpha^*_j,\beta_i^*),\mathbf{x}^*(\theta_r^*)) \mid z_{r-1}(\theta_{r-1}^*)). \quad (8.13)$$

When expressed as conditional probability distribution function, expression (8.13) takes the form (Hogg & Craig, 1965),

$$f_r = f_r[(z_r(\theta_r^*)\cap z_{r-1}(\theta_{r-1}^*))]/f_{r-1}(z_{r-1}(\theta_{r-1}^*)) \quad (8.14)$$

Expression (8.14) can be written as,

$$f_r = f_r(z_r(\theta_r^*).f_{r-1}(z_{r-1}(\theta_{r-1}^*))]/f_{r-1}(z_{r-1}(\theta_{r-1}^*)) = f_r(z_r(\theta_r^*)$$

In this way by further extension we can derive:

$$F_N=\Pi_r f_r(z_r(\theta_r^*); r = 1,2,\ldots,N \quad (8.15)$$

In a product form of the $\mathbf{x}(\theta)$ for process $r = 1,2,\ldots,N$ we write,

$$f_r(z_i)= [A_i(\theta)\Pi_i x_i(\theta)^{\gamma I}]_r \quad (8.16)$$

$r = 1,2,..,N$. 'i' denotes the numbered variables in the $\{z_i\}$-set.

$$\text{Hence, } F_N = \Pi_r[[A_i(\theta)\Pi_i x_i(\theta)^{\gamma i}]_r; r = 1,2,\ldots,N \quad (8.17)$$

If now F_N is interpreted as the wellbeing function, it is shown here as the non-linear and complex function in terms of all the variables inside $\Pi_r[[A_i(\theta)]_r.[\Pi_i x_i(\theta)^{\gamma i}]_r$. Besides, by that, F_N is formed in terms of the circular causation relations interlinking the f_r-functions by the co-evolution of θ-values. The limiting $\{\theta_r\}$is now expressed in its limiting form as

$$\lim_{\cup \text{interaction} \cap \text{integration}}\{\theta_r\}=\theta. \quad (8.18)$$

The topological property of events, E({θ},{z(θ)}) along the IIE-processes

While we have formalized regarding the compound f_r-functional forms to establish the ultimate inter-systemic wellbeing function F_N as shown in expressions (8.10), (8.16), and (8.17), it is equally true that every monotonic positive transformation of F_N is also a wellbeing function (Henderson and Quandt, 1971). Likewise, every monotonic opposite transformation along the 'de-knowledge' trajectory is equivalently a 'de-knowledge' evaluation function. These properties being true, the space of

$E(\{\theta\},\{z(\theta)\})$ forms a topology, maintaining its wellbeing inducing or 'de-knowledge' inducing properties defined on this set.

We now need to prove that circular causation method maintains such topological properties of the set of functionals and events, $E(\theta) = \{F_N, f_r, (\{\theta\},\{z(\theta)\})\}$.But first, we will define the topological mapping T on the setE(θ).

The principal premise of the event space is (Ω,S). From this is determined {θ}-vector by specific applications of the general worldview derived from (Ω,S) and denoted by {θ*}.The **IIE**-learning process regenerates knowledge from the entire evolutionary learning universe denoted by [Ω→E(θ)→Ω]. The *functional* ontology of primal derivation of knowledge is done bythe principal mapping 'S'. The operations, $\cup_{interaction}$, $\cap_{integration}$; thereby $\cup_{interaction}\cap_{integration}$, when applied to E(θ), satisfy the expressions (8.17) combined with (8.18). Hence the mapping T preserves the properties of the space of $E(\{\theta\},\{z(\theta)\})$ in the **IIE**-learning processes. These properties comprise, firstly, the pervasively complementary and participatory nature of the variables signifying the episteme of monotheistic unity of knowledge. Secondly, the choices represented by the variables must be in accordance with the monotheistic law of organic oneness between the variables representing the choices.

But even as the **IIE**-learning processes evolve, the dimensionality denoted by the number of choices and their complementary and participative relations, expand towards super-cardinality of the super-space of the monotheistic law by the advance of knowledge. This is to say that the large scale multi-universe self-actualizes in the final domain of Ω (hereafter).[4]

Likewise, the cardinality of the cumulative largest 'de-knowledge' domain at the time of unravelling the super-cardinality of Ω, attainsits zero value. There is no meaning of the cardinality of Ωbeing zero, and thereby, of the cardinality of cumulative 'de-knowledge' domain to be the largest. This is because the purpose of the multi-universes moving towards the fullness of knowledge conveys the meaning of the ultimate state of equilibrium and de-entropy.[5] Thus, simultaneously with the attainment of Ω, its dimension attains super-cardinality in the sense of the optimally accumulated knowledge domain. The dimension of the accumulated 'de-

---

[4] The *Qur'an* (57:3, 92:13) refers to this self-actualization of the multi-universes in the domain of Ω by the two verses that close the knowledge, and thereby the multi-universes in the dimensions of knowledge, space, and time.

[5]The *Qur'an* (781-5) refers to this ultimate event of the hereafter in its meaning of the Great Event.

knowledge' space then at that point of full knowledge attains zero cardinality. In other words, falsehood is vanquished; truth prevails. Such contrasting evolutionary moments of phenomenological experience are moments of the ultimate great equilibrium. The *Qur'an* (24:40)) declares in this regard: "For any to whom God gives no light, there is no light."

The topological properties of $E\{\theta,\mathbf{z}(\theta)\}$are now stated: The topological mapping T applies to the opposite knowledge and 'de-knowledge' domains by monotonically preserving the mappings within each of these domains by contrast, while satisfying the following properties:

1. $T(\cup\{E(\theta,z(\theta)\})$ belongs to the **IIE**-learning process for every$E(\theta,z(\theta))$ in the **IIE**-learning process across interactions. This is true of both intra-system and inter-system.
2. $T(\cap\{E(\theta,z(\theta)\})$ belongs to the **IIE**-learning process for every$E(\theta,z(\theta))$ in the **IIE**-learning process across integration. This is true of intra-system and inter-system.
3. $T(\cup\cap\{E(\theta,z(\theta)\})$ belongs to the **IIE**-learning process for every$E(\theta,z(\theta))$ in the **IIE**-learning process across interaction and integration. This is true of intra-system and inter-system.
4. Since Ω belongs to and generates the total $[\Omega\rightarrow_S$World-System$\rightarrow_S\Omega]$, therefore, T as by S, is denoted by $T(\Omega) \subseteq \Omega$. Likewise, $S(\Omega) \subseteq \Omega$.
5. $\Omega\cap\Omega\sim= \phi$, thereby, $T[\Omega\cap\Omega\sim] = \phi$, where, $\Omega\sim$ denotes the complete space of 'de-knowledge'. $T(\Omega) = \Omega$, likewise, $T(\Omega') = \Omega'$ denotes the closure ofΩ by itself, and of Ω' by itself. The closure property is necessary to establish the existence of evolutionary equilibrium; and steady-state equilibrium in each of these two cases, respectively (Nikaido, 1987).

The property of topological space of $\{E(\theta,z(\theta)\}$and topological mapping T defined on $\{E(\theta,z(\theta)\}$ including $[\Omega\rightarrow_S$World-System$\rightarrow_S\Omega]$, and the opposite category of 'de-knowledge' establishes the uniqueness of the two distinct forms of reality. These are namely the space of knowledge defined by (Ω,S) and the space of 'de-knowledge' defined by (Ω',R), where R denotes the domain of rationalism. The epistemology of unity of knowledge as of *tawhid* in the monotheistic law, and the epistemology of methodological differentiation as of rationalism, form opposite and unmixable realities. They define different worldviews and methodologies (Smart, 2000).

The result of the super-cardinal *tawhidi* super-space (Dewitt, 1992) also shows that a greater expanse of socio-scientific reality is explained in the knowledge-induced worldview than in the domain of 'de-knowledge'. Socio-scientific conception and application based on 'de-knowledge' produce a continuity of the world of methodological individualism and methodological independence in system-relations. The growing atomism of the concurrent differentiating relations causes the ultimate disappearance of dimensionality in the limit of the entities moving into singletons. On the other hand, the continuity of embedding of systems governed by pervasive complementarities under the epistemology of unity of knowledge causes increasing dimensionality.

The fact that the episteme of unity of knowledge, as in the *tawhidi* methodological worldview, increases its dimensionality, moving towards the terminal super-cardinal dimension of knowledge, space, and time, implies the conception and application of this worldview being universal. The episteme of rationalism is marked by its disability of finitude in dimensionality.[6] Rationalism is therefore unable to explain truth in its widest comprehension as is otherwise possible in the super-cardinal domain of (Ω,S).

The method of circular causation, which emerges from the epistemic worldview of pervasive complementarities (participation), applies to the universal domain of socio-scientific phenomena in knowledge, space, and time. The attribute of endogeneity persists in the circular causation relations. The same is not true of the nature of functional relations in exogenous variables. Exogenous variables cannot be expressed in terms of endogenous variables. Thereby, the number of equations of the exogenously structured system of relations is less than the number of equations in the endogenously structured system of circular causation relations. In the end, the generalized system of **IIE**-processes represented by their respective r-denoted expressions (shown above) in the circular causation relations brings together the wellbeing function, along with the circular causation relations. The transformation realized here marks the pervasive complementarities in the framework of endogeneity, complexity and non-linearity caused by θ-values and their influence on the socio-scientific variables $\mathbf{x}(\theta)$ along the evolutionary **IIE**-processes (Choudhury, 2012).Such transformations occur continuously and across continuums of socio-scientific systems that span the entirety of the intra-system and inter-system chains of relations in $[\Omega \rightarrow_S \text{World-System} \rightarrow_S \Omega]$.

[6] As a result it can be readily proven that $\Pi_i[x_i(\theta)]_r \geq [\Sigma_i\, x_i(\theta)]_r$. Thereby, with A > 1 as a result of increasing returns to scale and increasing economies-of-scope in the wellbeing objective function, $\Pi_i A_r(\theta).[x_i(\theta)]_r \geq \Pi_i[x_i(\theta)]_r \geq [\Sigma_i\, x_i(\theta)]_r$.

Finally, the uniqueness and universality of complexity, non-linearity, perfect endogeneity between variables of the circular causation relations, and economy-of-scope of the wellbeing function(Pindyck and Rubinfeld, 2001,imply the following result: The final terminal completion of knowledge is the nature of the largest scale multi-universe.This terminal state of the learning universe is governed by unity of knowledge as in the *tawhidi* case. Rationalism cannot fathom such a conception and method of quantitative application due to its constricted dimension of action and its ultimate measure of zero cardinality.

The implications here are vaster and deeper. The pervasive non-linearity, complexity, and endogeneity as characteristics of the intra-systemic and inter-systemic circular causation relations and wellbeing function, within the super-cardinality of the (Ω,S) multi-universe in knowledge, space, and time means that the universal socio-scientific structure reflects such properties. Linearity and paucity of relations is not even a local phenomenon, in as far as a subset of the topological space conceptualized above is also a topological space with its endowed topological mapping. For instance, the *qur'anic* multi-universes are epistemologically premised on the monotheistic unity of knowledge. Next, the derived consequences of this learnt state is justice. Justice now means a universal balance, purpose, and wellbeing in the generalized large structure of the human and non-human universes; and the known and abstract universes taken together. Now justice as balance means the balance, purpose, and wellbeing conveyed by the non-human domain and by the human domain on their own and via interaction across these inter-systems.[7]

[7] Take this simple example: $y = a.\ x + b$ is a linear equation in (x,y), with a and b as constants. But now transform this equation in the domain of knowledge, space, and time as endogenous system of relations as follows: $y(\theta) = a(\theta).x(\theta) + b(\theta) + c.\theta$. This equation cannot stand alone. It must have its circularly related equations: $x(\theta) = f(y(\theta),\theta)$, and $\theta = g(x(\theta), y(\theta))$. Each of these equations is non-linear, complex, and with endogenously related variables due to the **IIE**-process implications in the interactive variables arising from the presence of learning (i.e. θ-values), with $\theta \in$ large scale universe of (Ω,S) in the beginning and end of the *tawhidi* String Relation (TSR). Besides, the θ-function is of the identity form derived by the implicit function theorem of differential calculus, $\theta \equiv W(x(\theta),y(\theta))$.

Review of the literature in circular causation, cumulative causation and endogenously related complex and non-linear systems of relations.

The academic works of Myrdal (1958) and Schumpeter (1961) have been well summarized by Toner (1999a,b) and Cantner et al. (2009), respectively. These works bring out the social consequences of disequilibrium, or contrarily the cumulative passage of learning along the path of 'creative destruction' towards contributing to economic development.

For instance, the poor conditions for Blacks in America have been explained by Myrdal (1958) in terms of the social cumulative effect of social stigma. The result was a deepening of the adverse socioeconomic development conditions of the Blacks. This was reflected in the poor employment and income levels, low human resource development, social alienation causing delinquency, and social disenfranchisement over a protracted time period in American social and economic history. In this way, the depriving social conditions of Blacks in America took up a pattern of social alienation over a protracted time period. All this conveyed an adverse condition of equilibrium as a pattern of sustaining the social disequilibrium inter-relating the ensemble of factors causing evolution of social deprivation. The 'ought-to-be' historical ensemble is sought. In other words, the adverse social conditions maintained a certain deprived system of relationship to create the disequilibrium as an accepted social projection. The 'ought-to-be' situation rejects this condition and proposes ways and means of attaining a moral social reconstruction.

Likewise, Schumpeter's theory of creative destruction established no ethical parameters towards creating an equilibrium condition combining technology and ideas, and institutional interaction with markets to generate definitive directions of consciousness, control and regulation for attaining an ethically reconstructed future social and economic order. Understood in this way, Schumpeter's evolutionary development model was like Popper's (1965) open system conjectural universe of socioeconomic perspectives that are restricted to the domain of economic and social phenomena and no further. While both conflict and moral reconstruction can exist along the path of creative destruction, no prescription is pointed out for attaining a morally and ethically reconstructed world-system.

Consequently, even with the similarity of the **IIE**-learning process dynamics in Myrdal, Schumpeter, and Popper, the absence of a definitive epistemological prescription to attain certain normative ends, as of epistemic unity of systemic knowledge, cannot render self-actualization of the normative and ascertained goal. The result then is impossibility of aggregating ensembles of knowledge-induced and 'de-knowledge'-induced functions into one functional. This latter case is otherwise the result we find in respect of the **IIE**-process methodology of organic unity between the good things of life, as opposed to the linearly differentiated relations of systemic independence of variables and their relations. The evolutionary paths of creative destruction and of open-universe conjecture remain unresolved concepts.[8]

The conjectural universe of Popper is predated in Marx's conception of epistemological pluralism and conflict among multitudes of over-determined competing epistemologies. Resnick and Wolff (1987) comment on this problem of over-determination as one of anomie in the selection of a well-determined socio-scientific thought. Marxist political economy thus became a study of disequilibrium conditions caused by conflicting groups in society at large.

If the above-mentioned undetermined evolutionary dynamics in opposing event-sets is applied to the theme of technological change, which we can denote by the topological mapping T, the result is disequilibrium condition caused by the conflict between the opposing kinds of event-sets. Non-linearity and complexity abide. But there is no guarantee for the pervasive existence of endogeneity between the variables. The absence of endogeneity also rules out the principle of pervasive complementarities between the event-sets. Instead, the postulate of marginal rate of substitution abides. These results are also those of the conjectural spaces that are governed by heteronomy in rationalist reasoning. The idea is contrary to the continuity of relations in segregated spaces of the good and the bad choices defined by the universal and unique nature of the monotheistic law, as explained earlier.

In the case of economic dynamics as an example, the change in real output caused by technological change does not leave a clear picture on the nature of price stabilization and growth. In other words, there is no

---

[8] Consider the following sets of events in terms of their respective variables in the knowledge and 'de-knowledge' sets, $E(\{\theta\},\{\mathbf{z}(\theta)\})$, $E(\{\theta\sim\},\{\mathbf{z}(\theta\sim)\sim\})_r$, respectively. The symbols were defined earlier. Now according to Myrdal and Schumpeter's methodologies, $E((\{\theta\},\{\mathbf{z}(\theta)\})\cap(\{\theta\sim\},\{\mathbf{z}(\theta\sim)\sim\})_r \neq \phi \Rightarrow W(\theta,\theta\sim) = W(z(\theta),z(\theta\sim)\sim)$ is well-defined. This is a contradiction to the concept of wellbeing function as the measure of inter-variable complementarities by circular causation. Now it is impossible to find an Ω and Ω', such that $\Omega\cap\Omega' = \phi$. Therefore, ϕ does not belong to the topological set, which is governed by the topological mapping T. Consequently, the concept of truth and falsehood, good and bad, conflict and coordination, are lost in the absence of ϕ as an operation applied to members of the topological space, such as the two opposite kinds of events in truth and falsehood.

well-determined sign for the following change values: the relationship between the change in real output y_R and technological change, dy_R/dT can have undetermined signs, as T can swing either ways between the opposing event-sets. Likewise, it is true for $d\mu/dT$, for the same reason as mentioned above. Consequently, there is no well-determined sign for $dy_R/d\mu$.μ denotes the rate of change in price level. Now technological change of the type emerging from the idea of evolutionary dynamics mentioned above fails to expand the full-employment level of real output to higher non-inflationary levels. No policy implications can be derived from such anomie in the signs of the technological effects when no distinction is made between the opposite kinds of event-sets.

An example: technology in the IIE-process with complexity, endogeneity, and non-linearity contrasted with mainstream economic theory on money and fiscal dynamics

The non-linear, complex, and endogenous relations arising from circular causation in respect of evaluating the wellbeing function can be applied to the case of monetary and fiscal dynamics at and around the full-employment point of real output with non-inflationary technological induction on output. The idea to present here is this: The complementary use of monetary and fiscal regimes although much desired for economic expansion with price and growth stabilization, the resulting phenomenon remains plagued with uncertainty, unpredictability, and is subject to perturbations that adversely affect stable price and output relations. See *Wikipedia* (http://en.wikipedia.org/wiki/Interaction_between_monetary_and_fiscal_policies): Interaction between monetary and fiscal policy for the contentious issue of monetary and fiscal policy regimes.

For instance, the joint income multiplier effect of both fiscal and monetary liberalization near to the full-employment point of real output, despite that the full-employment point itself is evasive of attainment, pushes the economy into the inflationary region. Along the Keynesian aggregate supply curve and the monetarist classical aggregate supply curve the neutrality of monetary and fiscal policies to output causes the inflationary pressure.

Here we have equated the idea offiscalism with spending (aggregate demand stimulation) rather than with government spending alone. The reason for this is that, while fiscal stimulation proceeds on the consumption and investment functions, the net trade balance equation does not remain benign to change under economic stimulation by government expenditure. Consequently, fiscal expansion spurs total spending. This affects overall economic stimulation and its relationship with price stabilization.

Yet complementarities between monetarism and fiscalism as real sector spending regimes and policies[9] are much desired to engender long-run stable and non-inflationary economic expansion. The attainment of such complementarities in the stable and sustainable forms also unleashes sustainable consequences of the monetary and fiscal (spending) regimes on other critical variables of the money and fiscal functions. Among such variables are employment and real income and entitlements, real profitability and financial stability. Price stability along with the growth of output in the complementary monetary and fiscal regimes therefore, involves endogenous and knowledge-induced learning linkages between the variables underlying the monetary and fiscal functions in the absence of interest rates. Interest rate as impediment to spending by the choice of bank-saving is replaced by rates of profits, market turnover rates, or profitability yields in the real economy.

The attainment of non-inflationary economic growth with complementary monetary and fiscal (spending) regimes being much desired, results in the money (M), finance (F), fiscal (total spending) (S) and real economy (RE) – Money, Finance, Spending, Real Economy (MFSRE) complementary interrelations.Such interrelations form a system in circular causation. Now a systemic study of complementary interrelations in the circular causation system simulates wellbeing function normatively in the light of epistemic oneness.

By taking stock of the above-mentioned goal of growth with price stabilization, we can formulate the complete MFSRE model as follows:

Simulate wellbeing function, $W = W(y,M,f,P,E,\rho)$ (8.19)

Subject to the circular causation relations in respect of estimation followed by simulated levels of complementary relations between $\{y,M,f,P,E,\rho\}$.

Y denotes real output.
M denotes the quantity of money in circulation.

[9] Fiscalism here means total spending as the sum-total, Y_{GDP} = Consumption spending + investment + government expenditure in as much as any government expenditure ought to make the real sector grow by affecting consumption and investments positively in a growing and technologically induced real economy.

F denotes fiscal or spending measure.
P denotes asset prices.
E denotes employment.

ρdenotes profit-sharing rate replacing interest rate.ρcan be treated as a proxy for technological change due to its restructuring effect of the financial system, causing it to be away from interest rate, and moving the economy into a participatory system.

The circular causation relations to simulate the wellbeing function are as follows:

$y = F_y(M,f,P,E,\rho)$ in log-linear or non-linear form of the functional form of F_y; (8.20)
$M = F_M(y,f,P,E,\rho)$ in log-linear or non-linear form of the functional form of F_M; (8.21)
$f = F_f(y,M,P,E,\rho)$ in log-linear or non-linear form of the functional form of F_f; (8.22)
$P = F_P(y,M,f,E,\rho)$ in log-linear or non-linear form of the functional form of F_p; (8.23)
$E = F_E(y,M,f,P,\rho)$ in log-linear or non-linear form of the functional form of F_E; (8.24)
$\rho = F_\rho(y,M,f,P,E)$ in log-linear or non-linear form of the functional form of F_ρ; (8.25)
$\theta = \theta(y,M,f,P,E,\rho)$ in log-linear or non-linear form of the functional form of F_θ. (8.26)

The circular causation relations (8.20)-(8.26) imply either the existence of or the normatively reconstructive possibility for inter-variable complementarities. Such estimations are followed by simulation. The simulated learning coefficients in the epistemological light of unity of knowledge, hence meaning degrees of possible inter-variable complementarities, explain the endogenous nature of the variables in circular causation inter-relations.

How do we explain the passage from ‘estimation’ to ‘simulation’ in order to interpret the prevailing positivistic state followed by the normative reconstructive possibilities in terms of the MFSRE-model to explain complementarities between the sectors by circular causation method? Within these sectors reprcsented by the variables are embedded the measurement of wellbeing and the money-fiscal complementarities to establish price stabilization and economic expansion.

In the MFSRE-model the normative picture is that the quantity of money is brought to connect with real economic activities via suitable productivity-based financial instruments. The fiscal, i.e. spending activity takes place in the real economy to support productivity related activities with technical change. In the absence of interest rates and cost of capital, the mobilization of money into real economy activities, as is the case of spending in productive activities such as investment, causes increases in (y,f,E). Thereby, ρ increases as long as technological advance and endogenous relations between the variables realize increasing returns to scale (Toner, 1999b).

The above kinds of effects mean that as the technology inducing variable ρ increases, increasing returns and the interconnection between monetary and spending (fiscal) regimes cause prices to increase at rates lower than the rate of growth of real output. This is the meaning of stable prices in relationship with changes in real output. Consequently, $[(1/P)*(dP/dt)]/[(1/y)*(dy/dt)] = \varepsilon_{p,y}$ decreases with increase in y. That is, the growth rate of y increases more than the rate of inflation. This is equivalent to having the elasticity of P in respect of y to decrease with the increasing effect of technological change as represented by ρ-effect.The result in the end is price stability. This situation increases the real output and sustains technological change by a multi-directional causality between real output, price level, and technological change.

Besides, technological change is sustained endogenously by a learning process, as interactions proceed on between all variables. Equation (8.25) conveys the theoretical implication that positive coefficients of other variables, as shown, will have a net positive effect on technological advance. Likewise, positive coefficients of 'ρ' in the equations (8.20)-(8.26) will have positive effects on the other predictors.

The expectation on the signs of the estimated coefficients is though not guaranteed. The positivistic nature of data could prove otherwise. For instance, it is possible that interest rates and the cost of capital do not decline; yet the price level remains stable by the action of higher interest rate policy. It is also possible in this case for the financial sector to grow in opposition to the real sector. Consequently, output would grow under the force of financial growth.

Yet at the end, the wellbeing will be adversely affected; for endogenous technological change would fail to exist to complement increasing levels of employment and price stability. The intent of MFSRE-model will be lost by the loss of complementarities between the sectors.

Most importantly, the real economic sector and the financial sector will fail to complement, as resources move away from the real sector into the financial sector in the form of bank-savings. Bank-savings become withdrawals from the real economy, and hence impede productivity gains. This is shown both by the Keynesian comparative statics and the inter-temporal case of resource allocation. The role of knowledge dynamics in the generalized system of complementarities that need to be formed by endogenous circular causation relations as a total unification process between wellbeing-inducing possibilities becomes ineffective.

The positivistic results conveyed by 'estimation' of the system of circular causation (8.20)-(8.28) are therefore, simulated by correcting the unwanted signs of the coefficients. An example here will suffice to convey the approach to attain the normative alternative. Other cases can be explained and applied accordingly by their respective normative correctives.

Take the case of the log-linear form:

$$\log M = A + a.\log y + b.\log f + c.\log P + d.\log E + e.\log\rho \qquad (8.27)$$

$$\varepsilon_{M,f} = b = (f/M)*(dM/df) = \text{percentage change in M/percentage change in f.} \qquad (8.28)$$

A negative value or a small positive value of $\varepsilon_{M,f}$ that is statistically significant will imply a contractionary fiscal (spending) regime in the face of an expansionary monetary regime. By the usual use of Keynesian comparative static analysis, this situation can imply any of the following: crowding-out effect on real output y; or a drawdown of y. The way to arrest the drawdown of y is to keep 'f' (IS curve) as close as possible to M (LM curve). This means better complementarities between the monetary and fiscal (spending) regimes. Such is the normative case as to how closely the fiscal expansion should be to complement with the expansionary monetary regime.

Besides, the above-mentioned normative correction to attain complementary monetary and fiscal policy (with total spending) relationship, which is explained in reference to the IS-LM curves, the normative correction will also replace 'r' by 'ρ' marked on the vertical axis. The negative relationship between 'r' and 'y' yields the elasticity coefficients, $\varepsilon_{\rho,f}$ and $\varepsilon_{\rho,M}$. The shapes of the curves of (P,M), (P,F) are quite different from those of the LM-curve in (r,M), and the IS-curve in (r,F) taken together with increasing ρ (technology effect). In the ρ (technology)-induced case the (P,M) and (P,F) curves are overlapping positively sloped at a stable P-value with increasing ρ effect. In other words, the classical short-run perfectly elastic aggregate supply curve is indefinitely enhanced to overlap with the Keynesian elastic form of the aggregate supply curve. Monetarism and fiscalism (spending regime) are thus made to converge to a common interactive goal of price stability and expansion of real output.

The further result that arises from these kinds of inter-variable relations is that there is no constrained notion of full-employment level of output in the case of technologically induced consequences on price and output stability and sustainability caused by complementarities between monetary and fiscal (spending) regimes, as otherwise is the case contrarily in the IS-LM analysis of full-employment.

Normatively by simulation, the coefficient signs between the variables can be expected by the following relations:

$$M\uparrow \Rightarrow f\uparrow \Rightarrow r\downarrow \Rightarrow c\downarrow \Rightarrow (\mu \rightarrow 0) \Rightarrow y\uparrow \Rightarrow E\uparrow \Rightarrow \rho\uparrow, \quad (8.29)$$

μ denotes rate of change in price level (inflation rate); $(\mu \rightarrow 0)$ denotes convergence to price stability.

The system of feedback inter-relations (8.29) is circular everywhere, and thereby, there are pervasive inter-variable complementarities. This phenomenon is also shown by the equations (8.20)-(8.26). The circular causation chain (8.29) is similar to that given by Mishkin (2007), except that this is now used to explain the MFSRE type relationship in respect of real asset valuation. In our case, we note the complementarities between the monetary regime (M,r,c), fiscal (spending) regime (f), and the real economy (y,E,μ,ρ).

The message inherent in the circular causation relations (8.20)-(8.26) also points to the role of knowledge in this system of endogenously complementary relations. Knowledge in this case means the process of realizing unification (shown by positive signs of coefficients, or lessening negative signs) between the appropriate variables. This is necessarily a normative outlook, but turned into a positivistic one by empirical simulation and structural changes that correct the signs of the coefficients appropriately.

A wider perspective of circular causation in respect of tawhidi unity of knowledge and the world-system

This chapter and the subsequent ones that apply circular causation as the method derived from the *tawhidi* epistemology are empirically premised on received data. The results of 'estimation' are then 'simulated' to yield a progressively learned transformation into a unified worldview in the light of the constructs and instruments of the law of monotheism (*tawhid*), as by the *maqasid* choices. But such an approach although analytically desired is neither the best nor the most meaningful one to reveal the effect of knowledge-induced simulation of an estimated system. We therefore propose yet another approach here in the circular causation method.

This is the *discursive* method rather than the *ranking-of-knowledge parameter* shown by selection and revision of θ-values for a given problem under study. But the two methods can be combined. This would make the discursive and the empirical θ-ranking and averaging method complement each other in a more meaningful analytical undertaking.

A select number of responsible firms' representatives are surveyed byquestionnaires that represent how the firms' activities match the meanings of the attributes of *Allah* called the *asma al-husna* ranked from 1 to 10. The *asma al-husna* are attributes comprising the beatific names of God as they apply to goodness in belief, comprehension, and actions in worldly experiences. Examples here are the use of Islamic financing instruments in investment activities of a selected firm under study.[10]The result would then be represented as in the following table for k-numbered respondents (e.g. processes, time, individuals, regions, firms, etc.).

Table 8.1 can now be arranged for empirical work in Table 8.2. This approach brings out the combined results of survey (discourse) and empirical work (formalism). In Table 8.2 we take k to denote time, t = 1,2,…,T.

The data tabulation of Table 8.2 is now amenable for 'estimation' and 'simulation' of the wellbeing function by the circular causation method as formalized earlier (see expression (8.1) and Figure 8.1). The reference to *asma al-husna* in the assignment of θ-values, and tallying the socio-scientific variables with this over k-numbered observations, carries the *tawhidi* worldview into the socio-scientific world-system.

---

[10]The *Qur'an* (59:24) declares on the beatific names of *Allah*: "He is God, the Creator, the Evolver, the Bestower of Forms (of Colours). To Him belong the Most Beautiful Names: Whatever is in the heavens and on earth, doth declare His Praises and Glory: And He is the Exalted in Might, the Wise."

Table 8.1: Illustrative example: Assigning θ-values to survey results relating the attributes of *asma al-husna* to socioeconomic variables

Socioeconomics Variables: activities	attributes from *asma al-husna* (a_i)	responses by numbered responses	averaged to denote θ-values
x_1^k	i = 1	θ_{11}^k	
	2	θ_{12}^k	
	.	.	
	,	.	θ_1^k=Avg(θ_{11}^k,..,θ_{1n1}^k)
	n_1	θ_{1n1}^k	
x_2^k	i = 1	θ_{21}^k	
	2	θ_{22}^k	
	.	.	
	.	.	θ_2^k=Avg(θ_{21}^k,..,θ_{2n1}^k)
	n_1	θ_{2n1}^k	
.			
x_n^k	i = 1	$\theta_{n,1}^k$	
	2	$\theta_{n,2}^k$	
.		.	θ_n^k=Avg($\theta_{n,1}^k$,..,$\theta_{n,n1}^k$)
.		.	
.	n_1	$\theta_{n,n1}^k$	

Table 8.2: Tabulating survey tallying attributes of *asma al-husna* with variables

t	x_1^t	x_2^t	....	x_n^t	θ_1^t	θ_2^t	...	θ_n^t	θ^{t*} = Avg(θ_1^t,θ_2^t,..,θ_n^t)
1	x_1^1	x_2^1	...	x_n^1	θ_1^1	θ_2^1	...	θ_n^1	θ^1
2	x_1^2	x_2^2	...	x_n^2	θ_1^2	θ_2^2	...	θ_n^2	θ^2
.									
.									
T	x_1^T	x_2^T	...	x_n^T	θ_1^T	θ_2^T	...	θ_n^T	θ^T

Conclusion: Bringing together the *qur'anic* monotheistic law of unity of knowledge projected by organic pairing between diversities[11]

The precept of complementarities, caused by multivariate and multi-systemas well as intra-systemic pairing, conveys the evidential proof of the monotheistic law. This is the way the *Qur'an* explains the monotheistic law and the precept of the oneness of God in the order of things by the signs of God[12] in abstraction and evidences of the world-system. In this world-system are pervasively interacting, integrating, and evolutionary (**IIE**) learning entities and processes that unify thedomains of heart, mind and matter in our material choices. The proof of universality and uniqueness of the monotheistic law, through a super-cardinal topological argumentation, sets the pattern of the universe. In this are comprehended, observed, and applied the signs of God in the order and scheme of all things.

Thereby, the universal system and cybernetic properties of inter-variable and inter-causal complementarities join together with the non-linear, complex, and endogenous nature of evolutionary learning by unity of knowledge. The inductive and empirical translation of the deductive premise of unity of knowledge is realized by the method of circular causation. This method becomes the way of deciphering the unity of systemic knowledge between the good things of life, while also unravelling the separateness of the ethically fallen choices and states of positive evidences. These latter ones wait for simulative reconstruction into moral capability. We therefore conclude that the be-all and end-all of the entire of reality is premised on the monotheistic unity of knowledge. Unity is evidenced by the circular causation method of evaluation. That is,

---

[11] *Qur'an* (36:36): "Glory to God, Who created in pairs all things that the earth produces, as well as their own (human) kind and (other) things of which they have no knowledge."

Qur'an (13: 3): "Of every kind He made in pairs, two and two: He draws the Night as a veil over the Day. Behold, verily in these things there are Signs for those who consider."

[12] *Qur'an* (2:164-65): "Behold! In the creation of the heavens and the earth; in the alternation of the Night and the Day; in the sailing of the ships through the Ocean for the profit of mankind; in the rain which God sends down from the skies, and the life which He gives therewith to an earth that is dead; in the beasts of all kinds that He scatters through the earth; in the change of the winds, and the clouds which they trail like their slaves between the sky and the earth; -- (here) indeed are Signs for a people that are wise."

'estimation' is followed by 'simulation' of the wellbeing function as the criterion of organic pairing and relationship between the good things of life, and organic conflicts otherwise.

Yet for all this, the ultimate nature of the self (heart), mind (abstraction), and matter (world-system) interrelations within the circular causation relations of the large scale universe of *tawhid* from the beginning to the end of existence, the study of this method has remained marginal. Nonetheless, the universe is the theatre of grand interconnectedness unravelled creatively by evolutionary learning and represented by the circular causation method of concrescence. On this fact, the great philosopher Kant has written(See Ledger & Pickard op cit, p. 8): "Parts bind themselves mutually into the unity of a whole in such a way that they are mutually cause and effect of one another".

This chapter has formalized the *functional* ontological method of 'estimating' and 'simulating' the wellbeing function by means of the circular causation system in two subtle ways.These can be seen as original contributions in heterodox socio-scientific study. The question of value imputation in the socio-scientific variables has been carried out both by the formal approach and by the valuation approach of the beatific names of God in His divine Oneness -*asma al-husna*- in survey design for tabulating response data in formal application. We referred to this combination as the formal analytical approach with the discursive analytical approach.

Likewise, on the utter impracticality of linear forms and absence of circular causality in the form of methodological individualism and methodological independence between entities, Rousseau (trans. Cranston, 1968, p. 71) wrote: "It is said that Japanese mountebanks can cut a child under the eyes of spectators, throw the different parts in the air, and then make the child come down, alive and all of a piece. This is more or less the trick that our political theorists perform – after dismembering the social body with a sleight of the hand worthy of the foreground, they put the pieces together again anyhow."

In the end we note that, without the overarching universal conception of wellbeing, pervasive complementarities between the good things of life cannot be gained. Such pervasive complementarities are ordained by the monotheistic law. They are formally expressed by non-linearity of complex and endogenous relations between intra-systemic and inter-systemic variables. Yet the same methodology of unity of knowledge in *tawhid* explains both complementarities and its opposite marked by methodological individualism, methodological independence, differentiation, and rationalistic conjectures. Despite this case, transformation from the opposite state to the *tawhidi* world-system is made possible by returning the world-system to its true divine foundation.

We can now summarily explain the above-mentioned variant systems as follows (Choudhury, 2009): The true concept of system is conveyed only by the **IIE**-process delineation that arises from the *Qur'an* and is explained by the *sunnah*.[13] All other ideas of systems are either differentiated by

---

[13] A saying (*hadith*) of the Prophet Muhammad that explained the learning path through the world-system beginning from *tawhid* and ending in *tawhid* is this:

The socio-scientific interactions that define the directionally 'straight' but relationally complex perspective of *sirat al-mustaqim* are brought out in a reliable *hadith* of the Prophet Muhammad. The *hadith* is narrated by Abdullah, a companion of the prophet. The Prophet drew a square and then drew a line in the middle of it and let it extend outside the square and then drew several small lines attached to that central line, and said, "This is the human being, and this (the square) is his lease of life, encircling him from all sides (or has encircled him), and this (line) which is outside (the square), is his hope, and these small lines are the calamities and troubles (which may befall him), and if one misses him, another will snap (i.e. overtake) him, and if the other misses him, a third will snap (i.e overtake) him." (Sahih al-Bukhari, Vol. 8, *hadith* No. 426).

In this *hadith* the straight lines outside the square can be understood to represent the primordial nature of the righteous path (*sirat al-mustaqim*). The two protruding parts of the straight line outside the square explain the *qur'anic* verse (42:53), "The path of God to Whom belongs all that is in the heavens and all that is in the earth. Verily, all matters at the end go to God."

The *hadith* also conveys the self-referential methodology of *tawhidi* epistemology that establishes the unified interrelationships among the three parts, namely, the epistemological, the ontological, and the ontic. The process of interrelationships once again rises to new realization of *tawhid* and so on circularly along the incessantly process-based path. This kind of circular relationship, explained by the correspondence, 'from *tawhid* in the primal to knowledge-centered world-systems to *tawhid* in the hereafter', is shown in the *Qur'an* to function both within actual experience as well as in the terminal culmination of all knowledge-flows. Likewise, such a passage applies to knowledge-induced events. Together their final determination in the scale of just reward and retribution is in the hereafter (*akhira*).

The straight line inside the square perturbed by the smaller ones around it can be understood as signifying the worldly effects upon the primordial righteous straight path. The worldly lines distort and distract our worldly lives from the full comprehension of *tawhid* as the universal and unique worldview. The totality of the straight line (*sirat al-mustaqim*) 'from *tawhid* to *tawhid* in *akhira* through the process of knowledge-flows in actual experience', summarizes the unified perspective of the *tawhidi* episteme. Such a process forms the comprehension and internalization in actual experience by the process-based order described by cumulative knowledge-flows premised on *tawhid*.

methodological individualism and methodological independence or they form a disequilibrium system of dialectics. Such contrasting systems are shown in Figure8.2.

This author considers extension of the under-mentioned *hadith* of the Prophet to higher dimensions of mathematical topologies (Choudhury, 2013). By suchan extrapolation possibility, the stated*hadith* is inferred to apply to the domain of *tasbih* as consciousness in explaining the *res extensa* of the discursive process of *shura-tasbih* experience concerning the world-system. The *shura-tasbih* experience enables comprehension not only of the domain of mundane affairs, but also of the entire world-system along with its subtle and substantive relationship in the abstract and socio-scientific analytical entirety.

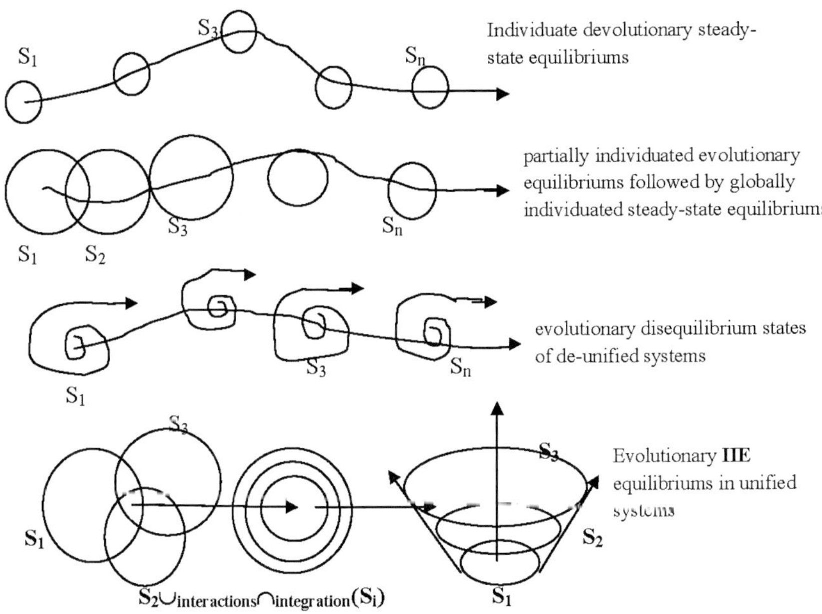

Figure 8.2: Kinds of evolutionary equilibriums with different systemic characteristics

Statistical Appendix: Explaining Socio-economic Development by means of Circular Causation Model involving GDP, Price Level, and Poverty: The Case of Indonesia

The wellbeing function in the measured form is estimated by the regression equation:

$$\ln\theta = 9.96 - 0.044 \ln G - 2.47 \ LnP - 0.150 \ln CPI \quad (8A1)$$

t-stats (3.10) (-0.32) (-3.01) (-0.88)
$R^2 = 52.3$; DW-stats = 2.395

Equation (8A1) is expressible as,

$$\Theta = \exp(9.96).G^{-0.44}.P^{-2.47}.CPI^{-0.158} \quad (8A2)$$

The estimated coefficients show that

$$\ln G = -4.09 - 0.192 \ln\theta + 1.24 \ln P + 0.369 \ln CPI \quad (8A3)$$

t-stats: (-0.46) (-0.32) (0.55) (1.05)
R^2=12.0; DW-stats = 1.961

$$\ln P = 3.90 - 0.174 \ln\theta + 0.0200 \ln G - 0.110 \ln CPI \quad (8A4)$$

t-stats: (17.70) (-3.01) (0.55) (-3.25)
$R^2 = 72.2$; DW-stats = 2.161

$$\ln CPI = 19.3 - 0.408 \ln\theta + 0.229 \ln G - 4.24 \ln P \quad (8A5)$$

t-stats: (4.41) (-0.88) (1.05) (-3.25)
R^2= 55.3; DW-stats = 1.224

The statistical results of estimation of the circular causation relations point out an absence of sustainable development in Indonesia. That is, while an increase in CPI reduces poverty, the growth is inflationary with a partial elasticity coefficient of 0.229 for CPI with respect to G, and 0.369 of G with respect to CPI. Poverty cannot be reduced in the presence of such perverse relationship between CPI and G, and recursively between G and CPI. This explains that, if an increase in government expenditure inflates prices, the result is transmitted to Gthrough such an inflationary effect of government expenditure.

On the other hand, if G increases under the combined effect of government expenditure and market forces, this ignites inflation, indicating that total real productivity is low. Consequently, the poor are not part of the productive process. Therefore, an increase in poverty increases G. The partial elasticity coefficient of G to P is high at 1.24. On the other hand, an increase in G increases poverty by an elasticity of 0.02. The conclusion from such relationships is that there is no empowerment generating productive participation of the poor in economic growth. All these effects may also be creating resource curse in the economic system in Indonesia.

The joint effects of poverty P, CPI, and G are projected in the wellbeing function. The estimated result of the wellbeing function points to a dire need for the correct forms of causality to engender wellbeing. Wellbeing is found to be distant from its attainment in the estimated case of the relationships between the mentioned variables and the wellbeing proxy by θ-variables in expression (8A1).Likewise, there exist adverse relationships of θ to the (G,CPI,P)-variables as shown in the estimated equations (8A3)-(8A5) with different elasticity coefficients.

Expression (8A1) or (8A2)points out that, while the coefficients between P and θ, and between CPI and θ have the correct signs (-ve), the sign of G to θ is perverse for wellbeing. A good deal of coefficient simulation of each of the equations leading to the θ-simulated value is in place. This requires a substantive change in the structure of growth and development to generate the proper relations for attaining poverty alleviation, price stabilization, and participatory economic development.

The statistical results also reveal that the linear form of circular causation models adopted are not a good fit to the data. Hence non-linear forms of the circular causation models ought to be a better choice. In the modelling of simulation of wellbeing, such a model selection remains an open question. The model selection is also related with the epistemological theme of the knowledge-induced worldview of *tawhidi* unity of knowledge. For example, the combination of circular causation with pervasive complementarities in the **IIE**-learning process model must necessarily imply the prevalence of controlled non-linearity between the variables not allowing extreme forms of perturbations that would cause absence of predictability, measurement, and inference. Simulation out of estimation, which implies convergence to the state of evolutionary equilibrium, must therefore be based on complexity and non-linearity but of the type of controllability within perturbations.

Table 8.A1: Statistical Time-Series Data for Indonesia

Year	θ	G	P	CPI
1996	7.93	7	17.47	637
1997	8.52	8	16.3	401
1998	6.05	NA	24.23	398
1999	1.12	13.2	23.5	676
2000	5.64	0.4	18.95	416
2001	4.89	4.9	19.06	392
2002	6.07	3.5	17.6	424
2003	6.44	4.4	17.42	679
2004	6.99	4.9	16.66	1000
2005	7.2	5.1	16.63	1162
2006	5.69	5.7	19.45	1813
2007	7.43	5.5	16.58	2745
2008	8.16	6.3	15.42	1355
2009	7.84	6.4	14.15	2534
2010	9.25	4.5	13.33	3703
2011	8.24	6.5	13.33	3821

How are θ-values calculated – the empirical case?

θ-values are ranks for complementarities between the variables in the columns (G, P, CPI). The calculation of such ranks is also an open question on methods. One way is to distribute the column ranks from 1to10 in ascending (or descending) order of appropriateness of the corresponding variables. Hence, the highest value of G would be assigned 10; and then all other values prorated by interpolation or extrapolation between the values of the variables. On the other hand, the lowest value of P would be assigned 10 in this column, and all other variables prorated by extrapolation in descending order as P increases. This is the same method for CPI column values. The θ-values by columns so generated are then averaged across the three column θ-values to yield the final column of θ-values.

Following the computational method of generating rank values of θ-values by columns and average, a discursive method is adopted to tally the further set of appropriate values. The whole θ-setting is then a combination of empirical work and discursive validation as prompted by the **IIE**-evolutionary learning process methodology.

Other algorithmic ways of generating θ-values as ranks of complementarities across the row variables can be used. The example given above is illustrative, not complete. The complete empirical exercise will involve simulated values of the predictors by way of changing the coefficient values in the circular causation system of equations (8A2-8A6). These predictor values will then reflect the target values in a given learning process. Other processes in the same way can be generated by re-simulated predictor variables including the new θ-values over time. In this restarting process the *tawhidi* episteme is recalled in the form of *maqasid as-shari'ah* to form the choices of the new evolutionary learning process. Such a restarting of the new processes requires revisiting the *tawhidi* episteme [(Ω,S)→θ*]. In our phenomenological formalism revisiting the *tawhidi* episteme is termed 'recall'.

In every case, new processes are defined by the simulacra of new predictor values of the variables including the θ-values over time. These values get determined by simulation with fresh changes in the coefficient values in accordance with the principle of pervasive complementarities as the empirical sign of unity of knowledge between variables, and thereby, the measurement of wellbeing. Generating such simulacra of values is a tedious job using the statistical method as shown in this chapter. But the method of Spatial Domain Analysis (SDA) of the Geographical Information System (GIS) is a most suitable method that can be used to bring out the dynamic nature of generating simulacra of predictor values via the underlying learning processes. My students have used Autoregressive Estimation/Simulation methods in their doctoral dissertations.

In the end, the time-series of simulacra of predictor values of variables including θ-values can be traced along the process-oriented path of evolution by learning. A number of comparative evolutionary learning possibilities thus arise. Firstly, there is the comparative 'estimated' and 'simulated' time-series path of the variables and wellbeing function (8A1,8A2). This comprises learning within a given process. Secondly, the simulacra of similar learning paths of the variables and wellbeing function bring out the evolutionary learning processes in respect of changes in the coefficients in the light of [(Ω,S)→θ*].Thirdly, there is thepossibility of describing the time-series path of the simulacra of simulated values. Table 8A2 explains these comparative possibilities.

Table 8A2: Comparative estimated and simulated possibilities of predictor values by circular causation

(1) Estimation over time within a process $\{est(z_t = (G,P,CPI,\theta)_t\}$
↓

(2) Simulation over time within a process $\{sim.(z_t = (G,P,CPI,\theta$; changes in coefficients of $\{est(z_t = (G,P,CPI,\theta)_t\})_t\}$
↓

(3) Simulacra of simulations dynamic form of across processes $\{sim.(z_t = (G,P,CPI,\theta$; changes in coefficients of $\{est(z_t = (G,P,CPI,\theta)_t\})_t\}$
↓

(4) Evolutionary learning path: evolutionary wellbeing values as measured by θ-values over simulacra of processes *qua* processes

References

Barrow, J.D., 1991,*Theories of Everything, the Quest for Ultimate Explanation*, Oxford University Press, Oxford, Eng.

Bertuglia, C.S. &Vaio, F., 2005, "Dynamical systems and the phase space", in their, *Non-linearity, Chaos & Complexity, the Dynamics of Natural and Social Systems*, pp. 49-70, Oxford University Press, Oxford, UK.

Cantner, U. Luc Gaffard, J. & Nesta, L., (eds.), 2009,*Schumpeterian Perspectives on Innovation, Competition, and Growth*. Springer Verlag, New York, NY.

Choudhury, M.A., 2011, *Islamic Economics and Finance: an Epistemological Inquiry*, Emerald Group Publishing Ltd., Bingley, UK.

—. 2012, "Endogeneity and complexity in economic modeling", *Kybernetes, International Journal of Cybernetics, Systems and Management Science*,(42)2.

—. 2013, "The *qur'anic* universe in knowledge, time and space with reference to matrix game in Islamic behavioural financial decision-making", *Journal of Muamalat and Islamic Finance Research*, forthcoming.

Choudhury, M.A. & Hossain, M.S., 2006, *Development Planning in the Sultanate of Oman*, The Edwin Mellen Press, Lewiston, New York.

Dewitt, B., 1992,*Supermanifolds*, Cambridge University Press, Cambridge, England.

Einstein, A., n.d., "The laws of science and the laws of ethics", in his,*Lectures in Physics*, Philosophical Library, New York, NY.

—. trans. by Lawson, R.W., 1954, *Relativity, the Special and the General Theory*, pp. 154, Methuen University Paperbacks, London, Eng.

Gruber, T.R., 1993, "A translation approach to portable ontologies", *Knowledge Acquisition*, (5)2, 199-200.

Hogg, R.V. & Craig, A.T., 1965, *Introduction to Mathematical Statistics*, Macmillan Co., New York, NY.

Kant, I. quoted in Ledger, I. & Pickard, S. (eds.), 2004,*Creation and Complexity: Interdisciplinary Issues in Science and Religion*, ATF Press, Adelaide, Australia.

Lucaks, J., 1968,*Historical Consciousness*, Harper & Row Publishers, New York, NY.

Mishkin, F.S., 2007b, "The transmission mechanism and the role of asset prices in monetary policy", *Monetary Policy Strategy*, pp. 59-74, The MIT Press, Cambridge, MA.

Myrdal, G., 1958, "The principle of cumulation", in Streeten, P. (ed.), *Value in Social Theory, a Selection of Essays on Methodology by Gunnar Myrdal*, pp. 198-205, Harper & Brothers Publishers,New York, NY.

Nikaido, H., 1987, "Fixed point theorems", in J. Eatwell, M. Milgate & P. Newman (eds.),*The New Palgrave: General Equilibrium*, pp. 139-44, W.W. Norton, New York, NY.

Pindyck, R.S. & Rubinfeld, D.L., 2001, "The Degree of Economies of Scope", in *Microeconomics*, Fifth Edition, p. 231, Prentice-Hall Inc., Upper Saddle River, New Jersey.

Popper, K., 1965,*Conjectures and Refutations: The Growth of Scientific Knowledge*, Basic Books, New York.

Rousseau, J-J. trans. byCranston, M.,1968, *The Social Contract*, Penguin Books, London, England.

Resnick, S.A. &Wolff, R.D., 1987,*Knowledge and Class, A Marxian Critique of Political Economy*, The University of Chicago Press, Chicago, IL.

Schumpeter, J.A., 1961,*The Theory of Economic Development*, Chapter II, (trans.) by Opie, R., Harvard University Press, Cambridge, MA.

Smart, N., 2000, "The nature of morality", in his, *Worldviews*, pp. 114-116, Prentice Hall, Upper Saddle River, New Jersey.

Toner, P., 1999a, "Gunnar Myrdal (1898-1987): circular and cumulative causation as the methodology of the social sciences", in his, *Main*

Currents in Cumulative Causation, the Dynamics of Growth and Development, Chapter 5, Macmillan Press Ltd., Houndmills, Hampshire.

—. 1999b, "Conclusion", in *Main Currents in Cumulative Causation, the Dynamics of Growth and Development*, Chapter 7, Macmillan Press Ltd., Houndmills, Hampshire.

CHAPTER NINE

A QUANTITATIVE APPLICATION OF CIRCULAR CAUSATION METHOD IN EVALUATING *TAWHIDI* WELLBEING AND SUSTAINABLE DEVELOPMENT

M.A. CHOUDHURY, T. MARIYANTI AND M.S. HOSSAIN

Background

Economic models to date have sparsely matured in the area of encompassing the broader explanation of embedded social processes and events. Embedded systems are characterized by the complexity of system-dynamics and by the variables that represent the complexity of the embedded sub-systems. Instead, economic modelling has proceeded on as an isolated nicety within its own niche of specialization, but at the loss of social realism. Mathematics and statistics have thus continued on to be used in economic modelling in isolation of the greater outlook of social, cultural, and multifaceted decision-making processes (Beed & Kane 1991). These approaches together characterize social and economic interaction. This kind of deepening academic development in economics, as in science, has been to the detriment of studying and enriching the field of credible prediction of the events as we experience them (Soros, 1998).

Yet the system modelling and inferences gained in the field of an embedded system, being overarching across sub-systems of the human entirety, reflect a semblance of methodological universality of such broader formal modelling. And if the field of such overarching extensions across interdisciplinary sub-systems expands, the emerging models are likely to converge into uniqueness of the modelling enterprise by their capability for higher dimensional analysis. Boland (1991) writes in this regard that a higher level of falsification of a theory may supplant a lower level and thus comprise ever expanding domains of universality of emergent theories over previous ones.

Future of socio-scientific modelling

The formalism on convergence to a universal and unique theory in all the sciences is a project for realizing a model that can answer the nature of scientific arguments in general and of 'everything' (Barrow, 1991). The same methodical characteristics are extended to the derived particulars of the general-system model. Such a course of research invites a deluge of diverse issues and problems that are specific to different disciplines yet are embedded in the generalized system model. We therefore coin the term 'the socio-scientific', to represent the holistic systemic worldview of integrated science and society (Sztompka, 1974). Within this social embedding lies economics as a social science.

Also, since universality and uniqueness of such a model applies to all issues and problems across diverse disciplines, the modelling enterprise invokes the epistemology of unity of knowledge between the diversely emergent categories of issues, problems, and disciplines. The resulting theory of the socio-scientific 'everything' now combines a new substantive theory of the social sciences and the natural sciences taken together in one intellectual enterprise. The organic linkage and explanation of concepts and implications, emanating from the application of the unique and universal model, has its methodology premised on the epistemology of unity of knowledge to study the dynamics of organically unified systems. These by their fuzzy spaces of lack of determinateness reflect non-linear relations.

With such extensions of the modelling enterprise, the aspects of the overarching exercise combined with its emerging character of universality and uniqueness in studying the organic unity and process orientation of the embedded sub-systems, bring forth the investigation of the embedded social political economy. The corresponding theory of such a process-oriented extensively systemic study as social political economy, yields a study of political economy that is different from the mainstream one. Now the traditional definition of political economy ceases to be simply the study of differentiated and disequilibrium dynamics of competition in ownership, production, and distribution of wealth and resources (George, [1897]) between opposing agents in economy and society.

The field of social political economy is different. Social political economy as an embedded socio-scientific system of interactions is understood as the epistemological study of multitudes of organically unifying sub-systems of the human order. The forces underlying the meeting grounds of interaction between such systems show conflict. Interaction, integration, and organically relational unification remain absent (Sztompka, 1991). When conflicts exist, the epistemological groundwork of unity of knowledge between the embedded sub-systems becomes a normative moral and ethical field of social reconstruction out of the positivistic nature of an unwanted situation of conflicts and differentiation. Non-linearity in the case of an embedded system modelling bears the properties of interaction leading to integration and evolutionary intra-system and inter-systemic dynamics by the force of endogenous learning fired in the episteme of unity of knowledge. These properties regiment the whole of the modelled system for predictability and controllability. The sub-systems now form unity in the sense of system-ensemble and convey analytical consequences that are premised on the epistemological worldview of the unified social whole.

Now evolution as history of the future of such a system-ensemble represents a socially reconstructed possibility of sustainability that is driven by the epistemological nature of organic unity of systems. We explain such extensively organic unity of relations in terms of pervasive complementarities between the variables and agencies of the embedded sub-systems. The principle of pervasive complementarities in social embedding of the economic, social, and other forces is equivalent to having intra-systemic and inter-systemic participation between agents, agencies, and their characteristic variables (Choudhury, 2007).

Objective

In this chapter, carrying over from the previous ones, we continue to introduce the substantive area of new research of systemic interaction, integration, and evolutionary dynamics driven by the epistemic worldview of unity of knowledge. Here we take up an additional application of this unified concept to the field of sustainability in development. The *tawhidi* methodological worldview becomes the foundational premise to derive the methodical working of this monotheistic worldview through the application of the method of circular causation. The monotheistic episteme of unity of knowledge as derived from *tawhidi* epistemology overarches across economy, science, and societal interrelations. The epistemological groundwork of such organic interrelations is based on unity of systemic knowledge. It addresses the phenomenon of organic linkages between all the disciplines in respect of all issues and problems that are represented by selected system-variables and their interrelations. Here deductive reasoning leads into inductive analytics; inductive reasoning re-emerges as deductive continuity of learning across processes of organic unity of knowledge and materiality. This unified and recursive inter-causal relationship between the deductive and inductive reasoning describes the total field of unity of knowledge and its induced forms. The governing worldview of unity of knowledge in non-linear spaces presents complex learning dynamics. Nonetheless, the emergent complex processes are characterized by predictability and controllability.

Explanation

The inherent unifying methodology expresses two kinds of participative organic unity of being and becoming (Prigogine, 1980). Firstly, there is the inner dynamics of interaction within sub-systems. This leads into Integration (convergence). Interaction leading to Integration continues on into Evolutionary learning processes. This chain of regenerated cause-effect circularly completes the **IIE**-process dynamics. Such interactive, integrative, and evolutionary dynamics appear and melt away within and across the disciplines in reference to the holistic approach while investigating the problems under study. All these properties comprise intra-system dynamics. Secondly, simultaneously by continuous type mathematical functionals, there comes about evolution of the interactive and integrative processes into new phases of evolutionary learning systems (Whitehead, 1978). Such emergent processes are referred to as evolutionary learning processes across systems over time as the recorder of events.

The resulting organically unifying phases within any learning process are universalized and remain unique in the interdependent socio-scientific issues by virtue of the dynamics of interaction leading to integration and thereby to evolution. Such dynamics occur continuously in phases of learning and repetition of the same kind of inter-causal functional relations between the selected variables.

Knowledge-flows arising from the systemic understanding of embedded sub-systemic interrelations become the foundational force of consequences and change. While knowledge is epistemic in nature, relating to the system-ensemble concept (Hubner, 1985), its degree of incidence to form organic unity of embedded systems is evaluated by positivistic methods of analysis. The estimated results point out the normative alternatives that ought to be simulated, as opposed to the socially unwanted estimated ones.

In such evolutionary learning dynamics of embedded sub-systems, 'time' enters in a peculiar way. Time *does not cause* change or reconstruction. It simply plays the deterministic role of recording events and results of evaluations. Yet in the **IIE**-process methodology, any state of the socio-scientific system is evolved into newer ones by knowledge-flows that are endogenously generated and continued on along the **IIE**-learning processes over time. 'Events' by definition are thereby a concrescence of knowledge induction in space and time. Consequences of the events, as by economic valuations, actualize in the dimensions of knowledge, space, and time (Choudhury, 2009).

All events in such an epistemic framework of learning dynamics are probabilistic in nature. They span the self-same patterns of circular causality between embedded systems. Thereby, there arise extensively complementary organic relations between the variables representing specific sub-systems. All variables are induced by knowledge-flows. Hence knowledge-induced variables remain endogenous in interrelating sub-systems by the **IIE**-evolutionary learning processes.

A brief review of the literature in the thematic field of embedded system modelling

In this brief section (see Choudhury & Hossain, 2007 for extensive coverage) we point out a formalism of the type of **IIE**-process modelling. The emergent non-linear models generate perturbations caused by the interdisciplinary nature and the inherently complex aggregation that emerge (Bertuglia & Vaio, 2005). Mathematical functionals of non-linear topological spaces arise (Kupka & Peixoto, 1993).

Such inferences on the nature of non-linear modelling that emerge by system embedding go beyond Chichilnisky (1990), Gelfand (1961), and Debreu (1990). But the idea of complex aggregation of topological cells into higher dimensional manifolds was started by Smale (1990). The multilinear economic relations forming tensor variations of the coefficients of the manifold functionals is referred to here as 'foliation'.

In the end, the normative study of reconstructed systems is made amenable to complex events in interactive sub-systems. Consequently, convexity of optimal surfaces and the assumptions of perfectly competitive markets, and steady-state equilibrium together with the postulate of optimization, cannot mark the field of such mathematical applications in economic theory. On the other hand, linearity of the mathematical equations that characterize all of mathematical applications in econometrics is due to the parametric constant coefficients or assumed patterns of probabilistic variations in the estimated coefficients. At best, assumed Bayesian probability distributions are assigned to the estimated coefficients.

Contrary to the linear approach, inter-system complexity caused by embedding is exhibited by the learned values of the 'simulated' coefficients of the model. The estimated coefficients are probabilistic in nature (Choudhury, 2012). But the probability distribution function of the coefficients in the case of modelling sub-system embedding is determined not by pre-assignment, such as by normal distribution. Rather, the probability distribution of 'simulated' coefficients in the **IIE**-process models of intra-systemic and inter-systemic embedding is determined by the normative socio-scientific states desired. In such states of the socioeconomic data, the unified organic relations between them appear in all the sub-systems of the grand design. This is the topological result that spans *res extensa* across knowledge-induced embedded sub-systems.

IIE-model formalism in non-linear topological space

We construct here the salient features of the evolutionary learning process model in Figure 9.1. By the recursive effect (circular causation) of interaction and integration between the variables (Myrdal, 1958) $(x_1(\theta),x_2(\theta))$ by way of f_1 and $\beta.f_1^{-1}$; f_2 and $\alpha.f_2^{-1}$, an evaluation functional follows. It is referred to as the wellbeing function by virtue of its descriptive functional based on unity of knowledge. The knowledge-flow variables determined in terms of the foundational episteme of unity of knowledge are the assigned θ-values.

The wellbeing function is the evaluative criterion that normatively measures degrees of 'estimated' and 'simulated' complementarities that are possible between the selected variables. Such degrees of complementarities represent the epistemic sign of participatory interrelationship between the selected variables. The degrees of positivistic estimated and normatively simulated complementarities are empirically set on the basis of given observations. The 'estimated' circular causation equations are next simulated by assigning new values to the estimated coefficients. The simulated coefficients and thereby the predictor-variables reflect the normative perspective of change in the light of systemic unity of knowledge attainable at possible levels. Such simulated functionals are denoted by g_1 and g_2 in Figure 9.1. There are as many circular causation relations as there are variables. The circular causation system of relations is thus uniquely solvable for any set of assigned predictor-values of the variables that are simulated.

The wellbeing functional criterion that is simulated by the recursive relations intra-system (i.e. in a single process) is formally denoted by $W(x_1(\theta),x_2(\theta))$. The recursive relations, i.e. the circular causation equations to estimate and simulate the circular causation relations between the variables are the following ones:

$$x_1 = f_1(x_2(\theta),\theta);\ x_2 = f_2(x_1(\theta),\theta); \tag{9.1}$$

and the recursively generated knowledge-value given by,

$$\theta = G(x_1(\theta),x_2(\theta)). \tag{9.2}$$
$$i = 1, 2$$

Note that since the simulated θ-function shown by G(..) is a monotonic positive empirical representation of the wellbeing index, therefore by the implicit function theorem of continuously differentiable functions of calculus, we can write, $\theta = G(x_1(\theta),x_2(\theta))$. We note that this derived function is a 'similar' functional representation of $W(x_1(\theta),x_2(\theta))$. Thus the measured $\theta \equiv W(.) = G(..)$ represents the 'measurable' objective functional of wellbeing. The ordinal assignment of θ-values are computed as ranked ordinal numbers. Such ordinal ranks are derived by noting the trends in the $(x_1(\theta),x_2(\theta))$-values by virtue of the need for complementarities between them. Such complementarities are deduced in reference to the episteme of unity of knowledge as the ethical consequence of organic relationship between the knowledge-induced variables.

Next, evolutionary organic relations generate new knowledge-flows. Evolutionary knowledge-flows continue on regenerating across processes of learning. Each process is 'evaluated' by 'estimation' followed by 'simulation'. These appear continuously along the simulacra of evolutionary learning processes in the (knowledge, space, and time)-structure. Such emergent evolutionary learning processes of inter-systemic θ-values etc. are formalized in the following way:

A completed intra-system process is denoted by:

$$[\theta \rightarrow (x_1(\theta),x_2(\theta)) \rightarrow \text{Simulated } W(x_1(\theta),x_2(\theta)), \tag{9.3}$$

$$\text{subject to } x_1 = f_1(x_2(\theta),\theta);\ x_2 = f_2(x_1(\theta),\theta). \tag{9.4}$$

$$\theta = G(x_1(\theta),x_2(\theta)) \text{ reflects } W(x_1(\theta),x_2(\theta))]. \tag{9.5}$$

The end of a process is followed by the evolution of new θ-values, etc. Note that intra-system (processes) type recursive θ-values represent simulated wellbeing indexes by the improvement of the estimated coefficient values in reference to actual $(x_1(\theta),x_2(\theta))$-values, followed by the simulated vector, say $(x_1^*(\theta),x_2^*(\theta))$. On the other hand, evolutionary θ-values across processes are inter-systemic in nature. They represent continuously recursive learning over the dimensions of knowledge, space and time.

Non-linear transforms

The monotonic positive mappings, say F_i, across repetitively interactive, integrative, and evolutionary (**IIE**-processes) intra-systems and inter-systems denoted by 'i' preserve the self-same kind of **IIE** learning processes along with their circular causation mappings in evaluating wellbeing. Yet they do not necessarily converge to the identity map. That is, recursion of knowledge-flows does not form *linear* mappings. *Non-linearity* of the functional relations (mappings) between the variables remains permanent by the induction of knowledge-flows $(\{\theta\})$-values.

We can therefore write the following results with all forms of composite mappings:

$$F_i o f_2^{-1} = F_i o \alpha.I = \alpha'.I. \tag{9.6}$$

F_i here denote arbitrary mappings of the f-functions at the ith round of **IIE** within a given learning (recursive) process. α' is scalar in non-linear mappings. It is therefore a function of $(\{\theta\})$-values in the evaluation of wellbeing function.

Likewise,

$$F_i o f_2 = F_i o \beta.I = \beta'.I. \tag{9.7}$$

β' are compounded (composite) scalar functionals of $(\{\theta\})$-values on β carrying the implication like α' as scalar.

$$F_i o f_4 = F_i o \gamma I = \gamma'.I. \tag{9.8}$$

γ' are compounded scalar functionals of $(\{\theta\})$-values on γ.

It is likewise the same kinds of recursive mappings for chains of mappings along the **IIE**-learning processes. The Figures 9.1 and 9.2 can then be extended by an indefinite number of integrated mappings, now explaining as many interrelations as there are emergent variables in the compound maps.

For inter-system learning following evaluation of W(.), the results will be as follows: $F_i(W)$ is a monotonic positive transformation of W(.) by the positive mappings F_i in the ith **IIE**-simulation process. Thus, $F_i(f_1) = F_i(x_1(\theta))$ represent simulated forms of the estimated functional with $x_1 = f_1(x_2(\theta),\theta)$. $F_i(f_1)$ as arbitrary monotonic positive transformation is recursively set by the simulated θ-value in the ith round of **IIE**-learning process. $F_i(.)$ thus denotes simulacra of non-linear transforms (Fitzpatrick, 2003; Wallerstein, 1998) with i = 1,2,…,n..

F_i are non-linear by virtue of the density of {θ}-values in its ith simulated set of variables. That is,

$$\text{plim}\{\theta\} = \theta^* + \varepsilon(\theta), \tag{9.9}$$

$$d\varepsilon(\theta)/d\theta > 0. \tag{9.10}$$

These relations define evolutionary equilibriums (Grandmont, 1989; Burstein, 1991).

It can be readily shown by a diagram with 'θ' on the vertical axis and the socio-scientific variable on the horizontal axes that, the area under the non-linear surface with {plim{θ}} will include all the sequences of {plim{θ}} under the linear surface, but not vice-a-versa. Consequently, the positive non-linear transformation above the linear domain of learning will yield higher values of $\{x_1(\theta,x_2(\theta),\theta\}$. Consequently, $F_i(W(x_1(\theta,x_2(\theta))))_{\text{non-linear learning}} > F_i(W(x_1(\theta,x_2(\theta))))_{\text{linear learning}}$, for $\theta_{\text{non-linear}} > \theta_{\text{linear}}$. Linear transformations form deconstruction of non-linear functional.

By virtue of the positive monotonic transformation of the **IIE**-learning processes, the sets $\{\mathbf{x(\theta)}\} = \{(x_1(\theta,x_2(\theta),\theta)\}$, $\{\mathbf{W(\theta)}\} = \{W(x_1(\theta),x_2(\theta))\}$, $\{\mathbf{F(x(\theta),\theta)}\} = \{F_i(W(x_1(\theta),x_2(\theta)))\}$ and their more elementary functionals form topologies. This is proved simply by noting that the continuously differentiable functionals establish neighbourhood evolutionary learning points intra-system and inter-system. This implies that $\cap\{\mathbf{x(\theta)}\} \neq \phi$. Thereby, by the property of continuous positive monotonic transformations, $\cap\{\mathbf{W(\theta)}\}\neq\phi$; $\cap\{\mathbf{F(x(\theta),0)}\} \neq \phi$. Also, in the open learning space of evolutionary {θ}-values, any of the mathematical intersections and unions of the given class of sets form similar classes in the learning domain.

Consequently, there are monotonic positive mappings that preserve the nature of the transformations. In the open space of set-theoretic unions and intersections, the universal set of all possible positive monotonic transformations form the universal set of all non-linear possibilities. Such a domain of solutions is referred to as the space of socio-scientific 'everything'.

Finally, the higher density of the non-linear functionals implies that linear spaces appear as exceptions. They can therefore be contained in a set of finite measure, leaving the rest of the complex set of non-linear functionals mathematically 'measurable almost everywhere' - Æ (Friedman, 1982). Thereby, the null-set ϕ separates the space of non-linear mappings from the space of linear mappings. Then by the positive monotonic transformation, the space of non-linear mappings remains above the space of linear mappings – at a higher level in the dimensions of knowledge, space, and time. In this way, the definition of topology as a mapping that preserves these properties of mappings is established (Maddox, 1970).

Yet the topology we have described here is over non-linear mappings $\{F_i\}$ appearing as compounding, shown by 'o' of non-linear functionals (shown above). Besides, since $\{F_i\}$ explain simulations out of simulacra of changes in the coefficients of the functionals such as {f's} and $\{F_i\}$, therefore, every such functional transformation has probabilistic coefficients that are subject to continuous variations.[1] This makes the simulated mappings $\{F_i(f's)\}$ non-linear 'foliation' of 'simulated' relations (shown by the simulated version of the estimated coefficients – predictor coefficient values). In mathematical tensor language, the evolutionary learning spaces define unions of such evolutionary learning spaces. Such set-theoretic unions signify linear aggregation of non-linear relations caused by simulated relations in terms of knowledge-induced dynamic coefficients (continuous variations by simulated predictor values) and their non-linear specifications of the elementary functions of the compound maps.

---

[1] In respect of the pervasively probabilistic nature of events in the universe Hawking and Mlodinow (2010, p. 72) write: "According to quantum physics, no matter how much information we obtain or how powerful our computing abilities, the outcomes of physical processes cannot be predicted with certainty because they are not determined with certainty."

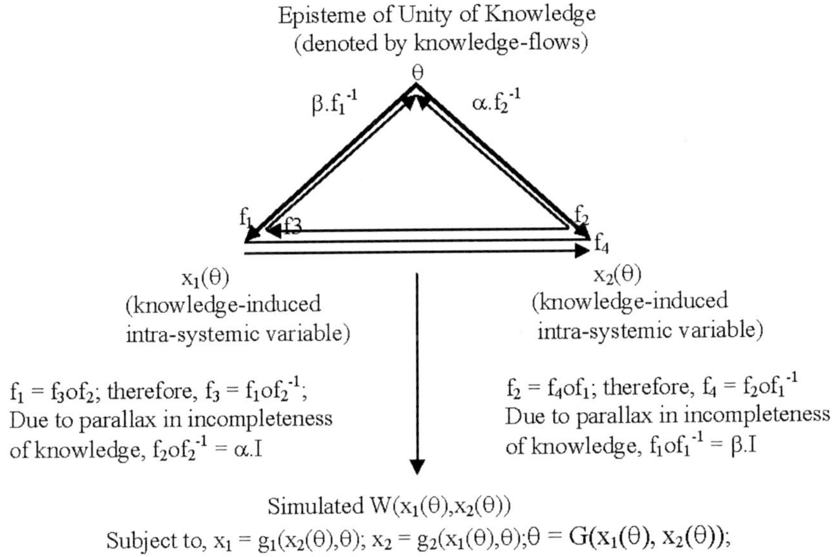

Figure 9.1: The intra-systemic IIE-learning process dynamics

Let $F_i(.)$ denote the simulated representation of W(.) in ith learning process Now Figure 9.1 assumes the dynamics shown in Figure 9.2.

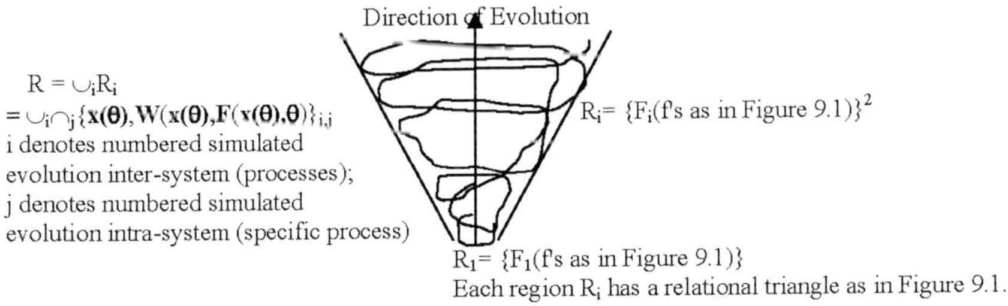

Figure 9.2: Evolutionary learning dynamics in non-linear spaces

Generalization

The non-linear character of the evolutionary learning model as described above has properties and formalism that are purely of mathematical nature. The emergent **IIE**-model of learning in participative organism of unity of knowledge as the episteme thereby, applies universally and uniquely to all the issues and problems intra-system and inter- systems. This means that diversity of disciplines can be studied uniquely by the same evolutionary learning formalism with the epistemic unity of knowledge in 'everything'. This is true despite the variation in the emergent problems of diverse but embedded systems.

The result is a unique one, besides being universal by virtue of its purely mathematical nature extending to 'everything' in the sense of evolutionary learning systems. Methodological uniqueness is explained by virtue of its global nature of participative complementarities between variables, their topological transformations, and the underlying agencies being represented by the variables and their relations.

This result is contrary to the postulates of resource scarcity, opportunity cost of resource allocation, and marginal rate of substitution between competing alternatives in mainstream economic theory. A strong example of the participative case is the knowledge-induced treatment of appropriate complementarities between growth rate and poverty reduction rate. We take up this illustration as an empirical case for Indonesia in the appendix.

There is no endogenous (learning) theory and process model of the kind in mainstream economics. In the natural sciences too the endogenous meaning of Gaia remains an epistemological aspiration (Primavesi, 2000). In theoretical physics the words of Hawking (1988, p. 33) in respect of reverse (recursive) causality are worth noting to put in place a cosmological meaning of uniqueness of methods in our model: "Space and time not only affect but also are affected by everything that happens in the universe." Social and biological Darwinism is disposed of by the logical consequence of pervasive complementarities (Xuemou & Dinghe, 1999).

Empirical illustration of non-linear complexity in circular causation relations

The importance of representing changes in the socioeconomic variables caused by knowledge-induced variables and the knowledge-flows is a concept quite different from the trends in time-dependent observations of socioeconomic variables. We have taken here the comparative trends in the growth rate of real GDP and the poverty rate as proportion of the poor in the total population in Indonesia. These variables are induced by the ranked knowledge values responding to degrees of complementary interrelations caused by the ranked knowledge-variables. See the appendix for the development of ordinal parametric data – the ranked θ-values. The comparative time-dependent trends in these variables are shown to bring out the difference in the understanding of the causality effects in these variables.

The important matter to note is that in the circular causation case between poverty rate, growth rate of real GDP, and the ranked knowledge-values by averaging over complementarities in these two variables, the expressions for the variables are given as follows:

> $G(\theta,P(\theta);t)$ denotes the growth rate of real GDP in terms of the endogenously related poverty variable $P(\theta)$. Both variables are induced by θ-ranked values (see appendix).
>
> Likewise, $P(\theta)$ is specified.

These transforms are like the F(f)-functional transformations shown earlier in respect of explaining non-linearity caused by systemic embedding.

In the sheer time-dependent case of specifying these variables the diagrams show the comparative time-trends of $G = G(t)$; $P = P(t)$.

Figures A9.1 and A9.2 (appendix) present a comparative view between t-dependent values and θ-dependent values as obtained by estimation. In the simulation part of the total **IIE**-process, empirical work can be developed from the Spatial Domain Analysis. See appendix in this respect. The empirical work presented here establishes the substantive difference in the interpretation and measurement of the socioeconomic variables by time-dependence and θ-dependence. Such a difference in the meaning and measurement of the socioeconomic variables over knowledge-induced domain of embedding and circular causation relations presents the inherent non-linear character of the socioeconomic variables in circular causation relations. It signifies systemic embedding by unity of knowledge as signified by the attributes of pervasive complementarities (and thus participation) between the variables.

Implication of tawhidi methodological worldview in non-linear socio-scientific modelling by circular causation

The non-linear property is imputed in complex and endogenous type of socio-scientific modelling by way of the continuity and continuums of knowledge-induction. Such knowledge-flows destroy the demarcation problem between deductive and inductive reasoning of the type discussed by Popper (2009) and others. Continuity of knowledge-flows and their induction on unifying the diversity of world-system is possible only by invoking the good things of life and the ontological combination of heart, mind, and world in the seat of reason, knowledge, and application. These are attributes conveyed into the law of choice of the good things of life in the light of the purpose and objective of the *shari'ah* – *maqasid as-shari'ah*. This in turn is derived from the *tawhidi* epistemological foundation.

The same kind of a premise cannot be found in a sheer monotheistic law that has no medium and instruments to translate the law into worldly action for the wellbeing of all. If this is to be the function of the monotheistic law, then the divine law remains ontologically removed from living experience of the possibilities of life. Consequently, neither rationalist conjecture nor the concept of God as a metaphysical reality can make the world and well-define the objective of wellbeing.

The divine ordainment of the scientifically benign type was rejected in the Eighteenth Century Enlightenment of the Schoolmen of the Church at that time. The same event did not happen in the Muslim World. In fact, the result of Muslim scholarship of the earlier times that was disseminated into Europe fired the spirit of the Renaissance.

The rigorous formalism of *functional* ontology of monotheism is not a formalism *of* God Himself. Rather, it is the *law* of oneness of God that establishes the grand design of oneness in the precincts of reason and construction of the world-system. This objective reasoning and construction takes place through a discursive and applied medium taken together. Through this process the deductive and the inductive realms of reasoning are unified together to provide a knowledge-induced circularity of cause and effect. The result is the knowledge-induced transformation of all entities into relational forms. The underlying process in this transformation unifies the cause-effect circular relations. Yet God, His law of monotheism, and the conveying of the monotheistic law through the prophetic guidance, the *sunnah*, remain the sole exogenous premise – the driving *numeraire* of the entire system comprising the generality and its specifics.

For this reason the result follows that knowledge-flows of the socio-scientific world-system emanate from the invariant divine epistemic premise. The knowledge-flows and the evolutionary learnt design of the unifying world-system are then generated and continued by organic reproduction of knowledge induction across continuums, for advancing on moral reconstructions. The whole mathematical functional dynamics is explained by the **IIE**-process, which we have explained. In the end we note that,

$[\theta^* \in (\Omega,S)] \rightarrow_f \{\theta\} \rightarrow \{(\theta,\mathbf{x}(\theta)\} \rightarrow \text{Evaluate}\{W(\theta,\mathbf{x}(\theta))\}$, subject to circular causation relations → continuity across continuums (i.e. intra- and inter- systems; generality and specifics of the world-system issues)

This kind of dynamics, called the **IIE**-learning process, is unique and universal in the scheme and order of things. The arguments in regard to this contention were provided earlier. They will be taken up further in the form of theorems.

Conclusion

The search for a unified theory of nature is alive not only in the natural sciences. The grand unified theory of 'everything' ought to encompass the social sciences as well. The result then would be a purposive and meaningful construction of the economy-science-society embedded interrelationship. The result will be a unified theory of inter-causality in ‘everything’. Now in the social sciences there arises the structure of a socially embedded political economy by systemic embedding (Sztompka, 1974).

This chapter has been a pointer in that direction. Economy shares this interactive unity richly by its immanent new theory of social political economy and the endogeneity of ethics and economics in economic modelling. Sociology shares it by a new theory of the world-system. Mathematics shares it by its emergent theory of complexity, systems and cybernetics. Philosophy of science shares it by its demand for a new epistemological outlook (Thayer-Bacon, 2003). The formalism introduced in this chapter thereby breaks new ground of novelty for further investigation in mathematical socio-scientific field of intellection. This totality includes, importantly, economics and social sciences.

Statistical Appendix: Sustainability Question in Indonesia by SDA Simulation

The empirical work presented below is for a one-process learning model for the case of growth-poverty circular relations in Indonesia. The *actual* case of the interrelationship is statistically estimated over *time*. The normative case of knowledge-induced change over the dimensions of knowledge, space, and time is implied in reference to the episteme of unity of knowledge. This normatively points out the need for economic, social, and policy changes that can establish coterminous relationship between increasing real growth rate (G↑) and decreasing poverty rate (P↓), and thereby, to define the wellbeing index in its positive and normative forms in terms of 'θ' as a function of (G,P).

The conclusion gained from the empirical results is this: Reading the relationship between growth rate and poverty rate in the normative scale reveals the internal dynamics of 'ought'-against-'is' states of such relations. The endogenous formulation of such normative changes in the perspective of unity of knowledge, as explained earlier, while revealing such internal 'ought-to-be' relations between G and P as read out by the θ-ranks of knowledge variable over the prescribed time-period, shows different statistical spread in the predictor values of the estimated and simulated variables in terms of their knowledge-induced values and time-dependent values of (G,P). Knowledge-induced predictors form endogenous policy directions of change. These directions of change are termed 'Events'. Time-dependent values present states of the predictors as they are found in reality by way of observations.

Yet in all these relations of causality and differences between the two forms of predictor values, the outlier 'Black Swan' point remains almost identical. This singular observation can be explained by the fact that extreme forms of uncontrollability and lack of predictability are rejected in the knowledge-induced case of the circular causation results. All endogenous variables are thus interrelated. Exogenous variables do not comprise the variables in the circular causation relations. θ-values corresponding to (G,P)-values over a one-process ethical learning under unity of knowledge are thus attained by rejecting the outlier as a non-learning entity in respect of its absence of inter-causal dynamic complementarities.

An outlier is therefore an exogenous case in both the θ-dependent and t-dependent systems. But in the latter it can be a case of an exogenous policy variable that remains devoid of a functional relationship with the (G,P)-variables. An example of this case is the fiscal policy variable of charity of the Indonesian Government for poverty alleviation. Yet charity in this case does not generate productivity in the recipients to influence economic growth.

On the other hand, the circular causation system of inter-relations necessarily requires complementary relations between all the endogenous variables. Their inner dynamics combined with evolutionary learning across processes over time explain the nature of complexity in the embedded system modelling – growth, poverty, and wellbeing.

Part I: Circular Causation by Regression Equation

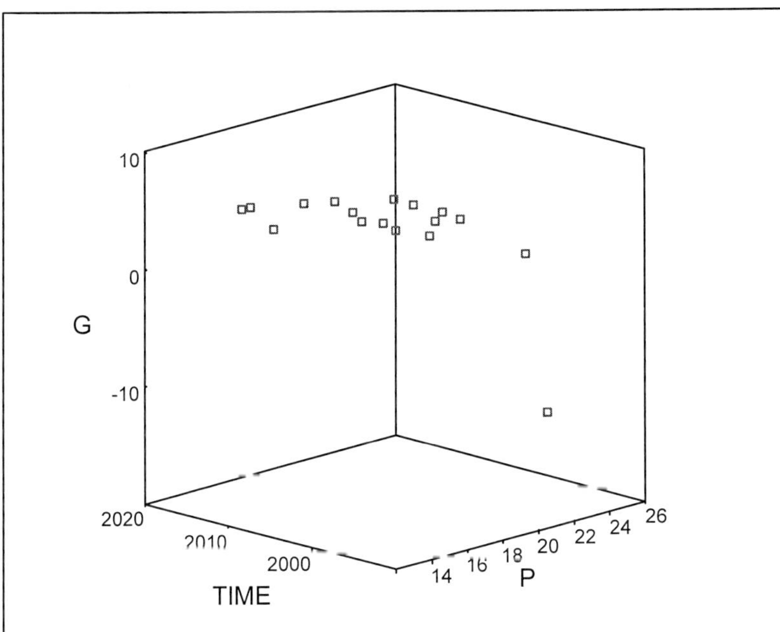

Figure 9A1: 3-Dimensional representation of the scatter relationship between ln[Real Economic Growth Rate (G)], ln[Poverty Rate (P)] over time.

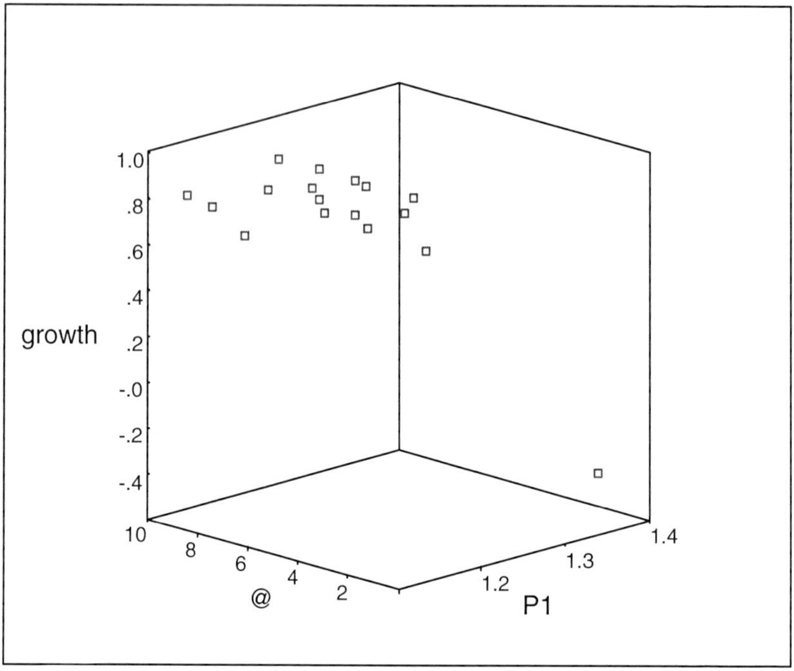

Figure 9A2: Representation of ln[Real Growth Rate (G) and ln[Poverty Rate, P1] over θ (learning) - values (@) corresponding to Time Points

Statistical Results

$$\ln G = -2.632 + 1.564\ln P + 1.737\ln\theta \qquad (9A1)$$

t-stats: -7.735 6.554 24.362

$R^2 = 0.986$

$$\ln P = 1.618 + 0.482\ln G - 0.895\ln\theta \qquad (9A2)$$

t-stats: 44.109 6.554 -8.615

$R^2 = 0.904$

$$\ln\theta = 1.573 + 0.562\ln G - 0.940\ln P \qquad (9A3)$$

t-stats: 10.860 24.362 -8.615

$R^2 = 0.991$

Table 9.A1: Time (t), θ, lnθ, lnG and lnP values, Indonesia

Year	θ lnθ	lnG	lnP
1994.00	6.65 0.82	.76	1.26
1995.00	6.92 0.84	.80	1.26
1996.00	7.93 0.90	.87	1.22
1997.00	8.52 0.93	.88	.37
1998.00	6.05 0.78	.63	.92
1999.00	1.12 0.05	-.40	.98
2000.00	5.64 0.75	.67	1.49
2001.00	4.89 0.69	.57	1.28
2002.00	6.07 0.78	.68	1.27
2003.00	6.44 0.81	.71	1.23
2004.00	6.99 0.84	.74	1.23
2005.00	7.20 0.86	.77	1.21
2006.00	5.69 0.76	.77	1.21
2007.00	7.43 0.87	.71	1.22
2008.00	8.16 0.91	.79	1.46
2009.00	7.84 0.89	.80	1.13
2010.00	9.25 0.97	.71	1.13
2011.00	8.24 0.92	.80	1.17

Source: Bank Indonesia databank.

Part II: Possible Simulation Results by Spatial Domain Analysis (SDA)

The range of 'simulated' values of the coefficients presently shown as 'estimated' coefficient values based on actual data, lies between the regions dividing the three variables as shown by their differently coloured regions. The SDA-contours are the results of computation of continuous sequences of values of possible simulation of coefficients in the divided regions. Thus, if a value of the coefficient of lnP can be chosen in the divided region (lighter green) this would imply a better relationship for (G↑,P↓), and thereby, better coefficient values to represent corrected (i.e. normatively changed) relationship for (G↑,P↓,θ↑).

$$\ln\theta = 1.573 + 0.562\ln G - 0.940\ln P$$

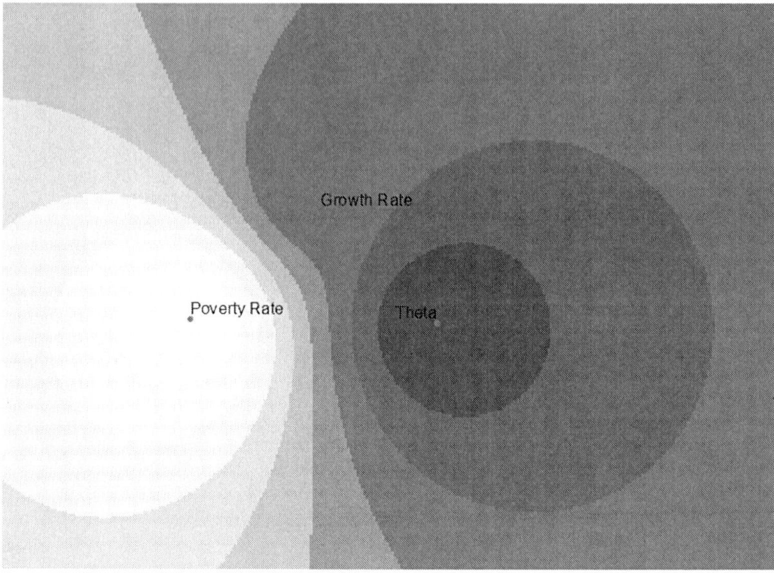

Figure 9A3: Interaction of θ with Poverty Rate and Growth Rate

Such simulated choices of coefficient values that are generated in SDA-fields involve resource allocation questions, which in turn give rise to policy questions to be endogenously determined by institutional discourse and formal simulation.

Consider the following implication: In Figure 9A3 we note the simulated possibilities:

Simulated θ Elasticity of G > 0.562 ;
Simulated θ Elasticity of P > - 0.940 (up to positive values)

That is, [%change in (θ)/%change in G]/[%change in (θ)/%change in P] = [%change in P / %change in G] = in the neighbourhood of -0.562/0.940 = -0.5978. (9A4)

Therefore, a one percent increase in the growth rate will decrease the poverty rate in the neighbourhood of 0.5978%. For this better development situation to be realized, appropriate relations must be maintained between the G and P variables that are induced by the θ-ranks. Such inter-variable relations for simulation purposes are implied by the results in (9A5) and (9A6).

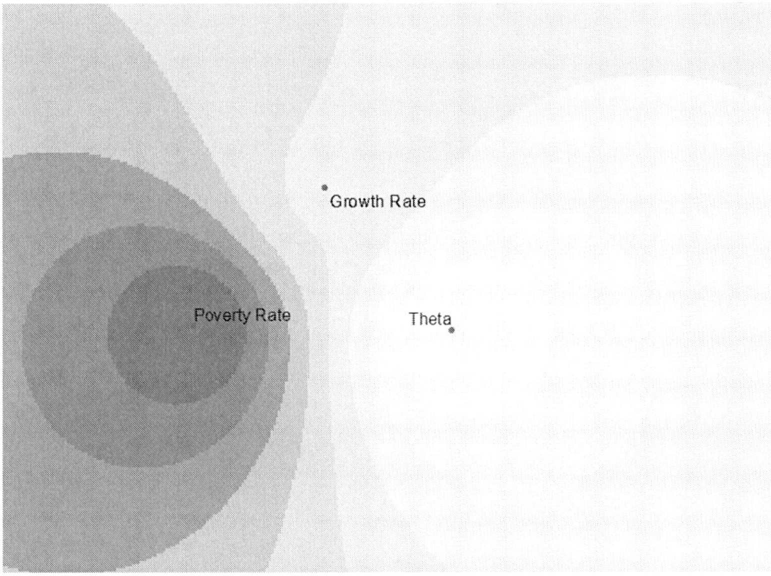

Figure 9A4: Interaction of Poverty Rate with Growth Rate and θ

$$\ln P = 1.618 + 0.482\ln G - 0.895\ln\theta$$

By the method of SDA as explained in Figure 9A3, the simulation implications of Figure 9A4 can be drawn up. The calculations in this case are the following ones:

Simulated P Elasticity of G < 0.482 (ought-to-be on normative policy scale to a negative value);
Simulated P Elasticity of θ < -0.895 (up to positive values on a normative policy scale).

That is, [%change in (P)/% change in G]/[%change in (P)/%change in θ] ought to be simulated to take values in the neighbourhood of a positive simulated value.

[%change in θ / %change in G] = in the neighbourhood of a positive around -0.482/-0.895 = 0.5385.

That is, a simulated value should be affixed in the neighbourhood of +0.5385 to indicate an increase in ‘θ’ by this percentage for a 1 percent increase in G. (9A5)

Therefore, a one percent increase in the growth rate will improve wellbeing by a value in the positive neighbourhood of +0.5385 per cent in order to affect a decrease in poverty rate in the neighbourhood of 0.5978% (expression 9.A4). For this to be realized, appropriate relations must be maintained between the G and P variables and the θ-ranks.

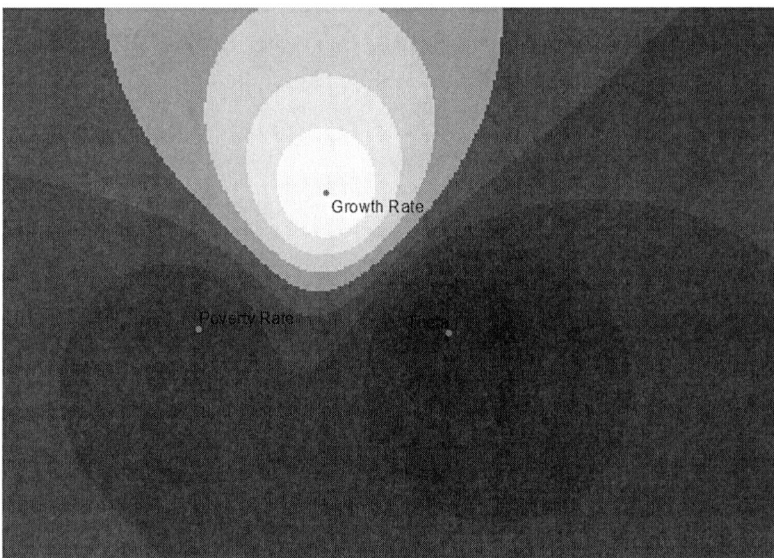

Figure 9A5 : Interaction of Growth Rate with Poverty Rate and θ

$$\ln G = -2.632 + 1.564\ln P + 1.737\ln\theta$$

In the same way as expressions (9.A4) and (9.A5) we obtain:

[%change in θ / %change in P] = in the neighbourhood of -1.564/1.737 = -0.9004 (9A6)

Therefore, a one percent decrease in P will improve wellbeing by a value in the neighbourhood of 0.9004 per cent in order to affect an increase in G and θ (wellbeing) relationship as indicated in expressions (9.A4) and (9.A5).

References

Barrow, J.D., 1991, *Theories of Everything, the Quest for Ultimate Explanation*, Oxford University Press, Oxford, Eng.

Beed, C. & Kane, O., 1991, "What is the critique of the mathematatization of economics?" Kyklos, (44)4.

Bertuglia, C.S. & Vaio, F., 2005, "Dynamical systems and the phase space", in *Non-linearity, Chaos & Complexity, the Dynamics of Natural and Social Systems*, pp. 49-70. Oxford University Press, Oxford, UK.

Boland, L.A., 1991, "On the methodology of economic model building", in his, *The Methodology of Economic Model Building,* pp. 39-63, Routledge, London, Eng.

Burstein, M., 1991, "History versus Equilibrium: Joan Robinson and Time in Economics", in Rima, I.H. (ed.), *The Joan Robinson Legacy*, pp. 49-61, M.E. Sharpe, Inc., Armonk, New York.

Choudhury, M.A., 2007, *The Universal Paradigm and the Islamic World-System: Economics, Ethics, Science and Society*, World Scientific Publishers, Singapore.

—. 2009, "Which comes first? – knowledge or time", *Philosophical Papers and Review* (1)4.

—. 2012, |"A probabilistic evolutionary learning model with epistemological meaning in Islamic economics and finance", *Journal of Financial Reporting and Accounting*, Special Issue.

Choudhury, M.A. & Hossain, M.S., 2007. *Computing Reality*, Aoishima Research Institute, Tokyo, Japan.

Chichilnisky, G., 1990, "Topology and economics: the contribution of Stephen Smale", in Hirsch, M.W. Marsden, J.E. & Shub, M. (eds.), *From Topology to Computation: Proceedings of the Smalefest*, pp. 147-161, Springer-Verlag, New York, NY.

Debreu, G., 1990, "Stephen Smale and the economic theory of general equilibrium", in Hirsch, M.W. Marsden, J.E. & Shub, M. (eds.), *From Topology to Computation: Proceedings of the Smalefest*, pp. 131-146, Springer-Verlag, New York, NY.

Fitzpatrick, T., 2003, "Postmodernism and new directions" in Alcock, P. Erskine, A. & May, M. (eds.), *The Student's Companion to Social Policy*, pp. 127-136, Blackwell Publishing, Oxford, UK.

Friedman, A., 1982, *Foundations of Modern Analysis*, Dover Publications, Inc. NY.

George, H., 1897, *The Science of Political Economy*, Robert Schalkenbach Foundation, New York, NY.

Gel'fand, I.M. & Shenitzer, A., 1961, "Introduction to tensors", in their *Lectures on Linear Algebra*, New York, NY: Interscience Publishers, Inc.

Grandmont, J-M. 1989, "Temporary equilibrium", in Eatwell, J. Milgate, M & Newman, P. (eds.) *New Palgrave: General Equilibrium*, pp. 164-185. W.W. Norton, New York, NY.

Hawking, S.W., 1988, "Space and time", in his, *Brief History of Time*, Bantam Books, New York, NY.

Hawking, S.W. & Mlodinow, L., 2010, *The Grand Design*, Bantam Books, New York, NY.

Hubner, K. trans. by Dixon, P.R. Jr. & Dixon, H.M., 1985, "Foundations of a universal historistic theory of the empirical sciences", in his *Critique of Scientific Reason*, pp. 105-122, The University of Chicago Press, Chicago, ILL.

Kupka, I.A.K. & Peixoto, M.M., 1993, "On the enumerative geometry of geodesics", in Hirsch, M.W. Marsden, J.E. & Shub, M. (eds.), *From Topology to Computation: Proceedings of the Smalefest*, pp. 243-253, Springer-Verlag, New York, NY.

Maddox, I.J., 1970, *Elements of Functional Analysis*, Cambridge University Press, Cambridge, Eng.

Myrdal, G., 1958, "The principle of cumulation", in Streeten, P. (ed.), *Value in Social Theory, a Selection of Essays on Methodology by Gunnar Myrdal*, pp. 198-205, Harper & Brothers Publishers, New York, NY.

Popper, K., 2009, *The Logic of Scientific Discovery*, Routledge, London, Eng.

Prigogine, I., 1980, *From Being to Becoming*, W.H. Freeman, San Francisco, CA.

Primavesi, A., 2000, *Sacred Gaia*, Routledge, London, Eng.

Smale, S., 1990, "The story of the higher dimensional Poincare' conjecture (what actually) happened on the beaches of Rio)", *Mathematical Intelligence*, (12)2, 44-51.

Soros, G., 1998, "Fallibility and reflexivity", in *The Crisis of Global Capitalism*, pp. 3-45, Public Affairs, New York, NY.

Sztompka, P., 1974, "Systemic models in functional analysis", in his, *System and Function, Towards a Theory of Society*, pp. 47-57, Academic Press, New York, NY.

—. 1991, *Society in Action, The Theory of Social Becoming*, The University of Chicago Press, Chicago, ILL.

Thayer-Bacon, B., 2003, "Why (e)pistemology?" in her, *Relational (e)pistemologies*, pp. 14-48, Peter Lang New York.

Wallerstein, I., 1998, "Spacetime as the basis of knowledge", in Bordo, O.F. (ed.), *People's Participation, Challenges Ahead*, pp. 43-62, Apex Press, New York, NY.

Whitehead, A.N., 1978, *Process and Reality*, Griffin, p. 7, p. 24, 41-42, D.R. & Sherburne, D.W. (eds.), The Free Press, New York.

Xuemou, W. & Dinghe, G., 1999,"Pansystems cybernetics, framework, methodology and development", *Kybernetes, International Journal of Systems and Cybernetics*, (28)6&7), 679-694.

CHAPTER TEN

TAWHIDI CIRCULAR CAUSATION MODEL OF MALAYSIAN ECONOMY

The Malaysian economy is an interesting topic for studying the application of the *tawhidi* circular causation method in generating endogenous economic and social linkages. One such examination with circular causation is the quantitative example in unity of knowledge between organically interrelated variables. The immanent model shows the complexity and endogenous nature of organic unitary relationships across the diversity of evolutionary learning between variables and socioeconomic goals. The circular causation model is a methodological representation of the *tawhidi* epistemology of knowledge and of its knowledge-induced world-system exemplified by macroeconomic relations. Malaysia has recently experienced an explosion of rich experiences in Islamization of knowledge. This is shown by Malaysia's expanding Islamic education system, Islamic capital markets, innovating on diversified secondary Islamic financing instruments in its Islamic banking, especially during the times of recent global recession. Malaysia is also promoting the idea of the Islamic gold currency, called the Islamic Dinar (Billington, 2002).

Endogenizing the macro-economy

The concept of value and valuation of economic transactions in relation to social perspectives is done with the knowledge-induced configuration of prices and quantities. But since an essentially *tawhidi* perspective of a morally meaningful economy is characterized by dynamic basic needs of development, the market of such a system interacts, integrates, and evolves through the market for dynamic basic needs or life-fulfilling needs. The growth, development, consumption, and investment patterns of the Islamic economy are thereby characterized by the threc kinds that exist in stages of their progressive evaluation. This is the idea of dynamic basic needs or life-fulfilling needs. The types of good in such a dynamic life-fulfilling basket of needs comprise necessaries (*dhururiyath*), comforts (*hajiyyath*), and refinements (*tahsaniyyath*). The markets that transact in such a basket make up the *shari'ah* market. The macro-economy represents a complex aggregation of preferences and market exchange at the microeconomic level. Yet there is no methodological legitimacy for adding up market equilibrium prices and quantities to arrive at a macroeconomic conception of price level and output level. Likewise, there is no transference of individual consumer or investor preferences to a macroeconomic equivalent concept. Instead, in all such cases the aggregation makes up a complex compounding of relations between variables and entities to form wider preferences, baskets of goods for choices, and the price level.[1]

Because of the central endogenous functions of knowledge-induced price and output in dynamic basic needs or life-fulfilling regimes of socioeconomic development we denote the vector $(\mathbf{p}(\theta),\mathbf{q}(\theta),\theta)$ as representing the endogenous complementarities in organically coordinated markets. This phenomenon emulates the *tawhidi* phenomenological model of unity of knowledge via the learning linkage between them caused by unity of knowledge (life-fulfilling needs regime of development).

In our study of the Malaysian economy in the light of the *tawhidi* phenomenological model of unity of knowledge, including in it the characteristics of complexity, endogeneity, and non-linearity of relations, we will treat $(\mathbf{p}(\theta),\mathbf{q}(\theta),\theta)$ along with its multi-sectoral aggregative implications. Such an aggregation is done by interconnecting the endogenous variables and generating endogenous circular causation relations between them and increasingly with other selected variables.

In the list of the endogenous variables, policy variables also turn out to be endogenous by virtue of the knowledge-induced participatory dynamics. This takes up the learning character of a pervasively complementary socio-scientific system. But we will allow for adaptation of knowledge over lagged time of the variables. Here are variables for

---

[1] As an example, $x_1 + x_2 = y$ forms a lateral addition as a linear form of aggregation. But complex aggregation means, $y = A.x_1^{\alpha}.x_2^{\beta}$. The aggregation is both non-linear and complex but endogenously related if $(y,x_1,x_2)[\theta]$ are interrelated via the knowledge-variable denoted by 'θ'. In that case furthermore, we have the circular causation relationship in evaluating (estimating and simulating) the wellbeing function. All this means that, $(y(\theta),x_1(\theta),x_2(\theta))$ forms the knowledge-induced vector with circular causation between the elements. Finally, the proxy representation of the wellbeing function appears as the knowledge-flow equation, $\theta = F(y(\theta),x_1(\theta),x_2(\theta))$. More complex forms of the functions can be selected. Note that α and β are also functions of θ-values in the complex representation of $(y,x_1,x_2)[\theta]$.

consideration in describing the nature of the Malaysian economy and its evaluation in the light of the *tawhidi* phenomenological model. The reason for such a specific kind of evaluation, contrary to the mainstream economic evaluation, is the need for endogenously integrating the economic and social perspectives of the socioeconomic variables. Without this particular focus, neither the wellbeing objective criterion can be addressed nor can the sustainable development be attainable. Thereby, the interactive, integrative, and evolutionary nature of the continuous relationship between the life-fulfilling variables (*maqasid as-shari'ah* variables) forms the properties of the learning system according to the epistemology of unity of knowledge.

Objective

This chapter will formalize a general equilibrium system of the Malaysian economy in terms of the interrelationship between its equations on aggregate demand, aggregate supply, monetary and real-sector interrelationship based on the conception of endogenous money, and being interconnected endogenously by the $(\mathbf{p}(\theta),\mathbf{q}(\theta),\theta)$-vector. The price vector is further disaggregated into the elements (yields, profits, and rates-of-return). In this way we will also bring out the conceptual issues of micro-macro interface in terms of the endogeneity of complex and non-linear macroeconomic relations that are induced by the knowledge-flow of organic relational unity of knowledge. We will also build into the conceptual analysis in this chapter a post-Keynesian and post-monetarist theory of money and the real economy by using the evolutionary general-equilibrium economic system that arises from the endogenous, complex, and non-linear generalized system model. All these are derived in the light of the *tawhidi* phenomenological methodology.

The selected economic variables

The following variables will be used to establish the generalized-system model for evaluating the Malaysian economy in the light of the *tawhidi* phenomenological model of unity of knowledge:

Q_s: aggregate output in the sth sector
K_s: net capital expenditure in the sth sector
L_s: employment (or labour force) in the sth sector
$NE_s = X_s$-Y_s: trade balance in the sth sector; X_s denoting export value, Y_s denoting import value

M_s: quantity of money required for satisfying transactional demand in the sth. sector; M_s plays a catalytic role in money-real economy linked development, and through the asset-link in the production function of the sth sector

FR_s: financial resources in the sth sector appearing as loans, grants, advances, and deposits

HR_s: human resource development expenditure in the sth sector

FDI_s: foreign direct investment in the sth sector

PD_s: price deflator of production in the sth sector

r_s: portfolio aggregate yield rate on investment and assets of the sth sector

i_s: index of inter-bank loan rates advanced for production in the sth sector

$r_s/i_s = q_s$ is the form in which the relative rates can be studied with an economy-wide suitable index of such relatives; for example $^n\sqrt{\prod_s(r_s/i_s)}$ as the nth geometrical root of the compound index, s = 1,2,3,..,n.

p_s: price level by sectors

e: exchange rate

T_s: terms-of-trade for goods of the sth sector

P_s: unit value of production in the sth sector

Pop_s: potential labour force in sth sector

θ: knowledge-flow affecting all variables in terms of the *tawhidi* epistemology of unity of knowledge.

While the entire vector of variables would set up endogenous relations between them, we are interested here with the endogenous effect of the price and output vectors with the other variables. Such interrelationships are studied in terms of the specific circular causation relations between the price-vector as the endogenously affecting sub-vector influencing the other variables. The endogenous, and thereby knowledge-induced price-vector is denoted by $p_s(\theta) = (1/PD_s,r_s,i_s,T_s,e)$ for the sth sector. We re-write this price-vector as, $(1/PD_s,r_s/i_s,T_s,e)$. $(1/PD_s)$ denotes the discounted value of an annuity flow of \$1.00 in perpetuity.

The relative price variable (r_s/i_s) points out that, as rates-of-return r_s relative to interest rates i_s increases, financial resources are increasingly mobilized into the real sector in the production of goods and services. Besides, with the induction of this price relative by θ-values the production of goods and services are according to the *maqasid as-shari'ah*. That is, the increasing trend in (r_s/i_s) is sustained by a deepening interrelationship between money and the real economy via the financial sector. Bank-savings, thereby, lose their role in favour of resource mobilization, and the economy progresses faster towards the potential level of output due to the resulting income multiplier. Besides, with the further effect of decreasing i_s and increasing r_s, the demand for investment increases. This brings about technological change, which sustains the rounds of technologically related income multiplier effect. The aggregate supply curve shifts right-wards in the Keynesian type general macroeconomic equilibrium model. The aggregate demand also shifts, generating higher levels of potential output, employment, factor use, and national income (Mankiw, 2003).

Now PD_s declines increasingly as (r_s/i_s) increases. Likewise, with declining PD_s the rate of inflation remains low. Hence there is conformity between an expansionary aggregate supply curve and an expansionary aggregate demand curve in setting ever-deepening effect of endogenous technological change on the regeneration of potential output, employment, factor use, and price stability. Finally, the exchange rate is now regulated by the ever-deepening interrelationship between money and the real economy through the financial instruments. Consequently, exchange rate is determined not by interest rate policy. Rather, the stabilizing relationship between price level, increasing output, technological change, and money and real economy by participatory financing instruments cause exchange rate to be determined by the terms-of-trade in an open economy.[2]

The above-mentioned relationship in the elements of the $\mathbf{p}(\theta)$-vector points out the complementary relationship in these price-elements. It is therefore expected that the $\mathbf{p}(\theta)$-vector will have a uniform positive effect on all the other endogenous variables. We therefore state that the price-vector acts endogenously to interrelate with the rest of the variables of the general-system relations of the circular causation in the midst of the

---

[2] $e = (p_X.X/p_Y.Y)$, p_X, p_Y being price of exports and price of imports, respectively. But p_X/p_Y is the term-of trade, say T. Therefore, $e = (X/Y),T_s$,. In an advancing trade environment with an expanding economy, X/Y stabilizes by way of reciprocal interrelations in the trade environment, Say, $X/Y = a$. Thereby, $e = a.T_s$. With a further unifying effect of 'θ' on the variables, the stabilizing effect between the variables is enhanced. Now, $e = a.T$ becomes better established and the exchange rate policy in trade and real economic development is enhanced. This result on stabilizing exchange rate is readily proven by noting the stabilizing effect of θ-value on 'a' and 'T'.

tawhidi induced complementarities between the variables of *maqasid as-shari'ah.*[3]

We note the following set of relations among the full system of circular causation relations that we need to examine in terms of the price vector as the endogenously interconnecting variable:

$$z_s(\theta)= f_s(\mathbf{x}_s(\theta)) \quad (10.1)$$

Here, s denotes the economic sectors between which complementarities of the variables are to be evaluated and simulated to appropriate levels following estimation using the actual observations of the existing relations.

$z_s(\theta)$ denotes any one of the variables in the vector, $\mathbf{z}_s = (Q_s, K_s, L_s, NE_s, M_s, FR_s, HR_s, FDI_s, q_s, p_s, P_s, Pop_s; \mathbf{p})[\theta]$. $\mathbf{p}(\theta)$-vector can be expressed as a price index to form a composite variable that endogenously relates with the z_s-variables.

$\mathbf{x}_s$ denotes the vector $\mathbf{z}_s$ without the selected z_s-variable in expression (10.1)

$f_s(.)$ is a functional relationship in the $\mathbf{x}_s(\theta)$. (10.2)
$s = 1,2,\ldots,n$

The final relationship is a prototype of the wellbeing function,

$$\theta = W(\mathbf{z}_s). \quad (10.3)$$

The estimated equations followed by the coefficient-simulated whole system comprising (10.1) and (10.2) as the circular causation relations and the empirical version of the wellbeing function in (10.2) yield the wellbeing function in the predictor values of the variables. The predictor values are denoted by $\mathbf{z}_s'$. The simulated version of the wellbeing function is given by, $\theta' = W(\mathbf{z}_s')$, with $\partial W/\partial \mathbf{z}_s = (\partial W/\partial\theta)/(\partial \mathbf{z}_s/\partial\theta) > 0$.

Finally, the above set of relations can be sector-specific, in which case the system is evaluated (estimated and simulated) for each sector, s = 1,2,..,n. Otherwise, the variables can be aggregated by geometrical averaging over sectors to denote the economy-wide integrated variables. In the latter case of aggregation natural log-linear forms can be used in order to readily interpret the coefficients as inter-variable elasticity coefficients.

---

[3]The θ-value arising from *maqasid as-shari'ah* is derived from the epistemic core of the *tawhidi* string relation shown by, $[(\Omega,S)\rightarrow\theta^*]\rightarrow\theta$ etc.

Thereby, the coefficients can be interpreted as the wellbeing elasticity coefficients of the individual variables.

The wellbeing effects of the stated variables

In the *tawhidi* implication of circular causation with pervasive endogeneity between the variables representing the wellbeing function, the following relationships can be noted for the Malaysian economy. For that reason the project of Islamization of knowledge and socio-scientific transformation in the light of the *tawhidi* worldview plays a significant transformational role. The resulting transformation occupies a matter of vast proportion in the modern world many years after what Ibn Khaldun laid down as his philosophy and outlook of the philosophy of history. But beyond Ibn Khaldun (Choudhury, 2004; 2008), the Malaysian socio-scientific transformation can be considered in the essentially Islamic perspective on the basis of the *tawhidi* methodological worldview. The critical result is the negation of Ibn Khaldun's one directional causality that explains the disintegration of the frugal Islamic grassroots of *assabiyya* (community) as nations rise towards *hadara* (civilization) through the process of *umran* (nationhood). But the explanation of social transformation under the *tawhidi* concept of Islamization for Malaysia presents inter-causality through the interaction, integration and evolutionary (**IIE**) dynamics. This takes place between epistemology, *tawhidi* Islamization of knowledge, and the rise of a modern and cultured social order encompassing economic and social change. Within these are also included Islamic financial developments, peaceful co-existence of a multi-racial society, and advanced intellectual cultivation (Mahathir Mohammad, 2000; Ibrahim, 1996).

Economic growth for Malaysia has been poverty-centred. Malaysia records a substantial success in poverty alleviation along with robust real economic growth. Even during this time, Malaysia's investment climate was significantly demand driven with a consistent demand for investment exceeding available bank-savings. This is a significant fact for sustainability of Islamic financial climate, which establishes itself in the midst of active resource mobilization by complementarities between the variables reflecting *maqasid as-shari'ah*, and thereby, the unity of knowledge in the good things of life by the epistemology of *tawhid*. Such meaningful Islamic socioeconomic transformation along with the excess demand for investments has not adversely fuelled inflation in the country. That is because healthy resource mobilization in the social and economic and financial outlets for generating economic growth complemented government positive policies in alleviating poverty and sustaining investments in the good things of life that cause wellbeing through inter-causal and inter-variable organic linkages. The advance and sustainability of wellbeing in the Malaysian nation was thus affirmed.

Employment has remained robust for all citizens, Malays and non-Malays, in Malaysia. Innovation has spearheaded this absorbability of the potential labour force into the productive and meaningful sectors that can be promoted by degrees of learning towards the social transformation process as of *maqasid as-shari'ah*. Innovation was the cause of technological change in Malaysia. It created an endogenous growth and social transformation in organic complementarities with each other. The favourable climate for such transformation added to the inter-causality between a vibrant external sector and internal socioeconomic sustainability. The Malaysian Islamic financial transformation can be fuelled by the growth of Islamic secondary financial instruments and an active discourse to innovate on this front, particularly in the direction of issuing Islamic bonds, *sukuk*.

Consequently, certain very encouraging inter-variable circular causal relations pervaded in the Malaysian socio-scientific transformation and its sustainability. The monetary sector aided the private sector transformation and maintained steady exchange rate. Monetary policy was complemented by government fiscal stimulation, particularly for social development as of poverty alleviation, and in improving the socioeconomic conditions of the poor Malays by its New Economic Policy within the development plans. Such complementarities between monetary policy and fiscal policy were instrumental in the human resource mobilization and empowering by inter-sectoral participation. Such complementarities also brought about the inverse relationship between sectoral rates of return and interest rates. The rates of return to investment relative to interest rates on bank savings increased due to the impact of the monetary-fiscal complementarities, resource mobilization towards innovation by technological change, human resource development, and economic growth.

The contrary would have been the case if interest rate was active in monetary policy and if fiscal stimulation for growth and poverty alleviation generated inflationary pressure, and thus higher interest rates relative to mobilization of resources with higher yield rates. The result would then be contrary to all the positive consequences of a participatory economic and social order by way of organic interrelations between the variables.

Furthermore, Malaysia extended its growth and social change program to the benefits obtained from a vibrant open economy. Exchange rate remained stable in the face of a strong Ringgit currency value. Thus, terms-of-trade of Malaysian commodity exports remained healthy. In the face of good terms-of-trade causing a strongly innovative and growth oriented economy, foreign capital was in free flow into Malaysia. Finally, the value of net exports remained high due to a low discount factor in the face of low inflationary pressure. This situation yielded a further enhancement to Malaysia's growth and social development and sustainability.

Such interactions turning into complementary effects by the organic interrelations between the variables spell out the nature of inter-causality in inter-variable unity of knowledge that the *tawhidi* worldview establishes. Wellbeing was thus simulated effectively by circular causation relations in the Malaysian economy.

We represent such a unifying interactive, integrative, and evolutionary (**IIE**) pattern of circular causation relations between the variables of the vector, $\mathbf{z}_s = (Q_s, K_s, L_s, NE_s, M_s, FR_s, HR_s, FDI_s, q_s, p_s, P_s, Pop_s, \mathbf{p})[\theta]$ in Figure 10.1:

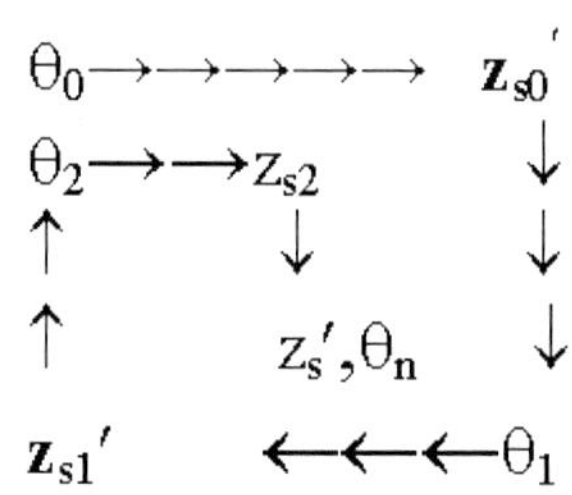

Figure 10.1: Recursive simulation of wellbeing and estimated predictor values of inter-causal and inter-variable circular causation relations

The **IIE**-properties of Figure 10.1 are explained by the Process 1 formation of $(\theta_0,\mathbf{z}_{s0}'(\theta_0))$; that is, by 'estimation' yielding next to 'simulation' of coefficients of the estimated circular causation equations. The empirical version of the conceptual wellbeing criterion is next given by $\theta_0' = W(\mathbf{z}_{s0}'(\theta_0'))$. The recalling of the episteme of unity of knowledge takes the values of Process 1 and starts up Process 2. The same approach to 'evaluation' is followed up towards yielding $\theta_1' = W(\mathbf{z}_{s1}'(\theta_1'))$. In this way, Process 'n' yields $\theta_n' = W(\mathbf{z}_{sn}'(\theta_n'))$ along with the simulated predictor values of variables in every such evolutionary process.

The most subtle case of **IIE**-properties across learning processes is shown by the trend in the θ_n'-values *across* processes. Such processes can be taken equivalent to knowledge-induced progress recorded over time.

Likewise, the knowledge-induced process-based and time-dependent predictor values of variables can be constructed. Such co-evolutionary $\{\theta',\mathbf{z}'(\theta'),t(\theta')\}$-values point out the 'simulated' trends enacted by the episteme of unity of knowledge over time recording the impact of knowledge, $t(\theta')$. The simulated values can then be compared with the corresponding 'estimated' $\{\theta,\mathbf{z}(\theta),t(\theta')\}$-values. Thereby, policy issues and possibilities for targeted levels of wellbeing can be pointed out and the possibility of attaining them can be determined.

Systemic interaction between the endogenous variables of circular causation

Table 10.1 points out the signs of the inter-variable coefficients in the Malaysian economy for the year 2000 (Choudhury, 1995). The interactions point out the complementary linkages between the critical variables that existed. Such a relationship signifies a systemic participatory development scenario in the circular causation relations, as pointed out by the arrow below.

The same kind of interactions between inter-causal variables are shown in terms of the knowledge induction by θ-variable in Figure 10.2. The two directional arrows point out that the tuple denoted by $\{\theta,\mathbf{z}(\theta)\}$is inter-causal in its elements across evolutionary processes. At the same time, the θ-value induces the vector $\mathbf{z}(\theta)$ to make it interactive and inter-linked (integrated) by circular causation.

Table 10.1: Inter-variable circular causation results expected of the nature of the Malaysian economy, year 2000

←	Q_s	K_s	L_s	NE_s	M_s	FR_s	HR_s	FDI_s	q_s	p_s	P_s	Pop_s	**p (Islamc)**
Q_s	**1**	+	+	+	+	+	+	+	+	-	+	+	+
K_s	+	**1**	+	+	+	+	+	+	+	-	+	+	+
L_s	+	+	**1**	+	+	+	+	+	+	-	+	+	+
NE_s	+	+	+	**1**	+	+	+	+	+	-	+	+	+
M_s	+	+	+	+	**1**	+	+	+	+	-	+	+	+
FR_s	+	+	+	+	+	**1**	+	+	+	-	+	+	+
HR_s	+	+	+	+	+	+	**1**	+	+	-	+	+	+
FDI_s	+	+	+	+	+	+	+	**1**	+	-	+	+	+
q_s	+	+	+	+	+	+	+	+	**1**	-	+	+	+
p_s	+	+	+	+	+	+	+	+	+	**1**	+	+	+
P_s	+	+	+	+	+	+	+	+	+	-	**1**	+	+
Pop_s	+	+	+	+	+	+	+	+	+	-	+	**1**	+
p	+	+	+	+	+	+	+	+	+	-	+	+	**1**

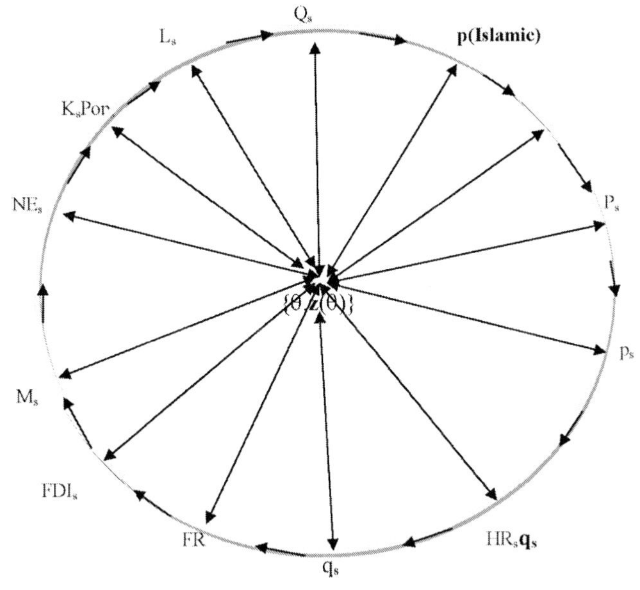

Figure 10.2: Inter-variable circular causation generated by knowledge induction by θ-values derived from the epistemic *tawhidi* unity of knowledge

Further focus on the Malaysian economy in the light of circular causation outlook of tawhidi episteme

Stability of the Malaysian economy

Stability of the macroeconomy expressed in terms of non-inflationary economic growth is given by the relationship of real productivity growth being higher than either the inflation rate, or the rate of money supply being less or equal to the rate of real productivity growth. For the Malaysian economy it was noted that a high savings gap calling forth demand for capital, and this combined with an accelerated financial resource mobilization both from the domestic and foreign sectors, created a climate of the quantity of money being absorbed in economic growth. Thus the absorption factor combining the expenditure side of gross domestic product closed upon the quantity of money. The result was complementary relationship between spending and monetary effects.

When such a complementary relationship is combined with technological change caused by the financial and human resource mobilization, the result is a positively shifting aggregate supply curve. This yields the sign of expanding employment and gross domestic product with enhancing technological change and productive spending for economic growth. Price level remains stable as a result. Non-inflationary economic growth is attained.

Interest rate versus real productivity effects on economic stabilization

Because of the robust growth of the Malaysian economy with investment demand (capital formation) and stable economic growth, the ratio of interest rate to change in capital productivity declined for quite some time. This indicates that interest rate policy of the central bank in controlling the quantity of money for sustaining non-inflationary economic growth did not play a major role. The inference from this is that there was endogenous response to stable economic growth by private sector activity. Monetary and fiscal (spending) effects complemented each other in the climate of private sector expansion. Technological change adds to this expansion. Besides, in the light of *maqasid as-shari'ah*, good things of life are for worth spending on, and life-sustainability comprises wellbeing (*maslaha*). The wellbeing as knowledge-flow (θ-value) comes to acquire its fusion-type income multipliers (Choudhury & Malik, 1992). Such multipliers exemplify the complementary effects of spending, money, and technological change as endogenously interrelated effects on sustainable non-inflationary economic growth.

Even though Malaysia has not yet experienced a robust accomplishment in Islamic socioeconomic change, a low interest-rate regime followed by expansionary monetary and spending complementarities promoting private sector expansion signalled the practice of low reserve-ratio setting in monetary policy. Consequently, only open-market operations as monetary policy remained the active one along with the market-determined endogenous socioeconomic variables. But during the process of transformation of the private sector into an Islamized one, open-market operations would signify a deepening role, though not exclusively. Now buying and selling of bonds remains an active policy with low rates of interest. This must mean that the bonds must provide non-interest rates for their popularity in an Islamization agenda. Such Islamic bonds are called *sukuk*. They have become popular in many countries. Malaysia has pioneered the issuance of *sukuk* Islamic bonds.

The combination of endogenous socioeconomic factors in non-inflationary economic growth in Malaysia is a strong indicator of the appropriate complementary policies promoting private sector development with the outlook of *maqasid as-shari'ah*. The Malaysian government ought to sustain such a social transformation. The private sector then ought to learn from such endogenous participatory development practices to drive the economy along the path of such endogenously self-governed transformation (Krugman, 1996).

It is no wonder that during the recent global financial crisis and recession in many developing countries where Islamic banks operate, their contribution toward stabilizing the economies and performing exemplary resilience in the capital market got established. There is every reason to adopt similar policies hinging on the complementary and participatory type endogenous socioeconomic indicators. Among these are monetary policies, spending (fiscal) policies, technological advancement, human resource development, and participatory financing instruments replacing interest-rate and fractional reserve-requirement policies of the central bank. In the end, out of the evolutionary dynamics of such an endogenously learning economy, the fractional reserve requirement monetary policy can be replaced by the 100 percent reserve requirement monetary system. Such a great transformation in the end can be backed by the gold standard. Malaysia has been a pioneer, albeit on an experimental basis, to introduce the gold-dinar as currency asset for holding to support trade transactions (Billington, 2002; Mydin and Larbani, 2004).

Labour market situation in Malaysia and its circular causation relations under the tawhidi episteme

The small population size and large capital stock, as evidenced by investment demand outstripping the supply of savings in Malaysia, places pressure on the use of capital in preference to labour. But is this scenario of technological change necessary? The *tawhidi* epistemic implication on complementary relationship between labour and capital in economic growth and participatory development leads to an endogenous growth model of the 'capital-labour augmenting' (Solow, 1980) form of the growth model.

In such a model, the first-order differential, dK/dL remains positive. But the second order differential can assume any possible sign including zero.[4] Priority of growth and development is now built along the path that combines the two properties. These are namely, $dK/dL > 0$. Yet $(d/d\theta)(dL/dK)$ assumes any possible sign, depending upon the relative size of factor endowments of given regions, sectors, technological change, and state of socioeconomic development.

It is perfectly possible for the factor augmentation to be different according to their technological impacts. That is, labour and capital inputs are now augmented by resource capability. Such resource-augmented inputs are denoted by,

$$L^* = L.\exp(\alpha.t); \quad (10.1)'$$

$$K^* = K.\exp(\beta.t), \quad (10.2)'$$

All parameters are induced by θ-value.

Now therefore, the real growth function (F(.)) takes the form,

$$y = F(k.\exp(\beta\text{-}\alpha).t) = (\exp(\beta\text{-}\alpha).t).F(k), \quad (10.3)'$$

$$\text{where } k = K/L; \quad (10.4)'$$

y = (aggregate Y)/L* in the aggregate endogenous production function,

$$Y = F(L^*,K^*)[\theta]. \quad (10.5)$$

By differentiation we can write in terms of rates of change caused by variations in θ-value and denoted by g(.):

$$g(y) = \{[d(\beta\text{-}\alpha)/d\theta].t\}+(1/F(k)).dF(k)/d\theta \quad (10.6)$$

[4] Let the endogenous growth model (Romer, 1986; Turnovsky, 1995) be, $Y = F(L,K)[\theta]$, such that, $dY/d\theta > 0$ by the evolutionary learning processes in the growth of output implies, $(\partial Y/\partial L).(dL/d\theta) + (\partial Y/\partial K).(dK/d\theta) > 0$. The positive nature of the L and K relationship in the complementary form of circular causation between these variables under the impact of learning in epistemic oneness (i.e. evolutionary θ-values), implies also that individually, $dL/d\theta > 0$, $dK/d\theta > 0$. Therefore, $dL/dK > 0$.

But consider now the following: $(d/d\theta)(dL/dK)$ can take all possible signs including zero. Such possibilities are caused by the evolution of the endogenous positive interrelations between (K,L) along different evolutionary paths caused by the impact of the θ-variables, while yet maintaining $dL/dK > 0$.

By positive endogenous relationship between K and L under the impact of θ-value,

$$dF(k)/d\theta > 0. \tag{10.7}$$

$$\text{Therefore, } g(F(k)) > 0. \tag{10.8}$$

$$\text{We now obtain, } g(y) = \{[d(\beta\text{-}\alpha)/d\theta].t\} + g(F(k)) \tag{10.9}$$

$$\text{If } g(y) \geq 0, \text{ then, } g(F(k)) \geq \text{absolute value } \left| d(\beta\text{-}\alpha)/d\theta].t \right| \tag{10.10}$$

That is, $g(y) \geq 0$ according to the comparatively higher degree of technological augmentation of either K or L. Yet under positive endogeneity of learning relationship between the factor inputs of production, the following condition would hold: $dK/dL > 0$. We refer to the term, g(F(k)), as the first-order effect on real economic growth rate g(y). We refer to the term, {[d(β-α)/dθ].t} as the second order effect by virtue of its specific response to the state of supply of factor inputs and the resource endowment of the growth system.

The meaning of 'priority' in resource allocation in the regime of pervasive complementarities

Here the meaning of 'priority' of factor utilization is established in the positive endogenous sense of participatory development under the unifying learning effect of θ-value. 'Priority' in such a development regime means the conjoint use and development of all factors simultaneously, given that the differential allocation of resources between them as a result of the evolutionary learning path of the factor uses due to their unequal augmentation based on the natural endowment of productive factors.

The above explanation of the meaning of 'priority' in choices is contrary to how most Islamic economists of mainstream leaning understand this concept. The mainstream idea has been borrowed by the Islamic *shari'ah* scholars (Qaradawi, 2000). These developments in Islamic thought point out the difference between the understanding of the ideas of *shari'ah*-compliance and *maqasid as-shari'ah*. Yet the central epistemology of *qur'anic* thought pervading across the socio-scientific field is premised on *tawhid*. As the monotheistic law the *tawhidi* methodological worldview is unravelled by the principle of pervasively complementary pairing between the good things of life. This principle has been abandoned by Islamic economists in their understanding of priority. Consequently, the mainstream postulates of resource scarcity and marginal rate of substitution that hinge on such a concept of priority have entered lock, stock, and barrel into Islamic economics in its garb of mainstream thought.

Contrarily, the abundance of resources made available for spending in the cause of God, self, and the world-system rejuvenates the flow of knowledge. Knowledge-flows then establish inter-causality with the growing abundance of the world-system with all its diversity in the framework of unity of knowledge and its induced artefacts. On this point the *Qur'an* (2:265) declares: "And the likeness of those who spend their substance, seeking to praise God and to strengthen their souls, is as a garden, high and fertile: heavy rain falls on it but makes it yield a double increase of harvest, and if it receives not heavy rain, light moisture suffices it. God sees well whatever you do." This verse explains the two parts of the priority definitions that we have derived from the *qur'anic tawhidi* implications as explained above.

In respect of the distribution of the total economic output into factor payments in the neoclassical and endogenous economic growth theory, the idea of marginal products, which has been borrowed by Islamic economics, Islamic finance, and Islamic social theory abounds. This aberration of thought is contrary to the *tawhidi* implication of unity of knowledge and the continuous regeneration of resources by knowledge-induction in a pervasively complementary regime of *maqasid* goods and services.

Expression (10.9) points out the two parts of the *qur'anic* verse mentioned above. The first part comprises the first-order effect that adds to g(y) by virtue of the positive endogenous relationship of the prioritized (K,L)-complementarity. The second order effect is the choice of technology to further enhance the growth rate g(y). The right-hand side of expression (10.9) is monotonic positive under the induction by θ-values along the **IIE**-learning processes. Therefore, a fusion-type income multiplier works by the compound effects of spending and the average propensity of spending (Choudhury, 1993). The resulting continuous expansion in incomes augments resources and factor payments. The inter-causality between knowledge-induction, growth, and technological change altogether enhances the complementary system of reproduction of resources, output, and inputs. This in turn annuls thc constriction otherwise created by scarcity, which then causes the misplaced idea of choices by priorities.

To further explain the important concept of abundance and pervasive complementarities versus scarcity, marginal rate of substitution, and subjection to the idea of priorities, we consider the following formalism. We formalize in the context of the pervasively complementary evolutionary learning model of unity of knowledge relating to the problem of factor payments and resource endowment. We use the endogenous growth concept, yet with a substantive difference due to the epistemic axiom of unity of systemic knowledge between the input, output, and technology variables. All are induced by knowledge-flows. We formalize as follows:

$$\text{Let } Y = A(\theta)\prod_{i=1}^{n} x_i(\theta)^{\alpha i} \quad (10.11)$$

This transforms into natural log-linear form,

$$\ln Y = \ln A(\theta) + \Sigma_i \alpha_i \ln x_i(\theta) \quad (10.12)$$

In mainstream growth theory with the exogenous role of technology, the expression (10.12) converts to,

$$\ln Y = \ln A(\theta) + T(\theta) + \alpha_i \ln x_i(\theta) = F(\theta) + \Sigma_i \alpha_i . \ln x_i, \quad (10.13)$$

$T(\theta)$ denotes exogenous technology effect; x_i is independent of the endogenous effect of θ-value. Consequently, expression (10.11) has been log-linearized into two independent components: technological change and the input and output variables.

Now the measure of factor payments in respect of changes in θ-value (technology) is given by,

$$g(Y)/d\theta = dF(\theta)/d\theta + \Sigma_i \alpha_i . g(x_i)/d\theta \quad (10.14)$$

Because of the exogenous relationship of x_i to θ-values, the change in growth rate $g(Y)$ is only due to the effect of technological change. Yet the technological effect of this type does not revert to its circular causality with x_i and $Y(.)$. Consequently, no enhancement of factor payments can take place endogenously by the inter-causal effect of θ-value.

An example that proved to be disastrous for Malaysia, but was soon after resolved, was the racial civil riots of the seventies. The entire technological stock then was concentrated in the hands of non-Malays. Economic disparity arose, leading to deep dissent by the Malays. Riots broke out. To stem the tide of social and economic discontent, the

Malaysian Government formulated the New Economic Plan. It called upon all Malaysians to interactively integrate their relations between the contending groups. Thereby, endogenous relations were realized between economic growth and distributive equity. The labour-market problems were thereby brought to a resolution. But its sustainability today depends on mutual relations, which Dr Mahathir briskly worked towards, promoted, and realized.

In the light of such **IIE**-relations in the national context of complementarities between economic efficiency and distributive equity arising from the labour market, expression (10.14) changes into circular causation relations concerning the simulation of the Malaysian wellbeing function in the midst of pervasively endogenous knowledge-induced prescriptions. We formulate the underlying social and development model as follows:

$$\text{Evaluate/simulate } W = W(Y,\mathbf{x},T,P)[\theta] \qquad (10.15)$$

Subject to circular causation relations,

$$Y = f_1(\mathbf{x},T,P,\theta) \qquad (10.16)$$

$$\mathbf{x} = f_2(Y,T,P,\theta) \qquad (10.17)$$

$$T = f_3(Y,\mathbf{x},P,\theta) \qquad (10.18)$$

$$P = f_4(Y,\mathbf{x},T,\theta) \qquad (10.19)$$

$$\theta = f_5(Y,\mathbf{x},T,P) \qquad (10.20)$$

T denoting technological change is signified here by the θ-induced values of the parameters, α and β, and hence by α_i in the expressions (10.9) and (10.11).

Y denotes output; **x** denotes the vector of factor endowments; T denotes technological change of the capital-labour augmenting type; P denotes participatory policies based on inter-racial and inter-sectoral discourse. The interaction and integration between such variables representing the discursive groups can be promoted by Pusat Islam (The Islamic Center) in Malaysia. Yet presently, the pursuit in this learning direction remained absent and neglected. Pusat Islam continued on to be an overly religious authority, rather than an advisory for nation building on the basis of the Islamic unitary worldview. Contrarily, a positive advisory role of Pusat Islam could have synergized the relations between contending groups as they are represented by the variables when induced by θ-values.

In such a comprehensive way, factor payment would be determined by the extension of similar circular causation relations as (10.15)-(10.20). A practical way to compute factor payments (w_i) is given by the system of computable circular causation relations,

$$w_i = Y(\theta)/x_i(\theta) \qquad (10.21)$$
$$i = 1,2,\ldots,n$$

Y and x_i are firstly 'estimated' and then 'simulated' by the circular causation system denoted by expressions (10.15)-(10.20).

Average productivity, instead of marginal factor productivity, becomes the correct measure of factor payment in the system of equations (10.21). Such is also the case with factor payments in the Walrasian general equilibrium model (Chang, 2006). This makes sense, because the average cost curve is never at its minimum point due to the θ-induced technological learning effect. Likewise, the productivity curve is never at its maximum point for the same reason. Thereby, the marginal cost and marginal productivity values cannot exist in the evolutionary learning conditions with technological progress. Such were also the viewpoints of the Austrian school of economists, notably Hayek.

Malaysian economy is therefore prone to 'prioritizing' capital formation and technological change in the sense of capital-labour complementarity. This happened in a situation where human resource development was still in its early stages, particularly for the native Bumiputeras. The Government of Malaysia had placed an affirmative action program of labour-market adaptation for the disadvantaged in its New Economic Policy. NEP was built into the Malaysian development plan. The capital formation priority in the above-mentioned sense, while complementing it with labour-market adaptation, established two important perspectives of the development plan. Firstly, distributive equity became possible. Secondly, foreign direct investments (FDI) were encouraged in Malaysia. In this way, a multiple complementary scenario of sustainable development was possible, namely the recursive feedback in circular causation fashion between growth (denoted by the real economic growth rate), capital formation (investment demand), FDI, simultaneous human resource development, and labour-market adaptation of target groups. The result was a remarkable poverty reduction in Malaysia.

There were other important linkages that came out of the above-mentioned kinds of sectoral interrelations. Gradual indigenous human resource development in the agricultural sector caused positive shifts in the (Q_{agric}/Q_{manuf})-ratio of outputs (Qs). This caused labour-market adaptation while it also made it possible to diversify the economy by manufacturing-agriculture growth linkages. To all of such linkages in the form of joint sectoral production function there came about a vast system of complementary linkages. Sustainability of such a system of growth-oriented linkages required market-friendly policies. Thereby, policies interactively integrated with the whole system of positively endogenous inter-causal relationships in the growing and learning Malaysian economy. This was a remarkable example of the *tawhidi* form of the **IIE**-learning process model of growth and development in operation.

The components of aggregate demand in Malaysian growth and development

The endogenous structuring of Malaysian economy requires circular causation linkages to attain simulation of wellbeing. The goal of pervasive complementarities between economic growth and distributive equity, development of human potential, and a caring and empowering discursive society also led to a participative functioning and structuring of Malaysian social economy. On this outlook, the expenditure accounting and income version of measuring the gross domestic product and its derived results are replaced by an appropriate dynamic form of the input-output model of the economy. Consequentially, the components of consumption expenditure, investment expenditure, government expenditure, and net exports, all change into interaction between these activities, as if they were sectors of activities with inter-causality between them.

In the Islamic social and economic perspective some critical activities for the structuring and functioning of the economy are needed. Whether Malaysia followed these directions needs to be examined. The critical variables, and thereby the relevant ones for productive sectoral activities are the following: phasing out the interest-rate regime, enhancing trade activities by way of participatory financing instruments, implementation of the zakat fund (Islamic wealth tax fund) to alleviate poverty and establish distributive equity among deprived groups, and the usual expenditure activities of the macroeconomy. These activities are taken up in the sense of their interactive, integrative and learning by way of dynamic linkages.

The implication of IIE-learning process on the generalized meaning of the shari'ah

The social objectives in their endogenous interaction and integration with the economic and financial domain require the extension of the *maqasid as-shari'ah* to the economy as a whole. This type of extensive objective and goal of the *shari'ah* requires a general equilibrium understanding of the *shari'ah*, and not the segmented contractual idea (*aqad*) between the financing instruments. A generalized worldview of the *shari'ah* has not been understood by Islamic scholars except sparingly in contemporary times, as by Asad (1967). The absence of a generalized worldview has caused the *shari'ah* to remain oblivious of the divine law in the perspective of its overarching comprehension as the universal law (*sunnat Allah*). The universal law interactively integrates the phenomenological universe with public affairs (*muamalat*). Without such a generalized systemic worldview, the contrary *shari'ah*-compliance idea now being promoted in the Islamic economic, financial, and social circles, has failed to comprehend the understanding of the divine law *res extensa* as given by the *Qur'an* and *Sunnah* in the formulation of *maqasid as-shari'ah* choices.

Consider integrating by interaction the following verses of the *Qur'an* in the light of establishing the phenomenological worldview of *tawhidi* unity of knowledge *res extensa*. Keep in mind the systemically unifying relations pointed out in the verses in respect of the diversity in the universal scheme of things. The *Qur'an* (13:1-4, selective parts with author's emphasis on exegesis) declares: ".... He has subjected the sun and the moon (to His Law) [cosmological]... He does regulate all affairs, explaining the Signs (observations and experience) in detail that you may believe with certainty in the meeting with your Lord [universality comprising worldly affairs and socio-scientific phenomenology]. And it is He who has spread out the earth,...[ecology] .... Of every kind He made in pairs two and two [pervasive complementarities and endogenous inter-relations]." The *Qur'an* (48:23) then establishes: "(Such has been) the practice (approved) of God already in the past: No change will you find in the practice (approved) of God (irreducibility and invariance of the divine law, *sunnat Allah*)". In this way, the *Qur'an* establishes the overarching meaning of the relational universe in unity of knowledge. The segmented contractual idea of *shari'ah*-compliance is a detached one. It does not form the generalized worldview. In its segmented meaning, the *shari'ah* as we understand it presently, fails to be the universal law, which otherwise needs to be premised on *tawhid*. A comprehensive perspective of the *shari'ah* would be able to study the resulting unified world-system.

Here we take the generalized overarching meaning of the *maqasid as-shari'ah* and configure the following general dynamic input-output relational system called the economy: We particularize the explanation of the *Tawhidi* String Relation (TSR) connected with the case of *zakat*-Islamic bank-economy circular causation interrelationship in the light of an objective wellbeing function that interactively integrates these tripartite interrelationships and causes evolutionary learning dynamics to occur in a sustainable developmental framework.

Zakat is a levy of 2.5 per cent on net wealth and asset value existing in liquid form. Let the *zakat* variable in financial units be denoted by Z.

Let *zakat* be levied on wealth and asset value at source in the Islamic Bank by the consensus of shareholders. Thereby, Z is mobilized through the Islamic Bank into *maqasid as-shari'ah* projects in the economy to generate GDP (Y) through the dynamic form of the input-output model that ensues in the light of the circular causation relations between the sectors.

The Islamic bank mobilizes the *zakat* at source by participatory forms of development financing instruments. These are well known in Islamic economics and finance to be *qard hasanah* (interest-free grants and loans), *mudarabah* (shares based on profit and loss sharing projects in which the poor can participate as shareholders by mobilizing their portion of *zakat* received), trade financing (by which zakat can be made to work for the benefit of the *zakat* recipients). There is also the equity-participation financing instrument called *musharakah*, and the popular mark-up financing on hire-purchase called *murabaha*. Then there is a host of secondary financing instruments that revolve around the primary ones. Let the vector of such development financing variables be denoted by P.

The economic variable is therefore GDP (Y). But this is further disaggregated into C as consumption expenditure, I as investment expenditure, and G as Government expenditure.

The question we face now is whether Z can be linearly added to the national income and expenditure accounting identity to yield GDP in an interactive sense between its components and the *zakat* variable. If we accounted for Z in this way, the linearity of the relationship between the variable will merely be an accounting relation. It would not explain the circular causation relationships between the critical variables of the input-output model with dynamic coefficients. Yet circular causation between systemic entities in the framework of learning is the essence of *tawhidi* unity of knowledge in world-systems. The interactively generated integrative states (consensus by convergence of interaction), followed by further regenerative knowledge formation and its induced newly cognizing entities in world-systems and in the problems under attention together form the immutable properties of the **IIE**-processes.

In other words, in as much as *zakat* affects GDP through C, I, G variables and the development financing instrumental variables (P), so also these latter variables affect the growth and flow of *zakat*. Besides, the variables {Z, C, I, G, P} are themselves interrelated by circular causation relations in the simulation problem of the wellbeing function

$$W(Z, GDP, P) = W(Z, C, I, G, P).$$

All these variables are knowledge-induced in reference to the **IIE**-process generated complementarities (unity of relations) between the variables, the medium of development financing and resource mobilization instruments and by the knowledge of such complementarities gained in the institutional setting of the circular zakat-Islamic bank-GDP (economy) interrelations. The discourse and *functional* ontology underlying such a dynamic input-output relationship along with the epistemology and ontology of knowledge formation is referred to in the *Qur'an* as comprising the worldly learning process in *shura-tasbih* experience. The **IIE**-process underlying this institutional-ontology learning process in the light of the *tawhidi* worldview of unity of knowledge is referred to here as the *shuratic* process.

Hence a linear aggregation of zakat with the GDP relation is merely an accounting identity. Such an identity does not explain the interactive contributions between the variables (Z, C, I, G, P) in the formation of economic value with ethical induction as by the **IIE**-processes.

The dynamic input-output method of evaluating the zakat-Islamic bank-economy inter-relationships

We note the following forms of feedback relationships that exist between the mentioned variables in order to build the dynamic input-output model interconnecting *zakat* (Z), Islamic bank (policy vector 'P' for generating interaction between the mentioned variables), and economy (C, I, G). The input-output model is dynamic in the sense of its learning coefficients. That is, the I-O coefficients turn out to be dynamic coefficients under the impact of learning in the **IIE**-process methodology emanating from the *tawhidi* unity of knowledge as the relational epistemology.

Zakat causes augmentation in consumption through the amelioration of the very poor and deprived. Investment is enhanced by directing some of the *zakat* funds into grassroots development projects for ameliorating the very poor. Islamic banks direct *zakat* funds into projects for the very poor and deprived in which the government participated. In all such project financing Islamic banks use a mix of participatory development financing instruments. The Malaysian Government is known to have used a unit trust called *amanah saham* to build grassroots shareholding. Thus the *zakat* expenditure can be seen to belong to a specific sector of the economy where its activities abound. We will name the sector that directly uses a portion of the *zakat* fund in servicing current needs as the ZS-sector. The rest of the *zakat* then goes into the consumption goods sector, investment goods sector, and government sector, where respective kinds of goods are produced and *zakat* funds are used to participate in such productions.

On a feedback relation, all forms of expenditure, including C, I and G generate spending in the good things of life according to *maqasid as-shari'ah*. Such spending promotes economic growth and development in dynamic basic-needs regimes of development (Choudhury & Hoque, 2004). Consequently, increasing levels of sector-specific GDP connected with projects are channelled in turn into more *zakat* collection and disbursement. We will refer to the Spending Sector separately as the Consumption Goods Sector (CS), Investment Goods Sector (IS), and Government Sector (GS). In each of these sectors, waste is avoided by selecting the proper *shari'ah* projects and direction of *zakat* funds into dynamic regimes of life-fulfilling goods and services.

The Islamic policy variables (P) are embedded in all such relations as means of resource mobilization. The implication is that the poor are capable of and induced into ethical and productive relationship with others (e.g. dynamic basic-needs regime of development). Projects so chosen are those that complement the mainstream projects for the ultimate goal of attaining wellbeing through social and economic complementarities. A good example is the Underprivileged Children Educational Program (UCEP) in Bangladesh, where panhandlers are taken off the streets and put in fast-track education and vocational training programs. Students of this program end up servicing certain technical outlets of mainstream enterprises and multinational companies.

With the above named sectors, the input-output model interrelating the sectoral flows between them takes the form:

Table 10.1: Input-Output Table of Zakat-Islamic Bank-Economy Interrelations

Total Output	ZS	CS	IS	GS	VA
Z	$Z_{Z,Z}$	$Z_{Z,C}$	$Z_{Z,I}$	$Z_{Z,G}$	z
C	$C_{C,Z}$	$C_{C,C}$	$C_{C,I}$	$C_{C,G}$	c
I	$I_{I,Z}$	$I_{I,C}$	$I_{I,I}$	$I_{I,G}$	i
G	$G_{G,Z}$	$G_{G,C}$	$G_{G,I}$	$G_{G,G}$	g

Z+C+I+G = Accounting Total Output
z+c+i+g = National Income in the Zakat-Related Sectors

In Table 10.1 the variables X_{kl} denote the inter-sectoral flow of resources to generate intermediate output in sector l by the inputs of the contributing sector k; k,l = ZS, CS, IS, GS. Xs are the various inter-sectoral variables.

VA denotes value added for the sectors. z denotes the value added of the direct *zakat*- using sector.

z denotes the residual amount of *zakat* after the use of total Z inter-sectorally in productive projects for the appropriate recipients of *zakat* (*Qur'an*, 2:177). Indeed, there are *shari'ah* rules approving that in certain cases surplus *zakat* fund can be transferred for later use. An example is the case of the use of *zakat* proceeds in building Tabung Haji as a charitable lending institution in Kuala Lumpur, Malaysia.

c denotes the residual consumption spending after the inter-sectoral usage of C. Such residuals are known to build up stocks for future use. The idea of *takaful* (insurance) in foodstuff is an example.

i is the residual investment spending after its inter-sectoral usage in the investment goods sector. An example is of delayed developments of *zakat* related projects.

g denotes the residual government spending. An example is a postponement of G to future years in the form of foodstuff and insurance.

Now, in terms of the I-O coefficients we write,

$$A_{kl} = X_{kl}/X_l;$$

k,l = ZS, CS, IS, GS. X's are the various sectors as explained.

An example is of $A_{ZC} = Z_{ZC}/C$, denoting the proportion of Z used in the development of projects for poverty alleviation in the consumption goods sector relative to the total spending in the consumption goods sector pertaining to the projects. An example is of paddy production by means of Z funds as a proportion of the total consumption spending in the grains production sector. This is the case of Malaysia paddy production where *zakat* is used as an ameliorative input to help out poor farmers.

Since all X_{kl} and X_l, as the $X(\theta)$–vector variables are induced by the knowledge-flow variable $\{\theta\}$, therefore all respective coefficients A_{kl} become learning coefficients. In regards to the extensively ameliorative effect of charity (Z) the *Qur'an* (2:261) declares: "The parable of those who spend their substance in the way of God is that of a grain of corn: it grows seven ears, and each ear has a hundred grains. God gives a manifold increase to who He pleases: and God cares for all and He knows all things."

Yet the enactment of the learning process by means of $\{\theta\}$-values simulated in the progressive **IIE**-processes is not automatic. It is partly intrinsic and partly guided. Learning as the experience of unifying participation and complementarities is embedded in all things according to the *Qur'an*. Note the model of the 'paired universes' that the *Qur'an* mentions (*Qur'an*, 13:3). Thus all things learn, just as the human world learns in unity of knowledge in the good things of life. But there is also the central role of moral guidance in such an evolutionary learning system. The policy and development financing variables denoted by P are careers of the moral transformation through the **IIE**-processes.

Islamic banks thus perform a central role in resource mobilization in ways that the social and economic objectives of social wellbeing are simultaneously realized by activating the development financing instruments pertaining to the *shari'ah*. We also note that in the above kind of formalization regarding the economy-wide resource mobilization with inter-sectoral linkages by *zakat*, the very nature of project-specific spending of the *zakat* fund linking up with spending in the other sectors, reveals the microeconomic nature of *zakat*-accounting in the *zakat*-Islamic bank-economy interrelationship. We thereby note that the ethical focus of the Islamic economy changes the aggregation basis of the variables into microeconomic forms.

Estimation procedure of the learning input-output coefficients

Take two particular circular causations with zakat variables, in the forms:

$$Z = A.C^{\alpha}.I^{\beta}.G^{\gamma}.P^{\delta} \text{ (nominal values)}$$

$$z = B.c^{q}.i^{r}.g^{s}.P^{v} \text{ (real values)}$$

These are readily estimable equations along with their counterpart equations in the other variables determined by circular causation relations.

For a particular case we define,

$$\Delta A_{ZC} = [\%\Delta Z/\%\Delta C].\ \Delta C = \alpha.\Delta C;$$

$$\Delta a_{ZC} = [\%\Delta z/\%\Delta c].\ \Delta c = q.\Delta c$$

The rest of the parameters and the I-O coefficients can be estimated likewise. These coefficients describe the dynamic path of sectoral linkages as a sign of unity of knowledge. It can be seen that the dynamic components of the I-O coefficients are now readily estimable in terms of the variables {Z, C, I, G, P}. A and B are learning shift-coefficients.

Since the estimated regression coefficients, even in their random forms (Bayesian probabilities), would not explain the dynamic nature of such coefficients, it is recommended to use other statistical methods for the simulation of such coefficients so as to arrive at desired simulated values. Every such desired set of estimated values of the coefficients such as ΔA_{ZC} [Δa_{ZC}] and its counterparts is policy induced by P, though this is not necessary to explicitly exhibit.

Such statistical programs that were used for a similar empirical work (Choudhury, 2012) are SPSS (for estimation of regression coefficients) combined with Spatial Domain Analysis of GIS (to simulate a random field of the estimated I-O coefficients similar to ΔA_{ZC} [Δa_{ZC}]). The field of possible estimates of the latter was interpreted as the domain of policy-induced values of the regression coefficients. Such simulated estimates reflect interesting policy meanings in the development context. Once the dynamic versions of the I-O are so estimated we can transform the I-O Table 10.1 into its coefficients form and then re-estimate the dynamic and policy induced values as in Table 10.1. This formalism is not shown here but can be seen elsewhere (Choudhury & Hossain, 2005). Other empirical methods and their comparative effectiveness in circular causation method are shown in Chapter 13 of this book.

The Simulated Wellbeing Function

In the end, the wellbeing function can be estimated as follows. Let the wellbeing function be in the form,

> Z/GDP = a, a parameter simulated to 2.5 per cent, as the rate of *zakat*. 'a' at any instance cannot equal 2.5 per cent in this case.

Alternatively, this equation can be expressed as,

$$Z = a.C^{a'}.I^{b'}.G^{c'}.P^{d'}$$

The implication here is that the Islamic economy in dynamic life-fulfilling goods and services, and the endogenous existence of ethical values, enjoy increasing returns to scale in production. This occurs as unit cost of risk and production progressively declines with enhanced learning in complementarities generating participatory opportunities. a', b', c', d' are elasticity coefficients of Z with respect to C, I, G and P, respectively. 'a' is a learning shift-parameter. Other similar coefficients for the circular causation equations in the other variables can be treated in like manner.

The comprehensive wellbeing simulation problem interlinking the variables {Z, C, I, G, P} in respect of their respective sectors as shown in Table 10.1 is now given by,

> $\text{Simulate}_{\theta}\ Z(\theta) = [a.C^{a'}.I^{b'}.G^{c'}.P^{d}][\theta]$, induced throughout by θ-values. with circular causation expressions and along with the remaining similar relations between the recursive variables {Z, C, I, G, P}.

A given range of simulation stops within a given **IIE**-process when Z/GDP is approximated to 2.5 per cent. The nearness of this simulated value is decided upon by the institution of *shuratic* discourse in development planning.

The above simulation model shows that two dynamics are constantly at work, namely the setting of the elasticity coefficients, α, β, γ, δ; q, r, s, v; a', b', c', d' by virtue of using the appropriate statistical methods of dynamic simulation of these parameters. Secondly, there is continuous institutional guidance along *shari'ah* ways for the *shuratic* process to evolve. This requires the central role of Islamic bank in resource mobilization with positive feedback with the economy sustaining along the life-fulfilling regimes of development.

Contrasting views on the meanings of aggregate demand and aggregate supply in Keynesian, monetarist and tawhidi ethico-economic contexts

The heyday of Malaysian socioeconomic development during the late eighties showed that the Keynesian aggregate demand curve and aggregate supply curves were almost perfectly elastic and intertwined. The implications of such macroeconomic situations have important bearing on the Malaysian economy (Choudhury, 1999) despite a misnomer in the understanding of macroeconomics as a field of aggregation distinct from microeconomics (Choudhury, 2006).

Firstly, if a strict abidance with Keynesian and monetarist implications of perfectly elastic aggregate demand and aggregate supply curves was made, then the macroeconomy remains perfectly well coordinated, expanding, and stable in non-inflationary economic growth. The *tawhidi* form of evolutionary learning appearing in its **IIE**-processes is fully effective through the complementarities gained between fiscal policies, monetary policies, and non-inflationary growth, employment, productivity, efficiency, and innovation.

Secondly, because the aggregate demand curve cannot be positively sloped, and the aggregate supply curve cannot be negatively sloped in the fiscal-monetary version of macroeconomic coordination, only the perfectly elastic form of these curves could be possible. There is no other alternative. Such a binding macroeconomic case establishes perfect complementarities among the stated variables, namely, fiscal policies, monetary policies, and non-inflationary growth, employment, productivity, efficiency and innovation. Incidentally, the macroeconomic state of general equilibrium is now extended to both the aggregate demand and aggregate supply inter-causal relations, and the investment-savings (IS) relationship inter-causally related with liquidity-money (LM) curves. But the relationships have been transformed into an evolutionary learning form with the endogenous induction of the knowledge-variable in the Malaysian macroeconomy of the eighties in respect of the above-mentioned consequences of *tawhidi* dynamics in relationship with the complementary evolutionary learning perspectives of macroeconomic relations. These relationships are depicted in Figure 10.3.

The result establishes the necessary and sufficient conditions for the existence of pervasive complementarities in a fully participative economy. Such a pervasively complementary situation can be actualized only in the limiting case of the *tawhidi* macroeconomic complementary relations as the especial situation of the usual macroeconomic dynamics. Yet the endogenous effect on how knowledge-flow explains such substantive change is absent from explanation.

In Figure 10.3 fiscal-monetary dynamics are caused by the exogenous effect of innovation. Consequently, there is no presence of knowledge-flows to cause continuously complementary relations between IS and LM (likewise aggregate demand and aggregate supply curves). Such endogenous, complex, and non-linear changes are caused by the continuous production of knowledge and the knowledge-induced variables by circular causation among (θ, y_r,$\rho_r \geq i_r$). Here y_r denotes real output. $\rho_r \geq i_r$ means that the evolutionary learning dynamics of the endogenous variables is actualized by the force of innovation that causes indicators such as dynamic productivity, profitability, and efficiency (ρ_r) not to remain less in value than the real interest rate i_r. The evolutionary learning effect is conveyed by circular causation relations between (θ, y_r,$\rho_r \geq i_r$). This case is shown by the direction of arrows towards the flat surfaces of the boxes in Figure 10.3. Without the endogenous explanatory effect of 'θ' on the other circular causation variables, the self-augmenting effect of technological change and innovation remains costly and halting.

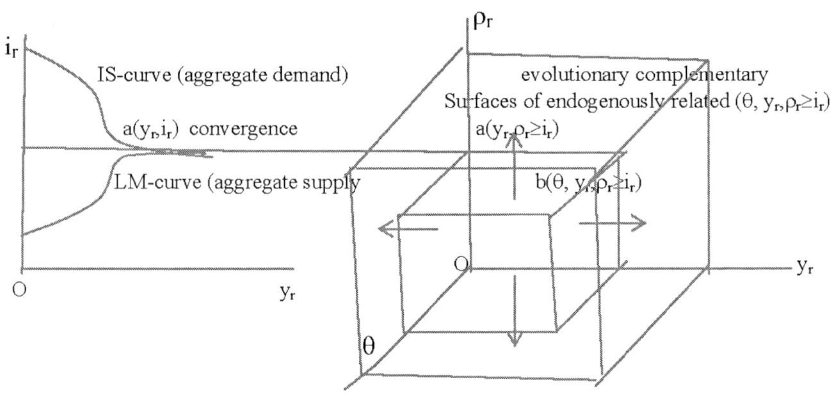

Figure 10.3: Conversion of exogenously innovation induced fiscal and monetary complementarities into endogenously induced knowledge-flows in the IIE-processes of *tawhidi* methodology

Conclusion: Malaysian economy yesterday, present, and tomorrow in tawhidi perspective

The broad perspective of pervasive complementarities that ensue along with those between fiscal and monetary policies, as mentioned above, open up the possibilities of stable organic relations for effective macroeconomic coordination with microeconomic foundations. Thus for example, one can relate the reversal of the Malaysian Ringgit (currency) to stability after its runoff during the South-East Asian financial crisis in the late nineties. One can examine the nature of the problem that was reverted due to stability of the Ringgit in the light of the *tawhidi* methodological worldview applied to economics and finance.

On the principal cause of the currency runoff, Dr Mahathir Mohammad (2000, p. 20), the then celebrated Prime Minister and architect of modern Malaysia in global affairs, writes:

> Malaysia was involved in a very complex socioeconomic restructuring. In the hands of the IMF, the need for equitable distribution of economic wealth between the races would not receive the attention that was needed. Merely recovering would not be enough for Malaysia. Recovery must be accompanied by the equitable distribution of the economic pie between the *Bumiputeras* and non-*Bumiputeras*.

Thus, for overall stabilization of the economy, Malaysia's model of socioeconomic transformation was seen as being based on the complementary balance between moral, ethical, social, and economic forces for establishing wellbeing. The model of reverting to stability thus constituted a wellbeing function as was formalized in the case of the *tawhidi* methodological worldview.

When stability was established, currency values stabilized out of the virtues of moderation in imports and the currency control on the outward flight of capital. The result was an inward looking policy for the benefit of national investment and improved asset-valuation, which otherwise was running down in value due to the devaluation of the Malaysian Ringgit. The currency runoff otherwise would allow currency and financial speculators to take advantage of buying assets cheap until such time when the Ringgit would be re-valued and the price of assets would accordingly increase. Assets would be valued upwards.

The resulting profitability of domestic investments in such re-valued assets would stop the flight of capital and maintain the Ringgit currency value as USD1.00 = MR3.80. This was an endogenous effect of market adjustment but linked with the policies of currency control, import moderation, and balance of complementarities between the good possibilities that arise with policy induction and are continued on with endogenous relationship between polity and markets. Such a kind of endogenous continuity in recovery and macroeconomic stabilization implicates the presence and intensification of induction of organic unity of knowledge in the knowledge-induced variables, indicators, and institutional entities.

Islamic banks, which performed well in the early days of the financial crisis of 2005-2007 failed to protect themselves from large losses in the following years as the financial crisis deepened (IMF, 2010). The cause is attributable to a failure of matching excess liquidity with real sector asset-investments. Resource mobilization by Islamic banks could not be linked with a sufficient number of assets. Real sector financing was only marginally asset-backed.

It therefore remains incumbent on Malaysia for its sustainability of growth, stabilization, and wellbeing of the socioeconomic conditions, to adopt policies of the polity-market organically linked type. Such policies can centre on asset-backing participatory fiscal, monetary, financial, and real economy interrelationships along with their other socioeconomic synergies. The prospect for sustainability thus rests on the understanding and applications of the *tawhidi* methodological worldview in the case of economy and finance. Malaysia today has taken a bold step in this direction through its Islamic banks domestically and with international networking. At present, about 20 per cent of the Malaysian stock market is supported by *shari'ah* financial instruments. This makes Malaysia the global hub for Islamic finance (internet version of news, Monday 7 January, 2013).

Yet the Islamic financial market remains a concentrated rather than a diversified market. *Sukuk* as Islamic bonds, and *murabaha* as cost-plus pricing mark-up, take up the highest shares of Islamic financing. The primary Islamic financing instrument, such as *mudarabah*, profit-sharing, is on the decline. *Musharakah*, equity participation has held its own.

References

Al-Qaradawi, Y., 2000, *Priorities of the Islamic Movement*, Awakening Publications, Inc. Birmingham, AL, USA.

Asad, M., 1987, *The Law of Ours*, Dar Al-Andalus, Gibraltar.

Billington, M.O., 2002, "Gold Dinar: an economic and strategic response to chaos", *Executive Intelligence Review* (internet version), Nov. 15.

Chang, A. 2006, *Fundamental Methods of Mathematical Economics*, McGraw-Hill, New York, NY.

Choudhury, M.A., 1993, "Postscript" in "Consumer demand", Chapter 5 (pp. 81-99) of his, *Comparative Economic Theory: Occidental and Islamic Perspectives*, Kluwer Academic, Norwell, MA.

—. 2006, "Islamic Macroeconomics?"*International Journal of Social Economics*, (33)2.

—. 1995, "A system model of the Malaysian macro-economy", *Kybernetes, the International Journal of Cybernetics, Systems, and Management Sciences*, (24)7, 75-90.

—. 1999, "A critique of econometric modeling for development studies: a political economy approach with special reference to Malaysia:, in Ghosh B.N. and Salleh, M.S. (eds.), *Political Economy of Development in Malaysia*, pp. 105-123, Utusan Publications and Distributors Sdn. Bhd., Kuala Lumpur, Malaysia.

—. 2004, *The Islamic World-System, a Study in Polity-Market Interaction*, Routledge Curzon, London & New York.

—. 2008, "A critique of Ibn Khaldun's causality concept", *Journal of King Abdulaziz University – Islamic Economics*, (20)1, 49-72.

Choudhury, M.A. and Malik, U.A., 1992, *The Foundations of Islamic Political Economy*, Macmillan Press Ltd., London, England & St. Martin's Press, New York.

Choudhury, M.A. and Hossain, M.S., 2006, *Development Planning in the Sultanate of Oman*, Edwin Mellen Press, Lewiston, New York.

Choudhury, M.A. & Hossain, M., 2012,"A probabilistic evolutionary learning model with epistemological meaning in Islamic economics and finance", *Journal of Financial Reporting and Accounting*, (11:1), Special Issue.

Ibrahim, A., 1996, *The Asian Renaissance*, Times Editions, Singapore.

International Monetary Fund, Oct. 4, 2010, "Islamic banks: more resilient to crisis?" *IMF Survey Magazine online*, IMF Research, online link: http://www.imf.org/external/pubs/ft/survey/so/2010/RES100410A.htm

Mankiw, G., 2003, "IS-LM as a theory of aggregate demand", *Macroeconomics*, pp. 291-295, Worth Publishers, New York, NY.

Krugman, P., 1996, *The Self-Organizing Economy*, Blackwell Publishers, Cambridge, MA.

Mohammad, Mahathir, 2000, *The Malaysian Currency Crisis, How and Why It Happened*, Pelanduk Publications, Sdn Bhd., Kuala Lumpur, Malaysia.

Mydin, A.K. & Larbani, M., 2004, "The Gold Dinar: The Next Component in Islamic Economics, Banking and Finance", *Review of Islamic Economics*, (8)1, 5-34.

Romer, P.M., 1986, "Increasing returns and long-run growth", *Journal of Political Economy*, 94:1002-37.

Solow, R., 1980, *Growth Theory, an Exposition*, Oxford University Press, Oxford, Eng.

Turnovsky, S.J., 1995, "An introduction to endogenous growth", in his, *Methods of Macroeconomic Dynamics*, pp. 391-425, The MIT Press, Cambridge, MA.

CHAPTER ELEVEN

THE CONTRASTING *TAWHIDI* WORLDVIEW OF SOCIO-ECONOMIC DEVELOPMENT: THE CASE STUDY OF THE SULTANATE OF OMAN

The methodology of system and cybernetic dynamics in the context of a unified or relational epistemology of a multidimensional circular causation model most appropriately explains the complex process of socioeconomic development and development planning. Development *is* indeed a complex process. The South Commission (1990, p. 13) defines the meaning of socioeconomic development in the broad sense encompassing economic, social and human factors as follows: "To sum up: development is a process of self-reliant growth, achieved through participation of the people acting in their own interests as they see them, and under their own control."

Objective

The objective of this chapter is to explain development as a system and cybernetic process of complementarities that explain socio-ethical transformations. These involve distinct features of interrelationships between the economies, markets, state institutions, communities, and the global order. Thus development while being a systemic process of complementary relations at the rejection or correction of contrary forces by endogenous forces and policy effects can be considered as a perspective in politico-economic worldview. The meaning here conveys the complex aggregation of the small elements to form the sustainable super-structure of development. The immanent systemic and cybernetic processes in turn derive their theories of structure and function from underlying epistemologies that are embedded in the complementary interrelations that arise.

In this chapter we will discuss the nature of such systemic and cybernetic interrelations, thus contrasting the emergent theory with mainstream thought on socioeconomic development. While undertaking this critical investigation we will also refer often to the alternative development paradigms that 'ought to be' premised on the complementary processes between human preferences and values, socioeconomic variables, and their institutional meanings.

This chapter is presented in three parts. Part I introduces our new perspective of participatory socioeconomic development in the framework of what we term as system and cybernetic approach to study development. Part II is an extensive review of the literature in contrasting paradigms of development to bring out the singularity of the new proposed methodology. Part III is a return to the contrast between our system and cybernetic model of relational epistemology in development and contrasting paradigms. Part IV is a conclusion highlighting the contrasting new perspectives of this chapter.

Part I: The importance of participatory or complementary process in socioeconomic development: the system and cybernetic worldview of development

We note from the social systemic and cybernetic perspective of socio-economic development the central role that the participatory process plays in the understanding of development as a complementary process of unifying dynamics. Such dynamics and their construction of the knowledge-induced world-system present the singular and indispensable core issue of the *tawhidi* worldview. Furthermore, the development process penetrates the microeconomic levels of the grassroots where problems of poverty, entitlement, and empowerment abound. Upon such focus of development study there are also the issues of human development (UNDP, 1997-2000) and a further disaggregation of development at the levels of industrial sectors and institutional decision making. Thereby, the complexity of development study increases by the extension of such microeconomic issues to participatory dynamics. The emergent model of complexity, non-linearity, and endogeneity was explained in Chapter 9. In all of these and more the development as a process of human and value determination is linked with economic and social factors. The result is the participatory approach to decision-making as the central endogenous force in socioeconomic development. It is also this participatory process having a systemic meaning that becomes coterminous with the epistemology of unification of knowledge across diverse sub-systems. The moral, ethical, social, and economic change and reconstruction are thus studied.

The World Bank (2000, op cit p. 12) remarks with respect to the participatory scope of development:

> The strategy in this report recognizes that poverty is more than inadequate income or human development -- it is also vulnerability and a lack of voice, power, and representation. With this multidimensional view of poverty comes greater complexity in poverty reduction strategies, because more factors—such as social and cultural forces—need to be taken into account.
>
> The way to deal with this complexity is through empowerment and participation—local, national, and international....

On the same topic UNDP (1999, p. 75) remarks:

> Participation in the process must be widened. Knowledge is needed not only of the latest technologies but also of local ecosystems and food chains, local culture and systems of exchange, socioeconomic conditions and political and market stability. This calls for broad collaboration.

Furthermore, the socioeconomic development worldview is now combined with the development planning process. Planning in such a context may be defined as the management of development in its broad context encompassing economic, social, and human factors. This kind of an overarching study comprises a systemic politico-economic worldview. The importance of such a multidimensional perspective of development planning as systemic management of development is only recently being understood as a 'globally' embedded perspective for all developing countries and development organizations (Choucri & North (1995, p. 477).

Development planning is a way of attaining targeted output levels by setting price relatives. This means that market processes are intervened by political and social priorities in determining such price relatives of goods and services (Gerber, 2002). Accordingly also, the levels of employment, and thereby, the wage relatives between sectors are all determined on the basis of the development planning targets on total and sectoral outputs. The variables of the closed and open economies, such as cost, production, trade-offs in resource allocation, relative prices, imports and exports, exchange rate and interest rate regimes, technological choices and social goals are set together in a deterministic way to attain both economic as well as social goals. Thus planning can waiver between extremes of socialist central planning and the attaining of capitalist transformation by adopting the particular kinds of policy-theoretic approach that the determinism of the political, social, and economic interests would demand. Development planning is thus a carrier of perceived structural transformation that the political engines and technocracy demand.

While development planning is an extensively interactive exercise across decision-makers and sectors, and economic, public and social goals, it is the centralized nature of its enactment that causes the regimentation of the targeted goals. The United Nations (1987, p. 22) states: "The formulation of national development plans is basically a process of public policy-making in the economic field at central government levels. Its purpose is to identify and define the policies best suited to achieving general economic and social objectives."

Now combining the meanings of socioeconomic development with planning in the context of incorporating together the economic, ethical, human and global perspectives of social transformation, brings about the same kind of functional aggregation in the structural formation of system dynamics. Functionalism is micro-oriented; structure is the aggregation of the functional organisms. A special case of the entities of such an aggregation comprise the economic sectors. The variables we are interested in are inter-sectoral distribution of output, employment, employment/population ratio, profitability indicators, investment, and policy variables like distributive equity, price stabilization, risk and cost diversification instruments in the choice of technology and the financial sectors, etc.

Contrarily, the parameters of the underlying models explain the complementarities between these variables according to systems and cybernetic learning between functional entities, variables, and their relations. A structural econometric system arises. In this the elasticity coefficients and the input-output coefficients in a two-phase model system between a regression system and the input-output analysis are estimated and simulated. The extension of such a system model addresses micro-issues at the grassroots (Choudhury, 2011).

Examples of such micro-issues are poverty alleviation, integrating the microenterprise in development planning, promoting institutional knowledge diffusion by discourse (participation), formation of appropriate economic and financial instruments that make it possible to attain complementarities between distributive equity and economic efficiency in their various forms. All these and other additional socioeconomic factors aim at attaining higher levels of human development taken in its multidimensional functional form combining poverty alleviation, entitlement, empowerment, food sufficiency, equitable income and resource distribution, sustainability, fair and honest corporate and global governance, and policy enactment in the context of comprehensive human wellbeing.

The IMF (1995, p. 48) writes on such global ethics that enter the programs of development planning in comprehensive perspective:

> .... An ethical dimension to global governance requires a three-fold approach:
>
> - Enunciate and encourage commitment to *core values* concerned with the quality of life and relationships, and strengthen the sense of common responsibility for the *global neighbourhood.*
> - Express these values through a *global civic ethic* of specific rights and responsibilities that are shared by all actors, public and private, collective and individual.
> - Embody this ethic in the *evolving system of international norms*, adapting, where necessary, existing norms of sovereignty and self-determination to changing realities.

In general we note from all the current thinking on development paradigms that the globally co-determined and participatory framework stands out as the most impressive and newest way of understanding and realizing development from the bottom up. The central implication and context of the South Commission's definition of socioeconomic development is to construct a vastly relational process characterizing social and politico-economic systemic dynamics for determining those human choices that are appropriate within an ethically codetermined perspective of development. Such a principle is particularly prescribed for the developing countries in view of the potential that they can jointly share in, and can be enacted to realize justice in the global arrangement of ownership and management of resources towards determining self reliance. Such a relational view of dynamic complementarities, among the various potentials that the developing countries can together render, now becomes the premise of our new praxis of socioeconomic development. Within the immanent systemic and cybernetic worldview, the interactive and discursive phenomena of markets, economies, institutions and policies assume their nature and viability to embed and coexist by the inherent endogenous synergies that they commonly share.

Part II: Contrasting views on the comprehensive perspective of development planning

In Figure 11.1 we describe a trajectory of development paradigms. Multidimensional indicators are shown to impinge on the trajectory AB.

The economic theories explaining assumed relations of such indicators along the development trajectory are briefly explained (Meier, 1995).

We first examine the mainstream economic explanations of the socioeconomic development relations in two ways. First, the relations are seen as linear optimal processes in mainstream economics, particularly in neoclassical economic theory and its prototypes. Secondly, in some other development doctrines the relations are found to be intra-system dynamic, but are not dynamic inter-systems other than showing time-trends.

In either of these two cases, systemic learning ceases to experience interrelations that would otherwise explain inter- *and* intra- system multidimensional interaction in the framework of a co-evolutionary relational epistemology that is explained by unity of systemic knowledge and the recursive evolution caused by the circular causation methodology between knowledge-induced variables and the wellbeing function. Such is the essential nature of the system and cybernetic social worldview that is now converted into an explanation of participatory socioeconomic development.

Mainstream development paradigms: the neoclassical methodology

Mainstream socioeconomic development paradigms are entrenched in neoclassical economic theory, only with marginal variations between them. The principal axioms of all of mainstream economic thought led by neoclassicism is that the world can be well-ordered by the flow of full or bounded information. The axiom of economic rationality, which is assumed to pre-order resource allocation by given preferences of the decision makers or production menus of the producers and structures of institutions (Buchanan, 1954), underlie the assumption of full information and perfect preordering of choices (preferences). The axiom of rationality is causally linked with that of resource scarcity. The natural corollary is competition between alternatives. This in turn causes the pursuit of self-interest. In such a development system, markets and institutions aim at attaining optimal profits and utility, given full or bounded information within these situations (Simon, 1987).

In the special case of perfect competition, the assumed existence of atomistic consumers and producers leads to the state or resource allocation that remains optimal by virtue of the perfect information that is disseminated in the absence of policy intervention and independently between the neoclassical entities. As a result of such *laissez faire* situation of economic choices, mainstream economics remains silent on the *process* of attaining optimal goals. Goals are treated as terminal attained states of optimal resource allocation. No process explanation of attaining the goals is given. Consequently as well, the axioms of scarcity of resources, economic rationality, full-information, competition, optimality and steady-state resource allocation (Shackle, 1972) towards attaining the goals of socioeconomic development, remain unexplained by way of social process.

Scarcity of resources is thereby an unexplained condition in optimal resource allocation, except that it is *necessary* in order to establish the optimality and equilibrium for 'solving' economic problems. In the absence of a process-oriented allocation of resources all endogenous impact of interacting agents, markets, dynamic changes in human preferences, and productive menus, institutional rules, ecological and technological effects of the endogenous type, are ignored. In such an axiomatic state of 'solving' technical economic problems the neoclassical axioms remain causally interconnected between them. These are namely, self-interested human behaviour, scarcity of resources, competition and economic rationality explained by transitivity of preferences as datum. All of these attributes result in 'solving' the economic problem of constrained optimization and attaining the corresponding state of equilibrium in resource allocation.

The neoclassical methodology of 'solving' economic problems out of the technical need for optimization and equilibrium, results in the necessary conditions of prescribed preferences to be consistent and transitive. Likewise, production menus, and the existence of substitutes at large negate the possibility of pervasive complementarities. The possibility of optimal and steady-state equilibrium resource allocation is determined by the principle of marginal rate of substitution in both perfect and imperfect competition, and in states of perfect and bounded economic rationality (Simon, 1987). This principle is a non-dynamic concept. It cannot hold in the same manner in the dynamic case of intertemporal resource allocation with learning (Robinson, 1961). Thereby, the neoclassical postulates have no room in explaining the nature and properties of resource allocation, and social and economic change in knowledge-induced learning systems (Stehr, 2002).

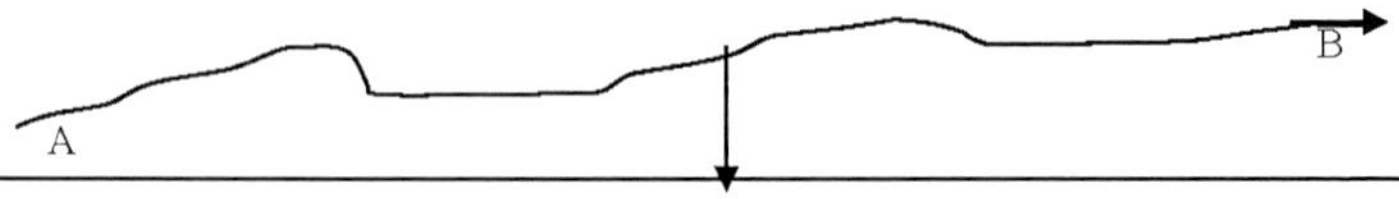

Socioeconomic Variables	Institutional Variables	Wellbeing Globalization
Economic	Technology choice	Mainstream
Output	aggregate production	Social Welfare
Income	capital vs. labour intensity	and Utility
Wealth	Policy variables	Function
Profitability	macroeconomic policy analysis	
Efficiency	(fiscal, monetary)	(competition,
Direct cost	Stabilization policies	substitution &
Savings &		marginalization)
Investment		
Capital formation		vs.
Markets	Technology choice	the ethico-economic
Goods	production menus	Social Wellbeing
Services	joint production	(complementarities
Imponderables	Preference formation	by learning in
(knowledge &	consumer preferences	interactively
information)	collective decision making	co-evolutionary
Prices	Prices: substitutes or	systems)
Capital Markets	complements	
Shares, bonds	Composition of portfolio	Both of the above
Interest rates	ratios by volume & value	concepts involving
Yields or turnover	ratios of yields/interest rates	contrasting ways
	(r/i)	of treating all the
Social	Discursion	
Population	interaction between the	variables mentioned here.
Employment	social variables: global	
Human resources		
Interdependence:		
Distributive equity	ethics and sustainability	sectoral &
Sustainability	questions and issues	corporate relations
Trade		
Merchandise ←	Management of: →	trade relations
Goods	balance of payments imbalances	all incorporating
Services	debt ratios and debt-service payments	global ethical
Imponderables	consumption & production choices	goals & critical
Capital		policies:
Foreign Direct Invest.	Targeted of FDI/Portfolio	discourse on
Portfolio savings	choices	the policies of
Exchange rates	Exchange rate-interest rate relations	develop.Finance
↑	↑	↑

DIFFERENTIATION BETWEEN DEVELOPING & INDUSTRIALIZED ECONOMIES

Figure 11.1: Schema of the socioeconomic development planning study

The trade-off between economic efficiency and distributive equity as a neoclassical consequence

One of the critical issues of marginal substitution and competition in resource allocation to reach a growth driven economic development is the economic efficiency-distributive equity trade-off. Subsequent to this perception it is found that development planning of the neoclassical genre has come to influence institutional and policy making in the development organizations. What is implied here is that the neoclassical type preferences at the individual level are aggregated laterally to form neo-liberal institutional choices. Thereby, the implications of the neoclassical axioms are built into both the institutional behaviour and the policies that are enacted. These in turn influence the kind of markets and global order that emerge. A grand causality is generated in this pattern of interaction and interrelationships. But such interactions evolve within given segmented systems that are made to compete. This behaviour isolates the systems from each other. We would like to refer to such a co-evolution of interactive entities within given systems but not across systems, as the endogenously formed segmented systems caused by the force of competition. The result is causing the sub-systems to become exogenous to each other. Thus, technology, population change, preferences, ecology and institutions remain exogenous between them. Their endogenous behaviour is only within systems, not across systems (North, 1981; Srinivasan, 1985).

In treating the issue of economic growth with its coexisting attributes, namely economic efficiency and total factor productivity, we find that these concepts and their measurements have been treated in certain ways in the economic literature. Here the neoclassical model of resource allocation and economic growth predominates.

The neoclassical model represents the postulate of efficient allocation of scarce resources into competing ends. The causality among variables shows that competition and economic rationality become coterminous with the concept of optimal resource allocation and with the competing nature of resources in markets and among the competing alternatives so generated. Consequently, resource scarcity, rationality, economic competition, optimization, and steady state equilibrium are made to establish specific interrelationships among themselves. These lead to a perpetuation of the neoclassical paradigm.

Within such a paradigm there is assumed to be a universal nature of agent-specific behaviour based on the same rationality concept that pervades through markets, as through human preferences, and into the formation of institutions, and the organization of economic life (Buchanan, 1999 reprinted). Such a generalization is found to be embedded in individual, national, and global relations either by virtue of market forces generated by such Hobbesian forms of human preferences or by enforcing them through the role of institutions and powerful governance. In respect of such a deepening relationship between human preferences formed by obsession for ownership and control, Heilbroner (1985) saw in capitalism a form of organic development of ownership and control and their perpetuation through the medium of market order. Hayek (1990) wrote on the idea of the role that democracy as a political philosophy and its institutions play in perpetuating market capitalism. Marx (see Carchedi, 1991) pointed out the problem of over-determination processes of extensive interrelationships between wealth, ownership, power, institutions and markets under capitalism.

Capital formation and economic development in the neo-liberal and neoclassical methodologies

While the above discussion is a remark on neoclassical economic perspective and its relationship with capitalism, there are also similar relationships to be found with the classical conception of economic growth. Economic growth comes about through capital formation. This in turn is a conversion of savings into capital accumulation over time by means of the rate of interest as the medium encouraging saving and the optimal allocation of scarce resources intertemporally. In the resulting relationships among interest rate, bank savings and capital formation, there arise capital markets and economic policy that promote the required allocation of financial resources for attaining economic growth.

Banks play a specific role in promoting the underlying forms of resource allocation through intertemporal savings for generating capital and economic growth. Tisdell (1989) referred to such a pattern and medium of resource mobilization in favour of capitalism as the neo-mercantilist praxis. Despite the institution-polity-market interconnection underlying the classical growth outlook, the singular goal of economic growth in these paradigms has made them narrowly objective and socially unacceptable. Todaro (1977) refers to such an exclusive outlook of economic growth and of all the agents serving it as the one-dimensional linear economic phenomenon.

Hence we find that the place of material power and its extensive entrenchment in global capitalism have coloured the nature of the 'bread' basket of economic growth as an exclusive goal. This is pursued as an objective goal for attaining, though through complex interrelationships. Problems of economic growth and capital formation arise because of their singular objective criterion that remains focused on material acquisition alone. A civil society now gets subsumed in a competitive race. Here the resulting win-lose situation narrows down many of the social benefits due to the powerful, the acquisitive, and the capitalist agents.

Sullivan (1982) points out this problem of the liberal society in this regard. In perpetuating the acquisitive, competing and self-interested preferences confronted by the spectre of scarcity, institutional behaviour is depicted by the aggregation of similar kinds of preferences as an average datum at the level of the liberal democratic order. Such is the model of industrial democracy presented by public choice theory according to Buchanan (1954) and Nordhaus (1975). In the perspective of this singular goal of economic growth and capital formation with polity-market interactions that address this goal through market medium, it is appropriate to call such models as being linear in themselves. Such models and their implementation do not address the complexity involving wider social reproductive processes that abound in the interaction among moral, social, and economic forces.

On the side of the moral and social issues we find a similar problem in theories of Fabian socialism (Fusfeld, 1994) and the welfare state, where governments abound to undertake the distributive process. The result has been a large degree of inefficiency with high costs in the production and delivery of services that ultimately cause social costs to increase. Examples here are of the imposition of population control in developing countries under the UNDP Program that proved to be costly, socially resisted, and ineffective (Bhattacharya, 1991). Another result of the welfare state is providing free-ridership to the employable. Yet this causes welfare trap for the discouraged workers. The productively employable abscond from work when wage levels turn out to be lower than their welfare payments.

Rejection of developmentalism has given rise to the exclusiveness attitude among the extreme environmentalists and some indigenous people in the name of community and self-identity. This attitude too is found to have been associated with anti-development in many parts of the world (Choudhury & Noor, 1997). Consequently, we find that increasing opposition against globalization has carried with it both loss of objectivity and extremism. Many of the good prospects of globalization seem to have been overshadowed by such resentment. This is found to be true especially in the areas of trade liberalization and capital flows. It has been pointed out by Bhagwati (2 April 2000) that while dangers truly exist with free-market operations in the unbridled capitalism model, yet institutional guidance and economic restructuring could be used to develop the needed guidance and control for the proper management of trade and liberalization of capital flow.

The result of utter rejection of economic growth and development and of the outcomes that these bring about, importantly human resource development and institutional development, there is still the perpetuation of poverty and deprivation. Sen (1986) has pointed out that, among the various factors causing entitlement failure, are deficiency of human resource development and failure of tradability of ones skills and merchandise. While Sen recognizes the limitations of markets in establishing morals of distribution and equity, there still exists a mechanism whereby markets can be mobilized to realize ethical ends. The emergent area of investigation comprises endogenous preference transformation and the institution building caused by such organic transformation. Examples in this area are the actualization of consciousness centred on moral sustainability (Hawley, 1986) along with the resulting process of social becoming of the individual and communities within knowledge-induced market processes (Sztompka, 1991).

In the economic and social history of the orient the above-mentioned forces have often been found to work at the mutual exclusion of each other. The result was a certain kind of neoclassical model of competition and moral excludability. Popkin (1979) explains one such delineation of a mutually excludable model of the neoclassical genre using cultural phenomenon. In recent times, under the drive for globalization, the developing countries are found to be in the grips of the neoclassical transformation by way of their deepening individualism and political and corporate hegemony.

Examining Figure 11.1 for neoclassical trade-offs

Several trade-offs can be identified in the neoclassical perspective with respect to Figure 11.1. Firstly, the path AB is an optimal path with respect to the neoclassical perspective of development *ceteris paribus*. Here each of the variables as shown, remains independently distributed, following what is known as the Normal Probability Distribution. This assumption enables economic 'solving' of problems by the use of methods such as linear regression models, even though these may be of the complex type intra-systemically (Nelson, 1996, Rossi, 1996). Besides, the probability measures for the variables in their expected forms must be mono-causal by virtue of statistical independence. Otherwise, the expected values would not make sense.

Consider now the population, output, employment, savings, investment or rate of change in capital formation, exchange rate and interest rate variables in one such set of neoclassical trade-offs between these variables. The neoclassical aggregate production function basing its efficiency and productivity arguments on marginal rate of factor substitution must see to it that savings and spending are in trade-off with each other. The key variable in this system of trade-offs is the rate of interest, or at best the ratio of interest rate to productive returns (i/r). As (i/r) increases more financial resources are driven into savings. As (i/r) decreases, more financial resources are driven into spending (hence investment). Thus savings appear as withdrawal in this trade-off. Yet over time, i.e. over the economic planning horizon, neoclassical economic theory places the burden of capital formation on the growth of savings. In the real economy and its financial linkage, the savings and interest rate as the assumed medium of capital accumulation remain in trade-off with the growth of real output. Thereby, savings and interest rate form a trade-off with employment. Thereby, the employment/population ratio, which measures the manpower or human resource development and utilization is adversely affected in the given savings-interest rate and spending-real output relationship.

Finally, the trade variables are affected by similar arguments when the bulk of the capital flow is made to depend upon the competing allocation of the total FDI between real FDI and portfolio savings. The latter has been found to experience phenomenal growth in recent times. On the side of the trade-off between merchandise trade and capital movements, higher exchange rate acts as a price favouring capital inflow, but adversely affecting merchandise trade. Yet both can be negatively affected in the case of lower productivity gains.

When exchange rates remain low to promote net exports, while the capital inflow into portfolio savings remains depressed, interest rates are driven up to attract the needed capital inflow. Higher interest rates and lower exchange rates oppose the macroeconomic policies of fiscal stability and monetary expansion. Consequently, the real output suffers. Along with this, spending and employment are adversely affected. The ratchet effect from the side of the exchange rate and interest mechanism to savings and output and employment are repeated.

For developing countries with large population that absorbs much of the national output and depend additionally on imports, lower exchange rates militate adversely against both exports and capital inflow. This causes a worsening of the balance of payment deficits, which turns out into debt. On these grounds of adverse effects of volatile exchange rate movements and high interest rates, the nineties are well known as the lost development decade (Raymond, 1992).

Furthermore, on the social counterpart of economic development planning, high debt burden, lower output and adverse export revenues in the face of low exchange rate-high interest countries except for commodities that are under a long-run low terms of trade, the social safety net remains vulnerable. Consequently, governments cannot allay their development expenditure on the social front to look after the goals of poverty alleviation, human resource development overall, particularly at the grassroots. The entire range of factors like entitlement, empowerment and other social expenditures needed to uplift the total human development suffers. The compound complex of all the microeconomic levels of development indices measures this total human development. The well-known trade-off between economic efficiency (economic growth) and distributive equity (employment, ecology, social expenditure) is now found to deepen.

Microeconomic neoclassical trade-offs between economic efficiency and distributive equity

Certain estimated structural regression equations were found to yield either trade-offs or statistically insignificant results for interrelations between Gender Development Index (GDI), Human Poverty Index (HPI), Human Development Index (HDI) and GDP (Choudhury et al, 2001). Trade-off or weak relationship was found to exist between the rate of change in HPI and the rates of change in HDI and GDP per capita. The relationship between the rate of change in HDI and the rates of change in HPI and GDP per capita was found to be very weak. The rate of change in GDI was found to be weakly related with the rate of change in GDP per capita. The relationship of GDP with HPI was found to be weak. The rate of change of GDP per capita had a trade-off with the rates of change in HPI and GDI.

We conclude that in both of the estimated relations referred to here: There is no strong explanatory relationship of complementarities between the rates of change of GDP, HDI and GDI. Importantly, we observed that, while a percentage change in GDI has a strong positive relationship to percentage change in HDI, as is expected, yet there is a weakly negative relationship between GDI and GDP. That is, after correction for multicollinearity in the relationship between HDI and GDP, there would be a suspected negative relationship between such a corrected relationship between HDI and GDP in terms of their percentage rates of changes.

In our analysis, GDP and HDI are macroeconomic variables, whereas GDI is a microeconomic variable in the sense of its capacity to study microeconomic problems of socioeconomic development at the gender level. If neoclassical traces of development paradigm were found in the relationship between GDP and HDI, one would expect to find trade-off between GDP and GDI. That is, we are deriving a macroeconomic trade-off from microeconomic GDI-relationship. Conversely, when GDI is explained by GDP, we are in fact deriving microeconomic trade-off from macroeconomic relationship.

Since we found trade-offs in both of these cases, our conclusion of an overall trade-off between microeconomic and macroeconomic relations is upheld. In other words, our theoretical premise is proved. That is, according to neoclassical economic theory of development, trade-offs exist not simply at the macroeconomic level but also at the microeconomic level, which itself can be further disaggregated.

Indeed, in the estimated results our inference is a reliable one in view of the overall statistically significant levels of the regression coefficients and the good fit of the regression equations. We thereby infer that there is either a trade-off or independence in the relationships among the development variables used here both at the macroeconomic level and in its disaggregation at the microeconomic levels.

Of late, the school of endogenous growth theory argued that human capital induction in the growth model would make the trade-off variables evolve in a codetermined fashion. The theory claims that it would then be possible to get out of diminishing marginal returns on resource use, which is a principle that underlies the trade-off perspective (Romer, 1986).

Our contention against the endogenous growth model in the literature continues on along lines of the neoclassical debate. We claim that since diminishing marginal rate of return and the marginal trade-off are coterminous concepts, it is impossible to replace such a trade-off by complementary relations without completely taking off the pre-condition of scarcity of resource allocation, and hence of competition and perfect or bounded foresight. All of these conditions are retained in the endogenous growth model. Endogenous growth model is like the neoclassical public choice theory of endogenous institutions (Buchanan, 1954, op cit). All these approaches translate a model of marginal substitution and diminishing marginal returns of production into a technologically induced one having conflicting market-polity interactions that we have discussed above. The attenuating methodological problems of the neoclassical economic paradigm persist.

Other development paradigms: their neoclassical roots

Besides the methodological problem encountered in the entitlement and empowerment relations of Sen's neoclassical formulation with respect to the alleviation of poverty and deprivation, we have similar problems of the neoclassical postulate of marginal rate of substitution as trade-off and optimality of resource allocation in most other development planning paradigms. We will consider a few of these in the light of the variables and institutional implications of Figure11.1.

Some development economists, notably Hirschman (1958), Lewis (1954, 1979), Myrdal (1989), Prebisch (1950), Singer and Ansari (1988) and more recently Stiglitz (1974) have emphasized the inflexibility of relative prices, which in turn is known to be associated with neoclassical type smooth production possibility, and thereby, with the postulate of marginal rate of substitution. Causes attributable to this price distortion were inflexible factor prices, information incompleteness, excess supply of labour, inability for factor markets to adjust, and imperfect economic adjustments caused by demand-supply mismatch of tradable commodities with low terms of trade.

Issues relating to the mismatch between technological change in the urban sector versus its absence in the rural sector, and the capitalist control of resources by such a technological divide and its perpetuation in the global scene, were also attributed as manifestation of the power and hegemony of capitalist ownership of resources and technology. This problem is extended to explain also the disequilibrium between the modern sector and the traditional sector in terms of their unequal organizational structures of the goods, capital and factor markets (Myint, 1985, 1987). In the end, the neoclassical models applied to explain growth and resource allocation for industrialized economies and sectors were found inadequate for the developing economies and their under-developed sectors.

Sustainable development

The other side of the development paradigm belongs to the sustainable development theory and practice. Brundtland (1987) had in her mind the win-win situation caused by the complementary functions of economic and social factors each reinforcing the other in the total context of balanced use of global resources for the present and future generations. But according to Goulet (1995) sustainability is far more than an issue concerning environmental conservation and sustained growth of the economy. It is causally intertwined with deeply ethical causes to make such a sustainable paradigm realizable.

From the coterminous order of sustainable development comes a strong criticism of the development paradigms that either bases development on aggregate growth and the measurable variables of economic progress and prosperity or takes a linear and dissociated view of the old World Bank formula, "Development = Economic Growth + Social Change". Goulet (1996) warns against an unquestioned acceptance of this perception, for he argues that not any kind of economic growth and social change will do. What is required in the context of sustainability is a coterminous existence of complementarities between the growth and social ends to define a development paradigm for human wellbeing. This would at once require not simply the predominant presence of the ethical code to instil the sustainability principle but also a re-structured institutional, economic, and social planning in a wide context. Such an approach is our microeconomic orientation of functionalism to define the superstructure, which is structural in nature.

Radical models of development and their neoclassical basis

Lewis' model depends upon this marginalization and contesting movement of population between the rural and urban sectors, and between the modern and traditional sectors. The inability of the total cost of production is dichotomized between direct cost and transaction cost, instead of having a coherent way of explaining them in the framework of an integrative and interactive cost relationship. Hirschman's argument against the flexibility of relative prices of the neoclassical smooth production possibility does not unravel the coterminous nature of economic and social forces that can be encapsulated within a polity-market interactive and evolutionary process giving the measurement alternative for observing prices, quantities, costs and benefits. Such a paradigm belongs to the system and cybernetic unified worldview.

The state of dualism between the social and the economic, polity and the communal order, labour and capital, corporations and microenterprises, global hegemony and the grassroots etc. is emphatically depicted in the words of Nitzan and Bichler (2000, p. 67):

> And so from Smith onward, it became increasingly customary to separate human actions into two distinct spheres, 'vertical' and 'horizontal'. The

> vertical dimension revolves around power, authority, command, manipulation and dissonance. Academically, it belongs to the realm of politics. The horizontal axis centers around wellbeing, free choice, exchange and equilibrium – the academic preoccupation of economists. The consequence of this duality was to make modern political economy an impossible patchwork: its practitioners try to re-marry power and wellbeing, but having accepted them as distinct spheres of activity to begin with, the marriage is inherently shaky.

Examining neoclassical trade-offs in Figure 11.1 according to development paradigms with hidden neoclassical ideas

We can now examine the nature and expected relationship of variables of Figure 11.1 in the light of our above critique of the development paradigms beyond the neoclassical one. In the modern vs. traditional sector development perspective we note that the variables as mentioned are now divided into two microeconomic parts, one belonging to each of these competing parts. Upon this a transaction opportunity cost appears, which measures the foregone social development priorities.

Now in the absence of a methodology followed by the emergent technical methods of analysis we find two kinds of measurement tools. First, each of the opposing microeconomic units has dynamics *within* its own that are explained in a systemically coordinated way. On the other hand, the neoclassical principle of marginal rate of substitution prevails *between* the disparate microeconomic units. The transaction opportunity cost exists in this latter case, but it is now assumed to be measurable even though the imponderables of transaction cost and benefits prevail. The magic is accomplished with the method of probability theory and mathematical expectation. The essence of process-related configuration of the transaction costs and benefits that could otherwise be done within a discursive environment is lost. The place of institutions, hence policy, technology, and social interaction are left out as exogenous factors of what should otherwise be coherently interactive, integrative and co-evolutionary entities both within as well as across the microeconomic units.

Within this microeconomic differentiation by groups on opposite sides we consider the relationship between capital formation, output, spending, international trade, social factors, technology, and the role of institutions. We find here a number of segmented approaches, once again emulating the neo-liberal and neoclassical approach or of their subtle prototypes as mentioned above. Thus we face the impossible and undaunted task of making these exogenously segmented units of inquiry connect in any manner of co-determination other than that explained by their own inward looking theories of methodological individualism and independence.

The question of capital formation again in radical development argument

Capital accumulation in other than neoclassical development theories is caused by the advantage that capitalists assume through the capital and financial markets according to the well-known M-C-M model of money and commodities (Heilbroner, 1985 op cit):

Money (M) – Commodification of Money (C) – Production, Goods (Q) – Roundabout ways of production (Σ_Q Q(M,i)) – More Commodification of Money (C') – More Money (M' = a.C') (11.1)

In symbolic terms, this relationship is expressed as follows:

$$M \rightarrow C = M + i.M \rightarrow Q(C) = Q(M,i) \rightarrow \Sigma_Q Q(M,i) \rightarrow C' = M(1+i)^2 \rightarrow a.C' = M'(Q,i) \text{ etc.} \quad (11.2)$$

Here 'i' is the rate of interest, which defines the savings path as withdrawal from the productive economy, to be spent in the future. It is noted that 'i' gives the central driving force to this M-C-M relationship of capital accumulation.

In other than neoclassical paradigms that we are considering here, the issues of conflict and disengagement between opposing microeconomic units, is centrally premised on the rate of interest and its role on the evolution of economic output over time. But 'i' is an exogenous variable of the M-C-M relationship at its source, which is the central bank. Hence the resolution of the conflict rests upon management of an exogenous factor. That is, the ethical issues of equality, equity, participation by entitlement and empowerment, availability of development capital and the capitalistic animal spirit linked with interest rate, all remain exogenous factors.

International institutional implications in development paradigms

International institutionalism is formed by the underlying cultural preferences. This means that if the preferences are formed on the basis of a neo-liberal and neoclassical worldview, this would be the epistemology of institutional conduct in the global order. If the preferences are formed on the basis of any other epistemological premises, the nature of policies and the ensuing development agenda will be accordingly diverse.

The extension of the neo-liberal and neoclassical paradigms of economic, social, trade, and development structures means a form of utilitarianism of the global order. The social objective criterion in this case turns out to be a lateral aggregation of national utility functions into global welfare function, just as national utility function is constructed by the lateral aggregation of individual or group-specific utility functions. On this issue of aggregation of indices and variables Ruggie (2003a, p. 7) refers to the work of Waltz (1979).

International institutionalism in the perspective of neo-liberalism is seen as emulating microeconomic preferences, consumer utilitarian behaviour, market exchange in seeking self-interest, and hegemony through competition and maximization of self-constructed rules. These conditions imply the prevalence of methodological individualism as being transported intact to international institutionalization. The constitutional economics of globalization in the neo-liberal and neoclassical sense is premised on the postulate of such methodological individualism (Buchanan, 1954 op cit) of nation states.

The utilitarian perspective of international institutionalism is methodologically incapable of incorporating any ethical, cultural, technological, institutional, and policy preferences, all taken as endogenously interrelated learning factors. This inference comes out of the work by Hammond (1987), which despite its claim on altruism, fails to depart from the linearly aggregated social welfare function invoking in it what is termed as the principle of fundamental Benthamite utilitarianism.

Part III: Alternative criteria of socioeconomic development in the system and cybernetic framework: the Social Wellbeing criterion and human development

To move away from the concept of utilitarian type social welfare in neoclassical economics and into the concept of social wellbeing, and thus to see both the conceptual and policy-theoretic consequences of this substantive change, we will use the indicator of the Human Development Index. We formulate the HDI as a composite index differently from its UNDP construct.

We recommend formulating an HDI in terms of composite index comprising the indexes of HPI, GDI and GDP. These are now all taken in their log-linear form. We can then interrelate them by a system and cybernetic form of interrelated index in which the component indexes exist in circular causality. Thus our simple version of the social wellbeing criterion function would be the relationship of log-linear rate of change in HDI in terms of the log-linear rates of change in the other variables as mentioned. We can then circularly interrelate each of these indexes in terms of the remaining ones in a system of structural regression equations.

The World Development Report has proposed a similar form to be developed so as to express a more comprehensive outlook than is presently possible at the aggregate level. The World Development Report writes on this topic (World Bank, 2000, op cit, p. 19):

> One approach to addressing comparability is to define a multidimensional welfare function or a composite index. An alternative is to define a poor anybody who is poor in any one of the dimensions—without attempting to estimate trade-offs among the dimensions …

By circularly interrelating the composite indexes of the comprehensive index we are addressing this topic of multidimensionality in human development. Yet it must be observed that, if it is possible to disaggregate the composite measures of human development by their additional microeconomic components, then a more comprehensive multidimensional system can be formulated for studying causality among these indexes in reference to circular causation relations. The idea of such a large-scale endogenous system of interrelationships is now conveyed in the emergent system and cybernetic complex model assuming the nature of social synergy. They form systems that nearly correspond with the complex nature of the interactive, integrative and evolutionary relations. We have referred to this as the unified, evolutionary learning system model. It is different from the neoclassical model in addressing the phenomenon of relational complementarities.

Problem of indexing various microeconomic aspects of Human Development Index

Demarting (op cit, pp. 469-470) has pointed out various problems with the HDI. He suggests that the HDI is too aggregate an index to bring out the differences in problems such as, ethnicity inequality, gender inequality, income inequality, and levels of corruption in government. The example given is of the quantitative measure of ethnicity index for white population and black population in South Africa. If this differentiation was made, South Africa's rank for 1992 according to the ethnicity index would be

24th in the world and that of the Black South Africans would be 123rd in the world.

The nature of unweighted averaging of the HDI index based on very broad measures, namely life expectancy index (LEI), the educational attainment index (EAI), and the adjusted real GDP per capita, is bound to hide many of the needs for weighting according to social classes. This is proved in the above-mentioned case for South Africa. Thus as it presently stands the problem of inequality, which can be addressed by generating weighted averaging according to social differentiation, and thus proper indexing of the macroeconomic form of HDI by several microeconomic components, is missing.

Consequently, although a country can show weak complementarities between the component indexes of the HDI, yet at the micro-level there can be severe trade-offs between the social equity goal and the goal of economic growth. This is a methodological problem inherited in the study of development from neoclassical roots.

In bringing microeconomic indexes to bear upon the aggregate HDI measure with appropriate weighting, there is dire need for data at these microeconomic levels. Factual data at these levels should be collected by means of organized community actions rather than by macro sampling, as is usually done. The UNDP should look into ways and means of implementing such community-based data banks. This can be realized by including such data-bank development projects within the machinery of non-governmental organizations and national development banks.

The indexes concerning gender, ethnicity, and race, about which Demarting discusses, can be empirically estimated to reach policy inferences. Such an empirical study is too elaborate to be included in this chapter. We refer here to Choudhury (2001) and Choudhury, Seyyed & Korvin (2001). Very briefly, the kinds of compounded wellbeing indexes yield empirical and policy-oriented estimation in terms of diverse indexes for which data can be found. This would allow for the sectorally diversified social and economic variables along with their international compositions to be included in the explanation of the social wellbeing index, now represented by the composite HDI.

Tawhidi implications of the extensively participatory development paradigms: the case of Sultanate of Oman according to her Sixth Development Plan

The method of circular causation, applied to the issue of economic development, is a natural methodical corollary of *tawhidi* epistemology. Such applications extend the domain of issues studied by *tawhidi* epistemology to the generality and specifics of diverse world-systems. All such studies reveal the same theoretical, quantitative, and policy implications premised in unity of knowledge. Thereby, a participative and complementary methodological worldview emerges. In the theory of economic development and development planning the embedded interactive, integrative, and evolutionary learning nature of the *tawhidi* worldview is unravelled in extensively participatory development as relational epistemology in the good things of life. The *maqasid as-shari'ah* characterizes the good and relationally unified entities of the organic interrelationships. Markets, institutions, polity, and the variables representing the entities, remain endogenously interactive, integrative, and evolutionary in the emergent embedded organic interrelationships by unity of knowledge. *Tawhid* as the epistemology of unity of knowledge is thus brought to bear upon the theme of participatory development theory and development planning. Such a conceptual and policy-theoretic study is of a most natural, logical, and analytical type. This fact proves that the *tawhidi* epistemology and its applications are not constrained by religious and cultural constrictions. It is a universal theory with substantive meaning and applications for all.

Emerging trends in Omani participative economic development studied by *tawhidi* worldview of circular causation

Table 11.1 points out the general inference we derive from the emergent trends in Omani development. The background log-linear regression equations interrelating the sectoral output provide the signs of the coefficients as indicated. Such coefficients denote inter-sectoral output related elasticity coefficients. Table 11.1 likewise represents the signs of the coefficients of the inter-related investments denoted by capital expenditure.

Table 11.1: Circular causation regression coefficients signs between sectoral GDP

Dependent GDP	Independent sectoral GDPs
Ma	P, G, Mi, C, U, F, L (+), (+), (+), (-), (-), (-), (+)
P	Ma, G, Mi, C, U, F, L (+), (-), (+), (+), (+), (-),(-)
G	Ma, P, Mi, C, U, F, L (+), (-), (+), (+), (+), (+), (-)
Mi	Ma, P, G, C, U, F, L (+), (+), (+), (+), (-), (+), (+)
C	Ma, P, G, Mi, U, F, L (-), (+), (+), (+), (-), (+), (+)
U	Ma, P, G, Mi, C, F, L (-), (+), (+), (-), (-), (+), (+)
F	Ma, P, G, Mi, C, U, L (-), (-), (+), (+), (+), (+), (-)
L	Ma, P, G, Mi, C, U, F (+), (-), (-), (+), (+), (+), (-)

Table 11.2: Circular causation regression coefficients signs between sectoral capital expenditure (K)

Dependent K	Independent K-variables
Ma	P, G, Mi, U, H, L (-), (-), (+), (+), (-), (+)
P	Ma, G, Mi, U, H, L (-), (-), (-), (+), (-), (+)
G	Ma, P, Mi, U, H, L (-), (-), (-), (-), (-), (+)
Mi	Ma, P, G, U, H, L (+), (-), (-), (-), (+), (-)
U	Ma, P, G, Mi, H, L (+), (+), (-), (-), (-), (+)
H	Ma, P, G, Mi, U, L (-), (+), (-), (-), (-), (+)
L	Ma, P, G, Mi, U, H (+), (+), (+), (-), (+), (+)

Legend: s : (Ma) manufacturing sector, (P) petroleum sector, (G) gas sector, (Mi) minerals sector, (U) utility sector, (C) construction sector, (F) finance sector, (H): human resource expenditure, (L): total employment, (+,-) coefficient signs of estimated circular causation equations.

Policy analysis between presently existing ('estimated') and the future ('simulated' = normative, policy induced) states of Oman development planning

Tables 11.1 and 11.2 provide a summary of the sectoral output and capital expenditure trends in the Omani economy in the perspectives of sectoral diversification and linkages on the one hand, and sectoral trade-offs on the other hand, as two distinct outlooks of resource allocation in *tawhidi* development perspective. The case of marginal substitution negates sectoral complementarities due to specific underlying forces that need to be explained. The coefficients of marginal rates of substitution can be changed into better semblance of complementarities by appropriate policy simulations concerning the inter-variable relationships.

The case of complementarities versus trade-offs, better known in neoclassical economic theory as marginal rate of substitution, is explained by the signs and magnitude of the partial elasticity coefficients in the estimated log-linear Cobb-Douglas functional forms of sectoral GDPs and capital formation (K). These variables are considered in the circular causation sense of the relational epistemological *tawhidi* model of development planning.

A negative value of the partial elasticity coefficient implies that the percentage changes in the interrelating variables move in opposite directions. In the sense of partial elasticity coefficients, the same implication points out that the changes of the corresponding interrelating variables move in opposite direction. Hence the case of marginal rate of substitution of resource allocation is established.

Why does this negative result happen? How can the negative partial elasticity coefficient be corrected by policy measures? What does a positive partial elasticity coefficient (inter-causal inter-variable complementarities) imply in development planning?

The negative value of the partial elasticity coefficient, implying marginal rate of substitutions between interrelating variables, means that scarcity of resource allocation between the sectors may be driven by policy priorities differentiating between sectoral development focus. The same result can be due to market driven allocation of resources through the private sector, or budgetary constraint, or privatization goal of the Government of Oman in attaining targets. The targets are of economic efficiency, growth and productivity that maximize on the economic goals. In the neoclassical model that Oman development closely adopts, such goal oriented pursuits of development planning would cause trade-offs between the economic, social, and institutional driven forces.

Privatization as a market-oriented economic transformation itself calls for minimal government presence. This would cause erosion of policy intervention while the private sector is promoted in market setting. Government policy intervention would otherwise have social goals. In the perspective of *tawhidi* resource allocation the public and private sectors would coexist in their allocation of. In the neoclassical perspective of development planning these two sides would compete for scarce resources competing between sectors in terms of profitability, growth, efficiency, and productivity purely on economic grounds at the cost of social priorities.

Negative partial elasticity coefficients can be caused also by policy conflicts between sectors and by given macroeconomic policies, particularly monetary and fiscal policies affecting the sectors in conflicting ways. In the neoclassical economic literature, the notion of permanent scarcity of available resources inevitably causes trade-off between monetary and fiscal policies. This in turn is a macroeconomic cause of opposite movements of the relationship between money supply and government expenditure. This situation can result in crowding out effect on GDP either at high or low rates of interest. At low rates of interest savings remain low, whereas resources are also not sufficiently mobilized, as bond prices and share prices remain high. Between the low and high rates of interest, particularly of the short-term interest rates, the instability of the term structure of interest rates causes capital market volatility and investment uncertainty.

Technological change can be a major cause of sectoral trade-off in resource allocation. If a production factor is relatively less productive compared to another factor there will be a marginal rate of technical substitution between such factors across sectors. Consequently, the trade-off will show up in the contribution of the factors to their own sectoral outputs. Businesses will substitute more productive factor-driven sectors for the lower productive sectors.

The role of a productive form of Omanization in human resource development is central to the development of indigenous labour market and choices of appropriate technology. All these will reinforce the process of human resource development i.e. Omanization. In the absence of such complementarities between technological choice and human resource development by sectors, the important goal of development with growth and equity simultaneously cannot be attained. Consequently, the negative partial elasticity coefficients imply unequal and uneven Omanization program between sectors. Human resource development for effective and productive Omanization will therefore depend importantly on the pace of matching up HRD with appropriate technological change.

In the case of the open-economy, world prices of critical commodities will influence the marginal rate of sectoral substitution in output and capital expenditure. In the case of Oman the critical commodity is petroleum but development planning cannot overlook the critical importance of emergent prices of manufactures. Indeed, manufacturing will be a significant contributor in sustaining economic diversification in Oman.

In the regime of fixed exchange rates (as for the Omani Riyal vis-à-vis the U.S. Dollar) the trade-off between monetary policy (effective) and fiscal policy (ineffective) will increase as the foreign direct investments are given easy access into Oman. However, since many of the trading partners of Oman experience flexible exchange rates regimes vis-à-vis the U.S. dollar, therefore Oman faces a flexible effective rate of exchange. This will again accentuate the trade-off problem between monetary and fiscal policies. Besides, in such a case of globally compared flexible exchange rate regime for Oman, a move towards expansionary monetary policy for the sake of privatization will be costly for external sector stabilization in respect of economic growth and productivity. Higher economic growth can still come about but at a higher cost of resource use derived from oil revenues, and thereby, by its linkages with other sectors in targeting economic growth.

These are some of the uncertain forces that cause opposite movements in output (GDP) and investments (K) between economic sectors. Thereby, the inter-sectoral trade-offs prevail, even though the *tawhidi* perspective of development planning recommends a complementary way of realizing inter-sectoral allocation of development resources and circular causation interrelations between critical socioeconomic and policy variables.

Part IV: Conclusion

The relational epistemology and the neoclassical methodology along with its prototypes in development theory are opposite perspectives of world-systems. The global discursive change by the participation of nation states and all sectors and groups of peoples within and across nation states, gives a true idea of participatory development with sustainability. Yet the development paradigms that emerged following the Marshall Plan of Europe and found their roots in developing countries out of internal academic, political, and institutional self-interests, while being driven by foreign powers and international development organizations, was a copying of the model of global capitalism.

Yet this global state has now neared its aging decline. Along with this capitalist maturation has also come about deep conflicts that cannot be explained by the linear and optimal world-system of neoclassicism. This is despite the fact that, at the expense of human liberty to participate at all stages of society, what global capitalism has created is a hegemonic imposition of powerful will and the attenuating preferences. These forces are carried through by the institutionalization of such egos.

The question then is this: Can mankind hope for the utopian goal where zero capitalism will be replaced by an egalitarian society? Will the kinds of trade-off persist between distributive equity and economic efficiency along with the variables that characterize either side of these spectrums?

The relational world-system of participation provides the answer to these questions on the basis of shared and discoursed realities between the actors in the total development debate, while keeping the ultimate goal of human being in focus within these discoursed possibilities. Ruggie (2003b, p. 38) writes on this foundation of the relational worldview for attaining an epistemic institutionalization of the interactive, integrative, and co-evolutionary preferences of polity, market, and the small with the large groups in the economic and social arenas: "Epistemic communities, then, may be said to consist of interrelated roles that grow up around an episteme: they delimit, for their members, the 'proper construction of social reality."

We have discussed that development planning is an exercise that carries over a given epistemological thinking in economic, social and political ordering into their institutionalization nationally and globally. Since the bulk of economic theorizing has centred on neoclassicism in its direct or indirect forms with multiple ways of thinking out socioeconomic development, therefore, the methodology and the methods used in such paradigms are captured by the institutionalization of sustainable development. In this regard, the policies and programs emanating from development planning and development institutions in the context of the development paradigms discussed in this chapter, intensify the same groundwork of theory and application. Here we have contended that reality is not necessarily enforced application of a body of thinking. We termed this state of capitalist globalization as global capitalist governance by hegemony. Contrarily, it is the participatory nature of discoursed values that essentially defines a globally accepted functional ontology of ethics and values. These in turn enter the world-system, along with the inherent economic, social, ethical, and political forces to describe socioeconomic development as a process of knowledge formation and its co-evolutionary enhancement across national and international 'epistemic communities'.

Palan (2002, p. 215) writes in regards to the axiomatic nature of neoclassicism and its prototypes vis-à-vis prescribed preferences and their enforcement by corporate and political governance versus the discursive worldview:

> Modern institutionalist thought in particular is united in rejecting rationalist, progressivist and crude-materialist explanations of social processes and practices. Rather than adopt a simple ideas versus practice type of theory, they view 'the materiality of social institutions and their dynamics (as product) of evolving interrelated systems of institutions and discourse rather than as grounded in externalised and objective social realities' (Cameron and Palan, 1999).

To neoclassicism the externally imposed and institutionally enforced 'objective external realities' are its axioms of choices premised on the assumption of economic rationality. To other paradigms, the premise is one of assumed conflict and engagement between opposing sides in development paradigms. Such conflicts are construed as a form of marginal substitution appearing on the social versus economic planes with the intervening medium of institutions and polity. Even when discourse is promoted, it centres on one or the other form of such contending epistemologies of the development debate.

The participatory worldview of development, designs development sustainability around the political economy of a unified world-system in the good things of life. Thereby, an altogether new paradigmatic methodology emerges.

References

Bhattacharya, D., 1991, "A review of zero population growth", *Middle Eastern Business and Economic Review*, (3)1, 36-50.

World Commission for Environment and Development (Brundtland, G.H. Report), 1987, *Our Common Future*, Oxford University Press, Oxford, Eng.

Buchanan, J.M., 1954, "Social choice, democracy, and free markets", *Journal of Political Economy*, 62: 114-23.

—. 1999 (reprinted), "The domain of constitutional economics", in *The Collected Works of James M. Buchanan, the Logical Foundations of*

Constitutional Liberty, Vol. 1, pp. 377-95, Liberty Fund, Indianapolis, IN.

Cameron, A. and Palan, R., 1999, "The imagined economy: mapping transformations in the contemporary state", *Millennium*, (28)2, 267-89.

Carchedi, G., 1991, "Production as a social process", in his, *Frontiers of Political Economy*, pp. 7-41. Verso, New York, N.Y.

Choudhury, M.A., 2001, "Relationship between military expenditure and social spending", in B.N. Ghosh (ed.), *Contemporary Issues on Development Economics*, Routledge, London, Eng.

—. 2011, *Islamic Economics and Finance: an Epistemological Inquiry*. Emerald Publication, Bingley, UK.

Choudhury, M.A., & Noor, H.M., 1997, "A policy-theoretic analysis of sample survey of the Mi'maq people of Cape Breton in the light of the knowledge-based worldview", *International Journal of Social Economics, Socioeconomics of community development in global perspectives II, Festscrift in honour of Immanuel Kant, the Great Eighteenth Century Epistemologist*, (24)12, 1939-70.

Choudhury, M.A. Seyyed, F. and Korvin, G., 2000, "Discovering micro-level tradeoffs in economic development and studying their fractal character", *Indonesian Management and Accounting Research Journal*, (1)1.

Choucri, N. & North, R.C., 1995, "Global accord: imperatives for the twenty-first century", in Choucri, N. (ed.), *Global Accord*, pp. 477-508, The MIT Press, Cambridge, MA.

Demarting, G., 1999. "Human development index", in O'Hara P.A. (ed.), *Encyclopedia of Political Economy*, London, Eng.: Routledge.

Fusfeld, D.R., 1994, "English philosophers of the welfare state", in his, *The Age of the Economist*, pp. 92-96, HarperCollins College Publishers, New York, N.Y.

Gerber, J., 2002, *International Economics*, pp. 415-16, Addison Wesley, New York.

Goulet, D., 1995, *Development Ethics*, The Apex Press, New York.

—. 1996, " 'Development' …. Or Liberation", in Jameson K.P. & Wilber C.K. (eds.), *The Political Economy of Development and Underdevelopment*, pp. 539-42, McGraw-Hill, Inc., New York, N.Y.

Hammond, P.J., 1987, "On reconciling Arrow's theory of social choice with Harsanyi's fundamental utilitarianism", in Feiwel G.E. (ed.), *Arrow and the Foundations of the Theory of Economic Policy*, pp. 179-221, Macmillan, London, Eng.

Hawley, A., 1986, *Human Ecology, a Theoretical Essay*, University of Chicago Press, Chicago, ILL.

Hayek, F.A., 1990 (reprint), "The use of knowledge in society", pp. 183-200, in Spechler, M.C. (ed.), *Perspectives in Economic Thought*, McGraw-Hill, New York, N.Y.

Heilbroner, R., 1985, *The Nature and Logic of Capitalism*, W.W. Norton, New York, NY.

Hirschman, A.O., 1958, *The Strategy of Economic Development*, Yale University Press, New Haven.

IMF, 1995, "Global civic ethic", in *Our Global Neighbourhood, a Report of the Commission on Global Governance*, pp. 55-67, Oxford University Press, New York, N.Y.

Lewis, W.A., 1979, "The dual economy revisited", *The Manchester School*, 37:212-17.

—. 1954, "Unequal development with unlimited supplies of labour", *The Manchester School*, pp. 139-91.

Meier, G.M., 1995, "Dualistic development", in his, *Leading Issues in Economic Development*, 113-160, Oxford University Press, New York, NY.

Myint, H., 1985, "Organizational dualism and economic development", *Asian Development Review*, (3)1, 25-42.

—. 1987, "The neo-classical resurgence in development economics: its strength and limitations", in G.M. Meier (ed.), *Pioneers in Development*, Oxford University Press, New York .

Myrdal, G., 1989, "Utilitarianism and modern economics", in Feiwel, G. (ed.), *Arrow and the Foundations of the Theory of Economic Policy*, pp. 273-280, Macmillan Press, London, Eng.

Nelson, D.B., 1996, "Modeling stock market volatility changes", in Rossi, P.E. (ed.), *Modeling Stock Market Volatility*, pp. 3-15, Academic Press, Inc. San Diego, CA..

Nitzan, J. and Bichler, S., 2000, "Capital accumulation: breaking the dualism of 'economics' and 'politics', in Palan, R. (ed.), *Global Political Economy, Contemporary Issues*, pp. 67-88, Routledge, London, Eng.

Nordhaus, W.D., 1975, "The political business cycle", *Review of Economic Studies*, 42:169-90.

North, D.C., 1981, "A neoclassical theory of state", in his *Structure and Change in Economic Theory*, pp. 26-30, W.W. Norton, New York, N.Y.

Palan, R., 2002, "The constructivist underpinnings of the new international political economy", in Palan, R. (ed.), *Global Political Economy, Contemporary Theories*, pp. 215-28, Routledge, London, Eng.

Popkin, S.L., 1979, *The Rational Peasant: The Political Economy of Rural Society in Vietnam*, University of California Press, Berkeley, CA.

Prebisch, R., 1950, *The Economic Development of Latin America and Its Principal Problems*, United Nations, New York, NY.

Raymond, N., 1992, "The 'Lost Decade' of development: The role of debt, trade, and structural adjustment", pp. 1-14, The U.S. National Committee for World Food Day, Washington, D.C.

Robinson, J., 1961, "Prelude to a critique of economic theory", *Oxford Economic Chapters*, 13: 7-14.

Romer, P.M., 1986, "Increasing returns and long-run growth", *Journal of Political Economy*, 94:1002-1037.

Rossi, P.E. (ed.), 1996, *Modelling Stock Market Volatility*, Academic Press, Inc., San Diego, CA.

Ruggie, J.G., 2003a, "Introduction: What makes the world hang together? Neo-utilitarianism and the social constructivist challenge", in his, *Constructing the World Polity*, pp. 1-40, Routledge, London, Eng.

Ruggie, J.G., 2003b, "The new institutionalism in international relations", in his *Constructing the World Polity*, pp. 45-61, Routledge, London, Eng.

Sen, A., 1986, "Exchange entitlement", in his *Poverty and Famines, an Essay on Entitlement and Deprivation*, pp. 167-73, Clarendon Press, Oxford, Eng.

Singer, H.W. and Ansari, J.A., 1988, *Rich Nations and Poor Nations*, Unwin Hyman, London, Eng.

Shackle, G.L.S., 1972, *Epistemics and Economics*, Cambridge University Press, Cambridge, Eng.

Simon, H., 1987, "Decision making and organizational design", in Pugh, D.S. (ed.), *Organizational Theory*, pp. 202-23, Penguin Books, Hammondsworth, Middlesex, Eng.

South Commission, 1990, *The Challenge to the South*, Oxford University Press, Oxford, Eng.

Srinivasan, T.N., 1985, "Neoclassical political economy, the state and economic development", *Asian Development Review*, (3)2, 38-58.

Stehr, N., 2002, "Knowledge societies", in his, *Knowledge & Economic Conduct, the Social Foundations of the Modern Economy*, pp. 63-73, University of Toronto Press Toronto, ON, Canada.

Sullivan, M.W., 1982, "The contemporary crisis of liberal society", in his, *Reconstructing Public Philosophy*, University of California Press, Berkeley, California.

Sztompka, P., 1991, "The model of social becoming", in his, *Society in Action, the Theory of Social Becoming*, pp. 87-199, Chicago University Press, Chicago, ILL.

Tisdell, C., 1989, "Imperialism, economic dependence and development: a brief review of aspects of economic thought and theory", *Humanomics*, (5)2, 3-21

Todaro, M.P., 1977, "The meaning of development", in his *Economic Development in the Third World*, pp. 50-68, Longman, New York, N.Y.

United Nations Development Program (UNDP), 1997, 1998, 1999, 2000 issues, *Human Development Report*, Oxford University Press, New York, NY.

UNDP 1998, op cit. p.16.

United Nations, 1987, *Guidelines for Development Planning, Procedures, Methods and Techniques*, New York: Department of Technical Co-operation for Development, United Nations.

Waltz, K.N.,1979, "Theory of International Politics, Addision-Wesley, Reading, MA.

The World Bank, 2000, *World Development Report 2000-2001*, Oxford University Press, New York, N.Y.

—. 2000. op cit, p. 38.

CHAPTER TWELVE

CIRCULAR CAUSATION METHOD APPLIED TO FISCAL/SPENDING AND MONETARY COMPLEMENTARITIES IN *TAWHIDI* UNITY OF KNOWLEDGE

This chapter will firstly undertake a literature review of the underlying issues and problems of the complementary nature of monetary and fiscal regimes on the theme of sustainability of long-run non-inflationary growth with the attainment of wellbeing in an embedded social economy. The chapter will thereby develop a new model of the unified (complementary) synergistic linkages between money, spending, and the real economy through the choice of proper financial instruments that enable such complementarities to sustain with interest rates being replaced by productivity rates. This study gives rise to yet another applied implication of the *tawhidi* methodological worldview.

The literature review pointing to the problems of monetary and fiscal complementarities leads to the formulation of a money-fiscal-financial-real economy model (referred to as MFSRE-model, mentioned earlier) in a system of circular causation between these sectors with endogenous technology and growth. The result shows the attainment of wellbeing by way of non-inflationary economic growth and its stabilization, predictable, and long-term sustainable effects in the embedded social economy.

The chapter makes a selective review of the literature on the problems of instability, unpredictability, and perturbations caused by the traditional approaches to the study of monetary and fiscal regimes. The alternative perspective of a theory complementing monetary and fiscal regimes in a socially embedded stable and sustainable economy is pointed out in the literature review. Such a social economy with complementary monetary and spending functions and the critical socioeconomic variables in these functions has a distinctive epistemological background of its own. Note here that fiscal spending is extended to mean *all* spending variables. The reason for this inclusiveness is that when government fiscal expenditure increases (decreases), then along with this the economy is stimulated in all of its spending components, such as consumption, investment, and net exports. The income multiplier is then spurred by the total marginal propensity to spend (= marginal propensity to consume, marginal propensity to invest, marginal propensity of net trade, along with complementarities between these). Fiscal policy variables are thereby endogenously linked with all the spending variables, thus causing complementary relations among all such variables.

Throughout this chapter the mention of fiscal will mean the fiscal induction on *all* the spending components, thus spending and fiscal expansion (contraction) take coterminous meaning throughout this chapter.

The chapter goes on to present the salient features of the alternative model of money, fiscalism, financial and real economy (MFSRE) having its distinctive *tawhidi* epistemological and formal analytical implications. The MFSRE model (Mufeedh Choudhury, 2009) takes the form of simulation of a wellbeing objective criterion in the complementary variables representing M, F, S, RE sectors in a system of circular causation relations between the variables representing the sectors.

The chapter analyses the theoretical and policy ramifications of the MFSRE-model in the light of a new theory of monetary and spending (fiscally induced) complementarities with technologically induced non-inflationary economic expansion. In this section, the endogenous theory of economic growth and technological change invoking money and fiscal complementarities in the MFSRE-model is developed. It is proved that fiscal and monetary complementarities with unity of knowledge and its driving force in innovation and economic stabilization, non-inflationary growth, and sustainability is possible only in the *tawhidi* alternative to Keynesian and monetarist versions of the aggregate demand, aggregate supply, and thereby, in the dynamics combining Investment-Savings (IS) curve and Liquidity-Money (LM) curve.

The chapter deals with a prescriptive direction for the MFSRE-model in the light of the microeconomic foundation of the macroeconomic theory underlying the model. It finally examines, though in a rudimentary way, the applicability of the MFSRE-model to Malaysian macroeconomic data.

Review of Literature

In the history of economic thought monetary policy and fiscal policy mechanisms have remained opposed to each other on the issue of stable, sustainable, non-inflationary economic growth. Blaug (1993, p. 29) has pointed out such opposing consequences of the two approaches on non-inflationary economic expansion in the following words: "The great debate between Keynesian and monetarists over the respective potency of fiscal and monetary policy has divided the economic profession, accumulating what is by now a simply enormous literature.". But among the most distinctive cleavages that Blaug points out between monetarism and Keynesianism as the fiscal domain is the important role of knowledge that becomes the causal element of economic change. Knowledge is treated as being more than simply the determination of the signs of coefficients of critical variables in economic models.

This determining factor of knowledge that we will explain comprehends the epistemology and the ways arising from it in endogenously generating adjustments towards stability, though not steady-state equilibrium in the economy. The economy is now understood as a circular causation *system* of *inter*relations. The theme of causality that underlies the inherent system of interrelations that encompass an integrated economy is strongly pointed out by Blaug (1993, pp. 221): "Monetarism never succeeded in clarifying the causal mechanism that produced its empirical results, sometimes even denying that these results required interpretation in the light of a supporting causal theory, and it failed to refute any but a crude travesty of the Keynesian theory it opposed. Keynesianism on the other hand, proved to be capable of absorbing monetarist ideas in a more sophisticated brand of macroeconomics that appears to be emerging from the fifteen-year-old melee."

We point out the distinct oppositeness and important substance on the issue of causality related with knowledge concept in the economic system in the footnote in a cursory way.[1] The issue is of a vastly elaborate,

---

[1] In a simple time-dependent version of the quantity theory, MV = P.y; where M denotes quantity of money. V denotes the velocity of money supply. P denotes price level; y denotes real output. Over time in terms of growth rates denoted by g(.), g(M) + g(V) = g(P) + g(y). In the simplifying case, let V=constant, and assume the presence of real interest rate 'r', and fiscal spending 'f'. The above equation then assumes the form, g(M(r,y)) = g(P(r,y,f,M) + g(y(r,M,f)).

By time derivatives we obtain the following results:

$g(M(r,y)) = (1/M)*[(\partial M/\partial r)*(dr/dt) + (\partial M/\partial y)*(dy/dt)]$. This expression has no definite sign by theory; for monetary demand may decline sufficiently by the r-effect in order to displace the monetary equilibrium into a declining trend with increasing 'r'. Yet there can also be a positive effect of 'r' on M over time on the contrary. Likewise, depending upon the relative effects of various monetary components, increasing change in y over time can be linked to decreasing monetary effect if the effect of money in circulation is weaker than that of other interest-bearing monetary components.

systemic, and rigorous nature. See (Bartalanffy, 1974; Skyttner, 2005; Maturana and Varela, 1987) on system study of socio-scientific phenomena.

We will examine the formalism of the MFSRE-model in this chapter. The end result is that the randomness, perturbations, volatility and uncertainty caused by the indeterminateness of the combination between monetary and fiscal dynamics (policies and mechanism) do not allow the study of causality and complementarities that help to attain economic stabilization. There remain permanently inflationary pressures caused by the plethora of short-term rates of interest that plague all the critical variables.

From the above-mentioned nature of the oppositeness of approaches between monetarism (Friedman) and Keynesianism (fiscalism and spending) there arises the problem of permanent instability in economic growth. This confusion is caused by the inconsistency interrelating price level, output, and employment in respect of the expansion of the economic system by means of monetary and fiscal/spending policies together or by piecemeal applications of one without the other of them. Instead, it is necessary to understand the theoretical and policy-institutional paradigm that can combine the two approaches together to generate the possibility of expansionary aggregate supply and aggregate demand curves without inflationary pressure. This kind of a sustainable economic growth involves a gamut of other consequences, such as employment and technological change on the economic side, and development issues such as participation, empowerment and poverty alleviation, and thus social justice and social balance on the ethical front. The complementarity question between monetary and fiscal approaches to economic expansion in a

---

In the same way, there is no definite theoretical sign of $g(y(r,M,f)) = (1/y)*(dy/dt)$. In this case, if the source of generating y is the productive one, then $\partial y/\partial r < 0$ with $dr/dt > 0$. Contrarily, if the growth of y depends more on the financial source of income generation, then $\partial y/\partial r < 0$, with $dr/dt > 0$. Yet, theoretically, $\partial y/\partial M > 0$; $dM/dt > 0$ together; $\partial y/\partial f > 0$ and $df/dt > 0$ simultaneously.

Hence in the end, the sign of $g(P(r,y,f,M))$ remains indeterminate. A degree of uncertainty in price variations along with variations in 'r' and M relationship is introduced in the system of interrelations between the variables (r,y,f,M). The interrelationship between M and f mechanisms remains uncertain. Besides, the result is uncertainty due to the extensive variations in the term structure of a labyrinth of short-term interest rates. The effect is felt both on the aggregate demand curve and IS curve of the expenditure sector; and on the aggregate supply curve and LM curve by the kind of indeterminateness of the signs of the terms as mentioned above.

regime of price stability also results in complementarities between the gamut of economic and social variables. The interrelations in such a complementarity concept share fully the principle of cumulative causation that was invoked by Myrdal (1958).

On the same point, Toner (1999a, p. 124) writes on bringing out the distinction between mainstream economic theory, principally neoclassical economics, and the theory of circular causation that endogenously integrates with economic and non-economic elements for a comprehensive understanding of economic theory for attaining total wellbeing: "The notion of complementarity in production and consumption is central to CC (circular causation in the process of cumulative causation) theory. For Kaldor, given his concern with growth and dynamics as opposed to the allocation of fixed resources, complementarity in production and consumption is far more pervasive and significant than the neoclassical principle of substitution." The same kind of strong circular causation between economic and non-economic complementarities is discussed by Kaldor (1975).

The interference of knowledge-induced dynamics in terms of information-flow taken in its wider sense of technological change of the participative nature in the economic system with a vast span of interactions between variables representing socioeconomic and policy goals and sectors is considered by Lucas (1975) in his theory of rational expectations. Yet the debate against the existence of steady-state equilibrium in knowledge-induced systems of interrelations between diverse variables is not invoked in Lucas' model (Minford & Peel, 1983). Instead, the monetary model of rational expectations is based on the assumption of adaptive dynamics in information-flow.[2] This kind of an

---

[2] The following three equations on money (m) and price (p) movements in terms of output (y*) and given interest rate with all variables in natural logarithmic form:

$$m_t = p_t + y_t;\ p_t = E(p_{t-1}) + \gamma(y-y^*)$$

with y* being targeted y; m = m* + ε, m* being targeted m and ε being normally distributed error term, are solved by Rational Expectation method to yield the final result,

$$y = y^* + (1/(1+\gamma)),\ p = m^* - y^* + (\gamma/(1+\gamma))\varepsilon.$$

Here (m*-y*) is the anticipated part of adjustment of m to output as in M1 form of money or the transaction demand for money. The unanticipated part $(\gamma/(1+\gamma))\varepsilon$ is unpredictable due to its probabilistic nature.

Thus, output and the quantity of money are related in an unpredictable nature. Consequently, price and output stability remains untenable. Such unpredictable quantity of money for real economic growth has proved to be problematic even for industrialized economies, such as the EU (Trichet, 2008).

approach to the solution of the monetary model in rational expectation, changes the monetary dynamics into a steady-state one, with steady-state equilibrium once again replacing the endogenous dynamics of evolutionary equilibriums (Shakun, 1988).

Thus the paradigm of evolutionary equilibrium as the obverse side of the picture of perturbations by interaction and evolutionary knowledge-induced change has prevailed always. Consequently, in the case of monetary and fiscal debate the goal of full-employment and the nature of analysis centred in aggregate demand, aggregate supply, IS and LM curves, have continued on. Thereby, the possibility of endogenous effects has remained foreign in the development of a robust model of monetary and fiscal/spending complementarities with sustained stabilization.

On the other hand, endogenous circular causation results from factors such as the following ones: knowledge-induction, perturbations, technological change, and a negation of the relationship between money, spending, output and interest rate in the IS-LM analysis. In the extended quantity theory equation of exchange (Friedman, 1989, 1960), the replacement of diverse kinds of variables depending on interest-rates for attaining sustainable non-inflationary economic expansion gives rise to an altogether new perspective in monetary and fiscal (spending) theory. A new category of thought and its formalism arises.

Mishkin (2007a) writes on this issue. But Mishkin's theory has a weak pointer to the above-mentioned problem caused by the non-conformity between monetary and fiscal dynamics. Only the time-dynamics, as opposed to the knowledge-dynamics, which considers time only as recorder, is maintained. Yet it is true that the policy futures for the activities of central bank results in the breeding of a knowledge background for the reform of the monetary transmission mechanism.

The result ensuing from Mishkin's monetary policy strategy in stabilizing prices and sustaining growth without inflation is as follows: In his chapter on the role of the Central Bank on stabilization issue, Mishkin's ideas are taken to mean the independence of the Central Bank role in the management of the key goal that we are concerned with. This is that price stability ought to be maintained along with output stability. Stability means holding inflation rate low while expanding the real output. Monetary and fiscal policies ought to be aligned. The short-run goal of employment-price level trade-offs to build upon long-term employment and a stability goal are not recommended. Central bank should have independence in setting its monetary goals and the development of financial instruments.

The instability of the financial sector is the most problematic one. It ought to be given priority. The principal priority for central banks to follow is as Mishkin writes (op cit, p. 41): “Price stability should be the overriding, long-run goal of monetary policy”. In this chapter we emphasize that monetary policy should not be independent of fiscal policy in attaining price and output stability with endogenous learning and technological change. Consequently, economic stabilization with complementary monetary and fiscal policies by a change in formalism away from monetarism (Friedman) and Keynesianism (fiscalism/spending) is needed.

And why is this simultaneous policy application needed? The need for simultaneity of policy impacts arises from the fact that monetary policy focuses on privatization and market oriented developments, such as the stock market, and from thereon to the private savers across the board. On the other hand, government management of fiscalism is necessary for swerving investment and social objectives away from too much reliance on the market performance. Indeed, such was Keynes’ original motivation when he was driven by implicating G.E. Moore’s ethical views in economic stabilization with Government expenditure effects expressed in the aggregate demand, aggregate supply, and the IS-LM policy-induction method for attaining stabilization.

Mishkin (2007b, p. 59-73) furthermore points out an issue that is of interest for this chapter. That is the topic on studying the combined effects of monetary (M) and fiscal/spending regimes and policies (f) on asset prices (P). Here we proxy fiscal (spending) effect by investment (I) and the growth of real assets. These can be read off by the net worth of firms (NW) with the cost of capital (c) and the rate of interest (r), both declining. Such a chain relation between monetary and fiscal regimes affecting productive increase in prices in the presence of declining interest rates and cost of capital, which finally affect output Y, is marked out as follows: $M\uparrow \Rightarrow c\downarrow \Rightarrow r\downarrow \Rightarrow P\uparrow \Rightarrow I\uparrow \Rightarrow NW\uparrow \Rightarrow Y\uparrow$.

This relationship has an important bearing on our formulation of the MFSRE-model. That is a quantity of money M is combined with spending such as ‘I’ and valuation of economic performance in terms of NW and Y. These variables *inter*relate through the route of decreasing 'c' and 'r'. P increases via the productivity effects of I and of NW on Y. In the MFSRE-model of money, fiscal policy, financial instruments, and the real economy we will show how such a model establishes linkages between the variables marking these activities via phasing out interest rate and cost of capital, while price stability in an expanding economy is reflected in the growth rate of Y remaining higher than the rate of change of P, and at least equal to the rate of increase in the quantity of money.

Money-fiscal/spending endogenous relations

We commence this section by definitions of some critical terms and concepts that we use in this chapter to study the theme of complementarities between monetary and fiscal/spending mechanisms for maintaining price stability with sustained economic expansion. The positive interrelations between the variables of the monetary and fiscal domains when studied by circular causation between them, which is by feedback, are termed as being endogenous between them. Some such variables are pointed out in the footnotes.

Because the presence of 'r' causes perturbations in the other variables, including the price level, therefore, 'r' must be replaced by a variable that causes at least short-term predictability and stabilization. One such candidate is the profit-sharing rate denoted by 'ρ'. By its relations with productivity and social selection of the kinds of goods in production diversification along with risk diversification, and thereby technological change, the derivatives $\partial y/\partial r > 0$ with $dr/dt > 0$; $\partial y/\partial M > 0$; $dM/dt > 0$ together; and $\partial y/\partial f > 0$ and $df/dt > 0$, simultaneously. Consequently, predictability and price stabilization are established along the path of economic expansion when technological change works endogenously in the money-fiscal/spending interrelations.

However, since knowledge-induction over time marks the learning nature of the circular causation relations between the variables, a special form of dynamics based on evolutionary epistemology of the interacting variables to form and explain complementarities between them defines the learning domain of complementarities gained by interaction in the light of evolutionary epistemology of the system of interrelations.

A system is defined here by the circular causation relations that evaluate the degree of complementarities or simulated reconstruction towards complementarities between the endogenously related variables. The vector now is {y,M,f,P,ρ}, which is now induced by the knowledge-flow, {θ}, arising from the epistemological roots. The Austrian School is highly acclaimed of taking up such an approach (von Mises, 1976). Out of the endogenous relations between money, spending, and all the socioeconomic variables that best occurs in the free-market venue, Yeager (1997) referred to endogenous money in the relational sense of interaction and evolution occurring by a *laissez faire* concept of money.

The degree of complementarities between the variables reflects the premise of unity of knowledge (*tawhidi* epistemology). This in turn conveys the epistemological meaning of wellbeing. In the money-fiscal/spending complementary relations such wellbeing is formulated in terms of the degree of price-stability and economic growth attained with technological advance that enhances the knowledge-flow. But technology while being a carrier is not the totality of epistemic knowledge.

By denoting the knowledge-flows in the epistemological sense we obtain the entire knowledge-induced vector. This is now denoted by $\{y,M,f,P,\rho\}[\theta]$, meaning that each of the bracketed variables is induced by the epistemology of a complementary or participative meaning of wellbeing in unity of knowledge. Such a wellbeing criterion in its measurable form indicating the degree of complementarities that exist or can be normatively constructed, is denoted by $\theta = F(y,M,f,P,\rho)$. This criterion is simulated in the sense of the learning process by means of circular causation between the variables of the vector. We denote any of all such relations as, $x_i(\theta) = F_i(z|x_i)[\theta]$. 'i' denotes the specific of the **x**-variables in the vector $\mathbf{x} = (y,M,f,P,\rho)$. '$z|x_i$' denotes the vector excluding the particular x_i-variable. All variables are epistemologically driven by the normative outlook of unity of knowledge in the complementary system. Such a consequence is of the *tawhidi* genre.

In the especial case of complementarities between money and fiscal/spending variables the equations are as follows: $M = F_m(y,f,P,\rho)[\theta]$; $f = F_f(y,M,P,\rho)[\theta]$. The consequential price and output variables to determine the degree of stability with economic growth in the system are as follows: $P = F_P(y,M,f,\rho)$; $y = F_y(M,f,P,\rho)$. The productivity relation, and synonymously the technology relationship, is given by $\rho = F_\rho(y,M,f,P)$. Thus all the equations are firstly 'estimated'. Thereafter, the 'estimated' relations are normatively 'simulated' by affecting changes in the estimated coefficients so as to generate overall complementarities, especially between M and f, as suggested by the epistemological meaning of θ.

The system of feedback inter-relations is everywhere circular, and thereby, there are pervasive inter-variable complementarities. This phenomenon is also shown by the equations in the footnote.[3] The resulting

---

[3] Evaluate $W = W(y,M,f,P,E,\rho)$ (12.1)

Subject to, $y = F_y(M,f,P,E,\rho)$ in linear or non-linear form of the functional form of F_y; (12.2)

$M = F_M(y,f,P,E,\rho)$ in linear or non-linear form of the functional form of F_M; (12.3)

$f = F_f(y,M,P,E,\rho)$ in linear or non-linear form of the functional form of F_f; (12.4)

circular causation chain (footnote) is similar to that given by Mishkin to explain the MFSRE type relationship in respect of real asset valuation. In our case we note the complementarities between the monetary regime (M,r,c), fiscal (spending) regime (f), and the real economy (y,E,P^,ρ).

The message inherent in the circular causation relations also points to the role of knowledge in this system of endogenously complementary relations. Knowledge in this case means the unification (shown by positive signs of the coefficients) between the appropriate variables. This is necessarily a normative phenomenon, but it can also be a positivistic one if the expected correct signs of the coefficients exist.

A diagrammatic explanation of the circular causation results interconnecting money and fiscal/spending regimes

Figure 12.1 summarizes much of the theoretical results mentioned above in the contrasting paradigms of circular causation in terms of the stability relations between the monetary regime, the fiscal/spending regime, price stability, and economic expansion with technological change and growth of productivity. On the side of the theory of complementary endogenous relations between the various sectors of the MFSRE-model, Figure 12.1 points out the following dynamics: The P level replaces the interest rate because of the monotonic relationship between inflation targeting and the old Keynesian and monetarist comparative statics (Benanke & Mishkin, 2007). That is to say, a certain price target is set towards which inflation is to gravitate and spell out the monetary policies needed to maintain the inflation target.

In the case of the complementary dynamics of circular causation of endogenous interrelations between the selected variables, as in the circular causation system, the price variable is not set *ad hoc* by the central bank independence of functions and policy targets. Rather, the normative direction by simulation, if the positivistic results do not show up by estimation, ought to drive the inter-variables circular causation relations in such a way so as to result endogenously in price stability around a point, but not exactly *at* a given point. There is the matter of imperfect knowledge, adaptive knowledge as in rational expectations, and incompleteness of knowledge as organic inter-variables linkages in the

---

$P = F_P(y,M,f,E,\rho)$ in linear or non-linear form of the functional form of F_p; (12.5)
$E = F_E(y,M,f,P,\rho)$ in linear or non-linear form of the functional form of F_E; (12.6)
$\rho = F_\rho(y,M,f,P,E)$ in linear or non-linear form of the functional form of F_ρ; (12.7)
$\theta = \theta(y,M,f,P,E,\rho)$in linear or non-linear form of the functional form of F_{θ}: (12.8)

system of circular causation learn to complement. The appearance of P (rate P^) on the vertical axis in place of 'r' is therefore acceptable.

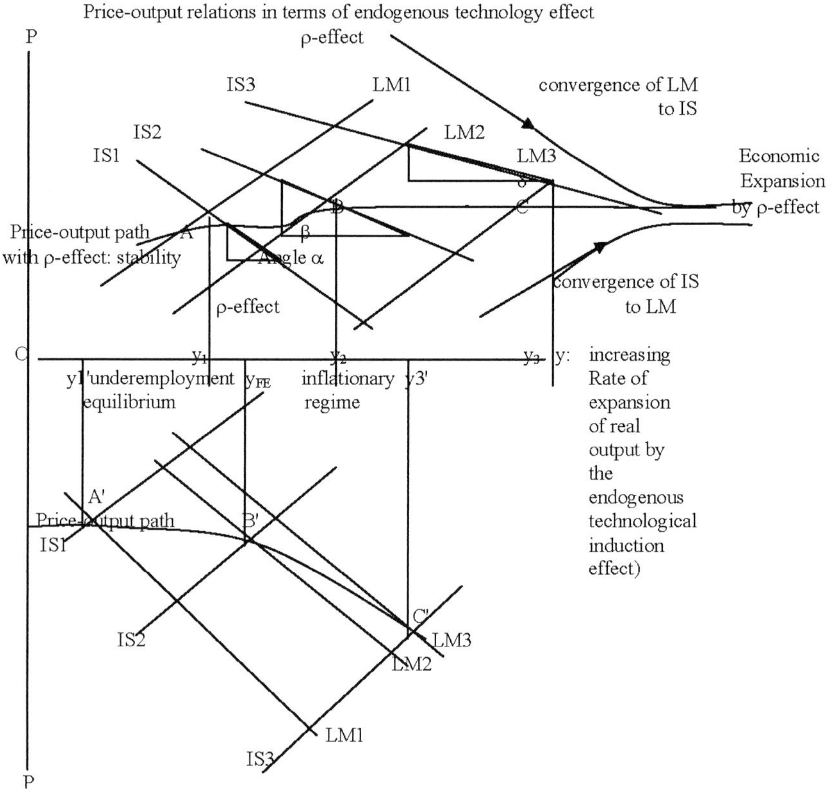

Figure 12.1: Price-output stability by money-fiscal/spending complementarities contrasted with the monetarist-Keynesian case

In the diagram on complementarities the shifting of the spending curve (IS) and the monetary curve (LM) is enhanced by the effectiveness of technology (ρ-effect). As this takes effect, the slopes of the IS curve decrease; and the decreasing angles, α, β, δ etc. show the convergence between the IS and LM curves. The price-stability is thereby attained across increasing real output levels with the technology effect causing increasing returns to scale. The convergent price-output path to an approximated form of stability in this case is shown.

The lower diagram of Figure 12.1 is of the monetarist-fiscal/spending case. It shows that, after a non-inflationary expansion of the economy along the Keynesian underemployment levels of output, income multipliers work towards slowing down, but not eliminating the income multiplier effect, as the IS curves narrows down towards the LM curve near to the full-employment level of output. At this level, the temporary price stability gives way to inflationary regime with growing neutrality of monetarist and fiscal/spending regimes on the growth of real output. The price-output path is thus shown.

Clearly then, the two diagrams can become identical with the flattening of the IS and LM curves under the impact of technological advancement but of the endogenous type. In such a case, it is possible to introduce the effectiveness of circular causation with the technological effect on monetarist and fiscal/spending relations causing complementarities, and thereby, establishing and sustaining price-stability over the long run.

The effect of endogenous growth on technological advancement and price-output stability caused by monetarist and fiscal/spending complementarities

It is noted from our formalism in this chapter thus far that technological advance plays the critical role in the expansion of output along with price stability. In this way, all the critical variables are made to function in complementary ways with positive coefficients. Such signs are either determined by estimation (prevalent economic state) or by simulation (economic state as it ought to be). We have examined the circular causation interrelations between money and fiscal/spending relationship, employment, and investment. Other critical variables related to economic expansion and attainment of wellbeing can be tried out and studied in similar ways.

The expansion of technology is like the expansion of knowledge and information in the system of circular causation relations expressed by the circular causation equations. The appearance of systemic knowledge as interaction leading to simulated complementarities, and followed by evolutionary expansion of similar complementary relations, is an epistemological issue on unity of systemic knowledge. The emergence of such a learning system of evolutionary interrelations between the critical variables invokes the study of endogenous growth and development models. Such models take up specific characteristics of learning equilibriums along epistemological lines.

Myrdal, who we have referred to earlier, Schumpeter (see Cantner et al, 2009), the Austrian School of Economics (Kirzner, 1997), and in respect of the moral economy by Boulding (1971), and recently new (endogenous) growth theory of Romer (1986) have left a legacy in the development of evolutionary socioeconomic growth and development. This chapter follows along the same directions. There is a difference in the methodology though. Our objective criterion is not growth, development, economic expansion, wealth maximization, price-stabilization, and the like. This chapter treats all such goals to be instruments to attain the principal objective criterion of simulating wellbeing. The wellbeing criterion is defined as a measure of the degree to which complementarities exist or are attained by simulation under normative perspectives of ethical and policy futures.

Therefore, while Myrdal (1957) wrote on circular causation and cumulative causation in respect of the problems of destitution of Blacks in the United States, he multiplied such socially disruptive causations in his disequilibrium model. Boulding's perspectives of ecological futures in his model of social causation did not treat morality and ethics as endogenous forces of moral-social reconstruction, although he invoked these in his evolutionary model of the social economy (Boulding, 1981). Romer's new growth model is a neoclassical model but without the assumptions of marginal rate of substitution and diminishing return, both of which represent scarcity of resources in the face of human wellbeing and choices. But it can be readily inferred that a multiplicative form of the capital and labour knowledge-augmenting growth model must necessarily imply marginal rate of substitution between these variables. Substitution is a concept contrary to that of pervasive complementarities, as was pointed out in the works of Myrdal and Kaldor (Toner, 1999c).[4]

---

[4] Note that technological augmentation of labour (say γ, thus γL) must carry with it a similar augmentation of capital (say η, thus ηK) in the growth model. The supply of nominal output is given by,

$$Y(t) = F(\gamma L, \eta K) = A.\ (\gamma L)^{\alpha}*(\eta K)^{\beta} = [A_1*\gamma^{\alpha}*\eta^{\beta}*]*[A_2*L^{\alpha}*K^{\beta}] = T(t)*L^{\alpha}*K^{\beta}.$$

Here, L(t) denotes labour input; K(t) denotes capital input both at time t. 'A' now becomes the technological factor influencing output. In this form, Romer's model is identical with Denison's model. Consequently, all the trappings of marginal rate of substitution and marginal productivity of factor inputs are retained in this form of the technologically induced growth model. The endogenous effect of technological change on factor inputs, and thereby on output growth, remains benign.

It is not possible in Romer's concept of endogeneity to obtain the result $dL(t)/dK(t) > 0$ unless L(t) and K(t), and thereby Y(t), are induced by T(t). In other

The evolutionary learning model of endogenous complementarities via circular causation relations in this chapter shares with, but yet differs from, the genre of models in the Austrian vintage, specifically Schumpeter's model of development with creative destruction. The major difference is on the issue of continuity of technological enhancement in the evolutionary model of circular causation in this chapter. Opposed to this is Schumpeter's discontinuity property in the growth of spending (investment), and the need for monopoly to cover up the slack caused by such temporary slowdown. On this issue Gaffard (2009) writes: "As shown with the model used by means of numerical simulations, the introduction of the new technology generates an initial fluctuation, which brings about temporary unemployment as well as a temporary fall in productivity. However, this fluctuation very soon damps down and the economy converges to a new steady-state corresponding to the superior technology, with a higher level of productivity—which allows lower prices and higher real wages—and full employment". This problem of a temporary halt in economic expansion causing disequilibrium in the Schumpeterian perspective of economic growth and development is overcome in the MFSRE-model by the continuous simulation of wellbeing with circular causation relations by learning, which represents appropriate technological change.

In the end, the MFSRE-model is not a model of jumping the tides of growth and development in the 'wants' economy. Instead, it is a model of

---

words, the time variable, 't', cannot act as the medium to mobilize human resource as technological effect. Human resource must be induced on the expansion path. Thus, HR becomes exogenously induced in the growth model.

The concept of endogenous circular relations in this paper avoids the above kind of treatment that beleaguers new growth theory. Instead, knowledge (technology) is induced in the variables. The above mentioned problem of allocation of resources for attaining output maximization is replaced by the simulation model, in which all variables remain complementary by the appropriate choice of technology.

In the end, any maximization objective is replaced by the wellbeing simulation. The wellbeing function is a monotonic technological function expressed in terms of the complementary variables and then revised by coefficient changes according to the demand and possibility of complementarities between the circular causation variables as shown in the circular causation system of equations.

Toner (1999, p. 166) writes in regards to the externality property of technological change in new growth model, which once again gives a neoclassical semblance to the new (endogenous) growth model that wants to overcome the postulate of diminishing returns to scale: "This abandonment is achieved by invoking some externality that offsets any propensity to diminishing returns".

appropriate technology that enhances the *dynamic changes and sustainability* of dynamic basic-needs regimes of development. Conformably, the nature of money as a value of spending[5] in the real economy brings about the dynamic changes by appropriate technology and financial instruments that interlink the sectors. Such inter-sectoral dynamics present the sign of systemic learning, and also the epistemological content of the MFSRE worldview. Cooperation and coordination by way of sectoral and inter-variable complementary linkages, and by way of sectoral inter-flow of resources, replace the competitive and dismal cumulative causation model of the Austrian genre, especially that given by Myrdal and Schumpeter.

In MFSRE worldview, old and failing industries are not replaced. They are integrated into new industries by innovation and development. Nascent industry protection is carried on in the MFSRE model of evolutionary learning for interactively integrating and followed by innovation. This feature is found in the Schumpeterian model but with a caution. Schumpeter writes: “There is certainly no point in trying to conserve obsolescent industries indefinitely; but there is a point in trying to avoid their coming down with a crash and in attempting to turn a rout, which may become a centre of cumulative depressive effects, into orderly retreat”.

---

[5] Quantity of Money = Total Spending by the equation of exchange with a subtle meaning: $MV=Py$. This implies that a portion of the total quantity of money denoted by MV equals the value of its expenditure in transactions on real things denoted by Py = nominal value of output. However, if we further assume that direction of money is into projects appearing in various interlinked sectors (say, $i = 1,2,\ldots,n$) then, a micro-quantity of money (say M_i) flows fully to equate to the spending (P_iy_i) requirements of that project. Thereby, $M_i=P_iy_i$. In this case $V_i = 1$ because a quantity of micro-money flows fully into specific projects.

Furthermore, because of the interlinked nature of the sectoral projects, total quantity of money arising from the micro-foundations is equal to $M = [{}^n\sqrt{\prod M_i}] = [{}^n\sqrt{\prod P_iy_i}] = [{}^n\sqrt{\prod P_i}]*[{}^n\sqrt{\prod y_i}] = P*y$. This expression is more appropriate than the simple case of disjoint projects, and therefore disjoint sectors that are spanned by such projects. In that case, total quantity of money circulating in given independently distributed projects would be the uninteresting case, $M = \Sigma_{i=1}{}^nM_i = \Sigma_{i=1}{}^nP_i*y_i$.

The micro-foundations of the quantity theory of money expressed in terms of the disaggregate forms of the equation of exchange implies direct complementarities between money and spending with the real economy via projects. In such a structure of the economy there is no role for rates of interest and the cost of capital, for resources must be mobilized; not held back as time-distributed savings as withdrawals. Interest rates on bank-savings are replaced by real yields, rates of returns, profit rates, and profit-sharing rate in the project-specific case.

Thus there are profound similarities and some dis-similarities between the MFSRE and Schumpeterian-Austrian development dynamics.

Along with the continuous nature of increasingly enhancing effect of technology and innovation on the growth of output, the MFSRE-model by its formulation of the dynamic basic-needs approach to growth, development and wellbeing, also establishes the money-fiscal/spending complementarities. In such a case, the MFSRE becomes similar to the case that Schumpeter wrote about (Gaffard, 2009):"Active monetary and banking policies allow productivity gains associated with the introduction of a new and superior technology to be captured. As Schumpeter pointed out, money forces the economic system into new channels and allows a quasi-steady state to be re-established."

Yet in the case of MFSRE the complete interconnectivity between money and spending that brings about complementarities along moving and evolutionary equilibriums caused by the organic forms of the circular causation relations implies money as well as fiscal/spending activities to flow along new channels of innovation and economic progress by creating total wellbeing. It is therefore possible that the evolutionary perspectives of MFSRE and Schumpeterian model can converge in the dynamic basic-needs regime of development. But this will not be possible in a 'wants' economy for reasons of the failure to adopt appropriate technology and innovation that establish continuity of the endogenous relationship between complementary variables. The basic-needs regime instead, can attain what Schumpeter envisioned, and as Gafford (2009) points out: "Schumpeter addresses the question of the intensity and the speed of structural changes and pleads for gradualism."

An economy with endogenous induction of knowledge as technology in the money-fiscal (spending) evolutionary relationship with non-inflationary stable growth yielding wellbeing

In the MFSRE-model the effectiveness of technological change as knowledge-flows acting over the growth of capital accumulation continuously in spending, and the growth of efficient units of labour by HRD, requires the micro-foundation of relationship between monetary and fiscal/spending expansion. We have dwelled on this topic in this chapter thus far. We are now to investigate the financial consequences of such relations on the money-fiscal/spending complementary effect on economic expansion.

Our arguments in this chapter showed that, when monetary and fiscal/spending regimes become complementary then only the expansion of the real economy generates productive value. The financial sector now becomes a bridge -- to carry money efficiently, subject to the level of knowledge available in the economic system -- into spending. Now with the perfect money-fiscal/spending complementarities realized with appropriate financial resource mobilizing instruments for the sole benefit of real sector growth and the variables in this sector that matter, the rate of interest 'r' and the cost of capital 'c' will run down to zero. In other words, there is no price of financial capital like the rate of interest for valuation of financial flows. Only prices in the real economy matter in yielding the value of the financial flows by the profitability from the real transactions.

The result then is the perfect working of the equation of exchange of the Fisher-type in the light of circular causation relations. To explain this point we note the identity, $M(\mu,\rho)*V = P*y(\mu,\rho)$, where μ is the yield rate. We differentiate with respect to P assuming that V = constant to start with. The result yields the following simplification:

$$d\log(M)/dp = d\log P/dp + d\log y/dp \quad (12.9)$$

$$\text{That is, } g(M).dM/dp = g(p) + g(y).dy/dp \quad (12.10)$$

The g(.) symbols denote growth rates of the specified variables.

By holding the target of price stability we obtain,

$$g(p) \sim 0, \text{ yielding } g(M).dM/dp \sim g(y).dy/dp \quad (12.11)$$

That is, $dM/dp \sim dy/dp$; or $M \approx a + b.y$, meaning that the value of a quantity of money approximates to the value of real output, subject to the evolutionary learning capacity available.

$$\text{Next by extension we write } M(\mu,\rho) = y(\mu,\rho) \quad (12.12)$$

M and y are positive functions of (μ,ρ).

By a further extension we write in reference to the wellbeing concept of the circular causation equations,

$$M(f,y,P,E,\mu,\rho) = a + b.y(M,f,P,E,\mu,\rho) \quad (12.13)$$

Each of the bracketed variables has a positive relationship with M and y in the context of complementarities and wellbeing with the target of price stability within a given range, as can be accommodated by evolutionary learning in the variables. This is true either as a positivistic fact or a normatively reconstructed case of simulation, as explained earlier.

Next we look at the specific form,

$$M(f,y,P,E,\mu,r,c,\rho) = a + b.y(M,f,P,E,\mu,r,c,\rho), \quad (12.14)$$

where 'r' is the real rate of interest; 'c' is the cost of capital.

Clearly, 'r' and 'c' have negative relationship with each of the other variables. Therefore, these rates cannot be acceptable in sustaining the effect of technological change on increasing non-inflationary growth and development with wellbeing. A financial system is necessary, and has arisen, that replaces the 'r'- and 'c'- based financial instruments by the 'μ'-based ones. The positive complementarities between variables representing the sectors of the MFSRE model explain the efficacy of the 'μ'-based financial instruments.

The economic example of such a case is the Islamic economy with its financial and banking system (Choudhury, 2011a). The Islamic system works on the basis of the epistemology of unity of knowledge (*tawhid*).This stands on organically learned complementarities between the good things of life as determined by *maqasid as-shari'ah* and are represented by the variables of the sectors in the integrated MFSRE-model. Wellbeing is the natural corollary of the complementarities between Money (M), Finance (F), Fiscal or spending (S), and Real Economy (RE) as the interacting, integrating, and evolutionary sectors by virtue proceed by their inherent learning.

The Islamic financial instruments promoting resource mobilization (Mankiw and Rashwan, 2012) as spending into the real economy are principally the primary ones, such as, profit-sharing (*mudarabah*), equity participation and joint venture (*musharakah*), and mark-up asset pricing or hire-purchase pricing (*murabaha*). Besides these, there are the secondary financing instruments such as, rental (*ijara*), deferred asset valuation (*bay' muajjal*), contractual payment in manufactures (*wadia*), Islamic bonds in mega-projects (*sukuk*), and charitable donations (*qard e-hasana*). The integrated nature of MFSRE-model advocates a mixed portfolio with diversification between all the financing instruments mentioned here and more (Mufeedh Choudhury, op cit).

The yields in the above-mentioned kinds of asset pricing, even during the financial crisis, have remained approximately at 7 per cent annually in Islamic banks world-wide; and projects have flourished at the micro-level (Mankiw & Rashwan, 2012). Demand for the Islamic portfolio has remained resilient. This is proved by the Malaysian Islamic capital market with its 20 per cent of capitalization of the stock market; and by the highest number of depositors of all Bangladeshi banks in the Islamic Bank Bangladesh. Indeed, IBBL has earned her reputation of being the best Islamic bank worldwide by the Global Finance Forum.

In the Arab Gulf and MENA region, the demand for Islamic financial portfolio can be seen by the following evidence (Mega Middle East Advisors, 2006): The number of rich households and their wealth in the GCC region. CAGR for liquidity was 7% between 2003 and 2006; number of wealthy households increased by 6 per cent CAGR between 2003 and 2006 increased even as GDP and privatization picked up. CAGR of nominal GDP was 19 per cent between 2002 and 2006. Within the wealth formation there was a 40 per cent share of the capital market that preferred Islamic over conventional funds. There was preference for high returns over stable return among this class of investors. Additionally, 20 per cent of the market share in the GCC region was made up of investors that preferred pure Islamic funds. These investors preferred *shari'ah*-compliant investments over conventional ones, no matter what was the performance of Islamic funds. The rest of the 40 per cent share of the capital market was of investors in the GCC region preferring conventional funds.

The composition of the Islamic capital market was made up of portfolios of equity: *sukuk* CAGR 232 percent between 2002 and 2006; private equities CAGR 36 per cent between 2000 and 2006; real estate CAGR 36 per cent between 2002 and 2006; and Islamic insurance *takaful* CAGR 13 per cent between 2002 and 2005. In general, Islamic funds increased by CAGR 22 per cent between 2000 and 2006, but with a focus on medium to small scale enterprises.

The Islamic investment picture for the MENA region is similar. Forty per cent of MENA Islamic investments were in real estate. This is followed by 17 per cent in financial services; 14 per cent in travel and tourism; and 29 per cent in private equities. In all, Islamic funds in MENA experienced a CAGR of 130 per cent between 2002 and 2006.

Our implications of money-finance-real economy circular causation relations are reflected in the choice of Islamic diversified portfolio contrary to the independence of the financial sector as a competing one with the real economy. Thus our results concerning the nature of MFSRE-model are supported by the evidence of the GCC and MENA regions.

Estimation and simulation of circular causation relations in money and real economy relations, the case of Malaysia

The following results point out how the estimation and simulation (evaluation) of wellbeing subject to circular causation relations are carried out and the results obtained therefrom in order to analyse the inter-variable complementary issue for attaining wellbeing.

Estimated equations[6]

$$(1)\mathbf{ln\theta = -0.514 + 0.792\ lnM - 0.244\ lnIN + 0.123\ lnTRADE} \quad \mathbf{(12.15)}$$

$$(2)\mathbf{lnTRADE = 6.53 - 1.63\ lnM - 0.022\ lnIN + 1.57\ ln\theta} \quad \mathbf{(12.16)}$$

$$(3)\mathbf{lnM = 1.20 + 0.244\ lnIN - 0.176\ lnTRADE + 1.09\ ln\theta} \quad \mathbf{(12.17)}$$

$$(4)\ \mathbf{lnIN = 1.32 + 2.27\ lnM - 0.022\ lnTRADE - 3.11\ ln\theta} \quad \mathbf{(12.18)}$$

Simulated equations (using the SDA numerical choices for selected coefficients)

$$\mathbf{(2')}\quad lnTRADE = 6.53 - 1.417.lnM - 0.022\ lnIN + 1.57\ ln\theta \quad \mathbf{(12.15')}$$
$$\mathbf{(3')}\quad lnM = 1.20 + 0.103\ lnIN - 0.103\ lnTRADE + 1.09\ ln\theta \quad \mathbf{(12.16')}$$

$$\mathbf{(4')}\quad lnIN = 1.32 + 1.672\ lnM - 0.022\ lnTRADE - 3.11\ ln\theta \quad \mathbf{(12.17')}$$

$$(5)\quad \mathbf{ln0 = -0.514 + 0.792\ lnM - 0.244\ lnIN + 0.123\ lnTRADE} \quad \mathbf{(12.18')}$$

Tables 12.1 and 12.2 give the estimated and simulated values, respectively, for all the variables over the time-period 1990-2008 for Malaysia. These values are charted in Figures 12.2, 12.3, 12.4 and 12.5.

[6] This section is adapted from Noreha Halid, Mohammad Saleh Ahmed, Masudul Alam Choudhury, and "Circular Causation Relations using Malaysian Data on Money and Real GDP", Chapter 10 of Choudhury, M.A., (2012), *Islamic Economics and Finance: an Epistemological Inquiry*, Emerald, Bingley, UK.

Table 12.1: Estimated values of the natural logarithm variables and the wellbeing index ‘θ’

YEAR	lnM	lnIN	lnTrade	lnθ
1990	3.028729	2.281141	4.474355	1.89087
1991	3.016001	2.271952	4.493234	1.838109
1992	2.934276	2.435738	4.436823	1.77571
1993	3.04094	2.249392	4.480648	1.903995
1994	3.034887	1.741766	4.756527	2.047363
1995	2.937106	1.93596	4.695302	1.927509
1996	2.952987	1.958982	4.698482	1.84772
1997	2.769532	2.219091	4.626825	1.735273
1998	2.657149	2.162338	4.742497	1.577921
1999	2.902974	1.17243	5.151269	2.01929
2000	2.785608	1.304155	5.083616	2.103191
2001	2.809719	1.332004	5.067209	2.085399
2002	2.892835	1.137896	5.149293	2.123856
2003	2.987651	0.967619	5.214237	2.159127
2004	2.949029	0.951494	5.223702	2.184113
2005	2.959712	0.895367	5.249401	2.198976
2006	2.928511	1.111181	5.130819	2.168849
2007	3.000422	1.10347	5.097477	2.222949
2008	2.921725	1.169502	5.081687	2.218552

Table 12.2: Simulated (Predictor) values of the natural logarithm variables and the wellbeing index 'θ'

YEAR	lnM	lnIN	lnTrade	lnθ
1990	3.033362	0.460517	5.122838	1.8785
1991	3.008144	0.474554	5.133444	1.872984
1992	2.915919	0.671824	5.065107	1.761356
1993	3.046929	0.420285	5.132153	1.896692
1994	3.132733	-0.076	5.403994	2.049692
1995	3.007119	0.172046	5.323586	1.917336
1996	2.993872	0.217396	5.318813	1.924687
1997	2.803798	0.553654	5.220033	1.70711
1998	2.683936	0.60593	5.29687	1.646178
1999	3.082529	-0.5183	5.753487	2.132689
2000	3.008451	-0.39361	5.68834	1.999273
2001	3.019396	-0.36925	5.673175	2.009555
2002	3.10907	-0.58386	5.762562	2.132842
2003	3.204128	-0.78043	5.83687	2.257472
2004	3.182752	-0.79333	5.845187	2.231982
2005	3.199642	-0.85268	5.872034	2.257299
2006	3.14622	-0.64327	5.755731	2.165343
2007	3.214216	-0.69688	5.738739	2.220077
2008	3.149172	-0.60986	5.715475	2.139696

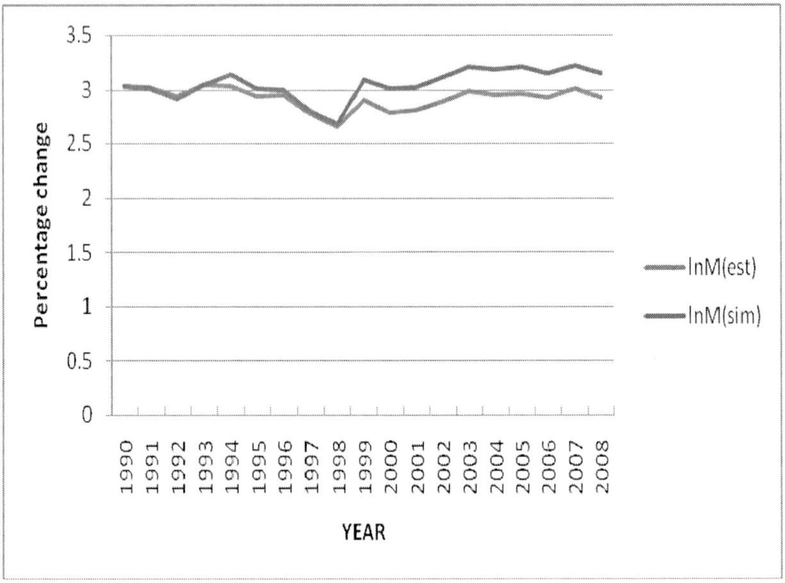

Figure 12.2: Percentage change of estimated lnM and simulated lnM over a period of 1990-2008

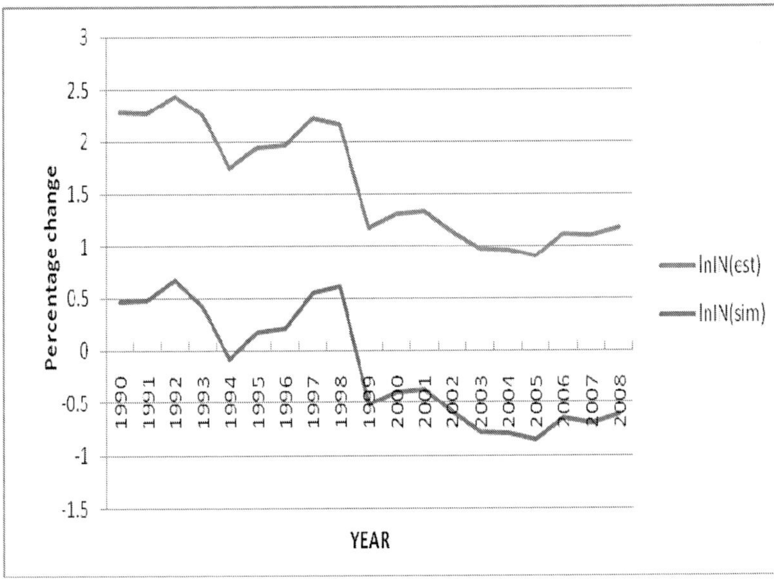

Figure 12.3: Percentage change of estimated lnIN and simulated lnIN over a period of 1990-2008

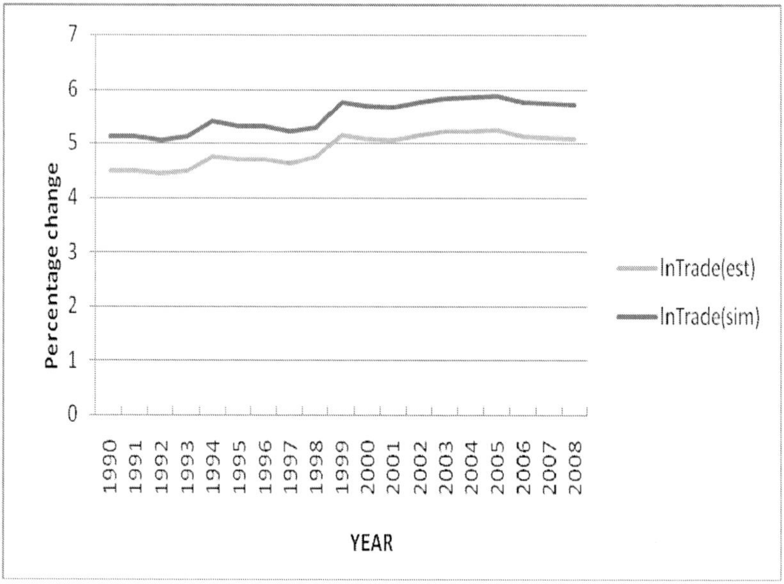

Figure 12.3: Percentage change of estimated lnTrade and simulated lnTrade over a period of 1990-2008

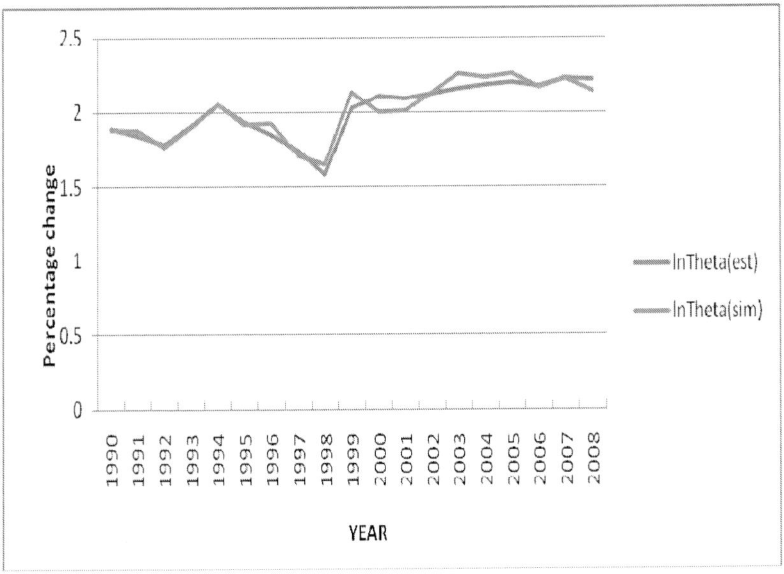

Figure 12.4: Percentage change of estimated lnθ and simulated lnθ over a period of 1990-2008

Regression Analysis

Regression analysis: lnM*100, lnIN%, lnTRADE*100, lnθ

1. Regression Analysis: lnM versus lnIN, lnTRADE, lnθ

The regression equation is

$$\mathbf{lnM = 1.20 + 0.244\ lnIN - 0.176\ lnTRADE + 1.09\ ln\theta} \quad (12.\ 19)$$

Predictor	Coef	SE Coef	T	P
Constant	1.2043	0.5362	2.25	0.040
lnIN	0.2444	0.0564	4.33	0.001
lnTRADE	-0.1763	0.0715	-2.46	0.026
lnθ	1.0860	0.1129	9.62	0.000

S = 0.0408542 R-Sq = 88.1% R-Sq(adj) = 85.8%
Durbin-Watson statistic = 1.57629
2. Regression Analysis: lnIN versus lnM, lnTRADE, lnθ

The regression equation is

$$\ln IN = 1.32 + 2.27 \ln M - 0.022 \ln TRADE - 3.11 \ln\theta \qquad (12.20)$$

Predictor	Coef	SE Coef	T	P
Constant	1.317	1.859	0.71	0.490
lnM	2.272	0.525	4.33	0.001
lnTRADE	-0.022	0.259	-0.08	0.935
lnθ	-3.106	0.454	-6.84	0.000

S = 0.124582 R-Sq = 96.0% R-Sq(adj) = 95.1%
Durbin-Watson statistic = 1.45823

3. Regression Analysis: lnTRADE versus lnM, lnIN, lnθ

The regression equation is

$$\ln TRADE = 6.53 - 1.63 \ln M - 0.022 \ln IN + 1.57 \ln\theta \qquad (12.21)$$

Predictor	Coef	SE	T	P
Constant	6.532	0.8467	7.71	0.000
lnM	-1.635	0.6632	-2.46	0.026
lnIN	-0.022	0.2577	-0.08	0.935
lnθ	1.568	0.8266	1.90	0.077

S = 0.124388 R-Sq = 87.1% R-Sq(adj) = 84.5%
Durbin-Watson statistic = 0.887537

4. Regression Analysis: lnθ versus lnM, lnIN, lnTRADE

The regression equation is,

$$\ln\theta = - 0.514 + 0.792 \ln M - 0.244 \ln IN + 0.123 \ln TRADE \qquad (12.22)$$

Predictor	Coef	SE	T	P
Constant	-0.5142	0.5125	-1.00	0.332
lnM	0.7923	0.0824	9.62	0.000
lnIN	-0.2437	0.0357	-6.84	0.000
lnTRADE	0.1234	0.0651	1.90	0.077

S = 0.0348958 R-Sq = 97.2% R-Sq(adj) = 96.6%
Durbin-Watson statistic = 1.87454

SDA results[7]

Note that the ethical index remains almost unchanged in the estimated and the normative equations because of the correct signs of the variables related to $\ln\theta$. But predictor (simulated) values are different from the estimated values. A simulated view of selected the wellbeing index and circular causation equations can be shown by the use of the Spatial Domain Analysis. The results in this regard are shown and explained below. Note that only needed simulation values of the coefficients of specific variables are given. The coefficient values of other variables are retained as in the estimated case.

[7] Spatial Domain Analysis (SDA) is a methodology within Geographical Information System (GIS) that maps the interrelations between variables (hence entities), which can be represented in the real space. But when we treat the socioeconomic and abstract socio-scientific cases by means of SDA, we take the real space to be represented by measured variables. Such measurements can be actual data or ordinal numerical representations. By so representing the variables and abstract relations between variables visually by means of SDA technology, this is dealing with modelling capability of the spatial interaction of the entities in their spatial domains.

GIS is a technology that facilitates the study of spatial cause-effect relations between $\{(\theta,x(\theta))$-domains and their entities. Thereby, spatial domain analysis stores the requisite data into computer memory for doing SDA-work. The **IIE**-methodology of *tawhidi* worldview of systemic unity, which is central to the learning model of unity of knowledge and is formalized by the significance of complementary relations in circular causation relational system, can be simulated by SDA in connection with the econometric estimation methods. Consequently, **IIE**-model as a real-world system can be represented in a 'computer-world' according to SDA and GIS. The spatial analysis capability of GIS facilitates the manipulation of spatial information and helps generate various "what if" scenarios as being necessary for evaluating decision-making processes on real-time basis. In this way, GIS becomes an appropriate tool to deal with the heart of the theme of relational epistemology, which is given by the Interactive (I), Integrative (I) and Evolution (E) – **IIE**-learning process.

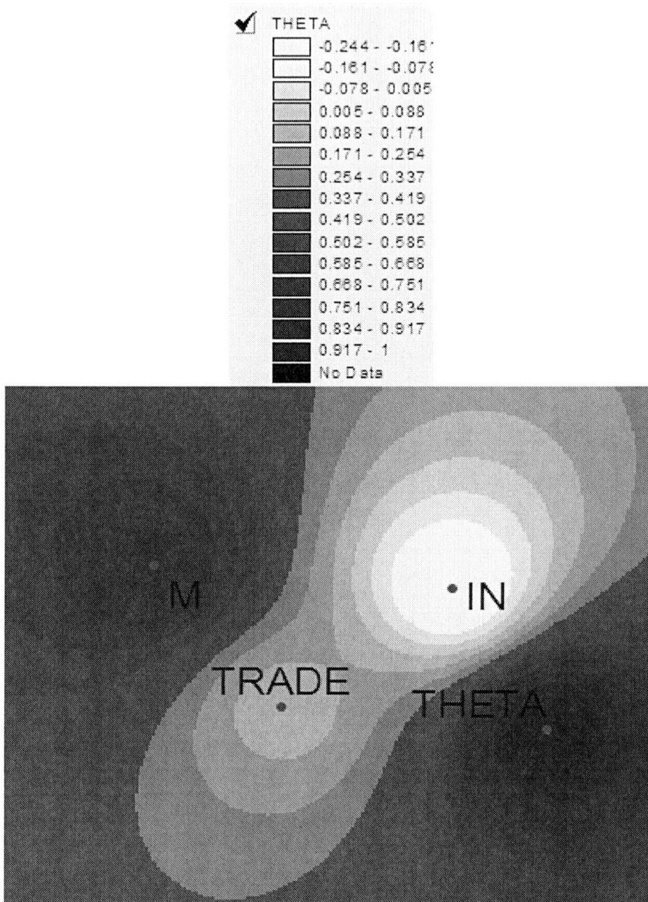

Figure 12.5: SDA Analysis in lnθ versus InM, InIN, InTRADE
$\ln\theta = -0.514 + 0.792 \ln M - 0.244 \ln IN + 0.123 \ln TRADE$

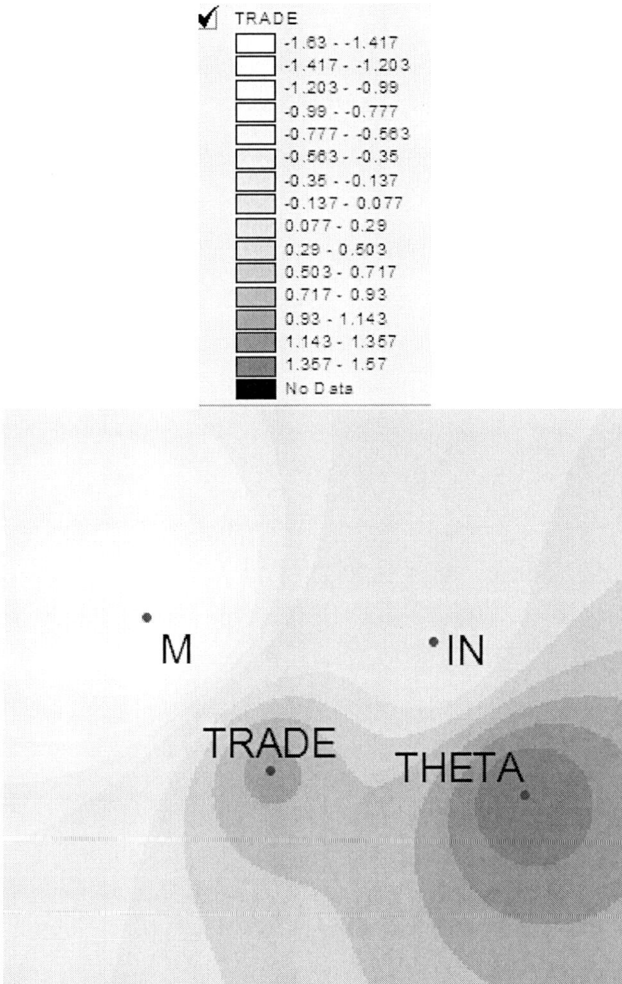

Figure 12.6: SDA Analysis lnTRADE versus lnM, lnIN, lnθ
$\ln TRADE = 6.53 - 1.63 \ln M - 0.022 \ln IN + 1.57 \ln\theta$
simulated value (-1.417)

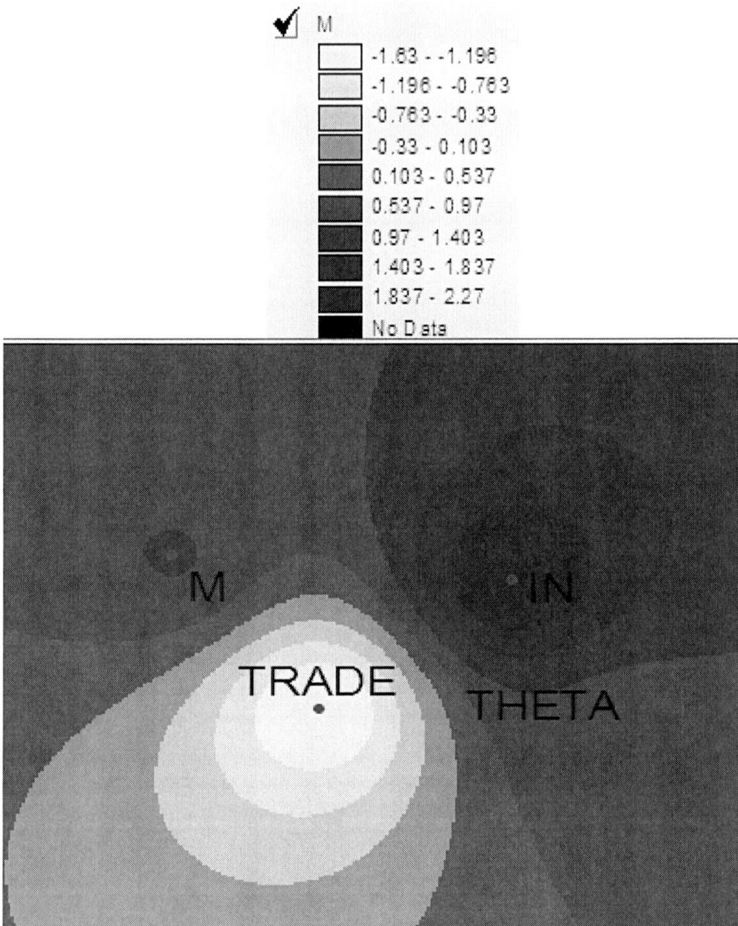

Figure 12.7: SDA Analysis lnM versus lnIN, lnTRADE, lnθ
$\ln M = 1.20 + 0.244 \ln IN - 0.176 \ln TRADE + 1.09 \ln\theta$
simulated value (0.103) (0.103)

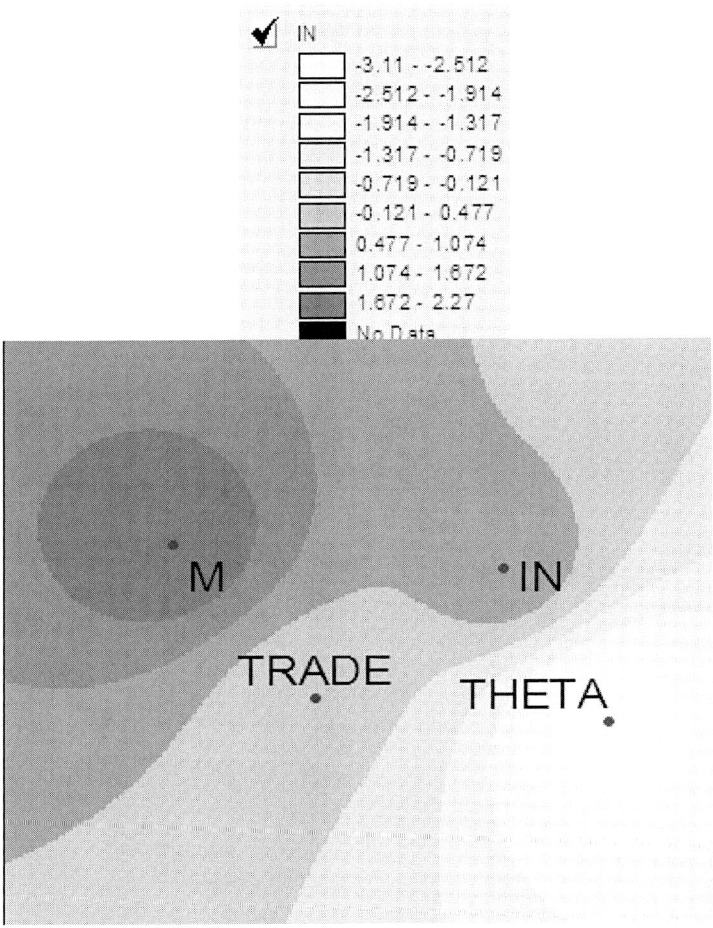

Figure 12.8: SDA Analysis lnIN versus lnM, lnTRADE, lnθ
$\ln IN = 1.32 + 2.27 \ln M - 0.022 \ln TRADE - 3.11 \ln\theta$
simulated value (1.672)

Conclusion

The principal contribution of this chapter has been to extend the thinking on the macroeconomic stabilization by monetary and fiscal/spending regimes and policies to the controversial area of complementarities between these two 'good' ways for macroeconomic coordination, and by means of implementing suitable policies. The complementarities between monetary and fiscal/spending regimes have raised controversies traditionally due to the post-Keynesian criticism of fiscalism/spending regime using Friedman's monetarism theory on price stability. Blaug wrote on this point (1993, p. 216): "The great debate between Keynesian and monetarists over the respective potency of fiscal/spending and monetary policy had divided the economic profession, accumulating what is by now a simply enormous literature." Blaug continues on (p. 221): "... monetarism never succeeded in clarifying the causal mechanism that produced its empirical results, sometimes even denying that these results required interpretation in the light of a supporting causal theory, and it failed to refute any but a crude travesty of the Keynesian theory it opposed. ... Keynesianism on the other hand, proved to be capable of absorbing monetarist ideas in a core sophisticated brand of macroeconomics that appears to be emerging from the fifteen-year-old melee."

Such opposing reflections on either side have led to the dismay in economic thought and in macroeconomic policy coordination at the level of industrial countries and its followership by developing countries. The emergence of a sustainable or at least a search for a universal theory of macroeconomic policy coordination, politico-economic institutionalism, and economic stabilization, has failed.

But a consequence of even more concerning nature is the deepening missing and exogenous treatment of the topic of wellbeing. Thus, the macroeconomic divide has caused a methodological impossibility on several fronts. Firstly, the issue runs deep into the problem of demarcation between deductive and inductive reasoning in scientific thought that always remained intrinsic to occidental mind. It was championed by Popper and joined in by Samuelson (Boland, 1989).

In the classical age of scientific thought in the West the origins can be traced down to the methodological approach to reasoning laid down by Kant (1964, 1977), the deductive champion; and by Hume (1992), the inductive champion. The possibility and search, leave alone the discovery of at least a way towards a universal theory of macroeconomic coordination, has failed. To this failure also adds on those of loss of well-defining the micro-foundation of macroeconomic methodology, the nature of relationship between money and fiscalism (spending), and their total effects on total wellbeing. Thereby, the understanding of endogenous ethics in economics, and the emergence of a new epistemology, that of unity of systemic knowledge in these directions, have not dawned. Such a grand failure has occurred despite the great minds of the scientific economic tapestry.

Economic stabilization, gained simply by short-run policies and remedial instrumentation of economic disturbances lost between monetary and fiscal/spending regimes by themselves, is inadequate in addressing the ultimate goal of wellbeing. Contrarily, such a goal is deeply moral, ethical, social, and holistic in nature. Such forces are embedded in the endogenous nature of ethics in economic reasoning at the most rigorous level and depth of intellection (Sen, 1990).

We overcome such epistemological limitation of economic theory despite the works of the Austrian School of Economics (von Mises, 1960) to relegate the ultimate premise of economic reasoning to rationalism. The search and the possibility for a methodological theory of 'everything', and the quest for universality even by the most rigorous of argumentation have been left out in economic theory (Choudhury, 2011b). In this chapter such a meta-epistemology of socio-scientific reasoning has been addressed. That is to show the methodology towards unification of the deductive and inductive episteme, and thus to organize socio-scientific reasoning upon the emergent episteme of moral and ethical endogeneity in the morally and socially embedded sense.

The ultimate premise of this new socio-scientific argumentation taken up in economics has been presented in this chapter in terms of the episteme of unity of knowledge (*tawhid*i worldview). This has been made to work through the micro-foundation of macroeconomic stabilization theme using the objective criterion of wellbeing defined by pervasive complementarities between the 'good' things of life. The most elemental one of such good things is the knowledge to gain unity of being and becoming along the evolutionary learning process. Monetary and fiscal/spending regimes are thus studied by the principle of pervasive complementarities. The empirical examples given in this chapter, point out that such an ultimate epistemology of 'everything' is possible.

For the last words, we borrow from Gaffard who eulogizes the great Schumpeterian legacy: "On the other hand, industrial policy must create incentives for firms to engage in co-operation, which is the key to the viability of such a complex process as innovation. It is characterized by interaction among multiple actors. This is not meant to eliminate the competitive character of the market, but to strengthen the coordinating role of competition."

In this chapter we have fully replaced competition by systemic complementarities as the sure sign of the *functional* ontology of unity of knowledge and participatory dynamics. The obvious corollary is replacement of competition by cooperation everywhere. In circular causation system this phenomenon is explained by organic unification of relations.

Such is the worldly manifestation of organic unity of knowledge that *tawhidi* methodology projects in 'everything'. The methodological foundation and its result is of a general-system understanding as opposed to a general equilibrium approach to economic modelling (Skyttner, 2005). The general-system structure is holistic, combining ethics, evolutionary learning, and wellbeing. This is specified in this chapter in yet another application. That comprises the theme of money and fiscal/spending complementarities in attaining wellbeing.

References

Benanke, B. & Mishkin, F.S., 2007, "Inflation targeting: a new framework for monetary policy", in Mishkin, F.S., *Monetary Policy Strategy*, pp. 207-226, The MIT Press, Cambridge, MA.

Blaug, M., 1993, *The Methodology of Economics*, Cambridge University Press, Cambridge, Eng.

Boland, L.A., 1989, "On the methodology of economic model building", in his, *The Methodology of Economic Model Building,* pp. 39-63, Routledge, London, Eng.

Boulding, K. E., 1971, "Economics as a moral science", in Globe, F.R. (ed), *Boulding Collected Papers Vol. 2*, Association of University Press, Boulder, CO.

Boulding, K.E., 1981, *Evolutionary Economics*, Russell Sage, New York.

Cantner, U. Luc Gaffard, J. & Nesta, L. (eds), 2009, *Schumpeterian Perspectives on Innovation, Competition, and Growth*, Springer, New York, NY.

Choudhury, M.A., 2011a, *Islamic Economics and Finance: an Epistemological Inquiry,* Emerald, Bingley, UK.

—. 2011b, "A critique of economic theory and modeling: a meta-epistemological general-system model of Islamic economics", *Social Epistemology*, (25)4, 423-44t6

Choudhury, Mufeedh. U.A., 2009, *Money, Finance, and the Real Economy in Islamic Banking and Finance: Perspectives from the*

Maqasid as-Shari'ah, unpublished MSC dissertation, Department of Economics, University of Stirling, UK.

Friedman, M., 1960, *A Program for Monetary Stability*, Fordham University Press, New York, NY.

—. 1989, "Quantity Theory of Money", *New Palgrave: Money*, pp. 1-40, W.W. Norton, New York, NY.

Gafford, J., 2009, "Innovation, competition, and growth: Schumpeterian ideas within a Hicksian framework", in Cantner, U. Luc Gaffard, J. &Nesta, L. (eds.), *Schumpeterian Perspectives on Innovation, Competition, and Growth*, pp. 7-24, Springer, New York, NY.

Hume, D., 1992, "Of the understanding", in his *Treatise of Human Nature*, Prometheus Books, Buffalo, N.Y.

Kaldor, N., 1975, "What is wrong with economic theory?" *Quarterly Journal of Economics*, (LXXXIX)3, 347-357.

Kant, I., 1964, 1977, *Groundwork of the Metaphysics of Morals*, (trans.) Paton, H.J., Harper & Row Publishers, New York, 1964. See also Kant, I., "Critique of pure reason", in Friedrich, C.J. (trans.), *The Philosophy of Kant*, The Modern Library, New York.

Kirzner, I., 1997, "Entrepreneurial discovery and the competitive market process: an Austrian approach", *Journal of Economic Literature*, (XXXV)1, 60-85.

Lucas, R.E., Jr., 1975, "An equilibrium model of the business cycle", *Journal of Political Economy*, 83:1113-1144.

Maturana, H.R. & Varela, F.J., 1987, *The Tree of Knowledge*. New Science Library, London, Eng.

Mega Middle East Global Advisors, 2006, *The Islamic Funds and Investments Report 2006*, UAE.

Minford, P. & Peel, D., 1983, *Rational Expectations and the New Macroeconomics*, pp. 15-21, Martin Robertson, Oxford, Eng.

Mishkin, F.S., 2007a, "What should Central Banks do?" *Monetary Policy Strategy*, pp. 37-58,The MIT Press, Cambridge, MA.

—. 2007b, "The transmission mechanism and the role of asset prices in moentary policy", *Monetary Policy Strategy*, pp. 59-74, The MIT Press, Cambridge, MA.

Mankiw G. & Rashwan, M.H., 2012, "Islamic Finance", in their *Principles of Economics Middle East Edition*, pp. 575-592, Cengage Learning, Hampshire, UK.

Myrdal, G., 1957, "An unexplained general traits of social reality", in his, *Rich Lands and Poor, the Road to World Prosperity*, Harper & Row, New York, NY.

—. 1958, "The logical crux of all science", in Streeten, P. (ed.), *Value in Social Theory, a Selection of Essays on Methodology by Gunnar Myrdal*, pp. 231-236, Harper & Brothers Publishers, New York, NY.
—. 1958, "The principle of cumulation", in Streeten, P. (ed.), *Value in Social Theory, a Selection of Essays on Methodology by Gunnar Myrdal*, pp. 198-205, Harper & Brothers Publishers, New York, NY.
Romer, P.M., 1986, "Increasing returns and long-run growth", *Journal of Political Economy*, 94:1002-37.
Sen, A., 1990, "Freedom and Consequences", in *On Ethics and Economics*, Basil Blackwell, Oxford, Eng.
Shakun, M.F., 1988, *Evolutionary Systems Design, Policy Making under Complexity and Group Decision Support Systems*, Holden-Day, Inc., Oakland, CA.
Skyttner, L., 2005, *General Systems Theory*, World Scientific Publishing Co., Singapore.
Toner, P., 1999a, "Nicholas Kaldor (1908-1986) "The marriage of Young and Keynes", in *Main Currents in Cumulative Causation, the Dynamics of Growth and Development*, Chapter 6, Macmillan Press Ltd., Houndmills, Hampshire.
—. 1999b, "Gunnar Myrdal (1898-1987): circular and cumulative causation as the methodology of the social sciences", in *Main Currents in Cumulative Causation, the Dynamics of Growth and Development*, Chapter 5, Macmillan Press Ltd., Houndmills, Hampshire.
—. 1999c, "Conclusion", in *Main Currents in Cumulative Causation, the Dynamics of Growth and Development*, Chapter 7, Macmillan Press Ltd., Houndmills, Hampshire.
Trichet, J-C., 17 Jan. 2008, "The creation of economic and corporate wealth in a dynamic economy – contribution to the panel", speech delivered at Banque de France and the Conference Board, Frankfurt, Germany.
Von Mises, L., 1976, *The Ultimate Foundation of Economic Science*, Sheed Andrews & McMeel, Kansas City, Kansas.
—. 1960, *Epistemological Problems of Economics,* Princeton University Press, Princeton, NJ.
Wikipedia, internet version. "Interaction between monetary and fiscal policy", http://en.wikipedia.org/wiki/Interaction_between_monetary_and_fiscal_policies
Yeager, L.B., 1997, *The Fluttering Veil, Essays on Monetary Disequilibrium*, The Liberty Press, Indianapolis, IN.

CHAPTER THIRTEEN

QUANTITATIVE ISSUES RELATION TO THE *TAWHIDI* EPISTEMOLOGY IN CIRCULAR CAUSATION

M.A. CHOUDHURY, M. SHAHADAT HOSSAIN,[1] AND JADI SURIADI[2]

The objective of this chapter is to establish some important mathematical properties of the *tawhidi* methodological worldview in a scientific treatment of the generalized and specific cases of study. The conclusion thereby derived from this technical treatment provides a further proof of universality and uniqueness of the *tawhidi* methodological worldview. The treatment is mathematical for reason of the rigorous analysis that is required on the imminent substantive issues. The ensuing mathematical treatment appears as a series of theorems.

Part I

Theorem 13.1: The *tawhidi* evolutionary learning system is non-linear, complex, and endogenous in the inter-relations between the variables. This property abides continuously along the interactive, integrative, and evolutionary (IIE) learning processes.

Consider the wellbeing function, W(x,y,a)[θ]. (13.1)

[1] Professor of Computer Science, University of Chittagong, Bangladesh.
[2] Lecturer, Postgraduate Program in Islamic Economics and Finance, Faculty of Economics, Trisakti University, Jakarta, Indonesia.

W(.) is a non-linear functional because of the continuous functional dependence of each of the variables shown on knowledge-flow $\theta \in (\Omega,S)$, the *tawhidi* episteme. The resulting method of circular causation between the variables yields the following inter-causal relations:

$y = a(\theta).x(\theta)$. This is a non-linear form because of the knowledge-induced parameter $a(\theta)$. (13.2)

We can write, $y = f_1(\theta,a(\theta),x(\theta))$ as a mathematical functional form. (13.3)

Then by circular causation idea:

$$x = f_2(\theta,a(\theta),y(\theta)) \quad (13.4)$$

$$a = f3(\theta,x(\theta),y(\theta)) \quad (13.5)$$

By the principle of 'similar' functions the following expression is a monotonic positive transform of the wellbeing function W(.):

$$f(\theta) = F(x(\theta),y(\theta),a(\theta)) \quad (13.6)$$

Hence, expression (13.6) is the empirically evaluated form of the wellbeing function conceptualized in expression (13.1).

We write:

$$df(\theta)/d\theta = (\partial F/\partial x).(dx/d\theta)+(\partial F/\partial y).(dy/d\theta)+(\partial F/\partial a).(da/d\theta) > 0, \text{ identically} \quad (13.7)$$

by the positive value of each term

Expression (13.7) establishes the monotonic positive expressions of each of the terms, proving thereby, the process-based evolutionary learning effect of interaction and integration (formation of θ-values) and post-wellbeing evaluation into evolutionary learning processes. Hence, non-linearity (θ-functional effect), complexity (process-based learning), and endogeneity (recursive relations in circular causation) properties of wellbeing evaluation are established through the interpretation of expressions (13.1)-(13.7).

We write the process-based evolutionary learning in the stochastic knowledge-flows and the corresponding selected induced variables in expressions (13.8) and (13.9); bold $\mathbf{x}_i(\theta) = (x,y,\ldots,a)[\theta\}$, $i = 1,2,3,\ldots,n$. The outside bracket indicates θ-induction of all the inside variables:

$$\begin{array}{ccccccccc} \theta_1 & \rightarrow & \theta_2 & \rightarrow & \theta_3 & \rightarrow \ldots\ldots \rightarrow & \theta_n \\ \downarrow & & \downarrow & & \downarrow & & \downarrow \\ \theta_1^* & \rightarrow & \theta_2^* & \rightarrow & \theta_3^* & \rightarrow \ldots\ldots \rightarrow & \theta_n^* \\ \downarrow & & \downarrow & & \downarrow & & \downarrow \\ \theta_1^{**} & \rightarrow & \theta_2^{**} & \rightarrow & \theta_3^{**} & \rightarrow \ldots\ldots \rightarrow & \theta_n^{**} \\ \text{etc.} & & & & & & \end{array} \quad (13.8)$$

The knowledge-induced variables have similar trends:

$$\begin{array}{ccccccc} \mathbf{x}_1(\theta_1) & \rightarrow & \mathbf{x}_2(\theta_2) & \rightarrow & \mathbf{x}_3(\theta_3) & \rightarrow \ldots\ldots \rightarrow & \mathbf{x}_n(\theta_n) \\ \downarrow & & \downarrow & & \downarrow & & \downarrow \\ \mathbf{x}_1^*(\theta_1^*) & \rightarrow & \mathbf{x}_2^*(\theta_2^*) & \rightarrow & \mathbf{x}_3^*(\theta_3^*) & \rightarrow \ldots\ldots \rightarrow & \mathbf{x}_n^*(\theta_n^*) \\ \text{etc.} & & & & & & \end{array} \quad (13.9)$$

By repeated simulations with different choices of the simulated coefficients of the system of circular causation relations (13.2)-(13.7) we write:

$$\begin{array}{ccccccccc} \mathbf{x}_1^*(\theta_1^*) \rightarrow & & \mathbf{x}_2^*(\theta_2^*) \rightarrow & & \mathbf{x}_3^*(\theta_3^*) \rightarrow \ldots\ldots \rightarrow & & \mathbf{x}_n^*(\theta_n^*) & & \\ \downarrow & & \downarrow & & \downarrow & & \downarrow & & \\ \mathbf{x}_1^{**}(\theta_1^{**}) & \rightarrow & \mathbf{x}_2^{**}(\theta_2^{**}) & \rightarrow & \mathbf{x}_3^{**}(\theta_3^{**}) & \rightarrow \ldots\ldots \rightarrow & \mathbf{x}_n^{**}(\theta_n^{**}) \\ \text{etc.} & & & & & & \end{array} \quad (13.10)$$

The arrow (↓) denotes *intra*-process knowledge formation and induction. The arrow (→) denotes *inter*-process knowledge formation and induction.

The same interpretation can be given for intra-system and inter-system knowledge formation and induction. These can be combined with time-specific values. Hence the non-linearity, complexity, and recursive endogeneity of the process-based relations revealed by the principle of pervasive complementarities (participation) continues across continuums of simulations, referred to as simulacra (Fitzpatrick, 2003).

The simulacra of emergent wellbeing functionals out of repeated simulations (intra-process and inter-process) are represented in the generalized form as,

$$F_i(\mathbf{x}_i^{m}*(\theta_i^{m}*)), \quad (13.11)$$
$i = 1,2,..,n$ for each specific processes (intra-systems by processes).

The inter-systemic evolutionary learning effect is shown by expanding expression (13.11) laterally across inter-systemic vector-variables that are combined together along **IIE**-processes. Thus the 'measured' wellbeing functionals and their overall circular relations may be represented by,

$$\Pi_{i=1}^{n}F_i(\mathbf{x}_i^{m}*(\theta_i^{m}*)) \quad (13.12)$$

The data for valuation, that is 'estimation' of the existing state, and followed by 'simulation' for ethical construction in the light of *tawhidi* unity of knowledge, meaning pervasive complementarities and participation, comprises the following vector. These vectors assume column values of the elements:

$$\mathbf{x}_{ij}(\theta_i), \quad \mathbf{a}_{ij}(\theta_i), \quad \theta_i \quad \theta = \text{Avg}\{\boldsymbol{\theta}_i\} \quad (13.13)$$

θ-values are generated by scaling or ranking in accordance with the numerical complementarities observed to exist between the selected $(\mathbf{x}_{ij}(\theta_i),\mathbf{a}_{ij}(\theta_i))$-vectors.

Example: How is endogenous functional relations treated differently from technologically induced ones?

Consider the following Cobb-Douglas production function in which human capital variable H augments labour (X_1) and capital (X_2) inputs:

$$Q = A.X_1^{\alpha 1}.\ X_2^{\alpha 2}.H^{\alpha 3} = A.(X_1H_1)^{\alpha 1}.(X_2H_2)^{\alpha 2}, \quad (13.14)$$

$$\text{where, } H^{\alpha 3} = H_1^{\alpha 1}.H_2^{\alpha 2} \quad (13.15)$$

By logarithmic transformation we write,

$$\ln(Q) = \ln(A) + \alpha_1(\ln X_1) + \alpha_2(\ln X_2) + \alpha_3(\ln H) \quad (13.16)$$

$$\ln(H) = (\alpha_1/\alpha_3)(\ln H_1) + (\alpha_2/\alpha_3)(\ln H_2) \quad (13.17)$$

From the equation (13.16) it can be deduced that,

$\alpha 1 + \alpha 2 + \alpha 3 > 1$, implying economies of scale caused by technological change.

The resource (R) equation is written as,

$$R(X_1,X_2,H) = w.X_1 + r.X_2 + h.H, \quad (13.18)$$

$$\text{with, } \partial Q/\partial X_1 = \alpha_1.(Q/X_1) \quad (13.19)$$

$$\partial Q/\partial X_2 = \alpha_2.(Q/X_2) \quad (13.20)$$

$$\partial Q/\partial H = \alpha_1.(Q/H) \quad (13.21)$$

The expressions (13.18)-(13.21) show that the factor payments including payment for technological change (human resource, H) become independent of each other in the production function (13.14), and which is also shown by the linearly independent resource form (13.17). Therefore, the induction of the production function by the exogenous input of the technology variable to induce the factor inputs does not change the nature of exogeneity of the technology variable and independence of relationship of each of the input variables of the production function.

To understand the meaning of endogenous relationship between the input variables by induction of the knowledge-flow derived in the *tawhidi* epistemic sense we proceed on to Theorem 13.2.

Theorem 13.2: Augmentation of resource mobilization by *tawhidi* knowledge-flow rejects the core postulate of scarcity in mainstream economics and establishes the principle of pervasive complementarities.

Consider the resource equation of a perfectly competitive production system with labour (L) and capital (K); and respective payments being w (wage rate), r (cost of capital):

$$\text{Resource, } R(\theta) = w(\theta).L(\theta) + r(\theta).K(\theta) = Q(\theta), \quad (13.22)$$

which like in expression (13.2), is non-linear, complex, and endogenous in the variables. The variables of the wellbeing function, of which one embedded sub-system is the production system, are,

$$\mathbf{x}(\theta) = \{Q(\theta),R(\theta),w(\theta),r(\theta),L(\theta),K(\theta),\theta\} \quad (13.23)$$

The complete evaluative system is given by,

Wellbeing, $W(Q(\theta),R(\theta),w(\theta),r(\theta),L(\theta),K(\theta)\}$ (13.24)

Circular causation relations:

$\mathbf{x}_i = f_i(\mathbf{x}_j(\theta))$, where $(\mathbf{x}_i,\mathbf{x}_j)[\theta\}$ are elements of $\mathbf{x}(\theta)$ with $i \neq j = 1,2,\ldots,n$ (13.25)

$\theta = F(\mathbf{x}(\theta)\}$ (13.26)

Consider, $dW/d\theta = (\partial W/\partial \mathbf{x}(\theta)) \bullet (d\mathbf{x}(\theta)/d\theta) > 0$, (13.27)

identically by vector multiplication terms.

As particular cases, $(dr(\theta)/d\theta) > 0$; $(dw(\theta)/d\theta) > 0$; thus, $(dr(\theta)/dw(\theta)) > 0$ (13.28)

Now as a result of expressions (13.22) and (13.28),

$(dR(\theta)/d\theta) = (dQ(\theta)/d\theta) = \{(dr(\theta)/d\theta).K(\theta) + r(\theta).(dK(\theta)/d\theta)\} + \{(dw/d\theta).L(\theta) + w(\theta).(dL(\theta)/d\theta)\} > 0$, (13.29)

by the principle of complementarities under the effect of θ-value and the result of expression (13.2).

Hence, $dR(\theta)/d\theta > 0$; $dQ(\theta)/d\theta > 0$. (13.30)

Expression (13.30) is true for simulacra of changes in the coefficients of the circular causation relations.

Thus, continuous knowledge production and its augmentation of the production variables augment resources and output. The core principal of scarcity is annulled in such a case of continuous knowledge-induced augmentation of resource, output and the rest of the endogenous variables.

Figure 13.1 brings out the inherent case of evolutionary learning under the impact of *tawhidi* unity of knowledge.

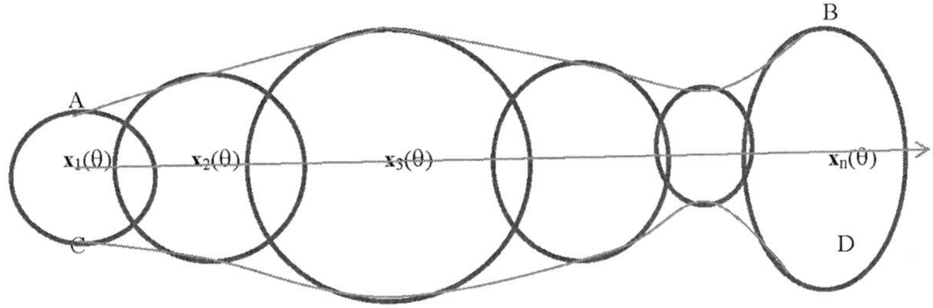

Figure 13:1: Circular causation inter-relationships intra-process and inter-process in unified continuums recursively augmenting each other

The $\mathbf{x}_i(\theta)$, i=1,2,…n processes are vectors of the production variables as in the vector (13.23). The circles denote intra-systemic dynamics that evolve subsequently into the next phase of evolutionary change denoted by the circular causation relations between the variables. The trajectories AB, CD, and the arrow denote the field of simulacra of simulation possibilities by changes in the coefficients, as explained earlier.

Theorem 13.3: Evolutionary equilibriums opposed to steady-state equilibriums appear along the interactive, integrative, and evolutionary trajectories of evolutionary learning

Let θ^* denote the unknown equilibrium point of convergence of the inter-process and systemic **IIE** trajectory defined by simulacra of θ-values. The *Qur'an*[3] permanently hides away θ_1^* from human cognition. It is known and is referred to as the state of *ghayb* (unseen). *Ghayb* may also be a shifting phenomenon, such as $\theta \rightarrow \theta_1^* \rightarrow \theta_2^* \rightarrow$etc. (*Qur'an*, 7:57)[4].

---

[3] *Qur'an* (27:65): "Say: None in the heavens or on earth, except God, knows what is hidden: Nor can they perceive when they shall be raised up (for Judgment)."

[4] By implication of the verse (*Qur'an* 7:57) we find the systemic diversity of equilibriums in their systemic states of *ghayb*. Each such *ghayb* as ultimate equilibrium is driven from one system to another in an interconnected way to explain the causality process involved: "It is He Who sends the Winds like heralds of glad tidings, going before His Mercy: When they have carried the heavy-laden clouds, We drive them to a land that is dead, make rain to descend thereon, and produce every kind of harvest therewith: thus shall We raise up the dead: perchance you may remember.

Therefore, there exists a value, $\varepsilon(\theta,\theta^*)$ in the open interval, (α,β)[5], and not being indefinitely small nor very large, as otherwise is the case in the theory of limits (see any graduate mathematics book). Now,

$$|\theta - \theta_1^*| > \varepsilon(\theta,\theta_1^*),\ \theta1^* \in (\alpha_1,\beta_1) \qquad (13.31)$$

Likewise, $|\theta_1^* - \theta_2^*| > \varepsilon(\theta,\theta_1^*,\theta_2^*) \in (\alpha_2,\beta_2)$ suitable open interval; etc.

In the end we obtain,

$$|\theta - \theta_n^*| = \Sigma_i\varepsilon_i(\theta,\theta_1^*,\ldots,\theta_i^*) > \varepsilon^*(\theta,\theta_1^*,\ldots,\theta_n^*) \in (\alpha_n,\beta_n) \qquad (13.32)$$

Having the property, $d\varepsilon^*/d\theta \neq 0$, in the knowledge-induced evolutionary sense of moving into different stages of evolutionary learning (> 0) or decreasing in learning to move into terminal optimal learning with stead-state equilibrium of the objective criterion of wellbeing and the constituent variables (< 0).

In terms of the corresponding knowledge-induced variables we obtain,

$d\varepsilon^*/d\theta = (d\varepsilon/d\mathbf{x}(\theta)).(d\mathbf{x}(\theta))/d\theta) \neq 0$ $\{(d\varepsilon/d\mathbf{x}(\theta)).(d\mathbf{x}(\theta))/d\theta) > 0$
$\Rightarrow$ if $d\mathbf{x}(\theta)/d\theta > 0$, then $d\varepsilon/d\mathbf{x}(\theta)) > 0$, implying $\{$evolving into higher **IIE** stages
$\{(d\varepsilon/d\mathbf{x}(\theta)).(d\mathbf{x}(\theta))/d\theta) < 0 \Rightarrow$ if $d\mathbf{x}(\theta)/d\theta > 0$, then (13.33)
$\{d\varepsilon/d\mathbf{x}(\theta)) < 0$, implying evolving into lower **IIE** stages

Similar scenarios of $(\theta,\mathbf{x}(\theta)\}$ can be deduced if the following case is studied in the wellbeing function: (1) $\mathbf{x}(\theta)$ is a mix of good and bad choices according to the *maqasid as-shari'ah*. That is, θ is derived from the *tawhidi* episteme of unity of knowledge.

[5] Because *ghayb* as terminal equilibrium point is indeterminate, therefore the open interval (α, β) cannot be measured numerically. Instead, it is judged by observing the degree of better complementarities simulated for ethical reconstruction of the learning relationship between the variables of the wellbeing function. The deeper are the complementarities gained as the sign of *tawhidi* unity of knowledge the better is the non-parametric estimate of the respective intervals in which a particular event and knowledge-flows lie.

Examples of the evolutionary equilibriums in asset-valuation in the *tawhidi* IIE-process trajectories over time

Consider the trajectory shown in Figure 13.2. One asset-case is represented by the curve AB. AB is non-linear, complex and endogenously related in the variables of the background wellbeing simulation, subject to the circular causation relations of complementarities and participation between the variables. But due to the random field of $\{\varepsilon,\varepsilon^*\}[\theta]$-values in the generalized structure of knowledge, space, and time, denoted by $(\theta,\mathbf{x}(\theta),t(\theta))$ (Choudhury, 2009), many possible **IIE**-trajectories can evolve out of the evolutionary learning spaces denoted by S_1, S_2, ... Thereby, inter-process and inter-system evolutions are generated by the various **IIE**-trajectories.

Of these spaces, S_3 for instance, yields $d\varepsilon/d\theta < 0$ indefinitely. That is, with $d\mathbf{x}(\theta)/d\theta > 0$, it must be that $d\varepsilon/d\mathbf{x}(\theta) < 0$. Steady-state equilibrium is reached and innovative evolutionary learning ultimately comes to an end when wellbeing function in this case attains an optimal state. Such a state of convergence is rejected along the **IIE**-trajectory of evolutionary learning. Therefore in the latter case, for $d\mathbf{x}(\theta)/d\theta > 0$, it is necessary that $d\varepsilon/d\mathbf{x}(\theta) > 0$.

Point of evaluation of assets in IIE-process trajectory

Now the concept of 'nearest' evaluation point along the mutually **IIE**-trajectory between diverse assets and evolutionary conditions in unity of knowledge is defined in the following way: $\{\theta_i,\mathbf{x}_i(\theta_i),t(\theta_i)\} \in S_i$, $i=1,2,\ldots,n$ are nearest points as probabilistic observable points at given points of time, and being subject to the **IIE**-learning dynamics among the $(\theta,\mathbf{x}(\theta))$-values at the specific points of time. Thereby, $(\theta,\mathbf{x}(\theta))$ as a geometrical coordinate is observed at various points of time, but not formed by any action *of* time. Only knowledge causes change in its epistemic sense of reference with the world-system. Time only records such epistemic change in the dimensions of knowledge, space, and time.

$$\text{Now, Prob. } E\{\theta^*_i,\mathbf{x}_i^*(\theta^*_i),t(\theta^*_i)\} = E\{\theta_i,\mathbf{x}_i(\theta_i),t(\theta_i)\} + \varepsilon(\theta,\theta^*), \quad (13.34)$$

with $d\varepsilon/d\theta > 0$ (evolution by epistemic unity of knowledge) to allow for an increasing domain of interaction, integration and co-evolution. Such a domain of $\{d\varepsilon/d\theta > 0\}$ generates simulacra of **IIE**-trajectories. E(.)

denotes the event of occurrence of $\{\theta_i,\mathbf{x}_i(\theta_i),t(\theta_i)\}$, as in the case of mutually exclusive and interdependent asset-valuation.

The system S_2 shows excess capacity in evolutionary learning. The system S_3 shows the trend to the end of learning. Thus there are the implications concerning $d\varepsilon/d\theta$.

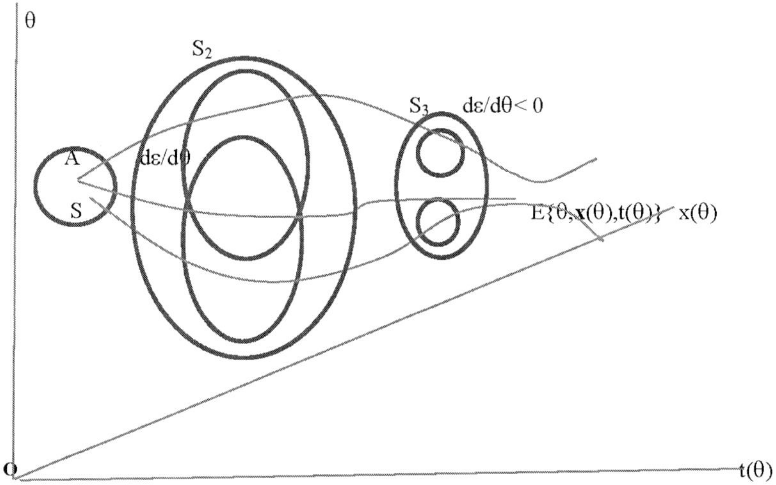

Figure 13.2: Evolutionary equilibriums opposed to steady-state equilibrium in IIE-trajectories

Theorem 13.4: How to generalize the wellbeing results to a mix of good (g) and bad (b) choices?

The *tawhidi* assumption implicated in *maqasid as-shari'ah* is that God's mercy on creation always places a good with a bad, so that complete entropy is non-existent. Even the great event of *akhira*, when the doomsday (*kiyamah*) as the entropy of universal destruction of the bad and false will happen, so also simultaneously the rise of order and de-entropy, and a blissful world will arise perfectly demarcating the good from the evil (*Qur'an*, 24:38): "That God may reward them according to the best of their deeds, and add even more for them out of His Grace: for God does provide for those whom He will, without measure."

Thus the worldly version of the generalized evaluation of the wellbeing function in the vector of good choices (**g**) and the vector of bad choices (**b**) is now written as,

Evaluate $W = W(\mathbf{g},\mathbf{b})[\theta]$ (13.35)
Subject to circular causation relations,
$g_i = f_i(\mathbf{g}_j,\mathbf{b},\theta)$, $i \neq j = 1,2,3,\ldots,n$; and $\mathbf{g}_j$ being the vector $\mathbf{g}$ without g_i.
$b_q = f_q(\mathbf{g},\mathbf{b}_r,\theta)$, $q \neq r = 1,2,3,\ldots,m$; and $\mathbf{b}_r$ being the vector $\mathbf{b}$ without b_q.
$\theta = F(\mathbf{g},\mathbf{b})$, which is the measured version of the conceptual $W(\mathbf{g},\mathbf{b})[\theta]$

Note the familiar properties:

$dW/d\theta = (\Sigma_i(\partial W/\partial g_i).(dg_i/d\theta)) + (\Sigma_q(\partial W/\partial b_q).(db_q/d\theta)) > 0$, identically by the terms in this expression.

Therefore, $(dg_i/d\theta)/(db_q/d\theta) < 0 \Rightarrow dg_i/db_q < 0$

Corollary: *The principle of pervasive complementarities is the permanent property of the* tawhidi *world-system in epistemic unity of knowledge. Marginal rate of substitution is the permanent property of the rationality postulate of mainstream economics*

I. Expression (13.40) implies that, if good and bad choices are mixed in the wellbeing function because of incompletion of knowledge of tawhidi epistemic unity of being then the necessary relationship between **g** *and* ***b*** *is given by,*

$dg_i/db_q < 0$, for all (i,q)

with incompleteness of learning expressed by,

$\lim \{\theta\} = \theta^* + \varepsilon(\theta,\theta^*)$

On the other hand,

$dg_i/dg_j > 0$, for all (i,j), subject to the condition (13.34) abiding.

Also, $db_q/db_r > 0$, for all (q,r), subject to the condition (13.37) abiding.

Expressions (13.43) and (13.44) comprise the necessary condition of substitution between **g** and **b**. Yet such a choice being inside a fuzzy system like S's in Figure 13:2, there is no exact point determining the substitution, as would otherwise be the case with marginal rate of substitution in resource allocation of mainstream economics.

The conditions (13.43) and (13.44) subject to (13.36) and (13.37) altogether establish the principle of pervasive complementarities between both good choices and bad choices. Yet in either case, the steady-state equilibrium conditions for **g** and **b** do not hold. Besides, **g** and **b** remain opposite to each other (expressions (13.43) and (13.44); and in expressions (13.36) and (13.37)).

II. Next, for the sufficient condition of permanent oppositeness between tawhidi principle of pervasive complementarities (PPC) and marginal rate of substitution (MRS), the following result will hold:

If conditions (13.41)-(13.44) hold then PPC permanently characterizes learning (truth) and de-learning (falsehood) criteria in **g** and **b**, respectively in the *tawhidi* epistemic sense, then g and b remain permanently opposite to each other.

The existence of expressions (13.41) – (13.44) implies the following sufficiency result:

$(dg_i/d\theta)/(db_q/d\theta) < 0 \Rightarrow$ by *maqasid as-shari'ah*, $dgi/d\theta > 0$; and $db_q/d\theta < 0$.

Thus g and b are permanently opposite to each other in the *tawhidi* epistemic sense.

By a logical continuation, the following result is true:

If θ' denotes de-knowledge flow, then, $dg_i/d\theta' < 0$; $dbq/d\theta' > 0$. Hence, $(dg_i/d\theta')/(db_q/d\theta') < 0 \Rightarrow$ by *maqasid as-shari'ah*, $dg_i/d\theta' < 0$; and $db_q/d\theta' > 0$.

In the end, the necessary and sufficient conditions for the oppositeness between g and b in fuzzy sets of choices by θ and θ', respectively, are given by expressions (13.41)-(13.43) [necessary]; and by expressions (13.45) and (13.46) [sufficient].

The following are the conclusions of Theorem 13.2 and its corollary in the light of *tawhidi* epistemology:

(1) PPC is the permanent property of the evolutionary learning worldview according to *tawhidi* epistemology acting in the world-system with incomplete knowledge formation causing progressive evolutionary learning.

(2) PPC is the permanent property of the evolutionary de-knowledge worldview according to *tawhidi* epistemology acting in the world-system with incomplete de-knowledge formation causing continuously evolutionary de-learning by way of demarcation between deductive and inductive reasoning (Popper, 2004; Resnick & Wolff on Marx, 1987).

(3) MRS is the permanent property of the steady-state condition of equilibrium and optimality of the world-system.

Theorem 13.5: The idea of 'priority' imminent in marginal rate of substitution of resource allocation is a methodological error

In the *tawhidi* methodological worldview the meaning of priority in resource allocation is explained in the following way: PPC established the permanent result of unity of knowledge (unity of de-knowledge devolving into methodological individualism) (Choudhury, 2000). That is,

$dX_i/dX_j > 0$, for every (i,j). Thus X_i and X_j are both augmented continuously by learning to augment resources as formalized earlier.
But, $(d/dX_j)(dX_i/dX_j) =$ (13.47)
{> 0, no priority shift of resources exists by virtue of θ-induction
{< 0, priority in the increased allocation of X_i while maintaining complementarities
{between(X_i,X_j)
{0, the assigned increased allocation of (X_i,X_j) remains constant while maintaining
{complementarities between (X_i,X_j).

Figure 13.3 shows the three forms of complementary resource allocations pointed out by expression (13.47). Resource allocation in (X_i,X_j) along $a_1a_2$describes the case of (> 0). Resource allocation along a_2a_3 describes the case of (< 0). Resource allocation along a_3a_4 describes the case of (= 0). The multiple possibilities of systems, domains, and learning processes are shown by S_i. The **IIE** trajectories arising from these fuzzy spaces of evolutionary learning equilibriums and perpetual simulacra are shown by the multiple trajectories. These may not preserve the trends of each other. But in every case they are governed by the principle of pervasive complementarities, defying marginal rate of substitution in the light of *tawhidi* epistemic worldview.

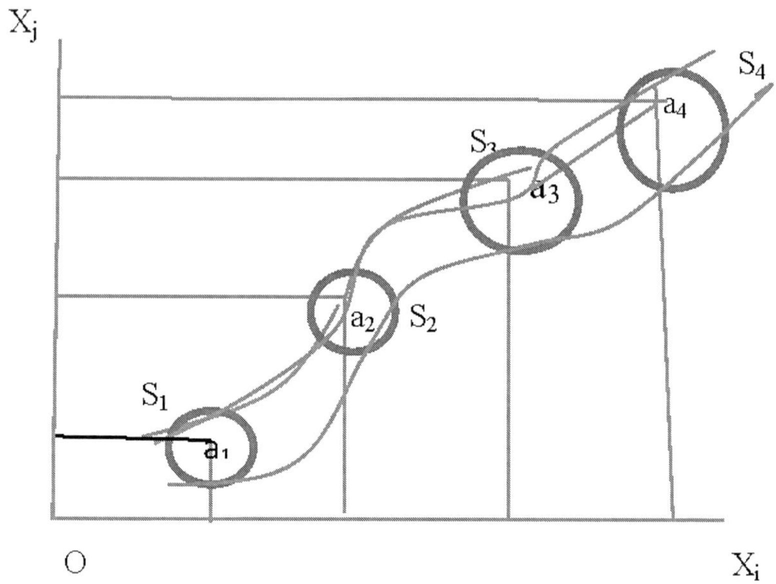

Figure 13:3. Knowledge-induced resource allocation between (X_i,X_j) in the complementary space defying the MRS concept of priority

Theorem 13.6: The universality and uniqueness of the *tawhidi* methodology of unity of knowledge (hence of 'de-knowledge' but evolving into methodological individualism) are established conclusively.

Whether we take the generalized case of wellbeing in **g** and **b** together or in the particular exclusive cases of **g** and **b** taken separately, the properties of circular causation abide with the conditions given in expressions (13.41) to (13.47). In other words, the contrary condition of $dg_i/db_q > 0$ for any and all of (i,q) does not exist. However, it is necessary to invoke the *maqasid as-shari'ah*[6] to differentiate between **g** and **b** as truth and

---

[6] Islamic traditionalists usually associate five characterizing elements with the objective and purpose of the *shari'ah* (*maqasid as-shari'ah*). These are namely, (i) preservation and promotion of belief in *tawhid*; (2) preservation of the rational faculties; (iii) preservation of the family; (iv) preservation of progeny; (v) preservation of life and property rights. But this is a traditional understanding. In the generalized extended purview of the *qur'anic* meaning of criterion between truth and falsehood (*furqan*), multi-criteria and multi-system emergences can be

falsehood, respectively. Expressions (13.41)-(13.47) therefore comprise the universal conditions of the *tawhidi* epistemic oneness across everything.

Is it possible that $dg_i/db_q < 0$ universally, in any epistemic construct other than the *tawhidi* epistemological methodology? The answer is in the negative. Thus the mix of good and bad cause no exact predictability and ethical future. We now take examples here to explain the failure of uniqueness in the differentiation between truth (good) and false (bad) in any other doctrine other than the *tawhidi* methodology.

Firstly, take the case of inflation (μ) and unemployment rate (u) relationship. Three versions of their interrelations have been pointed out in the economic literature in the context of economic stabilization and non-inflationary economic growth.

The Phillips Curve of long-run relationship yields the relationship, $du/d\mu < 0$ (Phillips, 1958). Yet $(u,\mu) = \mathbf{b}$. Friedman's accelerationist hypothesis shows $du/d\mu = 0$ with increasing values of μ See Ruggeri (1981) on Friedman's version of the Phillips Curve. Likewise, in the long-run evolution of the economy to the full-employment real output level, $d\mu/d(1\text{-}u) \geq 0$ (Burnside, 2005).Thus, $db_q/db_r \leq 0$ or ≥ 0; and $d\mathbf{b}/d\mathbf{g} > 0$, are both possible. Thus there is no demarcation between the good choices and bad choices in all of mainstream economic theory. Only relative truth applies between goods by way of marginal rates of substitution, or by the choice of a lesser bad for a very bad choice. The matter of priority in resource allocation by using MRS predominates. Any precise differentiation between **g** and **b** is annulled in mainstream economic

---

associated with *maqasid as-shari'ah*. This is true by virtue of the *res extensa* spanning of events in the inter-causal multi-dimensions of knowledge, space, and time. A cursory example is the intertemporal outlook of the five components. Events that now become extended elements of the *maqasid as-shari'ah* are preservation of the wider field of the meaning of life and resources, such as properties (Inglott, 1990); and the substantive meaning of social justice, such as the balanced composition of the five elements further complemented by a wider precept of the social contract; and the establishing of a discursive society of knowledge and learning (Foucault, 1972, 1983). Such extended elements of *maqasid as-shari'ah* truly belong to the generality of the *qur'anic* law (*sunnat Allah*). Yet they have not been given adequate attention in the history of the science of *shari'ah* (Mahdi, 1964).

The above kind of extension of *maqasid as-shari'ah* to the entire domain of the socio-scientific universe also implies that the *shari'ah* is not simply a narrowed down Islamic law of economy, society, and a personal law. In fact, the *shari'ah* is a cognitive Islamic law of understanding the monotheistic law at work in the universal entirety (*sunnat Allah*).

theory. Indeed, this is equally true of the entire epistemological background of mainstream socio-scientific worldview (Nozick, 2001).

In the *tawhidi* epistemic sense of the extended generality of *maqasid as-shari'ah*, a precise differentiation is established between **g** and **b**. Hence the continuous knowledge augmentation of complementing possibilities (PPC), as opposed to the idea of alternatives in Theorem 13.5 annuls the meaning of 'priority' between (X_i,X_j), otherwise caused by marginal rate of substitution (MRS). The properties given by expressions (13.41)-(13.47) now apply 'universally' and 'uniquely' in establishing well-determination between **g** and **b**.

Theorem 13.7: Particularization of wellbeing function to separable functions of 'g' and 'b' preserves the conditions of universality and uniqueness of the tawhidi methodological worldview in 'everything'

We write the total wellbeing criterion[7] as a separable function, W(**g**,**b**) = W(**g**) + W(**b**). The treatments of W(g) and W(g,b) have been done earlier. We turn now to the exclusive function W(**b**). We have explained above that the *Qur'an* expresses God's mercy by a balancing of entropy with de-entropic reversal by placing some element of good even in the worst situation of the bundle of bad choices[8].

The conditions (13.41)-(13.47) can readily be proved for the exclusive case of, $W(\mathbf{b}) = W(b_1,b_2,\ldots,b_m) = W_g(\mathbf{g}) + W_b(\mathbf{b})$. Yet we need to invoke the ruling of the *tawhidi* epistemic law in the *maqasid as-shari'ah* to clearly differentiate between **g** and **b** in everything to the limits of evolutionary θ-values derived from the completeness of the monotheistic law, (Ω,S), and therefore, appertaining to the *tawhidi* foundation of *maqasid as-shari'ah*.

On the other hand, for θ', the de-knowledge flow, $db_q/db_r \Rightarrow (db_q/d\theta')/(db_r/d\theta') > 0$.

Here, $(db_q/d\theta') > 0$; $(db_r/d\theta') > 0$.

---

7 We retain the terminology of wellbeing because of the meaning of the criterion separating **g** and **b** (*furqan*).

8 *Qur'an* (6:54): "When those come to thee who believe in Our Signs say: "Peace be on you: Your Lord hath inscribed for Himself (the rule of) Mercy: eerily, if any did evil in ignorance, and thereafter repented, and amended (his conduct), lo! He is oft-forgiving, Most Merciful."

Hadith al-Qudsi: "My Mercy rules over my wrath" (Ibrahim & John-Davies (undated)).

The following condition holds: $\lim[\cap\{\theta'_{qr}\}] = \phi$, as interaction give way to the pervasively placed utilitarian type methodological individualism. This condition is true universally in all of mainstream economic theory (Buchanan, 1971). Integration between alternatives converges into the optimal and steady-state case of linear addition, even with ethical overtones (Hammond, 1989). Therefore, $\cup_{interactions}\cap_{integration}\{\theta'\} = \Sigma\{\theta'\}$, an independently distributed utilitarian form of inter-systemic de-knowledge flows.

Consequently, by the condition of functional correspondence in the knowledge, space, and time dimensional multi-variables $(\theta,\mathbf{x}(\theta),t(\theta))$, likewise $(\theta',\mathbf{x'}(\theta'),t(\theta))$, the limiting state of the latter case leads to optimality as end of learning in steady-state equilibrium; or this state remains in perpetual conjectural equilibrium (evolutionary epistemology, Campbell, 1988). We then write in such two forms of $W_b(\mathbf{b})$,

$$W_b(\mathbf{b}) = \{\Sigma_q W_{bq}(b_q) \text{ in the utilitarian case}\}; \quad (13.48)$$

or

$\{W_b(b_1,b_2,..,b_m)$, with $db_q/db_r = (db_q/d\theta')/(db_r/d\theta') > 0$.
Because there is
$\{$no well-definition of **b** and $\{\theta'\}$ in conjectural models of evolution,
$\{$therefore, $(db_q/d\theta')$, $(db_r/d\theta')$ could have any sign randomly in pairs.
$\{$Consequently, $\{\theta'\}$ does not converge to any specific limiting point.[9]
$\{$The resulting kind of the $W_b(b)$criterion function not having a limiting point
$\{$becomes a model of disequilibrium. (13.49)

Thus steady-state equilibriums are of the only type that describes the optimal state of the utilitarian model, which is the cause and effect of methodological individualism of independently distributed agents and entities. In any other functional form the criterion function is either in states of evolutionary disequilibrium; or a dictatorial rule needs to be imposed to cause equilibrium and optimality to be attained (Arrow, 1951; Sen, 2002).

---

[9] The underlying intervals for the evolutionary $\{\theta'\}$-values do not contain convergent values even in the evolutionary sense.

Figure 13.4 shows the contrasting forms of the evolutionary learning and 'de-learning' systems according to *tawhidi* epistemology and rationality of methodological individualism, respectively. The two curves are completely opposite to each other, being premised differently -- on unity of knowledge in *tawhidi* epistemology; and by methodological heteronomy in rationalism, respectively.

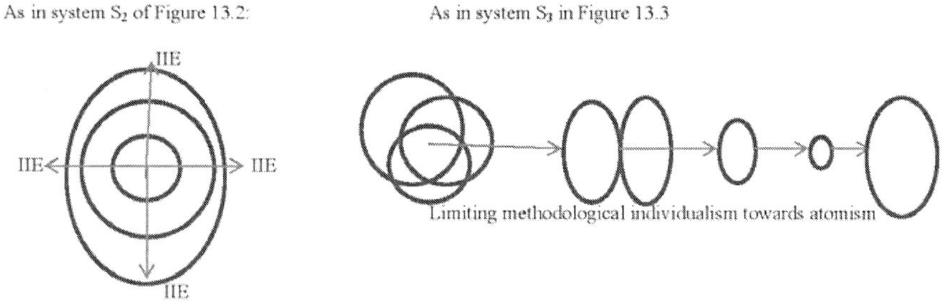

Figure 13.4: Contrasting evolutions between *tawhidi* methodology and methodological individualism

Part II: Some Statistical Methods for Circular Causation

Evaluation[10] of the wellbeing function subject to the system of circular causation equations between the variables can be carried out by various statistical methods. This proves the fact that although the *tawhidi* epistemological methodology for the generality and specifics of the world-system is universal and unique, yet the method of circular causation in the light of the *tawhidi* methodology remains diverse. This fact proves that methodology and methods are distinct facts of socio-scientific inquiry. But even so, the methods that arise in empirical socio-scientific inquiry are derived from the epistemological meaning. This in the *tawhidi* worldview means the development and use of methods springing from and reflecting the nature of unity of knowledge in *tawhidi* epistemology as methodology.

This Part II is a technical note on the diversity of methods that have been used to unravel the role of *tawhidi* unity of knowledge in evaluating the degree of such unity to be explained as the positive state followed by

---

[10] Evaluation means firstly 'estimation' to check out the degree of complementarities or absence of these between the *maqasid as-shari'ah* related variables in the wellbeing function. The coefficient 'estimates' are next 'simulated' to generate desired and possible levels of complementarities between the variables.

the normative possibility of reconstructing the socioeconomic order of complementarities between the variables related with *maqasid as-shari'ah*.

The problem studied is of circular causation interrelations between the following variables. Of them the microenterprise variable is focused upon.

ME: proportion of total number of microentrepreneurs of the labour force in Indonesia
TP: index of education level
TM: total national private savings (trillions of Indonesian Rp)
PB: commercial bank funding to ME (in trillions of Indonesian Rp)
KP: number of bank offices
KM: annual consumption per capita
PDB: per capitareal gross domestic product

The following are the circular causation equations relating to the wellbeing of microenterprises in Indonesia in terms of the other variables. Each variable is taken in relation to the other variables for evaluating the degree of complementarities between the variables. Circular causation provides the measured sign of unity of knowledge arising from the principle of pairing (organic unity) given by the *tawhidi* precept in everything.

Equation system (13.50) here is written as,

$$\left.\begin{array}{l} ME=f(TP, TM, PB, KP, KM, PDB) \\ TP=f(ME, TM, PB, KP, KM, PDB) \\ TM=f(ME, TP, PB, KP, KM, PDB) \\ PB=f(ME, TP, TM, KP, KM, PDB) \\ KP=f(ME, TP, TM, PB, KM, PDB) \\ KM=f(ME, TP, TM, PB, KP, PDB) \\ PDB=f(ME, TP, TM, PB, KP, KM) \end{array}\right\} \qquad (13.50)$$

Figure 13.5 shows the circular causation relations of inter-causal pairing between variables by way of double-directional arrows.

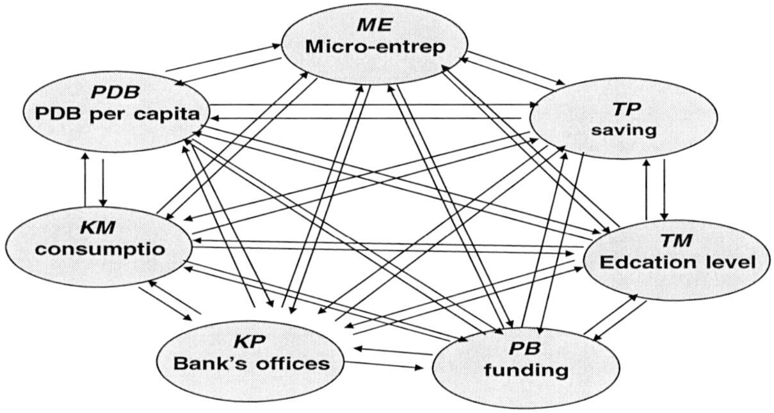

Figure 13.5: The complexity and endogenous relationships of circular causation

The following statistical models were used. The results are interpreted in order to point out the possibility for simulation of the coefficients to realize ethical reconstruction of the underlying wellbeing function.

1. Simultaneous equations regression model is estimated as,

ME=-5.4503+3.3479*TP+0.1497*TM-0.0577*PB-0.0994*KP+0.0566*KM- 0.1368*PDB (13.51)

TP=1.8551+0.1670*ME-0.0320*TM+0.2927*PB+0.0273*KP-0.0009*KM+0.0234*PDB (13.52)

TM=4.5565-4.0195*TP+0.9357*ME-0.2264*PB+0.6475*KP+0.0080*KM+ 0.6817*PDB (13.53)

PB=-0.8443-0.8117*TM+0.0131*TP-1.2939*ME+0.7332*KP+0.1101*KM+ 0.9970*PDB (13.54)

KP=-2.8865+0.2509*PB+0.7942*TM+4.2071*TP-0.7618*ME+0.0020*KM-0.4253*PDB (13.55)

KM=-2.2543+0.0164*KP+0.2995*PB+0.0783*TM-1.1358*TP+3.4526*ME+1.3717*PDB (13.56)

PDB=-4.7353+0.1613*KM-
0.3977*KP+0.3190*PB+0.7818*TM+3.3654*TP-0.9804*ME (13.57)

We note from the estimation results that negative coefficients exist between ME and 'number of bank offices' KP, and real GDP. The implication is that ME are being financed and developed weakly by bank financing and government assistance.

Likewise, private savings are negatively affected by per capita consumption level and ME funding. This result affirms the previous one that ME are at the mercy of their own non-conventional national private savings by keeping consumption rate constant.

Other results can be deduced by examining the coefficient signs and values. These results point out adverse effects of variables like educational levels, bank funding PB, and PDB as critical variables on the development of MEs in Indonesia. In these, TP simulation possibilities exist by way of developing policies that will turn the negative coefficients into near or fully positive coefficients. Thereby, a new trajectory of simulated relational paths in the variables can be developed, as formalized in theorem 13.1.

2. Vector Autoregression (VAR)

VAR model regresses the difference variables (D(**x**)) on each other variables, which are lagged by 1 and 4 lags as shown below. Here only the main equation under study, namely the ME dependent variable equation is shown:

DME = 1.0056*DME(-1) - 0.3343*DME(-2) - 0.1761*DME(-3) +
0.8616*DME(-4) + 0.7194*DTP(-1) + 1.8430*DTP(-2) -
2.1158*DTP(-3) - 5.0932*DTP(-4) - 0.1281*DTM(-1) +
0.1275*DTM(-2) - 0.0426*DTM(-3) + 0.0149*DTM(-4) -
0.1031*DPB(-1) - 0.0485*DPB(-2) + 0.1372*DPB(-3) -
0.0898*DPB(-4) + 0.0298*DKP(-1) + 0.0608*DKP(-2) -
0.1452*DKP(-3) + 0.1282*DKP(-4) + 0.0956*DKM(-1) -
0.1582*DKM(-2) - 0.0265*DKM(-3) - 0.01931*DKM(-4) +
0.8025*DPDB(-1) - 0.3942*DPDB(-2) - 0.9593*DPDB(-3) +
0.7787*DPDB(-4) + 0.0723 (13.58)

Such a result of VAR is very complicated. Too many independent variables are involved to give rise to different lagged variables coefficients for the same variable. In the presence of many endogenous variables of circular causation relations, the VAR method becomes untenable. Interpretation of the results of estimation to lead into appropriate simulation by changes of coefficients in the light of *maqasid as-shari'ah* requirements and the principal epistemology of *tawhidi* organic unity by complementarities where variables are compliant with *maqasid as-shari'ah,* becomes very difficult.

Statistical Results of Goodness of Fit for Multiple Regression Equations of Circular Causation

The coefficients C(i)s refer to the estimated equations (13.59)-(13.60). *C* appearing alone is the constant value of the various equations.

The secondary data are given in Table 13.1. For the units of these secondary variables see text.

Equation: ME=C(1)+C(2)*TP+C(3)*TM+C(4)*PB+C(5)*KP+C(6)*KM−C(7)*PDB

Instruments: ME TP TM PB KP KM PDB C
Observations: 35

R-squared	0.907799	Mean dependent variables	2.314490
Adjusted R-squared	0.888042	S.D. dependent variables	0.589740
S.E. of regression	0.197327	Sum squared residuals	1.090268
Durbin-Watson stat	1.623186		

Equation: TP=C(8)+C(9)*ME+C(10)*TM+C(11)*PB−C(12)*KP+ C(13)*KM− C(14)*PDB

Instruments: ME TP TM PB KP KM PDB C
Observations: 35

R-squared	0.938724	Mean dependent variables	2.491472
Adjusted R-squared	0.925593	S.D. dependent variables	0.161581
S.E. of regression	0.044075	Sum squared residuals	0.054394
Durbin-Watson stat	1.646227		

Equation: TM=C(15)−C(16)*TP+C(17)*ME+C(18)*PB+C(19)*KP+ C(20)*KM− C(21)*PDB

Instruments: ME TP TM PB KP KM PDB C
Observations: 35

R-squared	0.995273	Mean dependent variables	9.736163
Adjusted R-squared	0.994261	S.D. dependent variables	6.510840
S.E. of regression	0.493251	Sum squared residuals	6.812314
Durbin-Watson stat	1.295593		

Equation: PB=C(22)+C(23)*TM+C(24)*TP−C(25)*ME+C(26)*KP+C(27)*KM− C(28)*PDB

Instruments: ME TP TM PB KP KM PDB C
Observations: 35

R-squared	0.986270	Mean dependent variables	10.72916
Adjusted R-squared	0.983328	S.D. dependent variables	7.232324
S.E. of regression	0.933833	Sum squared resduals	24.41723
Durbin-Watson stat	0.858679		

Equation: KP=C(29)−C(30)*PB+C(31)*TM−C(32)*TP+C(33)*ME+C(34)*KM+C(35)*PDB

Instruments: ME TP TM PB KP KM PDB C
Observations: 35

R-squared	0.982132	Mean dependent variables	11.36860
Adjusted R-squared	0.978303	S.D. dependent variables	3.708448
S.E. of regression	0.546245	Sum squared residuals	8.354747
Durbin-Watson stat	1.246883		

Equation: KM=C(36)−C(37)*KP+C(38)*PB−C(39)*TM+C(40)*TP+C(41)*ME+C(42)*PDB

Instruments: ME TP TM PB KP KM PDB C
Observations: 35

R-squared	0.992067	Mean dependent variables	22.98726
Adjusted R-squared	0.990368	S.D. dependent variables	15.68992
S.E. of regression	1.539884	Sum squared residuals	66.39479
Durbin-Watson stat	0.578266		

Equation: PDB=C(43)−C(44)*KM+C(45)*KP+C(46)*PB−C(47)*TM+C(48)*TP+C(49)*ME

Instruments: ME TP TM PB KP KM PDB C
Observations: 35

R-squared	0.996837	Mean dependent variables	11.60360
Adjusted R-squared	0.996159	S.D. dependent variables	8.523228
S.E. of regression	0.528207	Sum squared residuals	7.812068
Durbin-Watson stat	0.753746		

Table 13.1: Biannual data for the circular causation variables as shown, Indonesia

No.	Mid-year	ME	TP	TM	PB	KP	KM	PDB
1	1994-1	0.89	2.16	1.48	3.06	6.41	4.36	2.00
2	1994-2	1.25	2.19	1.70	3.42	6.52	4.59	2.15
3	1995-1	1.43	2.22	1.85	3.76	6.75	4.82	2.35
4	1995-2	1.37	2.26	2.15	4.09	6.96	5.05	2.57
5	1996-1	1.30	2.29	2.42	4.42	7.29	5.27	2.73
6	1996-2	1.47	2.30	2.82	4.93	7.63	5.85	2.84
7	1997-1	1.60	2.31	3.03	6.42	8.08	6.43	3.17
8	1997-2	1.52	2.33	3.58	6.87	10.00	7.07	3.95
9	1998-1	1.62	2.37	5.74	5.01	9.71	7.70	4.76
10	1998-2	2.20	2.40	5.74	4.74	9.89	10.72	5.14
11	1999-1	2.67	2.42	6.09	3.96	9.54	13.75	5.42
12	1999-2	2.45	2.45	6.26	3.97	9.66	13.31	6.01
13	2000-1	2.11	2.46	6.58	4.32	9.09	12.87	6.75
14	2000-2	2.36	2.47	7.24	6.07	9.18	13.71	7.38
15	2001-1	2.80	2.47	7.68	6.54	9.28	14.55	7.89
16	2001-2	2.88	2.47	8.15	6.81	9.38	17.59	8.28
17	2002-1	2.74	2.48	8.04	6.56	9.75	20.63	8.59
18	2002-2	2.62	2.50	8.54	7.05	9.97	21.56	8.94
19	2003-1	2.59	2.52	8.62	7.79	10.99	22.49	9.36
20	2003-2	2.70	2.55	8.62	8.83	11.35	23.01	9.91
21	2004-1	2.83	2.57	8.91	8.87	10.66	23.53	10.61
22	2004-2	2.82	2.59	9.45	11.70	11.91	25.10	11.49
23	2005-1	2.73	2.59	9.93	12.52	11.60	26.68	12.56
24	2005-2	2.67	2.63	11.05	13.71	11.87	27.99	13.75
25	2006-1	2.62	2.62	11.64	14.29	12.38	29.30	14.90
26	2006-2	2.65	2.65	12.64	14.70	12.87	32.32	15.97
27	2007-1	2.61	2.65	13.45	15.55	13.29	35.34	17.36
28	2007-2	2.60	2.48	15.10	17.37	13.68	36.99	19.37
29	2008-1	2.65	2.66	15.65	18.12	14.27	38.64	21.43
30	2008-2	2.68	2.68	17.41	19.54	15.23	40.82	22.82
31	2009-1	2.59	2.68	18.36	21.23	17.09	43.01	23.91
32	2009-2	2.64	2.65	19.93	22.20	17.70	46.25	25.27
33	2010-1	2.58	2.69	21.40	23.45	18.12	49.48	26.90
34	2010-2	2.78	2.71	24.19	26.07	19.50	54.43	28.77
35	2011-1	2.99	2.73	25.33	27.59	20.30	59.37	30.80

Badan Pusat Statistik (BPS), for ME, TP, KM and PDB
Bank Indonesia (BI), for TM, PB, KP

Part III: The Spatial Domain Method of Circular Causation: Evaluating Coefficient Values from Computer Representation

Spatial Domain Analysis (SDA) is a contour representation of Geographical Information System (GIS) over a topography. In our work we have extended the application of SDA of physical contour into socioeconomic topography. A most useful and ready application has been made by us in the area of circular causation to allow the generated SDA figures to display levels of interrelationships, positive or negative, between the variables. The SDA field generated out of the distribution of 'estimated' coefficients of the multiple regression equations generates a continuous domain of all possible numerical value of the coefficients around their position according to the estimated value. Thus movement across the coloured field around the estimated values of the various coefficient variables as shown, causes movements into positive or negative directions. The simulated coefficients of the selected variables in the light of the implications of the *maqasid as-shari'ah* (positive or negative) can be read off the continuous fields in reference to the tabulation of the coefficients, as shown.

Thus the SDA method presents the visualisation of interaction between the variables in a graphical way, which is very user-friendly. The same approach is not possible in sheer statistical domain, where the interaction can be recognised in terms of a given estimated value and then this is changed by step-wise simulation.

Because of the greater domain of interactive possibility generated by the visual representation, the Interaction component of the **IIE**-learning process model can be perceived. In addition, it is possible to see the space where the negative value of interaction (shown by negative coefficients) can be changed into positive values. Underlying policy changes are implied in such simulations. Hence integration resulting from interaction between the variables can be explained. Thus, the interactive and integrative components of the **IIE**-process model can be depicted in the SDA domain. In this way, the concept of circular causation, which is used to ensure the relational complementarity between the domain of the variables, can be understood in the SDA domain representation. Yet this is not possible in the statistical domain all by itself.

In equation (13.50) – and all other equations interpreted similarly -- it can be observed that the interaction between the variables ME and PDB is negative (-0.9804).This is depicted in Figure 13.1 with the lightest colour. On the other hand, complementary interaction between TP and PDB is highly positive (3.3654); and this is illustrated with deep colour.

In this way, the SDA approach allows the visualisation of interaction between the variables in a graphical way. In this way, the interactive and integrative components of the **IIE**- process model can be perceived. In addition, it is possible to see the space where negative value of interaction can be changed into positive value as the consequence of changing policy scenarios. Hence a complementary form of integration result between the variables in the light of the implications of *maqasid as-shari'ah* can be understood.

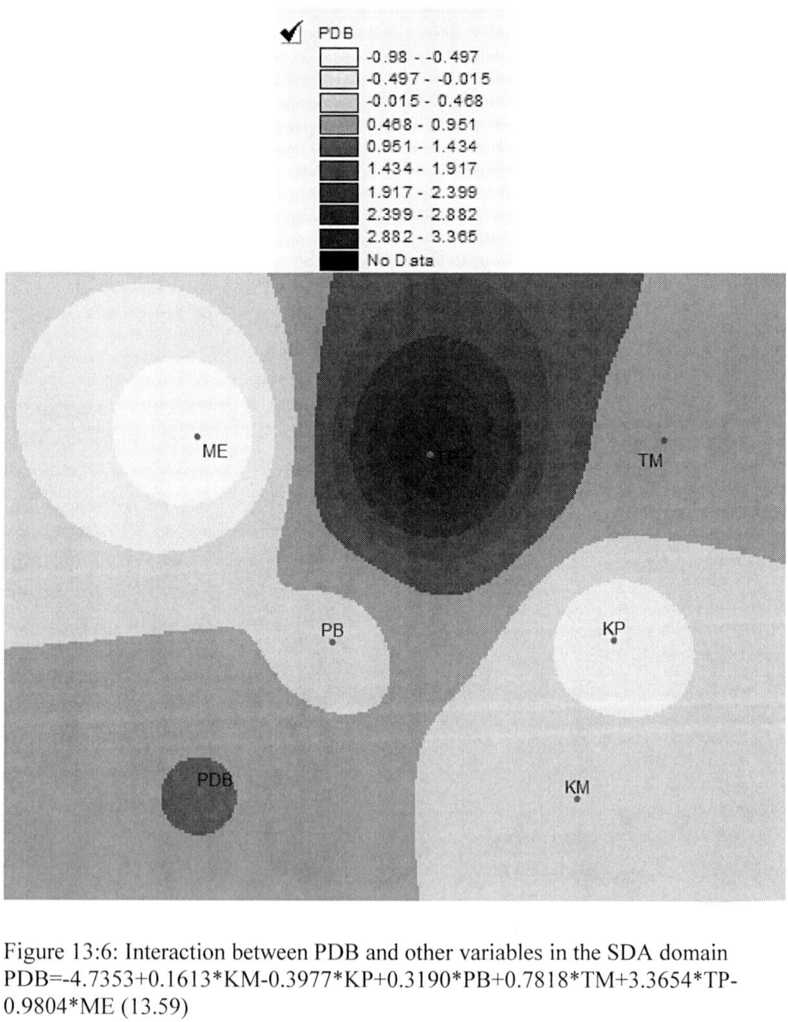

Figure 13:6: Interaction between PDB and other variables in the SDA domain PDB=-4.7353+0.1613*KM-0.3977*KP+0.3190*PB+0.7818*TM+3.3654*TP-0.9804*ME (13.59)

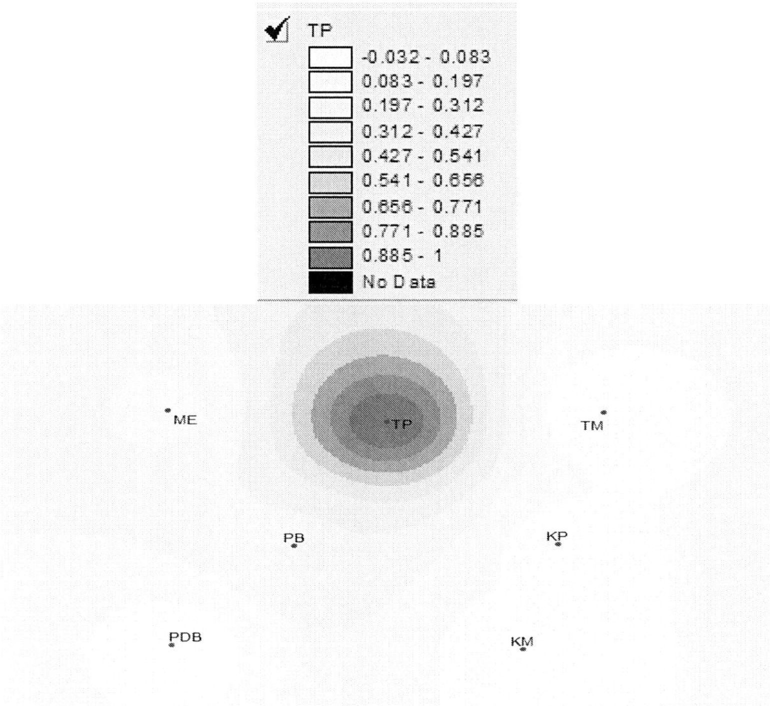

Figure 13:7: Interaction between TP and other variables in the SDA domain
TP=1.8551+0.1670*ME-0.0320*TM+0.2927*PB+0.0273*KP-0.0009*KM+0.0234*PDB (13.60)

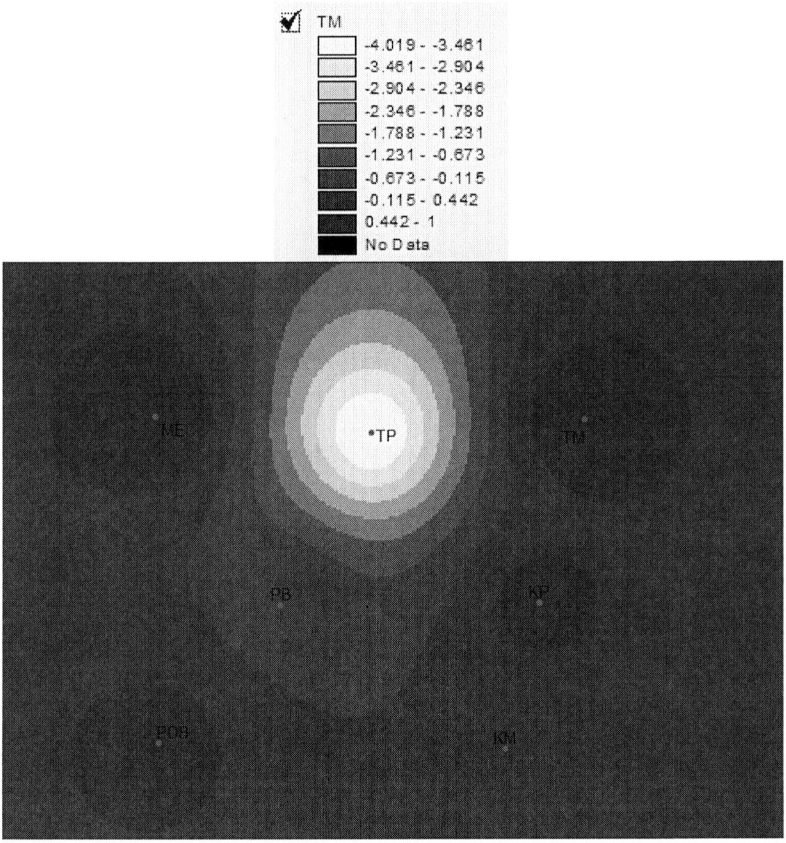

Figure 13.8: Interaction between TM and other variables in the SDA domain
TM=4.5565-4.0195*TP+0.9357*ME-0.2264*PB+0.6475*KP+0.0080*KM+0.6817*PDB (13.61)

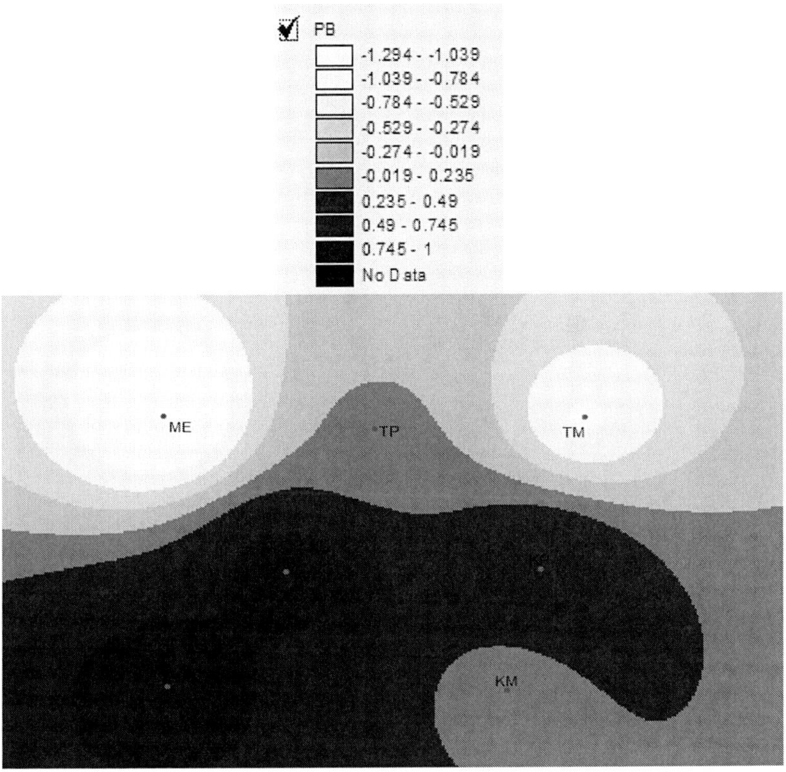

Figure 13:9: Interaction between PB and other variables in the SDA domain

$$PB=-0.8443-0.8117*TM+0.0131*TP-1.2939*ME+0.7332*KP+0.1101*KM+0.9970*PDB \qquad (13.62)$$

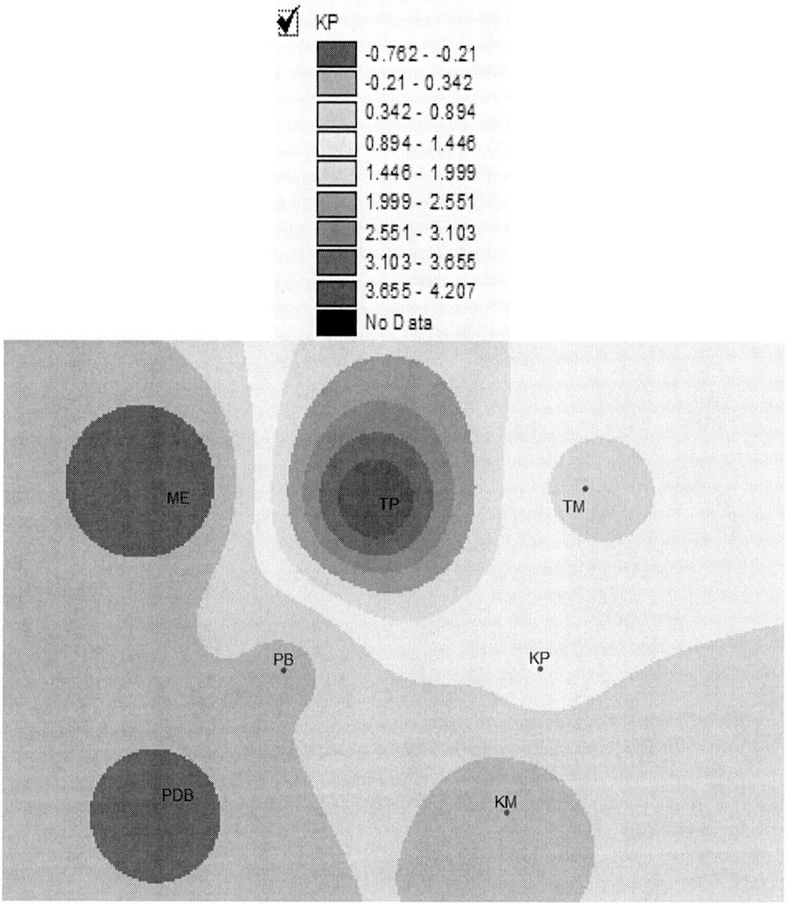

Figure 13:10: Interaction between KP and other variables in the SDA domain

KP=-2.8865+0.2509*PB+0.7942*TM+4.2071*TP-0.7618*ME+0.0020*KM-0.4253*PDB (13.63)

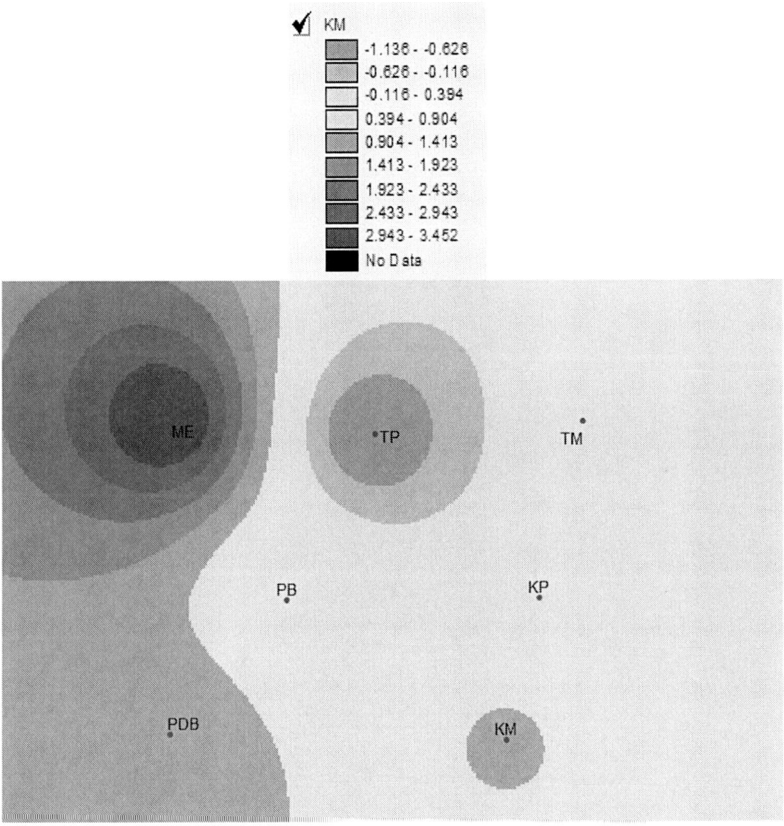

Figure 13:11: Interaction between KM and other variables in the SDA domain
KM=-2.2543+0.0164*KP+0.2995*PB+0.0783*TM
1.1358*TP+3.4526*ME+1.3717*PDB (13.64)

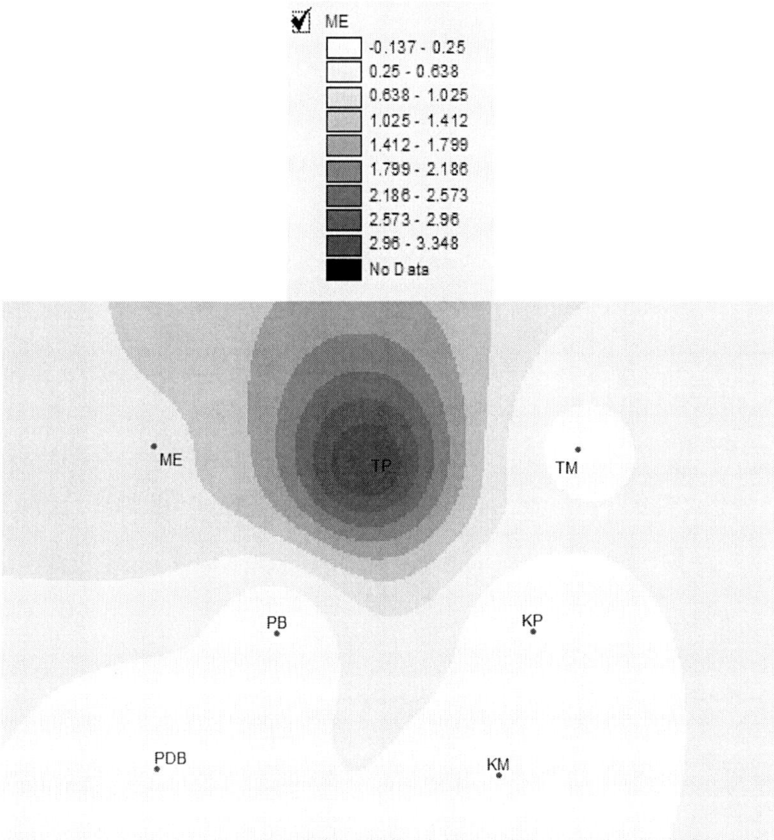

Figure 13:12: Interaction between ME and other variables in the SDA domain
ME=-5.4503+3.3479*TP+0.1497*TM-0.0577*PB-0.0994*KP+0.0566*KM-0.1368*PDB (13.65)

References

Arrow, K.J., 1951, *Social Choice and Individual Values*, John Wiley & Sons, New York, NY.

Buchanan, J.M., 1971, *The Bases for Collective Action*, General Learning Press, New York, NY.

Burnside, C., 2005, “Theoretical prerequisites for fiscal sustainability analysis”, in his (ed.), *Fiscal Sustainability in Theory and Practice, a Handbook*, pp. 11-33, esp. p. 20, The World Bank, Washington, D.C.

Campbell, D., 1988, Evolutionary epistemology”, in his, *Methodology and Epistemology for Social Science, Selected Papers*, Chapter 16, edited by Overman, S., The University of Chicago Press, Chicago, ILL, USA.

Choudhury, M.A., 2000, *The Islamic Worldview, Socio-Scientific Perspectives*, Kegan Paul International, London, Eng.

—. 2009, “Which of the two? – knowledge or time”, *Philosophical Papers and Review* (1)4, 2009.

Fitzpatrick, T., 2003, “Postmodernism and new directions”, in Alcock, P. Erskine, A. & May, M. (eds.), *Social Policy*, pp. 125-133, Oxford, Eng.: Blackwell.

Foucault, M. trans. by Sheridan, A.M. 1972, *The Archeology of Knowledge and the Discourse on Language*, Harper Torchbooks, New York, NY.

—. 1983, *The Archaeology of the Human Sciences*, pp. 44-78, The University of Chicago Press, Chicago, IL.

Hammond, P.J., 1989, “On reconciling Arrow’s theory of social choice with Harsanyi’s Fundamental Utilitarianism”, in Feiwel, G.R. (ed.), *Arrow and the Foundation of the Theory of Economic Policy*, pp. 179-221, Macmillan, London, Eng.

Ibrahim, E. & John-Davies, D. (u.d). *Forty Hadith Qudsi*, privately published.

Inglott, P.S., 1990, “The rights of future generations: some socio-philosophical considerations”, in Busuttil, S., Agius, E., Inglott, P.S., & Macelli, T., (eds.), *Our Responsibilities Towards Future Generations*, pp. 17-27, Foundation for International Studies & UNESCO, Malta.

Mahdi, M., 1964, *Ibn Khaldun’s Philosophy of History*, The University of Chicago Press, Chicago, IL:.

Nozick, R., 2001, *Invariances, the Structure of the Objective World*, The Belknap Press of the Harvard University Press, . Cambridge, MA.

Phillips, W.W. 1958, "The Relation between Unemployment and the Rate of Change in Money Wages in the United Kingdom, 1861-1957",

Economica, Vol. XXV.
Popper, K., 2004, *The Logic of Scientific Discovery*, Routledge, London, Eng.
Ruggeri, G.C., 1981, "The Inflation-Unemployment Trade-Off", in Ruggeri G.C., (ed.), *The Canadian Economy, Problems and Policies*, Gage Publishing Ltd., Toronto, Ont.
Sen, A., 2002, “Rationality and social choice”, .In his, *Rationality and Freedom*, pp. 261-291. The Belknap Press of Harvard University Press, Cambridge, MA.

CHAPTER FOURTEEN

CONCLUSION

The focus of this book has been on the understanding of the law of monotheistic oneness in Islam as given by the epistemological foundations of the *Qur'an* and the *sunnah* in respect of socio-scientific formalism and construction of the generality and details of the world-system in such a unified worldview. The concept of oneness is explained in terms of relational epistemology of unity of knowledge in the form of functional formalism; and not as metaphysical formalism. The latter is the precept that remains hidden in quiddity. Yet it is presented in terms of the unity of the signs of God in the order and scheme of 'everything'. Throughout the book, the relational unity of interaction, integration, and creative evolution (**IIE**) by learning has been presented in the rigorous scientific language encompassing everything of the socio-scientific entirety; but being focused on economics, finance, and society.

The *tawhidi* methodology with its worldview and functional ontology explaining the field of rigorous formalism deepens into philosophy of science, mathematics, analysis, and moral reconstruction. Thus the book has taken its due expression in the exegesis of the *Qur'an* and the *sunnah*. These are studied by recourse to the rigorous socio-scientific language and analysis, inferences, and possibilities of moral reconstruction for establishing the *functional* ontology of the unity of knowledge in 'everything'. By the same approach we have also studied the contrary methodology of falsehood as 'de-knowledge'. 'De-knowledge' comprises all that contradict the monotheistic law of oneness and its application – the *tawhidi* epistemology and its applications in the generality and specifics of the world-system.

In the attempt to attain its rigorous socio-scientific goal of formalism and moral reconstruction in the light of the *tawhidi* methodological worldview, this book has considered the derivation and formulation of the unique and universal message by human volition in reference to the *Qur'an* and the *sunnah* along with the interactive, integrative and evolutionary (**IIE**) dynamics of the Islamic discursive society as derived from the same epistemological source of authentic Islamic knowledge.

This formalism termed as the *Tawhidi* String Relation (TSR) was emphasized in every chapter. The purpose behind this was to bring out the application of this unique and universal methodology with methods of monotheistic oneness to specific issues and problems in economics, political economy, world-system study, finance, and society,

The moral essence of the *tawhidi* worldview was shown to lie in the purpose and objective of the Islamic law, referred to as *maqasid as-shari'ah*. Yet in the *tawhidi* worldview of unity of knowledge, purpose, and objective of wellbeing and unity of inter-causal, inter-variable relations, the domain of *maqasid as-shari'ah* was shown to extend over the dimensions of knowledge, space, and time. *Maqasid as-shari'ah* as concept was thereby used to apply equally to worldly affairs (*muamalat*) and to hard core scientific thought as well. The foundation of the *maqasid as-shari'ah* was thus explained at length to comprise the *tawhidi* epistemological worldview. The contrary ideas of *shari'ah*-compliance and traditional *fiqh* approach to interpretation of the *shari'ah* were annulled and replaced by discursive recalling the *Qur'an* and the *sunnah* in every issue -- new, old, and futuristic -- for understanding moral sustainability.

The central method emanating from the *tawhidi* methodology of relational concept of balance and organic unity of inter-causal and inter-variable relations was referred to as circular causation. This method has been established methodologically and applied effectively to various practical problems of economics, finance, society, religion, and science. The circular causation method following the ideas of many great scholars but presented in its empirical form, is a substantive application of this work.

The blueprint of the ummah (world-nation of Islam) and the tawhidi methodology

The final phenomenological model in its analytical shape and form incorporating the most central issues of the Islamic world-system is summarized in Figure 14.1. This figure represents the ultimate nature of inter-causal and inter-variable relations between various central sectors of the Islamic world-system called the *ummah*.

The summary of the grand design of monotheistic oneness in the formalism of the world-system is brought together in Figure 14.1 in the form of the blueprint of the *ummah*. The salient most important issues of the *ummah,* in the midst of complex and endogenous yet meaningful implications of the blueprint, encompass its mind-space and application on the central issues. These comprise the left-hand-side and the right-had-side, respectively, as shown in Figure 14.1.

The two sides of Figure 14.1 together, through their **IIE**-process relationship, exemplify how the epistemic realm of consciousness (*tasbih*) together with discourse (*shura*) in unity of knowledge (*tawhid*) establishes the ultimate phenomenology of unity in 'everything' of the good things of life (*maqasid as-shari'ah*). This book has investigated this rigorous theme in terms of the theorems of universality and uniqueness of the *tawhidi* methodological worldview of unity of knowledge across systemic holism.

Concluding the tawhidi implications for the generalized world-system

Tawhid as the law of monotheism in its precept and functional ontological formalism and application establishes the generalized system of thought, worldview, methodology, and application for all people, not only for Muslims. Such a theory of 'everything' finds its resting place in the deepest of the sciences. Here philosophy of sciences and rigorously analytical thought are bliss. The *tawhidi* epistemic methodology also establishes the grand design of the knowledge-induced worldview that comes naturally to the mind. Its application through the methods of unity of knowledge, balance of relationship in pervasive complementarities and systemic participation, wellbeing, and their signification by the circular causation method of relational unity, altogether form the profound domain of everyone's substantive concern. It embraces scholarly activities, high thinking, and the perspective of moral transformation.

When by Figure 14.1 the concept of the *ummah* is invoked, the emergent model, as shown, is equally applicable to the world-system of the common future of mankind. It is a model of coexistence between Islam and others by a common social contract and consensus. It offers equally for diverse modalities of trade, development, sustainability, human resource development, and an ethical social transformation through the medium of a discursive society and the common good (Global Governance, 1995). Yet the unique model is presented in the framework of evolutionary epistemology for all discursive participants across cultural diversity in unity of knowledge. This is a scholarly and sustainable project for all people.

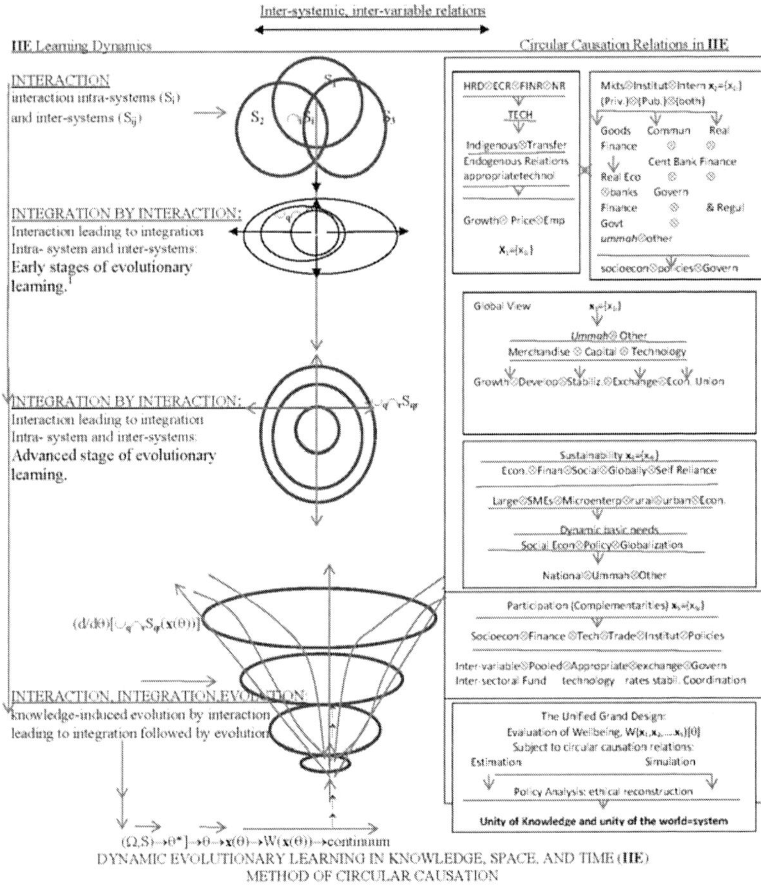

Figure 14.1: Summary: Global View of *IIE*-learning process model and the blueprint of the *ummah*

Yet the phenomenology of monotheistic unity of knowledge and the world-system articulated and formalized in this book does not present a perfect and optimal state of any system that is under socio-scientific investigation. The learning condition of the evolutionary knowledge-induced system is bound to raise conflicts and polarity as part of the inevitable historical deviations. But these will be temporary rather than permanent features of the progressive model of unity of knowledge and unity of the world-system. The modern world that mankind has inherited, in the words of Anthony Giddens (1983, p. 44), is characterized as follows:

> Functionalist theory conceives of society as a system of 'present' parts, analogous to the parts of an organic system. What is lacking in this view, in addition to deficiencies previously noted, is the idea of the duality of structure as 'binding' the interplay of absence and presence in the *duree* of social interactions. This is indeed a notion which links the moments or instantiation of social activity to the properties of collectivities or social wholes (the structural properties of social systems).

The rigorous socio-scientific language of tawhidi methodological worldview

This book has proved the rigorously mathematical inherent features of the *tawhidi* methodological worldview in terms of the structure and functions of its phenomenological model. In this regard, Figure 14.2 summarizes the mathematical and substantive underlying meaning of the generalized *tawhidi* model and its worldview. It is important to note in this figure the pervasiveness of the topological mathematical structure and function that were formalized in various ways in this book. Together with this, the very same topological mathematical nature of the phenomenological worldview establishes the universality of the *tawhidi* worldview. It brings out the potentiality for application in both the empirical and practical venues of human experience. All this is taken up in the evolutionary sense of the learning and unfolding universe of knowledge, while discarding the inconsistency of falsehood or ‘de-knowledge’ model of rationalism and its prototypes.

<*maqasid as-shari'ah*>	Functionalism & Formalism		Continuity	…… Hereafter
Fundamental deriving Epistemology (exogenously prescribed)	deriving rules of the moral law generality and specifics	application unity of knowledge of evolutionary learning universe	knowledge, and inference topology with non-compact world-systems	closure in knowledge, space, and time

<structuralism><functionalism: mathematical, philosophical><the universality property>:
and applied evaluation of the general and specific issues of world-system>
evolutionary epistemology: closure in large universe

Super-cardinality epistemic (large topology) embedding (see Rucker, 1982) of the moral Maxwell, 1962) law: determining rules and evaluation	Mathematical formalism in the midst of mathematical and epistemological embedding of the moral law; its application	emergence and repetition of processes	knowledge, space, time systemic continuity and closure

$[(\Omega \rightarrow S \equiv (\Omega,S)) \rightarrow \theta^*]$ $\rightarrow (\theta \rightarrow x(\theta) \equiv (\theta,x(\theta)) \rightarrow$ evaluate $W(x(\theta))$ $\rightarrow$

Subject to Circular causation Relations between the Variables $x(\theta)$ and the Evaluation of the measured Wellbeing index, θ in terms Of the simulated predictors Of the circular causation Equations.

continuity of knowledge-induced processes by unity of knowledge.[2]

<mathematical, philosophical, quantitatively applied and empirical formalism by *tawhidi* unity of knowledge in the generalized and specific issues of the world-system sustained by evolutionary learning in the dimensions of knowledge, space, and time>

Figure 14.2: Summarizing the comprehensive methodological nature of the *tawhidi* worldview in the dimensions of knowledge, space and time

Last words

The nature of the conscious, cognitive, and phenomenological world of 'everything' has a commonly ingrained message of unity of knowledge and entities for all. This is the worldview explained by *tawhid* – the oneness of God and the unity of knowledge induced by the monotheistic law in understanding relational epistemology of unity. In this work we have exemplified this universal and unique fact by conceptual insight, analysis, and formalism; and by applying the same to diverse issues of economics, finance, political economy, society, and science. Indeed, the world-system is for everyone as a commonly shared gift of God through His divine law. The grand design and message of *tawhid* is thereby for everyone and for everything since time immemorial. Even in the case of the *ummah* model of Figure 14.1, this model can be applied to the case of globally participated cooperation between the industrialized world and the developing world; and within the goals and objectives of all economic unions (Choudhury & Mohammad, 2011)

Two very touching voices now help us to state the last and permanent words of that universal message of *tawhid* and its structural and functional worldview of consciousness for all:

Bruteau (1997) writes:

> If you can see the God you love present in, even as, this world, then feel that union and rejoice in that. And be active in it, contribute to it, participate in the building, in the artwork, in the healing, in the understanding. This is where Reality is. You yourself are both a member of the Finite and a member of the Infinite….

Gulen, M.F. (2006) writes:

> We use 'the horizon of hope' to mean traveling beyond the visible dimension of existence, and considering existence as an interrelated whole in the absence of which things and events cannot be perceived as they really are. Nor can its essence and relation with the Creator as well as the relation between them and humanity be grasped. Scientific disciplines that conduct their own discourse largely in isolation from one another and the prevailing materialistic nature of science that has compartmentalized existence and life cannot discover the reality of things, existence, or life.

References

Allen, R.G.D., 1967, "Technical progress", in his, *Macroeconomic Theory*, pp. 236 258, Macmillan, London, Eng., and St. Martin's Press, New York, NY.

Bruteau, B., 1997, *God's Ecstasy*. p. 179, The Crossroad Publishing Co., New York, N.Y.

Choudhury, M.A., 1997, "Policy conclusion", Chapter 10 in his, *Reforming the Muslim World*, Kegan Paul International, London, Eng.

Choudhury, M.A. & Mohammad, L.S., 2011, "Sustainability by interrelating science, society and economy in embedded political economy– an epistemological approach" in Pachura, P. (ed.),*The Systemic Dimension of Globalization*, pp. 3-26, Rijeka, Croatia: InTech.

Commission on Global Governance, 1995, "Global Civic Ethic", in *Our Global Neighbourhood, a Report of the Commission on Global Governance*, Oxford University Press, New York, N.Y.

Giddens, A., 1983,*A Contemporary Critique of Historical Materialism, Vol. 1: Power, Property and the State*, particularly pp. 26-48, University of California Press, Berkeley, CA.

Gulen, M.F., 2006, *Toward Global Civilization of Love & Tolerance*, The Light, Inc., Somerset, New Jersey.

Maxwell, G., 1962, "The ontological status of theoretical entities", in Feigl, H. & Maxwell, G. (eds.),*Minnesota Studies in the Philosophy of Science, Vol. II: Scientific Explanation, Space and Time*, pp. 3-27, University of Minnesota Press, Minneapolis, Minnesota.

Rucker, R., 1982, "Large cardinals", in his. *Infinity and the Mind*, pp. 273-286, Bantam Books, New York, NY.

GLOSSARY OF ARABIC TERMS

Ahkam	rules derived on issues in the light of the *Qur'an*, sunnah, and ijtihad
Amanah saham	unit trust
Aqd	contract
Asma al-husna	beatific names of *Allah*
Ayn al-yaqin	certainty gained through observation
Ayath-Allah	signs of God (*Allah*)
Ayath al-kursi	*qur'anic* verses of the divine Throne
Asabiyya	primitive stage of community
Burhan aqli	evidences based on rationalism
Dhimmi	the trusted ones in an Islamic state
Fana	self-annihilation
Fitra	essence of divine goodness and truth
Hadara	civilization
Haqq	truth
Haqq al-yaqin	certainty by way of divine truth
Hayath at-tayyabah	life-sustaining good things
Ijma	consensus

Ijtihad	exerting effort to derive rules and meanings from the epistemological sources of the *Qur'an* and *sunnah*
Ilm al-yaqin	knowledge by way of divine belief (faith)
Istawa	God's Throne (the most High, the most elevated, supreme, complete)
Istidlal	interference by rational processes of reasoning
Istihsan	public purpose
Jihad	struggle to discover truth by various means of both faculty and war
Maslaha wal-istihsan	wellbeing for the public purpose
Mizan	balance
Mubah	indeterminate
Qiyas	analogy
Riba	interest (as financial or excess)
Shahadah (*tawhid*)	declared submission to Oneness of God
Shari'ah	Islamic law
Siffat	divine attributes
Sirat al-mustaqim	straight path (path of truth and righteousness)
Taffaqur	consciousness
Taqlid	blind submission to authority
Tawhid al-rububiyyah	*tawhidi* law in respect of the Oneness of God as Creator

Tawhid al-uluhiyyah	*tawhidi* law in respect of the Oneness of God as Sustainer of the universe
Umran	city-state

INDEX